Violence and New Religious Movements

Violence and New Religious Movements

EDITED BY

JAMES R. LEWIS

OXFORD
UNIVERSITY PRESS

Oxford University Press, Inc., publishes works that further
Oxford University's objective of excellence
in research, scholarship, and education.

Oxford   New York
Auckland   Cape Town   Dar es Salaam   Hong Kong   Karachi
Kuala Lumpur   Madrid   Melbourne   Mexico City   Nairobi
New Delhi   Shanghai   Taipei   Toronto

With offices in
Argentina   Austria   Brazil   Chile   Czech Republic   France   Greece
Guatemala   Hungary   Italy   Japan   Poland   Portugal   Singapore
South Korea   Switzerland   Thailand   Turkey   Ukraine   Vietnam

Copyright © 2011 by Oxford University Press, Inc.

Published by Oxford University Press, Inc.
198 Madison Avenue, New York, New York 10016

www.oup.com

Oxford is a registered trademark of Oxford University Press.
All rights reserved. No part of this publication may be reproduced,
stored in a retrieval system, or transmitted, in any form or by any means,
electronic, mechanical, photocopying, recording, or otherwise,
without the prior permission of Oxford University Press.

Library of Congress Cataloging-in-Publication Data
Violence and new religious movements / edited by James R. Lewis.
   p.   cm.
Includes bibliographical references and index.
ISBN 978-0-19-973563-1; 978-0-19-973561-7 (pbk)
1. Violence—Religious aspects. 2. Persecution. I. Lewis, James R.
BL65.V55V55   2011
200.086'92—dc22   2010017422

9 8 7 6 5 4 3 2 1

Printed in the United States of America
on acid-free paper

To Evelyn Dorothy Oliver—the Spirit and Inspiration behind this volume

Contents

Introduction, 3

Part I. THEORIZING NRM VIOLENCE

1. Deciphering the NRM-Violence Connection, 15
   David G. Bromley

2. Minority Religions and the Context of Violence:
   A Conflict/Interactionist Perspective, 31
   James T. Richardson

3. Reciprocal Totalism: The Toxic Interdependence of
   Anticult and Cult Violence, 63
   Dick Anthony, Thomas Robbins, and Steven Barrie-Anthony

Part II. THE "BIG FIVE" (PLUS ONE)

4. Narratives of Persecution, Suffering, and Martyrdom: Violence in
   Peoples Temple and Jonestown, 95
   Rebecca Moore

5. Revisiting the Branch Davidian Mass Suicide Debate, 113
   Stuart A. Wright

6. Explaining the Murder-Suicides of the Order of the Solar Temple:
   A Survey of Hypotheses, 133
   Henrik Bogdan

7. Religion and Violence in Japan: The Case of Aum Shinrikyo, 147
   Martin Repp

8. The Euphemization of Violence: The Case of Heaven's Gate, 173
   Benjamin E. Zeller

9. "There Will Follow a New Generation and a New Earth": From Apocalyptic Hopes to Destruction in the Movement for the Restoration of the Ten Commandments of God, 191
   Jean-François Mayer

Part III.   SELECT RELIGIOUS GROUPS INVOLVED IN VIOLENCE

10. Murder in Knutby: Charisma, Eroticism, and Violence in a Swedish Pentecostal Community, 217
    Jonathan Peste

11. Modern Pagan Warriors: Violence and Justice in Rodnoverie, 231
    Kaarina Aitamurto

12. Ananda Marga, PROUT, and the Use of Force, 249
    Helen Crovetto

13. Knocking on Heaven's Door: Violence, Charisma, and the Transformation of New Vrindaban, 275
    E. Burke Rochford Jr.

Part IV.   RHETORICS OF VIOLENCE AND PEACEFUL DENOUEMENTS

14. The Nation of Islam and Violence, 295
    Martha F. Lee

15. Cultural Capital, Social Networks, and Collective Violence at Rajneeshpuram, 307
    Marion S. Goldman

16. "Strong as Steel, Steady as Stone": Skirting Pitfalls in 3HO/Sikh Dharma, 325
    Constance Elsberg

17. "Smite Him Hip and Thigh": Satanism, Violence, and Transgression, 351
    Jesper Aagaard Petersen

Part V.   VIOLENCE AGAINST NRMS

18. State-Fostered Violence against the Falun Gong in China, 379
    James T. Richardson and Bryan Edelman

19. Deprogramming Violence: The Logic, Perpetration, and Outcomes of Coercive Intervention, 397
    Anson Shupe

Afterword, 413

Index, 425

Contributors

Kaarina Aitamurto is a postgraduate student at the Aleksanteri Institute at Helsinki University. Her research interests include new religious movements in Russia and the relationship between religion and nationalism. She is the author of several articles on the various aspects of contemporary Slavic Paganism, Rodnoverie, and is currently writing her doctoral dissertation on this subject.

Dick Anthony is a research and forensic psychologist specializing in the psychological and sociological concomitants of involvement in new religious movements. His research has been supported by United States government agencies such as the National Institute of Mental Health, the National Institute of Drug Abuse, and the National Endowment for the Humanities, and he has published its results in many articles and books. He frequently testifies or serves as a trial consultant in cases involving allegations of coercive or harmful religious influence, and also provides consultation to groups and individuals with respect to optimizing social or individual adjustment.

Steven Barrie-Anthony is a PhD student in Religious Studies at the University of California, Santa Barbara. His research focuses on contemporary religious innovation and change, such as new spirituality movements in relation to broad cultural shifts, and on the relationship between pluralism and shifting styles of solidarity. He has authored or coauthored several scholarly articles, as well as many essays in periodicals such as the *Los Angeles Times*.

Henrik Bogdan is professor of religion at Göteborg University, Sweden. His main areas of research are Western Esotericism and new religious movements. He is secretary of FINYAR (Swedish Association for Research and Information on New Religious Movements). Bogdan is the author of *Western Esotericism and Rituals of Initiation* (SUNY, 2007).

David G. Bromley is professor of sociology at Virginia Commonwealth University. Among his recent books on religious movements are *Cults, Religion, and Violence* (Cambridge University Press, 2002), *Toward Reflexive Ethnography: Participating, Observing, Narrating* (Elsevier Science, 2001), and *The Politics of Religious Apostasy: The Role of Apostates in the Transformation of Religious Movements* (Praeger, 1998). He is former president of the Association for the Sociology of Religion; founding editor of the annual series Religion and the Social Order, sponsored by the Association for the Sociology of Religion; and former editor of the *Journal for the Scientific Study of Religion*.

Helen Crovetto is an independent scholar of new religious movements within Hindu Tantrism. She studied tantra yoga and related disciplines in Kolkata, Varanasi, and Sweden in the late 1970s. Her publications include "Embodied Knowledge and Divinity: The Hohm Community as Western-style Bāuls," *Nova Religio* (2006) and "Ananda Marga's Tantric Neo-Humanism," in *The Encyclopedia of Religion and Nature* (2005).

Bryan Edelman (BS, Florida State University; PhD, University of Nevada, Reno; LLM, University of Kent, Canterbury) is senior trial consultant at the Jury Research Institute in northern California. His articles have appeared in *Journal of Church and State* and *Nova Religio*. Special interests include jury behavior, social control, and application of international conventions and customary law to religious belief and expression.

Constance Elsberg is a professor of sociology and anthropology at Northern Virginia Community College. She is the author of *Graceful Women: Gender and Identity in an American Sikh Community*, which examines women's lives in 3HO/Sikh Dharma, as well as several articles on this subject. Her interest in Sikh Dharma has extended to a more general interest in Sikh and Punjabi studies and to study and fieldwork there.

Marion S. Goldman is professor of sociology and religious studies at the University of Oregon. Her research focuses on new religions, the sociology of gender, and cultural innovation. Her *Gold Diggers and Silver Miners* (1981) won the Hamilton Prize for research on gender and society. *Passionate Journeys* (2000) considered the accomplished women who followed Rajneesh. Her recent work examines the Esalen Institute and its contributions to the spiritual marketplace.

Martha F. Lee is professor of political science and Stephen Jarislowsky Chair in Religion and Conflict at the University of Windsor, Canada. Her publications focus on the link between religion and politics in millenarian movements. Her work has been most recently published in the *Journal for the Study of Radicalism*, and her new book, *Conspiracy Rising: Conspiracy Thinking and American Public Life* (Greenwood, 2011), includes an examination of the role of conspiracy theory in millenarian movements.

James R. Lewis is associate professor of religious studies at the University of Tromsø (Norway). He is the editor of a dozen scholarly anthologies in the field of new religious movements and has authored both a major reference book, *The Encyclopedia of Cults, Sects, and New Religions*, and a textbook, *Odd Gods: New Religions and the Cult Controversy*. Additionally, he is the editor of *The Oxford Handbook of New Religious Movements*, and, most recently, *Scientology*.

Jean-François Mayer is director of Religioscope Institute (Fribourg, Switzerland). He is the author of more than ten books and many articles published in several languages on contemporary religious movements and trends. He is the editor of the bilingual website Religioscope (http://www.religion.info). Additional biographical and bibliographical information are given at http://www.mayer.info.

Rebecca Moore is chair and professor of religious studies at San Diego State University. She has written and published extensively on Jonestown and Peoples Temple and maintains an educational website on the subject: http://jonestown.sdsu.edu. She is also coeditor of *Nova Religio: The Journal of Alternative and Emergent Religions*, which covers new religions around the globe.

Jonathan Peste, PhD in religious studies and lecturer at Göteborg University, has written on late antique hermetism and gnosticism, religious radicalism, and modern Judaism.

Jesper Aagaard Petersen is a PhD student and teaching assistant at the Norwegian University of Science and Technology. He is the editor of *Contemporary Religious Satanism* (2009), and coeditor with James R. Lewis of *Controversial New Religions* (2004) and *The Encyclopedic Sourcebook of Satanism* (2008).

Martin Repp is a lecturer at Heidelberg University and the editor of the journal *Japanese Religions*. Since 1988 he worked at the NCC Center for the Study of Japanese Religions in Kyoto. From 2004 to 2009 he was Professor for Comparative Religion at Ryukoku University (Kyoto). His research focuses on Japanese Pure Land Buddhism, Aum Shinrikyô, and forms of communication between religions. He is the author of *Das religiöse Denken Hônens-Eine Untersuchung zu Strukturen* *religiöser Erneuerung* (2005), *Aum Shinrikyô-Ein Kapitel krimineller Religionsgeschichte* (1997), and a number of articles on these and other themes.

James T. Richardson, JD, PhD, is professor of sociology and judicial studies at the University of Nevada, Reno, where he directs the Grant Sawyer Center for Justice Studies, as well as the judicial studies degree programs for trial judges. He is the author or coauthor of nearly two hundred articles and chapters, as well as seven books, including his latest, *Regulating Religion: Case Studies from Around the Globe* (Kluwer, 2003).

Thomas Robbins is a semiretired sociologist of religion (PhD from the University of North Carolina, 1974). He is the author of *Cults, Converts, and Charisma* (Sage, 1988) and the coauthor of six collections of original papers, including *Millennium, Messiahs, and Mayhem* (Routledge, 1997) and *Misunderstanding Cults* (University of Toronto, 2001). He has published numerous articles, essays, and reviews in social science and religious studies journals.

E. Burke Rochford Jr. is professor of sociology and religion at Middlebury College in Vermont. He has researched the Hare Krishna movement for the past twenty-eight years and written numerous articles on it. His most recent book is *Hare Krishna Transformed* (New York University Press, 2007).

Anson Shupe is professor of sociology and anthropology at the joint campus of Indiana University and Purdue University in Fort Wayne. He is the author of numerous professional articles and more than two dozen books, including *Six Perspectives on New Religions*; *Born Again Politics and the Moral Majority*; and *Wealth and Power in American Zion*.

Stuart A. Wright is assistant dean of graduate studies and research and professor of sociology at Lamar University. He is the author of *Leaving Cults: The Dynamics of Defection* (Society for the Scientific Study of Religion, 1987) and editor of *Armageddon in Waco* (University of Chicago Press, 1995). He has published more than thirty articles or book chapters in scholarly venues and has become a widely recognized expert and legal consultant.

Benjamin Zeller is assistant professor of religion at Brevard College. He is the author of a number of articles and book chapters on Heaven's Gate. His new book is *Prophets and Protons: New Religions and Science in Late Twentieth-century America* (New York University Press, 2010).

Violence and New Religious Movements

Introduction

Those who dwelled on God's Name, shared their earnings with others, wielded the sword in battle, distributed food, offered their heads at the altar of Dharma, were cut up limb by limb, skinned alive, boiled and sawed in half, but did not utter a sigh nor faltered in their faith, kept the sanctity of their hair until their last breath and sacrificed their lives for the sanctity of the Gurdwaras; remember their glorious deeds O Khalsa and utter Waheguru!

—From the *Ardas*

During the early to midseventies, I was a member of Yogi Bhajan's Healthy, Happy, Holy Organization, better known as 3HO (Elsberg 2003; Jakobsh 2008; Laue 2007). In my capacity as a local 3HO leader, I organized a small community of some eighteen people living together in an ashram (as 3HO centers were referred to, at least back in the seventies), plus a larger number of informally affiliated participants in the Tallahassee, Florida, area. I eventually disaffiliated from 3HO after a three-year membership period (a defection I describe in Lewis 2010).

A thumbnail description of 3HO would be that it represents a blend of highly orthodox Sikhism, a diverse set of yogic practices that Bhajan collectively referred to as kundalini yoga, and an eclectic selection of other ideas and practices drawn from the larger spiritual subculture of the 1970s. Because of mainstream Sikhism's valorization of its history of martyrdom and militant resistance to Mughal oppression, 3HO inherited a martial tradition that, one might reasonably anticipate, would be used to legitimate violent actions. (It should be stressed here that Sikhism's martial dimension is but one part of a complex, noble religion.)

Moreover, 3HO did not shy away from this tradition. For example, as part of the Tallahassee ashram's morning *sadhana* (a generic South Asian term for one's daily spiritual routine), I led residents in a recitation of the *Ardas*—a traditional Sikh prayer that, among other components, includes descriptions of the tortures endured by Sikh martyrs (see the chapter epigraph). The core membership of 3HO also embraced the Sikh "uniform"—the so-called Five Ks—many components of which have martial associations.

When Guru Gobind Singh, the tenth Guru of the Sikh tradition, introduced the Khalsa brother- and sisterhood to the Sikh community, he also introduced the distinctive regalia that distinguish Sikhs from non-Sikhs. The five Ks are as follows: Kesh, uncut hair (a traditional Indian sign of saintliness); Kangh, a comb for keeping the hair neat; Kach, short pants for quick movement in battle (in later times, commonly interpreted as an admonition to wear underwear, which, in India, is associated with sexual self-control); Kirpan, a sword (later generations were permitted to carry Kirpans symbolically, such as by carrying a miniature steel emblem of a sword embedded on their Kangh); and Kara, a steel bracelet worn around the right wrist. Many contemporary Karas are light pieces of jewelry, but the older style of Karas were (at least for men) thick, heavy rings that looked like something out of a diesel truck engine. Though one can find diverse interpretations of the significance of the Kara, the original Karas were pieces of armor designed to help protect one's forearm from an opponent's sword blows. Thus, three of the five Ks originated from Guru Gobind Singh's desire to remold his Sikhs into a community of warriors. During my 3HO years, I wore the full Sikh uniform and owned several (nonsymbolic) Kirpans.

The symbol of Sikhism, comparable to Christianity's cross and Islam's star and crescent, is the Adi Shakti, which consists of two swords, a dagger, and a circle. There are a number of interpretations of what the circle means. When Sikhs went into battle in the old days, they would wear large metal rings around their turbans that would protect them from downward-slashing sword blows to the head. This, according to some sources, is where the circle comes from in the Adi Shakti.

Members of 3HO were also encouraged to purchase guns, and firearms training eventually became a regular part of the annual gatherings that took place around the summer solstice. In her contribution to the present volume, Constance Elsberg recounts that, "In the early years . . . women received handgun training at their 'Ladies' Camp.' . . . The summer (1983) when I attended a 3HO camp for women, Bhajan always had security guards around him, and we took turns being on night guard duty." I was part of the security detail in 1973 and 1974 for the annual winter 3HO gatherings that took place in Florida. Though I did not carry a gun, I knew where the guns were hidden—"in the event they were needed."

I should finally add that, particularly in the first decades of its existence, 3HO contained all of the key internal traits that many analysts have deemed essential for a new religion to become violent. These "endogenous factors," which are the focus of David Bromley's chapter in the current collection, typically include a charismatic leader, a millenarian belief system, and a totalistic social organization that is insulated from the surrounding culture to a greater or lesser degree. In her chapter Elsberg discusses how 3HO fulfilled (before Bhajan's passing in 2004) these characteristics.

Given the martial dimension of the Sikh tradition in combination with all of the traits of a potentially dangerous new religion, we have what seems to be a potent recipe for disaster. However, the group has never been involved in violence, either external or internal. So the question becomes, why not?

As the 3HO example demonstrates, seemingly straightforward, commonsense criteria for predicting which new religion might commit an act of violence are inadequate. And, unfortunately, the more nuanced criteria developed by scholarly specialists are also not decisive. The problem boils down to one of the issues of law enforcement approaches: predictability. Researchers can generally agree on the combinations of certain factors that are "'necessary' for the eruption of major incidents of cult-related violence, although they are not 'sufficient' to predict this violence" (Dawson 2006, 145–46).

Certain critics of new religious movements (NRMs)—the critics who are often collectively referred to as the anticult movement (ACM)—regularly portray a wide variety of alternative religions, if not all NRMs, as potentially violent. Such an approach is frequently just fearmongering, similar to the claim that Iraq possessed weapons of mass destruction during the period leading up to the Iraq invasion.

The good news is that far and away the great majority of NRMs are not violent and show little or no propensity to become violent. However, a number of major incidents involving alternative religions have raised public concerns. Violent incidents involving NRMs have been making international headlines at least since the People's Temple murder-suicides at Jonestown in 1978. After a fifteen-year period of relative quiescence, four major incidents took place within the short span of five years: The ATF/FBI raid on the Mount Carmel community (1993), the Solar Temple murder-suicides (1994, 1995, and 1997), the Tokyo subway poison-gas attack (1995), and the Heaven's Gate suicides (1997).

The earliest approaches to NRM-related violence, especially those influenced by anticult sentiments, focused on the (explicitly or by implication socio/psychopathological) personality of the leader and emphasized the role of the group's totalistic organization. In the wake of the four major violent events that took place in the nineties, many studies shifted emphasis to these groups' millennialist beliefs, implicitly or explicitly portraying millennialism as the key to understanding their violence. The near approach of the new millennium in the 1990s seems to have influenced this perspective, and the violence associated with the implosion of the Movement for the Restoration of the Ten Commandments of God (MRTCG) in the year 2000 seemed to confirm the validity of this focus.

In the last decade, the tendency has been to incorporate external forces such as hostile apostates and intrusive governmental agencies and to construct general models that take both internal and external factors into account. This newer perspective also calls attention to the relational nature of violence and to the developmental stages that lead up to extreme actions. This multifactor view is the underlying orientation of David G. Bromley and J. Gordon Melton's anthology, *Cults, Religion, and Violence* (2002). The Bromley-Melton volume has been the field's state-of-the-art theoretical statement on NRMs and violence since it appeared in 2002.

The relatively mature state of the literature on new religions and violence puts contemporary researchers in a position to ask different sorts of questions and to undertake different kinds of analyses than were previously possible. For example, rather than attempting to construct a general model of all NRM-related violence, what if one focused instead on more specific kinds of violence, such as group suicides? Alternately, what if, instead of focusing exclusively on the "big five"—Jonestown, Heaven's Gate, Aum Shinrikyo, the Branch Davidians, and the Solar Temple (the Bromley-Melton volume focuses exclusively on the latter four)—we examined violence in other, less prominent new religions? Yet another theme that calls out for examination is violence *against* new religions.

The current collection does not attempt to pursue all of these possibilities. What it *does* do is to bring together essays on violence in a wide variety of alternative religions, including groups such as the Nation of Islam and the Knutby community, that are not normally studied under the NRM rubric.

Part I consists of three general theory chapters. In the area of NRM violence, David G. Bromley is best known for his analysis of such violence in terms of what he refers to as "dramatic denouments." The core structure of dramatic denouements is a four-stage processual model of interactive conflict amplification: (1) latent tension, (2) nascent conflict, (3) intensified conflict, and (4) dramatic denouement. In "Deciphering the NRM-Violence Connection," he focuses attention on internal movement traits—sometimes referred to as endogenous (as opposed to exogenous) factors—that have been linked to NRM-related violence: millennial ideology, totalistic organization, and charismatic leadership. Bromley's finely tuned analysis throws new light on these movement characteristics.

In James T. Richardson's "Minority Religions and the Context of Violence: A Conflict/Interactionist Perspective," violence associated with the recent rise of newer religious groups or "cults," as well as older minority religions, is examined using a conflict orientation. The interactional nature of such violence is discussed, and accusations of violence concerning minority and newer religions are placed in a conflict perspective that stresses the interdependency of religious groups and their opponents. Special attention is given to allegations of (1) violence derived from group teachings and practices, with a focus on major recent tragic events involving religious groups and (2) violence directed against members and groups by others, including private individuals and organizations, as well as governmental entities.

Religio-ideological totalism entails an absolute division of humanity into dual categories such as saved/damned, human/subhuman, godly/demonic, and so on. Totalistic "cults" are not necessarily violent, but the psychology of totalism does feature an impulse to validate an absolute worldview by confronting demonized exemplars of evil as contrast symbols. Anticult confrontations of totalistic movements may themselves take a totalistic and hence persecutory form. In "Reciprocal Totalism: The Toxic Interdependence of Anticult and Cult Violence," Dick Anthony, Thomas Robbins, and Steven Barrie-Anthony discuss research that documents a cycle of increasing totalization of both the group and the countergroup response, which may escalate out of control to the point of triggering a violent denouement.

Part II covers the major groups that have been the focus of analyses of new religions and violence: Peoples Temple, the Branch Davidians, the Order of the Solar Temple, Aum Shinrikyo, and Heaven's Gate. This section ends with a chapter on the Movement for the Restoration of the Ten Commandments of God, a group that is sometimes considered on a par with the "big five."

Among other things, the Jonestown murder-suicide established a point of reference for all subsequent discussions of violence and NRMs. In "Narratives of Persecution, Suffering, and Martyrdom: Violence in Peoples Temple and Jonestown," Rebecca Moore begins by presenting a brief history of Peoples Temple and the events leading up to the final day in Jonestown. It first discusses examples of four types of violence that existed in the Peoples Temple and then looks at the rhetoric of persecution, suffering, and martyrdom that prevailed within the group. The chapter examines other studies of violence in Peoples Temple and considers analyses of contemporary religious violence. Finally, it examines the world stage upon which the drama was enacted: the players, the goals, and the ultimate purpose in the decision to die.

Stuart A. Wright's "Revisiting the Branch Davidian Mass Suicide Debate" revisits the controversy, recently revived by Kenneth C. G. Newport, that the Branch Davidians had a theological rationale for mass suicide and likely set fire to their own home. Newport couples the theological argument with assertions of "unassailable evidence" regarding the government's reports. Wright's chapter challenges this claim. Despite Newport's largely uncritical acceptance of the official version of events, the reliability of the government's case is hampered in a number of ways. Wright also contends that the tragic denouement at Waco has to be viewed in the cultural context in which it emerged. When examined against the backdrop of these disturbing machinations and conditions, the evidence supporting mass suicide at Mount Carmel is hardly unassailable.

The Order of the Solar Temple caught the attention of the public in October 1994, when fifty-three members of the order in Switzerland and Quebec were murdered or committed suicide. These tragic events were later followed by two group suicides, and the Solar Temple quickly became one of the most notorious and discussed "cults." Henrik Bogdan's "Examining the Murder-suicides of the Order of the Solar Temple" surveys the most important scholarly theories about the violence of the Solar Temple. It also addresses the broader discussion of sects and violence using the Solar Temple as a case study.

Martin Repp's "Religion and Violence in Japan: The Case of Aum Shinrikyo" investigates violent acts committed by the new religious movement Aum Shinrikyo during the 1980s and 1990s. Most studies portray Aum Shinrikyo's development from the hindsight of the poison-gas attack, thereby suggesting that it was an internal and consequent process caused from the very beginning and "necessarily" by its leader, Asahara Shoko, and his teachings. In contrast with such monocausal explanation attempts, the present study traces the internal (organizational and doctrinal) developments of the group in historical order and in its social context. It is the process of reciprocal interactions with contemporary society in Japan that triggered and accelerated the group's violent potential.

In 1997, Heaven's Gate, a small UFO religion, committed mass suicide in southern California. Given the group's original teaching of bodily ascension into waiting UFOs, analysts have often called attention to the contradiction between their early eschatology and their later valorization of suicide. In "The Euphemization of Violence: The Case of Heaven's Gate," Benjamin E. Zeller takes a new approach by considering what he refers to as the "euphemization of violence," the rhetorical transformation of (self-)violence into a more benign act. After providing an overview of the group's history, he traces this transformation across the course of three phases of the movement's twenty-year history.

Jean-François Mayer is one of the few Western scholars of NRMs to investigate the Movement for the Restoration of the Ten Commandments of God, the Ugandan group that, in 2000, exploded in an incident of mass suicide-murder. In "'There Will Follow a New Generation and a New Earth': From Apocalyptic Hopes to Destruction in the Movement for the Restoration of the Ten Commandments of God," he pieces together the fragments of available information about the MRTCG and considers various alternative explanations of the group's fiery end in terms of what we know about other incidents of NRM violence.

In contrast to other treatments of new religions and violence that focus on the "big five/six," the present volume (as noted earlier) brings together essays on violence in a wide variety of alternative religions, including groups that are not normally studied under the NRM rubric. Part III presents four chapters on a selection of other new religions that have been involved in violence.

With the exception of the Order of the Solar Temple, analysts do not usually consider other examples of new religion violence in Europe. In "Murder in Knutby: Charisma, Eroticism, and Violence in a Swedish Pentecostal Community," Jonathan Peste recounts the narrative of a series of murders that took place in the Knutby Filadelfia community. He concludes that the violence should perhaps be understood as a combination of lack of external control, social interaction among a tight community of charismatic ministers, a theology of eroticism and death, and the egoism and psychopathology of the murderers.

The study of Russian contemporary Slavic Paganism, Rodnoverie, has tended to focus on the ultranationalist, racist, and anti-Semitic features of the movement. Rodnoverie is, however, an extremely heterogeneous movement, and, as several recent studies show, there are also those who renounce aggressive nationalism. Furthermore, the most radical Rodnovers form a relatively small minority within the movement and are excluded from the mainstream organizations. Kaarina Aitamurto's "Modern Pagan Warriors: Violence and Justice in Rodnoverie" analyzes Rodnoverie morality and perceptions of the usage and justification of violence and also examines the idea of the Pagan as a "warrior." While liberal Rodnovers emphasize the interconnectedness of life and the ethic of reciprocity, in xenophobic interpretations "justice" easily turns into aggression and a scapegoat mentality. Additionally, the way "confrontation" is understood varies within the movement. It can range from a pacifist conviction to the acceptance of the law of "an eye for an eye."

Ananda Marga is an international movement that claims over a million adherents in more than one hundred countries. The progressive utilization theory (PROUT) is its socioeconomic philosophy and the name of its political branch, whose organization is officially called PROUTist Universal. Ananda Margiis are perceived by some as terrorists, while much of their social service work, positive environmental philosophy, and effective system of tantric spiritual practices is overlooked. It would be more accurate to call Ananda Margiis and PROUTists revolutionary sociospiritual utopians rather than terrorists. There are several allegations against them concerning the murder of apostates. In "Ananda Marga, PROUT, and the Use of Force," Helen Crovetto concentrates on the well-founded doctrinal basis for Ananda Marga and PROUT's association with the use of force and examines their moral arguments justifying it.

In "Knocking on Heaven's Door: Violence, Charisma, and the Transformation of New Vrindaban," E. Burke Rochford Jr. considers the relationship between violence, charismatic authority, and the development of one of the more significant new religious communities that emerged during the 1960s in the United States—New Vrindaban. Located in West Virginia, New Vrindaban was founded and led by Kirtanananda Swami, one of the early members of the Hare Krishna movement. New Vrindaban represents an interesting case study precisely because Kirtanananda's charisma was never institutionalized, a fact that ultimately had devastating consequences for the community in the face of violence. Rochford considers how two acts of violence in 1985 and 1986 directly and indirectly undermined Kirtanananda's authority and resulted in mass defection, financial collapse, and the decline and subsequent transformation of New Vrindaban's purpose.

Part IV examines a set of religious movements that articulate discourses about militancy and violence without actually becoming violent (or that have been involved in limited violence). One of the chapters in this section also examines a case study of a group that seemed set on a trajectory of violence but whose activities ultimately culminated in a peaceful denouement.

In the United States, the African American struggle for identity, freedom, and equality was expressed in a variety of religious and political movements throughout the twentieth century. In "The Nation of Islam and Violence," Martha F. Lee examines one of the most important of those movements—the Nation of Islam, which emerged in the late 1920s and continues to exist today. American society has often perceived this religious organization as a violent threat to its stability and security, while the Nation of Islam, in its outspoken criticism of white America, has often implied that it would not hesitate to use violence to achieve its goals. Despite this context, however, the actual incidents of violence in which the Nation of Islam was involved have been limited in both number and intensity.

Despite possibilities for bloodshed, members of Rajneeshpuram, the short-lived communal city in central Oregon, violence never escalated to the point of mass murder, suicides, or large-scale collective attacks. In "Cultural Capital, Social Networks, and Collective Violence at Rajneeshpuram," Marion S. Goldman uses data from Bhagwan Rajneesh's temporary community to explore the utility of Pierre Bourdieu's theories of culture in adding another dimension to theory and research about collective religious violence. An important factor in the dynamics of the Oregon group was its class background. Members' ongoing contact with networks outside Rajneeshpuram, their personal and family resources, and their knowledge of the legal system all contributed to a relatively peaceful resolution of external and internal tensions.

Yogi Bhajan's 3HO group can briefly be described as a blend of kundalini yoga and Sikhism. Due to the strongly martial dimension of Sikhism, the group is thus heir to a militant tradition, which, one might suppose, could easily be used to justify violence. Also, particularly in the first decades of its existence, 3HO contained all of the key ideological and organizational characteristics that have been associated with violent new religions. However, the group has never been involved in violence, either external or internal. In "'Strong as Steel, Steady as Stone': Skirting Pitfalls in 3HO/Sikh Dharma," Constance Elsberg surveys the various factors that have mitigated against violence in 3HO.

In "'Smite Him Hip and Thigh': Satanism, Violence, and Transgression," Jesper Aagaard Petersen approaches the issues of Satanism and violence by elaborating on his earlier classification of modern Satanism—rationalist, esoteric, and reactive—in a "satanic milieu." By analyzing various discourses on Satanism and violence, he expands on the trait of antinomianism or nonconformity through the concept of transgression. The important point is how to *discern* the actual violence of serial killers, neofascists, and marginalized teens using Satanism as an alibi (a demonological use of violence and transgression that in essence is confirming social mores) and distinguish it from the "symbolic violence," "aesthetic terrorism," or "transformational psychodrama" that satanic groups and individuals use to challenge the self-evident and decondition the self.

Part V consists of a pair of chapters that deal with violence against NRMs. One represents a case study of state violence against a new religion. The other examines vigilante violence against a wide variety of groups labeled "cults." The Branch Davidians, who were victims of state violence, could have appropriately been included in this section as well.

The key question of James T. Richardson and Bryan Edelman's "State-fostered Violence against the Falun Gong in China" is how such high levels of violence against members of a minority religious group are justified by those in positions of power in China and how the apparatus of the state is used to effect this violence. It is one thing for a state to *allow* discriminatory behavior toward minority faiths that are out of step with dominant values and parties in a society. That happens with regularity around the globe. However, when the state itself becomes an instrument of violence toward minority faiths, this demands an explanation of how and why this occurs.

A considerable literature, popular/academic and/or laudatory/condemnatory, has grown up surrounding *deprogramming*, a once prolific but now rare practice of forcibly extricating persons from unconventional religious (but not always religious) groups. However, other than images of this vigilante behavior recounted as "atrocity stories" by civil libertarians or "heroic" interventions by supportive anti-cultists, the violence associated with deprogramming has rarely been sifted for behavioral patterns, nor has deprogramming been examined as violence per se. In "Deprogramming Violence: The Logic, Perpetration, and Outcomes of Coercive Intervention," Anson Shupe, drawing on forty years of case studies, considers deprogramming violence along three axes or typologies: deprogramming agents; facilitating, broker agents; and harms incurred by deprogrammees from this radical intervention tactic.

REFERENCES

Bromley, David G., and J. Gordon Melton, eds. 2002. *Cults, Religion, and Violence*. New York: Cambridge University Press.
Dawson, Lorne. 2006. *Comprehending Cults*. New York: Oxford University Press.
Elsberg, Constance Waeber. 2003. *Graceful Women: Gender and Identity in an American Sikh Community*. Knoxville: University of Tennessee.
Jakobsh, Doris. 2008. "3HO/Sikh Dharma of the Western Hemisphere: The 'Forgotten' New Religious Movement?" Religion Compass 2(3): 385–408
Laue, Thorsten. *Kundalini Yoga, Yogi Tee, und das Wassermannzeitalter: Religionswissenschaftliche Einblicke in die Healthy, Happy, Holy Organization (3HO) des Yogi Bhajan*. Münster: LIT.
Lewis, James R. 2010. "Autobiography of a Schism." *Marburg Journal of Religion* 15: 1–19.

PART I

Theorizing NRM Violence

1

Deciphering the NRM-Violence Connection

David G. Bromley

It is frequently observed that religion and violence are no strangers to one another. History is replete with religious wars and crusades, persecution of heretics and nonbelievers, witch hunts, violence by and against religious leaders, religious theologies that legitimate and sometimes glorify violence, and countless cases of individuals from a myriad of religious traditions who engage in interpersonal violence (Iadicola and Shupe 2003). Around the globe currently there are numerous cases of violent clashes within and between religious traditions, such as Protestant-Catholic violence in Northern Ireland, Israeli-Palestinian violence in the Middle East, Hindu-Christian violence in India, and Sunni and Shiite Muslim violence in Iraq. This chapter focuses on a particular kind of violence that has attracted a great deal of public and scholarly attention, collective violence involving new religious movements (NRMs).[1] More specifically, I am concerned here with extending the theory of dramatic denouements that was initially developed in *Cults, Religion, and Violence* (Bromley 2002).

The theory of dramatic denouements analyzes conflicts that culminate in climactic moments when movement and/or society conclude that the requisite conditions for their coexistence are being subverted and one or both parties embark on a project of violent final reckoning that is intended to reestablish appropriate moral order. The historically based theory argues that specific sociocultural contexts are more or less conducive to an escalation toward a violent resolution. Outcomes are contingent throughout the escalation sequence as either or both sides in the conflict can, and often do, choose a variety of alternatives to violent resolution. Because violence is a social relationship, both parties play a role in the direction that the relationship moves. As articulated in the original statement, dramatic denouements can be understood as involving four levels of historically situated disputation that involve an increasing breadth and seriousness of claims making by the respective parties: (1) latent tension, in which the foundational logic and organization of movement and society stand in contradiction to one another, although there may not be direct engagement; (2) nascent conflict, in which emergent, bilateral conflicts are not articulated in ideological terms, future adversaries have not mobilized organizationally, and parties therefore orient toward one another as "troublesome"; (3) intensified conflict, in which there is heightened mobilization and radicalization of movements and oppositional groups, entry of third parties, and orientation by parties toward one another as "dangerous" (Sarbin 1967); and (4) dramatic denouement, in which polarization and destabilization of dangerous relationships lead to orientation by parties as "subversive" and to projects of final reckoning intended to reverse power and moral relationships (Emerson and Messinger 1977; Emerson 1981).

The dramatic denouement model describes the interactive process of conflict escalation from nascent conflict through dramatic denouement, but a number of other issues need to be addressed in order to more fully articulate the dynamics of the process of conflict escalation toward dramatic denouement. In this chapter I consider the role of internal movement characteristics—endogenous factors—that have been linked to NRM violence. Three specific endogenous factors are examined: millennial ideology, totalistic organization, and charismatic leadership. The objective is to distinguish between factors that are associated with movement radicalization and those that contribute more directly to violence. I argue that many of the factors that are currently being linked to violence are actually more predictive of radicalization of parties to the conflict than they are of violence. Additional specification of directly related factors is therefore necessary.[2] I explore these issues by first summarizing some of the most important theoretical work that identifies key endogenous factors on the NRM-violence connection and then drawing on that work to propose a more closely articulated relationship between the factors incorporated in those theories and NRM violence. The set of proposed characteristics describes movements that are organized and predisposed toward undertaking a moment of final reckoning and feel a sense of urgent necessity toward that end.

Analyses of the NRM-Violence Relationship

The impetus to understand the participation of NRMs in violence has arisen out of a series of episodes of collective violence involving NRMs during the last half of the twentieth century. Benchmark cases referred to by various scholars include the Manson Family murders in 1969, the murder-suicide of 914 members of the Peoples

Temple at Jonestown in 1978, the death of 80 people during the standoff at the Branch Davidian compound outside of Waco in 1993, the murder-suicide of 74 members of the Solar Temple in Switzerland and Quebec in 1994, 1996, and 1997, the Aum Shinrikyo murders of about 23 members and opponents, as well as 12 other innocent subway passengers in Tokyo in 1995, the collective suicide of 39 members of Heaven's Gate in California in 1997, and the murder-suicide of about 780 members of the Movement for the Restoration of the Ten Commandments of God in Uganda in 2000.[3]

Theoretical analyses of these cases can be broadly divided into those that focus on one or several endogenous factors and those that propose more interactive models that incorporate both endogenous and exogenous factors. The same set of endogenous factors, although sometimes conceptualized and labeled somewhat differently, are repeatedly identified as putatively related to violence involving NRMs—millennialism/apocalypticism, charismatic/prophetic leadership, and high-demand/radical/totalistic organization (Dawson 2006, 2010; Robbins and Anthony 1995; Robbins 2002; Walliss 2005). It is typically acknowledged, as Dawson does in considering these three factors, that "No single factor will generate violent behaviour, nor will the simple combination of the three. Instead, they constitute some of the prime conditions 'necessary' for the eruption of major incidents of cult-related violence, although they are not 'sufficient' to predict this violence" (Dawson 2006, 145–46).

Marc Galanter's social systems model, developed in *Cults: Faith, Healing, and Coercion* (1999), exemplifies a more internally oriented approach in analyzing the Peoples Temple, Branch Davidian, Aum Shinrikyo, and Heaven's Gate cases. He concludes that these episodes contain four conditions in common, three of which are internal: group isolation, leader grandiosity and paranoia, absolute dominion, and government mismanagement. Isolation can lead to extreme actions because groups reduce the possibility of external feedback to their actions and operate solely on the basis of internally constructed definitions of events. Movements can isolate themselves from conventional society either through geographic separation or constant mobility. Galanter argues that another dynamic in violent episodes is leaders' need to maintain absolute control. The result can be to produce paranoid fears that others inside or outside the movement will usurp their power. In order to protect their positions, leaders create a siege mentality within the group in order to maintain solidarity and loyalty. Movements may also exercise centripetal control mechanisms that closely regulate members' lives, leading to absolute domination of individuals' thoughts and behavior. Finally, governmental mismanagement refers to agencies' failure to immediately control illicit activity and to prevent young adults from being enticed into these movements. In the Galanter model, then, all of the factors except governmental mismanagement refer to attributes of movements, and the one external factor specifies government inaction, apparently excluding the possibility of overreaction. The emphasis is on the interaction of internal factors related to radicalization and conflict.

Several more interactively oriented explanatory models containing both endogenous and exogenous factors have also been proposed to account for violence involving new religious movements. These models incorporate many of the same endogenous factors but also incorporate exogenous ones and emphasize the interactive nature of violent episodes. The John Hall, Philip Schuyler, and Sylvaine Trinh model detailed in *Apocalypse Observed: Religious Movements, the Social Order, and Violence in North America, Europe, and Japan* (2000) acknowledges internal factors but emphasizes external ones. John Walliss's model, developed in *Apocalyptic Trajectories: Millenarianism and Violence in the Contemporary World* (2005) considers the role of both endogenous and exogenous factors and their interrelationship. David Bromley's model, outlined in *Cults, Religion, and Violence* (2002), incorporates both internal and external factors while emphasizing an interactive process of conflict escalation.

Hall, Schuyler, and Trinh base their analysis on the Peoples Temple, Branch Davidian, Aum Shinrikyo, Solar Temple, and Heaven's Gate cases. They identify a number of movement characteristics that may create a proclivity toward violence—an apocalyptic worldview, charismatic leadership, a high level of internal control, and high internal solidarity/high isolation from conventional society. However, it is not these characteristics in themselves that result in conflict but rather the movement-society interaction. According to Hall, Schuyler, and Trinh, conflict is likely to move in one of two directions. A "warring apocalypse of religious conflict" describes a situation in which conflict escalates between a movement and a coalition of movement opponents, governmental agencies, and media representatives. The second type, a "mystical apocalypse of deathly transcendence," involves flight from external opposition. The group elects collective suicide and from its perspective moves to another realm of existence. The Hall, Schuyler, and Trinh model thus emphasizes movement-societal conflict in which movements respond to external opposition.

John Walliss considers six cases: Peoples Temple, Branch Davidians, Aum Shinrikyo, Solar Temple, Movement for the Restoration of the Ten Commandments of God, and Heaven's Gate. He pinpoints three primary sets of factors related to episodes of violence: the actions of cultural opponents, challenges to leadership authority or charismatic authority, and internal threats to movements' millennial goals. Cultural opponents were present in all but one case (Heaven's Gate), although they had different levels and types of impacts on conflict dynamics. Challenges to charismatic authority include loss of movement reputation, exposure of fraudulent claims by charismatic leaders, and deteriorating personal health of the charismatic leader, which throws the future of the movement into doubt. Internal challenges to millennial goals include dissent within and defection from the movement and failure of the movement to realize its goals. For each set of factors Walliss is careful to explore both the internal implications for the movement and the implications for movement-societal interaction.

In his analysis of the Peoples Temple, Branch Davidian, Aum Shinrikyo, Solar Temple, and Heaven's Gate episodes, Bromley argues that movement-society conflicts develop through three stages—latent tension, nascent conflict, and intensified conflict. Most conflicts do not reach an intensified level because all of the parties have the options of contestation, accommodation, or retreat. In most cases conflict is resolved at a lower level. At the intensified level, movements and opponents engage in heightened mobilization and radicalization, coalitions of allies and opponents form, and parties mutually begin to define one another as dangerous rather than merely troublesome. It is when conflict reaches the intensified stage that what Bromley terms dramatic denouements occur. *Dramatic denouements* are climactic moments when movements and/or society conclude that the requisite conditions for their existence are being subverted. The parties to the conflict polarize as they engage in threatening actions, symbolic degradation of opponents, and internal radicalization. The conflict relationship destabilizes as a result of secrecy of actions, elimination of mediating third parties, and organizational consolidation or fragmentation. With polarization and conflict destabilization, one or both parties embark on a project of final reckoning that is intended to reestablish appropriate moral order. The likeliest projects are either "exodus, "collective withdrawal from the realm in which the conflict is taking place," or "battle," in which the initiating party rejects the prospect of mutual existence and seeks to restore appropriate moral order through coercion. Each of these two responses is thus premised on a position of moral superiority and on a repudiation of continued mutual existence in the same social space. In the dramatic denouement model, episodes of violence are clearly interactional, and either movement or societal units may precipitate a dramatic denouement.

Toward Theoretical Convergence on Endogenous Factors

In exploring the role of millennialism, totalism, and charismatic leadership in the occurrence of episodes of violence, I am primarily concerned with distinguishing between factors that produce movement radicalization or volatility and those that are more closely related to the occurrence of violence (Melton and Bromley 2009). The latter appear to be considerably fewer in number but of central theoretical importance in understanding the outbreak of movement-societal violence.

Millennialism

Among NRM cultural characteristics, the most frequently cited is millennialism/apocalypticism (hereafter, millennialism). Millennial religious ideologies typically reinterpret and thematize human history as a progressive separation of humanity from original creative intent, denigrate the conventional social order as corrupted, idealize the religious group as a faithful remnant, and anticipate a transformative moment (or process) of final reckoning in which the existing social order will be swept away. Groups with millennial ideologies often assign themselves a privileged role in the transformation process. Different versions of millennial ideology are shared by many millions of Americans in mainstream Christian churches. Both the Seventh-Day Adventists and the Jehovah's Witnesses, for example, emerged out of the millennial Millerite movement during the nineteenth century. Given the pervasiveness of millennial doctrines in mainstream churches, it seems clear that millennial ideologies are not in themselves predictive of either radicalism or violence.

Since NRMs envision some type of world transformation, millennial expectations are rather commonplace. Because NRMs are religious protest movements, their ideologies rise to the level of sacred narratives with supernaturally authorized mandates. That is, movement protest is sacralized. Certain features of millennial ideologies potentially move a group toward a more radical posture. For example, Wessinger (2000) distinguishes between "progressive" millennialism and more radical "catastrophic" millennialism, with the former envisioning a more peaceful, gradual transformation and the latter an imminent, violent change. Millennial ideologies that intensify movement-societal polarization, which Robbins and Anthony refer to as "exemplary dualism," (1997) and profess a profound and pervasive disregard for societal norms, "antinomianism," detach the movement from the established social order. This kind of symbolic detachment is likely to radicalize standards of doctrinal purity. Further, once a movement has symbolically detached itself from the established social order, designating it as socially and morally irredeemable, a symbolic divide is created that heightens mutual misperception and mistrust between movement and host society. Since both movements and external groups base their actions on perceptions of the other's motives and actions, this symbolic divide is a significant factor in destabilizing movement-societal relationships. Millennial ideologies also shape members' motivation and expectations. To the extent that movement members are convinced that they are engaged in events with a predestined outcome and are supported by supernatural power, normal reinforcement schedule logic is reversed. Members are more disposed both to accept persecution and reversals of fortune and to confidently confront opponents with vastly greater earthly power.

Millennial ideologies do not merely produce a generically radical posture in NRMs but may also contain sacred mandates that are contentious and resist compromise, constitute self-sealing thought systems that may be relatively impervious to counterinterpretation, and articulate specific roles for movements during the millennial transformation. These elements of millennial ideology heighten the potential for violence. Movements may espouse unconventional beliefs and practices on many issues, but ideologies that permit or foster deviance in areas that are central both to a movement's sacred mandate and to a regulatory agency's central mandate are much more consequential. Coercion and sexuality are two such matters. Ideologies that legitimate the potential for using force, threats of force, or the actual use of force always pose a direct challenge to state authority and heighten state vigilance. Over the last several decades childrearing practices have become another highly charged political issue, particularly where punishment and sexuality are involved. Groups that have espoused corporal punishment or adult-minor sexual contact as an element of their religious mandate encounter a particularly volatile situation. It is no coincidence that force and sexuality have been central issues in NRM-state conflicts and played a significant role in all of the cases at hand.[4] The clash of core mandates may provoke a coercive response from either movement or control agency as either attempts to ensure the fulfillment of its mandate. In addition, millennial ideologies may serve not only as belief systems but also as self-sealing scripts. To the extent that NRMs move toward ideological depictions of the external environment that are hermetically sealed so that the ideology becomes the sole source of information about the external environment, a faux-interactional relationship is established that is self-reinforcing and not amenable to mitigation or correction. The movement essentially interacts with its own internally constructed image of the external world. Heaven's Gate appears to have approached this condition. Under these conditions radicalization within movements may spiral, and, in the limiting case, this may occur without significant external influence. Finally, movements may not only anticipate an apocalyptic moment but also prescribe a specific role for themselves in that script. It is relatively commonplace for movements to predict a calamitous ending to human history and to ascribe the avenging role to the gods, with the movement being a merely a spectator or beneficiary in these events. By contrast, movements that assign themselves the role of precipitating agent or combatant at least legitimate participating in violence and are also more likely to come into direct conflict with control agencies. Aum Shinrikyo and the Manson Family both sought to trigger major social conflagrations by undertaking campaigns of violence. The role of sacrificial victim is also available, of course, and may legitimate at least temporary capitulation.

Totalistic Organization

It is well established in the social science literature that conventional organizations use a variety of control systems and levels of control to regulate organizational conduct (Etzioni 1961). Organizations that are deemed high demand/radical/totalistic (hereafter, totalistic) are found throughout the social structure, and they vary in terms of the voluntarism of participants. Examples include therapy groups (London 1969), custodial mental hospitals (Goffman 1961), prisons (Etzioni 1961), military training academies (Dornbusch 1955), religious communities (Hillery 1969), and even corporations (Arnott 1999). Totalism in conventional organizations is legitimated when it presents itself as operating in the service of socially sanctioned objectives. Nonconventional organizations may also utilize totalistic organization, but they lack social legitimation and hence are likely to encounter greater resistance. One of the best documented cases is communes; an analysis of these groups reveals that the organizational characteristics of successful communes closely parallel the attributes of other types of totalistic organizations (Kanter 1972).[5]

New religious movements frequently exhibit a number of totalistic characteristics that increase their radicalization. During their formative years, when movement mobilization is most intensive, NRMs maintain high group boundaries that separate movement and external world. Boundary-maintenance mechanisms include geographical isolation, constant geographical mobility, meeting all individuals' needs internally and organizing individuals' activity within the group context, limiting and ritualizing contact with outsiders, and maintaining membership secrecy. Internal movement cohesiveness is increased by eliminating competing factions within the movement, eliminating relationships that mediate between individual and group (e.g., family), linking individual and group identity so that they move toward convergence, diminishing individual distinctiveness and prominence while enhancing the importance of the collective, and ritualizing daily life so that individuals are continuously embedded in sacralized group activity.

Movements also often create a multilayered set of groups internally, with a small, core decision-making group that consists of the most highly committed members at the center of movement. This is a particularly important factor as radicalization of a small, self-contained group is more easily accomplished. In the cases of Aum Shinrikyo and Solar Temple, for example, few grassroots members were aware of the plans for violence. Through these various mechanisms, movements can tightly link ideology and organization. The effect of such tight integration is to produce a movement organization that is completely dedicated to its ideological mission. There are two consequences of radical mobilization. The movement becomes more focused in pursuing its objectives, while the stakes in its success are simultaneously raised since the organization has a singular purpose. At the same time, the movement also presents a more threatening profile to the external world. Movements are much more likely to become capable of radical strategies and to be regarded as dangerous by external groups when they combine an ideology of rebellion, a protest organization dedicated to the furtherance of that ideology, and an organizational mandate that directly challenges the established social order.

These characteristics yield a more radical form of organization, but several other characteristics—acquisition of weapons, committed apostates, mandates that increase the movement's vulnerability, and impending failure of its mission—are more likely to move an NRM toward violence. The acquisition of means of violence is not an insignificant development in creating a basis for future violence. Movements that later became involved in episodes of violence at some point obtained weapons or other lethal products that could be used as means of either escape or attack. The Solar Temple, Peoples Temple, and Aum Shinrikyo all acquired means of violence that enabled the campaigns they subsequently undertook, and the Branch Davidians possessed the weaponry that enabled their resistance when raided by federal agents. While the possession of such means of violence did not guarantee violence, it did facilitate violent conduct when such a course had been legitimated.

The emergence of organized, committed apostates who threaten the movement's mission is another significant development (Bromley 1998). Such apostates infuriate their former movements by allying with movement enemies; frequently reveal movement secrets that render the movement more vulnerable to social control agencies; become a focus of media attention that can inflame public opinion against the movement; and play a major role in the legitimation strategy of opposition groups seeking to discredit targeted movements. It is not unusual for movements to feel compelled to lash out against those whom they regard as the worst type of traitors. The Solar Temple and Aum Shinrikyo both engaged in this type of campaign, placing themselves in direct confrontation with law enforcement agencies. When apostasy involves a significant number of movement members, it also results in more radical movement membership as the remaining members are likely to align more closely with movement leaders.

Another important characteristic is the method through which pursuit of the NRM's mandate is organized. Where the conduct of the movement's mission in itself increases the vulnerability of its sacred mandate, the probability of violence becomes substantially greater. For example, the Branch Davidian mandate to create the House of David by legitimating David Koresh's sexual relationships with girls who were legally minors left the group vulnerable to negligence and sexual abuse charges and Koresh himself to statutory rape charges. Finally, where the group's mandated mission is being subverted or failing, movements begin to consider violent responses. For example, members of Heaven's Gate undertook a concerted effort to make the outside world aware of the opportunity to save itself. The combination of unresponsiveness and ridicule led the group to conclude that further efforts to inform and assist others were futile and moved the group members in the direction of shedding their earthly vessels and undertaking a transit to the Next Level.

Charismatic Leadership

Theorists since Max Weber (1964) have repeatedly observed that charismatic leaders assert an independent claim to moral authority and do not operate within institutional constraints. As a result, charismatic authority has often been associated with movement instability and volatility, and there has been speculation that charismatic leadership may predispose groups to violence. However, numerous charismatic religious leaders of both established churches and religious movements—Billy Graham (Southern Baptist), Martin Luther King (Baptist), Oral Roberts (United Methodist), Jimmy Swaggart (Assemblies of God), Fulton Sheen (Roman Catholic)—regardless of whether they are respected and others reproved, have never been regarded as unstable or as harboring violent tendencies.

Charismatic leadership is pivotal in NRMs to the extent that a movement emanates from a revelatory/mystical experience by the leader and the leader's charismatic authority remains the primary internal power base. As Dawson (2002) points out, these leaders face a variety of internal management problems that can lead to leadership and movement volatility. These problems include maintaining the leader's image, moderating followers' identification with the leader, finding a mutually acceptable means of institutionalizing charisma, and creating new successes. Other management problems confront charismatic leaders because they usually function as the heads of movement organizations as well, and organizational success or failure can impact their charismatic standing. In that capacity, NRM leaders must maintain administrative control over developing movement organization, commitment of rank-and-file members, and loyalty of inner-circle confidants and organizational lieutenants. Further, charismatic founder-leaders of NRMs gain a following and build a movement by standing in opposition to the established social order while at the same time drawing upon and reworking elements of the established order in ways that violate existing understandings and practices. In this sense the charismatic leader creates a complex double threat to established social order. The inevitable result is some level of tension and instability associated with charismatic leadership in NRMs.

In maintaining charismatic and administrative control over their movements, NRM leaders may employ a variety of tactics that have the effect of radicalizing their movements. Among the commonly noted responses to leadership control problems are miracles or new revelations that buttress charismatic legitimacy and authority claims; withdrawal of the leader from contact with all but a handful of inner-circle followers to avoid erosion of charisma through overexposure; creation of crises of various kinds or imminent millennial/apocalyptic expectations to heighten movement solidarity; claims to higher charismatic status that require corresponding increases in followers' obligations; purges of potential competitors and intermediary relationships that eliminate alternative alliances and avenues for challenging leaders' authority; initiation of loyalty tests that demand greater sacrifice and displays of submission to leader authority; abrupt changes in members' status that leave followers dependent on leaders' favor for their personal stability, constantly shifting movement priorities so that goal achievement is more difficult to track and new challenges are created for members, and frequent geographic relocation to minimize lifestyle settling and maximize member deployability. All of these practices have the effect of radicalizing NRMs and increasing internal volatility. For example, enhanced charismatic status claims may require more dramatic demonstrations of charismatic power, withdrawal from contact with followers may produce isolation and loss of feedback, continual change within the movement may lead to membership defections, and purges can produce candidates for recruitment into the apostate role.

Because charismatic leaders are central to the development of movement ideology and organization, their authority is not independent of millennialism and totalism in its relationship to violence. Charismatic leaders often have already shaped an ideology and group organization that may be more or less predisposed to involvement in violence, even if this outcome is not anticipated at the time. The most significant factor predisposing charismatic leaders to violence is a sense of loss of control over personal and movement destiny. Through their lives charismatic leaders often come to personify NRMs, and their lives and movement existence may become inextricably intertwined. By their nature NRMs envision change at a cosmic level, and the charismatic leader is at the heart of this transformative process. Therefore, the perception that the movement's sacred mission is somehow being subverted or that the leader's life is ending, with the result that the movement will be unable to complete its sacred mandate, may lead to more dramatic actions designed to reassert movement control and bring about the moment of final reckoning. For example, the exposure of the Solar Temple's illegal weapons' purchases and fraudulent miracles left the movement's image and finances seriously damaged. In the cases of Peoples Temple, Heaven's Gate, and the Branch Davidians, both Jim Jones and Bo were experiencing significant deterioration of personal health, while David Koresh was suffering from a bullet wound incurred during the gun battle with federal agents.

Because leadership authority is highly centralized, charismatic leaders' authorization clearly increases the probability of group-level violence and may be essential for its occurrence. The cases at hand involve permission for violence by the charismatic leader. In the cases of Solar Temple, the Manson Family, and Aum Shinrikyo, leaders gave direct orders to initiate violence. A second way that leaders may promote violence is by guiding the violence-escalation process. Millennial movement ideology is initiated through charismatic vision and revelation. The process of violence escalation becomes more likely where the charismatic leader scripts the process through interaction with a supernatural source. This scenario was most dramatically on display during Jim Jones's White Night drills and the stand-off between the Branch Davidians and federal agents, during which David Koresh was in the process of opening the Seven Seals and attempting to determine whether this confrontation was the onset of the end-time.

Conclusions

Several theories have been formulated to explain the episodes of violence involving the Manson Family, Peoples Temple, Branch Davidians, Aum Shinrikyo, Solar Temple, Movement for the Restoration of the Ten Commandments of God, and Heaven's Gate. While there is, in fact, considerable agreement on factors related to radicalization and violence, theoretical advances require additional work on at least three important issues. First, comparison of cases of conflict that are resolved at lower levels and those that reach the stage of dramatic denouement will provide a broader perspective on conflict escalation and resolution processes. In most instances movement-societal disputation has been resolved without violence after one or both parties to the conflict made concessions that averted conflict escalation. Wright (2002) identifies 130 cases of government-religious movement confrontation of various types, only three of which resulted in some kind of violence. Comparative analysis may well offer additional insight into the most critical aspects of conflict dynamics (Shaw 2009). Second, most of the cases that have been the focus of analysis have occurred in economically developed, democratic societies. As a result, this set does not include instances in which external opposition has been more coordinated and aggressive, as it was, for example, in the Chinese government's response to the Falun Gong. Current theorizing may favor endogenous factors in explaining episodes of violence because external intervention has tended to be more restrained in developed, democratic societies. In a related vein, even in the cases at hand there has been a great deal more exploration of factors associated with movement radicalization than of those associated with control agency radicalization (Wright 2009). A third issue that invites further analysis, and the one that is the focus of this chapter, is identifying the endogenous factors in NRMs that are associated with the occurrence of episodes of violence and not simply movement radicalization. With that objective, various characteristics of millennialism, totalism, and charismatic authority have been examined.

New religious movements are religious protest movements and by virtue of this quality tend to exhibit millennial, totalistic, and charismatic characteristics. However, a number of qualities of millennialism, totalism, and charisma that have been identified are associated with radicalization of NRMs but not necessarily with violence. I argue that millennialism is most likely to be associated with movement-societal violence when movement ideologies permit or foster deviance on issues that are central both to movements' sacred mandates and to the mission of regulatory organizations, serve as self-sealing scripts that result in a faux-interactional relationship with the external social order, which can lead to a spiraling of movement hostility and is not amenable to correction or mitigation, and prescribe for the movement a precipitating agent or combatant role in moments of final reckoning. Totalistic organization and violence are most closely linked when the movement possesses a means of undertaking a strategy of violence; a group of organized, committed apostates emerges that threatens a movement's sacred mandate; the very conduct of the movement's mission increases the movement's vulnerability; and the group's mandated mission is perceived as being subverted internally or externally. Charismatic leadership is more closely associated with violence when charismatic leaders feel that they are losing control of the movement's destiny and either authorize or guide the use of force.

As religious protest movements NRMs inherently possess some radical attributes, and millennialism, totalism, and charisma often serve to heighten their radicalism. I have enumerated a number of endogenous factors related to millennialism, totalism, and charisma that I argue were more directly related to episodes of violence involving NRMs. These factors might be combined into two general sets: those that create specific kinds of radicalism within movements and those that create a sense of loss of control within movements. Movements that profess ideologies and promote strategies as sacred mandates that challenge the core mandates of established authority and render the movement more vulnerable in the process, eliminate feedback loops in their understandings of the external social order, and arrogate to themselves the power or authority to initiate a final reckoning have created a situation that may well become increasingly resistant to compromise or accommodation strategies. When this type and level of radicalism is combined with a sense—authorized or guided by the leader—that the movement and its leader are losing control over their ability to complete their sacred mandate, an urgent impulse to bring on the moment of final reckoning may ensue. This combination of factors produces a situation in which movements are predisposed, on the one hand, to undertake a final reckoning and, on the other hand, to feel a sense of urgency and necessity for that moment. Staging a dramatic denouement is a means of rescuing and reasserting a movement's mission, making a powerful public statement, and closing a chapter but not the entire narrative. Because violence is an interactive process, no complete theory of episodes of violence can be fashioned from endogenous factors alone; however, this set of endogenous factors is pivotal to an understanding of internal movement dynamics that are conducive to dramatic denouements.

NOTES

1. By collective violence I refer to acts committed by individuals in the name of some religious movement or the acts committed against religious individuals or movements by agents of social control and legitimated by some organizational purpose. Collective violence may be internally or externally directed, and, in either event, it may or may not reflect group consensus. In the present context, multiple deaths are involved.

2. By radicalization I simply mean the transformation of a group in the direction of developing and promoting cultural and social ideologies and organizational practices that have as their objective creating extreme change in the existing in the social order.

3. There is some debate over which cases to include in analyses of collective religious violence. The Manson Family is sometimes mentioned, but there is disagreement about the extent to which the group, its ideology, and its actions should be categorized as religious. A primary problem with the Movement for the Restoration of the Ten Commandments of God is that very little scholarly analysis is available about the movement. In the Heaven's Gate case, while multiple deaths were involved, the participants did not interpret their own behavior as violent. One could argue that episodes where violence was intended would constitute a more theoretically relevant category.

4. These practices might include polygamy, marriage of underage children, corporal punishment, sexual relationships with children, and sexual abuse of women.

5. Kanter describes three major sets of dimensions—sacrifice/investment, renunciation/communion, mortification/transcendence—through which the community's significance is heightened and the individual's significance is diminished.

REFERENCES

Anthony, Dick, and Thomas Robbins. 1997. "Religious Totalism, Exemplary Dualism, and the Waco Tragedy." In *Millennium, Messiahs, and Mayhem*, ed. Thomas Robbins and Susan Palmer, 261–84. New York: Routledge.

Arnott, Dave. 1999. Corporate Cults: The Insidious Lure of the *All-consuming Organization*. New York: American Management Association.

Bromley, David G. 1997. "Constructing Apocalypticism: Social and Cultural Elements of Radical Organization." In *Millennium, Messiah, and Mayhem*, ed. Thomas Robbins and Susan Palmer, 31–46. New York: Routledge.

———, ed. 1998. *The Politics of Religious Apostasy: The Role of Apostates in the Transformation of Religious Movements*. Westport, Conn.: Praeger.

———2002. "Dramatic Denouements." In *Cults, Religion, and Violence*, ed. David G. Bromley and J. Gordon Melton, 11–41. New York: Cambridge University Press.

Dawson, Lorne. 2002. "Crises of Charismatic Legitimacy and Violent Behavior in New Religious Movements." In *Cults, Religion, and Violence*, ed. David G. Bromley and J. Gordon Melton, 80–101. New York: Cambridge University Press.

———. 2006. *Comprehending Cults*. New York: Oxford University Press.

———. 2010. "The Study of New Religious Movements and the Radicalization of Home-grown Terrorists: Opening a Dialogue." *Terrorism and Political Violence* 21: 1–21.

Dornbusch, Sanford. 1955. "The Military Academy as an Assimilating Institution." Social Forces 33: 316–21.

Emerson, Robert. 1981. "On Last Resorts." American Journal of Sociology. 87: 1–22.

———, and Sheldon Messinger. 1977. "The Micro-politics of Trouble." *Social Problems* 25: 121–34.

Etzioni, Amitai. 1961. *A Comparative Analysis of Complex Organizations: On Power, Involvement, and Their Correlates*. New York: Free Press of Glencoe.

Galanter, Marc. 1999. *Cults: Faith, Healing, and Coercion*. New York. Oxford University Press.

Goffman, Erving. 1961. *Asylums*. Garden City, N.J.: Doubleday.

Hall, John R., with Philip Schuyler and Sylvaine Trinh. 2000. *Apocalypse Observed: Religious Movements, the Social Order, and Violence in North America, Europe, and Japan*. New York: Routledge.

Hillery, George. 1969. "The Convent: Community, Prison, or Task Force?" Journal for the Scientific Study of Religion 8: 140–51.

Iadicola, Peter, and Anson Shupe. 2003. *Violence, Inequality, and Human Freedom*. Lanham, Md.: Rowman and Littlefield.

Kanter, Rosabeth. 1972. "Commitment and the Internal Organization of Millennial Movements." *American Behavioral Scientist* 16: 219–44.

London, Perry. 1969. *Behavior Control*. New York: Harper and Row.

Melton, J. Gordon, and David G. Bromley. 2009. "Violence and New Religions: An Assessment of Problems, Progress, and Prospects in Understanding the NRM-Violence Connection." *Dying for Faith: Religiously Motivated Violence in the Contemporary World*, ed. Madawi Al-Rasheed and Marat Sheterin, 27–42. London: Tauris.

Robbins, Thomas. 2002. "Sources of Volatility in Religious Movements." In *Cults, Religion, and Violence*, ed. David G. Bromley and J. Gordon Melton, 57–77. New York: Cambridge University Press.

———, and Dick Anthony. 1997. "Sects and Violence: Factors Enhancing the Volatility of Marginal Religious Movements." In *Armageddon at Waco: Critical Perspectives on the Branch Davidian Conflict*, ed. Stuart Wright, 236–59. Chicago: University of Chicago Press.

Sarbin, Theodore. 1967. "The Dangerous Individual: An Outcome of Social Identity Transformation." *British Journal of Criminology* 7: 285–95.

Shaw, Brent. 2009. "State Intervention and Holy Violence: Timgad/Paleostrovsk/Waco." *Journal of the American Academy of Religion* 77: 853–94.
Walliss, John. 2005. Apocalyptic Trajectories: *Millenarianism and Violence in the Contemporary World*. New York: Lang.
Weber, Max. 1964. *The Theory of Social and Economic Organization*, trans. A. M. Henderson and Talcott Parsons. New York: Free Press.
Wessinger, Catherine. 2000 *How the Millennium Comes Violently*. Chappaqua, N.Y.: Seven Bridges.
Wright, Stuart. 2002. "Public Agency Involvement in Government–religious Movement Confrontations." *Cults, Religion, and Violence*, ed. David G. Bromley and J. Gordon Melton, 102–22. New York: Cambridge University Press.
———. 2009. "Martyrs and Martial Imagery: Exploring the Volatile Link between Warfare Frames and Religious Violence." *Dying for Faith: Religiously Motivated Violence in the Contemporary World*, ed. Madawi Al-Rasheed and Marat Sheterin, 17–26. London: Tauris.

2

Minority Religions and the Context of Violence: A Conflict/Interactionist Perspective

James T. Richardson

Introduction

The relationship between religion and violence has been of considerable historical interest, with particular concern developing since the tragic events of Jonestown in 1978 in which over 900 people lost their lives. Since the Jonestown episode there have also been a number of other much-publicized occurrences of violence associated with newer religious groups, including the Waco tragedy, the mass suicides of 39 members of the Heaven's Gate group in San Diego, the Aum Shinrikyo murdering of critics and gassing of the Tokyo subway, the mysterious murder/suicides of the Solar Temple group in Europe and Canada, and the recent tragic deaths of nearly 1,000 people in the Ten Commandments group in Uganda. These tragedies have ignited interest in the issue of how religion and violence relate within the context of the growing concern over the proliferation of new religious groups, sometimes called "cults."[1] Also, there has been growing concern about potential religiously motivated violence associated with the advent of the millennium.[2]

A number of journalistic treatments of new religions have suggested that violence of various kinds is fostered by new religious groups in general, and some have used this notion and other allegations to define participation in new and other minority religions as a serious social problem. These journalistic treatments have contributed to a public mindset that associates violence and newer faiths.[3] Unfortunately, systematic attempts at comparing levels of violence in religious groups with that in other groups in American society have not been forthcoming, although the recent spate of books on the millennium have contributed to this effort because they sometimes include political movements.[4] The generally high level of "background violence" in American society[5] is usually ignored by detractors of controversial religions, as are studies indicating possible benefits or therapeutic effects of membership in such groups.[6]

Reports of widespread violence associated with contemporary religious groups (including millenarian ones), if true, would seem to warrant a program of systematic research and various official protective actions, while attempting to educate the public on the potential dangers of membership in such groups. Conversely, sound evidence generally indicating a low frequency of violence associated with minority religions could, if known and accepted, assuage current concerns about the safety of individuals who join these groups, as well as about the dangers to society of alleged violent practices by new religions.[7]

The Cultural and Interactional Context of Violence

The violence which surrounds some new religions appears to be related to a very basic conflict in values and vested interests between such new groups and conventional society.[8] Applying a *conflict perspective* reveals that the new religions and certain established segments of society are competing with one another for members, legitimacy and public acceptance, various sources of funding, and even political support.[9] New religions and more established groups are rivals competing for certain scarce resources (including members), and it is within this competitive context that violence, the potential for violence, and the labeling of certain behaviors as violent has occurred.

Work by Sandra Ball-Rokeach is relevant to understanding violence by, within, and against new religions. According to Ball-Rokeach, "Violence is a struggle to maintain, change, or protest asymmetrical social relations governing the distribution of scarce resources by the threat or the exertion of threat."[10] This emphasis upon the instrumentality and goal orientedness of violence helps us understand how normal, functioning social systems may contribute to and even cause violent behavior. We are directed toward assessing how violence is incorporated, maintained, and perpetuated in everyday systems of social action due to the asymmetry of particular social relations governing the distribution of scarce resources (including, of course, participants).

Ralf Darendorf has similarly contended that conflict results when different individuals and groups in society are locked into continuous competition for the power to dominate and impose their definitions of reality upon one another.[11] Darendorf suggests that this type of conflict may be conducive of violent behavior. His theorizing can explain, in part, the present situation of how new religions relate to other groups in society.

Still, there is another factor which we should consider in our discussion of the context of violence surrounding some of the new religions. Both new religions and anti-cult groups tend to label the beliefs and practices of the others as bizarre, unjust, and in some cases violent, and develop "accounts" of the behaviors of opponent groups that sometimes make use of violence.[12]

This general tendency seems to be a **political strategy** designed to delegitimate the methods and goals of the other, and ultimately even to destroy the opponent group. Whether one group or another's actions are labeled violent often seems to depend upon the values and sympathies of the observer. Thus, it should be apparent how organizations can employ labels, the making of claims, and attributions as **social weapons** to control, discredit, and minimize the influence of their adversaries.[13] Such theorizing has direct application to the area of new religions.[14]

Because of the competitive elements just described, a **context of violence** has engulfed some newer religious groups. This situation would suggest a truly perplexing problem in contemporary society: Does any group attempting to offer an alternative to the status quo for its members run the risk of being engulfed in a context of violence or labeled violent, thus invoking potentially violent efforts at social control?[15]

Previous discussions of violence of so-called "cults" have, for the most part, focused on presumed characteristics of cult members or the cults themselves to explicate violent practices. This **characterological approach** presumes some kind of autonomous psychopathic entity or entities promoting and using violence (i.e., violence erupting from violent persons or violent groups), and subsequently ignores the interdependencies of social action at either the individual or group level, or the extent to which each person's or group's response is shaped by and dependent upon, in large part, the response of the other.[16]

It is true that violence can flow from group beliefs, as scholars such as David Rapoport and Catherine Wessinger suggest.[17] Wessinger's typology of types of millennial groups involved in violence contains the category of "revolutionary millennial movements" possessing inherently revolutionary ideas that can motivate people to commit violence. This seems quite similar to Rapoport's description of religious believers who want an apocalypse so that the world can be redeemed. Also, however, Wessinger's other two types ("assaulted" and "fragile" millennial groups) invoke external factors as being crucial to outbreaks of violence. Others have also focused on the idea of **violence as reaction to external threats**.[18] Thus, it seems fruitful to focus attention on understanding the **interdependencies** of violent behavior and its social context.

Obviously, if a group's beliefs justify violence, then it is more prone to occur if external entities also expect violence and act on its inevitability. Thus an interactional spiral toward violence can develop as the two entities interact with each other either directly (such as through face-to-face negotiations) or indirectly (through media coverage or intermediaries such as covert informants or others). Thus the interactionist perspective is akin to Roy Wallis' provocative concept of the

amplification of deviance developed out of his study of Scientology.[19] What can develop through interactions based on shared views of the other's propensity for violence is an **amplification of violent expectations**, which in turn can lead to violence itself.[20]

Paul Secord and Carl Backman have argued that aggression be considered dependent upon the relation between individuals (or groups) and the location of that relationship within the larger social structure.[21] This same **relational or interactional perspective** can fruitfully be used to study violence. Thus, **violence can be viewed as a property of the interactional relationship between two or more persons or groups, and not just as a property of a person or group**. Secondly, **violence may be embedded in the interaction between religious groups and their opponents, and should not be viewed only as something necessarily inherent in the structure and organization of either**. The actual exercise of violence involves an **exchange** of sorts, and often depends on the **mutual dependency** of each social actor (group or individual) in relation to the other. Thus the **violence of some religions and their detractors** may be usefully considered not just as deriving from the violence of the social context, but also and importantly as a product of the interdependencies which they share. Those interdependencies may involve training and expectations for violence **on both sides.**[22]

The purpose of the present paper is to examine more frequent accusations of violence involving religious groups, particularly so-called "new" ones, and to assess the relational or interactional nature of actual instances of violence and allegations of violence. Two ways in which violence has been thought of in relation to new and other minority religions are considered herein: (1) an examination of whether or not some religions, through their actions and beliefs, deliberately or inadvertently foster violence among and toward members and others; and (2) the nature of violence which has been directed against particular members of religions and/or religious groups by outsiders.[23]

The definition of violence used herein is deliberately broad, incorporating **individual** acts of physical violence against others and against oneself (including suicide) done by opponents of religious groups, as well as by the groups themselves. The conceptualization also includes the notion of violence at a **collective level** by organizational entities, both private and governmental, which might be directed against individual members of religious groups or against the groups themselves. The possibility of collective level violence **by** religious organizations against opponents will also be considered, in light of events such as the Aum Shinrikyo gas attacks in the Tokyo subway.[24]

I. Violence Fostered by New Religions

There have been innumerable accusations that some of the new religions foster violence, either directly or inadvertently. Some new religious groups have been accused of treating members in violent ways, of teaching violence to their members, or at least sanctioning violence by members against themselves, other members, and non-members. Obviously, the most well-known modern case of such accusations is the tragic case of the Peoples Temple at Jonestown in 1978, which will be examined herein. While this group was not one of what is usually defined by scholars as a typical new religious movement,[25] most journalistic commentators and others viewed the People's Temple as "just another cult," and the Anti-Cult Movement was quick to use what happened at Jonestown as support for its own goals and purposes of social control of new religions.[26]

There have been other situations involving planning for violence or actual physical violence perpetrated on and by members of other groups. Since Jonestown we have seen the tragedy of Waco,[27] the collective suicides of the Heaven's Gate group,[28] the Aum Shinrikyo mass gassing in Tokyo and other acts of violence,[29] and the Solar Temple suicide/murder episodes in Switzerland and Canada,[30] and the Ugandan tragedy.[31] All these have been major media events that have structured public opinion about minority religious groups. And the tragic developments have raised important questions about how and why violence sometimes occur with newer religious groups.[32]

Other less publicized claims of violence or potential violence among newer religions include some members of The Way International being required to become expert marksmen, and allegedly stockpiling weapons.[33] Shortly after the Jonestown episode, members of the Unification Church were accused of teaching suicide training to new members so that they could avoid deprogramming by cutting their wrists if necessary.[34] The Alamo Foundation was accused at one time of beating opponents and of contributing to some deaths.[35]

Ananda Marga, a group centered mainly in Europe, has had several members commit suicide by self-immolation as a protest against the imprisonment of their leader in India. This group also has been accused of fostering violence by training members in para-military techniques and of stabbing an Indian diplomat in London.[36] They were accused, as well, of a bombing that caused two deaths in Sydney, and three members served five years in prison before they were finally freed for lack of credible evidence.[37]

Segments of the International Society for Krishna Consciousness (ISKCON) have been accused of building up stores of weapons, and there have also been accusations of culpability in two murders and other violence.[38] Members of the Divine Light Mission have been accused of physically assaulting a critic of the group, and the Children of God experienced several mysterious deaths early in its history of members (including a leader's son).[39]

Synanon, which claims to be a religion, was in the news with murder attempts against some of its critics.[40] Scientology has been accused of sanctioning law breaking of various kinds by some members, and some of its ranking officials have served prison terms for breaking into government offices.[41] The Church Universal and Triumphant (CUT) was accused of stock-piling weapons, attracting considerable attention some years ago.[42]

Several of the groups, including the Children of God and Hare Krishna, have been criticized for negligence and abuse of children of members. Burke Rochford presented a report of Krishna children who had experienced abuse while in Krishna schools, which was published in an official Krishna journal, implying that ISKCON was accepting the validity of such claims.[43] Accusations of child abuse have led to mass removals of children from several of the newer communal groups, including the Children of God (now called The Family) in Australia, Argentine, France, and Spain, as well as the Island Pond group in Vermont.[44] These accusations concerning children have carried with them the implication that techniques of child-rearing used in some groups were doing permanent damage to children, or that other more deliberate harmful actions were being taken with the children in some new religions.[45] Such accusations about harm to children also influence public perceptions, and contribute to efforts to exert social control over new religions.[46]

Many more such accusations of violence within newer religions could be listed, but these will suffice to make the point that accusations of violence are prevalent in journalists' accounts (and hence public perceptions) of these controversial religions. What is common to most of these allegations of violence by new religions is their **noninteractionist character**. Violence is generally considered a **trait of the group or group member, resulting from the acting out of group beliefs and values against group members (including sometimes children) and outsiders.** The violence is usually viewed as a **characteristic of group culture** which threatens their own members as well as citizens of outside society.

Journalistic reports of "cult violence" are generally **contextless accounts** about people who seemingly cannot function in ordinary society, but who have become a danger to society because of their involvement with a "cult." These accusational narratives usually can be considered "atrocity tales" or "negative summary events" used by those who are opposed to the groups and want to see them controlled or stamped out entirely.[47]

Yet, even in spite of the limited perspective of such accounts, as indicated above, it is not reasonable to dismiss all such accusations. History reminds us that many different religious groups have at one time or another sanctioned violence, including such tragic events in the history of Christianity as the Crusades, the Inquisition, and the burning of tens of thousands of people accused of being witches. Also, Rapoport's discussion of Thugs, Assassins, and Zealots-Sicarli reminds us that religiously based violence has occurred historically in other religious traditions, including Islam, Hinduism, and Judaism.[48] Recent events involving the Aum Shinrikyo, the Solar Temple, Heaven's Gate, the Branch Davidians in Waco, and the Ten Commandments group in Uganda demonstrate this, as well. Also recall historical examples such as the Mormon's "Mountain Meadows Massacre" that occurred in the late 1850s,[49] and more recently the relentless war between groups of Catholics and Protestants in Ireland.

Responding to Cultural Expectations of Violence

Based on work by social scientists and writers who have done participant observation studies and had considerable contact with some of the groups in question, incidences of violence within most new religious groups seem minimal, the aforementioned several recent sensational events notwithstanding.[50] There are hundreds, perhaps thousands, of newer religious groups, but the vast majority do not teach or practice violence, even if they accept millennial beliefs.

This general finding suggests that many new groups expend effort in **overcoming** cultural expectations for using violence to solve problems. the values of most such groups appear to countermand the "violence expectation" of American culture, and most groups apparently teach and practice nonviolence. An examination of the doctrines and teachings of major groups yields some evidence for this more peaceful approach being adopted. The Jesus Movement groups, for example, tend to emphasize the "turn-the-other-cheek" philosophy, and stress the idea of Jesus as a peacemaker,[51] and many Eastern-oriented groups de-emphasize violence with explicit teachings that refute violence as a way to solve problems.[52]

Exacerbation of Violent Tendencies

Even if we accept that violence is minimal within most newer religious groups, obviously some violence still occurs. Furthermore, the tendency toward violence can be exacerbated in certain situations, as a number of scholars have shown.[53] One such situation would be when direct conflict exists between these new groups and the more established groups in society over the allocation of scarce resources, including members or participants.[54] Another situation conducive of violence would occur when members and leaders **perceive** the presence of a direct attack on the group and its members, as occurred with the Branch Davidians and as was assumed by the residents of Jonestown.

Sometimes a particular group may develop explicit teachings and practices to justify the use of violence—a "theology of violence," or a revolutionary ideology that motivates believers to violence.[55] Or perhaps a "true believer" syndrome develops in a group to such an extent that violence seems implicitly if not explicitly justified against those with whom the group disagrees.[56] Such attitudes may develop or be given impetus in relation to the response(s) of others, and do not usually develop in a social vacuum.

A prototypical case to illustrate how violence might occur in relation to other groups in society is the Peoples Temple mass murder and suicide. Scholars such as John Hall have attached great historical and cultural prominence to this case, suggesting that this mass murder/suicide has influenced law enforcement reactions to religious groups ever since.[57] Thus this case will be examined in more detail. To close this next section other prominent instances of violence involving newer religious groups will be briefly discussed.

Peoples Temple

Peoples Temple is a clear example of violence by a religious group, both directed outward (killing Congressman Ryan and others) and inward (e.g., mysterious deaths of some defectors, violent internal social control of members, plus the mass murder/suicides of over 900 people in Guyana).[58] These shocking events demand an explanation beyond journalistic and academic treatments that often assume a completely psychological perspective.[59]

Peoples Temple was, in the words of Rebecca Moore, a scholar who had two sisters and a nephew die at Jonestown, "as American as Cherry Pie."[60] Peoples Temple developed within American culture, and as such is was potentially violent,[61] even if it developed as a reaction against the racism of American culture. Peoples Temple developed an absolutist theology in reaction to the overwhelming forces of racism and inequality it perceived. Many "true believers" consequently evolved within the group, especially among the leadership. An "if you are not for me, you are against me" mentality prevailed, especially among Jim Jones and his small circle of leaders in the later California setting.[62] An "all or nothing" ideology characterized the organization, as sometimes happens with groups attempting to challenge the dominant social order.[63]

Jones' teachings involved considerable attention to action in general, and to violence in particular. His "theology of suicide," which apparently derived from Black Panther leader Huey Newton's idea of "revolutionary suicide," was especially crucial.[64] The ritual practice of partaking of supposed poison that Jones required of his followers furnished a link between belief in their ultimate cause and actual behavior. As Wessinger notes, these rituals forged strong bonds among group members, as they contemplated ways to defend their "ultimate concern" of maintaining the community in the face of persecution, both real and fabricated.[65]

Interestingly, both People's Temple and the Black Panthers developed within the context of New Left politics, and were influenced by the work of Franz Fanon.[66] Fanon essentially argued that the only way to mobilize the oppressed masses against their oppressor was to directly link belief, behavior, and identity. Fanon, the French-educated psychiatrist, believed the only way for the Algerians to be freed of the French was to cast off the mental as well as the economic chains that bound them. By fighting the French and even dying for the cause of liberation, the oppressed Algerian could both liberate his or her countrymen and at the same time establish a positive sense of self respect. According to Fanon, to counter the "slave mentality" the Algerians needed to employ violence, and it was this "purifying act" which gave life, even if short-lived, a new meaning and the spirit of freedom and liberation.

Wessinger treats Peoples Temple as an example of a "fragile" millennial group.[67] When such groups are attacked (or perceived to be attacked), and if they are suffering severe internal problems (as was Peoples Temple, especially after the hasty move to Guyana), this may lead directly to violent reactions, as happened with Peoples Temple. Moore documents the many efforts to destroy or at least limit the activities of Peoples Temple, including especially many official governmental programs by various agencies of the federal government.[68]

Whatever the value of such apparently violent ideologies to mobilize oppressed peoples, which was Fanon's aim, or the therapeutic value of such discourse to the oppressed, we must appreciate the contextual nature of such ideologies when such ideas are found within the subcultural world of a religious group. Such situations can arise when particular individuals and groups who are caught up in a subservient relationship with the dominant society develop a keen sense of their worsening situation amidst rising hopes and expectations, or when such individuals experience a growing difference between what they perceive they have a right to and what they will probably get.[69] We should also recognize that the way Jones led his people to believe they were doing a glorious thing for their cause, and that they should be willing to sacrifice themselves at any expense indicates that the tragedy might be thought of as a mass form of what Emile Durkheim called "altruistic suicide."[70] Their actions were a way to make a very loud point on behalf of their ultimate concerns to a nonaccepting, hostile and oppressive society. Mary Maaga says the choice for members was one of loyalty to the group (through joining in the collective suicide) or betrayal of the group, which would mean physical survival, and the choice was made for loyalty.[71]

Besides the perceived oppressed/oppressor relationship that existed between Peoples Temple and the dominant culture, there is no doubt that Jones felt he was under direct attack. Child services authorities were trying to obtain custody of a young boy Jones thought was his son, and media attacks had increased, organized in considerable part through efforts of the Concerned Relatives group.[72] Jones may not have accepted completely the ideas he espoused about the groups and individuals supposedly attacking him and Jonestown, but he certainly promoted this paranoid interpretation among his followers. This was particularly the case after he arrived in Guyana, following persistent legal efforts to take custody of the young boy he thought of as his son, as well as widespread negative media coverage.

The presence of perceived external threat tended to isolate Jones, and probably made him feel increasingly under attack. Certainly there was a battle between Jonestown and the dominant American society over individual members. Jones did not like people to defect, and he apparently made life miserable for those who tried. Some who left indicated real fear for their safety, and there were a number of unexplained deaths among ex-members. One such case that contributed to Congressman Ryan's decision to go to Guyana involved the son of a friend of Leo Ryan who was found dead in a railroad yard the day after saying that he wanted to leave the group.[73]

Jones' battle with society was also one for control of approximately fifty foster children who had been made a part of the group. Jones rapidly and illegally removed nearly all such children to Guyana, where they were killed in the mass murder/suicide.[74] The same tragic fate befell a large number of elderly that Jones had influenced to become members. People's Temple was receiving regular checks from governmental agencies for support of the foster children and the elderly, and thus the people represented, among other considerations, economic resources that Jones fought for and defended, until the fateful decision to commit mass murder and suicide.[75]

However, Jones' battle with the forces of the dominant society was more than just a fight over members. The conflict involved a fight for power and credibility on Jones' part. He had managed to achieve a position of some political power in the San Francisco area, but when the negative media coverage started all that he had gained was jeopardized. He fought back by removing his members to Guyana, where he was able to isolate and encapsulate them, thereby solidifying his authority over the group.[76]

Thus, with People's Temple we saw a downward spiral toward violence, with the "ideology of oppression" taught by Jones to a mostly Black membership (many of which had experiential reasons for accepting the message) and his views about "revolutionary suicide" both being reinforced by Jones' views of the actions of others which Jones promoted to his followers. The interaction of Jones' ideas and beliefs with perceptions of the external activities of others led directly to the **amplification of violence** that occurred.

What About Other Instances of Violence?

A conflict/interactionist and contextual analysis of violence also can be applied to other religious groups involved in violence. This statement should **not** be viewed, however, as a prediction that such violence will occur frequently. Indeed, there seems little possibility that many similar events will develop within most of the hundreds (some would say thousands) of new religious groups known at present, the episodes involving Solar Temple, Aum Shinrikyo, Heaven's Gate, the Branch Davidians, and the Ugandan Ten Commandments groups notwithstanding. There is an open question about the possible effects of the coming of the millennium on the occurrence of violence, which has special meaning for some religious groups.[77]

All the instances of violence that have occurred in the time since Jonestown have differed considerably, and all are complex episodes not amenable to simple explanations. The Waco tragedy certainly demonstrates the importance of a conflict/interactionist approach, which highlights the on-going relationship between law enforcement groups and the Davidians. Most scholars seem to think that violence could have been averted if law enforcement officials in charge had used different tactics.[78] This view is widely held in spite of the fact that the Davidians were a millennial group with some strongly held "end-time" beliefs. Those end-time beliefs were reinforced by law enforcement actions assaulting the Davidians which helped convince them that the predicted end was near, contributing to the spiral of violence that occurred.

The conflict/interactionist perspective can also be applied to other violent episodes, such as with the Aum Shinrikyo in Japan and the Solar Temple episodes in Switzerland and Canada. Although there was some basis for the perception of external attacks against these groups, they were not overtly assaulted as were the Davidians. This leads to the conclusion that internal factors, including beliefs and ideology, but also such matters as the mental and physical health of the leader, may have played a large role.[79]

Both Jean-Francois Mayer and Catherine Wessinger have suggested that such is the case with the Solar Temple, which, while experiencing some attacks from outside, was suffering severe internal difficulties.[80] Massimo Introvigne writes of the interaction of external and internal factors, claiming that both were important, and that the persecution felt by the Solar Temple had a real basis in fact.[81] Introvigne says that the development of apocalyptic beliefs in the Solar Temple contributed directly to the development of external opposition, led by Swiss and French anti-cultists, and that this opposition interacted with the internal dissension in the group and with the health problems being experienced by Solar temple leader Joseph DiMambro. Introvigne says, "(W)hen internal factors are sufficiently strong, even moderate external opposition is easily translated into a narrative of cosmic persecution."[82] By His reference to internal factors being strong, Introvigne seems to be referring to what Wessinger would call "fragileness," which makes a group vulnerable to violence under certain conditions.[83]

Some external individuals and groups were mounting attacks on Aum Shinrikyo as well, but Japanese authorities have actually been criticized for **not** taking action against the group in the face of evidence that Aum Shinrikyo leaders were possibly involved in violence against outsiders and some members.[84] So, external factors alone can not explain the tragic tale of Aum Shinrikyo, as several scholars note (the lack of apparent concern by law enforcement was, of course, an external factor facilitative of other violence). It is obvious that Aum leader Asahara developing such beliefs, oddly enough provoked in considerable part by his reading of the apocalyptic prophecies from the Book of John in the Bible,[85] was derivative of a growing sense of failure on his part to save the world (his prophecy that 30,000 devotees could result in the world being saved was not even close to being met). His sense of failure, coupled with growing external opposition and internal dissension over the cover up of the first death of a member, contributed to the spiral of conflict that developed.

The case of Heaven's Gate seems most anomalous, and appears at first glance to refute the conflict/interactionist thesis. Balch focuses on internal factors in his analysis of the group's odd set of beliefs and their culture.[86] Certainly the internal factor of the death of Applewhite's long-term partner, Bonnie Nettles, to cancer in 1985 played a role in altering views about how to achieve the "next level" of existence, as did the often disproved predictions that a space ship would pick up the "fragile" group. Also, Applewhite's health was failing, giving impetus to his taking some major action while he was still alive and in control of the group. One important factor of note was the appearance of the Hale-Bopp comet, which Applewhite interpreted as being the way to achieve higher state for himself and the members (Applewhite apparently thought that a space ship containing his long-departed partner was hiding behind the comet). Thus it seems that the beliefs and certain internal developments may have been paramount in explaining the mass suicide of 38 people, but Robert Balch, who has studied the group for over two decades, admits that he does not know what prompted the tragic event.[87]

Winston Davis builds a case that Applewhite had managed to develop an internal dynamic of total obedience to Applewhite, a situation that allowed him to work his will with the members when he decided to achieve the "higher level" through the "transit" of collective suicide.[88] Davis stresses the public ridicule that was heaped upon Applewhite and the group as being a major catalyst, which does offer support for the conflict/interactionist view espoused herein.[89] This interpretation meshes well with the view of Wessinger who refers to the Heavens' Gate group as a "fragile millennial group" subject to violence as they sought to achieve their "ultimate concern," that being "to enter the Kingdom of Heaven."[90]

The controversy in Oregon some years ago concerning the Rajneesh group also presented a possible illustration of the conflict/interactionist hypothesis. Massive efforts by the state and federal governments, sanctioned by the courts, to force the group out of the state contributed to a strong reaction that involved direct attacks on people.[91] The attacks by a few followers of Rajneesh, which involved mostly the poisoning hundreds of people with salmonella (apparently none died), might have occurred anyway, but perhaps not without the concerted and successful efforts of authorities to exert strong social control over the group, which had taken over a small town in Oregon, upsetting many in the area. Lewis Carter gives considerable detail about interactions between authorities and the Rajneesh group, and the spiral into violence by the group, in a chapter entitled, "Desperation Defenses of Rajneeshpuram."[92] James Richardson discusses the open coordination of federal and state authorities in the judicial and legal systems, as well as other actions taken to exert control over the Rajneesh group once it had settled in Oregon and started exerting its own power in the local region.[93]

The continuing controversy over the Church Universal and Triumphant development of a rural community close to Yellowstone Park is another test of the conflict/interactionist hypothesis.[94] Violence might have developed in this situation, which has involved considerable friction between the group and the outside community over use of property, alleged stock-piling of guns, and other matters. However, these conflicts seems to have dissipated a bit in recent years, and relations between the CUT and their neighbors seem improved, hopefully thereby averting violence.[95] Somehow the downward spiral toward violence was arrested, a development worthy of more study. Wessinger makes the point that the CUT has made efforts to reach out to the media and the surrounding community in a nonthreatening manner, as well as respond to critical queries and questions from outsiders.[96]

She suggests that the way CUT has handled itself illustrates some of the major ways that violence can be averted.[97]

II. Violence Against New Religions

While the majority of public reports of violence and new religions tend to focus on violence within and by these groups, there is another dimension to the violence issue worthy of consideration. This dimension concerns the possible use of various forms of violence **against** the new religions and their participants, or taking actions that **justify** violence against the groups by others. Such activities can be defined as deliberate attempts to destroy, weaken, or suppress the organization itself. Violence against newer religions has developed in numerous ways: (1) creation of stories, sometimes referred to as "atrocity tales," or "negative summary events" alleging violent or other unconventional practices by new religions, thereby justifying the need for possibly extreme counter actions;[98] (2) implementation of "deprogramming" to forcibly remove thousands of new religious group members from their membership group; and (3) explicit organizational tactics designed to thwart, suppress, and even eradicate some new religions.[99]

Atrocity Tales: Ideas as Weapons

The issue of "atrocity tales," or to use James Beckford's less evocative term, "negative summary events,"[100] might seem unimportant to a discussion of violence, but such stories have sometimes served as a **justification** for attacks against individuals (including deprogrammings) and against even the presence of such groups in a society. David Bromley and colleagues defined an atrocity as an event that is perceived as a flagrant violation of a fundamental cultural value, generally characterized by the following elements: (1) some sense of moral outrage and indignation in relation to the perceived value violation; (2) the authorization of some sort of punitive sanction; and (3) the mobilization of control efforts by the offended or injured against the apparent perpetrators.[101] The veracity of such tales and stories is not the issue.[102] Instead, the major purpose of such allegations is to make the target group stand out from the ordinary by providing dramatic evidence of sinister and bizarre actions. Such tales then serve both to justify the assignment of negative labels and as a warrant for extreme actions.

Bromley et al., point out that atrocity tales have been used in propaganda campaigns, lynchings, racial tensions, wartime massacres, and "degradation ceremonies." They examine a sample of articles published on the Unification Church between 1974 and 1979 which suggest that use of atrocity tales to attack new religions is not uncommon. The atrocity tales concerned alleged loss of personal freedom and autonomy, the loss of private property rights and fair exchange, and threats to conventional patterns of relationships.[103]

Beckford's "negative summary event" concept is similar, if less provocative.[104] He includes five different elements in that he says characterize most media stories about new religions. These include (1) their **strangeness** in terms of beliefs, practices, dress, and lifestyle; (2) their alleged use of **trickery** to get people to join and participate, and to directly benefit leaders; (3) the **misery** from poor living conditions in the group for the "cult victims," and the psychological damage they may experience, as well as the disruption that comes to their families; (4) the **anger** toward the new religions of family members of participants and the way that anger may fuel public campaigns against new religions that may even involve political parties or churches working with concerned parents; and (5) the **threat** that "cults" pose toward normal society and even economically, as they supposedly amass large amounts of money and other resources.

The tragedy at Waco discussed earlier also illustrates the significance of such interpretations. The claim that "babies were being beaten" apparently provoked Attorney General Janet Reno to authorize the CS gas attack that culminated in the burning of the building, with great loss of life, and media stories about such claims helped prepare the general public to accept the eventual tragic outcome of this episode.[105] Although child abuse is a state crime and does not come under federal jurisdiction, that fact did not preclude the affidavit that supported the initial warrant developed by the BATF from discussing allegations of child abuse by David Koresh at some length.[106] Thus the Waco tragedy illustrates the power of accusations of child abuse (including sex abuse) that is now being used as justification for social control efforts toward new religions.[107] Such accusations have sometimes replaced the dominant themes of "brainwashing" and exploitation that have fueled such efforts for nearly three decades.

Other atrocity tales can also be found to have served the purposes of social control agents involved in the Waco situation. Questionable claims of various kinds were produced by the BATF initially, including the alleged presence of a meth lab at Mt. Carmel, which allowed the BATF to secure federal assistance such as training for the raid and weaponry that would have been otherwise unavailable[108] Such claims of drug use and manufacture, however unfounded, served to contribute to the broad atrocity-filled picture being painted by law enforcement officials involved with the Davidians. These tales were readily accepted by the media covering the episode, and thus helped justify among the general public the efforts taken against the Davidians.[109]

Other scholars have presented evidence of "atrocity tale" attacks against new religions.[110] Such allegations are a form of indirect violence against such organizations and the entire landscape of newer and smaller nonconventional religions. The implication of such tales is that these groups threaten society, and therefore they should be subject to possible retaliation for advocating different lifestyles, roles, relationships, and alternative value-orientations.[111]

The larger meaning of the use of atrocity tales is most apparent historically when we consider the responses of many sectors of American society to unconventional religious ideas. Such ideas generally have not been well received, and usually have been responded to with a typical pattern of stereotypic charges. We see historical evidence of members and leaders being attacked, movements labeled as political threats, children considered brainwashed or abused, allegations of submissiveness to leaders, and other atrocity tales told by apostates.[112] There was considerable anti-Catholic sentiment in early American society, as well as campaigns against the Shakers, but perhaps the prototypical historical case involved the lengthy period of persecution over a hundred years ago of the Mormons.[113]

Brock Kilbourne and James Richardson suggest that the new religions may be viewed as especially threatening in today's "psychological society," since the new groups often challenge the growing authority of psychiatrists and psychologists (i.e., our "secular priests") to define what is healthy and unhealthy, moral and immoral.[114] The high status and power relations enjoyed by these professionals is explicitly challenged by some of the newer religions. And some members of the psychological and psychiatric communities (and the occasional sociologist or legal scholar) seem ready to spread negative information about participation in new religions.[115] Such tales help justify more overt attacks on the groups, such as deprogramming.

Deprogramming

One major way violence against the new religions has occurred is through **deprogramming**, a tactic promoted for years by some segments of the Anti-Cult Movement.[116] Coercive deprogramming, the process of forcing disaffiliation from a new religion, has received much attention from scholars and others. The process involves abducting and incarcerating members of new religious groups, using physical force if necessary.[117] Once the abduction has taken place, the deprogrammer attempts to obtain control over important aspects of the deprogramming situation by isolating the person from sources of group support. The individual is, therefore, in a weakened position to resist forced influence attempts, and is sometimes overwhelmed both physically and emotionally.[118] Thousands of people have been deprogrammed from controversial newer religions in recent decades,[119] which means that the tactic may be viewed as a "success" from the perspective of those opposed to participation in newer groups.[120]

Brock Kilbourne, in a discussion of myths surrounding deconversion, observed that deprogramming generally entails captivity, forced participation, systematically induced frustrations, verbal attacks on the person's central beliefs and values, attempts to develop intense shame and guilt, and the explicit attempt to push the deprogrammee to the "breaking point."[121] The practice of coercive deprogramming suggests an "ideological ritual" designed to strengthen and to reaffirm, through force if necessary, conventional commitments to family, school, work, and community.[122] These practices therefore serve certain vested interests in society (i.e., perpetuation of the social control function of the "ideal form" of the middle and upper-middle class family and the various support professionals which have arisen to service its needs). Kilbourne adopts a conflict perspective to explain the deployment of such violent "stripping" rituals for the purpose of insuring the conformity of wayward and recalcitrant members of society, and in order to suppress the proliferation of some of the new groups. Such practices develop in relation to conflict between competing groups over different values, interests, and lifestyles.[123]

It is true that forcible deprogramming actions dropped considerably in number in the late 1980s the 1990s under the pressure of court decisions and negative publicity.[124] Now there is an emphasis on "exit counseling," which does not usually involve physical force, but depends on persuasion for its effectiveness. However, there are still reports of deprogrammings taking place on occasion in the U.S., and also in other countries, sometimes involving American deprogrammers.[125]

Organizational Level Violence Against Religious Groups

Another type of violence against religious groups occurs at the **organizational** level. Such violence against organizations can take the form of governmental action or private, self-help, action that may or may not be officially sanctioned. Mass media often play a major role in such campaigns against new religions, as they assist in determining what the general public thinks about a given group (see footnote 3). Such activities, which may include violence against individual members or leaders, is illustrated in U.S. history by efforts to stamp out new groups such as the Mormons and other devalued groups in the last century, and by periodic attacks against Jews in Western society. In more recent times explicit policies and strategies designed to hinder or even eliminate the new religions have been developed in some areas.

The organizational level attacks against certain new groups are explicitly indicated in the various activities of the Anti-Cult Movement in the U.S. and other countries, including former communist countries.[126] Anson Shupe and David Bromley contend the ACM functions in this capacity in several different roles.[127] It is most importantly as a disseminator of information, with the intent of denouncing and exposing the various groups. Updated reports on legal battles, recommended tactics, and interagency linkages are made available to the public in this manner, including in recent times through the use of the World Wide Web.[128] Thus, the ACM helps spread, using any means available, "atrocity tales" or "negative summary events" which were discussed above. Second, the ACM attempts to lobby directly before legislators and executives at local, state, and federal levels to restrict such groups both here and abroad.[129] Third, the ACM functions in a referral role to maintain ongoing files on deprogrammers and new groups, and to provide legal assistance, counseling services, and advice.[130] This referral role may facilitate attacks on the new religions because of actions taken by those referred toward the goal of controlling or even dismantling these groups.[131]

The Anti-Cult Movement, both here and abroad, is composed of numerous organizations, diverse in size and resources, intent upon controlling the proliferation of the new religions.[132] Some ACM groups have launched campaigns attacking the tax exempt status of certain groups, attempting to make the raising of funds more difficult by isolating the new religion from sources of popular support. These efforts have borne some fruit, leading scholars to discuss organizational level efforts by the IRS to define new religions as non-religious, which might have a predictable effect of encouraging the demise of some groups.[133] The most well-known of such efforts by the IRS is, of course, the tax evasion trial of Reverend Moon, which was appealed (unsuccessfully) to the U.S. Supreme Court. This case made Reverend Moon, who spent time in a federal prison as a result, something of a martyr in the eyes of many religionists, and did not lead to the demise of the organization.[134]

There are a number of scholarly treatments of other efforts to harm religious organizations through governmental actions, often with the assistance of private ACM groups or individuals. Omar Garrison has discussed efforts of governmental agencies in the United States to suppress or control Scientology.[135] Lewis Carter offers considerable detail about governmental efforts to suppress the Rajneesh group in Oregon.[136] Jean Swantko describes in detail the interactions of anti-cultists and governmental agencies and personnel in Vermont in the mid-70s that culminated in a raid on the Island Pond community that took away all the group's children, even if temporarily.[137] Richardson describes the machinations of two Australian state governments as they apprehended of over 150 children of The Family in an ultimately unsuccessful effort to make them wards of the state.[138]

A number of scholars have also presented evidence on the various strategies for control of new religions by governmental agencies and other groups in Germany and France.[139] More recently a number of Western European governments, including France, Belgium, Germany, and Switzerland have produced reports critical of new religions, and which have been used to justify drastic actions against some groups by governmental entities as well as private organizations.[140] In France, for instance, the tax officials have used the fact that the Jehovah's Witnesses organization was placed on a list with dozens of other groups that were defined as not being religious to send the organization a tax bill equivalent to $50 million. It seems clear that French officials, working in conjunction with private anti-cult forces there, want the Witnesses and many other minority faiths to stop operating in France.[141]

Similarly, in Russia a drastic turn of events has led to many smaller faiths being banned or otherwise persecuted by the government.[142] This campaign, which is in sharp contrast to the euphoria over new found religious freedoms of the early 1990s in Russia, has been joined in by the media in Russia, and is apparently being informally coordinated by functionaries of the Russian Orthodox Church and conservative political forces in Russia, with the open involvement of Western anti-cult organizations and people.[143] The effort to exert control over newer faiths has often involved the Russian legal system, but with mixed success.[144]

Discussion and Conclusions

Evidence of violent practices committed either by new or minority religions or directed toward them by others abound in journalistic accounts and scholarly writings. Several major episodes of violence involving minority faiths have occurred in the past two decades or so, feeding the idea that controversial religious groups are by their very nature violent. However, there is relatively little evidence to justify generalized allegations of violent practices by the vast majority of these groups, the several well-publicized tragic examples discussed herein notwithstanding. There is some evidence, as discussed above, indicating occasional violence of others, both private individuals and organizations and public authorities, **toward** the new religions, especially when deprogramming and organizational level attacks are considered.

One factor important for understanding violence involving some new religions pertains to the **relationship** of the groups to the dominant culture. Although much of what violence does occur in relation to new religions is probably related to the struggle for organizational survival and power, **such violence is usually essentially embedded in the relationship between religions and their opponents, and should not be viewed as something necessarily inherent in the structure and organization of either.**[145] Certain resources are typically precluded for the new religions (e.g., use of community facilities, long-term property assets and funds, positive treatment in major media), and therefore newer religions may feel compelled to resort to unconventional means to raise funds, expand their ranks, or defend themselves from outside attacks. Sometimes the groups are successful in such defensive efforts, which contributes to a negative societal reaction and may even increase the likelihood for conflict that can escalate into violence.

To some degree, a **context of violence** has engulfed both new religions and their foes. This is evident in how such groups are labeled and the reactions they engender, as well as the polarization that exists in this field of study.[146] The implications of this social reality for minority religion group members in particular and society in general are profound. Whether we are addressing new religious ideas, radical political movements, or new values, roles and/or lifestyles, there is often a rather common negative response by dominant groups to strategies for social change. And sometimes that response may incorporate violence, both official and unofficial.[147] An examination of the circumstances of new and minority religions provides insight into the stereotypic and historical response to new social groups which would attempt to change the social fabric of American society (i.e., basic values, beliefs, norms, commitments, and patterns of vested interests).

This understanding of the conflict between new religions and their opponents raises a quandary for those opposed to religious experimentation. If detractors attack the new groups in various ways, and especially if they are perceived by the new groups as being successful in the attacks, then there is at least the possibility that this perception may trigger a potentially violent reaction. For example, the hundreds of deprogrammings and other efforts to exert control over new religions that have taken place in America could be a contributing factor to some violent reactions in those new religions under attack. Also, it is clear that the **perception** of attacks (even if the actual attacks vary greatly in seriousness), in interaction with other factors, has played a major role in tragedies such as at Waco.

If there is any credence to such an idea, then the question of responsibility for at least some violence involving newer religions takes a markedly different twist than that which is usually assumed. To complicate the picture even more, many of the organizational attacks by the ACM on new and minority religions are **legitimate actions** commonly taken by other individuals and groups in our society (i.e., media campaigns, lobbying, lawsuits, etc.) to protect and perpetuate their own vested interests in the normal course of everyday affairs. Nonetheless, such actions can, under a broad and collective level definition of violence, technically be considered violent actions against organizational forms even if they are legitimate and presupposed within the social system of which they are a part. The actions of those opposing new religions may elicit similar reactions by new religious groups, as they engage in legal and other types of conflicts with anti-cult groups and participants, as well as governmental authorities in places where governmental policy has been influenced by anti-cultist sentiments.[148]

In sum, a context of violence surrounds many of those involved in and opposed to the new religious groups. This context of violence is characterized by interdependency, conflict, and the use of atrocity tales and labels used on both sides of the conflict as social weapons. Recognition of this situation appears to be more important than many of the specious claims being made about minority religions and those opposed to them. This perspective suggests a more sociological and general approach to studying violence, especially in relation to new groups in American society which are attempting to change the social order.

This is a revision of an earlier essay to which Brock Kilbourne made significant contributions. Appreciation is expressed to an anonymous reviewer and to Catherine Wessinger for helpful comments on earlier drafts of this chapter.

NOTES

This chapter is reprinted with permission from Terrorism and Political Violence 13(1) (Spring 2001).

1. For a sampling of this literature see Thomas Robbins, "Religious Mass Suicide before Jonestown," *Sociological Analysis* 46(1) (1986): 1–20; Thomas Robbins, "Religious Movements and Violence: A Friendly Critique of the Interpretive Approach," *Nova Religio* 1(1) (1997): 13–29; Jean Rosenfeld, "The Importance of the Analysis of Religion in Avoiding Violent Outcomes: The Justus Freeman Case," *Nova Religio* 1(1) (1997): 72–95; James Tabor and Eugene Gallagher, *Why Waco?* (Berkeley: University of California Press, 1995; Stuart

Wright, ed., *Armageddon in Waco* (Chicago: University of Chicago Press, 1995); David Chidester, *Salvation and Suicide: An Interpetation of Jim Jones, the Peoples Temple, and Jonestown* (Bloomington: University of Indiana Press, 1988); Ken Levi, ed., *Violence and Religious Commitment* (University Park: Pennsylvania State University Press, 1982); Mary Maaga, *Hearing the Voices of Jonestown* (Syracuse: Syracuse University Press, 1998); Ian Reader, *The Poisonous Cocktail? Aum Shinrikyo's Path to Violence* (Copenhagen: Nordic Institute of Asian Studies, 1996); John Hall, *Gone from the Promised Land: Jonestown in American Cultural History* (New Brunswick, N.J.: Transaction, 1987); James Lewis, ed., *From the Ashes: Making Sense of Waco* (Lanham, Md.: Rowan and Littlefield, 1994); Rebecca Moore, *A Sympathetic History of Jonestown* (Lewiston, N.Y.: Mellen, 1985); Robert Lifton, *Destroying the World to Save It: Aum Shinrikyo, Apocalyptic Violence, and the New Global Terrorism* (New York: Metropolitan, 1999).

    2. See, for example, Thomas Robbins and Susan Palmer, eds., *Millennium, Messiahs, and Mayhem: Contemporary Apocalytic Movements* (New York: Routledge, 1997); Catherine Wessinger, *How the Millennium Comes Violently: From Jonestown to Heaven's Gate* (New York: Seven Bridges, 2000); Catherine Wessinger, ed., *Millennialism, Persecution, & Violence: Historical Cases* (Syracuse: Syracuse University Press, 2000), as well as the classic by Michael Barkun, *Disaster and the Millennium* (Syracuse: Syracuse University Press, 1986).

    3. On journalistic treatments and the role of the media see James Beckford, *Cult Controversies: The Societal Response to the New Religious Movements* (London: Tavistock, 1985); Barend van Driel and James T. Richardson, "Print Media Coverage of New Religious Movements: A Longitudinal Study," *Journal of Communication* 38(3) (1988): 37–61; James T. Richardson, "Manufacturing Consent about Koresh: A Structural Analysis of the Role of the Media in the Waco Tragedy," in Wright (note 1), 153–76; James T. Richardson and Barend van Driel, "Journalistic Attitudes toward New Religious Movements," *Review of Religious Research* 39(2) (1997): 116–36; James T. Richardson, "Journalistic Bias toward New Religions in Australia," *Journal of Contemporary Religion* 11(3) (1996): 289–302; and for a discussion of how new religions or "cults" became a social problem see Thomas Robbins and Dick Anthony, "Deprogramming, Brainwashing, and the Medicalization of New Religions," *Social Problems* 29(3) (1982): 283–97.

    4. See Wessinger, *Historical Cases* (note 2) and Robbins and Palmer (note 2).

    5. See Hugh Graham and Robert Gurr, eds., *Violence in America* (Washington, D.C.: U.S. Government Printing Office, 1969) and Rebecca Moore, "'American as Cherry Pie': Peoples Temple and Violence in America," in Wessinger, *Historical Cases* (note 2), 121–37.

    6. For discussions of therapeutic effects see Marc Galanter, "The 'Relief Effect': A Sociobiological Model for Neurotic Distress and Large Group Therapy," *American Journal of Psychiatry* 135 (1978): 588–91; Brock Kilbourne, "Equity or Exploitation? The Case of the Unification Church," *Review of Religious Research* 28(2) (1986): 143–50; Brock Kilbourne, "Psychotherapeutic Implications of New Religious Affiliation," in Marc Galanter, ed., *Cults and New Religious Movements* (Washington, D.C.: American Psychiatric Association, 1989), 127–44; Brock Kilbourne and James T. Richardson, "Cults versus Families: A Case of Misattribution of Cause?" *Marriage and Family Review* 4(3) (1981): 81–100; Brock Kilbourne and James T. Richardson, "Psychotherapy and New Religions in a Pluralistic Society," *American Psychologist* 39(3) (1984): 237–51; Brock Kilbourne and James T. Richardson, "A Social Psychological Analysis of Healing," *Journal of Integrative and Eclectic Psychotherapy* 7(1) (1988): 20–43; James T. Richardson, "Psychological and Psychiatric Studies of

Participants in New Religions," in Laurence Brown, ed., *New Perspectives in Psychology of Religion* (Elmsford, N.Y.: Pergamon, 1985); James T. Richardson, "Clinical and Personality Assessments of Participants in New Religions," *International Journal for the Psychology of Religion* 5(3) (1995): 145–70; John Muffler, John Langrod, James T. Richardson, and Pedro Ruiz, "Religion," in J. Lowinson, P. Ruiz, R. Millman, and J. Langrod, eds., *Substance Abuse: A Comprehensive Textbook*, 3d ed. (Baltimore: Williams and Wilkins, 1997; and Robbins and Anthony (note 3).

7. This analysis should not be taken to mean that I condone violence by religious groups or that I am attempting to "explain it away." For discussions of this and related issues see Robbins (1997) (note 1); Jeffrey Kaplan, "Interpreting the Interpretive Approach: A Friendly Reply to Thomas Robbins," *Nova Religio* 1(1) (1998): 30–49; and Ian Reader, "Scholarship, Aum Shinrikyo, and Academic Integrity," *Nova Religio* 3(2): 368–82. Taking the perspective on violence proposed herein will, I believe, yield better understanding for those who want to see less such violence, a large group in which I include myself.

8. See Steven Tipton, *Getting Saved from the Sixties* (Berkeley: University of California Press, 1982); James T. Richardson, Brock Kilbourne, and Barend van Driel, "Alternative Religions and Economic Individualism," in *Research in the Social Scientific Study of Religion*, ed. Monty Lynn and David Moberg, 33–56 (Greenwich, Conn.: JAI Press, 1989).

9. See discussion of this conflict in Kilbourne and Richardson (1984) (note 6).

10. Sandra Ball-Rokeach, "Normative and Deviant Violence from a Conflict Perspective," *Social Problems* 28(1) (1980): 45–62, 46.

11. Ralf Dahrendorf, *Class and Class Conflict in Industrial Society* (Stanford: Stanford University Press, 1959).

12. On labeling see Howard Becker, *The Outsiders* (New York: Free Press, 1973); Eric Goode, "On Behalf of Labeling Theory," *Social Problems* 22 (1975): 570–83; and on accounts see Marvin Scott and Stanford Lyman, "Accounts," *American Sociological Review* 33 (1975): 942–45; James T. Richardson, Jan van der Lans, and Frans Derks, "Leaving and Labeling: Voluntary and Coerced Disaffiliation from Religious Social Movements," in *Research in Social Movements, Conflicts, and Change*, ed. Kurt Lang and Gladys Lang, 97–126 (Greenwich, Conn.: JAI Press 1986); and James Beckford, "Accounting for Conversion," *British Journal for Sociology* 29 (1978): 249–62.

13. On claims making see Malcolm Spector and John Kitsuse, *Constructing Social Problems* (Menlo Park, Calif.: Cummings, 1977) and on attributions see R. C. Prus, "Resisting Designations: An Extension of Attribution Theory into a Negotiated Context," *Sociological Inquiry* 46(2) (1975): 127–34; Harold Kelley and J. L. Michela, "Attribution Theory and Research," *Annual Review of Psychology* 31 (1980): 457–501.

14. See discussion of ideas as social weapons against new religions in Thomas Robbins, Dick Anthony, and James McBride, "Legitimating Repression," in *The Brainwashing/Deprogramming Controversy*, ed. David Bromley and James T. Richardson (New York: Edwin Mellen, 1983).

15. See Gary Marx, "External Efforts to Damage or Facilitate Social Movements: Some Patterns, Explanations, Outcomes, and Complications," in *The Dynamics of Social Movements*, ed. Mayer Zald and James McCarthy, 94–125 (Cambridge, Mass.: Winthrop, 1979). For direct application to the area of new religions see Massimo Introvigne, "Moral Panics and Anti-cult Terrorism in Western Europe," *Terrorism and Political Violence* 12 (2000): 47–59.

16. See R. B. Cairn, *Social Development: The Origins and Plasticity of Interchanges* (San Francisco: Freeman, 1979).

17. See David Rapoport, "Fear and Trembling: Terrorism in Three Religious Traditions," *American Political Science Review* 78(3) (1984): 658–77; David Rapoport, "Messianic Sanctions for Terror," *Comparative Politics* 20(2) (1988): 195–213; Ian Reader (note 1); Catherine Wessinger (note 2); and Lifton (note 1).

18. See Wright (note 1) and Tabor and Gallagher (note 1) on what happened at Waco.

19. Roy Wallis, *The Road to Total Freedom* (New York: Columbia University Press, 1977).

20. See the fine discussion of such interactions in Michael Barkun, "Millennial Violence in Contemporary America"; in Catherine Wessinger, *Historical Cases* (note 2), 352–63; and in Michael Barkun, "Millenarianism and Violence: The Case of the Christian Identity Movement," in Robbins and Palmer (note 2), 247–60.

21. Paul Secord and Carl Backman, *Social Psychology* (New York: McGraw Hill 1974).

22. See Wessinger, *How the Millennium Comes Violently* (note 2), 275.

23. An earlier version of this chapter also contained a section on so-called brainwashing claims as a form of violence against newer religions in that such claims have been used to justify violence against these groups and their members (such as through deprogrammings). See Dick Anthony, "Religious Movements Litigation: Evaluating Key Testimony," in *In Gods We Trust*, ed. Thomas Robbins and Dick Anthony, 295–344 (New Brunswick, N.J.: Transaction, 1990); Dick Anthony, "Pseudoscience and Minority Religions: An Evaluation of the Brainwashing Theories of Jean-Marie Abgrall," *Social Justice Research* 12(4) (1999): 421–56; Eileen Barker, *The Making of a Moonie: Brainwashing or Choice?* (New York: Basil Blackwell, 1984); James T. Richardson and Brock Kilbourne, "Classical and Contemporary Applications of Brainwashing Models," in *The Brainwashing/Deprogramming Controversy*, ed. David Bromley and James Richardson (1983); James T. Richardson, "Cult/Brainwashing Cases and the Freedom of Religion," *Journal of Church and State* 33(1) (1991): 55–74; and James T. Richardson, "A Social Psychological Critique of 'Brainwashing' Claims about Recruitment to New Religions," in *The Handbook on Cults and Sects in America*, ed. David Bromley and Jeffrey Hadden, 75–97 (Greenwich, Conn.: JAI Press 1993), for an assessment of such attacks.

24. A collective view is not a usual way to conceptualize violence. Typical views of violence often treat it as an individual and even a psychologized concept. Even more sophisticated social psychological treatments such as William Gamson, *The Strategy of Social Protest* (Homewood, Ill.: Dorsey, 1975), Cairn (note 16), and Ball-Rokeach (note 10), which discuss the context of violence and its basic relational character focus mainly on acts of individual violence. Terms like *menticide*, *homicide*, and *suicide*—all individualistic terms—have their collective-level analogues. *Orgacide* might refer to the destruction of an organization (see Christine King, *The Nazi State and the New Religions* [New York: Edwin Mellen, 1982] and Peter Matheson, ed., *The Third Reich and the Christian Churches* [Grand Rapids: Eerdmans, 1981] for examples of the Third Reich's efforts to obliterate some minority religions). Another collective-level term is *genocide*, which sometimes involves attempts to destroy a religious community.

25. See Gordon Melton, "Violence and the Cults," *Nebraska Humanist* 8 (1985): 51–60; and James T. Richardson, "Peoples Temple and Jonestown: A Corrective Comparison and Critique," *Journal for the Scientific Study of Religion* 19(3) (1980): 239–55.

26. See Anson Shupe and David Bromley, "Shaping the Public Response to Jonestown: The Peoples Temple and the Anti-cult Movement," in Ken Levi (note 1), 105–32.

27. See Tabor and Gallagher (note 1), Wright (note 1), Wessinger (note 2), and the provocative article by Stuart Wright, "Anatomy of a Government Massacre: Abuses of Hostage-barricade Protocols during the Waco Standoff," *Terrorism and Political Violence* 11(2) (1999): 39–68.

28. See Robert Balch, "The Evolution of a New Age Cult: From Total Overcomers Anonymous to Death at Heaven's Gate," in *Sects, Cults, & Spiritual Communities*, ed. William Zellner and Marc Petrowsky, 1–26 (Westport, Conn.: Praeger 1998); Wessinger (note 2); Winston Davis, "Heaven's Gate: A Study of Religious Obedience," *Nova Religio* 3(2) (2000): 241–67; and Hugh Urban, "The Devil at Heaven's Gate: Rethinking the Study of Religion in Cyber-space," *Nova Religio* 3(2) (2000): 268–302.

29. See Ian Reader (note 1), Lifton (note 1), Wessinger (note 2), and David Rapoport, "Terrorism and Weapons of the Apocalypse," *National Security Studies Quarterly* 5(3) (1999): 49–67.

30. See John Hall and Philip Shuyler, "The Mystical Apocalypse of the Solar Temple," in Robbins and Palmer (note 2), 285–311; Jean-François Mayer, "'Our Terrestrial Journey Is Coming to an End': The Last Voyage of the Solar Temple," *Nova Religio* 2(2) (1999): 172–96; Jean Rosenfeld, "Response to Mayer's 'Our Terrestrial Journey Is Coming to an End,'" *Nova Religio* 2(2) (1999): 197–207; and Massimo Introvigne, "The Magic of Death: The Suicides of the Solar Temple," in Wessinger, *Historical Cases* (note 2), 138–57.

31. For the most up to date information on this recent tragedy see the CESNUR website at www.cesnur.org.

32. Other and more overtly political events such as the Oklahoma City bombing have also contributed to how the general public feels about the relationship between violence and religion. Since the tragic event in Oklahoma City was apparently motivated in part by the Waco episode, there is a religious nexus in the minds of many. Also, nonviolent events such as the eighty-one-day Freemen standoff in Montana, which eventually ended without bloodshed, was in the news for months, as America collectively held its breath to see whether this situation would also erupt in violence. See Jean Rosenfeld (note 1) and Wessinger (note 2) for convincing analyses supporting the idea that the ideology of the Freemen was religious at base. Also see James Aho, *The Politics of Righteousness: Idaho Christian Patriotism* (Seattle: University of Washington Press, 1990) for a convincing analysis that patriot movements are at base religious.

33. See *Detroit News* (Jan. 7, 1979).

34. See Jerry Carroll and Bernard Bauer, "Suicide Training in the Moon Cult," *New West* (1979): 62–63. The church, however, vehemently denied such accusations.

35. See Sen. Mervin Dymally, "Impact of Cults on Today's Youth," Hearing Report of California Senate Select Committee on Children and Youth (Aug. 24, 1974).

36. See stories in *Chicago Tribune*, (June 15, 1978); *The Observer* (Oct. 8, 1978); and *The Sunday Times* (Nov. 6, 1977).

37. See James T. Richardson, "Minority Religions ('Cults') and the Law: Comparisons of the United States, Europe, and Australia," *University of Queensland Law Review* 18(2) (1995): 183–207.

38. See John Huber and Lindset Gruson, *Monkey on a Stick: Murder, Madness, and the Hare Krishna* (San Diego: Harcourt Brace Jovanovich, 1988).

39. See stories in the *New York Times* (Apr. 9, 1973) and *The Daily Telegraph* (March 15, 1976).

40. See Richard Ofshe, "The Social Development of the Synanon Cult: The Managerial Strategy of Organizational Transformation," *Sociological Analysis* 41(2) (1980): 109–27, and R. S. Anson, "The Synanon Horrors," *New Times* (Nov. 1978): 28–50.

41. See Omar Garrison, *Playing Dirty: The Secret War against Beliefs* (Los Angeles: Ralston-Pilot, 1980), and Wallis (note 19).

42. See James Lewis and Gordon Melton, eds., *Church Universal and Triumphant in Scholarly Perspective* (Stanford: Center for Academic Publications, 1994).

43. Burke Rochford, "Child Abuse in the Hare Krishna Movement: 1971–1986," *ISKCON Communications Journal* 6(1) (1998): 43–69.

44. On "The Family" see James T. Richardson, "Social Control of New Religions: From 'Brainwashing' Claims to Child Sex Abuse Accusations," in *Children in New Religions*, ed. Susan Palmer and Charlotte Hardman (New Brunswick, N.J.: Rutgers University Press, 1999). On the Island Pond episode see Susan Palmer, "Frontiers and Families: The Children of Island Pond," also in Palmer and Hardman (1999) and Jean Swantko, "The Twelve Tribes Communities, the Anti-cult Movement, and the Government's Response," *Social Justice Research* 12(4) (1999): 341–64.

45. See John Rothchild and Susan Wolf, *Children of the Counter Culture* (Garden City, N.Y.: Doubleday, 1976); H. J. Wallenstein, "Final Report on the Activities of the Children of God" (New York State: Charity Frauds Division, 1974); Dymally (note 35); M. J. Gaines, M. A. Wilson, K. J. Redican, and C. R. Baffi, "The Effects of Cult Membership on the Health Status of Adults and Children," *Update* 8(3): 9–17. But also see the entire volume by Palmer and Hardman (note 44) for another persepctive.

46. For discussion of the role of accusations of child abuse in social-control actions at Waco see Christopher Ellison and John Bartkowski, "'Babies Were Being Beaten': Exploring Child Abuse Accusations at Ranch Apocalypse," in Wright (note 1), 11–149, and James T. Richardson (1995) (note 3). Recent research has shown that most of these claims of child abuse of various kinds in newer religious groups were not founded in fact, but the claims have persisted nonetheless. See William Smith, "The Impact of Communal Living on Children in the 1980s," *Syzygy: Journal of Alternative Religion and Culture* 3(1): 51–60; Lawrence Lilliston and Gary Shepherd, "Psychological Assessment of Children in The Family," in *Sex, Sin, and Salvation: Investigating The Family/Children of God*, ed. James Lewis and Gordon Melton, 47–56 (Stanford: Center for Academic Publications, 1994); Gary Shepherd and Lawrence Lilliston, "Field Observations of Young People's Experience and Role in The Family," also in Lewis and Melton (1994), 57–70; Palmer and Hardman (note 44); and Richardson (note 44).

47. See Beckford (note 3) on "negative summary events" and David Bromley, Anson Shupe, and J. C. Ventimiglia, "Atrocity Tales, the Unification Church, and the Social Construction of Evil," *Journal of Communication* 29(3) (1979): 42–53.

48. See Rapoport (1984) (note 17).

49. See Grant Underwood, "Millennialism, Persecution, and Violence: The Mormons," in Wessinger, *Historical Cases*, 43–61 (note 2).

50. See Levi (note 1), 3–4, and Barkun, "Millennial Violence in Contemporary America" (note 20).

51. See Robert Ellwood, *One Way: The Jesus Movement and Its Meaning* (Englewood Cliffs, N.J.: Prentice Hall, 1972), and James T. Richardson, Mary Stewart, and Robert Simmonds, *Organized Miracles* (New Brunswick, N.J.: Transaction, 1979).

52. See Stillson Judah, *Hare Krishna and the Counterculture* (New York: Wiley, 1974), and Ted Nordquist, *Ananda Cooperative Village: A Study of the Beliefs, Values, and Attitudes of a New Age Community* (Uppsala: Religionshistoriska Institutionen, 1978).

53. See Levi (note 1), 10–20; Wessinger (note 2); Barkun (note 20); Robbins and Anthony, "Sects and Violence: Factors Enhancing the Volatility on Marginal Religious Movements," in Stuart Wright (note 1), 236–59; and Lorne Dawson, *Comprehending Cults* (New York: Oxford University Press, 1998), 128–57, for insightful discussions.

54. See Ball-Rokeach (note 10) and Kilbourne and Richardson (1984) (note 6).

55. See D. C. Bock and N. C. Warren, "Religious Belief as a Factor in Obedience to Destructive Commands," in *Current Perspectives in the Psychology of Religion*, ed. Newton Malony, ed., 191–98 (Grand Rapids: Eerdmans, 1977); J. M. Starr, "Religious Preference, Religiosity, and Opposition to War," *Sociological Analysis* 36 (1973): 323–34. Also see Rapoport (note 17), Aho (note 32), and Wessinger (note 2).

56. See Wessinger's discussion of the Aum Shinrikyo in *How the Millennium Comes Violently* (note 2), 120–57, as well as Reader (note 1) and Lifton (note 1).

57. See John Hall, "Public Narratives and the Apocalyptic Sect: From Jonestown to Mt. Carmel," in Wright (note 1), 205–35, for a discussion of the importance of the idea derived from the People's Temple tragedy that minority religious groups are prone to commit suicide and how that notion may have influenced the actions of law enforcement in the Waco tragedy.

58. See Rebecca Moore (note 5), 123–26, 132–35.

59. See Richardson (note 25).

60. Moore (note 5).

61. See Graham and Gurr (note 5).

62. See Maaga's thoughtful discussion of the culpability of other Peoples Temple leaders in the tragedy that developed at Jonestown (note 1).

63. See Barkun (note 20).

64. Huey Newton, *Revolutionary Suicide* (New York: Harcourt Brace Javanovich, 1973). See Hall (note 1), Chidester (note 1), and Richardson (note 25) for discussions of the implications of this teaching of Jones.

65. Wessinger, *How the Millennium Comes Violently* (note 2), 30–55.

66. Franz Fanon, *The Wretched of the Earth* (New York: Grove, 1963).

67. Wessinger (note 2).

68. See Moore (note 1) and Moore (note 5), 126–32.

69. See James Davies, "Toward a Theory of Social Revolution," *American Sociological Review* 27 (1962): 5–19, and D. E. Morrison, "Some Notes toward a Theory of Relative Deprivation, Social Movements, and Social Change," *American Behavioral Scientist* 14 (1971): 675–90.

70. However, many of the several hundred children and elderly who were members of Peoples Temple did not commit suicide but were murdered "for the cause" and on behalf of "revolutionary suicide." Such cases go far beyond what Durkheim meant by altruistic suicide. See Kenneth Woodin, *The Children of Jonestown* (New York: McGraw-Hill, 1981).

71. Maaga (note 1).

72. Moore (note 5), 126–27.

73. See Phil Tracy, "More on Peoples Temple: The Strange Suicides," *New West* (Aug. 15 1977): 18–19.

74. Woodin (note 70).

75. Wessinger (note 2); Hall (note 1).

76. See Dawson (note 53), 148–52, for the impact of encapsulation.

77. See Robbins and Palmer (note 2) and Wessinger (note 2).

78. See Wright (notes 1 and 27), Wessinger (note 2), Tabor and Gallagher (note 1), and Richardson (note 3). Also see the special symposium in *Nova Religio* 3(1) (1999) on the topic "Scholars of New Religions and Law Enforcement Officials" for a thorough discussion of such issues.

79. See Rosenfeld (note 30), 202.

80. See Mayer (note 30) and Wessinger, *How the Millennium Comes Violently* (note 2).

81. Introvigne (note 30).

82. Ibid., 157.

83. Wessinger (note 2).

84. See Manuba Watanabe, "Reactions to the Aum Affair: The Rise of the Anti-cult Movement in Japan," *Bulletin of the Nanzan Institute for Religion and Culture* 21 (1997): 32–48; as well as Reader (notes 1 and 7), Lifton (note 1), and Wessinger, *How the Millennium Comes Violently* (note 2). Wessinger's analysis of the Aum episode is especially useful.

85. Reader (note 1), 170, and Wessinger, *How the Millennium Comes Violently* (note 2), 136.

86. Balch (note 28).

87. Ibid., 24.

88. Davis (note 28).

89. Ibid., 260.

90. Wessinger, *How the Millennium Comes Violently* (note 2), 243.

91. See James T. Richardson, "New Religions on Trial: The Case of the Rajneesh in Oregon," presented at the Pacific Sociological Association annual meeting, Spokane, Washington, and Lewis Carter, *Charisma and Control in Rajneeshpuram* (New York: Cambridge University Press, 1990).

92. Carter (note 91), 201–40.

93. Richardson (note 91).

94. See the *New York Times* (Mar. 23, 1988), A15.

95. See James Lewis and Gordon Melton (note 42), William Smith, "Environmental Impacts, Stewardship, and Development: The Building of a Religious Community in Montana," *Sygyzy: Journal of Alternative Religion and Culture* 3(3) (1994): 231–40, and Catherine Wessinger, "Millennialism with and without the Mayhem," in Robbins and Palmer (note 2), 47–59.

96. Wessinger, *How the Millennium Comes Violently* (note 2), 258. Also see her discussions of the Freeman standoff in Montana and the Chen Tao situation in Garland, Texas, both of which ended peacefully. Also see Rosenfeld (note 1) on the Freemen situation and Lonnie Kliever, "Meeting God in Garland: A Model for Religious Tolerance," *Nova Religio* 3(1) (1999): 45–53, on Chen Tao.

97. Wessinger, *How the Millennium Comes Violently* (note 2), 285n14.

98. See Bromley et al. (note 47) on "atrocity tales" and Beckford (note 3) on "negative summary events."

99. For examples of these three types see Bromley et al. (note 47) and Beckford (note 3), as well as Anson Shupe, Roger Spielman, and Sam Stigall, "Deprogramming: The New Exorcism," in *Conversion Careers: In and Out of the New Religions*, ed. James T. Richardson, 145–58 (Beverly Hills, Calif.: Sage, 1978); King (note 24); Bromley and Richardson (note 23); Anson Shupe and David Bromley, *The New Vigilantes* (Beverly Hill, Calif.: Sage, 1980); Massimo Introvigne, "Moral Panics and Anti-cult Terrorism in Western Europe," paper presented at the CESNUR Conference, Turin, Italy (Sept. 10–12, 1998); and Massimo Introvigne, "Anti-cult Terrorism on the Internet," paper presented at the annual meeting of the Association for the Sociology of Religion, Chicago (Aug., 5–7, 1999), as well as Introvigne (note 15).

100. Beckford (note 3), 237.

101. Bromley et al. (note 47).

102. Bromley et al. (note 47) are not saying that the subjects of atrocity tales are never true, and I concur. Indeed, as I have already admitted herein, sometimes atrocious things do occur in new religious groups. The issue is their frequency, generalizability, and the way in which a group's detractors and the media may use such instances for purposes other than a full and accurate description of life in a given group.

103. See van Driel and Richardson (note 3) for similar conclusions from a broader study.

104. Beckford (note 3).

105. See Ellison and Bartkowski (note 46), and especially Richardson (note 3).

106. See Tabor and Gallagher (note 1), 101, as well as Wessinger, *How the Millennium Comes Violently* (note 2).

107. See Richardson (note 44) and Swantko (note 44).

108. Tabor and Gallagher (note 1), 102.

109. See Richardson (note 46) and Rebecca Moore, *The Davidian Massacre* (Franklin, Tenn.: Legacy Communication, 1995).

110. See Harvey Cox, "Myths Sanctioning Religious Persecution," in *A Time for Reconsideration*, ed. M. D. Bryant and Herbert Richardson (New York: Mellen, 1978); Bert Testa, "Making Crime Seem Natural: News and Deprogramming," in Bryant and Richardson, 41–81; Barbara Hargrove, "Social Sources and Consequences of the Brainwashing Myth," in Bromley and Richardson (note 23): 299–308; and Introvigne (note 15).

111. For a discussion of how these ideas get acted out in the legal setting to the detriment of controversial newer faiths, see James T. Richardson, "Discretion and Discrimination in Legal Cases Involving Controversial Religious Groups or Allegations of Ritual Abuse," in *Law and Religion*, ed. Rex Ahdar, 111–32 (Aldershot: Ashgate 2000).

112. See David Davis, "Some Themes of Counter-subversion: An Analysis of Anti-Masonic, Anti-Catholic, and Anti-Mormon Literature," *Mississippi Valley Historical Review* 47(2) (1960): 205–24; Donald Miller, "Deprogramming in Historical Society," in Bromley and Richardson (note 23), 15–28; and Shupe and Bromley (note 99).

113. Davis (note 112); Miller (note 112); Massimo Introvigne, "Latter Day Revisited: Contemporary Mormon Millenianism," in Robbins and Palmer (note 2), 229–44; Underwood (note 49).

114. See Kilbourne and Richardson (note 6) and M. L. Gross, *The Psychological Society* (1978); on "secular priests" see Perry London, *The Modes and Morals of Psychotherapy* (New York: Holt, Rinehart, and Winston, 1964).

115. See Margaret Singer, "Coming out of the Cults," *Psychology Today* 12 (1979): 72–82; Louis West and Margaret Singer, "Cults, Quacks, and Nonprofessional Therapies," in *Comprehensive Textbook of Psychiatry*, 3d ed., ed. H. Kaplan, A. Freedman, and B. Sadock, 3245–58 (Baltimore: Williams and Wilkins, 1980); Margaret Singer and Richard Ofshe, "Attacks on Peripheral versus Central Elements of Self and the Impact of Thought Reforming Techniques,"*Cultic Studies Journal* 3(1): 3–24; Margaret Singer (with Janja Lalich), *Cults in Our Midst* (San Francisco: Jossey-Bass, 1995); Eli Shapiro, "Destructive Cultism," *American Family Physician* 15 (1977): 80–83; John Clark, "Problems in Referral of Cult Members," *Journal of the National Association of Private Psychiatric Hospitals* 9 (1978): 19–21; John Clark, Michael Langone, R. E. Schecter, and R. Daly, *Destructive Cult Conversion* (Weston, Mass.: American Family Foundation, 1981). Also see the work of a legal scholar who has assisted in legitimating anticult activities: Richard Delgado, "Religious Totalism: Gentle and Ungentle Persausion under the First Amendment," *University of Southern California Law Review* 51 (1977): 1–100, and Richard Delgado, "Cults and Conversion: The Case for Informed Consent," in *Cults, Culture, and the Law*, ed. Thomas Robbins, Wiliam Shepherd, and James McBride, 11–128 (Chico, Calif.: Scholars Press, 1985),. Delgado even claimed that participation in a new religion was tantamount to slavery in Richard Delgado, "Religious Totalism as Slavery," *New York University Review of Law and Social Change* 9 (1979–1980): 51–68.

116. See Shupe and Bromley (note 99) and Anson Shupe and David Bromley, eds., *Anti-cult Movements in Cross-cultural Comparison* (New York: Garland, 1994); James T. Richardson, "Conversion, Brainwashing, and Deprogramming," *Center Magazine* 15(2) (1980): 18–24.

117. See Byong-Suh Kim, "Religious Deprogramming and Subjective Reality," *Sociological Analysis* 40 (1979): 197–207; Richardson, van der Lans, and Derks (note 12); John Biermans, *The Odyssey of New Religions Today* (New York: Mellen, 1988); Stuart Wright, *Leaving Cults: The Dynamics of Defection* (Washington, D.C.: Society for the Scientific Study of Religion, 1987); Trudy Solomon, "Integrating the 'Moonie' Experience: A Survey of Ex-members of the Unification Church," in *In Gods We Trust*, ed. Thomas Robbins and Dick Anthony, 275–303 (New Brunswick, N.J.: Transaction; James Lewis and David Bromley, "The Cult Withdrawal Syndrome: A Case of Misattribution of Cause?" *Journal for the Scientific Study of Religion* 26 (1987): 508–22; David Bromley, "Deprogramming as a Mode of Exit from New Religious Movements: The Case of the Unificationist Movement," in *Falling from the Faith*, ed. David Bromley, 185–204 (Beverly Hills,Calif.: Sage, 1988). See Bromley and Richardson (note 23) and Shupe and Bromley (notes 99 and 114) for more details on the early history of deprogramming.

118. The major movie by Academy Award–winning director Jane Campion, *Holy Smoke* (2000), supposedly illustrates an attempted "exit counseling." Some elements of the film may be typical, even if they were upsetting to some in the anticult movement. However, the deprogramee's ability to assert herself and take charge of the situation as did Kate Winslet, who starred, seems highly unlikely.

119. See the claim of one prominent deprogrammer to have deprogrammed more than twenty-five hundred people in Ted Patrick (with T. Dulak), *Let Our Children Go!* (New York: Dutton, 1976).

120. However, as a consequence of some deprogrammings, lawsuits have been filed against parents and others (see William Shepherd, "Constitutional Law and Marginal Religions," in Bromley and Richardson (note 23), 258–66, and charges of kidnapping have been brought against some of those involved. Evidence is building that indicates that some persons have been both physically and psychologically harmed by the actions of deprogrammers (see Solomon [note 117] and J. T. Ungerleider and K. K. Wellisch, "Coercive Persuasion [Brainwashing], Religious Cults, and Deprogramming," *American Journal of Psychiatry* 136[3] [1979]: 279–82), and some have developed apparently severe psychological problems as a result (see John Clark, "Problems in Referral of Cult Members," *Journal of the National Association of Private Psychiatric Hospitals* 9[4] [1978]: 19–21). The efforts may also solidify religious groups against the perceived external enemies—the deprogrammers (see Eileen Barker, "With Enemies Like That ... Some Functions of Deprogramming as an Aid to Sectarian Membership," in Bromley and Richardson [note 23] 329–44). Thus, as a tactic of social control of the cults, deprogramming cannot be viewed as an unqualified success. The process of coercive deprogramming that has led some to claim that it is deprogramming, and not the recruitment practices of the newer religions, that most resembles purported "thought reform" and "mind control" techniques (see Richardson [note 116]). See Gamson (note 24) for the most thorough discussion available on the idea of violence as a tactic of social protest and the "success" of using violence in social conflict situations.

121. Brock Kilbourne, "Deconversion: The Conversion out of Religions," paper presented at the annual meeting of Pacific Sociological Association, San Jose, Calif. (1983).

122. See Anthony F. C. Wallace, *Religion: An Anthropological View* (New York: Random House, 1970).

123. Kilbourne (note 121).

124. See David Bromley, "Conservatorships and Deprogramming," in Bromley and Richardson (note 23), 267–94, and John LeMoult, "Deprogramming Members of Religious Sects," in Bromley and Richardson (note 23), 234–57.

125. See Shupe and Bromley (note 99).

126. Ibid.; also Richardson (1996) (note 3); Introvigne (note 15); Massimo Introvigne, "Blacklisting or Greenlisting? A European Perspective on the Cult Wars," *Nova Religio* 2: 16–23; Swantko (note 44); Wright (note 1); Tabor and Gallagher (note 1); Bromley et al. (note 47); Marat Shterin and James T. Richardson, "Effects of the Western Anti-cult Movement on Development of Laws concerning Religion in Post-Communist Russia," *Journal of Church and State* 42 (2000): 247–71; Marat Shterin and James T. Richardson, "Religious Minorities and Religious Freedom in Russia: Examining a Major Legal Case," Religion in Eastern Europe 22: 1–38.

127. Shupe and Bromley (note 99).

128. See Introvigne (note 99).

129. See Frank Flinn, "Criminalizing Conversion: The Legislative Assault on New Religions," in *Crime, Values, and Religion*, ed. James Day and William Laufer, 153–91 (Norwood, N.J.: Ablex, 1987); Jeremiah Guttman, "The Legislative Assault on New Religions," in Robbins, Shepherd, and McBride, *Cults, Culture, and the Law* (note 115),

101–10; James T. Richardson, "Consumer Protection and Deviant Religion," *Review of Religious Research* 28(2) (1986): 168–79; Introvigne (note 15); and Shetrin and Richardson (2000) (note 126) for examples of direct attempts to influence legislation on new religions.

130. See Shupe and Bromley (note 99).

131. Attacks on minority religions by entities of the anticult movement can fruitfully be viewed as a form of violence, but these, too, should *not* be considered as indicating a "violent character" of participants in the anticult movement. Similar to violence that seems at first glance to be an inherent part of the new religions, anticult "violence" (in the form of organizational attacks and deprogramming) is better viewed as arising out of the competitive and conflictual relationship between new religions and the dominant culture (see Kilbourne and Richardson [1984] [note 6]). Both deprogramming and acts of violence by cult members, for instance, appear to arise from the conflictual relationship between religious groups and external forces in dominant society, including the anticult movement.

132. Much of the information in this paragraph is derived from Shupe and Bromley (notes 99 and 114).

133. See Meade Emory and Lawrence Zelenak, "The Tax-exempt Status of Communitarian Religious Organizations: An Unnecessary Controversy?" in Robbins, Shepherd, and McBride, *Cults, Culture, and the Law* (note 115), 177–201; James T. Richardson, "The 'Deformation' of New Religious Groups," in Robbins, Shepherd, and McBride, *Cults, Culture, and the Law* (note 115), 163–75; James Richardson, *Money and Power in the New Religions* (New York: Mellen, 1988); James T. Richardson, "Changing Times: Religion, Economics, and the Law in Contemporary America," *Sociological Analysis* 49 (suppl.) (1988): 1–14.

134. This effort may have backfired since a number of mainstrean religious organizations came to the defense of Reverend Moon because they organized their own finances similarly to the methods used by the Unification Church. Also, the effort attracted the attention of major legal scholars, as evidenced by the fact that Harvard law professor Lawrence Tribe carried the appeal to the U.S. Supreme Court. See Herbert Richardson, ed., *Constitutional Issues in the Case of Rev. Moon* (New York: Mellen, 1984); James T. Richardson, "Public Opinion and the Tax-evasion Trial of Reverend Moon," *Behavioral Sciences and the Law* 10 (1992): 53–63; and Carlton Sherwood, *The Inquisition: The Persecution and Prosecution of the Reverend Sun Myung Moon* (Washington, D.C.: Regnery Gateway, 1991).

135. See Garrison (note 41).

136. See Carter (note 91) and also Richardson (note 91).

137. See Swantko (note 44).

138. See Richardson (note 44).

139. See Beckford (note 3); James T. Richardson and Barend van Driel, "New Religions in Europe: A Comparison of Developments and Reactions in England, France, Germany, and the Netherlands," in Shupe and Bromley (1994) (note 114), 129–70; Anson Shupe, Bert Hardin, and David Bromley, "A Comparison of the Anti-cult Movement in the U.S. and Germany," in *Of Gods and Men: New Religious Movements in the West*, ed. Eileen Barker, 177–91 (Macon, Ga.: Mercer, 1983).

140. See James T. Richardson and Massimo Introvigne, "'Brainwashing' Claims in Official Governmental Reports in Western Europe," *Journal for the Scientific Study of Religion* (forthcoming, 2000), as well as Introvigne (note 15). Also on Belgium see Willy Fautre, "Belgium's Anti-sect War," *Social Justice Research* 12(4) (1999): 353–64; and on

France see Massimo Introvigne, "Holy Mountains and Anti-cult Ecology: The Campaign against the Aumist Religion in France," *Social Justice Research* 12(4) (1999): 365–75, and Swantko (note 44). On Germany see Hubert Seiwert, "The German Enquette Commission on Sects: Political Conflicts and Compromises," *Social Justice Research* 12(4) (1999): 323–40, and Irving Hexham and Karla Poewe, "'Verfassungsfeindlich': Church, State, and New Religions in Germany," *Nova Religio* 2(2) (1999): 208–27.

141. For more on the situation in France see Massimo Introvigne and Gordon Melton, *Pour en finir avec les sectes* (Milano: Di Giovanni, 1996), and Introvigne (note 15).

142. See Galina Krylova, "The Jehovah's Witness Case in Moscow," paper presented at CESNUR conference, Bryn Athyn, Penn. (1999), and Marat Shetrin and James T. Richardson, "Local Laws Restricting Religion in Russia: Precursors of Russia's New National Law," *Journal of Church and State* 40 (1998): 319–41.

143. See especially Shetrin and Richardson (2000) (note 126).

144. See James T. Richardson and Marat Shetrin, "Court Cases Involving New Religions in Russia," *Social Justice Research* 12(4) (1999): 393–408.

145. Obviously, situations such as occurred with the Aum Shinrikyo in Japan represent something of a limiting case for this assertion. As noted herein and in Reader (notes 1 and 7) and Wessinger, *How the Millennium Comes Violently* (note 2), this group became extremely violent as its failure to accomplish its goals interacted with growing opposition from external forces.

146. See the special issue of *Nova Religio* 2(1) (1998), which contains the comments of several scholars on this conflict and polarization. Also see James T. Richardson, "Sociology and the New Religion: 'Brainwashing,' the Courts, and Religious Freedom," in *Witnessing for Sociology: Sociologists in Court*, ed. Pamela Jenkins and Steve Kroll-Smith, 115–34 (New York: Praeger, 1996); Robbins (1997) (note 1); and Kaplan (note 7), as well as Reader (note 7), for illustration of the seriousness of the conflicts over how to interpret the phenomenon of newer religions. The conflict, which has also engulfed this field of study in Europe and elsewhere, has involved personal attacks and lawsuits against scholars and professional associations by other academics and has moved well beyond friendly differences of opinion.

147. See Marx (note 15).

148. Richardson (note 133) claims that the diverting of significant resources into defensive efforts by new religions is one of the major ways that they are "deformed" from their original goals and organizational structure.

RECENT REFERENCES:

Bromley, David (2004). "Violence and New Religious Movements." In James Lewis (ed.), *The Oxford Handbook of New Religious Movements*, (pgs. 143–162). Oxford: Oxford University Press.

Bromley, David and Gordon Melton (2002). *Cults, Religion, and Violence* (Cambridge: Cambridge University Press.

Chang, Maria (2004). *Falun Gong and the End of Days*. New Haven: Yale University Press.

Dawson, Lorne (2002). "Crisis of Charismatic Legitimacy and Violent Behavior in New Religious Movements." In D. Bromley and G. Melton (eds.), *Cults, Religion, and Violence*(pgs. 80–101). Cambridge: Cambridge University Press.

Juergensmeyer, Mark (2009). "Religious Violence." In *The Oxford Handbook of Sociology of Religion*, edited by Peter Clarke (pgs. 890–908). Oxford: Oxford University Press.

Juergensmeyer, Mark (2003). *Terror in the Mind of God: The Global rise of Religious Violence, rev. edition.* Berkeley: University of California Press.

Juergensmeyer, Mark, and Margo Kitts (2008). *The Princeton Reader on Religious Violence.* Princeton: University of Princeton press.

Krakauer, Jon (2003). *Under the Banner of Heaven: A Story of a Violent Faith.* New York: Doubleday.

Oleson, Theodore and James Richardson (2007). "The Confluence of Research Traditions on Terrorism and Religion: A Social Psychological Examination." *Psicologia Politica* 43: 39–5.

Rahn, Patsy (2002). "The Chemistry of a Conflict: The Chinese Government and the Falun Gong." *Terrorism and Political Violence* 4: 41–65.

Robbins, Thomas (2003). "Comparing Incidents of Extreme 'Cult Violence': A Comment on' Is the Cannon on Jonestown Closed?'," *Nova Religio* 6: 365–575.

Walliss, John (2005). Making Sense of the Movement for the Restoration of the Ten Commandments of God." *Nova Religio* 9: 49–66.

Wessinger, Catherine (2006). New Religions and Violence." In Eugene Gallagher and Michael Ashcraft (eds.), *Introduction to New and Alternative Religions in America* (pgs 165–205). Westport, CT: Greenwood Press.

Wessinger, Catherine (2002). "New religious movements and conflicts with law enforcement." In Derek Davis and Barry Hankins (eds.), *New Religious Movements and Religious Liberty in America.* (pgs. 115–139). Waco: Baylor University Press.

3

Reciprocal Totalism: The Toxic Interdependence of Anticult and Cult Violence

Dick Anthony, Thomas Robbins, and Steven Barrie-Anthony

Introduction

Millenarian movements have been involved in a number of episodes of collective homicidal or suicidal violence. One result has been an intensification of the stigma that had already been attached to "cults" and to the menace of cultic "mind control" or "brainwashing," which is viewed in some quarters as a linchpin of such groups' violent proclivities.[1] The stigma seems presently to be particularly powerful in Western Europe and in China, where the prosecutorial cult/brainwashing discourse, imported (like many "cults") from the United States, has become influential. This discourse has been taken up by official public commissions of inquiry and has influenced legislation in France.[2] A variety of heterogeneous and nonviolent groups have been assumed in Europe to be similar to the sensationally violent Order of the Solar Temple, which is viewed as the "quintessential cult."[3]

Several social scientists have argued that while sensational claims about "brainwashing" in "cults" are misleading and (to use legal jargon) more prejudicial than probative, nevertheless religio-ideological *totalism*, which is a frequent element in claims about "mind control," certainly exists and can in certain circumstances and in conjunction with other elements have dysfunctional and polarizing consequences and may sometimes be related to violence and other problems.[4] This chapter builds on discussions by the authors of the psychology of apocalyptic totalism and the issue of violence (see note 4), and also extrapolates the statement of Robert Lifton that "totalism begets totalism,"[5] to develop our view that militant reactions against totalistic sects that are perceived as menacing can acquire a totalistic (and thus a persecutory) quality of their own. We also argue that, when such attacks upon deviant beliefs have been combined with physical force either through kidnapping and deprogramming or through the imposition of the power of the state to punish such beliefs through conservatorships or civil actions, they constitute a form of violence.

Totalism is a relative rather than an absolute characteristic, and such persecution may take the form of overstereotyping and the tendency to treat a broad range of esoteric groups as equivalent to a tiny minority of notorious and sensationally violent sects. Totalistic anticult ideology treats a bewildering spiritual diversity as polarized between legitimate churches and sinister cults, autonomous and nonautonomous devotees, and so on. Anticult activities based upon such dualistic ideology may in turn play a role in triggering the further totalization of a group; and a cycle of increasing totalization between both the group and the countergroup response may escalate out of control to the point that it triggers the violent denouement that was formerly only one of a variety of possible outcomes of the group's development. Thus, a number of factors, including totalistic oppositional provocation, may determine whether and when violence in a totalistic group actually ensues.

Totalism

The totalism concept was originally defined by Lifton's mentor, psychoanalyst Erik Erikson, who developed it in a seminal article[6] describing the affinity between totalitarian ideologies and the personality makeup of individuals who are predisposed to respond favorably to such ideologies.[7] When people think of "totalism," they sometimes think of institutional or communal totalism: comprehensive regulation or regimentation of participants' activities in "total institutions." In this chapter, on the other hand, we are concerned with totalism as it was defined by Erikson and later by Robert Lifton;[8] that is, we focus on totalism as a composite sociopsychological structure or "milieu," resulting from the interaction between a certain type of individual identity (i.e., individual totalism), on the one hand, and totalistic ideology on the other.

Lifton applied Erikson's totalism concept to the experiences of forty interview subjects who had undergone Chinese thought reform. He found the concept useful in explaining why only two of these forty subjects, Father Simon and Miss Darrow, were significantly influenced by thought reform. (These two subjects did not actually convert to communism; at most they had become, in the terminology of the McCarthyist period, "fellow travelers" of communism.)

Lifton follows Erikson in viewing the totalism concept as a way of explaining why such totalistic individuals are differentially responsive to totalitarian ideologies. Lifton refers to such people as having been characterized by "individual totalism" before they even encountered the thought-reform milieu. Thus, Lifton states that by "ideological totalism," he means "to suggest the coming together of an immoderate ideology with equally immoderate character traits—an extremist meeting ground of people and ideas."[9] In both Erikson's and Lifton's definitions of totalism, then, the concept refers to the sociopsychological structure resulting from the interaction between totalistic people and totalistic ideology, rather than simply to a sociological property of totalitarian organizations.[10]

In applying Erikson's totalism concept to the thought reform experiences of his subjects, Lifton famously identified eight "themes" of the totalistic milieu: *milieu control*, i.e., monopoly of the spatial and informational environment; *mystical manipulation of powerful symbols*; *demand for purity*, i.e., the experiential world is sharply polarized between the pure and the impure, the absolutely good and the absolutely evil with respect to ideas, feelings and actions; *the cult of confession*, i.e., the obsession with the personal confession of violations of the absolute division between pure and impure ideas, feelings and actions; *the sacred science*, i.e., the claim that the ideology provides the ultimate moral vision for the ordering of human existence and that it also expresses airtight logic and absolute "scientific" precision; *the loading of the language*, i.e., totalist ideology is expressed in clichés and verbal formulas that discourage independent thought; *doctrine over person*, i.e., the subordination of individual human experience to doctrinal claims; and *the dispensing of existence*, i.e., the totalist milieu draws a sharp distinction between people and nonpeople, between those true believers, who have a right to exist and those with a different worldview, who do not. With the notable exception of the sociological property of "milieu control," these totalist themes pertain primarily to beliefs rather than to patterns of group behavior.

Lifton notes the following with regard to these eight "psychological themes" of ideological totalism:

> Each has a totalistic quality; each depends upon an equally absolute philosophical assumption; and each mobilizes certain individual emotional tendencies, mostly of a polarizing nature. Psychological theme, philosophical rationale and polarized individual tendencies are interdependent; they require rather than directly cause, each other. In combination they create an atmosphere which may temporarily energize or exhilarate, but which at the same time poses the greatest of human threats.[11]

More recently Lifton has identified totalism as synonymous with "political and religious fundamentalism," because of fundamentalism's tendency to define the world in absolute (i.e., dualistic) terms. Lifton has stated that:

> the quest for absolute or "totalistic" belief systems . . . has produced nothing short of a worldwide epidemic of political and religious

fundamentalism—of movements characterized by the literalized embrace of sacred texts containing absolute truth for all persons and a mandate for militant, often violent measures taken against designated enemies of truth or mere unbelievers.[12]

"Fundamentalism," in Lifton's view, "can create the most extreme expressions of totalism, of the self's immersion in all-or-nothing ideological and behavior patterns."[13]

The core element of ideological totalism, in our view, is *the radical, absolute division of humanity into dual evaluative categories* such as saved/damned, real persons/false persons, human/subhuman, God's people/"mud people," and so on. Elsewhere we have linked ideological totalism with what we have termed *exemplary dualism*, an apocalyptic theme "in which contemporary sociopolitical or socioreligious forces are viewed as absolute contrast categories in terms not only of moral virtue but also of eschatology and the millennial destiny of humankind."[14] Exemplary dualism weds dualistic moral absolutism to history and social tension; that is, "The great temptation of apocalyptic eschatology is to externalize good and evil in terms of present historical conflicts."[15] Anthony and Robbins have noted that most of Lifton's eight motifs of ideological totalism "can be derived from a conception of close-knit, authoritarian movements with intense solidarity and adherence to a distinctly apocalyptic and dualistic worldview."[16]

In Erikson's and Lifton's usage, the totalism concept is heuristically suggestive but somewhat vague. In this chapter we extrapolate their development and application of the totalism concept into a more formal model of totalitarian influence by integrating it with contemporary research on millenarian movements, the psychoanalytic concepts of "splitting" and "projective identification," and the sociological concept of "deviance amplification."

Totalism and Splitting

As we have indicated, Robert Lifton's use of the ideological totalism idea in his thought reform research was an application and extension of the totalism concept originally developed by his mentor, Erik Erikson. Lifton found the concept useful in explaining why only two of these forty subjects were significantly influenced by thought reform. As we said earlier, Lifton accepts Erickson's position that the individual totalism concept explains why some people are responsive to totalitarian ideology whereas others are not.

Erikson viewed totalism as a proclivity or an inclination of some persons "under certain conditions to undergo . . . that sudden total realignment, and, as it were, co-alignment which accompanies conversion to the totalitarian conviction that the state may and must have absolute power over the minds as well as the lives and the fortunes of its citizens."[17]

Erikson saw the total alignments and realignments that characterize conversion and deconversion to totalistic ideology as similar to the affective vicissitudes of early childhood in which a child may suddenly—if only briefly—switch back and forth from total love to total hate of "primary objects" (e.g., mother/father figures). Psychoanalysts see such unstably polarized total responses to parental figures as the origin of the ego defense of "splitting," i.e., the tendency to view the world dualistically in terms only of all-bad or all-good categories.[18] Splitting relates to the trait of "intolerance of ambiguity," which is characteristic of "authoritarian" personalities. It also refers to the dissociative polarization of the self-concept or ego identity into all-bad and all-good components. Splitting of the object and splitting of the self are viewed as invariably correlated with one another.[19]

In Erikson's view, individuals who tend to split the world and the self into all-good or all-bad categories are prone to conversion to totalitarian ideologies. According to Erikson, in the psychology of some adults:

> [V]iolent loves and hates and sudden conversions and aversions share
> with the child's fetishism and fears such factors as the exclusive focusing
> of a set of (friendly or unfriendly) affects on a person or idea; the
> primitivization of all affects thus focused; and a utopian (or cataclysmic)
> expectation of a total gain or a total loss to come from this focus.[20]

Splitting, which may be normal in a child, is thus viewed as distinctively conducive to conversions to totalistic ideologies in an adult. Splitting is fundamental to totalitarian psychology and entails a tendency to divide all humanity into good and evil, saved and damned, human and subhuman, and so on, and to shift quickly back and forth between these polarized categories. In other words a person with a polarized, totalist sense of self may idealize a person, group, or idea today, and then vehemently repudiate and disapprove of it tomorrow.

Erikson also uses the term *totalism* to denote an all-encompassing belief system that conceptualizes the world in terms of a comprehensive set of evaluative polarities, with a central duality such as "Aryan/non-Aryan" or "capitalist/communist," which renders subordinate and auxiliary polarities compelling. (Such a division of the world into polarized all-good and all-bad categories is a more general manifestation of the concept of splitting discussed earlier.)

In his later writings, Erikson used the term *pseudospeciation* to denote what we consider a key aspect of totalism: the tendency for totalists to treat stigmatized categories of persons, identified in terms of race, class, creed, color, religion, sexual preference, and so on, as totally different, indeed radically inferior, species—in effect subhuman.[21] Although Lifton does not explicitly use this term in *Chinese Thought Reform and the Psychology of Totalism*, the pseudospeciation concept is convergent with his discussion of ideological totalism, particularly his notion of the *dispensing of existence*, which implies that nonbelievers have no compelling claims or rights, at least when apocalyptic push comes to shove.[22] Persons who belong to categories stigmatized by totalist ideologies may be treated as nonpersons, even as subhuman.

In addition, as we have already indicated, Lifton claimed that Father Simon and Miss Darrow—the two of his forty subjects who were influenced by Chinese thought reform—had totalistic personalities prior to their exposure to the indoctrination process.[23] Thus, for both Lifton and Erikson the core of ideological totalism is an immoderate, absolutist ideology, particularly attractive to immoderate, volatile, and alienated persons, which *radically divides the world into legitimate and illegitimate species.*

Confrontation, Violence, and Projective Identification

Totalistic movements are not necessarily violent, but elements of the psychology of totalism may place a premium on *confrontation* with perceived exemplars of evil. The role of *contrast symbols* is psychologically vital. An elect group is specified whose members are encouraged to define their collective and personal identities in terms of absolute contrasts with radically devalued, hostile categories of outsiders. The group envisions itself as an enclave of truth, purity, and virtue in a corrupt, evil, and doomed world, and it may anticipate or even welcome the world's hostility.

Ideological totalism/exemplary dualism, then, presents to adherents an idealized system of exemplary leaders and values contrasted with its radically devalued opposite. Followers with polarized self-constructs or "divided selves" can identify with heroic leaders and the ideals they embody, while they themselves can hope to become new, heroic exemplars of such ideals. At the same time, rejected feelings of weakness, failure, lack of worth, sinfulness, shame, and guilt, which were once part of dissociated or split-off self-images, can now be projected onto designated outsiders viewed as innate inferiors or vile "enemies"—*contrast symbols* perceived as alien to the idealized community of believers. Through the dynamics of "projective identification," converts actually become somewhat psychologically dependent upon the human scapegoats or personified contrast symbols, who symbolize evil.

The psychoanalytic/object relations concept of *projective identification* refers to a psychological defense mechanism that is associated with splitting. Splitting and projective identification are viewed as "primitive" ego defenses that complement one another in a flawed attempt to support self-esteem and a coherent sense of self:

> The primitive defense of "splitting," of seeing oneself and others as all good, and dumping the all-bad object [and dissociated bad component of the self] externally onto another person, can be viewed as the forerunner of the more mature defense of repression . . .

> The second primitive defense is "projective identification" which is a forerunner of the more mature defense of projection . . . with projection

being solely an intrapsychic defense, and projective identification both an intrapsychic and interpersonal defense mechanism. *One individual evacuates a good or bad, self or object image externally onto another person, who then serves as a container for this projection. However, the other is induced through verbal and non-verbal communication into thinking, feeling, or behaving in accordance with this projection.* Thus there is an attempt to transplant one's internal split image into another and to manipulate the other to collude with it. The other's evoked response is then reinternalized through identification, thereby serving as a negative feedback loop, so that objective reality reinforces the projector's internal world of images. (emphasis ours)[24]

Simple projection, then, describes a one-person activity, whereas projective identification involves an interactive, two-person activity. In simple projection, one avoids the person upon whom one has projected unconscious motives, so that the targeted person is not directly affected by this intrapsychic maneuver. In projective identification, on the other hand, one projects split-off, unconscious motives (sexuality, aggression) or self-attributions (inferiority, evil) onto others and also manipulates them in such a way that they come to identify with the projected motives or attributions as their own. The targeted persons then act out the projected motives or personal characteristics in relation to the person doing the projecting, with the result that the original projections come to constitute *a self-fulfilling prophecy*.

For instance, person X is hostile toward person Y and projects this emotion onto Y so that X comes to feel that Y is actually hostile toward him. Then X begins to treat Y as an enemy, which in turn leads Y to resent X and to defensively treat X as an enemy, thus apparently confirming the accuracy of X's original projection.

The *paranoid-schizoid* stage of development is the childhood stage at which splitting and projective identification are the primary defense mechanisms. Those who continue to be fixated at this stage are viewed by psychoanalysts as suffering from "personality disorders," i.e., as having polarized selves that are split between unrealistically positive and unrealistically negative self-concepts. Such polarized selves alternate in relation to the fluctuation of external circumstances, with even minor fluctuations tending to trigger a shift from a grandiose to a very negative sense of self.

Such people are prone to projecting in turn each side of this split sense of self onto others, and to interacting with them in such a way that such alternately positive and negative projections are confirmed by the behavior of the others toward them. Idealizing the other persons tends to produce positive attitudes toward themselves, but when minor disappointments lead them to demonize the others, negative attitudes and disruptions in relationships are triggered. Because such unstable splitting and projective identification tend to result in unstable personal relationships and vocational histories, those prone to such tendencies are continuously searching for some more stable solution to their unhappy lives.

One solution to such paradoxes of identity, which Erikson referred to as "identity confusion," may be to convert to totalistic religious or political movements in which (1) the negative self-images of members are split off and projected onto the mainstream world; (2) the grandiosely positive self-images of members are affirmed and stabilized by membership in a group viewed as embodying the solution to the world's evil nature; (3) the group through projective identification interacts with the outside world in a manner that tends to confirm such projections and identifications of the dualistically split selves of the members; and (4) totalistic ideology, often of an apocalyptic or millenarian type, rationalizes both the projective identification of the negative self-images upon the outside world, and also the projective identification of positive self-images within the group.

The resulting confrontations with the evil outside world may become essential for valorizing the system and reinforcing participants' heroic identities. A sense of taking dynamic action against the forces of evil and their human embodiments may become necessary to maintain devotees' sense of wholeness and to preserve the rigid boundaries of the totalist self.

Our explanatory account of splitting and projective identification as the sociopsychological mechanism underlying the volatility of totalistic confrontations is consistent with the observations—at a more global level of description—of Lifton and other students of the dynamics of millenarian development. For instance, Lifton maintains that fundamentalist totalism is "always on the edge of violence, because it ever mobilizes for an absolute confrontation with designated evil, thereby justifying any action taken to eliminate evil."[25]

Charisma, Projective Identification, and Instability

Totalist movements generally have charismatic leaders—"heroic" exemplars of the movement's ideals. Charismatic leadership is viewed by some social scientists as inherently volatile by virtue of both the absence of institutionalized *restraints* on the leader's arbitrariness, and the absence of institutionalized *supports for* the leader's authority. In the absence of institutionalized support for his authority, a charismatic leader may attempt to maintain his position by aggressively curbing dissent, expelling rivals, and provoking confrontations ("crisis mongering") to dramatically demonstrate his indispensability.[26]

Another factor encouraging charismatic volatility may be the tendency for the leaders of totalistic groups to be afflicted by personality disorders—and their constituent characteristics, which include the unstable polarized selves, splitting, and projective identification referred to earlier. According to some clinicians, charismatic prophets and gurus leading deviant sects often exhibit "narcissistic" personality syndromes, and tend to perceive the movement and its participants as *extensions of themselves,* which may lower inhibitions against risking their followers' lives.[27]

Followers, on the other hand, may narcissistically project their aims and aspirations onto the charismatic leader such that they may sometimes mislead themselves as to the (perhaps shifting) nature of his leadership, goals, and the direction in which he is taking the group. Some messianic leaders of totalist groups have grandiose identities that lead them to equate the fate of humankind with their personal aggrandizement and thus to demonize any internal or external opposition.[28]

It is likely, then, that at least the more extremely totalist/dualist movements tend to recruit persons with dissociated aggressive tendencies. The dualistic, pseudospeciating movement provides a setting in which such tendencies may be enhanced and, more important, *channeled* and directed toward the movement's ideological scapegoats and contrast symbols. Actual violence and other modes of aggressive acting out may also come to the fore. According to the author of a study of a racist Christian identity group, members engage in self-idealization and project weakness and deviance onto devalued outsiders, for "to perceive oneself as pure, impure feelings and impulses must be projected onto a world where they become embodied in others."[29] The charismatic racist leader can thus "empower" alienated, rebellious, or ambivalent recruits by legitimating their pent-up hostility and directing it to scapegoated contrast symbols: "As a transitional object, the cult leader helps members express hostile impulses . . . When the leader initiates an antisocial act . . . members become free to act in a guiltless and violent way."[30]

However, the solutions to identity problems provided by totalistic movements are often unstable. In part, such identity solutions are unstable because the "projective identifications"— which bond followers to the leader and also create a type of psychological dependency of the group on its devalued contrast symbols —are prone to *sudden reversal*. Beloved leaders and comrades can almost instantly become excoriated betrayers.[31] Exalted ideals must be embodied precariously in flawed and fallible leaders. The sacrifices that participants make in a highly disciplined, authoritarian sect feed into a buildup of latent resentment that may quickly erupt under certain conditions and induce apostasy.

According to Catherine Wessinger, various developments can enhance a group's volatility and thus the probability of a violent response to external threat, including disconfirmed prophecies, failure to achieve grandiose goals, traumatic high-level defections, internal conflicts, diminishing charisma of the leader, and lack of movement growth.[32] According to Lifton, similar vicissitudes and traumas can undermine the internalized psychological support system of "functional megalomania," which reinforces the grandiose self-concept of a messianic totalist leader such as Shôkô Asahara of Aum Shinrikyo, with the result that the psychological reinforcement system disintegrates under stress and becomes transformed into rampant and volatile delusions of persecution.[33]

Notwithstanding these dynamics, violent confrontations *arise only with respect to a small minority of totalist/dualist movements*. The urge to palpably confront evil may not always be overwhelming; moreover, there are other, more manageable and routinized ways of confronting evil's human objectifications. These include *proselytization*, which may produce a validating sense of "winning over the enemy"; *aggressive prayer*, e.g., Pentecostal "prayer warrior" mystiques; *political action*; or even just "*waiting for the end*," when the sense of an imminent cataclysmic finale produces a thrill of expectation and validation of heroic movement-based identities.

Unfortunately, such milder forms of the confrontation with evil may sometimes become less effective. For instance, proselytization may for various reasons be curtailed (e.g., the movement retreats to an isolated wilderness enclave) or may appear to be losing its efficacy; the same may be said of political action or activism.[34] Confrontation may sometimes actually be sought by the opponents of totalist movements e.g., as occurred in different ways at Jonestown, Ruby Ridge, and Waco.[35] The features often associated with totalist movements include messianic charismatic leaders, authoritarian regimes, strong internal pressures for conformity, social encapsulation and isolation of participants, rigid puritanism or occasionally wild antinomianism, nasty scapegoating of certain social groups and categories, utopiate or apocalyptic visions, and absolutistic condemnation of the status quo; these features generally ensure that there is no dearth of vehement opposition to such groups.

Such opposition may sometimes be confrontational and may even come to possess a somewhat totalistic and persecutory quality. Totalist groups make handy scapegoats and thus may sometimes be victimized. Occasionally, rival totalist movements will furiously fight it out, sometimes literally, as with Nazi storm troopers and communist cadres battling on the streets of the Weimar Republic. More recent examples include communists versus clansmen in North Carolina, and neo-Nazis versus their strident European opponents.

In our view, anticult totalism may be one factor that tends to initiate such cycles of escalating reciprocal totalism—a point we return to later.

The Breakdown of "Normal" Totalism

In the view of Erik Erikson, totalism presents a risk of violence or dangerous extremism, but it is not necessarily pathological relative to the individual totalist's emotional condition. Totalism can address "split self" and "negative identity" patterns by allowing a convert to identify with heroic virtues and externalize devalued personal attributes, thereby resolving identity confusion and imparting a sense of wholeness, personal integrity, and authenticity.[36] Thus, totalism, particularly in its milder forms, is often therapeutic. In this connection, involvement in a "charismatic group" not infrequently produces relief from symptoms of neurotic distress[37] and can, particularly if involvement is temporary, assist a young person in transcending a traumatic disruption of adolescent or postadolescent development and in negotiating the transition to adulthood.[38] The shrill articulation of strident dualistic values can actually provide an empowering transition to an adult sense of efficacy and self-confidence on the part of some withdrawn and inarticulate young persons.[39]

Totalism and dualistic moral absolutism are to some degree built into our culture and can be seen in various themes and orientations that are not necessarily combined with institutional-communal totalism.[40] Various dualistic orientations, including racism, sexism, homophobia, anticommunism, and even anticultism, have totalistic overtones.

The spread of multiculturalism as a social ethos has been associated with an aggressive attack on traditional quasi-totalistic, dehumanizing orientations such as racism, sexism, homophobia, and so on. It is arguable that the strident contemporary reaction against deplorable traditional prejudices may itself take on a somewhat totalistic quality. The relentlessly conformist quality of social campaigns against traditional invidious dualisms such as sexism, racism, or homophobia may occasionally actually work in favor of targeted totalisms that may benefit from an "individualist" reaction against conformist "political correctness."[41] In any case, the breakdown of "normal totalism," and dualistic norms against women, minorities, and some sexual preferences, can at least contribute to a transitional milieu of anomie or perceived moral ambiguity in which new totalist movements,[42] as well as strident antitotalist campaigns,[43] can emerge.

As archetypal enclaves of intolerant totalistic thinking, authoritarian "cults" have become prime targets of the attack on received dualistic moral absolutism and traditional totalistic pseudospeciation. The attack on cults is thus partly related to strident multiculturalist ideology and contemporary "intolerance of intolerance."[44]

Anticult Totalism, Violence, and Suppression of Religious Diversity

Lifton first articulated the principle that totalism begets totalism in the section of his book on Chinese thought reform that discusses the reciprocal escalation of totalistic themes in the conflicts between communism and American anticommunism (especially McCarthyism). He later expressed this same principle in commenting on the extremist tactics employed by the anticult movement against controversial new religions, in particular coercive deprogramming.[45] We will extrapolate and generalize this principle.

There is little question that coercive deprogramming, which employs kidnapping, is the type of totalistic violence that we define in the introduction, i.e., an action that employs physical force with the goal of suppressing religious diversity. Coercive deprogramming has been justified by its perpetrators on the grounds that the original conversion process (the alleged "programming") was itself a coercive and involuntary process, a mental kidnapping that could be undone only by rescues that employed retaliatory violence. However, in this section we argue that anticult totalistic violence is typically employed to undermine the freedom of religious groups that are not guilty of depriving their members of the freedom of religious choice. Rather, anticult coercive totalistic activities—deprogramming, as well as civil legal actions alleging involuntary influence—are typically employed against groups that express types of religious belief of which the anticult movement disapproves.

Totalism in the public mind and as employed by the anticult movement is a somewhat imprecise and not clearly bounded concept, confused as it has been with the very different "brainwashing" concept. It is not always employed very precisely even by Lifton, who popularized the term/concept, which had originated in Erikson's seminal article. The totalism concept thus lends itself to inaccurate application and to use as an ideological weapon against minority movements and heterodox ideologies. For example, an influential legal manifesto by Richard Delgado drew on Lifton's work to condemn "religious totalism" and justify coercive deprogramming as a legitimate therapeutic intervention when it transpired under guardianship or conservatorship orders issued by courts and not under vigilante auspices.[46] Delgado later backed off support of court-ordered coercive deprogramming, and shifted his focus to litigation by ex-members against the groups alleged to have psychologically imprisoned them.[47]

Delgado's treatise, which became the theoretical spearhead of legal measures and litigation tactics in the 1980s, was intendent to combat the alleged use of "mind control" in religious sects, and emphasized the pernicious use of deception by totalistic cults to lure recruits. Delgado treated deception as a functional equivalent to the raw physical coercion by which inmates are placed in POW camps. However, Delgado's analytical model entailed a wild generalization to "cults" per se of one notorious instance of unequivocal deception.[48] More importantly, in actual legal cases, the concept of deception and the coercively imposed loss of the free will of alleged cult victims is typically built around a brainwashing theory—developed by the U.S. Central Intelligence Agency (CIA) for use as a propaganda device—rather than the claimed theoretical foundation of Lifton's version of Erikson's totalism concept.[49] This strategy was originally put into play by the testimony of psychologist Margaret Singer and sociologist Richard Ofshe in a large number of legal cases in the 1980s and early 1990s, and has continued to be used by other anticult experts since then. Singer's and Ofshe's testimony and the legal strategy based upon it were initially largely successful in imposing substantial financial losses upon the new religions against which it was employed; in several cases, the imposed penalties were in the range of $20–30 million, and some groups were forced to declare bankruptcy.

In a 1990 book chapter, Dick Anthony systematically compared the cult brainwashing publications and testimony of Margaret Singer and Richard Ofshe to the Erikson/Lifton totalism concept, on the one hand, and the CIA brainwashing concept of Edward Hunter, on the other.[50] In doing so he established that (1) the totalism concept does not provide, either in its conceptual claims or its empirical applications, any scientific foundation for allegations of coercively imposed involuntary influence, loss of free will, and so on; and that (2) the brainwashing concept, which did claim a scientific status for coercively imposed loss of free will, mind control, and so on, had been repeatedly shown—in internal research programs of the CIA and in research on communist thought reform by Lifton and others—to have no scientific basis. Anthony also demonstrated that Singer's and Ofshe's claims to base their cultic brainwashing testimony on the theoretical foundation of Lifton's research on communist thought reform/totalism was inaccurate and that it was actually based upon the CIA brainwashing concept, which the research of Lifton and others had shown to be without scientific foundation.[51]

Discourse alleging religio-ideological totalism in anticult actions, then, is typically based upon the CIA brainwashing theory. In brainwashing formulations, the concept of "totalism" becomes entirely divorced from its Eriksonian origins as the individual predisposition of some persons with fragmented identities to convert to highly authoritarian movements and ideologies. Instead, brainwashing is conceived as a kind of *omnipotent psychotechnology* that destroys autonomy. The brainwashing concept expresses a duality between "cult slaves,"[52] who have lost their free will and thus their essential humanity, and free, autonomous citizens who are not enmeshed in evil cults.[53] When this distinction is absolutized, a kind of totalistic pseudospeciation emerges, i.e., by radically dividing humanity into those who have and those who do not have free will, cult/brainwashing theory represents a form of totalistic pseudospeciation and religious intolerance that may be particularly adapted to a multicultural milieu.[54] In its use in civil legal cases the effect is to coercively deprive new religions and their members of their constitutionally guaranteed freedom of religious belief.

In our view, then, cult/brainwashing discourse amounts to a form of dehumanizing pseudospeciation in that it radically divides humanity into those who are fully human, have free will, and deserve to be granted the freedom to believe in and practice their religion, on the one hand, and those who are not fully human—enslaved robots who do not deserve or are incapable of exercising religious liberty—on the other.[55]

Since anticult legal testimony is based upon the unscientific brainwashing theory rather than the Lifton/Erikson totalism theory upon which it claims to be based, what it boils down to is the claim that the religious *belief* rather than coercive *conduct* is inherently coercive, and thus should be forbidden by government action in the United States and European countries. Close inspection of the testimony of Margaret Singer and other anticult witnesses shows that such testimony does in fact almost exclusively target religious beliefs and the normal religious practices and rituals that symbolize and express them.[56] Such claims are the heart of anticult religious testimony and legal claims.

In this connection, it is worth noting that the totalistic absolutism of cult/brainwashing discourse inheres not only in the distinction between brainwashed and nonbrainwashed persons—cult slaves vs. real persons—but also in the absolute distinction between the brainwashing techniques of "destructive cults," and the legitimate, non-mind-controlling patterns of influence found in nonstigmatized spiritual groups. According to Philip Jenkins, when anticult writers in the 1980s "described the sinister methods used to induce and maintain personality change [in cults], they were often describing practices like repetitive chant and movement, which are commonly used in religious systems, including large sections of Eastern Orthodox Christianity and even American Protestant revivalism."[57] As two psychiatrists have noted, ritual sequences in nonstigmatized black Baptist and black Pentecostal churches are just as plausible candidates for having powerful, manipulative psychoactive effects as are somewhat similar rituals in allegedly coercive "cults."[58]

In the testimony and publications of Singer and other anticult experts, however, engagement in such rituals in alternative groups constitutes the coercive imposition of false beliefs. The CIA brainwashing theory popularized by Edward Hunter argued that involuntary conversion to communist ideology was achieved by inducing hypnotic states in which victims were highly suggestible, and then exposing them repeatedly to communist propaganda. Singer and other anticult experts typically transfer this argument to Eastern or New Age groups that practice various techniques, such as meditation or the chanting of mantras, intended to enable practitioners to achieve "higher states of consciousness" in which they are able to experience for themselves the truth of the religious beliefs central to the theology of the groups. The core of the disagreement between Singer and members of such groups about their beliefs is twofold: (1) Singer believes that so-called higher states of consciousness are actually primitive, hypnotically induced, dissociated states; 2) she believes that the mystical beliefs that seem self-evidently true to people in such states are valueless clichés, as is obvious to people in a more rational state of mind.

Attempts to Criminalize Religious Beliefs: Since anticult testimony targets religious belief and the traditional religious practices that express them rather than coercive conduct capable of causing involuntary conversion and commitment to religious movements, it seems undeniable that such legal actions are coercive attempts to suppress religious diversity; as such, they are forms of anticult totalism and violence in the sense described in the introduction. This point becomes even more obvious when one realizes that Singer was the leader of anticult activists who worked repeatedly for five years in the midseventies to convince members of Congress and officials in the U.S. Department of Justice to utilize federal kidnapping statutes to make speech and normal religious practices that express certain types of religious beliefs subject to criminal prosecution, and their alleged perpetrators subject to imprisonment. These activities were widely reported by journalists and also discussed in a book chapter by James T. Richardson and Mary White Stewart.[59]

According to a news story circulated by the New York Times Service, these efforts culminated in May 1977, when Representatives Leo J. Ryan and Robert N. Giamo met with Benjamin Civiletti, chief of the Criminal Division of the U.S. Department of Justice, to discuss brainwashing by cults and whether it could serve as the basis for kidnapping actions against several national cults. The representatives also brought to the meeting Margaret Singer and Professor Richard Delgado, who explained the alleged scientific and legal foundations for such charges. For at least five years before the meeting, the Justice Department and the FBI had been receiving complaints against several national religious cults who were allegedly using mind-control techniques to imprison converts against their will. Ten weeks after the meeting, Civiletti sent a letter to Representative Giamo, stating, among other things:

> It continues to be the position of the Criminal Division that allegations of "brainwashing," "mind-control," "thought reform" or "coercive persuasion" would not support a prosecution under the Federal kidnapping statute. . . . A prosecution could not be sustained based upon evidence that an adult of normal intelligence had been "brainwashed" into continued association with a religious sect. Religious proselytizing and the recruitment of and the maintenance of belief through a strict regimen, meditation, chanting, self-denial and the communication of other religious teaching cannot under our laws—as presently enacted—be construed as criminal in nature and serve as the basis for criminal indictment.

Civiletti's letter also said that the government was wary of passing legislation to deal with these problems because such laws could be "an infringement on the sect's free exercise of religion," and that allegations of this type would not support statutes covering "peonage, slavery and involuntary servitude."

Singer's and Delgado's effort to criminalize religious beliefs and traditional religious practices, such as meditation and the chanting of mantras, occurred at the same time that coercive deprogramming/kidnapping (which they never disavowed) and legally mandated coercive deprogramming under conservatorship laws (which they advocated) were also popular remedies for the religious diversity they wished to make illegal. This combination of the advocacy of both involuntary deprogramming and prosecution for kidnapping strongly suggests that the milder civil lawsuit form of anticult violence has been a tactic for which the movement has had to settle, rather than the more extreme forms that its most influential leaders preferred. Imprisonment for heretical beliefs is of course less extreme than extermination in gas ovens as a remedy for religious diversity, but it is certainly well up the scale of totalitarian enforcement of a nation's ideological or theological unanimity through violence.[60]

Finally, anticult totalism manifests in connection with extreme overgeneralization and stereotyping, e.g., the present tendency in continental Western Europe, especially France, to see the sensationally violent Solar Temple movement as the "quintessential cult" and thereby to see small, close-knit, esoteric spiritual movements as inherently suspect and requiring stringent controls.[61] It is worth noting that even the Branch Davidians at Waco, who shot federal agents and may have "suicidally" started a fire, are pointedly excluded by Robert Lifton from his rogues' gallery of highly dangerous groups willing to "force the end" by precipitating an apocalyptic scenario through sensational symbolic violence.[62] In addition, movements much less violent than the Branch Davidians have been stigmatized as potential "Jonestowns" and threatened with persecution.

In our view, then, crusaders against cults share a dualistic proclivity to see all such movements as more or less *interchangeable* malefactors in whom extreme violence is an inherent, fundamental property rather than a situated contingency. The error is not in the description of some movements as totalistic—such allegations may in some cases be accurate—but rather in the totalizing tendency to oversimplify spiritual diversity by the use of polarizing either/or categorizations and dualistic visions from which any ambiguity has been excluded.[63] In this area the totalist visions of cults—of apocalyptic prophets, gurus, and preachers—have their counterparts in the anathemas of their zealous antagonists.[64]

Deviance Amplification: Escalating Cycles of Totalistic Confrontation and Violence

As we have seen, stigmatizing a movement on the basis of a vague evocation of its internal milieu as constituting mind control can itself be a form of totalistic pseudospeciation. Moreover, under the principle that totalism begets totalism, stigmatization could lead a targeted group to enhance its internal totalism and apocalyptic paranoia. Given the principles of projective identification that we have already discussed, at times this can even lead to violence. This is all the more likely to the extent that such totalistic persecution is enforced through concrete activities that effectively limit the group's freedom of religious belief and conduct.

As we have seen, Lifton regards at least some anticult activities, such as coercive deprogramming, as themselves manifestations of totalism. Besides coercive deprogramming, which in the United States at least has declined since the 1970s and early 1980s, various other measures arguably prevent "cultists" from practicing their religion—a privilege restricted to putatively autonomous and nonbrainwashed "free" citizens. These measures include lawsuits seeking damages against religious movements for various alleged harms (e.g., intentional or negligent infliction of emotional distress) that are primarily defined in terms of alleged cultic brainwashing. Large damage awards in this area definitely have implications for destroying (for instance, bankrupting) certain minority religious organizations.[65]

Other legal actions seek custody of the children of devotees when a parent claims that an ex-spouse involved in a devalued sect is by virtue of brainwashing insufficiently mentally competent (i.e., human enough) to be allowed to raise the children or even to be granted extensive noncustodial visitation rights. Members of devalued sects often lose custody of their children—and sometimes substantial visitation rights—if their apostate ex-spouses contest custody. Finally, new legislation passed in France makes it possible for the state to actually disband religious organizations that are convicted of a single instance of alleged mind control. Religious belief of which the state disapproves is here criminalized.[66]

Given the ambiguity and lack of scientific meaning of brainwashing allegations, it is important to realize that these several means of suppressing alleged cultic brainwashing through legal action boil down to the use of state power to suppress the worldviews and shared lifestyles of certain religions or political movements. As we discussed earlier, Erikson defined totalistic ideology first of all as "the totalitarian conviction that the state may and must have absolute power over the minds as well as the lives and the fortunes of its citizens."[67] By Erikson's definition it would seem, then, that these various types of state action, designed to reduce or eliminate allegedly totalistic belief and conduct, are themselves intrinsically totalistic. If totalism begets totalism, through projective identification or other means, such totalistic state action is more likely to create or at least enhance totalism than it is to eliminate or reduce it. Such totalistic consequences may include the incitement of violence within social movements that otherwise would not have occurred.

The use of state power to suppress religious or political belief and conduct by these several means is itself, implicitly at least, a type of violence; if these groups were to refuse to cooperate with such state-imposed legal action, they would be compelled to submit to it by physical force. Targeted groups may come to feel that their only defense against such forceful suppression of their worldviews would be defensive violence directed against either the state or themselves. (Arguably, both types of defensive violence occurred at Jonestown, where the Peoples Temple responded to the congressional investigation of its activities by murdering Rep. Leo Ryan and members of his party, as well by carrying out both murders and suicides with respect to its own members.)

Brainwashing ideology arguably has influenced state action that is even more overtly totalistic, such as that which occurred in the United States at Waco, and in China against the Falun Gong. In these situations, the connection of such totalistic attributions to escalating reciprocal violence seems self-evident.

Brainwashing ideology has also colored U.S. and Canadian governmental reports on the potential for violence in millenarian religious and political movements. Predictions of millenarian violence in such reports may potentially constitute the sort of self-fulfilling prophecies we are discussing here.

The FBI *Project Megiddo* report relies substantially on the work of Margaret Singer, the most influential American theorist of this genre,[68] and its descriptions of the ominous internal totalitarianism of cults incline somewhat in the direction of inflammatory demonology. While the Canadian report on "Doomsday Religious Movements" is less perfervid, Jenkins has criticized the related stereotypical notion of "doomsday cults." According to Jenkins, the doomsday cult concept comes:

> close to making millenarian expectations *ipso facto* a token of cult-like behavior and even a warning symptom of likely mass suicide . . . There

are few limits to the force that can be levied against any group once it has been designated a doomsday cult, a self-fulfilling title if there ever was one. Invoking the specter of mass suicide almost ensures that mass deaths will ensue.[69]

This self-fulfilling prophecy, emergent from the allegation of being a doomsday cult, may actually have affected the escalation of the Waco confrontation into its violent denouement. Federal agents had been influenced in their aggressive response to the Davidians' refusal to admit them into the compound, by anticult conceptions of a fanatic, suicidal, mind-controlling cult.[70]

It has been argued that the eruptions of violence and other antisocial behavior in apocalyptic movements occur in part because the movements become "deformed" or "destabilized" by virtue of aggressive harassment from opponents, including "anticult" activists, recriminating apostates, sensationalist media, "concerned relatives" of devotees, and state officials.[71] Spiraling sequences of "deviance amplification" may ensue whereby the mutual antipathy and suspicion between deviant groups and the votaries of a governmental crackdown reinforce each other and gradually escalate out of control until a catastrophic denouement unfolds.

In the words of the Canadian report:

> Sanctions applied by authorities are often interpreted by a movement as hostile to its existence, which reinforces their apocalyptic beliefs and leads to further withdrawal, mobilization and deviant actions, and which in turn elicits heavier sanctions by authorities. This unleashes a spiral of amplification, as each action amplifies each reaction, and the use of violence is facilitated as the group believes this will ultimately actualize its doomsday scenario.[72]

The Canadian report concludes that "three factors (apocalyptic beliefs, charismatic leadership and [provocative] actions by authorities), whether inherent to the dynamics of a Doomsday Religious Movement or in response to the actions that it engages in, translates into a predisposition toward violent behavior."

James Richardson has discussed the convergence of "deviance amplification" and "conflict/interaction" perspectives in his analysis of cycles of escalating violence between new religions and their anticult antagonists in a wide range of empirical situations. His article is probably the most even-handed, theoretically sophisticated, and empirically detailed application of the deviance-amplification/conflict-interactionist perspective to new religions presently available. He states the following:

> Obviously, if a group's beliefs justify violence, then it is more prone to occur if external entities also expect violence and act on its inevitability. Thus an interactional spiral toward violence can develop as the two

entities interact with each other either directly (such as through face to face negotiations) or indirectly (through media coverage or intermediaries such as informants or others). Thus the interactionist perspective is akin to Roy Wallis' provocative concept of the amplification of deviance developed out of his study of Scientology. What can develop through interactions based on shared views of the other's propensity for violence is an amplification of violent expectations, which in turn can lead to violence itself.[73]

One should realize that such processes of "deviance amplification" or "conflict interaction" observed by sociologists may be the sociological manifestations of the clinical and sociopsychological processes of splitting, projective identification, and totalism begetting totalism that we have described. There may be considerable scientific and practical value in integrating these sociological, social-psychological, and psychological levels of description rather than in viewing them as competing explanations or independent processes.

Conclusion: Internal vs. External Causes of Violence

The relative salience of "endogenous" (internal or intrinsic) and "exogenous" (external or extrinsic, i.e., persecutory) factors in outbreaks of violence involving deviant sects has been described by scholars.[74] In this connection, the FBI Project Megiddo report distinguishes between "defensive violence" and "offensive violence" perpetrated by "cults."[75] According to the FBI report, defensive violence, epitomized by the Branch Davidians at Waco, "is utilized by cults to defend a compound or enclave that was created specifically to eliminate most contact with the dominant culture." In contrast, some "cults with an apocalyptic agenda . . . appear ready to *initiate* rather than *anticipate* violent confrontations to bring about the Armageddon or fulfill 'prophecy' [and] present unique challenges to law enforcement officials." Somewhat similarly, Robert Lifton sees certain groups, such as Aum Shinrikyo and the "Manson Family," as prepared to "force the end" in the sense of precipitating, through sensational violence, an anticipated apocalyptic scenario.[76]

From the point of view we have developed in this chapter, the distinction between endogenous and exogenous causes of violence in religious or political movements may represent an artificial dichotomy. In both Erikson's and Lifton's treatment of it, totalism and nontotalism are relative rather than absolute distinctions. All social groups are totalistic to one degree or another, and, thus, all religious or political movements have both an endogenous potential for violent acting out in relation to contrast groups onto which they project their disowned negative qualities, and a tendency to increase their own totalism and potential for violence as a response to totalistic persecution by outside groups.

As we have already discussed, projective identification in its original psychoanalytic usage refers to an interaction between two people, each reacting to the other (i.e., one who is doing the projecting and another who is identifying with the motives or self-attributions that are being projected). So described, projective identification has both endogenous and exogenous dimensions, which can vary independently but which are never entirely separate from each other.

The endogenous variable in projective identification, that is, the tendency to project disowned attributes and motives, may vary substantially from person to person, but is never entirely absent from any person's defensive functioning. Similarly, the exogenous variable—the tendency to identify with and to act out other people's projections—also varies from person to person but is never entirely absent from anyone's makeup.

In this chapter, we have suggested that the projective identification concept may be generalized from a description of the interaction between individuals to a description of the interaction between groups. So extended, it may help to explain Lifton's principle, that totalism begets totalism, as well as the sociological process of deviance amplification. Assuming such to be the case, an accurate explanation of any specific occurrence of group violence must include assessment of both the degree of endogenous causation, and the degree of exogenous causation. Some groups may be so highly totalistic that they are very vulnerable to the triggering effect, i.e., prone to identifying with and acting out, even very modest degrees of totalistic projection from the outside world. This may have occurred at Waco or Jonestown.

Other groups may be relatively nontotalistic and thus highly resistant to identifying with unflattering projections from the outside. That is, they can resist identifying with even relatively extreme attributions of evil or pseudospeciation and can continue to interact in a moderate manner even when they are being treated as the enemy to a relatively extreme degree. Nevertheless, given the interactive model we are proposing, even such a relatively nontotalistic group could be driven to become more totalistic, or even to undertake some form of totalistic violence, given sufficient totalistic persecution from the outside.

In either case, it is highly inadvisable to use the power of the state to attempt to restrict totalistic belief.

NOTES

The present chapter is an expansion and revision of an earlier one that was published as Dick Anthony, Thomas Robbins, and Steven Barrie-Anthony, "Cult and Anticult Totalism: Reciprocal Escalation and Violence," in *Millenarianism and New Religious Movements*, ed. Jeffrey Kaplan, a special issue of *Terrorism and Political Violence* 14(1) (2002), 10–50.

1. On "cults" and the controversies surrounding them, see Benjamin Zablocki and Thomas Robbins, eds., *Misunderstanding Cults: Searching for Objectivity in a Controversial Field* (Toronto: Toronto University, 2001), and Lorne Dawson, *Comprehending Cults: The Sociology of New Religious Movements* (New York: Oxford University Press, 1998).

2. James T. Richardson and Massimo Introvigne, "'Brainwashing' Theories in European Parliamentary and Administrative Reports on Cults and Sects," *Regulating Religion: Case Studies from Around the Globe* (New York: Kluwer Academic and Plenum Publishers, 2004, 151–178); Thomas Robbins, "Combating 'Cults' and 'Brainwashing' in the United States and Western Europe," *Journal for the Scientific Study of Religion* 40(2) (Summer 2001), 167–176.

3. Jean-François Mayer, "The Vain Hopes of the Tabachnik Trial," *La Liberté* (Apr. 30, 2001). Distributed by The Family. See also note 2.

4. Dick Anthony and Thomas Robbins, "Religious Totalism, Violence, and Exemplary Dualism," *Terrorism and Political Violence* 7(3) (1995): 1–30, reprinted in *Millennialism and Violence*, ed. Michael Barkun (London: Cass, 1996); Dick Anthony and Thomas Robbins, "Religious Totalism, Exemplary Dualism, and the Waco Tragedy," in *Millennium, Messiahs, and Mayhem*, ed. Thomas Robbins and Susan Palmer, 261–84 (New York: Routledge, 1997); Thomas Robbins, "The Sources of Volatility in Religious Movements," in *Cults, Religion, and Violence*, ed. David Bromley and J. Gordon Melton (New York: Cambridge University Press, 2002) 57–79; Dawson (note 1).

5. Robert Lifton, "Cults, Religious Totalism, and Civil Liberties," in *The Future of Immortality and Other Essays for a Nuclear Age*, ed. Robert Lifton, 219 (New York: Basic Books, 1987).

6. Erik Erikson, "Wholeness and Totality—A Psychiatric Contribution," in *Totalitarianism*, ed. Carl F. Friederich, 156–71 (Cambridge, Mass.: Harvard University Press, 1954). For a fuller discussion of Erikson's concept of totalism, see Anthony and Robbins, "Religious Totalism, Violence and Exemplary Dualism" (note 4). See also below.

7. Erikson's totalism theory is a member of the general class of "totalitarian influence" theories, which describe the affinity between totalitarian ideologies and the personality makeup of individuals. The best-known example of such a theory is that of the "authoritarian personality." See Theodor W. Adorno, Else Frenkel-Brunswick, Daniel Sanford, and R. Nevitt Sanford, *The Authoritarian Personality* (Boston: Norton, 1950). For a detailed discussion of the relation between Erikson's theory and other members of this class, see Dick Anthony, *Brainwashing and Totalitarian Influence: An Exploration of Admissibility Criteria for Testimony in Brainwashing Trials* (Ann Arbor: UMI Dissertation Services, 1996).

8. Robert Lifton, *Thought Reform and the Psychology of Totalism* (New York: Norton, 1961), 419–38 (ch. 22).

9. Ibid., 419. Prior to chapter 22, Lifton has repeatedly used the unqualified term *totalism* as Erikson does, without the adjective "ideological," to refer only to individual propensities to convert to totalitarianism. However, within chapter 22, Lifton begins using the phrase *individual totalism* (cf. pp. 419 and 436) to refer to the individual characteristic, and the term *ideological totalism* to refer to milieux resulting from a combination of individual totalism and totalitarian ideology.

10. The personal relationship between the two psychoanalysts probably made Lifton's use of Erikson's totalism concept more congruent with Erikson's own treatment of it. Erikson apparently served as a sort of professional role model for the younger man. Lifton describes his relationship with Erikson during the period in which he was working on the concept of totalism in Chinese thought reform as that between a "mentor" and a "close student." Robert Lifton, preface, in *Explorations in Psychohistory: The Wellfleet* Papers, ed. Robert Lifton, 12 (New York: Simon and Schuster, 1974). Moreover, Lifton discussed his

research and manuscript on totalism with Erikson as his work proceeded. In his preface to the 1961 thought reform book, Lifton (note 8, xiii) states: "Erik Erikson, during many memorable talks at Stockbridge and Cambridge, made stimulating and enlarging suggestions, both about specific case histories and problems of presentation." Lifton also here refers to Erikson as one of a "few . . . people whose direct personal assistance was indispensable to the completion of this study."

In view of the consultation between the two men as the work on thought reform proceeded, Lifton's citation of Erikson as the originator of the totalism concept without articulating any disagreement with his original formulation, and his acknowledgement of Erikson's more general theoretical influence on his thought reform study, it is unlikely that Lifton intended his use of the totalism concept to be significantly at variance with Erikson's.

11. Lifton (note 8, 420).

12. Robert Lifton, "Preface to the 1989 Edition" of *Thought Reform and the Psychology of Totalism* (Chapel Hill: University of North Carolina Press, 1989), vii.

13. Robert Lifton, *The Protean Self: Human Resilience in an Age of Fragmentation* (New York: Basic Books, 1993), 16l. See also Charles Strozier, *Apocalypse: On the Psychology of Fundamentalism in America* (Boston: Beacon, 1984), 153–66.

14. Anthony and Robbins, "Religious Totalism, Exemplary Dualism, and the Waco Tragedy" (note 4), 419. The report "Doomsday Religious Movements" by the Canadian Security Intelligence Service notes that, within the dualistic worldviews of some movements, "The world is fractured into two opposing camps of Good and Evil, which confers a profound significance on small social political conflicts as evidence of this great cosmic struggle, and which could precipitate a violent response." Canadian Security Intelligence, "Doomsday Religious Movements," in *Millenarianism and New Religious Movements*, ed. Jeffrey Kaplan, a special issue of *Terrorism and Political Violence* 14(1) (2002), 53–60. The latter is one of several reports prepared by national intelligence services intended to assess the possibility of violence by millennial religious movements in light of the change of millennia that occurred in the year 2000. These reports relied upon publications from both scholars of new religions and anticult authors/experts; they usefully reflect the theme of this chapter and are commented on herein. A second report that we refer to repeatedly was prepared by the U.S. Federal Bureau of Investigation, "Project Megiddo," in *Millenarianism and New Religious Movements*, ed. Jeffrey Kaplan, a special issue of *Terrorism and Political Violence* 14(1) (2002), 97–108.

15. Bernard McGinn, *Antichrist: Two Thousand Years of Human Fascination with Evil* (San Francisco: Harper, 1994), 32.

16. Anthony and Robbins, "Religious Totalism, Exemplary Dualism, and the Waco Tragedy" (note 4), 274.

17. Erikson (note 6), 159.

18. Erikson (ibid.) uses the term *splitting* on pp. 160 and 167.

19. For a discussion of the concept of "splitting" as used in contemporary psychodynamic psychology, see Manfield, *Split Self/Split Object: Understanding and Treating Borderline, Narcissistic, and Schizoid Disorders* (London: Aronson, 1992). For a discussion of intolerance of ambiguity as characteristic of authoritarian personalities, see Adorno et al., note 7. See also Else Frenkel-Brunswick, "Intolerance of Ambiguity as an Emotional and Perceptional Personality Variable," *Journal of Personality* (1949): xviii.

20. Erikson (note 6), 160.

21. Erikson's use of the "pseudospeciation" term is discussed extensively in Lawrence J. Friedman, *Identity's Architect: A Biography of Erik H. Erikson* (New Yorkt: Scribners, 1999), 54–55, 187, 352, 442–43.

22. Lifton (note 8), 433–35.

23. For a fuller discussion of the theme of individual predispositions to totalistic conversion in Lifton's early work, see Dick Anthony (1996; note 7). See also Dick Anthony and Thomas Robbins, "Brainwashing and Totalitarian Influence," in *Encyclopedia of Mental Health*, ed. Howard Friedman (San Diego: Harcourt, Brace, Jovanovich, 1998). Reprinted from the *Encyclopedia of Human Behavior* (Academic Press, 1984). See also Anthony and Robbins, "Religious Totalism, Violence, and Exemplary Dualism" (note 4).

24. S. Slipp, *The Technique and Practice of Object Relations Family Therapy* (London: Aronson, 1991), 86–87. Slipp reports extensive research on the roles of splitting and projective identification in causing dysfunctional family dynamics and related personality disorders. For other discussions of the interaction of splitting and projective identification as primitive defense mechanisms see T. Ogden, *The Primitive Edge of Experience* (London: Aronson, 1989), 19–30. See also S. Akhtar, *Broken Structures: Severe Personality Disorders and Their Treatment* (London: Aronson, 1992), 92–94.

25. Lifton (note 8), 202.

26. See Roy Wallis and Steven Bruce, "Sex, Violence, and Religion," in *Sociological Theory, Religion, and Collective Action*, ed. Roy Wallis and Steven Bruce, 115–27 (Belfast, UK: Queens University, 1987). See also Frederick Bird, "Charisma and Leadership in New Religious Movements," *Religion and the Social Order* 3A (1993): 75–92.

27. Len Oakes, *Prophetic Charisma: The Psychology of Revolutionary Personalities* (Syracuse: Syracuse University, 1997). See also Anthony Storrs, *Feet of Clay: Saints, Sinners, and Gurus* (New York: Free Press, 1996); and Robert Lifton, *Destroying the World to Save It: Aum Shinrikyo, Apocalyptic Violence, and the New Global Terrorism* (New York: Holt, 1999).

28. Interestingly, the FBI's Project Megiddo report (note 14) strongly plays up the importance of charismatic leaders and somewhat plays down ideology:

> The potential for violence on behalf of members of biblically driven cults is determined almost exclusivehly by the whims of the cult leader . . . Cult members generally act to serve and please their leader rather than accomplish ideological objectives . . . The cult leader's prophecies, preachings, orders and objectives are subject to indiscriminate change.

This viewpoint has some cogency, but it is certainly overstated. It may be recalled that during the 1993 Waco siege, an FBI official in a commanding field position reportedly referred to David Koresh's insistence on preaching to the agents as "Bible babble." However, charismatic prophets can be prisoners of ideological perspectives, and the latter can influence their and their followers' actions. On the other hand, prophets such as David Koresh can have sudden revelations that can alter doctrine. According to the Project Megiddo report, the premium should be on "examination of the cult leader, his position of power over his followers, and an awareness of the responding behavior and activity of the cult," which is more important than attention to formal beliefs and group goals. However, the Canadian report on *Doomsday Religious Movements* (note 14) claims that, in a crisis intervention, "negotiators dealing with the movement must understand its belief structure, as ignorance of the minor differences between the beliefs of respective groups can have drastic outcomes."

29. Thomas Young, "Cult Violence and the Identity Movement," *Cultic Studies Journal* 7(2) (1990): 150–57.

30. Ibid., 157. Young drew on an earlier important theoretical paper by Fred Wright and Phyllis Wright, "The Charismatic Leader and the Violent Surrogate Family," *Annals of the New York Academy of Science* 347 (1980): 226–76. As a "transitional" object and parental surrogate, the totalist charismatic leader helps (sometimes troubled or alienated) young persons manage their hostilities. This can be therapeutic and/or dangerous, depending upon the worldview and aggressiveness of the leader. A former German neo-Nazi leader remembers that he and his colleagues "spent a lot of time indoctrinating beginners—not necessarily to make them more violent but to take the violence that was already in them and channel it in a politically useful manner." Ingo Hasselbach and Tom Reiss, "How Nazis Are Made," *New Yorker* (Jan. 8, 1996), 36–57.

31. This point is explored in more detail in Anthony and Robbins, "Religious Totalism, Violence, and Exemplary Dualism" (note 4).

32. Catherine Wessinger, *How the Millennium Comes Violently* (New York: Seven Bridges, 2000). The Canadian *Doomsday Religious Movement* report (note 14) highlights the "early warning sign" of an apocalyptic movement being discomfited by the emergence of "a humiliating circumstance running counter to their supposed glorious salvation before the onslaught of the apocalypse," as particularly seen in the Solar Temple violence. Volatility can be enhanced "should a group be humiliated to the extent that either its leader or apocalyptic scenarios appears discredited." The psychological dependency of devotees and leaders on their contrast symbols gives authorities unappreciated leverage "over doomsday movements, which depend upon them to fulfill their apocalyptic scenarios. Failure to comprehend this symbolic role often results in actions that trigger violence." See also Anthony and Robbins, "Religious Totalism, Violence and Exemplary Dualism," and Anthony and Robbins, "Religious Totalism, Exemplary Dualism, and the Waco Tragedy" (both at note 4).

33. Lifton (note 27), 169–78.

34. Some reports concerning the violent Aum Shinrikyo sect in Japan have noted the decline of the movement's growth rate and the failure of the leader's political ambitions prior to the onset of major acts of collective violence. See Wessinger, *How the Millennium Comes Violently*, 120–57 (note 32). See also Ian Reader, *A Poisonous Cocktail: Aum Shinrikyo's Path to Violence* (Copenhagen: Nordic Institute of Asian Studies Book, 1996). Psychiatrist Marc Galanter has developed a social systems model of "cults" or "charismatic groups" in which curtailment of proselytization leads to a redirection of energy from goal attainment to internal control and surveillance, with the result that negative feedback is suppressed and the group becomes increasingly defensive and sensitive to the threat of external intrusion and violation of the group's boundary. Marc Galanter, *Cults: Faith, Healing, and Coercion* (New York: Oxford University Press, 1989, 1999).

35. The *Doomsday Religious Movements* report (note 14) warns against "hasty action" by authorities, which "can trigger violence on the part of the [millennialist] group by forcing it to act out its 'endtimes' scenario, especially when its grandiose apocalyptic scenario appears discredited under humiliating circumstances." A similar point has been

made by two of the present authors; see Anthony and Robbins, "Religious Totalism, Violence, and Exemplary Dualism" (note 4); and Anthony and Robbins "Religious Totalism, Exemplary Dualism, and the Waco Tragedy" (note 4).

36. Erikson (note 6). See also Anthony and Robbins, "Religious Totalism, Violence, and Exemplary Dualism" (note 4).

37. Research by psychiatrist Marc Galanter has pointed to a "relief effect" whereby significant mitigation of neurotic distress symptoms is experienced by recruits to totalistic movements such as the Unification Church. Galanter's research also indicates that approximately 30 percent of such recruits experienced serious distress shortly prior to joining the group. Recognizing that the powerful psychological forces for identity transformation that are mobilized by close-knit "charismatic groups" can also have dangerous (e.g., violent) and pathological consequences, Galanter develops comparisons between cults and therapeutic support groups. See Galanter (note 34).

38. Saul V. Levine, *Radical Departures: Desperate Detours to Growing Up* (London: Harcourt, Brace, Jovanovich, 1984); see also Saul V. Levine, "Radical Departures," *Psychology Today* 18(8) (August 1984): 20–29.

39. Thomas Robbins, Dick Anthony, Thomas Curtis, and Madalyn Doucas, "The Last Civil Religion: The Unification Church of Reverend Sun Myung Moon," *Sociological Analysis* 37(12) (1976): 111–23. There is a tradeoff here, e.g., we wouldn't applaud the creation of self-confident Nazis. On the other hand, a student of one of the authors, who joined the Unification Church as a college undergraduate, developed journalistic and organizational skills working in the movement's divisions and, after leaving the church, became an executive in an important media enterprise.

40. Lifton treats "nuclearism" as a pathological mode of ideological totalism, which was influential in the United States during the Cold War of the late-twentieth century. Robert Lifton, *The Future of Immortality and Other Essays for a Nuclear Age* (New York: Basic Books, 1989).

41. This appears to be an implication of an interesting Canadian movie, *White Lies* (1998). A college student, played by the young actress Sara Polley, innocently questions a dictum of a liberal instructor, who stigmatizes her in class as a possible racist. Reacting against the unfair implication and the stifling milieu of political correctness, the student increasingly associates with seemingly iconoclastic, anticonformist young persons who are really vicious "white power" racists. She is drawn into a violent neo-Nazi group, from which she eventually defects.

42. An analysis of the worldwide surge of "religious terrorism" identifies as a significant factor a reaction of young, pious males against sexual liberation and the related equality of women. Mark Juergensmeyer, *Terror in the Mind of God: The Global Rise of Violence* (Berkeley: University of California Press, 2000), 195–207.

43. Some sociologists have suggested that the surge of agitation against cults in Western Europe, although greatly intensified by the trauma of the Solar Temple murder-suicides, is also related to anxieties over national and cultural integration in a period of shifting ethnodemographic patterns, foreign in-migration, and the growth of Islam. Many religious movements that are viewed as problematic are also seen as "alien" imports and "religious multinationals" and thus make convenient scapegoats in a xenophobic or at least particularistic reaction against cultural globalization. See James Beckford, "'Cult' Controversies in Three European Countries," *Journal of Oriental Studies* 8 (1998): 174–84;

Beckford, "Religious Movements and Globalization," in *Global Social Movements*, ed. Robin Cohen and Shirin Rai, 166–83 (London: Athlone, 2000); Thomas Robbins, "Alternative Religions, the State, and the Globe," *Nova Religio* 4(2) (2001): 172–86; and Robbins (note 2).

44. This may be why, notwithstanding the significant phenomenon of (primarily evangelical) Christian anticultism or "countercultism," the attack on cults so often seems to come from the Left. For example, repressive legislation against minority religions accused of "mental manipulation" was introduced in the French National Assembly by the Socialists. The legislation was passed, although the mental manipulation term was removed. Other language in the final law arguably produces the same effect of criminalizing minority religious beliefs.

45. In *Thought Reform and the Psychology of Totalism*, Lifton states the following:

> Such political inquisitions occur—as in thought reform—when ideological totalists set up their own theocratic search or heresy. One example of this variety of totalism in recent American history would be McCarthyism, a bizarre blend of political religion and extreme opportunism . . . And among those most actively engaged in the McCarthyist movement were many former Communists turned anti-Communist—all of which again seems to confirm (at varying levels of politics and individual emotion) *the principle that totalism breeds totalism*. (Lifton [note 5], 457–58; emphasis ours).

In a later publication, Lifton applies this principle to the tensions between the anticult movement and the new religions. He states that "Totalism begets totalism—and there can be notable totalism in so-called deprogramming. What is called deprogramming includes a continuum from intense dialogue on the one hand to physical coercion and kidnapping on the other . . . I am against coercion at either end of the cult process" (Lifton [note 8], 219).

A somewhat similar point has been made more fervently by Lee Coleman: "New Religions and 'Deprogramming': Who's Brainwashing Whom?" in *Cults, Culture, and the Law*, ed. Thomas Robbins, William Shepherd, and James McBride, 71–80 (Chico, Calif.: Scholars Press, 1985). The tendency for totalistic attacks on movements to strengthen the internal totalism of targeted groups is illustrated by the effect of the fear of coercive deprogramming in the 1970s and early 1980s in increasing the suspicion felt by devotees toward outsiders. See Eileen Barker, *The Making of a Moonie: Choice or Brainwashing* (New York: Blackwell, 1984), 64.

46. Richard Delgado, "Religious Totalism: Gentle and Ungentle Persuasion under the First Amendment," *Southern California Law Review* 51 (1977): 1–99.

47. On the history of the legal "cult wars" in the United States, see Dick Anthony and Thomas Robbins, "Negligence, Coercion, and the Protection of Religious Belief," *Journal of Church and State* 37 (1995): 509–36. See also Anson Shupe, David G. Bromley, and Susan E. Darnell, "The North American Anticult Movement: Vicissitudes of Success and Failure," in *The Oxford Handbook of New Religious Movements*, ed. James R. Lewis, 184–205 (New York: Oxford University Press, 2001).

48. The Unification Church indoctrination center in Booneville in northern California, was notorious for "luring" targeted recruits without first informing them under whose

auspices the camp was being run. Delgado seems to have extrapolated this operation into a general model of cult recruitment and conversion.

49. See Anthony (1996; note 7) for a lengthy discussion of the distinction between the CIA brainwashing concept, which claims to define conduct capable of coercively inducing involuntary influence, and the Erikson/Lifton totalism concept, which does not. The CIA theory was popularized by Edward Hunter, a covert CIA operative. See Edward Hunter, *Brainwashing in Red China* (New York: Vanguard, 1951) and *Brainwashing: From Pavlov to Powers* (New York: Bookmaster, 1961). See also Dick Anthony, "Religious Movements and Brainwashing Litigation: Evaluating Key Testimony," in *In Gods We Trust: New Patterns of Religious Pluralism in America*, 2d ed., ed. Thomas Robbins and Dick Anthony (New Brunswick, N.J.: Transaction, 1990) 295–344. See also Dick Anthony, "Tactical Ambiguity and Brainwashing Formulations: Science or Pseudo Science," in *Misunderstanding Cults: Searching for Objectivity in a Controversial Field*, ed. Benjamin Zablocki and Thomas Robbins (Toronto: Toronto University, 2001). See also Anthony and Robbins (note 23).

50. See Anthony (1990; note 49).

51. Anthony's argument has subsequently been used—typically with the aid of Anthony's services as a consulting and/or testifying expert—as the usually successful basis of legal briefs arguing for the exclusion of anticult brainwashing testimony by Singer, Ofshe, and others on the grounds that such testimony is contradicted by its own claimed theoretical foundation and thus has no scientific basis. Anthony's argument, combined with his legal services, has since the mid-1980s been successful in almost all of the legal cases in which it has been used in the United States, which includes most legal cases of this type, and in several in Europe as well.

52. Congressman Richard Ottinger, "Cults and Their Slaves," *Congressional Record* (1980), E3578–79. Representative Ottinger proposed a national conservatorship law that would permit parents to forcibly remove adult children from totalist movements.

53. See Eileen Barker's discussion of dehumanization in "the construction of 'otherness' in cult conflicts." Eileen Barker, "Watching for Violence: A Comparative Analysis of Five Cult-watching Groups," in *Cults, Religion, and Violence*, ed. David Bromley and Gordon Melton (New York: Cambridge University Press, 2002) 123–148.

54. In a pluralistic society with a multicultural ethos, it is difficult to degrade persons by reference to either their innate characteristics, such as race, or their religious beliefs. However, the issue of personal autonomy/heteronomy provides a basis for stigmatization and control. Nonautonomous persons can be held subject to special controls, and rights and freedoms can be viewed as presupposing autonomy. On the focus upon autonomy as the key value motif in modern society, see Richard Sennett, *Autonomy* (New York: Random House, 1981). See also James Beckford, *Cult Controversies* (London: Tavistock, 1985).

55. Richard Delgado refers to cultists as "cheerful robots" who aren't aware of their actual enslavement and degradation. Richard Delgado, "Religious Totalism as Slavery," *New York Review of Law and Social Change* 4(1) (1979–1980): 51–68.

56. See Anthony (1990; note 49), and Anthony and Robbins (1995; note 47).

57. Philip Jenkins, *Mystics and Messiahs: Cults and New Religions in American History* (New York: Oxford University Press, 2000), 197.

58. John Young and Ezra Griffith, "A Critical Evaluation of Coercive Persuasion as Used in the Assessment of Cults," *Behavioral Science and the Law* 10(1) (1992): 89–101.

59. See Nicholas Horrock, "Justice Refuses Cult Probes," New York Times Service, *Times News*, Hendersonville, N.C., Nov. 24, 1978. See also James T. Richardson and Mary White Stewart, "Medicalizaton and Regulation of Deviant Religion: An Application of Conrad and Schneider's Model," in *Regulating Religion: Case Studies from around the Globe*, ed. James T. Richardson, 528 (New York: Kluwer Academic/Plenum, 2004).

60. Contrary to the claims of anticult experts, in practice it would be difficult to differentiate leaders from followers with respect to such kidnapping charges built upon brainwashing claims. If Singer and Delgado had gotten their way, the resulting kidnapping charges would likely have been filed against members who actually interacted with the allegedly kidnapped converts, which would in most cases have been lower-level members. In France, where alleged cultic brainwashing has been treated as a crime, lower-level members, but not upper-echelon leaders, have gone to prison on such charges.

61. See note 4.

62. Lifton (note 27), 329–30.

63. Thomas Robbins, "Balance and Fairness toward Alternative Religions," in Zablocki and Robbins, *Misunderstanding Cults* (note 1) 71–98.

64. Anthony and Robbins suggest that at the Waco siege, "federal agents were also thinking and acting in a dualistic and apocalyptic mode such that extreme inflexibility and machiavellian subtlety [were] attributed to a stressed sect leader, who was actually vacillating and confused." Anthony and Robbins, "Religious Totalism, Exemplary Dualism, and the Waco Tragedy" (note 4), 282. In his theoretical treatise on the rhetoric of apocalypticism, Stephen O'Leary comments that at Waco, "In the end the government's agents were probably motivated by the same sense of ending that governs the logic of apocalyptic drama: the need to control the script by seizing the initiative and seeking some form of narrative closure." Stephen O'Leary, *Arguing the Apocalypse* (New York: Oxford University Press, 1994), 228. Movement totalism and anti-movement totalism interact explosively and, reinforcing each other, contribute through deviance amplification to a catastrophe such as the tragedy at Waco.

65. Anticult activists and "experts" often testify to alleged cultic brainwashing on behalf of ex-devotee plaintiffs in civil suits against the movements that have allegedly enslaved them. See Anthony and Robbins (note 47). Other "experts" testify for the defense on the alleged scientific flaws of the cultic brainwashing theory, upon which the legal action is based. (Dick Anthony is the scholar who has most often performed this role.)

66. Richardson and Introvigne (note 2). See also "French Senate Passes Anti-sect Law with Amendments," Human Rights without Frontiers News Brief; http://www.hrwf.net (accessed May 17, 2001). The new legislation criminalizes mind control or the use of techniques that "aim at altering the capacity or judgment" to create a "state of subjection" (physical or psychological). Offenders can be imprisoned for five years and heavily fined. Religious organizations can be dissolved. For detailed coverage of legal and church-state vicissitudes involving alternative religions or "cults" from the late 1990s through 2000, see James T. Richardson, ed., "Justice and New Religious Movements," special issue of *Social Justice Research* 12(4) (December 1999); and Pauline Coté, ed., *Frontier Religions in Public Space* (New York: Oxford University Press, 2001.

67. See note 6.

68. The section of the Project Megiddo report (note 14) on "apocalyptic cults" has three citations to a work coauthored by Margaret Singer and Janja Lalich, *Cults in Our*

Midst: The Hidden Menace in Our Everyday Lives (San Francisco: Jossey-Bass, 1995). Another cited work emphasizes that the isolation of members in a totalistic cult undermines their capacity for critical thought: Kevin Gilmartin, "The Lethal Triad: Understanding the Nature of Isolated Extremist Groups," http://www.au.af.mil/au/awc/awcgate/fbi/leb_sept961.htm. In partial contrast, the editors of the Canadian report on *Doomsday Religious Movements* appear to have been less influenced by clinicians and "cult experts" and more open to the somewhat different views of sociologists of religion and students of millenarian movements. However, this is not an absolute contrast, and the Canadian report and the "cult" section of the Project Megiddo report manifest some conceptual and analytical overlay, particularly involving nuances of apocalyptic beliefs.

69. Jenkins (note 57), 222.

70. Hall, Schuyler, and Trinh argue that anticult activists and officials influenced by them conceptualized the problem posed by the Branch Davidians in terms of a mass suicide stereotype arising from the prior Jonestown catastrophe and were therefore led to take forceful actions that may have helped provoke the end they feared (i.e., the "dynamic entry" that federal agents planned at Waco was intended to transpire so rapidly as to forestall the emergence of mass suicide during a lengthy siege). Mass suicide and the threat of "another Jonestown" became a "narrative of law enforcement" that ultimately helped create the Waco debacle. John Hall, Philip Schuyler, and Sylvaine Trinh, *Apocalypse Observed: Religious Movements and Violence in North America, Europe, and Japan* (New York: Routledge, 2000), 44–67.

71. Ibid. See also James Richardson, "Minority Religions and the Context of Violence: A Conflict/Interactionist Perspective," *Terrorism and Political Violence* 13(1) (Spring 2001): 103–33.

72. Canadian Security Intelligence (Note 14). Sociologists have termed this the *deviance amplification* process, which entails a model of spiraling escalation between a deviant religious or cultural minority and alarmed public authorities. Both parties become enmeshed in mutual interpretive feedback loops that mediate concurrent increases in both sectarian alienation and official control. Neither party may thus be exclusively responsible for a culminating violent catastrophe. Although initially developed by British experts in crime and deviance, the classic application to cult/state conflicts is Roy Wallis' discussion of conflicts involving the Scientology movement in the United Kingdom and Australia. See Roy Wallis, *The Road to Total Freedom: A Sociological Analysis of Scientology* (New York: Columbia University Press, 1977). A more recent application has been made to Christian identity paramilitarists; see Michael Barkun, "Millenarians and Violence: The Case of the Christian Identity Movement," in *Millennialism, Messiahs, and Mayhem*, ed. Thomas Robbins and Susan Palmer, 247–60 (New York: Routledge, 1997). Thomas Robbins has made a somewhat cryptic application to huge, incendiary mass suicides in early modern Russia among the Old Believers. Thomas Robbins, "Apocalypse, Persecution, and Self-immolation," in *Millennialism, Persecution, and Violence*, ed. Catherine Wessinger, 205–19 (Syracuse: Syracuse University Press, 2000). See also Thomas Robbins, "Religious Mass Suicide before Jonestown: The Russian Old Believers," *Sociological Analysis* 41(1) (1986): 1–20. Finally, see Barker (note 45). The Canadian report includes *Millennium, Messiahs, and Mayhem* (note 4) in its bibliography and may have been influenced by the contribution by Michael Barkun dealing with deviance amplification and Christian identity, and the Anthony and Robbins chapter on exemplary dualism and Waco.

73. James Richardson, "Minority Religions and the Context of Violence: A Conflict/Interactionist Perspective," *Terrorism and Political Violence* 13(1) (Spring 2001): 103–33. Richardson cites and discusses the conflict-interaction perspective on violence by Sandra Ball-Rokeach, "Normative and Deviant Violence from a Conflict Perspective," *Social Problems* 28(1) (1980): 45–62. In the note attached to the passage we have quoted in our text, Richardson cites the "fine discussion of such interactions" in Michael Barkun, "Millennial Violence in Contemporary America," in Catherine Wessinger, *Millennialism, Persecution, & Violence: Historical Cases* (Syracuse: Syracuse University Press, 2000): 352–63; and Barkun (note 72), 247–60.

74. As noted earlier, the most complete and even-handed analysis of endogenous vs. exogenous factors in violence involving new religions is Richardson's article (note 73). For discussions of a debate about the relative salience of such factors, see Thomas Robbins, "'Quo Vadis': The Scientific Study of New Religious Movements," *Journal for the Scientific Study of Religion* 39(4) (December 2000): 515–23; and Robbins, "Sources of Volatility in Religious Movements" (note 4). In fact, the relative weight of internal or external inputs to millennialist mayhem appears to differ markedly from fiasco to fiasco, as does the role of the state. Action by the state was probably hasty and provocative toward the defensive Davidians at Waco in 1993, but tardy and belated in Japan with respect to the escalating criminality of Aum Shinrikyo in 1995 (i.e., less aggressive officials might have saved lives in Texas while more aggressive officials might have saved lives in Japan). Thomas Robbins, "Religious Movements and Violence," *Nova Religio* 1(1) (1997): 13–29. This contrast is related to the emergence of partly competing "post-Waco" and "post-Aum" modes of scholarly reaction and recrimination. This has been noted by Ian Reader, "'Scholarship,' Aum Shinrikyo and Academic Integrity," *Nova Religio* 3(2) (2000): 368–82.

75. Project Megiddo (note 14) cites the work of Jeffrey Kaplan, who distinguished between *defensive, revolutionary* (offensive), and *rhetorical* violence in the Christian identity subculture (rhetorical violence predominated). See Jeffrey Kaplan, *Radical Religion in America: Millenarian Movements from the Far Right to the Children of Noah* (Syracuse: Syracuse University Press, 1997).

76. Lifton (note 27), 59–88, 270–340. Charles Manson's "Family" actually "committed at least ten murders and probably many more as part of a project that was meant to destroy the 'bourgeois' world and bring about Armageddon" (274). Lifton also compares homicidal Aum Shinrikyo and the suicidal Heaven's Gate group (306–27), and appears to interpret the ideology of the latter group as a dualist-totalist worldview in which "Luciferians" or demonic space aliens/fallen angels/world conspirators represent the exemplars of ultimate evil (314). Lifton also discusses the Peoples Temple in terms of a lethal apocalyptic totalism led by an unhinged prophet (281–302). However, he treats the Branch Davidians, "an armed but not violent small apocalyptic religious sect," as primarily victims of the FBI's "tragically ill-advised assault after a long siege in Waco, Texas, in 1993" (329). They are exempted from the rogues' gallery of violent movements that aim to "force the end."

PART II

The "Big Five" (Plus One)

4

Narratives of Persecution, Suffering, and Martyrdom: Violence in Peoples Temple and Jonestown

Rebecca Moore

The world was shocked in 1978, when more than nine hundred members of Peoples Temple perished in a mass murder–suicide in their jungle community called Jonestown. The sheer numbers involved, coupled with the assassination of a U.S. member of Congress and the execution-style killings of three journalists, seemed unprecedented. The fact that a religious movement was involved in the deaths only heightened the horror. Coming at the close of the 1970s, the deaths in Jonestown were anomalous and inexplicable. Today, however, with the benefit of extensive analyses of terrorism and other instances of religious violence that have seemingly become commonplace, it is easier to see the meaning and purpose of what appeared at the time to be a senseless act.

The assassinations, murders, and suicides in Jonestown were acts of political theater that were played out on the world stage by members of a religious group called Peoples Temple. The victims or perpetrators—many adults were both—saw themselves as martyrs willing to die for the cause of socialism. They believed they were committing an act of "revolutionary suicide" to protest the heartless and unjust system of capitalism that existed in the United States. A rhetoric of martyrdom permeated the discourse in the community and had been a constitutive part of the Peoples Temple's narrative throughout the 1970s in its California centers of Ukiah, San Francisco, and Los Angeles. The dramatic end of the collective dream in Jonestown, Guyana, was intended to send a message: People would rather die than succumb to the injustices of a racist, classist, and capitalistic society.

In addition to the public performance enacted by those in Jonestown, however, private performances of violence occurred throughout most of Peoples Temple's twenty-five-year history. Focusing entirely on the final day neglects at least four varieties of physical and emotional violence that existed within the group for at least a decade. These included discipline, behavior modification, behavior control, and, in Jonestown, terror. While the first two are generally sanctioned by the wider society, the latter two are not. Moreover, with the exception of the attack on the congressman and the reporters, the violence enacted in Peoples Temple was directed entirely inward rather than outward. Indeed, this final attack served as the justification for implementing the plan for self-destruction. Thus, it seems fair to state that Peoples Temple turned all, or almost all, of its violence upon itself.

This chapter begins by presenting a brief history of Peoples Temple and the events leading up to the final day in Jonestown. It describes examples of four types of violence that existed in the group and then looks at the rhetoric of persecution, suffering, and martyrdom that prevailed within the group. The chapter discusses other studies of violence in Peoples Temple and considers analyses of contemporary religious violence. Finally, it examines the world stage upon which the drama was enacted: the players, the goals, and the ultimate purpose in the decision to die.

I want to caution the reader that this chapter centers on violence in Peoples Temple to the exclusion of many other aspects of the group. Had I focused upon communal organization or the role of women or African Americans, it would have taken a completely different shape. Moreover, I have examined elsewhere the violence perpetrated against members of Peoples Temple and the organization itself (Moore 2000). As a result, I am presenting a partial and, as a result, a distorted view of Peoples Temple because I am examining only this narrow facet of life within the movement. Unfortunately, this is the aspect most studied by scholars and the media, and so a lopsided view prevails. In order to truly understand Peoples Temple and Jonestown, one must consider all of the evidence, not just some. As Richard Tropp wrote on the last day of his life in Jonestown: "Collect all the tapes, all the writing, all the history. The story of this movement, this action, must be examined over and over. It must be understood in all of its incredible dimensions" (*Alternative Considerations of Jonestown and Peoples Temple*, FBI FOIA doc. X-1-A-54). This chapter looks at just a single dimension.

Background

Peoples Temple began in Indianapolis, Indiana, in the 1950s under the leadership of a charismatic preacher named James Warren Jones (1931–1978). The Temple attracted a range of members with its mixture of programs for poor people and its visible commitment to racial and social quality. After he had a vision of a nuclear bomb destroying Chicago, Jones exhorted his flock to move to California. About eighty-five people made the move in 1965 with Jones, his wife, Marceline, and his "rainbow family" of adopted and biological children, to Redwood Valley, in a rural part of northern California. It was there that he assumed the status of a prophet, emulating the style of Father Divine: He demanded that members call him "Father" or "Dad" and attend Temple programs to replicate in no small way the entrepreneurship and the heavenly banquets of Divine's Peace Mission. Once established in Redwood Valley, the group made forays into San Francisco and Los Angeles, eventually opening facilities in each city by 1972. Membership changed from a mix of poor working-class whites and blacks to the urban poor, predominantly African American, although a cohort of young, middle-class, college-educated whites served in the leadership. The group gained a reputation in San Francisco for being politically progressive and socially active, although its primary work for members was welfare advocacy: offering legal services, housing, child care, employment, and drug and alcohol rehabilitation. Jones preached a message of "apostolic socialism" and advocated a communal way of life as described in the New Testament book of Acts (2:44–46, 4:34–35). (For a complete history of Peoples Temple and Jonestown, see Hall 1987; Chidester 1988; Reiterman and Jacobs 1982; and Moore 2009.)

Wanting to escape what they saw as growing repression in the United States, Jones and the leadership group sought sanctuary abroad. In 1976 the group formally signed a lease with the government of Guyana, an English-speaking country sandwiched between Venezuela and Surinam. Two years earlier, a number of Temple pioneers had begun clearing jungle for an agricultural project in the country's Northwest District. Jonestown, named after Jim Jones, arose from the jungle with housing and public facilities, fields for the cultivation of crops, and barns for livestock like chickens and pigs. In 1977 an exodus of Temple members began filling the community, crowding the limited facilities. Jonestown's population grew to around one thousand. Spirits nevertheless remained high, as people believed they had escaped the problems of inner-city life: drugs, crime, poverty.

Stories of violence within the Temple emerged as early as 1972, when the religion reporter for the *San Francisco Chronicle* wrote that a member wanting to leave the group had died under suspicious circumstances. (The charges were never substantiated.) The group generally had a good relationship with the media until 1977, when reporters for *New West Magazine* successfully persuaded former members to come forward with accounts of beatings and other abuses. News stories after that time were uniformly critical. Goaded by a group of vocal and well-organized apostates, journalists and government officials investigated a number of charges against Peoples Temple. In April 1978, the apostate group, called the Concerned Relatives, publicized an "Accusation of Human Rights Violations," which detailed abuses that they believed were occurring in Jonestown. Eventually the Concerned Relatives persuaded Congressman Leo J. Ryan (D-Calif.) to travel to Guyana to investigate conditions in Jonestown.

In November 1978 the congressman arrived in Jonestown, accompanied by hostile reporters and members of the Concerned Relatives. Although Ryan and the reporters formed a favorable first impression of the community, the fact that several residents wanted to leave with the congressional party on November 18—and the fact that Jonestown leaders tried to keep them from going—raised alarms. Ryan and a group of fifteen defectors departed Jonestown later that afternoon and went to an airstrip at Port Kaituma, six miles away. While they were waiting for another airplane to arrive, a few young men from Jonestown drove up, motioned the local Guyanese to the side of the airfield, and then began firing on Ryan and his party. They shot and killed five people, including Ryan and one Jonestown defector, and wounded a dozen others before they returned to Jonestown.

After Ryan had left Jonestown, Jones gathered the hundreds living there into an open-sided pavilion in the center of the community. There, medical staff brought out a galvanized tub of potassium cyanide mixed with tranquilizers and fruit punch. Parents squirted poison into their children's mouths and then took the poison themselves. There was some dissent, notably from an older black woman named Christine Miller, who calmly asked Jones why the children had to die. Nevertheless, it appears that most of the adults died more or less willingly, although this is contested (*Jonestown Report* 2006). More than 200 children were murdered, however, and perhaps as many as 100 seniors were involuntarily injected. In Georgetown, the capital of Guyana, where the Temple maintained a residence for members who were en route to Jonestown or needed medical attention in the city, a Temple leader received the order to kill herself. She gathered her three children into a bathroom and killed them by cutting their throats before she cut her own. At the end of the day, 5 Americans had died on the Port Kaituma airstrip, 4 had died in Georgetown, and 909 had died in Jonestown.

Four Types of Violence

All societies try to hold their members accountable for individual actions. In smaller societies—whether a village in Africa, a farming community in North America, or a commune in South America—it is easy to determine responsibility because everybody knows everybody else. There are clear taboos and equally clear consequences for breaking them. In larger societies, however, we assign law enforcement the task of preventing or stopping crime and the courts the task of dispensing punishment for wrongdoing. There is socially sanctioned punishment, such as performing community service, paying fines, or losing one's freedom; and there is socially sanctioned violence, such as incarceration in violent, government-run jails and prisons, as well as capital punishment. Members of Peoples Temple endeavored to establish their own society with its own rules and system of justice, bypassing external systems in order to deal with problems internally. Thus, the Temple's efforts to exert discipline and behavior modification were not radically at odds with what occurs in the larger society. Drug abuse, stealing, and pedophilia were addressed within the confines of the Temple, not outside. What was different from the larger society, however, were the social crimes that needed to end.

While the last day represented the most shocking, extensive, and visible example of violence in Peoples Temple, members had engaged in increasingly severe forms of brutality for at least a decade. These ranged from socially accepted types of coercion, such as discipline and behavior modification, to less acceptable types, including behavior control and terror. They also varied as to technique, encompassing both physical violence (spankings, boxing, beatings, rape, and torture) and emotional violence (verbal abuse, threatening language, public humiliation, fantasizing about violent acts, and obligatory self-criticism). What is perhaps most perplexing is the fact that members of Peoples Temple participated in their own victimization. More often than not, they were both the perpetrators of the violence and the victims.

It is easy to see why people participated in violent acts if we begin with discipline, which has a clear causal relationship between crime and punishment. Adults and children alike were punished for lying, stealing, cheating, hitting, or committing other acts that society considers bad behavior. Sometimes the punishment fit the crime: A child who had bitten another would be bitten himself; a boy who hit his sister with a flyswatter would have to box with a girl. Edith Roller, a Temple member who kept an extensive journal detailing her life in the organization, describes a typical example of discipline:

> Several small boys were brought on the floor for stealing cookies in a supermarket. Jim warned them that if they stole, a policeman would catch them and they would go to juvenile hall where they would be beaten on the head. They were given twenty-five whacks. (*Alternative Considerations of Jonestown and Peoples Temple*, Edith Roller Journal, II, 113, August 6, 1975)

Others were "brought on the floor" to be chastised or fined for smoking or to box with others if they were caught using drugs. In one instance, those responsible for picking up children after school had to raise $500 each when they neglected their duties and the school principal informed the Temple leaders. Members confiscated a pistol from a young man on another occasion and assigned the penalty of going to church for two days, including a Friday, in order to distribute pamphlets about Peoples Temple. Other forms of punishment included being assigned more volunteer hours or given extra cleaning to do.

A corollary to discipline was behavior modification. Peoples Temple members sought to create a new, nonbourgeois community in which racism, sexism, classism, elitism, ageism, and capitalism were eliminated from human relations. The means of behavior modification were similar to discipline: corporal punishment or consequences to fit the infraction. But the purpose differed. Rather than being chastised for socially recognized infractions, Temple members also faced consequences for internally recognized crimes against the group. These offenses included being rude to senior citizens, making sexist or racist remarks, hoarding food or other items that the community needed, or displaying self-centered conduct. One couple was "called up on the floor," according to the Roller diary, because they were very uncooperative in the communal living arrangement that had been set up for them:

> Debbie is still following bad practices with her son, Todd, taking him in her bed, dressing him like a girl, objecting to Barbara Cordell's care of him. Rick does good work, but doesn't put in an eight-hour day, refused to help out Cathy [Kathy] Tropp with transportation during the present emergency, so that she had to go without food and clean clothes, though he and Debbie each have a car. Debbie wouldn't leave Todd with Shirley Smith, the other member of the commune. Debbie admitted she resented having to live communally. (*Alternative Considerations of Jonestown and Peoples Temple*, Edith Roller Journal II, 113–14, August 6, 1975)

Jim Jones gave the couple two weeks either to change or to leave and appointed a committee to discuss them. The punishment for their selfish behavior was to raise $100 each. A woman who made a racist remark was beaten by elderly black women wearing boxing gloves (Mills 1979, 279). Another young man was penalized with 120 blows for calling a woman with a disability a "crippled bitch." Jones commuted his sentence when the young man screamed after receiving 70 hits. A young woman accused of eating extra meals at the college cafeteria in Santa Rosa was forced to strip to her underwear and jump into the Redwood Valley pool so that the congregation could see her rolls of fat (Mills 1979, 258–59). Those who did not do their fair share of the work, did not clean their rooms, or did not meet the new standards required by a commitment to socialism, were "called up" before the group and punished in an effort to transform them into people who cared for others.

One of the most extreme cases of behavior modification was the beating of one member who was accused of being a pedophile. The first time he was caught, he confessed that he was attracted to young boys and had sought psychiatric help. "Perhaps where the psychiatrists have failed, a switch will succeed," Jones was reported as saying (Mills 1979, 269). The perpetrator took the beating as his victim looked on. In the next instance, the congregation still declined to turn the man over to the police but instead had someone strike his penis until it bled. This incident prompted several individuals to leave the Temple. Other members justified the treatment as being a better alternative than imprisonment. Rather than expel the man, they attempted to change his behavior.

While discipline and behavior modification might be considered more or less socially accepted (at least in theory if not in practice), two additional forms of violence existed within the Temple that did not mirror the larger society: behavior control and terror. Jim Jones, with the help of peer-group pressure, exerted control over the daily lives of Temple members. This chiefly affected those who lived communally in California and particularly influenced people once they moved to Jonestown. This control encompassed assigning living quarters even if it meant separating married couples or families with children, determining relationships (who could sleep with whom), and making work assignments. Meetings consumed the life of a committed member, with the group assembling several times a week, in addition to attending weekly worship services and traveling via Temple-owned buses from northern California to Los Angeles. Moreover, the meetings often lasted into the early morning hours, leaving members with little time for sleep.

Deborah Layton details the Temple's efforts to control every aspect of behavior (Layton 1998). Members were required to write up negative thoughts and criticisms of the Temple. They were told that all men except for Jim Jones were homosexual. "He intended to discourage any bonds with the opposite sex that might compromise our allegiance to him" (Layton 1998, 54). Sex was considered selfish, a form of treason to the socialist cause. Jones bragged that movement defectors met with accidents and claimed that the group had bombed a military supply train, and Layton believed him. "Father made me watch the beating [of the man accused of pedophilia] and had my photo taken holding the rubber hose, which paralyzed my questioning inner voice" (Layton 1998, 61).

Jones used guilt as the primary form of control in California. He reminded his flock that any purchases they made supported the oppression of others in the form of government taxes, which propped up unjust regimes in Rhodesia and South Africa. When he preached or discussed current events, he reminded his followers that children around the world were starving. His followers took this to heart, as indicated by remarks by Mike Prokes, the Temple's chief public relations spokesperson, in a shortwave radio conversation:

> It's a crime, when two out of three babies are going to bed hungry in the world, that we're wasting food. We have a picture up in our dining hall that shows a woman who is starving, her breasts are deflated, and her child is trying to get nourishment from them. And the child is obviously starving.... We don't put it up there to make people feel guilty, but I'm not so sure they shouldn't feel guilt. It may not be their responsibility or their fault that that person is hungry, but it seems to me that ... if we care about people, and, you know, we claim love as Jesus taught, then that love should reach out to everyone, including those who are hungry. So when we take a bite of food [and] know that there are so many who cannot, that I think a person who has any conscience would feel some guilt and want to do something about such conditions in their own small way, whatever way that might be. (*Alternative Considerations of Jonestown and Peoples Temple*, FBI Audiotape Q 630)

Residents of Jonestown had virtually no time to themselves. Even on their days off, they were expected to work on crafts to sell in Georgetown, to write letters to family members, or to engage in socialism studies or other constructive activities. Few could rebel against the control because they felt guilty over any form of what they'd been told was—and what they considered to be—self-indulgence. Moreover, group members criticized each other harshly in "People's Rallies," which were public forums held in Jonestown. Jim Jones and others attacked Stanley Clayton, a Jonestown resident, at one rally. Marceline Jones angrily said, "I'm getting so tired of excuses being made for Stanley. By God, he's had chance after chance after chance. I've sat with him and given him chance after chance after chance" (*Alternative Considerations of Jonestown and Peoples Temple*, FBI Audiotape Q 635). Jim Jones and the rest of the community then enumerated Clayton's sexual failings, condemned him for having sex in the middle of a community emergency, and berated him for his weaknesses. One man complained:

> Really, Stanley, you been a punk for so goddamn long. Dad got your ass out of jail. You lived in the church, you lived communally, you be smug, be messing around with young sisters, spieling on [flirting with] young sisters, and don't tell me you didn't, 'cause we confronted you about that shit. (*Alternative Considerations of Jonestown and Peoples Temple*, FBI Audiotape Q 635)

At the conclusion of the meeting, the savaging of Stanley Clayton ended with one man saying, "To kill you would be too good for you 'cause you wouldn't have to bear any responsibility or any guilt" (*Alternative Considerations of Jonestown and Peoples Temple*, FBI Audiotape Q 637). (Clayton was one of the few Jonestown residents to flee during the mass deaths.)

The final form of violence internal to Peoples Temple—and the most pernicious—was a pervasive feeling of terror. In California, Jones terrorized the group with relentless reminders of torture. He gave sermons on methods of torture used by the CIA. Concentration camps frequently came up in his lectures. Members watched films like *The Pawnbroker* (about Nazi Germany) and performed plays like *The Anguish* (about concentration camps). The Temple's drama group, the "Skitsophrenics," also performed plays in which the Ku Klux Klan lynched African Americans. In a sermon preached in 1972, Jones announced that the government was:

> gonna put people in this country in concentration camps. They're gonna put them in gas ovens, just like they did the Jews. . . . They're gonna put you in the concentration camps that're already in Tule Lake, California, Allentown, Pennsylvania, near Birmingham, outside El Reno, Oklahoma. They've got them all ready—Title II of the McCarran Act—they still have the concentration camps, they did it to the Japanese, and they'll do it to us if we don't quit preachin' this pie-in-the-sky. (*Alternative Considerations of Jonestown and Peoples Temple*, FBI Audiotape Q 162)

In the same sermon Jones claimed that doctors in prison were "making people living vegetables without their consent." He added that the jails were filled with poor people and said that Edward Brooke, an African American senator from Massachusetts, pointed out that the United States already had "concentration camps" in its prisons filled with minorities. "I tell you, we're in danger tonight from a corporate dictatorship," Jones warned the congregation. "We're in danger from a great fascist state or a great communist state" (*Alternative Considerations of Jonestown and Peoples Temple*, FBI Audiotape Q 162).

Articles in the *Peoples Forum*, the newspaper of Peoples Temple, provided details about torture occurring in Chile to supplement a graphic film Jones had shown the group about conditions under the dictator Augusto Pinochet. An article from a November 1976 issue headlined "Torture Epidemic" begins with a graphic description of state-sanctioned torture:

> [P]eople beaten, raped, electrocuted, burned with cigarettes . . . left to starve, placed in tiny, airless cells . . . aroused constantly by loud noises, made to wear helmets during beatings that amplify their screams, driving them insane . . . made to ingest their own bowel movement . . . made to witness their own loved ones brutalized and killed . . . an endless catalogue of horrors. ("Torture Epidemic," 1976; original spelling and punctuation)

The terror escalated when the group moved to Guyana. For a week in September 1977 residents believed they were under siege. The entire community, young and old alike, stood on alert along the perimeter of the settlement, armed with cutlasses and awaiting an imminent attack. Jones also used the fear of poisonous snakes and wild animals to terrorize his followers. On one occasion, Jones threatened two young boys with being tied up in the jungle so that tigers could get them. Their crime: They had sneaked out one night. The boys responded with tears and wails even though Jones assured them that "Dad never came to kill, he came to heal. Dad never came to hurt but to relieve pain" (*Alternative Considerations of Jonestown and Peoples Temple*, FBI Audiotape Q 743). When Jones eventually did send the boys out to be tied for the tigers to get them, the boys were in near hysterics. They returned in hysterics as well but thanked Jones for protecting them from a tiger that almost ate them. Jones and community members laughed until they realized the boys believed they had actually seen a tiger.

On a different occasion, a woman was punished by being forced to have a snake crawl on her: She was terrified. Jones finally removed the snake, saying to it:

> Hi, you old sweet fella. I like him . . . Look at that, look at that grip. That's a grip. You're a good guy. Boy, they love that snake dance. She went through the snake dance in Georgetown fantastic. She was fantastic. (*Alternative Considerations of Jonestown and Peoples Temple*, FBI Audiotape Q 781)

A final form of terror took the form of the White Nights, which occurred in Jonestown. About half a dozen occurred in 1978 (Moore 2009, 75–80). Although there were numerous alerts in which the whole group was roused in the middle of the night to prepare for an assault on the community, a White Night was qualitatively different. People believed they were about to die on these occasions and therefore had to decide what to do with their children in case the community was attacked. When some of the residents advocated armed resistance, Jones would ask them whether they wanted to fight their black brothers in the Guyana Defense Force. It seemed that suicide was the only option, but if so, the children would have to be killed first in order to save them from impending torture and enslavement. Members of the community lined up, took what they were told was poison, and waited to die. During these suicide drills, individuals would speak to the group and explain why they were eager to die for the cause. They also justified the need to kill their children and expressed a willingness to do so.

Infrequent White Nights, coupled with the numerous alerts, kept residents in a heightened state of terror, not knowing what to expect. When Leo Ryan announced his intention to visit, Jones told the community that an invasion was imminent. They believed him in large part due to the fear of outside attack with which they were living.

The Rhetoric of Persecution, Suffering, and Martyrdom

A persistent and pervasive sense of persecution existed almost from the earliest days of Peoples Temple. Reports of racist graffiti sprayed on church buildings, ground glass found in food, and harassment on the street emerged in Indianapolis. With the move to Redwood Valley, accounts of shootings, animal poisonings, and other forms of persecution escalated to the point that guards monitored the perimeter of the church grounds during Sunday services. Some stories were undoubtedly true since the racially mixed congregation drew derision and epithets in the largely white, rural area. Other stories fueled the sense of terror with which members lived.

The move to San Francisco did not ameliorate the sense of persecution. General repression exercised in society at large, coupled with targeted stalking of Temple members, focused the group's attention on dangers lurking around every corner. Temple members identified "spies" working on behalf of Sen. John Stennis (D-Miss.) listening in to a presentation by Mississippi activist Unita Blackwell Wright. Agents from the U.S. Treasury Department attempted to compromise Dennis Banks, an American Indian Movement leader who was being helped by the Temple. A mysterious fire at the Geary Street facilities raised concerns. The general political situation—with the murder of Black Panther Party members by police departments throughout the 1970s, the raid on the Symbionese Liberation Army's house in 1974, the revelation of the Nixon administration's COINTELPRO (Counterintelligence Program) of domestic surveillance, and other instances of state-sanctioned political violence—merely reinforced the sense of persecution. A sermon Jones gave in 1973 during the Watergate hearings shows the extent of the repression the group felt:

It's us against the world. It's us against the world. All the time, we see the horror of this society. We see it in the television, we see it on the streets, we see it in the jobs. You've got to be sick of it. That's our only hope. If we'll be sick of it sufficiently, that when they come after us, that whatever we do, we'll do it together. (*Alternative Considerations of Jonestown and Peoples Temple*, FBI Audiotape Q 1053 Part 4)

A subtheme of suffering accompanies the narrative of persecution as a leitmotif: The two travel in tandem in sermons, speeches, and testimonials. Persecution results in pain and suffering, and no one endured more agony than Jim Jones "[b]ecause I suffer to the depth of my bone[s] that no human being ever lived before in history that suffered like I suffer over people, because I care deeply about every blessed one of you" (*Alternative Considerations of Jonestown and Peoples Temple*, FBI Audiotape Q 191). A month before the deaths in Jonestown, the community doctor, Larry Schacht, told the group about just how much pain Jones was bearing for them:

Dad takes into his body, takes into his body, all of the pain, all of the pain and the suffering that those of you here who have been very sick have not felt and have not endured, and all the times that people who have not died, is because Dad took that pain into himself. (*Alternative Considerations of Jonestown and Peoples Temple*, FBI Audiotape Q 182)

In a sermon given in 1973, shortly after a group of eight young adults left the church in a group, Jones reminded the congregation of the sufferings of Jesus. Those who live a godly life are "going to suffer persecution," he told them. "You gonna suffer for righteousness, you'll inherit the kingdom of God. If you suffer persecutions, prosecutions, and they'll even kill you, thinking they do God a service," he said, quoting John 16:2. He assured them that they were in good company with Jesus but added, "We're going to have some suffering" (*Alternative Considerations of Jonestown and Peoples Temple*, FBI Audiotape Q 1057, part 3).

Carolyn Layton, one of the top leaders in Jonestown, explained the reason for the group's suffering in a letter written in August 1978: "What the real truth is—we are just out of due season" (Moore 1986, 273). Jones undoubtedly promoted this idea since it appeared a few months later on the tape made in Jonestown's final hours. He quoted Paul the Apostle: "I was a man born out of due season" (1 Corinthians 15:8). He continued: "I've been born out of due season, just like all we are, and the best testimony we can make is to leave this goddamn world" (*Alternative Considerations of Jonestown and Peoples Temple*, FBI Audiotape Q 042).

Coupled with the narrative of persecution and suffering was a violent rhetoric of confession (inner-directed violence) and of retaliation aimed at the persecutors (outer-directed violence). Temple members were required to write confessions to violent acts: assassinating President. John F. Kennedy, raping and murdering children, planting explosives. Ex-members believed these notes were designed to control people and keep them from leaving the group. Other notes express violent fantasies about what members will do for the cause: blow up buildings and bridges, kill political leaders, and even carry out suicide bombings in crowded areas. Tape recordings made in Jonestown depict children and adults making graphically violent threats against family members in the United States. One girl says that she thinks Mr. Tupper should die:

> I think that I should take a knife and cut Mr. Tupper all up real good and then ... put poison in him and invite all my relatives over there and then have 'em eat him, and then they all die. (*Alternative Considerations of Jonestown and Peoples Temple*, FBI Audiotape Q 594)

Other fantasies are still more violent, focusing on genital mutilation, sodomy, and torture.

Related to the rhetoric of persecution, suffering, and violence was a narrative of martyrdom, which Temple members rehearsed for many years. Members took their cue from Jim Jones, who frequently boasted of his self-sacrificing nature, while complaining of all the demands placed upon him by his followers. A letter written by Annie Moore in 1973 notes that while Jones could heal people's cancer and blindness, "What counts is that he gives his whole self for others. He averages 2 hours of sleep a week because he is up all night doing counseling and church work. I never saw any soul care and have so much love for all aspects of life as I have in Jim Jones" (Moore 1986, 94; also online at *Alternative Considerations of Jonestown and Peoples Temple*). Tests of loyalty occurred throughout the years and ranged from declarations of a willingness to die for the cause, to actually drinking what members were told was poison. In Jonestown, the intensity and frequency of testing increased due to external pressures from government and media investigations, coupled with lawsuits filed by the Concerned Relatives.

Heightened concerns about dissent, on the one hand, and trustworthiness, on the other, led to repeated affirmations of a willingness to die. "My name is Bill Oliver," announced one Jonestown resident:

> I made the decision to commit revolutionary suicide. My decision has been well thought out. I've been a member of Peoples Temple for seven years, and I know of the goodness. And in my death, I hope that it would be used as an instrument to further liberation. Thank you. (*Alternative Considerations of Jonestown and Peoples Temple*, FBI Audiotape Q 245)

Time and again, residents stood up and declared that they would rather die than see the community fail or fall to traitors. Jones had appropriated the language of revolutionary suicide from Huey Newton, a leader of the Black Panther Party, although with a twist. Newton believed that if one challenged an unjust political system, one faced the possibility of death; hence, political action was a form of suicide. In contrast, Jones argued for literally committing suicide (Harris and Waterman 2004). It is in the act of revolutionary suicide that the people of Jonestown most resemble those who are committing violence for religious reasons today.

Analyses of Religious Violence

Studying the violence in Jonestown reflects the history of analyses of religious violence. Jonathan Z. Smith likens Jonestown to Euripides' portrayal of a new, Dionysian religion in the *Bacchae* (Smith 1982). While Smith presents an alternative to this view, he does claim that the plot of the *Bacchae* brings to mind the events of Jonestown. Psychological explanations of the violence appear in Ken Levi's *Violence and Religious Commitment* (Levi 1982), and articles in psychological journals emerged throughout the 1980s that focused on individual needs and weaknesses. In *Gone from the Promised Land* (1987), John R. Hall describes the role that cultural opponents played in provoking violence in Jonestown; with Philip Schuyler he further develops the interactionist model of religious violence as an explanatory device (Hall and Schuyler 1998; Hall, Schuyler, and Trinh 2000). Catherine Wessinger's typology of fragile, assaulted, and revolutionary millennial groups helps differentiate among various groups and highlights the fact that not all religious violence is the same (Wessinger 2000). Thus, the 1993 collapse of the Branch Davidians in an attack by the FBI differs qualitatively and quantitatively from the demise of Peoples Temple in 1978, which Wessinger identifies as a fragile millennial group. David Bromley and Gordon Melton's book, *Cults, Religion, and Violence* (2002), reflects two decades of reflection on religious violence, and though it focuses on episodes from the 1990s, it includes essays that address Peoples Temple and Jonestown both directly and indirectly. Thomas Robbins's chapter in that volume analyzes the sources of volatility in religious movements and cites apocalypticism as a factor in violence, as well as totalism, encapsulation, and "mind control," all of which existed in Jonestown (Robbins 2002). Lorne Dawson's contribution examines charismatic leaders and describes Jones's use of terror to control the residents of Jonestown and thereby influence their decision to die (Dawson 2002).

The onset of terrorism and organized religious violence as a global phenomenon has resulted in new perspectives that also shed light on the horror of the last day of Peoples Temple. James Rinehart's book on prophets of terror investigates "the functional relationship between millenarian-inspired terrorism and the process of political change" (Rinehart 2006, 1). He notes that members of three movements—including Aum Shinrikyo, which he examines in detail—responded violently when their collective sense of identity was threatened. This surely relates to the people in Jonestown, who believed that Leo Ryan and the Concerned Relatives intended to destroy their community (see also Wessinger 2000). The fact that policy analysts must now consider religion and the durability of religious beliefs as they decide upon international courses of action is also a change since 1978. Mark

Juergensmeyer and many others have written about this remarkable transformation (Juergensmeyer 2003; Stern 2003; Rennie and Tite 2008). Again, a consideration of the beliefs and commitments of those undertaking violent acts today demonstrates the necessity of understanding the motivations of those in Jonestown.

One of the most relevant of the new studies on religious violence for gaining insight into Peoples Temple and Jonestown is Terry Eagleton's *Holy Terror* (2005), in which the English literary and social critic distinguishes between hunger strikers and suicide bombers. This is a useful distinction when considering violence in Jonestown because we have a similar division: violence directed against the self (but ultimately pointed at the oppressor) and violence directed at others (such as the murder of Ryan, the journalists, and one defector). Eagleton says of hunger strikers that "it is not just a question of dying but of laying one's death dramatically at someone's door." Suicide bombers, on the other hand, proclaim that even death is preferable to their current existence. "Laying violent hands on oneself is in this sense simply a more graphic image of what the enemy is doing to you anyway, and so converts your powerlessness into a public spectacle" (Eagleton 2005, 90).

I do not think that previous analyses of Jonestown have noted this concept of "spectacle." An audiotape made as the deaths were occurring indicates that people believed they were sending a message to the world by laying down their lives in protest. Eagleton notes that "those excluded from the public sphere thus act out a public drama of their own creation" (Eagleton 2005, 92). While Jim Jones created this drama, he also had help from his followers, who participated in their own victimization. Fleeing the injustices of the United States in an attempt to create a utopian society in Guyana and already marginalized by race and class, Peoples Temple members had opted out of the public sphere. In order to have an impact, however, or to have a say, they needed to "speak" in spectacle. Just as hunger strikers transform weakness into power, so the Jonestown victims deprived their enemies of conquest. "Nothing is less masterable than nothing," Eagleton says. "Victory and defeat are thus indistinguishable" (Eagleton 2005, 95). One's body is the only thing one has in the struggle, so laying it down is playing a card that trumps every possible tactic. "The flesh may be corruptible, but in the very process of its dissolution the Idea which spurs them on stands forth radiant, sublime, unkillable" (Eagleton 2005, 96). The idea for which Jonestown residents died was the principle of socialism. As one women said as she waited to take the poison, "It's been a pleasure walking with all of you in this revolutionary struggle. No other way I would rather go [than] to give my life for socialism, communism, and I thank Dad very, very much" (*Alternative Considerations of Jonestown and Peoples Temple*, FBI Audiotape Q 042).

The World Stage

The narrative created by Jim Jones in collaboration with the members of Peoples Temple served as the script for a production performed on the world stage. The drama had a hero (Jim Jones), many villains (reporters, relatives, government officials), and a large supporting cast (more than nine hundred persons). Although the scoundrels changed names, their basic natures remained the same: They were eternally bent on destroying Jones and his people. Many rehearsals practiced over the years revealed early on that the play would have a Shakespearean ending, with the stage littered with corpses.

Though we might call the White Nights dress rehearsals or sacred theater, I have written that the ritual behavior served as the "sacrament of suicide" in an online debate over whether or not people in Jonestown were murdered (other than children and some of the older adults in the community). When we couple Jones's emphasis on torture, dying, and death with the ritualized—and perhaps even sacralized—actions his followers took during loyalty tests, a playbook is scripted in the minds of the actors:

> We need look no further than military basic training to find that
> humans' natural aversion to killing one another is broken down in order
> to create a successful fighting unit. The "basic training" in Peoples
> Temple was to accept the reality of death, and death by one's own hand
> at that. (*Jonestown Report* 2006)

It was an active rather than a passive acceptance and one that was continually practiced in thought, word, and deed. Those in Jonestown embraced the idea of martyrdom and prepared for it for many years. No one who had not trained for a very long time could enact the ritual with the precision it required. Audiotapes made during White Nights prior to November 18, 1978, present individual after individual, young and old, declaring their intention to die.

It is significant, however, that they died in a very public way in a remarkably private place. Public performance of the ritual was an essential element of the production. As martyrs, those who died in Jonestown bore witness to the depth of their commitment to and faith in socialism, that is, in their community and its goals. Unlike traitors who had apostatized, the martyrs chose loyalty over survival and sent a message to an uncaring world. "The act signifies a hope for the future," writes Eagleton of martyrdom, "bearing witness to a truth and justice beyond the present. By turning his body into a sign of the absence of these things, the martyr reminds us that the world is not yet fit for them and thus helps to keep them alive" (Eagleton 2005, 99).

The deaths in Jonestown may be characterized as a morality play, though not as society usually sees it or as the community itself intended. The media and the world misunderstood this revolutionary suicide. "We will win," Jones announced during his final hours. "We will win when we go down." A woman joyously declared that "This is nothing to cry about. This is something we could all rejoice about." And Jim Jones had the last words on the tape—and the final lines in the drama:

We said—one thousand people who said, we don't like the way the world is. [Tape edit] Take some. [Tape edit] Take our life from us. We laid it down. We got tired. [Tape edit] We didn't commit suicide, we committed an act of revolutionary suicide protesting the conditions of an inhumane world. (*Alternative Considerations of Jonestown and Peoples Temple*, FBI Audiotape Q042)

Like any good work of art, the spectacle generated multiple interpretations. These included condemnations of the danger of cults, attacks on the evils of socialism, and reports of numerous conspiracies involving Jim Jones and Peoples Temple. The message sent by those who died became lost in the horror of the murders and suicides. That is the problem with staging one's own death: It is always open to an interpretation that may not be the one intended.

REFERENCES

Alternative Considerations of Jonestown and Peoples Temple. FBI Freedom of Information Act (FOIA) documents, FBI audiotape transcripts, and Edith Roller journals are available at this website, http://jonestown.sdsu.edu.

Bromley, David G., and J. Gordon Melton, eds. 2002. *Cults, Religion, and Violence*. New York: Cambridge University Press.

Chidester, David. 1988. *Salvation and Suicide: An Interpretation of Jim Jones, the Peoples Temple, and Jonestown*. Bloomington: Indiana University Press. Reprint, 2003.

Dawson, Lorne L. 2002. "Crises of Charismatic Legitimacy and Violent Behavior in New Religious Movements." In *Cults, Religion, and Violence*, ed. David G. Bromley and J. Gordon Melton, 80–101. New York: Cambridge University Press.

Eagleton, Terry. 2005. *Holy Terror*. New York: Oxford University Press.

Hall, John R. 1987. *Gone from the Promised Land: Jonestown in American Culture*. New Brunswick, N.J.: Transaction. Reprint, 2004.

———, and Philip Schuyler. 1998. "Apostasy, Apocalypse, and Religious Violence: An Exploratory Comparison of Peoples Temple, the Branch Davidians, and the Solar Temple." In *The Politics of Religious Apostasy: The Role of Apostates in the Transformation of Religious Movements*, ed. David G. Bromley, 141–69. Westport, Conn.: Praeger.

Hall, John R., with Philip D. Schuyler and Sylvaine Trinh. 2000. *Apocalypse Observed: Religious Movements and Violence in North America, Europe, and Japan*. New York: Routledge.

Harris, Duchess, and Adam John Waterman. 2004. "To Die for the Peoples Temple: Religion and Revolution after Black Power." In *Peoples Temple and Black Religion in America*, ed. Rebecca Moore, Anthony B. Pinn, and Mary R. Sawyer, 103–22. Bloomington: Indiana University Press.

Jonestown Report, The. 2006. "Was It Murder or Suicide: A Forum." http://jonestown.sdsu.edu/AboutJonestown/JonestownReport/Volume8/forumIntro.htm.

Juergensmeyer, Mark. 2003. *Terror in the Mind of God: The Global Rise of Religious Violence*, 3d. ed. Berkeley: University of California Press.

Layton, Deborah. 1998. *Seductive Poison: A Jonestown Survivor's Story of Life and Death in the Peoples Temple*. New York: Anchor.

Levi, Kenneth, ed. 1982. *Violence and Religious Commitment: Implications of Jim Jones' People's Temple Movement*. University Park: Pennsylvania State University Press.

Mills, Jeannie. 1979. *Six Years with God: Life inside Rev. Jim Jones's Peoples Temple*. New York: A&W.

Moore, Rebecca. 1986. *The Jonestown Letters: Correspondence of the Moore Family 1970–1985*. Lewiston, N.Y.: Mellen.

———. 2000. "'American as Cherry Pie': Peoples Temple and Violence in America." In *Millennialism, Persecution, and Violence: Historical Cases*, ed. Catherine Wessinger, 121–37. Syracuse: Syracuse University Press.

———. 2006. "The Sacrament of Suicide." The Jonestown Report, 8. http://jonestown.sdsu.edu/AboutJonestown/JonestownReport/Volume8/forumRMoore.htm.

———. 2009. *Understanding Jonestown and Peoples Temple*. Westport, Conn.: Praeger.

Reiterman, Tim, with John Jacobs. 1982. *Raven: The Untold Story of the Rev. Jim Jones and His People*. New York: Dutton. Reprint, 2008.

Rennie, Bryan, and Philip L. Tite, eds. 2008. *Religion, Terror, and Violence: Religious Studies Perspectives*. New York: Routledge.

Rinehart, James F. 2006. *Apocalyptic Faith and Political Violence: Prophets of Terror*. New York: Palgrave.

Robbins, Thomas. 2002. "Sources of Volatility in Religious Movements." In *Cults, Religion, and Violence*, ed. David G. Bromley and J. Gordon Melton, 57–79. New York: Cambridge University Press.

Smith, Jonathan Z. 1982. "The Devil in Mr. Jones." In *Imagining Religion: From Babylon to Jonestown*. Chicago: University of Chicago Press.

Stern, Jessica. 2003. *Terror in the Name of God: Why Religious Militants Kill*. New York: Ecco.

"Torture Epidemic." 1976. *Peoples Forum* 1(12) MS 4124(2). San Francisco: California Historical Society.

Wessinger, Catherine. 2000. *How the Millennium Comes Violently: From Jonestown to Heaven's Gate*. New York: Seven Bridges.

5

Revisiting the Branch Davidian Mass Suicide Debate

Stuart A. Wright

Nearly two decades removed from the deadly conflagration outside Waco, Texas, in 1993, which killed seventy-six members of the Branch Davidian sect, the controversy surrounding the origins and the cause of the massive fire persists. In the aftermath of what has been called the worst federal law-enforcement disaster in American history, the U.S. government has steadfastly maintained that the fire was the result of actions by sect members, essentially claiming that the Davidians committed mass suicide. This chapter revisits the controversy, recently revived by a British religious studies scholar, Kenneth C. G. Newport, who contends that the Branch Davidians had a theological rationale for mass suicide and likely set fire to their own home.[1] That the fire was an act of martyrdom/suicide in the face of a violent government siege is certainly a possibility, but the evidence is far from conclusive. Newport would have us believe otherwise, coupling the theological argument with assertions of "unassailable evidence" and "hard "facts" about some of the government's reports as if no alternative interpretation or explanation of events is plausible. Indeed, there are other explanations of the events surrounding the fire that do not comport with Newport's thesis and can be readily accessed in government reports, court documents, scholarly research, and the public domain. The most glaring deficiency in Newport's argument, I suggest, is the failure to address the valid documentation and evidence adduced in this body of record.

While I find Newport's arguments unconvincing, the appearance of this work provides scholars an important opportunity to reexamine the fateful denouement of this religious community with the advantage of some historical distance and perspective. Equally important, in the years following the Waco tragedy significant new developments and/or evidence have emerged. Though I do not think the new information ultimately resolves the question of how the fire started, together with the ongoing inquiry into this calamitous event, we move in a direction of better understanding both the factors and the circumstances that led to the sect's destruction.

Let me begin by stating what I do and do not cover in this chapter. I leave the theological argument advanced by Newport to others better trained in biblical exegesis and hermeneutics. However, I have deep reservations about imposing a literal reading upon what is essentially allegory and metaphor in the biblical texts, particularly with regard to end-time prophecy. Prophetic pronouncements about "signs and wonders" signaling the apocalypse are routinely read into contemporary social and political events by fundamentalist and sectarian leaders, and routinely they are wrong. As such, religious believers have learned to accommodate failed prophecy without serious challenge to the continuation of the faith.[2] This elasticity of prophetic interpretation has served the religious mission well. The accommodation to failed prophecy may take several forms that allow believers to explain away disconfirmation.[3] Scholars such as Gordon Melton and Diana Tumminia conclude from their studies of prophetic failure that, from the perspective of the groups in question, "prophecy never fails."[4] One may deduce from this peculiar kind of religious logic that there is little downside to making bold predictions, and, thus, prophetic beliefs should not be taken as literal formulas for action. Among many conservative fundamentalist, evangelical, charismatic/Pentecostal, and new religions, dire apocalyptic warnings and predictions are a vital part of the religious culture. The surge of prophetic activity leading up to the new millennium and the alarm surrounding the Y2K phenomenon attest to the enduring nature of religious groups to survive and even thrive in the face of failed prophecies.[5] Newport's method of post-hoc transliteration of Davidian prophetic teachings is suspect for this reason. To impute a motive of mass suicide from apocalyptic content in the message of a religious sect requires strong independent evidence, and this is where I focus my attention.

My chapter explores Newport's claim to the "unassailable evidence" found in government documents or reports that the Davidians set fire to Mount Carmel and committed mass suicide. Despite Newport's endorsement and largely uncritical acceptance of the official version of events, there has been substantial controversy and quite credible criticism surrounding the government's selective account of the Waco disaster. Among other things, the reliability of the government's case has been hampered by false or misleading statements by federal officials; lost, mishandled, and/or concealed evidence, including pyrotechnic devices that could have started the fire;[6] an independent arson report that challenges the conclusions of the government's reports on the origins and causes of the fire; the suppression of evidence through extensive redaction or dubious national security classification;

the use of procedural rulings and exclusion of evidence in the federal civil trial; and the unfortunate politicization of Waco as it became a proxy for culture war battles in the early-to-mid-1990s.[7] When examined against the backdrop of these disturbing and perplexing machinations and conditions, the "hard facts" supporting mass suicide at Mount Carmel are hardly certain or unambiguous.

Examining the Contested Evidence for Mass Suicide

Newport's case for mass suicide, which is based on relevant material and circumstantial evidence, is found in chapter 14 of his book. In chapter 15 he proceeds from a theological perspective to outline the case for mass suicide, drawing on discussions and analyses in earlier portions of the book. I address key assertions and claims made in chapter 14 with regard to the evidentiary arguments. To be sure, Newport makes clear from the outset of this chapter that he believes the Branch Davidians set the fire that precipitated the suicide:

> In this chapter and the next an account of the fire is given and a particular case is argued regarding its origin. It will quickly become apparent that the case advanced here is not the one that has in general been argued in scholarly circles, at least not at any length. Nevertheless, the case is both consistent with the unassailable evidence, and best able to account for that part of the evidence that is not so clear; it would not have been put forward otherwise. In essence the argument is that the Davidians set fire to Mount Carmel themselves, and did so with a clear goal in mind. . . . The evidence relied upon by the United States government that the Branch Davidians set fire to Mount Carmel themselves and did so intentionally is extensive, unequivocal and detailed.[8]

The certainty with which Newport endorses the government's account of the fire to buttress the argument for mass suicide is surprising in light of other conflicting material which I examine later. Newport suggests four plausible explanations of how the fire started: (1) The Davidians set it intentionally; (2) government agents set it intentionally; (3) the Davidians set it accidentally; and (4) government agents set it accidentally. He spends a substantial amount of space challenging option two in order to make a case for option one. Interestingly, his arguments principally address conspiracy theories and do not delineate those from the scholarly inquiry and research. There are some notable omissions regarding the latter. For example, in 1999 I published an article in the journal *Terrorism and Political Violence* identifying sixteen violations of basic hostage-barricade standards and protocols by the FBI at Waco that point to government culpability.[9] Newport is apparently unaware of the publication, for nowhere does it appear in his references. One of the key violations includes the conditions under which CS (tear gas) should be used, and I explore the medical research on its lethality. The manufacturers of CS post stern warnings against its use indoors, and extensive exposure to CS has been cited as a cause of death by Amnesty International.[10] According to one standard chemical reference text, CS forms "flammable vapor-air mixtures in larger volumes. *May be an explosion hazard in confined space.* Combustion may produce irritants and toxic gases. Combustion by-products include hydrogen chloride and phosgene."[11]

The use of CS must be considered in the calculus of the fire at Mount Carmel. The gas can be both an explosion hazard and a fire hazard under the conditions that were created by the FBI attack on Mount Carmel. These conditions specify high concentrations of CS in a confined space, which is precisely what the barricaded sect members experienced during the six-hour insertion of the chemical warfare agent. A single spark produced by the tracks of the twenty-nine-foot-long, fifty-two-ton M60 combat engineering vehicle (CEV) in metal-to-metal contact during the insertion and penetration of the Mount Carmel Center would have been sufficient to ignite the initial fire. Indeed, the first indication of a fire was observed in the FLIR (forward-looking infrared) at 12:07:41 in the second-floor window in the southeast corner of the Mount Carmel Center, less than two minutes after a CEV breached that area of the building.[12] By noon, Mount Carmel was a virtual tinderbox after the massive insertion of CS, which coated everything inside the building, producing a flammable vapor-air mixture. The CEV may have also knocked over a lit Coleman lantern in the vicinity, a possibility that I discuss later. My point here is that modified military armored tanks recklessly crashing through a structure with no consideration for potential metal abrasion that could produce a deadly spark under these circumstances is a formula for disaster.

I stress that the variable factors and conditions that may lead to the start of a fire when using CS are greater and more precarious than the official government reports on Waco admit. Consider the following account recorded by two FBI crisis negotiators in one barricade incident. In attempting to force suspects out of a building, the police fired a CS canister into the area where the men were thought to be holed up. However, when the SWAT team fired the CS into house, the "gas canister landed on a sofa and burned down the entire structure."[13] The agents do not offer any details about how the CS canister's contact with the sofa caused the fire, but they clearly attribute the fire to the CS. Because of the range of possible sources of combustion in such violent police confrontations involving destruction of property and CS insertion, absolute declarations to "unassailable evidence" of the fire source in the Waco case is tenuous at best. The mass suicide thesis, of course, has other problems.

Technically CS is not a gas but a particulate or powder, a riot-control agent designed for crowd dispersal in open spaces. Although it is designated as a nonlethal weapon for crowd control, a number of studies have challenged this classification.[14] The debate seems to center on the quantity used, whether it is deployed in confined space, and the length of exposure. In other words, the issue revolves around whether CS is used properly as prescribed by the manufacturer and responsible authorities. The quantity to which one is exposed is a significant consideration. In elevated concentration, CS can significantly damage the heart, liver, and lungs and even induce chemical pneumonia.[15] According to chemical weapons experts, there is a "mean lethal dose" of CS that occurs when exposure exceeds a specific quantity in cubic space.[16] Consider the following testimony of Frank Bolz in the 1993 Waco hearings before the Senate Committee on the Judiciary. Bolz pioneered hostage-negotiation techniques and procedures while with the New York City Police Department in the 1960s and later trained FBI hostage negotiators at Quantico:

> Well we know that chemical agents are supposed to be less than lethal. We also know that chemical agents kill. If people ingest too much chemical agent physically than their body medically can withstand, if they coat the alveoli sacs inside of the lungs and inhibit the exchange of oxygen and carbon dioxide into the blood, people get what is known as chemical pneumonia. Moisture forms in the lungs and they die.[17]

It is not uncommon for police and the military to misuse CS. A study of the effects of CS and published in the *Journal of the American Medical Association* concludes that the use of CS by law enforcement and the military is often "indiscriminate" and "not used correctly," resulting in "severe traumatic injury" and "lethal toxic injury."[18] One misuse of CS involves dispersal in closed spaces. Clarke and Robinson observe that "All the data available for CN . . . and CS are calculated for *low concentrations obtained by dispersion in the open air*. But it must be emphasized that when powder is thrown into a closed area much higher concentrations build up."[19] The distinction is not insignificant: "Inhalation toxicology studies at high levels of CS exposure . . . have demonstrated its ability to cause chemical pneumonitis and fatal pulmonary edema. In situations in which high levels of exposures have occurred, the same effects, as well as heart failure, hepatocellular damage, and death, have been reported in adults."[20] Further, "Oral toxicology studies have noted the ability of CS to cause severe gastroenteritis with perforation. Metabolic studies indicate that absorbed CS is metabolized to cyanide in peripheral tissues."[21] Engineers for an independent laboratory, Failure Analysis, calculated that the average concentration of CS inside Mount Carmel was ten to ninety times that necessary to deter trained troops.[22]

A retired U.S. Army expert who helped to develop the ferret round method to deliver CS reported that the concentrations of CS at Waco were "excessive" and likely "incapacitated" the Branch Davidians "to the point where they were physically unable to exit the gassed areas."[23] This is a critical point of contention I have with both Newport and the government reports. If the sect members were incapacitated by the high levels of chemical agent, by definition, their failure to escape was not a voluntary decision. One cannot call this suicide. It is well established in the training protocols for critical incidents that the use of CS is potentially lethal in closed spaces.[24] However, what is not often well monitored by enforcement officials is the degree to which security-force personnel comply with their training and codes of conduct to ensure that CS is used properly. At Mount Carmel, it appears that the use of CS was excessive, particularly considering that massive amounts were poured into enclosed spaces over a period of six hours.

Newport is dismissive about the lethal effects of CS and cites the 2000 government report issued by John Danforth's Office of Special Counsel (OSC). Newport repeats the government's claim that the gas was not lethal because the persons inside were able to leave the area where the gas was present. Thus, he concludes that a "short period of exposure to the gas, even in high dosage, would not have resulted in death."[25] He does not, however, examine the possibility that six hours of massive insertion of CS might inundate and saturate the interior of the building, leaving no place for the Davidians to flee and causing severe incapacitation. Rather, he repeats the FBI's disputable claim that strong winds on the day of the assault dissipated the lethal effects of the gas. Yet the inner rooms of the Davidian complex, where many of the sect members were gathered, had little ventilation. The kitchen and bunker areas,[26] where most of the children were concentrated, had no back door or windows to allow escape of the CS.

The delivery system for the insertion of CS is also a consideration. The FBI fired ferret rounds and used sprayers to insert CS inside Mount Carmel, both of which employ methylene chloride as a suspension agent. Methylene chloride is toxic and may be metabolized by the body to form carbon monoxide.[27] Combustion of methylene chloride can generate toxic gases, including phosgene, an extremely poisonous gas. Burning CS can also produce cyanide. Moreover, CS creates a severe burning sensation in victims and, if it comes into contact with water—a common reaction is to splash water on the burn—can form hydrogen cyanide fumes.[28] We know from survivors' reports that mothers inside Mount Carmel attempted to cover the faces of infants and children with wet towels since they had no gas masks small enough to fit children. Forty-four of the Branch Davidian corpses tested positive for cyanide, some with enough to reach concentration levels in the blood to produce a coma or death.[29]

Mixed with methylene chloride, CS also poses an explosion and fire hazard. Dow Chemical's material safety data sheet notes that methylene chloride forms flammable vapor-air mixtures; in closed spaces the vapors can build up, causing "unconsciousness and death."[30] The amount of methylene chloride used by the FBI at Mount Carmel reached 8,000 ppm—sixteen times the level needed to cause intoxication.[31]

It appears that full disclosure of the toxicity and lethal aspects of the CS insertion proposed by the FBI was not readily conveyed to the attorney general in seeking approval for the chemical assault plan. Dr. Alan Stone, professor of psychiatry and medicine at Harvard Medical School, was asked by the U.S. Department of Justice to review the actions of the FBI at Mount Carmel in the aftermath of the incident. He had the following comments on the government's use of CS on the Davidians, particularly the children:

> It is difficult to believe that the U.S. government would deliberately plan to expose twenty-five children, most of them infants and toddlers, to CS gas for forty-eight hours. . . . Based on my own medical knowledge and review of the scientific literature, the information supplied to the Attorney General seems to minimize the potential harmful consequences for infants and children. . . . The Attorney General's information . . . understated the potential health consequences in closed spaces.[32]

Stone also cites a study that "closely approximates the expected Waco conditions," in which a four-month-old male infant was exposed to canisters of CS fired by police into a house to subdue a disturbed adult. The exposure lasted two to three hours (roughly half the exposure endured by the Davidian infants and children). After the incident, the male infant was immediately taken to an emergency room, where he was found to suffer from life-threatening conditions, including "severe respiratory distress typical of chemical pneumonia. The infant had cyanosis, required urgent positive pressure pulmonary care, and was hospitalized for twenty-eight days. Other signs of toxicity appeared, including an enlarged liver."[33] Stone states that "the infant's reactions reported in this case history were of a vastly different dimension than the information given the AG [Attorney General] suggested."[34]

In 1996 a special report by the House Committee on Government Reform and Oversight in conjunction with the House Committee on the Judiciary concluded that the insertion of CS into the enclosed bunker at Mount Carmel "could have been a proximate cause of or directly resulted in some or all of the deaths attributed to asphyxiation in the autopsy reports."[35] The report contradicts claims by a Department of Justice expert minimizing the effects of CS, citing medical case studies showing CS can be lethal in closed quarters.

Finally, the length of exposure must be a consideration. Proponents of CS claim that high levels of exposure are precluded because people are averse to remaining where the chemical agent is present. Nonetheless, people may be placed in extenuating circumstances that do not permit flight or escape. As such, length of exposure must be examined together with concentration. Independent of the obvious problem that Branch Davidians may have been incapacitated by the chemical agent, there is ample evidence that suggests that the demolition of Mount Carmel by combat engineering vehicles (often described as "tanks") collapsed the stairwells and possible escape routes during the FBI assault on April 19, trapping some sect members within the structure.[36] Newport dismisses this possibility:

> The question of whether, in fact, there was a blocking of exit point either by accident or by design has been much discussed in the literature, and there is no space to deal with this issue in detail here. Suffice it to say,

however, that the evidence clearly points to the fact that there were numerous avenues of escape open to the Branch Davidians had they wished to leave the burning building, and some of the members of the community (though not those in the "bunker" area) probably had a good fifteen to twenty minutes to make their way out.[37]

In fact, there is clear evidence that the demolition of the building by CEVs *did* collapse stairwells and obstruct exits. At the civil trial several Branch Davidian survivors described in gruesome detail their desperate attempts to escape Mount Carmel in the face of the deadly firestorm and fallen debris all around them. I attended the federal Branch Davidian civil trial in Waco and heard firsthand the witnesses' sworn testimonies in the summer of 2000. Marjorie Thomas testified at the trial and told the jury that she was "trapped in the building when the fire broke out."[38] Unlike others, she managed to escape before the chemical agent and the fire was able to devour her. She said she was frantic and felt her clothes starting to melt. She saw a little bit of light from a window on the second floor, put her hands over her head, and leapt out the window. Thomas suffered severe burns over 70 percent of her body. By the time of the trial she had already endured thirteen operations to repair skin damage. She faced more operations in the future. Marjorie Thomas stated emphatically that there was no plan for suicide. She was asked by attorneys whether Koresh or the Davidians had a theological position on suicide. Contrary to Newport's claim, Thomas said, "It was unacceptable."[39]

Another Branch Davidian, Misty Ferguson, testified at the civil trial. Ferguson is the daughter of Rita Riddle, one of the Davidians who came out early during the standoff. Ferguson was badly burned in the fire but managed to escape. When Ferguson was sworn in, she raised her hand to the sounds of gasps in the courtroom. All of her fingers on both hands had been amputated. She also had extensive scarring on her face and arms. Ferguson described the events of April 19 as a desperate effort to make her way through collapsing structures and debris. She said the floors of the building began to buckle; the stairways were blocked by debris and cut off any exit routes. Smoke filled the air, and she was unable to see much of anything. The floor collapsed underneath her, and she held out her hands to stop the fall. He fingers and thumbs were burned off as she grabbed hold of something. She ran down a hallway and saw a glimmer of light left by a hole punched in the building by a tank. She jumped through the hole to the ground outside.[40] Ferguson was the youngest of nine survivors on April 19. She was seventeen years old.

Newport's claim that there were "numerous avenues of escape open to the Branch Davidians had they wished to leave"[41] is purely speculative and ignores the survivors' accounts and sworn testimonies. The few sect members who escaped described the frenetic efforts of people inside Mount Carmel trying to find their way through the blinding black smoke, the rubble, wreckage, and debris, not to mention the raging heat and burning CS by-products, phosgene and cyanide.

David Thibodeau, another survivor, provides an eyewitness account of April 19 in his book, *A Place Called Waco*, in which he describes encountering several escape routes blocked by collapsing structures, fallen beams, and piles of debris.[42] He reports following two other sect members, Jamie Castillo and Derek Lovelock, through an opening in a wall as they successfully escaped the inferno. Thibodeau also notes that sect members were anxious about jumping out of the building for fear that they would be shot by federal agents.[43] Even in the face of the intolerable heat, the Davidians deliberated, however briefly, the prospect of escaping only to be gunned down. This is a significant consideration since even a moment of hesitation may have been the difference between life and death for some inside Mount Carmel. My interviews with other Branch Davidian survivors also support Thibodeau's assertion that they believed they would be killed by federal agents if they came out.[44]

Newport cites findings from Danforth's OSC final report on the causes of the fire. This report concludes that three separate fires were started by the Davidians in the interior of the building, that they were intentionally set within a two- or three-minute span, and that there was no external source of the fires.[45] The report states its findings definitively and unequivocally without concession to alternative explanations. However, a declaration filed in the civil case by Richard Sherrow, a former fire and explosion investigator with the Bureau of Alcohol, Tobacco, Firearms, and Explosives (ATF) and retired senior explosive ordnance disposal technician with the U.S. Army, states that the evidence is entirely consistent with a fire that originated from a single point and spread throughout the Mount Carmel structure.[46] Sherrow contends that the evidence is not as certain as government investigators claim. The same evidence could be used to support an entirely different conclusion: "It is also consistent with evidence that the original fire was started by an M728 CEV striking the southeast corner tower of Mount Carmel."[47]

According to official records, a heat signature was observed on the FLIR in the second window of the southeast corner tower less than two minutes after a CEV made violent contact with that part of the building. Survivors reported that a lit Coleman lantern was located in that vicinity.[48] Sherrow explains how this could have been the source of the fire:

> A Coleman-type lantern becomes extremely hot in operation, reaching as much as 700 degrees Fahrenheit. This temperature is sufficient to cause ignition of combustible material even in the absence of an external flame source. Moreover, if the flame of the lantern had been extinguished, the fuel would continue to be expelled from the manifold under pressure from the tank.... If a lit Coleman-type lantern, which had been operating for some time, had been knocked over by CEV contact with the building or shaking of the building by vibration from the operation of the CEVs outside, the heat from the lantern chassis, the mantle flame, and the continued production of atomized fuel could cause a fire consistent with that observed on the FLIR at 12:07:41.[49]

The rapid spread of the fire was facilitated not only by thick clouds of methylene chloride but also by "large amounts of highly flammable and combustible materials" inside Mount Carmel, "including, but not limited to, gasoline, kerosene, lamp oil, Coleman lantern fuel, paint, petroleum distillates, tar and roofing materials, acetylene and oxygen containers, gunpowder, metal shavings and a large quantity of small arms ammunition."[50]

Sherrow offers another possible explanation for the government's claim that three separate fires were started by the Branch Davidians because they were detected by the FLIR in three separate parts of the building. Technically, the "heat signatures" revealed by the FLIR indicate infrared heat radiation that is hotter than the background. These differences may be interpreted as fire, but they may also have other explanations, he observes: "A FLIR camera cannot distinguish between reflection and emission or between visible flame and hot smoke and gas."[51] Uneven heat emissions may not be detected but still be part of a common combustible system or structure. Heat signatures in FLIR technology only detect the hot-to-cold contrast in radiation. However, "there are no industry-accepted standards for use of this technology in fire cause and origin determination."[52]

Finally, Sherrow observes that the velocity and direction of the ambient winds outside Mount Carmel are consistent with the lines of fire growth and propagation. Two large holes made in the front of the structure by the CEVs helped to create an airstream pulled from the southeast corner of the complex, where the first fire was sited.[53] The breaches created a "venturi" or wind-tunnel effect, possibly creating the "fireball" later described by some survivors.

Government Misfeasance and the Politicization of the Branch Davidian Case

A distinct and equally disquieting problem with the evidentiary material and arguments provided by the state is that its credibility has been undermined. The Branch Davidian case has been hampered by false or misleading statements from federal officials; lost, mishandled, or concealed evidence; and suppression of evidence through extensive redaction of official reports and documents and dubious national security classification. I have written about these disturbing machinations elsewhere in several peer-reviewed publications (of which Newport also seems to be unaware and does not cite in his book).[54] Space does not permit an extensive review of this material, but suffice it to say that, taken as a whole, these actions do not portend favorably for the reliability or veracity of statements by government officials. It is the government's incompetence and/or misfeasance in the case as a whole that has called into question the integrity of the evidence regarding the origins of the fire. A few examples of government missteps in the preservation and control of evidence should adequately convey the problem.

After the conflagration, the FBI placed the evidence in a secure storage facility under the command of the Texas Department of Public Safety in Austin but would not allow defense attorneys access to it. Joey Gordon, a Texas Ranger who inventoried the evidence, later testified in a videotaped deposition during the civil trial that a number of critical items (e.g., military or pyrotechnic rounds) were mislabeled or missing.[55] At least one of the military rounds photographed at the crime scene disappeared. Four or five pyrotechnic "flashbang" grenades used by federal law-enforcement agents and found in the storage facility were mislabeled or misidentified by the FBI Crime Lab as well, including Q1237 projectiles and Q379 and Q380 prototypes, all capable of starting a fire. The FBI also misidentified "cooked-off" rounds of ammunition.[56] This information was not made available to the jury in the criminal trial in 1994 and became known to the public in 1999 only through a serendipitous miscommunication between the U.S. Attorney's office in the Western District of Texas and the Department of Justice that allowed an investigator in the civil case to examine the evidence in the secure facility. Indeed, it is unlikely that the civil trial would have gone forward at all without the discovery of this new evidence. Bill Johnston, the Assistant U.S. Attorney who gave the investigator permission to examine the evidence, was forced to resign over the incident. Labeled a whistleblower, he quickly became a pariah and a target of reprisals by the Justice Department, even though the plaintiffs in the civil case had every legal right to see the evidence.[57] Justice officials turned on Johnston, claiming he had concealed information from the Danforth investigation about incendiary devices used at Mount Carmel. However, Johnston accused Danforth and the Justice Department of making him a scapegoat when the government's misdeeds were exposed.

A number of other items in the evidence record disappeared or were mishandled. While these items do not shed light on the origins of the fire, they are pertinent to the larger issue of the preservation and integrity of evidence. The right front door of the Branch Davidian complex was a key piece of missing evidence in the criminal trial because it would have shown whether the bullet holes were caused primarily by incoming or outgoing rounds. The Branch Davidians claimed that, on February 28, ATF agents shot first through the front door, initiating the shootout. However, ATF officials claimed that the Branch Davidians shot through the door from the inside. Preservation of the right front door would have allowed investigators and the jury to determine which account was accurate. Mysteriously, the door disappeared.

Another piece of missing or mishandled evidence was the videotape of the initial ATF raid. To record the raid, ATF agents mounted a camera on the telephone pole at the entrance of Mount Carmel. After the failed raid and heated disputes about who fired first, ATF officials reported that the videotape was blank. The videotape could have established several contested facts in the case, including whether federal agents fired first, whether David Koresh actually appeared at the front door to plead with agents not to fire, and whether agents shot through the front door, as the Branch Davidians claimed.

Still another missing piece of evidence was the videotape on board the Blackhawk helicopter that circled Mount Carmel prior to and during the initial ATF raid. The videotape was critical in determining whether federal agents fired weapons from the helicopter, strafing the Branch Davidian residence even before the ATF team arrived at Mount Carmel. Several Branch Davidians reported gunfire from the helicopters. Colonel William Petit was aboard the Blackhawk on the day of the raid and testified in the civil trial. He told the court that he never saw gunfire from the helicopters. However, when asked about the tape, he said he was aware of the tape but had not seen it and did not know what had happened to it.[58] The videotape made on board the Blackhawk, like the pyrotechnic military rounds, the flashbang grenades, the right front door, and the videotape from the camera on the telephone pole to record the initial raid, either disappeared or was mishandled.

A particularly egregious example of governmental misfeasance concerns the evidence of alleged illegal firearms recovered at Mount Carmel after the fire. As part of an agreement between the Department of Justice and congressional committee members prior to the 1995 Waco hearings, an independent analysis was to be conducted by Failure Analysis, a firm routinely used by federal agencies, to assess the gun-tampering charges (converting semiautomatic into fully automatic weapons) in the warrants.[59] When scientists from Failure Analysis arrived at the Department of Public Safety in Austin, however, officials declined to make the firearms available to them. According the 1996 final congressional report on the Waco hearings, "The [Justice] Department agreed instead to conduct the tests itself and present its findings to the subcommittees. A short time later, the Department urged, for cost considerations, that tests not be performed. As a result, no tests were [ever] performed on the firearms."[60] This is hardly an incidental matter. If the Departments of Justice and the Treasury thought they had material evidence to support the charges in the warrants that the Davidians were illegally converting semiautomatic rifles to fully automatic weapons (the rationale for the raid), it is inconceivable that they would prevent these findings from being made public. Indeed, they would have made every effort to broadcast this information to the media and the public because it would offer some vindication of the initial enforcement action.

Finally, a key record of evidence that disappeared was the after-incident reports based on interviews conducted with the crisis negotiators by Justice Department officials. It was evident to me and other observers that during the fifty-one-day standoff the negotiations between the Branch Davidians and the crisis negotiators were effectively undermined by the tactical strategies of the hostage rescue team (HRT), which employed a bewilderingly mixed message. Instead of rewarding the barricaded sect members for concessions made during the negotiations (e.g., sending children or adults out, providing a videotape), the HRT would "punish" them by turning off their electricity or destroying more of their property with the CEVs.

The effect of this mixed-message approach was a breakdown in both communication and trust between sect members and negotiators. In the preparation for the 1994 criminal trial, the defense attorneys believed that exculpatory evidence could be found in the after-incident reports and filed requests with the Justice Department to examine these materials. However, the defense attorneys were told that the reports did not exist. Nonetheless, years later, some of the complaints and grievances of the FBI negotiators were leaked, and in the 2000 civil trial, the Justice Department suddenly "discovered" the missing reports. Not surprisingly, they were damning. Several negotiators objected loudly to the HRT's threatening tactics and even predicted that the standoff would end in the deaths of the sect members.[61]

It is imperative to remember that the disastrous federal siege of the Branch Davidian community took place in a cultural and political climate of growing Far-Right political activity and antigovernment sentiment in the early-to-mid-1990s. For Far-Right militias and patriot groups, Waco became a political symbol of government abuse and tyranny. Indeed, the federal sieges at Ruby Ridge and Waco, only six months apart, were key factors in the mass mobilization of the Far Right, which eventually led to the Oklahoma City bombing by antigovernment insurgents on the second anniversary of the April 19 FBI assault.[62] In the three years following the Waco raid, the number of militia and patriot groups climbed from less than a dozen to 858.[63] In this context, the raids, the trials, and the congressional hearings and reports became heavily politicized, symbolizing a culture war between liberals and conservatives, big versus small government, gun enthusiasts versus gun-control advocates. I contend that the Branch Davidians never got a fair hearing in the courts or in the court of public opinion, largely because the incident could not be extricated from the politics. While the Branch Davidians were never Far-Right political militants, their plight was appropriated by the Far Right and came to represent a much larger conflict and cultural divide.

I testified in the 1996 House hearings on Waco and witnessed this firsthand as conservative Republicans used the hearings to attack President Bill Clinton and the Democrats.[64] On the other hand, Democrats on the House committees were defensive and eager to label critics of the Waco raid as right-wing reactionaries or antigovernment zealots. As a liberal Democrat and editor of a highly critical book on the federal siege,[65] I was unsettled by this peculiar development. My own objection to the federal raid was purely on civil liberties grounds, not as a gun enthusiast or right-wing patriot. Yet the battle lines were clearly drawn.

Behind the scenes, the White House staff assembled a damage-control team and retained the services of a public-relations specialist to deflect negative publicity.[66] Treasury Secretary Robert Rubin contacted at least one member of the joint committees, Rep. Bill Brewster (D-Oklahoma) and requested that he not ask any questions that would embarrass the administration.[67] President Clinton himself used the Oval Office as a bully pulpit and charged that the hearings were an "attack on law enforcement."[68]

Investigators for the House committees prior to the hearings reported a concerted lack of cooperation from the White House and the Departments of the Treasury and Justice.[69] Officials attempted to narrow the scope of the committees' requests and restrict access to information. According to the final congressional report, the first delivery of important documents requested by House committees arrived only three weeks before the hearings, and "tens of thousands of others were received after the hearings had already begun. This 'wait-and-dump' strategy rendered meaningful staff review of many key documents virtually impossible prior to commencement of the hearings."[70] In addition, the Treasury Department's documents arrived in no apparent order, making the retrieval of any single document extremely difficult. However, "in what became symbolic of the administration's uncooperative attitude," it was later discovered that the Democrats were provided an index for locating Treasury documents, whereas no such index was given to the Republicans.[71]

Many of the documents requested by the House committees of the White House, the Departments of Justice and the Treasury, and the FBI were eventually produced for the hearings but were heavily redacted. In some cases, entire pages were blacked out, making comprehension and discovery of events virtually impossible. The White House and the federal agency leaders claimed redaction was necessary for national security, but most observers recognized this strategy for what it was: a self-serving obstruction of the investigation.

Sadly, the real victims in this episode at the pinnacle of the culture wars were the Branch Davidians and their families. The Branch Davidians could not be vindicated, I suggest, because, in this polarized, political context, this would have symbolized a victory for Far-Right, antigovernment ideology and beliefs. I have argued elsewhere that the best explanation for the disproportionate federal response to the Davidians (the largest enforcement action in the history of the ATF) was that key federal actors *perceived* the group to be part of the Far-Right Posse Comitatus and Christian Identity networks.[72] Moreover, ATF officials developed an inflated martial image of the Branch Davidians as a violent extremist group bent on war with the government in part because they listened to the cultural opponents of David Koresh and in part because the ATF was receptive to a "warfare narrative" that served the interests of an opportunistic agency:

> ATF investigators and officials framed the information they received to fit the narrative of warfare, causing them to overlook or ignore contradictory, conflicting or ambivalent evidence. This explains the puzzling decisions by ATF officials who failed to consider less lethal options or opportunities as they arose in what the Treasury report later referred to as "steps taken along what seemed to be at the time a preordained road."[73]

The FBI uncritically adopted this warfare narrative in its operation of the standoff and final CS insertion. The pervasive disregard for and violation of standard hostage-barricade protocols—the "noose-tightening" approach of tactical pressure over the objections of crisis negotiators, the use of psychological warfare, provocation and intimidation, and the dangerous CS insertion and demolition of the Branch Davidian complex—all speak to the antipathy and contempt of the FBI and its HRT for those inside Mount Carmel. Even after it became apparent that the Branch Davidians were not part of either the Posse Comitatus or Christian Identity networks in the weeks and months following the conflagration, the government continued to exploit this narrative and frame the group as antigovernment extremists. The government could not or would not acknowledge this grievous miscalculation.

Newport discounts the idea of a government cover-up,[74] but I believe there is compelling evidence and a quite plausible argument to be made. The collapse of trust in government during a period of growing fear about "big government" and even broad swaths of antigovernment sentiment in the United States threatened to ignite a crisis of moral authority—an incalculable cost to bear, at least in the minds of some leaders. Moreover, the Clinton White House and Democrats in Congress saw the appropriation of Waco by right-wing leaders as a thinly veiled attack on liberal ideology in the context of the culture wars—and rightly so. Keep in mind that the hearings took place less than a year after conservative Republicans swept into power and seized a majority in both houses of Congress. Democratic leaders likely saw Waco as symbolic of a larger battle they could not afford to lose. My point here is that the question of mass suicide or the cause of the fire that destroyed the Branch Davidian community is inextricably tied to the profoundly polarized politics of the culture during this time. Thus, finding the truth about the conflagration is acutely obscured and filtered through layers of deeply held beliefs, values, and political passions.

As a British observer, Newport does not seem to be aware of the significance of the political environment that shapes and redefines the terms of the controversy at Waco. Independent of the actual cause of the fire is the broader social construction of meaning and the assignment of blame, an imputing of characteristics and motives, the identification of culpable agents, villains, and enemies. Control over the framing of the Waco disaster confers power because it represents a struggle over cultural ideas imbued with greater import. Given the seriously compromised custody of evidence, we may never know how the fire started at Mount Carmel. However, if and when any new evidence does arise or perhaps some principal actor in the tragedy comes forward to make a startling confession in the future, it is likely that the meaning of Waco for most people will still be construed through the cultural lens of the period. Not unlike other highly contested government actions (e.g., the invasion of Iraq, extraordinary rendition, warrantless surveillance of citizens), explanations tend to entail coded interpretations of ideological canons or principles. Waco has become something of a Rorschach test for social actors, telling us more about their politics and values than about the actual chain of events that led to the annihilation of this religious community.

NOTES

1. Kenneth C. G. Newport, *The Branch Davidians of Waco: The History and Beliefs of an Apocalyptic Sect* (New York: Oxford University Press, 2006).

2. See Jon R. Stone, ed., *Expecting Armageddon: Essential Readings in Failed Prophecy* (New York: Routledge, 2000); Diana Tumminia and William Swatos, eds., *The Failure of Prophecy: Fifty Years after Festinger* (London: Brill, forthcoming).

3. Lorne Dawson, "When Prophecy Fails and Faith Persists: A Theoretical Overview." *Nova Religio* 3(1) (1999): 60–82.

4. J. Gordon Melton, "Spiritualization and Reaffirmation: What Really Happens When Prophecy Fails," *American Studies* 26 (1985): 17–29; Diana G. Tumminia, "How Prophecy Never Fails: Interpretive Reason in a Flying-saucer Group," *Journal of Contemporary Religion* 59 (1998): 157–70.

5. In October 1991 the FBI issued alerts to law-enforcement agencies in the Unites States about potential Y2K violence involving "extreme cultists" together with militias and radical Islamist groups in the Project Megiddo report. The FBI also worked with its Israeli counterparts in formulating a threat assessment of millennial religious groups. Israeli authorities expelled members of two Christian millennial groups, House of Prayer and Solomon's Temple, and denied entry to a third group, the Denver-based Concerned Christians, citing suspicions of violence or possible mass suicide. None of these groups engaged in violence, and the millennium passed without incident. The furor associated with apocalyptic prophecy and Y2K was largely overblown. See "FBI Issues Alerts for Possible Y2K Threats," *ABC News* (Oct. 20, 1999); "Israel Arrests Christian Groups Accused of Planning to Harm Public Safety; Reawakens Fear of Millennium Violence," *ABC News* (Oct. 25, 1999); "Israel Detains Christian Group in Pre-millennium Sweep—The Christians Were Seized near Jerusalem's Mount of Olives," *CNN* (Oct. 25, 1999); Deborah Camiel, "Israel to Expel 20 Members of Christian Groups," Reuters (Oct. 25, 1999); "Christians Appeal to Israel Ministry to Prevent Deportation," Associated Press (Oct. 28, 1999). For response from the evangelical Christian community, see Douglas E. Cowan, "Confronting the Failed Failure: Y2K and Evangelical Eschatology in Light of the Passed Millennium," *Nova Religio* 7(2) (2003): 71–85.

6. Newport contends that the FBI did not conceal evidence of the pyrotechnic rounds in the CS (tear gas) assault and that the information was later covered up by Assistant U.S. Attorney Bill Johnston. This is misleading. The information supplied by the FBI to the U.S. Department of Justice was buried and obscured, referring only to "military rounds" or "bubbleheads." Johnston said he didn't know what military rounds or bubbleheads were, and a number of other experts said they were not familiar with these terms. I think this obfuscation by the FBI was deliberate and tantamount to concealment. Johnston complained that they were punishing him for allowing the plaintiff's investigator into the storage locker to find the pyrotechnic devices, some of which were mislabeled.

7. Stuart A. Wright, "Field Notes: *Isabel Andrade et al. v. U.S.*," *Nova Religio* 4(2) (2001): 157–64; Stuart A. Wright, "Justice Denied: The Waco Civil Trial," *Nova Religio* 5(1) (2001): 143–51; Stuart A. Wright, "A Critical Analysis of Evidentiary and Procedural Rulings in the Branch Davidian Civil Trial," in *New Religious Movements and Religious Liberty in America*, ed. Derek Davis, 101–13 (Waco: Baylor University Press, 2002); Stuart A. Wright, "A Decade after Waco: Reassessing Crisis Negotiations at Mt. Carmel in Light of New Government Disclosures." *Nova Religio* 7(2) (2003): 101–10.

8. Newport, *Branch Davidians of Waco*, 279.

9. Stuart A. Wright, "Anatomy of a Government Massacre: Abuses of Hostage-barricade Protocols during the Waco Standoff," *Terrorism and Political Violence* 11(2) (1999): 39–68.

10. *Amnesty International Report*, June 1, 1988. The report notes that CS and CN (both tear gases) contributed to the deaths of more than forty Palestinians in an attack by Israeli forces against persons in closed spaces.

11. Cited in Dick J. Reavis, *The Ashes of Waco* (Syracuse: Syracuse University Press, 1995), 268.

12. Fire Investigation Report, Branch Davidian Compound, Waco, Texas, Apr. 19, 1993. Prepared by Paul C. Gray et al., 5, *Report to the Deputy Attorney General on the Events at Waco, Texas, February 28 to April 19, 1993*. Washington, D.C.: U.S. Department of Justice, October 1993.

13. Michael J. McMains and Wayman C. Mullins, *Crisis Negotiations: Managing Critical Incidents and Hostage Situations in Law Enforcement and Corrections* (Cincinnati: Anderson, 1996), 313.

14. Howard Hu, Jonathan Fine, Paul Epstein, Karl Kelsey, Preston Reynolds, and Bailus Walker, "Tear Gas: Harassing Agent or Toxic Chemical Weapon?" *Journal of the American Medical Association* 262(5); http://www.zarc.com/english/tear_gases/jamateargastoxic.html (accessed July 23, 2010).

15. Ibid., note 8; see also Testimony of Frank Bolz, *Hearing before the Committee on the Judiciary, United States Senate: The Aftermath of Waco: Changes in Federal Law Enforcement, October 31 and November 1, 1995* (Washington, D.C.: U.S. Government Printing Office, 1997), 118, 134–35.

16. Testimony of Frank Bolz, 135.

17. Ibid.

18. Hu et al., "Tear Gas," 1.

19. Robin Clarke and Perry Robinson, "United Kingdom," in *CBW: Chemical and Biological Warfare: London Conference on CBW*, ed. Steven Rose, 91–92 (London: Harrop, 1968); emphasis added.

20. Hu et al., "Tear Gas," 3.

21. Ibid.

22. Declaration of Richard Sherrow, Fire Investigators' Civil Suit Affidavit on Origin of April 19, 1993, Fire at Mount Carmel, U.S. District Court for the Southern District of Texas, Houston Division, H-94-0923, Jan. 17, 1996, 4.

23. Rex Applegate, unpublished report on FBI Planning and Operations Relating to the CS Gas Assault at Waco, Texas, February 28 to April 19, 1993 (Scottsburg, Ore., 1995), 23.

24. McMains and Mullins, *Crisis Negotiations*, 313.

25. Newport, *Branch Davidians of Waco*, 289.

26. Federal agents termed the concrete room at the base of the central tower on the ground floor of the residence a "bunker." It was actually a vault constructed years earlier for the previous administration building, which stood on the site and burned to the ground in 1983. Clive Doyle has reported that printed pamphlets and journals published by the Branch Davidians, particularly Lois Roden, were stored in the vault at the time of the 1983 fire and that all of the contents of the vault were untouched by the fire. When David Koresh and his followers began building the large residence on the site, they

incorporated the concrete vault into the plan of the new building. Koresh's Branch Davidians moved out of individual houses at Mount Carmel into the new single residence in the spring of 1992.

27. J. Fagin, J. Bradley, and D. Williams, "Carbon Monoxide Poisoning Secondary to Inhaling Methylene Chloride," *British Medical Journal* 281(6253) (1980): 1461.

28. David B. Kopel and Paul H. Blackman, *No More Wacos: What's Wrong with Federal Law Enforcement and How to Fix It* (Amherst, N.Y.: Prometheus), 159.

29. Ibid.

30. Ibid., 158.

31. Ibid.

32. Dr. Alan A. Stone, *Report and Recommendations concerning the Handling of Incidents such as the Branch Davidian Standoff in Waco, Texas*. Report to the attorney general, Nov. 8, 1993, 30–31.

33. Ibid., 34.

34. Ibid.

35. *Investigation into the Activities of Federal Law Enforcement Agencies toward the Branch Davidians*, thirteenth report by the Committee on Government Reform and Oversight prepared in conjunction with the Committee of the Judiciary (Washington, D.C.: U.S. Government Printing Office, 1996), 4.

36. Wright, "Field Notes: *Isabel Andrade*"; Wright, "A Decade after Waco."

37. Newport, *Branch Davidians of Waco*, 280.

38. Stuart A. Wright, Waco trial journal, author's personal notes from the civil trial.

39. Ibid.

40. Ibid.

41. Newport, *Branch Davidians of Waco*, 280.

42. David Thibodeau, *A Place Called Waco: A Survivor's Story* (Washington, D.C.: Public Affairs, 1999), xvi–xvii.

43. Ibid., xvii.

44. Catherine Matteson, interview by author, Sept. 10, 1993; Rita Riddle, interview by author, Dec. 17, 1993.

45. Walter Wetherington, *Final Report concerning the Fire at the Branch Davidian Complex, Waco, Texas, April 19, 1993. Prepared for the Office of Special Counsel, Waco Investigation*, Sept. 12, 2000.

46. Declaration of Richard L. Sherrow, 2.

47. Ibid.

48. Newport criticizes me for making a case that a CEV may have knocked over a lit Coleman lantern and chides me for using "unreferenced survivor reports." I am not drawing on unreferenced survivor reports but on Richard Sherrow's sworn affidavit submitted to the court in the civil trial. The argument here is clearly in the context of Sherrow's affidavit, and the specific point Newport contests as "unreferenced survivor reports" is indeed referenced in this document.

49. Declaration of Richard L. Sherrow, 5.

50. Ibid., 2.

51. Ibid., 5.

52. Ibid.

53. Ibid., 5–6.

54. Wright, "Critical Analysis of Evidentiary and Procedural Rulings"; Wright, "Decade after Waco"; Wright, "Field Notes from Waco"; Wright, "Justice Denied."

55. Wright, "Field Notes from Waco," 352.

56. "Cooking off" refers to the explosion of ammunition as a result of surrounding heat.

57. Bill Johnston, letter to the editor and statement, *Dallas Morning News* (Nov. 9, 2000).

58. Wright, "Field Notes from Waco," 353.

59. *Investigation into the Activities of Federal Law Enforcement Agencies toward the Branch Davidians*, 9.

60. Ibid.

61. Wright, "Decade after Waco," 107–108.

62. Stuart A. Wright, *Patriots, Politics, and the Oklahoma City Bombing* (New York: Cambridge University Press, 2007).

63. Southern Poverty Law Center, "The Rise and Decline of the 'Patriots' "; http://splcenter.org/intel/intelreport/article.jsp?aid=195&printable=1 (accessed July 29, 2009).

64. I worked with Republicans on the House committees leading up to the hearings, and in my judgment this was largely their motive.

65. Stuart A. Wright, ed., *Armageddon in Waco: Critical Perspectives on the Branch Davidian Conflict* (Chicago: University of Chicago, 1995).

66. Ann Devroy, "Clinton Team Focuses on Damage Control on Waco," *Washington Post* (July 19, 1995), A12.

67. *Investigation into the Activities of Federal Law Enforcement Agencies toward the Branch Davidians*, 7.

68. Ibid., 7–8.

69. Ibid., 8.

70. Ibid.

71. Ibid.

72. Wright, *Patriots, Politics, and the Oklahoma City Bombing*, 155–65.

73. Stuart A. Wright, "Explaining Militarization at Waco: Construction and Convergence of a Warfare Narrative," in *Controversial New Religions*, ed. James R. Lewis and Jesper Aagaard Petersen, 75–97 (New York: Oxford University Press, 2005).

74. Newport, *Branch Davidians of Waco*, 282.

6

Explaining the Murder-Suicides of the Order of the Solar Temple: A Survey of Hypotheses

Henrik Bogdan

Every slander, lie or falsehood about our deed could only be translated, once more, as the refusal to understand and fathom the Mystery of Life and Death. Space is short, time is ending. It is with unfathomable Love, ineffable joy, and without regret that we leave this world.
—from "To All Those Who Can Still Understand the Voice of Wisdom"

The 1990s witnessed a number of spectacular outbursts of violence associated with new religious movements. Those that received wide media coverage were the burning of the Branch Davidian ranch outside Waco, Texas, in April 1993; the sarin gas attack on the Tokyo subway on March 20, 1994, by Aum Shinrikyo; the murder-suicides of the Order of the Solar Temple in October 1994; and the Heaven's Gate suicides in California on March 26, 1997. Of these acts of violence, those by the Order of the Solar Temple (l'Ordre du Temple Solaire, or OTS) have received the least attention by the academic community; in addition, the public is likely to know very little about the OTS.[1] However, if we examine the actual effect of the violence—the lethal outcome in terms of people who died—the violence of the Solar Temple was the deadliest: The ATF/FBI raid on the Mount Carmel community, the Branch Davidians, and the subsequent fire that engulfed the compound resulted in the death of 75 individuals (54 adults and 21 children); the Heaven's Gate suicides led to the death 39 members; the gas attack by

Aum Shinrikyo caused 12 casualties (but created more than five thousand reported injuries), while the murder-suicides of the Solar Temple left a total of 77 persons dead.

The first murders committed by the OTS occurred on September 30, 1994, when a three-month-old baby (Christopher Emmanuel) was killed, together with his parents, who were ex-members of the group. A wooden stake had been driven through his heart, as the OTS leaders apparently believed that the baby was none other than the Antichrist. Four days later, on October 4, five persons were stabbed to death at the villa of the group's leader, Joseph Di Mambro, and the villa was destroyed by fire. Another fire started at 1:00 A.M. on October 5 at an OTS center in Ferme des Rochettes, in the canton of Fribourg, Switzerland. The authorities later discovered 23 bodies, some of which had been shot, while others had been suffocated by plastic bags over their heads. A few hours later three additional vacation chalets at Les Granges sur Salvan, in the canton of Valais, were set on fire, and another 25 bodies were found, including those of the leaders of the Solar Temple, Joseph Di Mambro and Luc Jouret. The 53 victims (not counting the three homicides committed on September 30) were divided into three different categories.

The first category, consisting of 15 members who were referred to as the "Awakened," belonged to the inner circle of Di Mambro and his right-hand man, Luc Jouret. This inner group of members committed suicide by taking poison. The second category, the "Immortals," who formed the majority of the dead members (30 persons), were either shot or smothered. The 8 members of the final category were labeled as "traitors" and were found murdered. These initial murder-suicides were followed over a year later, on December 16, 1995, by another group suicide in the southeast of France, near Grenoble, where members of the OTS from France and Switzerland had gathered in a forest. Most of the members had been drugged, shot to death, and then placed in a circle, while two remaining members had poured gasoline over the bodies, set them on fire, and then committed suicide. The violence did not end here, however. Fifteen months later, on the vernal equinox (March 20, 1997), five remaining members committed suicide in Quebec, Canada. In sum, the violence of the Solar Temple led to the death of 77 individuals in Canada, France, and Switzerland between September 30, 1994, and March 20, 1997.

Naturally, the murder-suicides of the Solar Temple raise a number of important questions about the relationship between religion and violence in general and new religious movements and violence in particular. Why did the leadership of the OTS turn to violence to solve the problems the group was facing? What sorts of problems *did* the group face? What caused many of the members to obey Di Mambro and Jouret and either murder their fellow members or commit suicide? What motivated the remaining members to commit suicide in 1995 and 1997 in order to follow the others? While the anticult movement and the press have usually provided simplified explanations (e.g., brainwashing) of the violence of the OTS, scholars have argued that one has to take into account the complexities of the case and to eschew single-factor theories. In this chapter I first give an overview of the

Solar Temple and then discuss a number of theories that have been put forward to explain the violence of the OTS.

The Esoteric Worldview and Organizational Structure of the OTS

The worldview of the Solar Temple is firmly rooted in Western esotericism and, more specifically, in neo-Templarism, twentieth-century Rosicrucianism, and the New Age movement. Western esotericism is a scholarly construct that covers numerous currents that share a family resemblance and can be described as a form of holistic spirituality characterized by resistance to the dominance of either pure rationality or doctrinal faith. Instead, the importance of the individual effort to gain spiritual knowledge, or *gnosis*, is often emphasized (van den Broek and Hanegraaff 1998, vii). This gnosis is not limited to intellectual or rational knowledge but is based on experiential knowledge that is unconstrained by the limits of the intellect. The path to gnosis is often believed to pass through self-knowledge since humankind is seen as a microcosm of the universe—the macrocosm. Human beings are created in the image of God and therefore reflect the whole of creation. The created universe is usually regarded as an emanation of the godhead, and since humans are perceived as a microcosm of the macrocosm, the esotericist believes that the godhead can be found within people. The quest for self-knowledge is thus also a quest for the divine aspect of existence, just as knowledge about the godhead is of necessity knowledge about us. The holistic understanding of the universe to be found within Western esotericism is based on the idea that the entire universe is alive and traversed by a network of sympathies and antipathies that link everything in nature (Faivre 1994, 10). The network, which is often referred to as mystical links, constitutes the theoretical basis of esoteric "sciences" such as astrology and ritual magic.

The Templar tradition that the Solar Temple was part of is a modern interpretation and reconstruction of the medieval Knights Templar, founded early in the twelfth century as a military monastic order whose chief object was to protect pilgrims traveling in the Holy Land, Outremer. The Order of Knights Templar was disbanded by Philip IV, "the Fair," of Bourbon (1268–1314) and Pope Clement V (1264–1314) in the first decade of the fourteenth century. In 1310 fifty-four Knights Templar were burned at the stake, and, according to Introvigne (1995, 279), the first fifty-three OTS deaths were intended to mimic these fiery deaths (a Swiss ex-member, Thierry Huguenin, managed to escape before being killed, thereby frustrating the plan to reach fifty-four deaths). According to a Masonic legend, the Templars survived in the highlands of Scotland and later reappeared in public as the Order of Freemasons. The first person to present this theory of continuation in public was Chevalier Michael Ramsay (1686–1743), a Scot who lived as an expatriate in Paris. In a famous oration given at a lodge in 1737 he claimed that the Order of Freemasonry was founded in the Holy Land by medieval crusaders. Although he did not explicitly identify the crusaders as Knights Templar, the connection was certainly made by the Freemasons. Soon enough, perhaps as early as 1737, Masonic Templar degrees appeared (Bogdan 2007, 95–100). During the second half of the eighteenth century, templar degrees flourished on the Masonic scene, but soon the Masonic supremacy over the Templar degrees began to be questioned. If Freemasonry is nothing but the medieval Knights Templar in modern form, then why should Freemasonry be required at all if one wanted to be a modern Templar? As Massimo Introvigne (1995) has shown in great detail, the origins of independent neo-Templarism can be traced to Bernard-Raymond Fabré-Palaprat (1773–1838), who in 1805 proclaimed himself Grand Master of the Templar Order. During the 1950s, French esotericist Jacques Breyer and later Raymond Bernard revived the Templar tradition, and by 1980 more than one hundred rival Templar orders existed across a wide spectrum, ranging from social clubs to organizations that indulge in sexual magic (Introvigne 1995, 267–73).

To the members of the Solar Temple, death was a transition, something that Di Mambro had most likely picked up from his time in the Ancient and Mystical Order Rosæ Crucis (AMORC), which was founded by H. Spencer Lewis (1883–1939) in 1915 and quickly became the largest Rosicrucian group in the world. According to one source, the AMORC may now have as many as 250,000 members (Barrett 2001, 357). The highly eclectic teachings of the organization have a firm foundation in occultist spirituality. Death is seen as a transition in which the physical body (which is subject to change and decay) becomes separated from the soul. According to H. Spencer Lewis, "the soul of man, or the divine essence which animates him is the only part of man which is not subject to the law of change" (Lewis 1941, 238). The soul is thus eternal and not limited by the death of the physical body. These sentiments were later echoed in the rituals of the Solar Temple (Bogdan 2006).

A common characteristic of many new religious movements is that their organizational structure is in more or less constant change, and in that respect the Order of the Solar Temple was no exception. Introvigne has described the various layers of the organization as a "Chinese box" system (Introvigne 1995, 274). The outer shell consisted (at least for a period) of the semipublic Amenta Club (which later changed its name to Atlanta), in which Jouret lectured on New Age topics such as homeopathy, naturopathy, and ecology. This outer shell worked as a recruiting ground for members to the inner and semisecret Archédia Clubs, which were established in 1984. According to Introvigne, in this layer of the organization one could "find a definite ritual and an actual initiation ceremony, with a set of symbols taken from the Masonic-Templar efforts of Jacques Breyer" (Introvigne 1995, 274). The third and central layer of the organization, to which only the most trusted members of the Archédia Clubs were invited, was the secret International Order of Chivalry Solar Tradition (founded in 1984), which later changed its name to the Order of the Solar Temple. To further complicate matters, a fourth organization existed: the Golden Way Foundation (previously called La Pyramide), founded by Di Mambro, which served as the parent organization of the Amenta and Archédia clubs. The order was quite successful in French-speaking countries but failed to establish itself in the English-speaking world, particularly in the United States and Australia. In the English-speaking world the order was known by at least two names: the Order of the Solar Temple and the Hermetica Fraternitas Templi Universali. Compared to other Rosicrucian and Templar organizations, the Solar Temple was a comparatively small organization. At its height in 1989 the order had a total of 442 members: 90 in Switzerland, 187 in France, 53 in Martinique, 16 in the United States, 86 in Canada, and 10 in Spain (Mayer 1996, 54).

The Order of the Solar Temple was organized as a Masonic initiatory society with a strict hierarchy divided into different degrees. As in Craft Freemasonry, the Solar Temple had three degrees: Frères du Parvis, Chevaliers de l'Alliance, and Frères des Temps Anciens (Brothers of the Court, Knights of the Alliance, and Brothers of the Former Times, respectively). It is unclear whether these three degrees made up the Solar Temple or constituted an even more secret, inner group. At least one source suggests that in 1990 the Rule of the Solar Temple "described an order under the absolute authority of a secret inner group called the Synarchy of the Temple," which consisted of the aforementioned three degrees (Hall and Schuyler 1997, 294). In order to attain these degrees, members had to undergo a rite of initiation for each level. The number and titles of the officiants in the initiation rituals varied, and it is thus impossible to give a clear picture of how the local "sanctuaries" were organized. In the "Dubbing of a Knight" ritual of the OTS, the following officiants were mentioned: priest, deacon, ritual master, matre, chaplain, sentinel, master of ceremonies, guardian, and escorts.

The practice of rituals appears to have been the core activity of the Solar Temple. These ceremonies seem to have been highly elaborate and suggestive and were often enhanced by the use of opera music, visual effects, and possibly hallucinogenic drugs (Palmer 1996, 306). The visual effects included simulated lightning, in which apparitions of the masters appeared and objects such as the Holy Grail materialized (Mayer 1999, 217). The rituals of the Solar Temple can be divided into two categories: magical/mystical ceremonies and rites of initiation. The first category allegedly included sex magic practices (Introvigne 1995, 276), in which couples practiced "sperm drinking" (Palmer 1996, 311). The extent to which such practices actually occurred is, however, unclear. According to Susan J. Palmer, the Solar Temple constructed "special underground sanctuaries which were concealed behind false walls and reached by secret passages, requiring the ritual descent of 22 steps" (Palmer 1996, 311). She does not explain what the 22 steps refer to, but, given the esoteric context, they probably allude to the 22 paths on the kabbalistic Tree of Life.

Explaining the Murder-Suicides

Scholarly literature on violence and the new religious movements often center on the four well-known cases of the 1990s (OTS, Branch Davidians, Aum Shinrikyo, and Heaven's gate), as well as the Peoples Temple murder-suicides at Jonestown in

1978. Based on these cases, a number of theories have attempted to explain the use of violence. Although these cases differ in several significant aspects, the tendency has been to focus on the similarities in order to find common denominators that might explain the violent ends of these groups. Chief among these common denominators are a millennial/apocalyptic ideology, a high-demand organization, isolation from the surrounding society, and a charismatic leadership.

The millennial/apocalyptic ideology denominator signifies an end-of-days expectation, which in the case of violent groups is connected to a fierce condemnation of the existing social order. The apocalyptic view of history is combined with a radically dualistic worldview, in which the group is identified with the "good" side, while society, understood in its widest sense, is identified with the "evil" side. Identification with the good side affords a group with a cosmic purpose in the sense that its members perceive themselves as chosen by God for a specific task. However, millennialism and apocalypticism are not restricted to violent new religious movements but are integrated parts of many Christian traditions. In order to differentiate between the millennialism of more violence-oriented groups and traditional millennialism, Catherine Wessinger distinguishes between progressive and catastrophic millennialism. Common to these two types is the belief in collective salvation that may be earthly and allegiance to a "principle whose authority is greater than the authority of civil law" (Wessinger 2000b, 8). Progressive millennialism is the belief that humans, under the guidance of divine agents, can progressively build the millennial kingdom in harmony and peace, while catastrophic millennialism presupposes that the millennial kingdom will be accomplished by an apocalyptic catastrophe orchestrated by God or some other superhuman agent. The catastrophe will destroy the current evil social order and lead to the subsequent salvation of the elect. According to Wessinger, the Order of the Solar Temple adhered to a catastrophic millennialism expressed in New Age terminology. The basic premise of the New Age movement (in *sensu stricto*) is that humankind is about to make a spiritual evolutionary leap forward as we enter the Age of Aquarius. The transition from the Age of Pisces to the Age of Aquarius is generally considered in the New Age movement as a positive step and is often viewed as connected with a transition from a dualistic form of thought (as exemplified by ancient religions such as Christianity) to a monistic form of thought. However, the Solar Temple took a highly pessimistic view of the evolution of consciousness and stressed that evolution "had reached its end on Earth." Wessinger argues that as a result of internal weaknesses and the simultaneous experience of cultural opposition, the leaders of the Solar Temple developed a pessimistic theology that justified a transit in order to escape the imminent cataclysm on earth (Wessinger 2000a, 223–24). Catastrophic millennialism is made evident in a number of passages of the so-called testaments, four short texts that were sent to various scholars and the media at the time of the suicide-murders in October 1994 with the aim of justifying the members' last actions. One of these texts, "Transit to the Future," states the following:

> The race is heading irreversibly toward its own destruction. All of nature is turning against those who have abused it, who have corrupted and desecrated it on every level. Man will pay heavy tribute for he remains no less than the only one responsible for it.
>
> Awaiting favorable conditions for a possible Return, we will not participate in the annihilation of the human kingdom, no more than we will allow our bodies to be dissolved by the alchemical slowness of Nature, because we don't want to run the risk of their being soiled by madmen and maniacs. (Lewis 2006, 183)

Catastrophic millennialism is expressed even more forcefully in the second testament, titled "To All Those Who Can Still Understand the Voice of Wisdom . . . We Address This Last Message":

> The current chaos leads man inescapably to face the failure of his Destiny. In the course of time, the cycles have followed one another in accordance with precise rhythms and laws. Different civilizations disappeared in the course of cataclysms that were destructive but regenerative, nonetheless none of these reached a level of decadence such as ours.
>
> Subjected to the devastating effects of individual and collective egocentricity, marked by a total ignorance of the Laws of the Spirit and Life, this civilization will no longer escape sudden self-destruction. (Lewis 2006, 177)

In seeking to understand the violence enacted by groups such as the Solar Temple, the importance these groups attached to millennialism has been stressed by numerous authors (e.g., Robbins and Palmer 1997; Daniels 1999; Bromley and Melton 2002), as well as by Wessinger, *How the Millennium Comes Violently: From Jonestown to Heaven's Gate* (2000a), and the edited collection *Millennialism, Persecution, & Violence: Historical Cases* (2000b). However, millennialism (or even catastrophic millennialism) is not seen as the sole reason that groups such as the Solar Temple become violent. As already mentioned, Wessinger stressed the importance of internal weaknesses and the simultaneous experience of cultural opposition that the OTS exhibited prior to the transits. In a similar manner, Hall, Schuyler, and Trinh stress in *Apocalypse Observed: Religious Movements and Violence in North America, Europe, and Japan* (2000) that focusing only on millennialism might lead one to overlook the importance of the "apocalyptic tensions between the established social order and countercultural religious movements" (Hall, Schuyler, and Trinh 2000, 3). In the case of the Solar Temple, though, the external opposition did not pose any imminent threat, and it is argued instead that "the mystical apocalypse of deathly transcendence" was the primary impetus to the violence of the Solar Temple (Hall,

Schuyler, and Trinh 2000, 2000). Likewise, John Walliss argues in *Apocalyptic Trajectories: Millenarianism and Violence in the Contemporary World* (2004) that what triggered the leaders of the OTS to abandon their belief in survivalism and instead to adopt an apocalyptic worldview that emphasized the necessity of escaping from earth was the experience of cultural opposition—viewed as persecution—in combination with the crumbling of the charismatic authority of Di Mambro and Jouret, caused by various internal factors. Introvigne and Mayer, in line with the aforementioned scholars, argue that four factors might explain the OTS tragedy, namely, predisposing apocalyptic ideology, perception of external opposition, internal dissent and apostasy, and the crumbling charismatic authority of the leader (Introvigne and Mayer 2002, 178–83).

There has, however, been some criticism of the primacy of millennialism/apocalypticism in explaining the violent end of the Solar Temple and of the fact that discussion has lumped together the murder-suicides of the Solar Temple and Jonestown, the ATF/FBI raid on the Mount Carmel community, the Tokyo subway poison-gas attack by Aum Shinrikyo, and the Heaven's Gate suicides. James R. Lewis has questioned the often-assumed connection between violent movements (e.g., Solar Temple), millennialism, and external provocation in an essay with the telling title "The Solar Temple 'Transits': Beyond the Millennialist Hypothesis" (2005) and instead focused on internal factors, especially the failing health of the leader of the OTS, Di Mambro. Lewis argues that Di Mambro not only had a grandiose self-image (a common enough feature in many new religious movements) but also developed strategies of legitimacy that created an organization in which members had to be totally committed and in which dissenting views were not tolerated. Di Mambro was perceptive enough to realize that he lacked the necessary charisma to control the members directly, so he isolated himself from the majority of them, thereby creating an air of mystique and authority around himself. Direct dealings with the members on a day-to-day basis were transferred to the more charismatic and younger Luc Jouret, something that Di Mambro apparently later regretted as he grew increasingly paranoid. Furthermore, Di Mambro based his authority to a large extent on the fact that he was perceived as the sole source of communication with the "Cosmic Masters," who guided the Solar Temple. This would prove to be an unstable foundation for his authority when members began asking for proof that the Cosmic Masters existed. These factors led to the crumbling of Di Mambro's charisma and legitimacy.

More important, however, was Di Mambro's failing health. Apparently, Di Mambro was suffering from kidney failure, incontinence, and severe diabetes and believed he also had cancer. According to Lewis, the failing health of the leader is an essential factor in our understanding of "suicide cults." By distinguishing the three groups that imploded in suicide—People's Temple, the Solar Temple, and Heaven's Gate—from the other violent new religious movements such as Aum Shinrikyo and the Branch Davidians, Lewis stresses that these groups shared the fact that their leaders (Di Mambro, Marshall Applewhite, and Jim Jones) believed they were seriously ill or even dying—something that set them apart from Koresh and Asahara. Based on his analysis of People's Temple, the Solar Temple, and Heaven's Gate, Lewis presents a list of traits that are essential characteristics of a suicide group:

1. Absolute intolerance of dissenting views.
2. Members must be totally committed.
3. Exaggerated paranoia about external threats.
4. Leader isolates him/herself or the entire group from the nonbelieving world.
5. Leader's health is failing—in a major way, not just a transitory sickness; or, alternately, the leader believes he or she is dying.
6. There is no successor and no steps are being taken to provide a successor; or, alternately, succession plans have been frustrated.
7. The group is either stagnant or declining, with no realistic hopes for future expansion (Lewis 2005, 311)

Peter Åkerbäck (2008), a Swedish historian of religions, agrees with Lewis that it is problematic to view violent new religious movements as constituting a particular category by themselves since this approach emphasizes their similarities while downplaying their differences. While focusing on the suicide groups (the Solar Temple, People's Temple, and Heaven's Gate) in his discussion of previous research, as exemplified by John R. Hall, Catherine Wessinger, and John Walliss, Åkerbäck argues that even though these scholars emphasize the groups' religious ideology—especially an apocalyptic and millenarian worldview—their research is problematic from two perspectives. First, their discussions of the movements' apocalyptic worldviews are often too general in character. The analyses are superficial in the sense that they deal only with basic and general assumptions about apocalyptic and dualistic worldviews without actually discussing in detail the ideology of the movements themselves. Second, Hall, Wessinger, and Walliss attempt to understand the context of and reasons for the groups' collective suicides and overlook their religious foundation. Åkerbäck emphasizes that, as a consequence, parts of their ideologies have been neglected, while others have been highlighted. He argues that previous scholars have emphasized the groups' similarities while minimizing the differences in their ideologies. In fact, according to Åkerbäck, the reality is the converse: These groups are characterized not so much by their similarities as by the *differences* in their ideologies.

Åkerbäck describes these differences as an *ideology of opposition*, a *temporary ideology*, and an *ideology of metamorphosis*. The first category, the ideology of opposition, describes the ideology of the Peoples Temple, in which apostolic socialism was seen as an antithesis to capitalism. The temporary ideology is connected to the Solar Temple, whose ideology was based on the notion of a select few individuals who represented the temple, manifested throughout history, and assisted humankind in its spiritual evolution. After the mission had been accomplished, the group would withdraw and advance to a higher spiritual level. Åkerbäck uses the *ideology of metamorphosis* to denote the ideology of Heaven's Gate, which centered on reaching a level above human. These three forms of ideology give witness to three highly different forms of worldview and soteriology, and thus one is forced to question the often-assumed similarities of these groups' ideologies and their import to the understanding of the subsequent collective suicides.

In "Death as Initiation: The Order of the Solar Temple and Rituals of Initiation" (2006) I have taken a somewhat different approach to the murder-suicides of the OTS. The role of the leaders of a "suicide cult" is undoubtedly of particular importance in trying to understand the motivating factors for extreme groups like the Solar Temple. However, at the same time such a focus runs the risk of avoiding the question of what motivated the members to follow their leaders into death. Strategies of authority notwithstanding, suicide must appear as a plausible option for the members in order for them to carry out such a drastic action. In the case of the Solar Temple, I have argued that a close reading of the rituals of initiation and the esoteric context of the movement can afford us with at least a partial key to understanding why the members (at least some of them) chose to join the transit. Through the rituals it is possible to understand the symbolic universe of the members and thus to place the transit within a frame of reference. The practice of rituals of initiation was central to the Solar Temple, and members progressed higher up in the hierarchy by undergoing them. A central theme in these rituals is the notion of purification, which was connected with the element of fire. The idea of spiritual purification was also connected to death symbolism, which is a common theme in many Western rituals of initiation, such as the Master Mason degree of Freemasonry. However, in the case of OTS this was connected to a neognostic dualism in which the material body was seen as less important than the spiritual self. The highly ritualistic circumstances of the murder-suicides and the fact that all traces of the Solar Temple were to be erased by fire indicate that the murder-suicides were seen as a final ritual of initiation, a rite of passage that led from the profane world to the spiritually pure world of another planet. The following extract from one of the rituals of initiation (Ritual for the Donning of the Talar and the Cross) found at the OTS headquarters in Switzerland gives an idea of the content and symbolism of these rituals of initiation:

> Death is the same for us all./It is how we leave Life that makes the difference.
>
> But always remember/that Death is an illusion./In fact,/It is only another aspect of Life.
>
> At this Station, let me tell you/that you must also consider Life/as ephemeral as smoke passing by,/or a cloud drifting overhead,/and all its glory/is like a flower in the meadow/which unfolds in the morning and dies at eventide.
>
> In the world of illusions,/all must pass away.

Everyone must one day confront/The great problem of Death/which alone gives meaning to Life./You must be able to die to the profane world/in order to be born again to the Cosmic World.

Therefore, let the quality and the wholeness of Life/compensate for its shortness./You, wishing to be a Knight of the Temple,/Do not think of living according to Cosmic Good.

And since nothing is more uncertain/than the hour of Death . . ./prepare yourself each day to be FREE/to leave this Earth/and to continue/on a parallel Invisible plane,/free from all human and terrestrial chains/which keep you prisoner of yourself. (Bogdan 2006, 150)

Concluding Remarks

The murder-suicides of the Order of the Solar Temple stand out as one of the very few examples of a Western esoteric group that turned violent. The ritual purification of the soul strived for in the initiatory system of the Order, neo-Templar notions of chivalry and self-sacrifice, and Rosicrucian beliefs in the importance of secret societies and Hidden Masters, in combination with New Age notions of an evolutionary leap forward for humankind as we enter the Age of Aquarius, formed the basic components of the esoteric worldview of the Solar Temple. In contrast to other violent new religious movements—apart from Aum Shinrikyo—the members of the Solar Temple were not marginalized members of society. On the contrary, the members of the OTS were generally well integrated into society, well connected politically and socially, and affluent.

To sum up, the various hypotheses for the murder-suicides of the Solar Temple often emphasize catastrophic millennialism in combination with factors such as perception of external opposition, internal dissent and apostasy, and the crumbling charismatic authority of the leader. Furthermore, the explanations of violence offered by scholars are often reached by a comparison with other violent new religious movements, especially the well-known cases from the 1990s (the Branch Davidians, Aum Shinrikyo, and Heaven's Gate), together with the Peoples Temple murder-suicides at Jonestown in 1978. This comparative approach has, however, been criticized for its tendency to focus on the similarities of these different groups, while to a large extent ignoring their differences. A final criticism has involved the assumption that millennialism is essential to our understanding contemporary violent groups.

NOTES

1. While there have been numerous books published on Peoples Temple, the Branch Davidians, Heaven's Gate, and Aum Shinrikyo, only one academic volume in English

specifically devoted to the Solar Temple has been published: James R. Lewis, ed., *The Order of the Solar Temple: The Temple of Death* (2006).

REFERENCES

Åkerbäck, Peter. 2008. *De obeständiga religionerna: Om kollektiva självmord och frälsning i Peoples Temple, Ordre du Temple Solaire, och Heaven's Gate.* Stockholm: Stockholms universitet.

Barrett, David V. 2001. *The New Believers: A Survey of Sects, Cults, and Alternative Religions.* London: Cassell.

Bogdan, Henrik. 2006. "Death as Initiation: The Order of the Solar Temple and Rituals of Initiation." In *The Order of the Solar Temple: The Temple of Death*, ed. James R. Lewis, 133–53. London: Ashgate.

———. 2007. *Western Esotericism and Rituals of Initiation.* Albany: State University of New York Press.

Bromley, David G., and J. Gordon Melton, eds. *Cults, Religion, and Violence.* 2002. New York: Cambridge University Press.

Daniels, Ted, ed. 1999. *A Doomsday Reader: Prophets, Predictors, and Hucksters of Salvation.* New York: New York University Press.

Faivre, Antoine. *Access to Western Esotericism.* 1994. Albany: State University of New York Press.

Hall, John R., and Philip Schuyler. 1997. "The Mystical Apocalypse of the Solar Temple." In *Millennium, Messiahs, and Mayhem: Contemporary Apocalyptic Movements*, ed. Thomas Robbins and Susan J. Palmer, 285–311. New York: Routledge.

———. 1998. "Apostasy, Apocalypse, and Religious Violence: An Exploratory Comparison of Peoples Temple, the Branch Davidians, and the Solar Temple." In *The Politics of Religious Apostasy*, ed. David G. Bromley, 141–70. Westport, Conn.: Praeger.

———, and Sylvaine Trinh. 2000. *Apocalypse Observed: Religious Movements and Violence in North America, Europe, and Japan.* New York: Routledge.

Hanegraaff, Wouter J. 1998. *New Age Spirituality and Western Culture: Esotericism in the Mirror of Secular Thought.* Albany: State University of New York Press.

Introvigne, Massimo. 1995. "Ordeal by Fire: The Tragedy of the Solar Temple." *Religion* 25: 267–83.

———. 1999. "Une dérive vers l'homicide et le suicide: l'Ordre du Temple Solaire." In *Sectes et démocratie*, ed. Françoise Champion and Martine Cohen, 300–13. Paris: Editions du Seuil.

———. 2000. "The Magic of Death: The Suicides of the Solar Temple." In *Millennialism, Persecution, and Violence: Historical Cases*, ed. Catherine Wessinger, 138–57. Syracuse: Syracuse University Press.

———, and Jean-François Mayer. 2002. "Occult Masters and the Temple of Doom: The Fiery End of the Solar Temple." In *Cults, Religion, and Violence*, ed. David G. Bromley and J. Gordon Melton, 170–88. New York: Cambridge University Press.

Lewis, James R. 2003. *Legitimating New Religions.* New Brunswick, N.J.: Rutgers University Press.

———. 2005. "The Solar Temple 'Transits': Beyond the Millennialist Hypothesis." In *Controversial New Religions*, ed. James R. Lewis and Jesper Aagaard Petersen. New York: Oxford University Press.

———, ed. 2006. *The Order of the Solar Temple: The Temple of Death*. London: Ashgate.
Lewis, Spencer H. 1941 [1929]. *Rosicrucian Questions and Answers with Complete History of the Rosicrucian Order*. San Jose: Rosicrucian Press.
Mayer, Jean-François. 1996. *Les mythes du Temple Solaire*. Geneva: Georg Editeur.
———. 1999. "Les chevaliers de l'Apocalypse: L'Ordre du Temple Solaire et ses adeptes." In *Sectes et démocratie*, ed. Françoise Champion and Martine Cohen, 205–23. Paris: Editions du Seuil.
Palmer, Susan J. 1996. "Purity and Danger in the Solar Temple." *Journal of Contemporary Religion* 1(3): 303–18.
Robbins, Thomas, and Susan J. Palmer, eds. 1997. *Millennium, Messiahs, and Mayhem: Contemporary Apocalyptic Movements*. New York: Routledge.
Van den Broek, Roelof, and Wouter J. Hanegraaff, eds. 1998. *Gnosis and Hermeticism from Antiquity to Modern Times*. Albany: State University of New York Press.
Walliss, John. 2004. *Apocalyptic Trajectories: Millenarianism and Violence in the Contemporary World*. New York: Lang.
Wessinger, Catherine. 2000a. *How the Millennium Comes Violently: From Jonestown to Heaven's Gate*. New York: Seven Bridges.
———, ed. 2000b. *Millennialism, Persecution, & Violence: Historical Cases*. Syracuse: Syracuse University Press.

7

Religion and Violence in Japan: The Case of Aum Shinrikyo

Martin Repp

Introduction

This chapter treats a new religious movement in Japan that started out as a small group of young yoga practitioners. About ten years later, after a period of considerable growth, most of its leaders and some of its ordinary members ended up in court and prison after having been convicted of murder and indiscriminate mass murder. As the first poison-gas attack executed by civilians, it became an act of terror. Since then, many people, including journalists and scholars, have asked how this religious group, called Aum Shinrikyo, could commit such crimes and even a poison-gas attack. Of course, the answers were manifold since they were given from diverse positions and perspectives. The present study does not claim to provide a definitive answer to this problem, but it offers some substantial explanations. After all, attempts to understand have to be made again and again in order to learn from this tragic case and, hopefully, to help prevent similar crimes from happening in the future.

    This chapter first provides a brief chronological account of the institutional and religious developments of Aum Shinrikyo.[1] The second part introduces some typical reactions to the Aum incident, as well as two academic narratives of Aum's violence. The third part treats a few alternative approaches to the Aum incident.[2] In the fourth part I analyze the factors leading to violence.[3] In the final part I present a few basic deliberations about the subject "religion and violence."[4]

1. Brief Account of Aum's Developments

In 1984 young people began to gather around Matsumoto Chizuo[5] in the Tokyo area in order to practice yoga. For this purpose, they formed a group and called themselves Aum Shinsen-no-kai [Aum mountain ascetics group]. In 1985 the New Age journal *Twilight Zone* published an article on Aum and printed on the front page a picture of Matsumoto levitating during yoga practice. This publicity helped to attract more people to the group. In 1986 Matsumoto traveled to India in order to develop his yoga practice, and after his return he claimed to have attained religious awakening. In the fall of 1986, several members of the group decided to dedicate their lives completely to religious practice and therefore left their family and work in order to pursue renunciant life (*shukke*). In 1987 the group changed its name to Aum Shinrikyo (Aum teaching of truth). The word "truth" stands for Buddha's teaching. Thus, in addition to yoga, Buddhist beliefs and practices were henceforth emphasized. This is also indicated by the name of the journal *Mahayana*, which the group began publishing in August 1987. That same year Matsumoto changed his name to Asahara Shoko.[6] In 1986 and 1987, the group began publishing books by their leader, treating topics such as acquiring supernatural powers, transcending the cycle of birth and death, and religious initiations. As a result of Aum's proselytization efforts, the membership gradually grew, both ordinary members and renunciants.[7] Subsequently, branches were also opened in other places in Japan.

In September 1988 the first unnatural death occurred among Aum members when Majima Terayuki died due to excessive ascetic practice. In order to avoid police investigation, Aum's leaders ordered his body to be burned and then disposed of, which is illegal. Toward the end of 1988 Aum applied to the Tokyo metropolitan government for status as a legal religious body (*shukyo hojin*) in order to receive tax breaks. These two issues constitute the background of the first murder to be committed in Aum. Because of Majima's premature death, another member, Taguchi Shuji, wanted to leave the group. When he threatened to leak this information to police in February 1989, Aum's leaders ordered him killed. The procedure for legal recognition as a religious body took more time than usual; on August 25, 1989, the status was granted.

In July 1989 Sakamoto Tsutsumi, a lawyer, established a "lawyers' group for the victims of Aum Shinrikyo" (*Aum Shinrikyo higaisha taisaku bengo-dan*). On October 21 concerned family members formed the Association of Aum Shinrikyo Victims (*Aum Shinrikyo higaisha no kai*). On October 15 the tabloid *Sunday Mainichi* began publishing a series of articles under the title "The Madness of Aum Shinrikyo," which criticized the expensive donations to the group, the separation of parents and children, and strange practices such as the ritual of drinking Asahara's blood. Thus, Aum was portrayed as being "antisocial" (*han-shakaisei*). The articles were one sided, based only on reports by ex-Aum members and families of Aum followers, and they were written in a provocative and sensationalist style. The editors did not bother to ask Aum for comments. When an Aum official finally visited the Mainichi office and asked the tabloid to publish a response, his request was granted. The official emphasized that these practices concerned renunciants rather than ordinary believers and that the renunciants had left their families of their own free will. This distinction is crucial because it indicates that the introduction of the renunciant option was a major cause of the ensuing conflicts between Aum and society (see section 4).

Also in October 1989 the Tokyo Broadcasting System (TBS) interviewed Sakamoto, the lawyer, and aired the interview together with footage of Aum practices.[8] When the producer informed Aum of the plan, leading members requested a preview of the Sakamoto interview, which was granted at TBS facilities on October 26. On October 31 Aum representatives (including Aoyama Yoshinobu, also a lawyer) visited Sakamoto at his office and demanded that he retract his interview, which he refused to do. Then, Aum leaders and TBS officials agreed on the following compromise: Instead of airing the interview with Sakamoto, TBS would get an exclusive interview with Asahara. At the beginning of November, however, Sakamoto, his wife, and baby suddenly disappeared from their apartment. An Aum badge was found, but the police failed to investigate properly; subsequently, this case was not solved until the police investigation of Aum began in 1995. The apparent reason for such negligence was that Sakamoto's law office had represented a member of the Communist Party who had been illegally wiretapped by the same Kanagawa Prefectural Police in 1986.[9] As a consequence, Aum was able to escape police scrutiny at the time. It was only much later, during the post-1995 court trials, that several leading Aum members were convicted of murdering the Sakamoto family.

As already mentioned, Aum received legal recognition of its status as a religious body on August 25, 1989. The very next day its leaders established a political party called Aum Shinri-to (Aum Truth Party).[10] The following winter they ran for office in the February 1990 election for the Lower House. However, none of the Aum candidates won a seat. From this point on, Aum changed considerably. After having experienced harsh media criticism and failure in politics, Aum members became more and more withdrawn from society and self-protective. In May 1990, for example, envisioning the arrival of Armageddon in the form of nuclear war and other catastrophies, Asahara stated that "no matter what kind of weapons should attack us, we must protect ourselves and preserve a place for our practice" (Asahara 1992a, 104; cf. 103) On the doctrinal level, Asahara declared that Aum's teachings would change from Mahayana Buddhism[11] to tantric or esoteric Buddhism (Tantra, Vajrayana). According to Asahara, tantric Buddhism permits the suspension of conventional moral codes (cf. Asahara 1991, 65; 1992a, 95). It can also be used to justify murder for religious reasons.

In line with the emerging self-preserving attitude of the group, in May 1990 Aum acquired land in Namino-son (Kyushu) that was believed to be tectonically stable. Here, members began building the "Lotus Village," a utopian community that would function as an alternative to Japanese society. However, as in other places, these young people did not also cultivate good relationships with their neighbors and ended up provoking antagonistic reactions. When Aum members tried to register as citizens of the local community, the village officials in Naminoson refused to accept their applications in order to avoid a "foreign takeover." This was understandable but illegal. On the other hand, the village representatives accused Aum of having acquired the land illegally through a front company and initiated legal procedures against them. Thus, in October 1990 the police searched the Aum facilities for the first time and arrested three leading members. Aum perceived this as "suppression by the state." At the subsequent court trial, Aum was ordered to evacuate the place—after receiving considerable financial compensation.

By 1991 Aum had established eighteen centers in Japan and one in New York. Also in that year they saw an opportunity to expand into Russia. After Perestroika, Japanese and Russian politicians attempted to intensify cooperation between the two countries for their mutual benefit. One project arising from these negotiations was a plan to establish a "Russia-Japan University" in Moscow. Since an investor was needed, politicians of the governing Liberal Democratic Party (LDP) approached Aum. This provided Aum with access to high-level political and military circles in Moscow, including Oleg Lobov, the powerful secretary of the State Security Council. In the end, the building provided by the Russian government was not used as a university but provided accommodations for the Russian Aum branch and other organizations. Aum was also permitted to use radio broadcasts to proselytize in Russia. In June 1992 the Russian government granted Aum legal recognition as a religious organization. The connection with Lobov enabled Aum also to purchase a Russian helicopter and weapons. By 1995 Aum was said to have at least thirty thousand followers in Russia.[12]

In 1993 Aum established business enterprises that purchased, for example, computer parts in Taiwan, which were assembled in Aum facilities; the computers were then sold in Aum shops in Japan. These enterprises also allowed Aum to buy huge quantities of chemicals that, according to the police, were later used for the production of stimulant drugs and poison gas. In 1993 an Aum company purchased a large sheep ranch in western Australia, likely in order to mine uranium (Repp 2003).

Suddenly, in June 1994 the quiet city of Matsumoto in central Japan was hit by a poison gas attack that left 7 people dead and 147 injured. Kono Yoshiyuki, an ordinary citizen whose wife fell into a coma and who first reported the strange fumes to the police, was treated by police and the news media as the prime suspect for almost a year even though he could not possibly have produced poison gas.[13] It should be also mentioned that half a year later, in January 1995, a huge earthquake rocked the Kobe-Osaka area and left more than 5,000 people dead and more than 26,000 injured. At least 260,000 people lost their homes.

On February 26, 1995, the notary public Kariya Kiyoshi disappeared in Tokyo. His sister had been an Aum member and had donated considerable sums of money to the group. However, Aum also demanded the donation of an expensive piece of property in Tokyo which Kariya had refused. Since there were indications that Kariya was abducted by Aum members, the police had a pretext for searching Aum facilities later in March. They concluded that Kariya had been abducted and killed by Aum members.

About March 18 numerous journalists began gathering in front of Aum facilities. As a consequence, Aum knew well in advance that the police were preparing an investigation. In Japan the police force frequently leaks its plans to the media before searching suspects' premises. This remarkable procedure not only enables citizens to watch the raids live on TV but also provides the suspects with some time to destroy possible evidence. This time, however, matters turned out differently.

In the early morning of March 20, commuters on several subway lines heading toward government buildings and the national police headquarters in central Tokyo were hit by gas attacks. Twelve persons died, and approximately 4,000 were injured. On March 22, more than 2,500 police officers began searching all of Aum's facilities nationwide. A number of officers were equipped with gas-protection gear from the chemical warfare unit of the Self-defense Forces. Once they were inside the buildings, they took off the gear (personal information provided by an eyewitness). This was apparently a well-orchestrated mass media event. At the time, Aum's membership in Japan included about 1,000 monks and nuns and about 10,000 ordinary followers. In their raids, the police arrested about 150 Aum members, who were subsequently put on trial. Some of them received suspended sentences; others were jailed or even received death sentences (Repp 1997, 54; 2001).

2. Mainstream Strategies to Cope with the Aum Incident

The "Aum incident" raised many questions, and, depending on the respective standpoint, a variety of answers were given.[14] After all, one needs to understand this challenging issue in one way or another. The mass media were quick to characterize Asahara as a power hungry "madman" and his followers as completely "brainwashed." These and other labels demonized and dehumanized the group altogether. For the first time, recent translations of American anticult literature provided the Japanese mass media and the anti-Aum movement with this kind of rhetoric. Henceforth, they would apply labels such as "cult" (*karuto kyodan*, cult group), "mind control," and "brainwashing" (*senno*) to Aum.[15] As a result of the Aum incident, the English word "cult" became part of everyday Japanese vocabulary. Because of this label, Aum Shinrikyo was put into the category of an asocial and antisocial group.

The term *cult* also helped certain religious groups in their attempts to tackle the Aum riddle. Some of them claimed that Aum was "not a religion" at all, whereas others stated that it was "not Buddhism" (cf. Kisala 1995, 83, 84–86, 92). In the end, however, such labels could not prevent the negative consequences the religious establishment feared: Among many ordinary Japanese, the Aum incident created an even bigger distrust of religion than they already harbored.[16]

These public reactions to Aum all attempt to keep a threatening phenomenon at a safe distance. David Chidester (1991, xi, 24–46) refers to such strategies as "rituals of exclusion" and "cognitive distancing."[17] Depending on the circumstances, he distinguishes between religious, psychological, and political distancing. The same strategy is evident in popular books on the Aum incident written in a sensationalist style, such as those by Brackett (1996) and Kaplan and Marshall (1996). Even scholarly treatises have not avoided such negative labeling.

Next I introduce explanations of Aum's violence by two scholars whose narratives were influential in shaping public perceptions of the Aum incident. First, Shimazono Susumu (1995, 408),[18] a scholar of religious studies at Tokyo University, claimed in an early article that "the introspection of Aum Shinrikyo's universe of belief led the group to develop in a closed and violence-prone direction." In his opinion, "Aum exhibited the traits of a closed religious group *from the very beginning*, including aggressive recruitment, vigorous elicitation of donations, vehement self-justification, and the cutting-off of believers from outside human relationships and information" (Shimazono 1995, 400; italics added). The examples provided here are more or less identical with the aforementioned *Sunday Mainichi* narrative. Shimazono argues that, as early as 1985, Asahara claimed to have received a revelation from Shiva, according to which he was appointed "the god of light who leads the armies of the gods" in a fight between Buddhists and infidels, and who, after having attained victory, will establish "Shambala," the utopian Buddhist kingdom.[19] As the next step on Aum's violent path, Shimazono (1995, 397–98) considers Asahara's teachings, beginning in 1988, on Nostradamus and on the apocalypse of John, which led him from a focus on attempting to prevent Armageddon to an emphasis on "the survival of the chosen." Shimazono (1995, 403, 407–408) further blames "Guru worship" and techniques of "mind control" for the uncritical behavior of his followers.

Shimazono (1995, 404f, 407f, 411) also observes similarities between Aum and other new religious movements in Japan on issues such as guru worship, coercion of members, aggressive fund-raising, and hostility toward critics. However, he quickly plays down these obvious similarities in an attempt to demonstrate the unique character of Aum, namely its "closed and violent nature," from its very beginning (Shimazono 1995, 408). It is not clear what Shimazono's motives are in applying a double standard to Aum and other religious groups. Additionally, his argument that Asahara's early *talks* about war and so forth makes Aum de facto a violent group *from the beginning* is not convincing.

In the end, however, Shimazono blames not only the guru and his teachings and practices but, in general, "modern freedom" without self-restraint. What he apparently means is not freedom (which always includes responsibility) but libertinism.

According to Shimazono (1995, 412), the nation-state today "experienced a decline in its ability to preserve public order." Hence, his general conclusion is that "It was this background that Aum Shinrikyo was able to escape the watchful eye of the state authorities and arm itself for battle" (1995, 412). Later I will discuss whether or not there were more concrete reasons for the failures of the state's "watchful eye." In the end, Shimazono's narrative remains ambiguous: Did internal factors lead to Aum's violence, as he initially emphasizes, or, as he subsequently claims, was it the libertinism of contemporary society?

Another scholar of religious studies, Ian Reader, has written two books on Aum. Whereas his first publication is an independent study in its own right,[20] in his second book he follows Shimazono's lead in explaining the Aum incident primarily in terms of internal factors (Reader 2000, 4ff, 161, 230). At the beginning he states: "I have now come to believe that the seeds of Aum's violence were more deeply rooted in its basic doctrines, in the movement's image of itself, in its self-proclaimed mission and in the personality of its founder, than I had discussed in that [earlier] book."[21]

As a primary doctrinal source of information to explain Aum's violent activities, Reader considers not so much apocalyptic beliefs (as Shimazono does), but rather Asahara's understanding of esoteric Buddhism: "[I]t was from the world of Tibetan Buddhism that Asahara drew his inspiration and legitimation of violence" (Reader 2000, 139). Thus, Reader (2000, 128) declares Asahara's textbook for the course on the Vajrayana doctrinal system (*Vajrayana kosu kyogaku shisutemu kyohon*, a collection of sermons given between August 1988 and April 1994) as "the very heart of Asahara's teachings." First of all is the teaching of *poa* (Reader 2000, 128), which in Tibetan Buddhism means to guide a soul into higher dimensions after physical death. In Asahara's understanding, this term could justify murder for religious purpose e.g., to kill somebody who has evil plans in order to prevent the person from accumulating bad karma. One implication of esoteric Buddhism is also that it allows one to suspend ordinary morality (Reader 2000, 130). Thus, under certain circumstances, even a deed that according to conventional morality is bad can be justified in tantric terms.

Apart from doctrinal sources, Reader (2000, 41; cf. 232) also considers Asahara's personality—his short temper and inclination to violence—as another cause of Aum's violent acts. He refers to this euphemistically as a "culture of violence," which, in his opinion, "Aum produced . . . from within its own dynamic" (Reader 2000, 161; cf. 205, 226, 232). On the other hand, Reader quickly dismisses Aum's claims of having encountered "conspiracies," "spies," and "persecution" as "fantasies," "delusion," and "paranoia."[22]

These theories about Aum's violence as proceeding from internal causes are not convincing for a number of reasons. First, the hypothesis that Asahara and Aum had a *violent nature from its very beginning* (Shimazono 1995, 400, 408; Reader 2000, 32, 61) relies on shaky evidence. Even if Asahara explained the Tibetan term *poa* in terms of justifiable murder in a sermon in 1987, this does not prove that he or his followers were *in fact* violent from the very beginning. Such an understanding of Aum is the result of an anachronistic interpretation of selected Aum teachings and earlier actions that appear to align with later developments. This is the logical mistake of "post hoc reasoning" (Lewis 1995, 102) and a questionable generalization. The hypothesis of an inherent violent nature from the very beginnings does not fit Aum's early self-representations in its internal publications, which depict followers gathered around their leader, all meditating peacefully in natural surroundings and with happy faces.[23] Only in later internal publications, after conflicts with various groups of society had taken place, do dark images of death, wars, and catastrophes begin to be featured. Along the same lines, the Aum music written and performed in the beginning was peaceful and conducive to meditation, whereas later productions used military-style music. Such a dramatic change in self-representation indicates that Aum altered considerably during its development.

Second, when warfare, weapons, and poison gas were introduced in Aum publications, this was done within the framework of defensive strategies against perceived threats from the outside. Whether such threats were real or imagined cannot be known because they have not been properly investigated. Aum saw the necessity of protecting itself. To the best of my knowledge, there are no Aum publications that ask the membership to take up weapons and actively initiate a war or other violent acts. It seems that some authors and the public prosecutors have overlooked this significant difference between self-protective measures and the unilateral initiation of acts of violence.

Third, if Aum was violent by nature and if it really fostered a "culture of violence," as Shimazono and Reader claim, one must ask why Aum's followers did not react with violence when the police entered and searched their facilities during the widespread and drawn-out raids.

Finally, when both authors consider Aum's doctrines as the primary factor in understanding its violence, one must also ask whether they are not confusing primary factual causes and secondary ideological legitimation. In the case of the Branch Davidians, Tabor and Gallagher (1995, 9–11) have demonstrated how the leader, David Koresh, interpreted the actual events—the siege by the Bureau of Alcohol, Tobacco, and Firearms (BATF) and the FBI—in the light of the book of Revelation. The "text" functioned here as orientation in the changing "contexts." Similarly, when Taguchi, the Sakamoto family, and others were murdered, as a religious group Aum needed for its members a religious justification for actions that contradicted basic Buddhist beliefs.[24] Thus, the term *poa* served as a secondary justification. This mechanism can also be shown at work in Buddhist justifications for the wars modern Japan was involved in between 1894 and 1945.[25] These cases show that primary causes and secondary legitimations must be distinguished. In the Aum incident, the factual reason for most of the murders (except the subway gassing) was that for Aum leaders the victims posed serious threats to their group (see section 4).

Apart from the inconsistencies and contradictions in Shimazono's and Reader's hypotheses concerning Aum's violence, there are some important problems with the Aum incident that both neglect in a very similar manner. First, both authors either ignore or downplay striking commonalities of violent behavior with other contemporary (mostly new) religious movements, from extorting donations and incurring unnatural deaths due to excessive religious practices, to intimidation and even murder of opponents or "anticult" activists.[26] Second, both scholars also neglect or downplay the fact that a number of factors in society significantly contributed to the genesis of the Aum incident in one way or another. They do not investigate a society that, in its pursuit of economic interests, left a spiritual vacuum (especially among young people) that Aum tried to fill. Third, they ignore the grave and repeated failures of the police to properly and swiftly launch investigations, such as in the disappearance of the Sakamoto family or the first gas attack in Matsumoto (cf. Reader 2000, 152, 204, 211ff). Fourth, even though Reader (2000, 217ff) admits that the subway gas attack was a "reaction" or an "ad hoc action" with the purpose of disrupting the police force's plans to investigate Aum and to search its facilities, neither he nor Shimazono question the police strategy of leaking their raid plans to the news media, which triggered the poison gas attack on the passengers in the Tokyo subways.[27] Finally, the active involvement of the mass media in the Aum incident is not even considered as a problem or a factor that contributed to the violence. Reader's (2000, 149) treatment of the *Sunday Mainichi*'s one-sided and provocative articles lacks a critical attitude. Also, both authors ignore the problem of TBS's coverage of its involvement in Sakamoto's disappearance (see later discussion).

These five common characteristics of the two scholars' treatment of the Aum incident show a significant tendency to decontextualize Aum and the Aum incident in a variety of ways. By blaming Aum's internal dynamics in a monocausal way and by too quickly dismissing the close interaction between Aum and the rest of society, both authors isolate the Aum incident from its contexts. In other words, both follow the strategy of "cognitive distancing" (Chidester 1991). When all of the blame falls on a group of "paranoid," "brainwashed," and "violence-prone" "madmen," serious questions about the society and its religions obviously become superfluous. Moreover, in the end it is not surprising to find that these authors' explanations of Aum's violent acts are very similar to the hypotheses presented by the public prosecutors at the beginning of the Aum trials.[28] This is the narrative of a "supreme ruler" who derived his motive for violent acts from apocalyptic ideas and Tibetan esoteric Buddhism and who controlled and directed his followers in any way he wanted. John Hall's (1995, 230) comments on the FBI's narrative of the Branch Davidian tragedy in Waco apply, in certain ways, to the Aum incident as well:

> [E]ven a cursory examination of the FBI construct of mass suicide suggests that they viewed it as an inherent and static predisposition, rather than a sect's possible response to a dynamic and shifting situation. . . . This static view of predisposition is based on a tendency that governmental authorities share with the anticult movement, a

tendency to see the dynamics of "cults" as internal to such groups, rather than examine external social interaction in conflict between a sectarian group and opponents and authorities themselves.

It is also noteworthy that Shimazono and Reader do not mention the many human-rights violations committed since March 1995 by police, town officials, school representatives, employers, homeowners, and neighbors of Aum's facilities.[29] Once a group is dehumanized, it seems its members no longer deserve to retain their human rights.

3. Alternative Views of the Aum Incident

Apart from these mainstream accounts, several alternative descriptions of the Aum incident in Japan took into account the active involvement of society and avoided demonizing the followers of Aum. With regard to responses by religious organizations (cf. Kisala 1995), there were few alternative views to those mentioned earlier. For example, the report of a research group on Aum established by the two Zen schools Rinzai and Obaku states that the Aum incident was not a matter that concerned "other people" but one that immediately concerned each of the Zen priests, as well as the Zen-Buddhist institutions (Zen Bunka Kenkyusho 1996).

Another attempt at avoiding the dehumanization of Aum's members was the documentary film *A* by Mori Tatsuya, released in 1998. For more than two years (October 1995–January 1998), Mori accompanied Aum's deputy spokesperson, Araki Hiroshi, and other members with his camera inside and outside the facilities. He presented a different view of Aum members than the one the mass media produced. Without becoming pro-Aum propaganda, his documentary shows how Aum members held on to their beliefs after the police raids and faced the intrusions by mass media and the mean-spirited investigation methods of the police with dignity.[30]

Another empathetic approach was introduced by Richard Gardner (2002), who collected short humorous poems (*senryu*) on Aum written by ordinary Japanese that were published in newspapers between March and May 1995. A few examples illustrate these alternative views of the Aum incident. Some put it into historical context: "Aum is imitating the Imperial Japanese Army in waging bacteriological warfare" (Gardner 2002, 40). "There was a time when all one hundred million Japanese were brainwashed" (Gardner 2002, 51). Others situated the Aum incident in the immediate social context: "Even without headgear, I am controlled by my wife" (Gardner 2002, 55). "As a result of the love of money and material things, we have a society where Aum lives" (Gardner 2002, 50). Such expressions portray Aum not as a group isolated from society but as an integral part of it. Some authors reveal a considerable distrust of police and politicians: "I am worried about where the police are storing all the dangerous substances seized from Aum" (Gardner 2002, 49). "Aum got enough religious donations to make even a politician jealous"

(Gardner 2002, 53). One draws a parallel with the catastrophic earthquake in January 1995: "A government that can handle neither natural disasters nor man-made disasters" (Gardner 2002, 44). Some indicate similarities with the "brainwashing" of the mass media: "All the television channels have been abducted [and taken to] to Kamikuishiki" (Gardner 2002, 45). "Brainwashed by Aum specials with high ratings" (Gardner 2002, 41). "Television has put headgear on us" (Gardner 2002, 50). Also, suspicions of the reports given by the police and mass media alike were prevalent: "Television talks too much, police are too silent" (Gardner 2002, 54, revised according to original). Finally, one author reverses the dehumanization by mass media and police after the incident: "With their headgear removed, they begin to be the children of humans" (Gardner 2002: 45).[31]

In fall 1995 the NCC Center for the Study of Japanese Religions (Kyoto) chose yet another approach to understanding the Aum incident by inviting young people to talk about their understanding of Aum and the Aum incident (Maeda 1997; Miyai 1997). At least for some of these young people, Aum's ways of thinking and acting were not as strange and incomprehensible as adults and scholars had perceived and portrayed them. On the contrary, in the framework of their worldview, they made sense.

4. Explanation Attempts of Aum's Violent Acts

By proposing an alternative analysis of the genesis of Aum's violent acts, I do not intend to completely negate those factors suggested by the police and the scholars discussed earlier. Certainly, factors like Asahara's desire for power, the internal dynamics of the group, and religious teachings on apocalyptic ideas (e.g., "final war"), and esoteric Buddhist notions (e.g., *poa*) played a role. In my view, however, they did not constitute the primary causes. In history and at present we find many power-hungry religious leaders, as well as apocalyptic or esoteric movements that do not lead to violent conflicts. There must be additional, different factors to account for.

Rather than explaining Aum's violence mainly through internal causes, it is more appropriate to understand it as a process that developed in the interface between the group and outside agents. External interactions consisted of frequent miscommunications between Aum and people in the society, such as neighbors, families, mass media, and the police. Communication is here understood in the broad sense of mutual (verbal and nonverbal) exchanges between two or more agents that may be either constructive or destructive. As in most cases of human conflict, causes have to be sought on both sides, though the degree of responsibility may differ. If this is the case, without attempting to diminish the responsibility of Aum's members, the circle of responsibility in the Aum incident has to be drawn wider (see later discussion).

In the framework of a communicational approach, I identify the following primary factors that appear to have led to the violent conflicts between Aum and the surrounding society. Some were triggered by Aum, and there were others for which the various agents of society have to be held accountable. To begin with, factors on the Aum side were (1) control of its boundary as a way of protecting the group, (2) renunciation, and (3) the young age of the group members.

When elaborating the factors leading to violence from the Aum side, it is appropriate to begin with an analysis of the first murder case of Taguchi in February 1989. He wanted to leave Aum and threatened to report Majima's death (September 1988), which he had witnessed, to the police. Taguchi's murder took place at a very sensitive time for Aum, for it had just applied to the Tokyo metropolitan government for legal status as a religious body. Officials had visited Aum three times—in January, February, and March 1989—to make inquiries because of the negative rumors about the group.[32] Normally, the procedure for legal recognition takes about three months. Since the first official visit took place in January 1989, Aum must have submitted its application in December 1988 at the latest. In the end, it took about nine months before legal status was granted—in August 1989—three times longer than normal. Judging from this, the first murder was an attempt by Aum's leaders to protect the young group from official investigation and to remove any possible obstacle to legal recognition.[33]

This and subsequent violent acts committed by Aum can be understood in the following theoretical framework. In his research on the Peoples Temple and other new religious movements, Marc Galanter treats such groups as "social systems" that carry out various functions. One such function consists of what Galanter (1989, 111–16) calls "boundary control." For example, the leadership perceives intrusions by external agents as a threat (Galanter 1989, 124). The confrontations become hostile and can result in violent acts of self-defense. This was the case with the murders and mass suicide in Jonestown (1978), as well as with the tragic death of the Branch Davidians and police officers in Waco (1993).[34] Violence erupted when intrusions occurred and attempts were subsequently launched to protect the boundary. The case of Jonestown shows that attempts to prevent members from leaving the group also belong to the category of boundary control (cf. Chidester 1991, 153ff). Aum's leadership was often concerned with members "deserting" the group (cf. Asahara 1993, 59), as Taguchi's tragic case demonstrates.

When explaining the Buddhist precept that prohibits murder, in January 1988 Asahara stated: "What motivates one to kill many beings is self-preservation, or the karma of anger" (Asahara 1992b, 59). Most of the subsequent violent acts committed by Aum members served the purpose of self-protection or boundary control. The following cases may illustrate this matter: The purpose of Sakamoto's murder in November 1989 was to prevent him from damaging Aum in his public statements (such as his interview with TBS) and his legal actions as a representative of concerned parents. The murder and attempted murder of anti-Aum group leaders with VX gas and other means in 1994 and 1995 were attempts to silence their criticism and block actions that Aum perceived as threats. The gas attack in Matsumoto in 1994 was aimed at preserving property claimed by Aum. This case shows that boundary control applies not only to human agents but also to claimed property. Finally, the gas attack on the Tokyo subway passengers—assuming it was carried out by Aum members—served the purpose of disrupting a planned police investigation of Aum.[35]

The second major factor prompting Aum to commit violent acts involved conflicts erupting from its introduction of renunciation (*shukke*). The "boundary control" of a community of renunciants is much stricter than that of a religious group of laypeople who can move freely between their ordinary life at home and their activities at the religious center. The first murder cases emerged in conflicts taking place on the interface between Aum's religious institution of renunciation and the outside society. The first harsh public criticism of Aum voiced by concerned parents in the *Sunday Mainichi* articles (October 1989) focused mainly on issues related to renunciation. The aforementioned response by an Aum official published in this tabloid also makes this matter clear. The same is true for the criticism by Sakamoto and the group of concerned parents he represented.

Renunciation entails separation from one's family, termination of education or employment, transfer of family assets and/or property, and a religious practice more rigorous than that of ordinary people. When leaving a traditional group like a family, the renunciant enters a very different kind of community that has its own rules, bonds, and boundaries. When concerned parents try to communicate with their renunciant family member, they do not encounter just an individual but a whole community that functions according to its own laws and mechanisms, which are quite different from those of ordinary society. The implications of renunciation represent many different potential sources of conflicts.

The problem of renunciation also has to be understood in several contexts. Aum introduced the renunciant lifestyle at a time when most of the established Buddhist groups in Japan had abandoned this form of communal life due to political pressure at the end of the nineteenth century (Meiji period) and when most new Buddhist movements in the twentieth century had established themselves as lay Buddhist groups (*zaike bukkyo*). Hence, most Japanese people were not accustomed to Aum's introduction of renunciation with all of its social implications. In fact, the introduction of renunciation is a characteristic that distinguishes Aum from most other new religious movements in Japan. Seen in broader historical and geographical contexts, the introduction of renunciation was mostly accompanied by conflict. Since Shakyamuni Buddha established renunciation as the ideal Buddhist way of life some twenty-five hundred years ago in India, it has often caused conflict with families. The major obstacle to introducing Buddhism to China in the first century C.E. was renunciation. And in a more recent case, in September 1996 conflicts escalated in Taiwan between parents and about forty young women who had taken vows as nuns without their parents' consent. The parents tried to drag their daughters away from the Chung Tai Chan monastery and to bring them home by force (*JT*, September 19, 1996). With respect to Aum, Richard Young (1995, 239ff) has explained the conflict between renunciation and society as follows:

Wherever the world and its ways have been rejected and a separate community of renunciates has been established, Buddhism—or whatever goes by that name—has been denounced as economically unproductive and the Buddhist monks who have been sexually unreproductive have been traduced as unfilial. Productivity and reproductivity are the essential ingredients of the pervasive *musubi* (growth) mentality one finds in Japan. Aum was obviously a threat to both.

In most studies of Aum, renunciation has been neglected as an important and even the initial factor in the emerging violent conflicts between Aum and society. The same is true for the following factor.

A third major factor in the development of conflicts between Aum and society was the simple fact that most of its leaders and members were young people who were acting according to the mindsets of their age group.[36] Most Aum followers were young people who lacked the experience of what in Japan is called *shakai-jin* (person of society) (i.e., somebody who has matured beyond the carefree life of young people and learned to behave according to society's rules, such as assuming responsibilities at work and in the family). The immature behavior of the Aum members is evident, first of all, in the ways in which they dealt with their neighbors. When Aum adherents moved into a building or to a larger property, they paid little heed to the neighbors' concerns and complaints. Instead of attempting to communicate properly and to negotiate compromises, Aum members often behaved inconsiderately, which triggered hostile reactions from the neighborhood. This was the case with many buildings in cities and with larger facilities in the countryside, such as Namino-son and Kamikuishiki, where village communities felt offended and refused Aum members to register as residents.

The behavioral pattern of adolescent Aum members became especially clear when they traveled abroad, some of which have been documented (Repp 2003). One bizarre but characteristic incident is the hijack of an Air Lanka plane that Aum had hired to bring Asahara and a group of followers back to Japan in May 1992. The reason for the hijack was that two flight attendants (who were to serve the crew on their way home) were sitting in the first-class area, which Asahara claimed for himself alone. During the ensuing dispute, Aum members physically apprehended one of the pilots. In this emergency situation, the copilot flew the plane back to Colombo, where special forces were called to the airport. Their deployment was prevented only by intervention of the president, whose guests Aum had been.

One particular problem of young age in the case of Aum is evident in Asahara's statement that he had no teacher (Asahara 1988, 98). Hence, his mode of learning, like the development of his group, followed the crude method of trial and error. This is not only very elementary and time consuming, but it is also quite a risky means of human learning. A related problem concerns the role of the group of leaders (*kanbu*) around Asahara. According to Galanter (1989, 103–105), one activity of a social system consists of "monitoring" the functioning of the group from the inside. A specific form of monitoring is performed by senior advisors, who may prevent the leader from making hasty decisions that may result in negative consequences. Galanter (1989, 123) provides examples of such cases—also called "middle management"—in new religious groups. This can also be applied to new religious organizations in Japan. The monitoring function of senior advisors prevents a religious leader from engaging in actions that may later be regretted. There is, in fact, one group that many Japanese consider to be much more dangerous for a democratic society than Aum. Its leader also exhibits dictatorial behavior, but his advisory board seems to prevent him from committing major mistakes in public. Although Aum had a group of senior advisors, they were still quite young, and not all of them had experience in working and living as adults in society. Judging from the outcome of the Aum incident, these leaders were unable to prevent actions that ultimately resulted in a heavy blow for the group.

Thus far, with respect to the interface between Aum and society, the factors that have been introduced were triggered by Aum. In the following, the factors that are examined are the responsibility of various agents of society. These are (1) the mass media's provocations and involvements, (2) grave negligence by the police, (3) the involvement of politicians, and (4) the Japanese government's failure to control the trade of chemicals.

The one-sided and provocative *Sunday Mainichi* series on Aum (October 1989), as well as its impact and consequences, have not yet been properly researched. In the case of the Branch Davidians, the role of the media has been investigated, both the media's impact in the escalation of the conflict toward violence, as well as its construction of the popular account of the incident.[37] In the case of Aum, at least the fatal role of TBS in the murder of the Sakamoto family has been made public, even though no steps against the broadcasting network have been taken. When, in 1995, the police finally began to investigate the murder of the Sakamoto family, which took place in 1989, questions about TBS's involvement in the case were raised. In a government hearing in March 1996, the president of TBS denied any involvement. After being confronted with factual evidence, however, he admitted that he had lied. He subsequently resigned from his post. Then, in April 1996, the chairman of the National Association of Commercial Broadcasters in Japan acknowledged that showing the video of the Sakamoto interview to Aum members and cancelling its broadcast in exchange for an exclusive interview with Asahara could have led to the murder of the Sakamoto family (*JT*, April 4, 1996; cf. Repp 1997, 71f).

The second major factor was police negligence in fulfilling their duties. As mentioned earlier, the Kanagawa police failed to properly investigate the murder of the Sakamoto family because the lawyer's office had represented a plaintiff against the same police in a case of illegal wiretapping. It took nothing less than the poison gas attack in Tokyo in 1995 to prompt the police to properly investigate the case—after six years of ignoring the disappearance of the Sakamoto family. Later, the chief of the National Police Agency (NPA), Kunimatsu Takaji, publicly acknowledged that if police had acted promptly in the Sakamoto case, "the nerve gas attacks in Matsumoto and on the subway would not have taken place" (*JT*, September 9, 1995; cf. *JT*, September 10, 1995). Thus, we observe the following chain of serious failures: The actions of TBS contributed to the murder of the Sakamoto family, and the police force's neglect of its official duties contributed to the two poison gas attacks. Moreover, the police also failed to properly investigate the poison gas attack in Matsumoto and instead accused a man who could not possibly have produced and sprayed the gas. To my knowledge, this failure of the police has never been investigated and publicly clarified. This closes another link in the chain of negligence: If the Matsumoto attack had been properly investigated, the attack on the Tokyo subways system would likely never have occurred.

The third major external factor in the development of the Aum incident was involvement by politicians. As mentioned before, politicians of the then ruling Liberal Democratic Party (LDP) introduced Aum leaders to high government officials in Russia, who needed investors to establish the Russia-Japan University. This enabled Aum's leaders, for example, to trade in weapons. These politicians were never questioned about their responsibility for this development of the Aum case.

The fourth factor concerns the insufficient control of the chemical trade by the Japanese government. Based on assessments of the stockpiles of chemicals for drugs in Aum's compounds, the "International Narcotics Control Strategy Report" issued by the U.S. State Department's Bureau of International Narcotics and Law Enforcement Affairs stated in 1996: "This finding casts doubt on the ability to control precursors and raised the question of how many precursor chemicals may have been diverted to drug organizations in the past" (*JT*, March 5, 1996).

All of these factors demonstrate that those who blame Aum alone for the violent developments leading up to the Aum incident fail to comprehend its complex nature. Attempts to identify one suitable (and at that time weak) scapegoat only end up in simplifications and misconceptions that may prove fatal should similar conflicts involving new religious groups arise in the future.

Finally, I want to draw attention to another contributing factor, namely communication in a narrower sense. Aum members spoke a very different language from that of ordinary people. They spoke not only the language of young people, filled with words and images from *manga, anime,* and science fiction and not easily comprehensible to adults, but also a religious language consisting of Buddhist and apocalyptic imagery that neither Buddhists nor scholars clearly understood. This caused a significant amount of miscommunication since the same words (e.g., Shiva, *poa,* Armageddon) were understood by insiders and outsiders very differently. These basic problems of miscommunication, the lack of communication, and the absence of possible mediators in the Aum case have not yet been investigated.

In the Waco disaster, Phillip Arnold and James Tabor found a serious problem in the Branch Davidians' religious language, which could not be understood by agents of the BATF and the FBI. Scholars who were acquainted with biblical apocalyptic thought and Adventist beliefs offered assistance to the FBI by "translating" the Branch Davidians' communications for the officers (Tabor and Gallagher 1995, 4f, 52–96, 108–110). Unfortunately, the FBI soon decided on an aggressive strategy of intimidation, which ended in a terrible tragedy. Livingstone Fagan, one of the few surviving members of the Branch Davidians, stated: "[I]t was not inevitable that events had to end the way they did. The final outcome was contingent on our adversaries' response to our efforts to communicate our position of faith" (Tabor and Gallagher 1995, 78). This case shows the crucial role that communication plays and how miscommunication and breakdown of communication may end in violence.

Another related observation that has been obliterated by focusing mainly on the violent side of Aum is that Aum members communicated with outsiders not only in hostile but also civil ways. In the case of the *Sunday Mainichi* series, for instance, an Aum representative was successful in eventually getting Aum's side published despite the fact that the articles were provocative and insulting. Subsequently, Aum members at least attempted to convince Sakamoto to withdraw his TBS interview even though they were unsuccessful. However, they were able to negotiate with TBS representatives to cancel this critical interview.

In a broader sense, Aum's representatives also engaged in civil forms of communication when they followed the application procedure for recognition as a religious body. When Aum established its political party and began its election campaign, its style of political communication was civilized and honest even though its performances appeared strange and funny to outsiders. Additionally, in the conflict with the villagers over the Aum property in Namino-son, Aum's representatives followed the rules of a court trial in a civil manner and in the end accepted the court's decision. During an all-night TV show on September 28, 1991, Aum's representatives showed their communication skills in a debate with members of the rival new religion, Kofuku no kagaku. Finally, even after the gas attack in Tokyo, Aum's representatives attempted to communicate peacefully with citizens, officials, and the mass media in order to make their side of the story known and understood.[38] In this situation, the most gifted Aum communicator began appearing on television, spokesman Joyu Fumihiro, who very skillfully countered questions and criticism by journalists and explained the Aum side of the story. All of these examples show that the Aum incident consisted not only of violence but also of a number of attempts to communicate with the larger society in a civil manner.

Concluding Reflections

The Aum incident raises basic questions such as these: What makes a violent act "religious"? What does the expression "religious violence" signify? Is "religious violence" constituted only by religious motive, agent, and/or legitimation? What are the mundane factors at work in violent acts committed by a religious group? What is the relationship between such mundane factors and specifically religious ones?

When Ian Reader (2000) focuses on "religious violence," he limits the causes to internal or religious issues. The findings of the present study, however, have detected quite a number of other factors contributing to the Aum incident. These were not only religious but also psychological, social, political, institutional, and economic factors. Hence, the title of this chapter distinguishes between "religion and violence" and thereby avoids the simplistic implications of an expression like "religious violence."[39]

Historical considerations may help to clarify the problem. In a recent study of monk warriors (*akuso* and *sohei*) in medieval Japan, historian Mikael Adolphson (2007, 1–5) questions the adequacy of the term *religious violence* because the Buddhist monasteries' motives, objectives, and forms of warfare were not different from those of the aristocrats and the imperial court. Whereas monk warriors were employed by monasteries to protect their economic basis and thereby to maintain their social status, ordinary warriors (*bushi*) served the same purpose for aristocratic landlords. Mundane factors led to violent acts committed by religious individuals and institutions. Therefore, one cannot speak simply of "religious violence." Adolphson, though, does not investigate contemporary Buddhist texts that try to doctrinally justify violence committed by monks since this constitutes a contradiction of basic Buddhist teachings. The distinction between mundane and religious violence factors committed by Buddhist groups can be seen in other cases of medieval Buddhism in Japan. For example, when established monasteries violently attacked new Buddhist movements in the beginning of the thirteenth century, they did so under the ideological pretetxt of fighting "heresies." However, the real reason was that the popularity of these movements caused a considerable loss of donations and membership in the established monasteries (Repp, 2010). On the other hand, Buddhist teachings designed to justify violence and other abuses by monks and monastic institutions were not called "heresies"—even though they contradicted Buddhist doctrines in essential points—for the very reason that they helped to preserve the economic basis and social status of the monastic complexes.

These historical observations show that even in cases of violence committed by religious groups, nonreligious factors certainly play a major role. In the case of Aum, we observed the following mundane factors leading to acts of violence:

psychological: the young age of members and leaders
social: the establishment of a new group that was structurally still weak and therefore sensitive to outside criticism; the functions of internal monitoring and "border control"; the establishment of a renunciant community, which created conflicts with family members and neighbors
political: the failed attempt to participate in the political process; the cooperation of Japanese politicians and connections with the Russian government
institutional: involvement by TBS and sensationalistic media coverage; the failure of the police to properly investigate Aum crimes and the failure of the Japanese government agency to control the trade of chemicals

economic: financial contributions by Aum members; the establishment of trade companies; Aum's computer business; and the production of drugs There may be also military factors, as the Russian connection indicates.

Finally, typical religious factors consist of the agents on the side of Aum (its leader, individual members, and the group as a whole), the introduction of a renunciant and communal life style, and ideological legitimation of violence. Thus, there are first a number of significant mundane factors that may apply to any social group involved in violence. Then there are several characteristically religious factors. The combination and interaction of these factors together led to the violent development referred to as the "Aum incident." The ways in which each of these factors worked separately and interacted with others collectively may be described as forms and processes of communication and miscommunication, be they verbal or nonverbal.

Whereas most of the factors listed here may be called active or "initiating" causes of violence, the typical religious issue of doctrinal legitimation is a secondary, or reactive, factor. It is normally introduced only after an act of violence has already been committed or is just about to be committed for one or more of the reasons listed earlier. The function and purpose of religious justification is to help a believer (or a group) overcome the apparent contradiction between basic nonviolent religious beliefs and the "factual necessity" of violating them. Thus, religious legitimation first ideologically enables or assists acts of violence and then later contributes to their unhindered continuation. The function of the religious legitimation of violence, however, is basically the same as political, social, or economic justifications of violence.

My observations suggest that the expression "religious violence" should be used very cautiously in order to avoid failing to understand the real causes of violence committed by religious individuals or organizations. Aum's violent acts were "religious" only insofar as they were committed by religious individuals and a religious group and as they were justified by religious teachings. The latter, however, is only a secondary, legitimating, and thus sustaining factor.

NOTES

1. This is henceforth abbreviated as Aum. For technical reasons, Japanese words in this chapter are not romanized with macrons on vowels. Japanese names are written according to the Asian order (first, family name, then personal name) with the exception of quotations from English publications.

2. The expression "Aum incident" (in Japanese *Oumu jiken*) signifies the conflicts and criminal activities connected with Aum Shinrikyo. Other authors (e.g., Reader 2000; Watanabe 1997) use "Aum affair," which is somewhat misleading.

3. This analysis is based on my own research of this case in Japan from 1995 to 2009, many conversations with Aum members, cooperation with investigative journalists, and American research on violence in connection with other religious groups.

4. For more detailed accounts of Aum and the Aum incident, see Shimazono (1995), Reader (1996, 2000), and Repp (1995, 1997, 2005).

5. He was born in 1955 in Kyushu.

6. He did so because he believed that the strokes of these Chinese characters would bring good fortune.

7. In 1989 Aum had about 290 nuns and monks and in 1995 about 1,000 renunciants and 10,000 lay followers in Japan (Repp 1997, 23ff.).

8. The Tokyo Broadcasting System is a television network belonging to the Mainichi Newspaper group, which at that time was influenced by a powerful religious organization, an opponent of Aum.

9. Eleven years later, in 1997, the court found the Kanagawa Prefectural Police and the National Police Agency (NPA) guilty of illegally wiretapping the phone (JT, May 26, 1999).

10. During this time, Aum also purchased land in Kamikuishiki near Mount Fuji, where it planned to construct facilities.

11. Mahayana teaches religious engagement in the world. This phase of Aum's doctrinal development is indicated by its attempts to open itself to society, as the election campaign indicates.

12. For Aum's activities in Russia, see Kabanoff (2001).

13. For the tactics of the police to force a confession from Kono whereby they employed the mass media after having provided false information, see Gamble and Watanabe (2004, 136–63). According to later police investigation, Aum carried out this gas attack apparently because it targeted judges who had presided over a court trial involving property which Aum claimed for itself.

14. There were also disturbing questions posed by investigative journalists in *Japan Times Weekly* (see the issues following the gas attack in March and throughout the year 1995) and elsewhere, which have not been pursued and answered conclusively. These questions concern problems such as the dubious police identification of "sarin gas" and the probability that foreign secret agents carried out the gas attack because it requires significantly greater technical skills than Aum members possessed.

15. Cf. Watanabe (1997). Steven Hassan and Robert J. Lifton also visited Japan in 1995. Lifton (1999) wrote a book on Aum. See also Lewis (1999).

16. Distrust of traditional Buddhist schools is the result of their demand for substantial financial contributions. Suspicions of new religions also derive from their high financial demands, as well as from some criminal activities. Mass media and scholars have mostly neglected the fact that in these two respects Aum was not unique among Japanese religions as portrayed.

17. Chidester relies on his investigation of the Peoples Temple and the murders and mass suicide in Jonestown.

18. This article is a condensed version of Shimazono's 2005 booklet *Aum Shinrikyo no kiseki* [The Locus of Aum Shinrikyo] (Tokyo: Iwanami Shoten).

19. Shimazono (1995, 388). This belief derives from the Kalachakra tantra [the wheel of time tantra], an eleventh-century Buddhist text from north India, which solicits Hindu support for the fight against Moslems invading the country. For an introduction and translation of representative passages, see Newman (1995).

20. I do not discuss this book here because, for Reader, the second publication represents his more recent research.

21. Reader (2000, 4; cf. 42). He explicitly identifies the violent acts as being committed by a *religious* group (Reader 2000, title and p. 25).

22. Ibid., 190; cf. 140, 196, 203, 230, 247. Alleged attacks on Aum have been documented in some of its publications. The suspicion of spies and persecution can also be found in groups such as the Peoples Temple and the Branch Davidians. There is insufficient space here to discuss this topic.

23. Here I do not detect any "violent images intrinsic from first days" (Reader 2000, 161). It should be mentioned that internal publications intended for believers do not need to idealize the group as publications for public relations purposes generally do.

24. The same phenomenon occurred in Tendai Buddhism in medieval Japan, when its followers attempted to legitimate monastic abuse such as warfare by its doctrine of "inherent awakening" (*hongaku homon*), which suspends Buddhist morals and practices.

25. The prominent Zen priest Shaku Soen, for example, stated in 1904: "Even though the Buddha teaches not to take another's life, he also teaches that all sentient beings through the exercise of infinite compassion will be united and thereby obtain final and ultimate peace. As means toward the harmonizing of the incompatible, killing and war are necessary" (Ketelaar 1990, 171). For more examples, see Victoria (1997).

26. For a list of similarities between Aum and other new religions, reaching from significant donations to murder, see Repp (1997, 83–89). The only, though grave, difference is the alleged mass murder attempt by poison gas attacks.

27. Academic treatments of the tragedies in Jonestown and Waco quite openly discuss the problem of the responsibility of the officials due to their inadequate approaches to these groups. In the case of the Aum incident, this problem is widely ignored by scholars and journalists.

28. The text of Asahara's indictment is published in Kyodo tsushinsha shakai-bu (1997, 232–98). For an English summary see *Asahi Evening News* (Apr. 26, 1996). It seems that both authors depend too much on the mass media's accounts, which were provided by the police (cf. Miura 1999; Gamble and Watanabe 2004).

29. Cf. the special issue of *Syzygy: Journal of Alternative Religion and Culture* 8 (1999) on "Aum Shinrikyo and Human Rights."

30. Mori (2000) also published a book on this project.

31. Another attempt in this respect was made by *JT Weekly* (Apr. 29, 1995) when it published interviews with Aum members. The cover page introduced them as follows: "They came of age as Japan reached the heights of prosperity, but materialism couldn't provide meaning to life. Nor could traditional religion. So these Japanese youths broke with the past to become children of the future.

    The mass media portrayed the followers of Aum Shinrikyo as social deviants who had been subjected to mind control and were a threat to public security. Nonetheless, their own life stories reveal they were average Japanese youths trying to find a peaceful alternative to a conformist and polluted society devoid of spiritual values."

32. Information about this case comes from the court records. See Mainichi Shinbun Shakai-bu (1997, 99–112).

33. Reader claims: "It is important to note that Aum's initial turn to violence had not come about because of external pressures placed on Aum. When violence first was used in the movement with the beating of disciples, and when Aum first broke the law with the concealment of Majima's death and then the murder of Taguchi Shuji, it had experienced

little external pressure" (Reader 2000, 161). Because Reader neglects the fact that the application procedure for legal recognition had begun in December 1988 at the latest, his statement is wrong. Taguchi was murdered precisely because there was such tremendous pressure on Aum to obtain legal recognition. Reader also overemphasizes Aum's concealment of Majima's unnatural death because he does not take notice of other cases in Japanese society. Premature deaths due to excessive practice (or related reasons) frequently occur in religious groups. They become public only when members talk to the police or the media.

34. When the police surrounded the compound, David Koresh, the leader of the Branch Davidians in Waco, told them, "You have come and stepped on my perimeter" (Tabor and Gallagher 1995, 99). In the case of Jonestown, Chidester (1991, 93ff, 153ff) describes the mechanism of violence emerging from self-defense.

35. I refrain from calling the poison gas "sarin," as Shimazono and Reader, many other authors, and the mass media uncritically do. The police built their case against leading Aum members on this kind of gas apparently because Asahara mentioned it in his sermons. However, the odor and smoke that witnesses reported, as well as the victims' symptoms, do not match those connected with sarin. The plastic containers of the poison gas were placed on the ground; this would not be done in case of sarin because it is more heavy than air. For more on the poison gas, see the following articles: "The Rashomon Riddle" by Yoichi Clark Shimatsu and "Tabun, It's Tabun" by John Parker (*JT Weekly*, Apr. 1, 1995), "Zettai Tabun" by Yoichi Shimatsu (*JT Weekly*, May 27, 1995), and Miura (1999). Further, it is also questionable whether Aum's members were technically able to spread poison gas. It is even a question whether Aum produced poison gas in the facilities in Kamikuishiki. (See the article "Seventh Heaven: What Was Being Produced inside Satyam no. 7 Chemical Plant?" *JT Weekly*, May 27, 1995). When an investigative journalist and I went to Kamikuishiki in order to see Satyam no. 7 shortly before its destruction, he observed that this building had no chimney installed, which would have been necessary as exhaust for gas production. The pipes on the outside of the building were part only of a cooling system. Therefore, it seems more likely that this facility was used for the production of drugs. Since the Japanese police did not permit independent specialists to see the facilities and the confiscated items (including huge amounts of chemicals), independent judgments were rendered impossible. Also, the courts did not clarify the matter since the Aum trials were based not on factual evidence but on confessions only. Confessions, however, are not reliable in Japan because police officers often try to force suspects to confess, such as in the aforementioned case of Mr. Kono in Matsumoto.

36. According to an estimate by *Daily Yomiuri* (May 15, 1995), the average age of Aum members at that time was twenty-seven years. For figures, see also Reader (2000, 96f).

37. See Tabor and Gallagher (1995, 80–95). Refering to a work by Herman and Chomsky, Richardson (1995, 163) observes that mass media reports about such incidents consist of "simplifications" and "dichotomization of subjects", a process "whereby topics are defined in black or white terms." This leads also to the aforementioned dehumanization of "cult" members.

38. Around this time I met Aum followers personally for the first time at an information booth in downtown Kyoto, where they offered pamphlets, books, and their explanations of the Aum incident. I was surprised at their courage at this time of widespread Aum hysteria, which had been initiated by the police and the mass media.

39. I have already distinguished between violence and religion in my 1996 article, "Religion und Gewalt im gegenwärtigen Japan: Der Fall Aum Shinrikyo." The title of Reader's book *Religious Violence in Contemporary Japan: The Case of Aum Shinrikyo* (2000) strikingly resembles that of my article except for this small but significant difference between adjective and noun.

ABBREVIATIONS

JT Japan Times

REFERENCES

Adolphson, Mikael S. 2007. *The Teeth and Claws of the Buddha: Monastic Warriors and Sohei in Japanese History*. Honolulu: University of Hawaii Press.

Asahara, Shoko. 1988. *Supreme Initiation: An Empirical Spiritual Science for the Supreme Truth*. Ed. Fumihiro Joyu. Trans. Jaya Prasad Nepal and Yoshitaka Aoki. New York: AUM USA.

———. 1991. *The Teachings of the Truth: A Collection of Lectures*, ed. and trans. Aum Translation Committee. Fujinomiya: Aum.

———. 1992a. *The Teachings of the Truth*. Vol. 2, ed. and trans. Aum Translation Committee. Fujinomiya: Aum.

———. 1992b. *The Teachings of the Truth*. Vol. 4, *The Path to Absolute Happiness*, ed. and trans. Aum Translation Committee. Fujinomiya: Aum.

———. 1993. *The Teachings of the Truth*. Vol. 5, *The Law of the Karma*, ed. and trans. Aum Translation Committee. Fujinomiya: Aum.

Brackett, D. W. 1996. *Holy Terror: Armageddon in Tokyo*. New York: Weatherhill.

Chidester, David. 1991. *Salvation and Suicide: An Interpretation of Jim Jones, the Peoples Temple, and* Jonestown. Indianapolis: Indiana University Press.

Galanter, Marc. 1989. *Cults: Faith, Healing, and Coercion*. New York: Oxford University Press.

Gamble, Adam, and Takesato Watanabe. 2004. *A Public Betrayed: An Inside Look at Japanese Media Atrocities and Their Warnings to the West*. Washington, D.C.: Regnery.

Gardner, Richard T. 2002. "'The Blessing of Living in a Country Where There Are *Senryu*!' Humor in the Response to Aum Shinrikyo." *Asian Folklore Studies* 61(1): 35–75.

Hall, John R. 1995. "Public Narratives and the Apocalyptic Sect: From Jonestown to Mt. Carmel." In *Armageddon in Waco: Critical Perspectives on the Branch Davidian Conflict*, ed. Stuart A. Wright, 205–35. Chicago: University of Chicago Press.

Kabanoff, Alexander. 2001. "Aum Shinrikyo in Russia." *Japanese Religions* 26(2): 149–70.

Kaplan, David E., and Andrew Marshall. 1996. *The Cult and the End of the World: The Incredible Story of Aum*. London: Arrow.

Ketelaar, James Edward. 1990. *Of Heretics and Martyrs in Meiji Japan: Buddhism and Its Persecution*. Princeton, N.J.: Princeton University Press.

Kisala, Robert. 1995. "Aum Alone in Japan. Religious Responses to the 'Aum Affair.'" *Japan Mission Journal* 49(2): 80–98.

Kyodo tsushinsha shakai-bu, ed. 1997. *Sabakareru kyoso* [The Founder on Trial]. Tokyo: Kyodo Tsushinsha (Kyodo News Service).

Lewis, James R. 1995. "Self-fulfilling Stereotypes, the Anticult Movement, and the Waco Confrontation." In *Armageddon in Waco: Critical Perspectives on the Branch Davidian Conflict*, ed. Stuart A. Wright, 95–110. Chicago: University of Chicago Press.

———. 1999. "The Death of Mind Control." *Syzygy: Journal of Alternative Religion and Culture* 8: 187–203.

Lifton, Robert Jay. 1999. *Destroying the World to Save It: Aum Shinrikyo, Apocalyptic Violence, and the New Global Terrorism.* New York: Metropolitan.

Maeda, Daisuke. 1997. "The Revenge of the Children." *Japanese Religions* 22(1): 87–91.

Mainichi, Shinbun Shakai-bu, ed. 1997. *Oumu "kyoso" hotei zen-kiroku.* Vol. 2, *Watashi wa muzai da!!* [Complete Court Trial Records of the Aum "Founder." Vol. 2, I Am Not Guilty!!]. Tokyo: Gendai shokan.

Miura, Hideaki. 1999. "Some Questions about the Sarin Cases." *Syzygy: Journal of Alternative Religion and Culture* 8: 139–84.

Miyai, Rika. 1997. "A Voice from the 'Aum Generation.'" *Japanese Religions* 22(1): 91–96.

Mori, Tatsuya. 2000. *"A" satsuei nikki [Diary of Filming "A"].* Tokyo: Gendai Shokan.

Newman, John. 1995. "Eschatology in the Wheel of Time Tantra." In *Buddhism in Practice: Princeton Readings in Religion*, ed. Donald D. Lopez Jr., 284–89. Princeton, N.J.: Princeton University Press.

Reader, Ian. 1996. *A Poisonous Cocktail? Aum Shinriko's Path to Violence.* NIAS Special Report. Copenhagen: NIAS Books.

———. 2000. *Religious Violence in Contemporary Japan: The Case of Aum Shinrikyo.* Richmond, Surrey: Curzon.

Repp, Martin. 1995. "Who's the First to Cast the Stone? Aum Shinrikyo, Religions, and Society in Japan." *Japan Mission Journal* 49: 225–55.

———. 1996. "Religion und Gewalt im gegenwärtigen Japan: Der Fall Aum Shinrikyo." *Dialog der Religionen.* 6. Jg.: 190–202.

———. 1997. *Aum Shinrikyo: Ein Kapitel krimineller Religionsgeschichte.* Marburg: diagonal-Verlag.

———. 2001. "The 'Trial of the Century'? Legal and Illegal Treatments of Aum after the Aum Incident." *Religion-Staat-Gesellschaft* 2. Jg.: 289–313.

———. 2003. "'The Last Continent': The Involvements of Aum Shinrikyo in Australia." *Japan Mission Journal* 57: 55–66.

———. 2005. "Aum Shinrikyo and the Aum Incident: A Critical Introduction." In *Controversial New Religions*, ed. James R. Lewis and Jesper Aagaard Petersen, 153–94. New York: Oxford University Press.

———. 2010. "Socio-economic Impacts of Honen's Pure Land Teaching—An Inquiry into the Interplay between Buddhist Doctrine and Institution." In *The Social Dimension of Shin Buddhism*, ed. Ugo Dessi. Leiden and Boston: Brill Publishers, pp. 11-58.

Richardson, James T. 1995. "Manufacturing Consent about Koresh: A Structural Analysis of the Role of Media in the Waco Tragedy." In *Armageddon in Waco: Critical Perspectives on the Branch Davidian Conflict*, ed. Stuart A. Wright, 153–76. Chicago: University of Chicago Press.

Shimazono, Susumu. 1995. "In the Wake of Aum: The Formation and Transformation of a Universe of Belief." *Japanese Journal of Religious Studies* 22(3–4): 381–415.

Tabor, James D., and Eugene V. Gallagher. 1995. *Why Waco? Cults and the Battle for Religious Freedom in America.* Los Angeles: University of California Press.

Victoria, Brian A. 1997. *Zen at War*. New York: Weatherhill.
Watanabe, Manabu. 1997. "Reactions to the Aum Affair: The Rise of the 'Anti-cult' Movement in Japan." *Nanzan Bulletin* 21: 32–48.
Young, Richard. 1995. "Lethal Achievements: Fragments of a Response to the Aum Shinrikyo Affair." *Japanese Religions* 20(2): 230–45.
Zen Bunka Kenkyusho [Institute for Zen Culture], ed. *Rin-o oumu mondai kenkyu-kai hokoku* [Rinzai and Obaku Report of the Research Group on the Aum Problem]. Kyoto: Hanazono University.

8

The Euphemization of Violence: The Case of Heaven's Gate

Benjamin E. Zeller

Its entire active membership having committed ritualistic suicide in a San Diego–area mansion in 1997, the new religious movement popularly called Heaven's Gate is often considered a prototypical movement-ending case of cultic violence. Indeed, self-violence did end the history of this new religion. Yet suicide was not always a possibility within the group. As previous studies have noted, the movement experienced an evolution from its foundation during the mid-1970s as a New Age therapeutic group to its eventual position as a world-denying neognostic movement. As other scholars and I have previously argued, the group members initially eschewed any concept of self-violence, but their eventual suicides were enabled by theological shifts over time. This chapter takes a new approach to understanding the violent end of Heaven's Gate. Here I consider what I call the "euphemization of violence"—that is, the rhetorical transformation of (self-)violence into a more benign form. Accomplished over the movement's twenty-year history, the euphemization of violence, I argue, is what eventually permitted—even encouraged—the 1997 mass suicides. Rather than envision the suicides as a disconnect from the group's earliest phases, I trace a history of euphemization through the history of the movement, beginning with its understanding of bodily transformation, continuing through its approach to the concept of martyrdom and disease, and culminating in the mass suicides. Crucially, by the end of the movement, its leaders and adherents did not consider their final actions either self-violent or suicidal.

Introduction

With its purple shrouds, barbiturate-laced applesauce, rolls of quarters, and black uniforms, the terminus of the new religious movement known as Heaven's Gate[1] seemed made for a media sensation. Unsurprisingly, the suicides of the thirty-nine members of Heaven's Gate in 1997 in Rancho Santa Fe, California, led to a journalistic bonanza of coverage that focused on the material culture of death. Reporters focused on the clothing, precision, and uniformity of the Heaven's Gate dead, as well as the process itself. Representative of other media coverage, *Time* magazine led off its cover-story treatment of the movement with just such a focus:

> If a group of people are going to choose to die together, it is best to have a master plan: proper burial outfits, packed suitcases, lists, farewell videotapes, even recipes for death. The ghastly jumble of bodies piled upon bodies discovered in Jonestown, Guyana, in 1978 may have provided a stark lesson in how not to do it. That mass suicide was a disorderly, ungracious way to meet your maker, a study not in serenity but in chaos. So last week, in that spacious Rancho Santa Fe mansion, with the bougainvillea in full bloom outside, 39 bodies were laid out on their backs on bunk beds and mattresses, looking like so many laboratory specimens pinned neatly to a board. (Gleick 1997, 31)

Though *Time*'s Elizabeth Gleick adopted a far more jovial tone than might have been appropriate given the reality of thirty-nine dead human beings, her focus on the means and methods of the Heaven's Gate deaths, as well as her comparison of the dead to the nonhuman specimens of a sterile laboratory, reveal an important truth. The members of Heaven's Gate who ended their terrestrial existences at Rancho Santa Fe on March 27 did not see themselves as human beings about to commit suicide but rather as extraterrestrial souls freeing themselves from their biological confines. Ironically, they would concur that the process ought to be orderly, sterile, and planned and that whatever remains remained did not merit serious consideration. Given their own comparison of their human bodies to larval insects, even the reference to the dead as pinned laboratory specimens was apropos.

The adherents of Heaven's Gate took such a position because they had rhetorically and theologically transformed the concept of death and suicide, shifting it from representing the destruction and disrupture of life to embodying the purpose of existence and an espousal of life. This transformation permitted the leaders and members of Heaven's Gate to embrace their "departures"—what outsiders considered suicide—as the best solution to the vexing spiritual problem of human embodiedness. "The only proper application of the term 'death' is the termination of the soul," wrote the Heaven's Gate member who called herself Jnnody shortly before the suicides, "and only the Kingdom of God can kill a soul. Therefore, the human body does not experience 'death'—it can be terminated or 'dropped'" (Jnnody 1996, A95). Such rhetoric enabled Jnnody's decision to lay down her human body alongside her compatriots, believing that an eternal award awaited her in the hereafter.

Despite originating in the mid-1970s and existing for more than two decades, Heaven's Gate is known best for its end. Like the Peoples Temple, the Branch Davidian movement, and Aum Shinrikyo, a moment of violence marks the end of Heaven's Gate. However, unlike those other new religious movements (NRMs), Heaven's Gate ended on its own terms through a process of self-directed violence rather than turning outward or responding to a direct, outside, physical threat. While the movement surely experienced a sense of persecution and failure, as Catherine Wessinger has noted in her *How the Millennium Comes Violently*, these conditions are not themselves sufficient to cause self-violence (Wessinger 2000). Nor did the movement always consider suicide as an option. Though often categorized as a "suicide cult," the concept of suicide entered the movement's theology very late in its existence, during the mid-1980s at the earliest. For the first decade of the group's history it flatly rejected the very notion of suicide, arguing instead for the need to transition into the heavens while still embodied.

That Heaven's Gate engaged in the euphemization of violence explains how and why the group eventually ended in the mass suicides of its members. It also solves a problem that has long vexed scholars of the group. When Heaven's Gate began in 1972, its leaders had explicitly stated that the salvation they offered was bodily and performed while one was still alive. Yet, given Heaven's Gate's founders devaluation of the human body, euphemistic treatment of the death of Christ, and their own prophesied deaths, the founders of the movement lay the foundation for the later shift toward suicide.

Most scholars who have studied Heaven's Gate emphasize the disjuncture between the early and late phases of the movement. Robert W. Balch and David Taylor, who researched the group in its early days during the 1970s, wrote the following:

> The suicides were especially surprising because Ti and Do [i.e., Nettles and Applewhite, respectively] originally claimed that the only way to enter the Kingdom of Heaven was in a *living physical body*. They believed that death simply condemned one to another incarnation on Earth. How then did Do [Applewhite] conclude that suicide was a viable alternative to physical departure, and why did his followers believe him? (Balch and Taylor 2002, 209)

Though Balch and Taylor argue that the eventual choice for suicide built upon a "belief system that, with few modifications, dated back to Ti and Do's initial revelations," they nevertheless describe the choice for suicides as a late development born of such "modification" (Balch and Taylor 2002, 209–10). Other scholars have made similar arguments, notably James R. Lewis, who focuses on the later developments in the group's theological history that made the notion of suicide more palatable (Lewis 2003, 113–17). Janja Lalich similarly argues that the experience of rejection and a fortress mentality led the beleaguered group late in its history to consider suicide (Lalich 2004, 96–98). By understanding Heaven's Gate as engaging in a process of the euphemization of violence throughout its history, one can more easily understand the nature of the suicides as something other than modifications to an existing belief structure.

Background and History

Heaven's Gate began in 1972, when Bonnie Lu Nettles (1928–1985), a registered nurse and sometime-member of the Houston Theosophical Society, met Marshall Herff Applewhite (1932–1997), a choir director and former Presbyterian seminarian. Both were experiencing serious life changes, with Nettles in the midst of a divorce and Applewhite having gone through a series of failed hetero- and homosexual relationships. As they rapidly severed relationships with everyone else around them, Nettles and Applewhite formed a strong partnership predicated on a sense of shared mission. According to Robert Balch, who studied the group shortly after it formed, almost immediately after the two cofounders of Heaven's Gate met, both felt that fate had brought them together and had destined them for a particular religious undertaking (Balch 1982, 33).

Nettles and Applewhite soon abandoned their lives in Houston—a fact made easier by the completion of Nettles's divorce and Applewhite's workplace termination—and embarked on journey of self-exploration and discovery. Over the next three years the two read widely in the metaphysical, theosophical, and Christian traditions, ruminated on their religious quest, and began to develop a religious ideology that cemented themselves at the center of a salvific drama. When they emerged into the public in 1975, they had transformed themselves into "the Two" and proclaimed that they brought a message of how human beings could transform themselves into perfected extraterrestrial creatures, escape the confines of earth, and enjoy eternal life among the stars.

Nettles and Applewhite—who used a variety of names during this period—found few individuals willing to accept their message but eventually succeeded in attracting their first followers in April 1975 after meeting with a Los Angeles–area psychic group. They followed this up in October of that year by convincing twenty individuals living in a small Oregon town to join them. By mid-1977, they had spoken with hundreds of people at their public meetings and attracted at least a hundred followers. Over the next eight years the movement slowly shrank as it shied away from public appearances and proselytizing and instituted an increasingly regimented monastic lifestyle.

In 1985 Bonnie Lu Nettles died of liver cancer, inaugurating the second period of Heaven's Gate's history. During this time, the movement became increasingly apocalyptic and separatist. Nettles's death also ushered in a new theology of minimizing the value of the human body, a development that I explore in more detail later. After this point Applewhite functioned as sole leader of Heaven's Gate, and under his leadership the group made a concerted effort to reach out to potential converts in the ufologists, New Age practitioners, and other individuals outside the American religious mainstream. Between 1988 and 1994 the movement published a short booklet, broadcast a twelve-part series of satellite television shows, advertised in *USA Today*, and toured the country seeking new converts.

By the end of that second period in the mid-1990s, the notion of suicide was well cemented in the theology and rhetoric of Heaven's Gate, but it was not until late 1996 and the appearance of the Hale-Bopp comet that the members of the movement took definitive steps to prepare to end their terrestrial existences. Convinced of a massive government conspiracy to hide an extraterrestrial flying saucer trailing the comet, the adherents of Heaven's Gate prepared for the end. Its members wrote short essays about their commitments to the group, recorded "exit statements," published the movement's history in an anthology, and created a webpage to host their materials after their death. On March 22, 1997, Applewhite and the adherents of Heaven's Gate began the process of "leaving behind their vehicles," what outside observers and scholars call suicide.

Euphemization in the Early Period of Heaven's Gate (1972–1985)

Though suicide did not enter the theology of the movement until quite late in its history, a euphemistic treatment of the concept of bodily transformation laid the groundwork for the later euphemization of violence. In both cases, the movement rhetorically shifted the idea of ending bodily human existence from a profoundly negative concept to a positive one. As I have argued elsewhere, in the early period of Heaven's Gate, bodily transformation served as the movement's main approach to understanding human salvation, and only later did this shift to an understanding of salvation that required suicide (Zeller 2006). Therefore, just as the group's belief in the necessity of overcoming the human body through metamorphic transformation lay the groundwork for their eventual belief in the efficacy of suicide, their rhetorical approach to understanding that transformation served as the foundation of their later euphemization of suicide.

The notion of bodily transformation lay at the heart of Applewhite's and Nettles's teachings, a position that they made clear in all of their printed materials, public meetings, and interviews. The two believed that human beings possessed the ability to transform themselves into perfected extraterrestrial beings through a "metamorphic process" of overcoming one's human limitations. Or, as they wrote in a statement that they mailed to potential members, "When the metamorphosis is complete, their 'perennial' and cyclical nature is ended for their 'new' body has overcome decay, disease, and death. It has converted over chemically, biologically, and in vibration to the 'new' creature." The two founders of the movement even called the group "Human Individual Metamorphosis" during its first years of existence, recognizing this as their central religious claim (Human Individual Metamorphosis, 1975a).

Applewhite and Nettles declared that bodily transformation represented the only way that human beings could transcend the limits of humanity and achieve the highest state of existence. They explicitly compared their goal to that of both the Christian longing for heaven and the mystical aim of experiencing enlightenment or cosmic union, though they insisted that their own understanding was the only real way to achieve such salvation (Human Individual Metamorphosis 1975a, 1975d). Yet the Two insisted that individuals could not accomplish the transformation they taught after the death of the body, as many other religions teach. No divine being offered resurrection of the flesh or the entrance of the soul into a heavenly state. Nor did the Two support the embodied practices of mystics who sought enlightenment before death, such as one finds in Kabbalism and many forms of Hindu and Buddhist religious practice. Rather, the Two insisted that salvation required overcoming the human body during the present life and initiating the metamorphic transition on earth. In this regard, scholars such as Rosamond Rodman have noted similarities between Heaven's Gate and early Christian gnostics (Rodman 1999). Without entering into a debate on the nature of gnosticism or any possible historical connections to Heaven's Gate, I maintain that a resonance does exist between this modern-day UFO movement and the religious movements of antiquity that upheld a similar dualism and vision of worldly declension.

The Two insisted that this transformative process was not easy and in fact emphasized its difficulty. As they wrote in 1975, the process must:

> subject the person to all the experiences and circumstances necessary to overcome all his human needs. The painful and long-suffering experience of overcoming fear and desperation, which every seeker undergoes, actually converts the cells of the body, chemically and biologically, into a new body. Upon the completion of his conversion experience that new body will have overcome death and decay. (Human Individual Metamorphosis 1975c)

As the Two argue here, the painful and uncomfortable process of overcoming one's humanity are not only unpleasant side effects of the metamorphic procedure but necessary components of it. Through the adversity of overcoming one's humanity, the body physically transforms—"chemically and biologically," in the words of Applewhite and Nettles—into a new, perfected, alien creature. Humanity and the human body were fetters that the Two's followers needed to overcome.

This rejection of the human body and insistence on a metamorphic transition represents the first way that Applewhite and Nettles introduced a euphemistic denigration of human life into their worldview. While certainly not preaching suicide—the two were clear on multiple occasions that the metamorphosis occurred during one's terrestrial lifetime—they nevertheless rejected the underlying value of the human body and human life on planet Earth. The Two explained in the second of their written statements: "In the truest sense an individual becomes a *man* only upon his entry into the kingdom of 'God'—having overcome the human kingdom—after literally leaving the human level with his 'new' body belonging to the kingdom above human" (Human Individual Metamorphosis 1975b). One must overcome human life and everything connected to it in order to experience the salvific transformation into an extraterrestrial being. This approach laid a foundation for the group's later willingness to toss aside the human body in its pursuit of salvation.

Though the Two clearly stated that suicide was not an option and that the metamorphic process of overcoming one's humanity must occur during the present lifetime, their theology included a stark example of the euphemization of violence and a hint at the necessity of the death of the body in their salvific theme. The Two called this example of euphemistic violence "the demonstration." During the demonstration, Applewhite and Nettles taught, the two founders of Heaven's Gate would reveal the underlying nature of the human body and indicate how others can overcome their humanity and transform themselves into perfected extraterrestrial creatures. Specifically, the Two taught that their enemies would assassinate them on a street, leaving their bodies to decay for three and a half days. During that time, the Two would reconstruct their bodies using "metamorphic" and "chemical and biological" means (Human Individual Metamorphosis 1975a, 1975d). On the third day, the two would rise from the dead, ascend into heaven aboard UFOs, and thereby demonstrate the reality of their claims. The movement made a similar claim about Christ's resurrection.

As I have argued elsewhere, the demonstration represented a recasting of a particular New Testament prophecy (Rev. 11:3–12) in the language of science and ufology (Zeller 2010, 79). Yet it also reveals a euphemization of violence. The Two used multiple methods to temper the sense of actual violence. These included the clearly rhetorical, e.g., Applewhite's and Nettles's insistence that they were merely "actors" in a "theater," engaging in a kind of performance designed to instruct human beings (Human Individual Metamorphosis, 1975). Since actors do not actually die during their character's death scenes, this approach rhetorically transforms the impending violence of the demonstration into an act or illusion. Similarly, the Two's theology minimized the violence implicit in the demonstration since death became a merely temporary state in a metamorphic process and the result of the demonstration featured bodily departure from the planet onboard a UFO. Both of these euphemizing approaches laid the foundation for the later euphemization of suicide. The demonstration as predicted did not occur, but it created a symbolic platform on which the movement could later develop its ideology of suicide.

Euphemization in the Middle Period of Heaven's Gate (1985–1995)

The death of Bonnie Lu Nettles in 1985 ended the first formative period of Heaven's Gate. The movement had gone underground in 1976, and when it again emerged in the late 1980s, it offered an updated theology that took into account the death of the cofounder. Nettles's death represented a direct challenge to the group's early teaching since, rather than enter heaven in bodily form, her earthly remains persisted as precisely that. During this period, Heaven's Gate offered a theological understanding of the human self that minimized the nature of the body, effectively declaring the essence of the self to be nonphysical and therefore unaffected by the death of the body. This approach permitted the movement to euphemistically transform the concept of death into that of a new form of life, or rebirth.

The group's only major written document during this era, a short booklet titled *'88 Update*, indicates this theological shift. Its opening words make clear that the physical bodies of Applewhite and Nettles were mere containers, vessels that temporarily carry—or, in the case of Nettles, *carried*—the immortal spirits of Ti and Do: "In the early 1970s, two members of the Kingdom of Heaven (or what some might call two aliens from outer space) incarnated into two unsuspecting humans in Houston, a registered nurse and a college music professor who were in their forties" (Heaven's Gate 1988, 1). Since the bodies of Marshall Herff Applewhite and Bonnie Lu Nettles were not the true selves of the two aliens, the bodily demise of Nettles represented not death but the freeing of her soul to return to space. Though neither the *'88 Update* nor Applewhite made any mention of suicide, the text clearly permitted the euphemization of suicide that followed.

Additionally, the *'88 Update* transformed the human body from the seat of the soul to a mere container, a "vehicle," in the words of Applewhite. Referring to his and Nettles's experiences during the 1970s, Heaven's Gate's leader wrote that "the memory and the 'old programming' of their bodies—which they now referred to as their 'vehicles'—had to be kept at bay like an annoying puppy in order to sustain their Next Level consciousness" (Heaven's Gate 1988, 1). Interestingly, this short sentence includes three rhetorical methods of deemphasizing the value of the human body. First, Applewhite treated the body as a computer, a thing to be "programmed" but also capable of reprogramming. Since computers require periodic updating and even replacement, the movement implied that the human body might require similar treatment. Second, Applewhite called the body a "vehicle." As such, the human body existed to serve and transport its contents, much like a car, an airplane, or a boat. Moreover, like such vehicles, one might switch between them depending on need (e.g., driving to an airport, flying to one's destination, then continuing the trip by boat). The ease with which one changes vehicles—and their purposes as mere means of locomotion rather than as ends in themselves—rhetorically positions the body as temporary and ultimately only a means to an end. Finally, Applewhite dismissed the memories and programming of the body as an "annoying puppy" in need of keeping at bay. Such an approach clearly deemphasizes, if not delegitimizes, the value of bodily existence.

Applewhite's actual description of Nettles's death follows a similar pattern, implying that the human body represented a mere container for Nettles's true self, and as such the death of the body was not a true death:

> Some 3-1/2 years ago from the time of this writing, Ti left her human vehicle. To all human appearances it was due to a form of cancer. We could say that because of the stress, due to the gap between her Next Level mind and the vehicle's genetic capacity, that the cancer symptom caused the vehicle to break down and stop functioning. However, it was strange that she experienced no symptoms prior to the week she left her vehicle, and for the most part her vehicle slept through the transition. We're not exactly sure how many days it might have taken her to return to the Next Level vehicle she left behind prior to this task. (Heaven's Gate 1988, 12)

Here Applewhite engages in multiple rhetorical techniques to euphemistically transform the death of Nettles into a more benign transition. First, following the pattern set elsewhere in the '88 Update, Applewhite continued to refer to the body of the deceased cofounder as a vehicle. Applewhite marked Nettles's true nature as distinct from that body, noting that Ti left a "human vehicle" and returned to a "Next Level vehicle" in the heavens. Now embodied in outer space, Nettles, née Ti, remained alive, whereas the human body of Nettles remained as mere "remains," to use the common sense of the term. Second, the '88 Update's description of the death process also euphemistically transformed Nettles's death from cancer into a peaceful transition of consciousness. In his description of the process, Applewhite never referred to Nettles's body as Nettles, always as the vehicle of Nettles. Using language more commonly used with inanimate objects, Applewhite wrote that her vehicle had broken down and stopped functioning, reserving the more animate language to refer to Nettles's self, which journeyed on to the Next Level to occupy a new vehicle.

As I have argued elsewhere, the death of Nettles represented a turning point in the group (Zeller 2006, 87). Though Heaven's Gate had already engaged in extensive euphemistic denigration of the human body, with the exception of the demonstration, Nettles and Applewhite had stated very clearly during the first period of the movement's history that transition to a next-level body required the transformation of a living human body. When asked about death, they bluntly declared that "[y]ou do not have to die" and that the UFO would pick up only living beings (Hewes and Steiger 1976, 89). The sole exception to this approach, the demonstration, functioned pedagogically as an empirical verification of the Two's claims but not as an archetype of universal salvation.

After the death of Nettles, this approach changed. Though the '88 Update made no mention of suicide, it clearly upheld a view of the human body as a temporary physical container for a noncorporeal self or spirit. After the death of Nettles, the leader and members of Heaven's Gate began to understand themselves as thoroughly divorced from human identity and the human body, mere travelers who happened to possess human bodies for a brief time as part of their spiritual education. Borrowing the New Age concept of "walk-ins"—spiritual beings possessing a human body—as popularly presented by proponents of channeling, the members of Heaven's Gate declared themselves extraterrestrial spirits temporarily bound within human forms. They wrote the following, using the third person to refer to themselves:

> They were briefed as a crew aboard a spacecraft about how they would incarnate into human vehicles in order to do a task. They left their Kingdom "world" and came into this "world" beginning in the late 1940s. They feel that some left their Next Level bodies via so-called UFO "crashes." . . . That is to say, they were all in "spirit" from the late 1940s and possibly early 1950s until the mid-1970s before actually entering and taking charge of the human vehicles—or the human bodies—they are now in. (Heaven's Gate 1988, sec. 3, p. 18)

Since the human bodies that the members of Heaven's Gate possessed—and "possessed" seems an apt term, given their description of entering these bodies as spirits—functioned as mere containers, vehicles, or clothing, the *'88 Update* implicitly introduced the possibility of discarding these human bodies as part of the process of reversing the arrival of these Next-Level souls. However, it would take another decade before the movement would make this implicit theology explicit.

While the death of Nettles created a shift in the group's theology, one cannot view these changes as an abrupt disjuncture. The leaders of the group had laid the foundation that supported the eventual decision for suicides a decade earlier in their devaluation of the human body and euphemistic approach to violence in terms of the crucifixion and demonstration. One must therefore disagree with John Wallis, who wrote in his *Apocalyptic Trajectories*:

> [I]t would appear that the group's decision to 'exit' from planet earth was the end point of a chain of events that began in 1985 with the death of Ti from cancer. . . . Ti's death also brought into question one of the central aspects of the Two's message. Right from the beginning the Two had taught that the only way to enter the Next Level was with a living, human body and that, indeed, death would simply lead to reincarnation back to the human level. Ti's death, as would be suspected, brought this belief into question and necessitated an urgent theological rethink. (Wallis 2004, 159–60)

Though Wallis does admit that this "urgent theological rethink" culminated a longer process, he still emphasizes disjuncture (Wallis 2004, 167–68). Given the history of the euphemization of violence within Heaven's Gate, I disagree. The roots of the suicides reached to the founding of Heaven's Gate and its earliest period, not the death of Nettles.

Euphemization in the Final Period of Heaven's Gate (1995–1997)

Shortly before the March 1997 suicides, which terminated the terrestrial history of Heaven's Gate, its leader and members produced an anthology of the group's written materials, including some of those from its first and second periods (First Statement and *'88 Update*, respectively), as well as new material, namely a set of "exit statements" produced in 1995 and 1996, written statements by the adherents of the group produced in 1997, and reprints of more ephemeral materials (e.g., posters, advertisements) from 1994 and 1995. These sources indicate that the movement had firmly adopted a position in favor of suicide by 1995 and worked to euphemistically transform that notion into a more benign form through its rhetoric.

The transition from a purely bodily understanding of salvation to the promotion of suicide was a slow process. Documents produced toward the end of the movement's second period (the mid-1990s) continued the rhetorical rejection of the human body and utilized language exclusively focused on the soul or spirit but did not yet indicate any possibility of suicide in the ideology of the members of Heaven's Gate. The group's November 29, 1993, poster, "The *Only* Way out of This *Corrupt* World," assumed the already-developed positions but combined them with an approach that addressed only the *souls* of the readers, not their bodies. It stated that the group could explain the following:

> [h]ow human physical bodies are only containers (suits of clothes) for souls; how the soul is the true identity; and how invasive influences and discarnate spirits can be recognized, dealt with, and aborted. How the real question is, now that "test time" is here, are the souls who have received the "gift of recognition" willing to accept this Truth and these Representatives from that Kingdom? (Heaven's Gate 1993a)

Bodies being merely temporary vehicles or suits of clothing—an even more dismissive and ephemeral perspective since most people change clothing daily—Heaven's Gate addressed only the souls of potential adherents. Despite this approach, the group avoided any direct discussion of suicide or attempts to euphemistically transform the notions of suicide. Nevertheless, sources from the same time period indicate at least the possibility of suicide, as indicated by the group's 1993 *USA Today* advertisement, which argued that "[a] soul cannot end its own existence. Though it may incarnate many times and the body or vehicle it is wearing may be terminated, only the true Kingdom of God—the Evolutionary Level above Human—can terminate the soul. This termination of the soul is the only proper application of the term DEATH" (Heaven's Gate 1993b). Though not quite supportive of suicide, Heaven's Gate had thoroughly transformed the nature of human bodily death by the mid-1990s, euphemistically describing it as a mere transition such as changing clothes or trading in a used car.

By the autumn of 1995 the members and leader of Heaven's Gate clearly entertained the option of ending their terrestrial existences rather than waiting for the Next-Level UFOs to enter the earth's atmosphere. The group's November 1995 Internet posting, "Undercover 'Jesus' Surfaces before Departure," refers to the imminence of their final acts and euphemistically alluded to suicide. Written by Applewhite, the statement declared that the group would soon "prepare to 'lay down' our human bodies" (Heaven's Gate 1995). Though Applewhite might have conceivably rendered the group's long-standing belief that human beings must overcome their human bodies and transform them into new extraterrestrial ones as a "laying down" of the body, such a rhetorical move seems unlikely. Heaven's Gate had abandoned the notion of the bodily metamorphosis during the second phase of its history, and by this point the members looked to the soul alone as the means of entering heaven. Since the body was at best irrelevant and at worst a distracting fetter—or an annoying puppy, to use Applewhite's earlier language—members of the group looked to the abandonment of the body as a crucial means of entering heaven. The statement continues: "If my Father does not require this 'disposition' of us—[then] He will take us up into His 'cloud of light' [spacecraft] before such 'laying down of bodies' need occur" (Heaven's Gate 1995). (The group repeated the same basic claims in a terser manner on a 1994 poster, "The Shedding of Our Human Bodies May Be Required" [Heaven's Gate 1994].) While this statement reveals profound uncertainty about the necessity of suicide, it does make clear that the group members had at least considered the termination of their earthly bodies, which they euphemistically called the "laying down" of their bodies. In other words, though Applewhite and the other adherents of Heaven's Gate portrayed a willingness to abandon the human bodies they possessed, they hedged bets on whether their superiors in the Next Level would require such an action. Despite this hesitancy, the members of the group had already rhetorically transformed the notion of suicide from that of self-violence to self-salvation, building on the earlier denigration of the human body.

For reasons that scholars still debate, during the spring of 1997 Marshall Herff Applewhite advanced the timetable for the end of Heaven's Gate. Possibly the sixty-five-year-old Applewhite recognized that his body ("vehicle") was showing signs of age, though it is also possible that the years of rejection by outsiders had inculcated an extreme pessimism within the movement. Regardless, by late 1996 Applewhite and the members of Heaven's Gate had opted to shed their human bodies, end their terrestrial existences, and journey to the heavens in spiritual form. As part of this effort, the leader and members of Heaven's Gate engaged in an extensive rhetorical reconfiguration of the notion of suicide and of the word "suicide" itself. While the group made this rhetorical work a highlight of the March

1997 website, which made the group famous, two of the "statements by students," as the anthology called the written position statements by the group's members, began the process.

The Heaven's Gate member who called herself Wknody offered one of these two direct treatments of the concept of suicide. Her statement, "A Matter of Life or Death? YOU Decide," represented the first time that a member of the group faced the word "suicide" itself and attempted to rhetorically alter its meaning. Rather than ending one's life, Wknody wrote, suicide represented denying the truth of the teachings of Heaven's Gate and thereby failing to achieve heavenly salvation. She made this argument by first assuming the devaluation of the body, which had long been a staple of the group: "[W]hen I speak of I, I am only referring to the mind/soul. I am not referring to the body or, as we refer to it, the 'vehicle' that I am wearing. As I said earlier, this vehicle is just a container" (Wknody 1996, A18). Thus far, Wknody's statement mirrored the teachings of Applewhite from the late 1980s and early 1990s. However, she continued, directly considering the notion of suicide: "In fact, to lose this vehicle means absolutely nothing to me, and most of the time it is an encumbrance to me. But to lose my Next Level mind, this 'gift,' because of denying this knowledge and, subsequently, my Teachers, who bear the only real truth, is suicide in the truest sense of the word" (Wknody 1996, A18). Combining her rejection of the value of the human body with rhetorical devaluation of that body—calling it an "encumbrance"—Wknody set the stage for her redefinition of the nature of suicide. Rather than meaning the intentional bodily death of a human being, Wknody defines suicide as the turning away from the only real truth of the universe and from the heavenly salvation that it brought. In other words, to remain on earth in bodily form represented suicide, but to lay aside the human body and free the spirit (or "Next Level mind," as Wknody calls it) was not suicide but life.

Wknody's coreligionist Stmody made a similar claim in his contribution to the group's anthology. Titling his piece "Evolutionary 'Rights' for 'Victims,'" Stmody accepted that suicide also meant the death of the body (i.e., he accepted the word as it is normally understood but described that meaning as a distinct form of "human suicide"). He contrasted such human suicide with his plans to lay down his own body, which he euphemistically compared to a driver's leaving behind a car or a tree's shedding a leaf:

> It doesn't make any sense to me that the driver "dies" when his "car" (body) stops "running." To me, the body is just a "leaf" of the "tree," and the genetic strain (family tree) doesn't end when the leaf's function becomes impaired. When it is becoming a burden on me and others, and whenever my choices are so restricted that growth is impossible, or ridiculously difficult, it is part of the design to evacuate it like a tree sheds a leaf. In contrast, human suicide (identifying as the body and trying to "end it all" for the purpose of avoiding the growth pains of lessons) gets you nowhere. It seems clear that longevity, physical beauty,

and sex appeal are all Luciferian concepts based on identifying as only the body and its desires. (Stmody 1996)

Here Stmody combines the rejection of the body, support for the impending suicides of the Heaven's Gate members, and a grudging acceptance of the notion of other forms of suicide.

Wknody and Stmody were the first of Heaven's Gate's members to explicitly treat the notion of suicide and euphemistically transform it into a more benign concept. Yet before the movement began the actual process of laying down their vehicles (committing suicide), the group offered one final defense of their choice and one final euphemistic attempt to transform suicide into a gentler process. Most likely written by Applewhite, "Our Position against Suicide," posted on their website in December 1996, amplified all of the previous explanations of the nature of suicide and relied upon the same denigration of the body and physical form. If one takes the document at face value—which one should—the group had still not fully settled on the need to voluntarily discard their bodies. It began by noting the value of residing within a body in order to "learn the lessons" of overcoming the world and to bring the message of Heaven's Gate to the human population of planet Earth. It also directly stated the group members' hopes to board the spacecraft bound for the heavens while still embodied (Heaven's Gate 1996).

Despite this hopeful opening, "Our Position against Suicide" very quickly turned to pessimism. It noted that "before that spacecraft comes, one or more of us could lose our physical vehicles (bodies) due to 'recall,' accident, or at the hands of some irate individual." Further, the author of the document noted that the government might attempt to incarcerate or torture the group's members, explicitly comparing their possible fate to that of the Branch Davidians at Waco and the antigovernment Weaver family at Ruby Ridge. In both cases, members of those groups died during government sieges (Heaven's Gate 1996).

Yet the document also made clear that voluntary suicide remained an option. Though the group did not make the link explicit, following the document's treatment of the events at Waco and Ruby Ridge, it cited another example of a besieged religious minority—one that existed nearly two millennia earlier:

> For example, consider what happened at Masada around 73 A.D. A devout Jewish sect, after holding out against a siege by the Romans, to the best of their ability, and seeing that the murder, rape, and torture of their community was inevitable, determined that it was permissible for them to evacuate their bodies by a more dignified, and less agonizing method. (Heaven's Gate 1996)

As the author of this document correctly noted, the Jewish rebels at Masada, who numbered 960, according to the ancient historian Josephus, committed mass suicide in order to prevent their capture by Roman authorities. According to Josephus's account, the Jewish rebels at Masada represented a radical faction of the Zealots, who opposed both Jewish and Roman law and government because they considered them corrupt. Recognizing that their rebellion was doomed, they chose to end their lives on their own terms rather than permit the Romans to capture them. Importantly, Josephus described the Masada suicides as performed in orderly stages, a parallel to the way in which the adherents of Heaven's Gate would eventually end their own terrestrial lives.

On March 22, 1997, when the Hale-Bopp comet reached its perigee to earth, the members of Heaven's Gate began the process of laying aside their earthly bodies. They left for the world a brief press release that explained the nature of their movement, their fundamental beliefs and positions, and the reasons for their suicides. Probably written by Applewhite, or at least approved by him, the statement declared the following:

> By the time you read this, we suspect that the human bodies we were wearing have been found and that a flurry of fragmented reports have begun to hit the wire services. For those who want to know the facts, the following statement has been issued. . . . RANCHO SANTO FE, CA—By the time you receive this, we'll be gone—several dozen of us. We came from the Level above Human in distant space and we have now exited the bodies that we were wearing for our earthly task, to return to the world from whence we came—task completed. (Heaven's Gate 1997)

The exit press release, as the movement called the document, offered the final redaction of the basic tenets of the group and the manner in which it had euphemistically transformed the self-violence of suicide into a more benign and ultimately noble endeavor. No longer did the group endorse its claims from the first phase of its history that heavenly entrance required bodily transformation, nor did it allude to suicide as merely a means of avoiding persecution or an option that perhaps the heavens would not ultimately require, as it did during its second phase. Instead, the press release clearly stated the absolute requirement to lay aside the human body as a condition to enter heaven: "[B]odies are merely containers, suits of clothes—the true identity [of the individual] is the soul or mind/spirit residing in that 'vehicle.' . . . You must leave everything of your humanness behind. This includes the ultimate sacrifice and demonstration of faith—that is, the shedding of your human body" (Heaven's Gate 1997). In March 1997, twenty-five years after Nettles and Applewhite met in Houston and formed the inchoate movement that would become Heaven's Gate, the terrestrial history of Heaven's Gate ended, thanks to the twenty-five-year process of euphemization.

NOTES

1. The group used a variety of names during its history, including Human Individual Metamorphosis, the UFO Cult, and Total Overcomers Anonymous, in addition to

Heaven's Gate. For the sake of simplicity I refer to the movement as Heaven's Gate throughout this chapter, aware that this name is anachronistic when discussing other periods of the group's history.

REFERENCES

Balch, Robert W. 1982. "Bo and Peep: A Case Study of the Origins of Messianic Leadership." In *Millennialism and Charisma*, ed. R. Wallis, 13–72. Belfast: Queen's University.

———, and David Taylor. 2002. "Making Sense of the Heaven's Gate Suicides." In *Cults, Religion, and Violence*, ed. D. G. Bromley and J. G. Melton, 209–229. New York: Cambridge University Press.

Gleick, Elizabeth. 1997. "The Marker We've Been Waiting For." *Time* (April 7, 1997), 27–36.

Heaven's Gate. 1988. '88 Update. In *How and When "Heaven's Gate" (The Door to the Physical Kingdom Level above Human) May Be Entered*, ed. Heaven's Gate, sec. 3, 1–19. Mill Spring, N.C.: Wild Flower.

———. 1993a. The Only Way Out of This Corrupt World [poster]. In *How and When "Heaven's Gate" (The Door to the Physical Kingdom Level above Human) May Be Entered*, ed. Heaven's Gate, sec. 6, 3. Mill Spring, N.C.: Wild Flower.

———. 1993b. "UFO Cult" Resurfaces with Final Offer [*USA Today* advertisement]. In *How and When "Heaven's Gate" (The Door to the Physical Kingdom Level above Human) May Be Entered*, ed. Heaven's Gate, sec. 5, 3. Mill Spring, N.C.: Wild Flower.

———. 1994. The Shedding of Our Borrowed Human Bodies May Be Required [poster]. In *How and When "Heaven's Gate" (The Door to the Physical Kingdom Level above Human) May Be Entered*, ed. Heaven's Gate, sec. 6, 11. Mill Spring, N.C.: Wild Flower.

———. 1995. "Undercover 'Jesus' Surfaces before Departure." In *How and When "Heaven's Gate" (The Door to the Physical Kingdom Level above Human) May Be Entered*, ed. Heaven's Gate, sec. 1, 3–6. Mill Spring, N.C.: Wild Flower.

———. 1996. Our Position against Suicide (cited November 13, 1997). http://web.archive.org/web/97801997356314/www.heavensgate.com/misc/letter.htm.

———. 1997. Exit Press Release: "Heaven's Gate 'Away Team' Returns to Level above Human in Distant Space" (cited November 13, 1997). http://www.heavensgate.com/misc/pressrel.htm.

Hewes, Hayden, and Brad Steiger. 1976. *UFO Missionaries Extraordinary*. New York: Pocket Books.

Human Individual Metamorphosis. 1975a. Statement #1: Human Individual Metamorphosis. American Religions Collection, ARC Mss 1, Department of Special Collections, University Libraries, University of California, Santa Barbara.

———. 1975b. Statement #2: Clarification: Human Kingdom: Visible and Invisible. American Religions Collection, ARC Mss 1, Department of Special Collections, University Libraries, University of California, Santa Barbara.

———. 1975c. Statement #3: The Only Significant Resurrection. American Religions Collection, ARC Mss 1, Department of Special Collections, University Libraries, University of California, Santa Barbara.

———. 1975d. What's Up? American Religions Collection, ARC Mss 1, Department of Special Collections, University Libraries, University of California, Santa Barbara.

Jnnody. 1996. "Incarnating and Discarnating." In *How and When "Heaven's Gate" (The Door to the Physical Kingdom Level above Human) May Be Entered*, ed. Heaven's Gate, sec. A, 89–97. Mill Spring, N.C.: Wild Flower.

Lalich, Janja. 2004. *Bounded Choice: True Believers and Charismatic Cults*. Berkeley: University of California Press.

Lewis, James R. 2003. "Legitimating Suicide: Heaven's Gate and New Age Ideology." In *UFO Religions*, ed. C. Partridge, 103–128. New York: Routledge.

Rodman, Rosamond. 1999. "Heaven's Gate: Religious Otherworldiness American Style." In *The Bible and the American Myth: A Symposium on the Bible and Constructions of Meaning*, ed. V. K. Wimbush, 157–173. Macon, Ga.: Mercer University Press.

Stmody. 1996. "Evolutionary 'Rights' for 'Victims.'" In *How and When "Heaven's Gate" (The Door to the Physical Kingdom Level above Human) May Be Entered*, ed. Heaven's Gate, sec. A, 71–79. Mill Spring, N.C.: Wild Flower.

Wallis, John. 2004. *Apocalyptic Trajectories: Millenarianism and Violence in the Contemporary World*. Oxford: Lang.

Wessinger, Catherine. 2000. *How the Millennium Comes Violently: From Jonestown to Heaven's Gate*. New York: Seven Bridges.

Wknody. 1996. "A Matter of Life or Death? YOU Decide." In *How and When "Heaven's Gate" (The Door to the Physical Kingdom Level above Human) May Be Entered*, ed. Heaven's Gate, sec. A, 18–21. Mill Spring, N.C.: Wild Flower.

Zeller, Benjamin E. 2006. "Scaling Heaven's Gate: Individualism and Salvation in a New Religious Movement." *Nova Religio: Journal of Alternative and Emergent Religions* 10(2):75–102.

———. 2010. *Prophets and Protons: New Religious Movements and Science in Late Twentieth-century America*. New York: New York University Press.

9

"There Will Follow a New Generation and a New Earth": From Apocalyptic Hopes to Destruction in the Movement for the Restoration of the Ten Commandments of God

Jean-François Mayer

Religioscope Institute, Fribourg, Switzerland

In front of the police station at Rukungiri in southwestern Uganda, not far from the border with the Democratic Republic of the Congo (DRC), the police officer could not believe his ears as I told him the story of the Order of the Solar Temple in Europe and Canada. His face showed a mixture of both puzzlement and relief: "You have also had such a case? In Switzerland? In a rich country? Not among poor people?" He called the other police officers: "Come, listen to this story! They have had the same thing in Europe!"

It takes two hours by road from Rukungiri to reach Kanungu, the place where hundreds of members of the Movement for the Restoration of the Ten Commandments of God (MRTCG) were burned alive on March 17, 2000, in a chapel whose door and windows had been nailed shut from the outside. At least 331 people perished in the church, while 6 more, who had been killed before the fire, were found buried in a pit inside the church. Around 450 additional victims were subsequently discovered in secret mass graves at four different locations. Though figures are approximate and some graves may have remained undiscovered, the MRTCG tragedy possibly caused even more deaths than Jonestown.

I traveled to Uganda twice (in 2000 and 2001) to research the case. I am no expert in African studies or African religions, but I had already carried out and published research on the Order of the Solar Temple before the 1994 events that made its name famous (Mayer 1999; Lewis 2006, 7–17, 91–103). I became intrigued when I heard about the events in Uganda, and I wondered whether they could shed some light—from an entirely different context and in a comparative perspective—on the dynamics of violence and self-destruction in small religious movements, notwithstanding the cultural and doctrinal differences involved in the two cases. Indeed, I could assure the Rukungiri police officer that such events do not occur only in Africa but in affluent environments as well. If we are looking for ways to explain the events, there is no reason not to compare them (Introvigne and Mayer 2002, 183–86) at least to some extent: While circumstances may differ greatly, the human mind is not that different across cultures.

Something else had brought me to Uganda. In the weeks following events there, I expected scholars with a knowledge of the field to research what had occurred. While there was a welcome initiative by a team of researchers from Makerere University in the Ugandan capital, Kampala, to gather material and promptly produce a small collection of papers immediately after the events (Kabazzi-Kisirinya, Deusdedit, and Banura 2000), and while there have been also some other local initiatives such as a report by the Uganda Human Rights Commission (2002) and a book by a local clergyman who was familiar with the MRTCG (Bagumisiriza 2005), plus two books by Ugandans living in Europe (Atuhaire 2003; Bwire 2007), the few articles that appeared in scholarly publications were not based on firsthand research but made use of media resources and some of the movement's texts. No doubt the analysis of these texts and informed comments based on media reports brought useful insights, but this remains insufficient. I am aware of the limitations of my own insights about an African environment, but I understand something about religious dynamics, including violent ones, and I am also familiar with some international networks and ideas that the MRTCG interacted with.

Much remains to be done—if, indeed, it is ever done. In Uganda, forensic resources were very poor. Several police officers did their best to investigate the events surrounding the MRTCG's fiery end, but there was not the kind of systematic, long-term effort that such a case required, and, to be honest, even in a Western country, a case of such magnitude would have posed major challenges. The Judicial Commission of Inquiry, which was formed by the Ugandan government in December 2000, never received any financial support and consequently never met (Mubangizi 2009).

Thus, one of the most significant acts of violence by a new religious movement in recent decades might never be investigated properly. Himself the author of a book (Atuhaire 2003) based on personal experience (he lives abroad but lost several relatives in the movement), Bernard Atuhaire sadly remarked in an op-ed in a leading Ugandan newspaper: "The interest shown by researchers is . . . miserably low. In a normal setting, an incident of such magnitude and more so the manner in which it was carried out, should have attracted a substantial amount of research interest" (Atuhaire 2005).

African-Initiated Churches, Apparitions of the Virgin Mary, and Popular Catholicism in East Africa

When scholars of contemporary religious movements hear about groups in Africa, the concept of "African independent churches" (or, better, "African-initiated churches") immediately comes to their minds. Many of these groups—representing a highly diverse variety—have a shared background in missionary efforts by various churches in the Protestant tradition. Some of them, on the other hand, have roots in Roman Catholicism; such is the case of the Legio Maria in East Africa (Kustenbauder 2009).

The MRTCG, however, should not merely be categorized and explained in terms of the general pattern of African-initiated churches. Among the leadership figures of the movement one finds several people who had been Catholic clergymen in good standing. Moreover, the roots of the MRTCG partly go back to a regional milieu of Marian visionaries, connected with international apparitionist networks, both inside the Roman Catholic Church and on its fringes. This does not discount the presence of specific African elements in the group as long as they do not eclipse the other significant dimensions.

The MRTCG cannot be understood separately from the wider context of Ugandan Catholicism, as described by Ronald Kassimir in his article on "popular Catholicism" in Uganda (Kassimir 1999). Kassimir underlines the fact that scholars of "popular religion" in Africa have devoted too little attention to its variants "within the mainstream churches of mission origin, especially Catholic"; much more attention has been given to neotraditional or Christian separatist movements. Many elements of popular Catholicism have built upon practices actually encouraged by the official Catholic Church. The decline of older associations, such as the Legion of Mary (not to be confused with the independent, previously mentioned Legio Maria), "contributed to the creation of space for new expressions" (Kassimir 1999, 251). Indeed, during interviews in the valley of Kamwezi, it was confirmed to me that several adherents of the MRTCG were former members of the Legion of Mary; this appears to have been the case for other Marian apparitionist groups as well.

I hasten to add at this point that neither African nor supranational aspects provide in themselves satisfactory explanations of the violent end of the group. Apocalyptic views provide a convenient background for such events but in themselves do not explain anything: Most apocalyptic and millenarian groups remain peaceful, content with watching the signs of the times and attempting to understand the unfolding events of the divine scenario.

Both in Uganda and nearby Rwanda, Marian apparitions have blossomed in some circles during the past decades. The apparitions of the Virgin Mary in Kibeho, Rwanda, starting in 1981, drew crowds from Rwanda and neighboring countries. The widow of one of the leading figures in the MRTCG, Teresa Kibwetere, confirmed to me in a discussion at her home that she had gone on pilgrimage to Kibeho with her husband and a few people from Kampala in 1984. At the time of the genocide in Rwanda in 1994, it was understood that the events had been predicted in some of the messages received by seers in Kibeho. The apparitions in Kibeho were officially recognized as authentic in 2001 by the Roman Catholic episcopate in Rwanda; at the same time, Catholic bishops in Rwanda warned against a proliferation of other visionaries and largely discounted visions connected to the Kibeho phenomenon after 1983—a clear indication of the wider impact of Kibeho on the development of a variety of uncontrolled messages and groups.

Such efforts to circumscribe "authentic" visions to some visionaries and a particular period rarely succeed in convincing all of those who are fascinated by the Virgin's apparitions and messages. It is in the milieu of such visionaries that the MRTCG developed.

How Visionaries Became Prophets, Apostles, and Bishops

Before reconstructing the main steps in the history of the group, I introduce three key figures that would play a role—not the only ones but definitely the central ones.

Firstly, there was Credonia Mwerinde (b. 1952), considered as having been the most influential leader and largely described as the villain of the piece by local and international media. Coming from Kanungu, she is generally depicted as a person of evil repute, said to have been involved in prostitution, who had come "to epitomise the very heart of evil in Kanungu" (Bwire 2007, 53). It is difficult to separate truth from fiction: Despite the March 2000 events, one wonders whether all of the evils attributed to her—including sacrificing children and drinking human blood—matched reality or were just fantasies. Whatever the case, she was obviously a strong-willed woman who did not easily accept opposition. She reported having visions as early as 1981. We will see that her family came to play a central role in the group.

Quite different at first sight was Joseph Kibwetere (b. 1932), a man of some importance and means who had been active in politics as a member of the (Catholic) Democratic Party at some point during his life. He apparently had a vision of Jesus Christ and the Virgin Mary in 1984, at a time when he had gone underground due to political repression, but he had apparently claimed to have received earlier messages from Jesus (though not necessarily visions). According to several reports, he had undergone treatment for psychiatric problems. Several sources in the

Catholic Church report that even in the 1970s Kibwetere had attempted to promote his views and to pressure bishops to introduce changes that would in fact have meant reverting to some pre-Vatican II practices. He would revive these efforts in 1989, claiming to transmit messages from Jesus himself. Whatever the case, Kibwetere found congenial spirits in Credonia Mwerinde and her associates and invited them to his home. Originally, his wife, Teresa, followed the group, but the authoritarian behavior of Mwerinde, who started to run everything in Teresa's home and humiliated her, finally convinced Kibwetere's wife and her children to break with the group—in which she had been elevated to the status of an apostle—and to evict its members from the family property. This happened in 1992 and led to the group's moving to its new headquarters in Kanungu. Through a vision, Kibwetere was chosen as a bishop.

Three Catholic priests also joined the group: Fr. Paul Ikazire, Fr. Dominic Kataribaabo (b. 1936), and Fr. Joseph Kasapurari (b. 1961). At least the first two were already acquainted with Kibwetere. An old, educated priest, ordained in 1947 and still able to speak Latin, Ikazire would leave the group in 1994 over various issues, but the other two priests would persevere to the end, though excommunicated by the Roman Catholic Church. Kataribaabo was more than an average priest. He had received a good education, had been the principal of a minor seminary, and had had an opportunity to study in the United States from 1985 to 1987, earning a master's degree in religious studies from Loyola Marymount University in California. He was considered at some point to be a prospective bishop. However, he apparently had quite an authoritarian character, and some of his acquaintances also reported that he came back from his stay in the United States as a changed person, having become quite taciturn. It is possible that the lack of a prestigious position for him in the church after his return caused some bitterness. Kataribaabo was made an assistant bishop in the group at the same time Kibwetere was elevated to episcopal status in 1992—there is no trace of any consecration within an apostolic succession, a direct and divine intervention obviously making this superfluous.

This chapter focuses exclusively on these three figures (Mwerinde, Kibwetere, and Kataribaabo), though they were not the only ones within the leadership of the group. This is not only due to space limitations. There are also reasons to believe that the interpersonal chemistry among these three people created the circumstances that led to the violent end of the MRTCG. It is unlikely that it would have met the same fate if they had continued to follow their own, independent trajectories.[1]

Quite early in the history of the movement, twelve apostles were selected. Six of these were women, something explicitly connected to the Marian dimension of the movement:

> Jesus gave the reason for this arrangement, namely, that at the beginning of his first mission to redeem mankind, he chose from his disciples twelve men whom he called *Apostles*, because he was alone; but now he

says that at his second coming he has come with his mother and, that since she is the one who asked God the Father for this mission, it is appropriate that she gets people of her kind on the team of the Apostles of the new community, the second generation.[2]

From Marian Visionaries to Apocalyptic Schism

There are different versions of the genesis of the group, but let us look at the "official" one. In the rubbles of the compound in Kanungu, a Ugandan policeman managed to retrieve and safeguard an important document: the untitled, unpublished, handwritten history of the MRTCG.[3] Written in good English, obviously by Kataribaabo, the document is clearly structured, with chapters and sections, and describes the history of the MRTCG as its leaders wanted it to be perceived. Since the leaders of the movement are no longer here to tell us their own story, it is important to summarize it as they saw themselves.

This history traces the origins of the group to Credonia Mwerinde's father, Paulo Kashaku, who passed away on July 12, 1991, and said to be 101 years old at that time.[4] Kashaku was considered the "grandfather" of the movement. The school building at the compound in Kanungu was dedicated to him. His body was buried (along with the body of his wife) below the altar of the new church in Kanungu, which did not burn. Kashaku was obviously seen as a saint by the movement: The handwritten history presents him as having been the original leader, with Kibwetere succeeding Kashaku after his death and becoming "the Head of the team of the Apostles."

Paulo Kashaku had been a faithful and devout Roman Catholic: An old priest who ministered at Makiro parish (i.e., the parish of Kanungu) in the mid-1950s told me that Kashaku used to be his best catechist. This might also explain why he apparently met with strong opposition when the movement began, if we are to believe the handwritten history. According to the document, in 1960, Kashaku had an apparition of his daughter Evangelista, who had passed away in 1957. "She brought him a message to say that sometime to come he would receive in his home special visitors from heaven." Visions and apparitions are reported to be quite common in the area. The predicted visit reportedly took place eighteen years later:

> Paulo had just finished saying morning prayers at his home on 27.2.1988, when he saw three people from the sky coming towards him when he was in his bed-room. On arrival, they identified themselves as Jesus, the Blessed Virgin and St. Joseph, Patron of virgins. The Blessed Virgin Mary . . . said . . . that they had brought him "a special blessing," namely that his home would from that time remain "a holy family," until the end of the present generation. Jesus in turn told him that he was giving him [Paulo] also a "special blessing" by which he would receive powers

to take curses away from the people who would come to him, in the name of Abraham, and, that by the virtue of that blessing Paulo would become the father-in-faith of those who would believe in the message in the same way Abraham became the father-in-faith of all who believed, like himself, in the message he had received from God.

Paulo was also asked by Jesus to let him use his land as a place of gathering for those who would answer the call—the compound of the group in Kanungu was built on this piece of land, which Kashaku made available. It is for this reason that the group settled in Kanungu despite the fact that, outside of Kashaku's family, few local people converted. Several of his children and grandchildren also received apparitions, and some of them are said to have met with strong opposition from the local Roman Catholic parish. Local people report that Kashaku first rejected his daughter's visions but finally converted and became a pillar of the group (Bwire 2007, 66–67): His role may thus have been reinterpreted by the group following his conversion.

While the text found in the burned-out church mentions that the foundational revelation to Kashaku was received in February 1988, an important document dated January 15, 2000 (two months before the final events), a typewritten letter sent by the leadership of the group "on behalf of all the members of the organisation" to the residential district commissioner of Rukungiri District, as well as to various other officials, mentioned that the apparitions leading to the movement's founding started in January 1987. It is difficult to assess the exact chronology, but all sources tend to agree that the movement really took shape in 1989.

The handwritten history reports some persecution against Kashaku's family in late 1988 and early 1989: Some of his relatives, including Credonia Mwerinde, were jailed for some time, while children of the family were sent away from the school. It is unclear whether the reasons were only the alleged revelations or reflected other tensions.

In 1989 Kashaku's daughter, Credonia Mwerinde, and granddaughter, Ursula Komuhangi, were allegedly sent by Kashaku, upon instructions by the Blessed Virgin, to take the message to other parts of the country, to which they would be directed. The report of that initial apostolic travel—the accuracy of which can obviously not be confirmed—is fascinating since we see the two women encountering other people who had seen apparitions, one of whom was Joseph Kibwetere, who claimed to have had apparitions since April 1984. They met with him in June 1989, we are told: "Jesus and Mary directed them all to meet and thus the nucleus of the ... community was formed"; "Jesus and Mary then told them to go to Mbuye to meet one of their children and present to her 'a special message' given to Paulo Kashaku."

Mbuye is a place in the Masaka diocese where apparitions were said to have taken place since 1987, which were condemned by the local bishop in May 1989 (Gifford 1998, 150). The messages received in Mbuye put great emphasis on AIDS, exactly as the literature of the MRTCG would do; the Virgin was expected to reveal there a cure for the disease (Battiata 1988). There was also a connection between Mbuye and the already mentioned apparitions in Kibeho, Rwanda, since a visionary in Mbuye, Specioza Mukantabana, was a Rwandan girl who claimed to have been one of the seers of Kibeho, though her name is not found on the list of acknowledged visionaries there. The emerging MRTCG explicitly went to Mbuye in order to get a confirmation, which is a typical legitimation process in the milieu of Marian apparitions, functioning on a networking basis, with visionaries confirming each other's legitimacy, but without organizational control over one another.

It is reported in Kataribaabo's handwritten history that the first members were found in a lay apostolate movement in the Mbarara diocese, the so-called Reparatrix-group, "which was dedicated to the reparation of the Sacred Heart of Jesus, wounded by the sins of mankind." In a chapter of a thesis he was writing in 2001, which he kindly shared with me, Msgr. Edward Baingana-Muntu, currently the vicar general of the archdiocese of Mbarara and the foremost expert on Marian visionary networks in that area, indicates that several female groups promoting "prayer and fasting to stop God from inflicting punishment on humanity because of the sins in the world" appeared during the 1980s in the Mbarara diocese. One of those women was Hilda Ruhesi, a close friend of Kibwetere's family. Kibwetere visited Ruhesi's informal group at some point in 1989, Baingana-Muntu reports: He was impressed by their prayer sessions and came another time with a group of people, among them Credonia Mwerinde. Baingana-Muntu explains how they actually attempted to "hijack" the group, leading to tensions between the emerging MRTCG and Ruhesi and finally to a break between them in November 1989. The MRTCG was apparently more successful with recruitment in some other groups in the diocese; thus, the MRTCG initially developed on the basis of preexisting circles and networks that it attempted to win over to its cause.

According to several reports, such as the observations made by the research team from Makerere University (Kabbazi-Kisirinya, Deusdedit, and Banura 2000, 14–15), the MRTCG actually started at a place in the Rwanyabingi Hills, where a rock (called Nyabugoto rock) bore some likeliness to the Virgin (Rukungiri District). This place had been known since the 1930s. In the 1980s a woman named Gaudia Kamushwa claimed to have received a vision there; Credonia Mwerinde was said to have joined her. Mwerinde's former husband told journalists that she had gone there first in 1987 and upon her return had claimed to have seen an apparition there and that the Virgin Mary had given her instructions, including abstaining from sexual relations. It is difficult to determine whether (or to what degree) the Nyabugoto episode was as significant as reported in some articles. Teresa Kibwetere confirmed having visited Nyabugoto three times but did not seem to attach much importance to it. Curiously, the handwritten history does not give significance to Nyabugoto—possibly because an attempted takeover of the place did not work due to the resistance of the local people, who remain careful to this day to prevent the strangely shaped rock from becoming a place of pilgrimage and who were not willing to tolerate the settlement of an MRTCG community. According to the handwritten history, neighbors used the name "Nyabugoto" as a sobriquet to describe the pioneer community in a derogatory manner. However, since Kataribaabo was not yet part of the group, he obviously had to rely on information shared with him by Mwerinde and others regarding that period.

Like so many other visionaries, the founders of the MRTCG first attempted to get church leaders to accept their message. According to the January 15, 2000, letter to several Ugandan officials mentioned earlier, "we proceeded to report the matter to religious leaders as is commonly done, they accordingly advised that we should continue praying as usual and that they would tell us what to do next. We did what we were advised to do." It is difficult to know whether this was really the case, but the next step was predictable:

> In 1989 the Blessed Virgin Mary and our Lord Jesus Christ came to us again and said that we should take the massage [sic] to the people because, they said, the punishments, especially Aids [sic], are going to wipe them out before they know what God is asking them to do.
>
> We went back to the religious leaders, they told us that the message was correct and orthodox but that we should wait while they carry out investigations. In the same year 1989, our Lord Jesus Christ and his Mother, the Blessed Virgin Mary, ordered us with authority to take the message to the people. From then on, we started teaching the message slowly and gradually believers started coming, as a result there arouse [sic] a lot of persecutions and tortures of various types.

This may be a somewhat "soft" record of the events: It is far from certain that the small group of visionaries was so willing to submit to the judgment of the church hierarchy. Nonetheless, as far as some aspects are concerned, the scenario would be quite typical of the birth of such groups: The visionaries first attempt to gain official recognition; church officials attempt to convince them to keep quiet and wait in the hope of preventing the group from drifting away from the church, but the lack of fulfillment of the visionaries' expectations finally leads to a break and to the birth of a new movement—even if many members continued to consider themselves as Roman Catholics, something that is also quite common in such cases.

When a visiting priest asked two of the MRTCG clergymen why they did not carry out their mission under the supervision of their bishop and whether this was therefore not a breach of their promise of obedience, the reply—quite logically from the viewpoint of the MRTCG followers—was this:

> Not at all, Father; our Lord Jesus Christ himself came to us and said: "I have sent you to the Bishops several times to ask them to accept my message and also my Mother's, and they have rejected it"; he went on

"now, between me and those bishops you will choose whom to follow: either me, and I then send you to work for many creeds, or you follow the bishops, where you will work for one creed?" We obviously opted to give our allegiance to Christ consistently following the promise of obedience which we had made at our ordination (MRTCG 1996, 162–63).

The Message of the MRTCG: A Response to Changes in Church and Society

As the mention of working "for many creeds" in the preceding quotation indicates, the self-understanding of the group was that it was to be a movement carrying a universal message addressed to people of all beliefs—a message of salvation at a time when the world was heading toward destruction due to its lack of respect for the Ten Commandments, with AIDS being understood as a punishment for the breach of the sixth commandment (dealing with the sin of adultery) (MRTCG 1996, 2–3). Besides the preexistence of a Marian visionary culture and milieu that was conducive to the emergence of the MRTCG, several factors in the local environment certainly contributed to the impact of the group. According to an article by Emmanuel K. Twesigye and other researchers from Ohio Wesleyan University, the issue of AIDS should be seen as central in the doctrine of the group since it was declared to be God's eschatological plague punishing evil and sin (Twesigye, Aden, and Benedicts 2005, 457–58). Uganda had one of the highest rates of infection in the world. In such a context, the preaching of a strict observation of the Ten Commandments and celibacy in a group adopting some quasimonastic features would make sense. There is no doubt that AIDS was a factor in the development of the MRTCG, but the group was not alone in preaching that AIDS was a divine punishment.

Although the MRTCG emphasized that its message was not reserved for Catholics, Roman Catholic features were strong. There was also clear defiance of some of the modern developments within the Roman Catholic Church. In an interview with a Ugandan journalist, Fr. Paul Ikazire, who left the movement after a few years, confided the following:

> We felt things were going the wrong way. Our Church was reneging on its commitments to give moral leadership to her flock. There was a desperate need to change the manner in which Church business was being conducted. Joining Kibwetere and Credonia was done for the sake of generating ideas on how to rekindle fire in a dying faith.

Notwithstanding some possible retrospective self-justification on Ikazire's part, the statement is clear evidence of discomfort with trends within the Roman Catholic Church, already expressed by Kibwetere in the 1970s. As much as a matter of faith, it was an issue of changes in practices. For instance, the book published by the MRTCG under the title *A Timely Message from Heaven: The End of the Present Times* (MRTCG 1996) was critical of receiving communion in the hand (a practice introduced in the Roman Catholic Church at the time of the liturgical reforms accompanying the Second Vatican Council in the 1960s). A message "from Heaven" received by Ikazire stated that "reception of Holy Communion should be as it was in the past, the people should kneel down and receive Him on the tongue" (MRTCG 1996, 76). Similarly, the book contained a criticism of the practice of general absolution "without confessing your sins to a priest": This was seen as not conducive to true repentance: "The Sacrament of Penance ought to be restored to its proper state" (MRTCG 1996, 81). Another revelation instructed that clergymen and nuns should stop dressing "like ordinary people" and rather return to wearing religious habits such as cassocks (MRTCG 1996, 131). Traditional devotions such as the recitation of the rosary were strongly encouraged.

The overall ideology was what could be described as a "selective traditionalism." There was opposition to some aspects of the reforms brought about by the Second Vatican Council but no rejection of the council itself, and the pope was recognized as legitimate. The new church in Kanungu had an altar against a wall and not facing the people, but Mass was celebrated in the vernacular, not in Latin, while local people report that drums were used, too, as is common today at Roman Catholic Masses in Uganda. The idea of being open to people of other religions to the extent that they could become part of the movement without giving up their affiliation (which was rather theoretical since the group's daily practices were strongly derived from Roman Catholicism) also represented a view that no Catholic traditionalist could share. One could thus describe the MRTCG's approach more as reflecting elements of a traditional piety than Catholic traditionalism as such. Such a mixture of traditional piety and innovations can be found in other movements derived from Catholicism and based on visions and apparitions: Revelations provide a space for introducing changes with heavenly approval.

As is obvious, the apocalyptic dimension was strong, which is not surprising in the religious atmosphere that gave birth to the MRTCG: "Most apparition devotees have understood recent Marian apparitions as part of a pattern of divine activity in the 'last days' immediately preceding the Second Coming of Christ" (Zimdars-Swartz 1991, 246). I discuss the issue of date setting in the MRTCG later, but the messages received by visionaries in the movement are replete with somber prophecies: "There will be a great tribulation upon all people such that has never before been experienced by any person since the creation of the world. Those who will not have repented from their sins will experience it most" (MRTCG 1996, 46). There was also the promise that some places associated with the MRTCG (e.g., an "ark of salvation") would be safe in the last days—a notion that can be found in some other Marian groups. The following passage in the doctrinal book of the MRTCG deserves to be quoted in full since it appears to have partly set the stage for the scenario that would lead to the burning of the church in Kanungu with the faithful inside, though it does not mention a "rapture" of the elect—but such scenarios are usually adjustable. It follows prophetic descriptions of disturbance to come on earth:

> Suddenly there appeared three holy ones of God who made a sound which was heard by everybody, and it definitively said:
>
> THOSE OF YOU WHO HAVE BEEN REDEEMED, GO TO TAKE UP YOUR PLACES!
>
> After all this there came the three days of darkness, an event that has never been experienced since the beginning of creation.
>
> Those who had repented were told to go into hiding to the houses they had built for this purpose, these houses called "Ark" or "Ship." They were ordered to shut all the doors and not to open anything at all. All activities such as eating, praying . . . should take place inside for three days.
>
> Anything that remained outside in the dark turned into devil. These devils lamented and cried for three days after which they were thrown into hell. (MRTCG 1996, 59)

It was not enough for people simply to believe the message in order to be saved: They should also live in accordance with the Ten Commandments and preferably join the community. This was done in several steps. In a revelation Jesus had called Kanungu the "motherhouse," "the gate of heaven," and the place of refuge "during the days of chastisements." Before going to the holy place, people had to take four-to-six-day courses at regional "learning centers," where they listened to the whole message being read to them. According to the handwritten history:

> Presently Our Blessed Mother Mary has said that the student of the message will be required to make only ten rounds of the entire message under the supervision of a commissioned teacher. The readings that you do when you are alone do not count.

Life within the community was strongly regulated and included many hours of prayer, "recited at an extremely slow pace" (Atuhaire 2003, 51), and heavy work. Chastity, poverty, obedience, and silence were listed as the features of the community. Life there was reminiscent of that in some monasteries, with practices such as silence (except for prayer) and sign language, based on the idea that sin came into the world through speaking. As Atuhaire (2003, 48–49) observes, there were no gates or physical barriers, but people entering the compound entered another, silent world. Another similarity to monasteries was the encouragement of a life of celibacy, even among married people, which is something often connected to the imminence of apocalyptic events.

Members sold land and property in order to join, which created serious tensions with nonmember relatives (Atuhaire 2003, 69). Before settling at the compound, new members had to fill out a form and present it to the local authorities of their village in order to cut their links with their original surroundings, including the fact that, in case of death, they would be buried at Kanungu and not in the village: this marked a real break with the communities from which they came. Thus, it is not surprising that one comes across a number of instances of people attempting, sometimes repeatedly, to convince a family member to leave the group. In some cases, people vacillated, first leaving the group, then returning to it: Such cases are quite reminiscent of similar issues surrounding high-demand religious communities in the West.

In accordance with the message found in the book presenting the teachings of the MRTCG, the confession of sins was a serious matter. This is evidenced by a handwritten confession found at Kanungu and translated by Atuhaire. It contains statements such as "I broke each Commandment more or less 1 to 100,000 times," along with more precise statements (Atuhaire 2003, 115–17).

The group maintained its own school for children, something that would also create conflict. Apparently the school was closed down by the authorities in 1998 for reasons the MRTCG members claimed not to know. Moreover, according to a typewritten document dated May 12, 1995, and obviously intended for visiting officials, the group stated that it had not originally planned to open its own school, but they had decided to do so as a result of strong tensions with the local people, which had led to the mistreatment of MRTCG members' children at local schools and even their eviction. I return later to the issue of tensions between the MRTCG and its neighbors.

Reading Kataribaabo's handwritten history and the listing of the group's achievements, including material ones such as the establishment of a farm and a school, together with the spiritual ones such as having published their message in three languages and spread it to all parts of Uganda, one can see that the MRTCG's founders were quite proud of what they had managed to do solely through the work of the group's members. Strangely for a movement with such a strong emphasis on the imminence of the end-times (but maybe not so strangely if the place was to be an ark left untouched by the tribulation before the emergence of a regenerated earth), the document also listed ambitious future plans for material infrastructure, including more land, a health clinic, a secondary school, and so on.

The Events of the Year 2000

Expectations of dramatic events and an ascent of the elect to heaven were part of the group's beliefs. At some point during the months before March 17, something went terribly wrong, although this would only be discovered in the days after the March events. Either to get rid of followers who possibly had become rebellious or to force events toward a final scenario by helping people die,[5] hundreds of people were secretly killed at four locations around the country, at properties belonging to the MRTCG: in Buhunga (153 bodies); in Rugazi, at a house that used to belong to Fr. Kataribaabo (155 bodies); in Rushojwa (81 bodies); and in Buziga near Kampala (55 bodies). A majority of the victims were women and children. Many bodies showed signs of strangulation, according to the report of the Uganda Human Rights Commission, but there were also isolated cases of stabbing or fractured skulls. At Buziga, the 55 bodies were reported to have no signs of strangulation, and they were probably poisoned, according to the pathologist who examined them. This implies that not all of the people were necessarily killed in the same way—and probably not at the same time: Some of the killings had been recent, while others could have been committed up to six weeks earlier. The people buried in the mass graves were packed closely together in small spaces. At one place, possibly for reasons of convenience but possibly also for symbolic reasons, all of the bodies had been buried face down. Some people conjectured that the people killed before the fire had been members who started to become rebellious, while the elect died in Kanungu: This is possible, but it remains speculative as there is no proof supporting the thesis, and the lack of information about the people killed at the various locations (e.g., their identities and their status within the movement) prevents any attempt to classify members and the way they died according to different statuses within the MRTCG.

But all this was not yet known to the world on March 17, 2000. Hundreds of members of the MRTCG had gathered at Ishayuuriro rya Maria, as the headquarters of the movement was called. They prayed in the newly built church in their compound. Around 9:50 A.M., a relative of some of the members who was staying in the guesthouse at the entrance of the compound saw them leaving the church in a procession. They went to the old church, which had been converted into a dining hall. Around 10:30 A.M., an explosion was heard, and the old church was engulfed in flames. People working in nearby field hastened to the scene and heard the screams of people burning alive inside the church but could do nothing to rescue them.

Kanungu is a remote place not far from the border with the DRC. Uganda does not have forensic facilities like those found in Europe or North America. Police officers there work with poor infrastructure and equipment. Identifying charred bodies or decaying bodies found in mass graves, especially in such huge numbers, was beyond the capacity of Ugandan law enforcement and, indeed, would have posed major challenges in any other place in the world. A consequence was the impossibility of knowing whether all of the leaders of the movement had died in the conflagration. Several local people were fairly sure that they recognized the body of Fr. Kataribaabo near the door of the church, wearing a clerical collar, but there was no way of knowing about the other leaders. Interestingly, it became known later that Kataribaabo had been the one who had bought the material used to start the fire in the church; thus, he probably knew what would happen once the doors were closed, although some people conjectured that he had intended or attempted to flee at the last minute, but these are merely suppositions.

On April 6, 2000, international arrest warrants were issued for several leading figures of the MRTCG, and police offered a reward for finding them. However, to this day, there is no evidence either that they survived or died. Along with most investigators, I tend to believe that they perished (with Kibwetere possibly dying before the event), but due to the lack of certainty, we cannot entirely rule out that at least some of them survived, though this seems unlikely.

Some of the initial suspicions suggested that the "cult leaders" fled after defrauding their followers. While this would fit a popular stereotype, the facts about the events that took place in the weeks before March 17 do not match such hypotheses. Witnesses whom I interviewed, as well as several media reports and the report by the Uganda Human Rights Commission, confirmed that members of the community in Kanungu sold their belongings (e.g., their cattle) much below market prices in the days before the events:

> The local residents say that a cow that would have ordinarily been sold for about Shs. 300,000 was going for as little as Shs. 100,000 or less. They had two shops in the nearby Kanungu trading centre whose merchandise was also cheaply sold off before 17 March 2000.

Property outside of Kanungu was also sold at bargain prices. Debts were settled: On March 14 three representatives of the movement spent the entire day at the regional administrative headquarters paying the poll tax for each member of the community This does not really fit a "murder for profit" scheme, especially since the money was primarily used for settling all debts, including taxes: It was to be an ordered ascent to heaven, it seems.

Moreover, no reliable witness has seen any of the MRTCG leaders alive since. Still, some witnesses who were in the Kanungu area on the day of the event claim that some of the leaders departed shortly before the event. This was alleged again by one of the few survivors, who by chance had been out of the compound at the time of the fire: "Mwerinde and Kasapuri had left the camp during day time," and "they were going to prepare another branch for similar prayers. Kataribaabo had left in the morning ahead of the others" (Nkurunziza 2007). Regarding the three people who were seen nailing up the windows from the outside, a police officer claimed that they were members of the community. Did they join the others inside later? Since it is not clear whether the doors were bolted from the outside or the inside, this must be left as a question.

In 2009 the Ugandan police decided to "temporarily shelve" the file, although some investigators still believe "Kibwetere and the others implicated went underground and took a low profile" (Bogere 2009).

Depending on the survival of one or more leading figures, the events would be seen in a different light. However, it seems useful to list and discuss some of the hypotheses that were developed to explain the case since doing so might contribute to our general understanding of violent developments within a religious group.

Failed Prophecy—or Prophecy Fulfilled?

One hypothesis links the violence to growing discontent among members, possibly as a result of failed prophecy, but also to other complaints by people who had forsaken everything for the MRTCG, including selling their belongings, and who may have wanted their money back. Although we do not know all of the details, it is quite possible that such discontent created a growing pressure on the leadership and caused the violence or at least contributed to it.

The pressure created by failed prophecy would make perfect sense if the leadership of the group had announced that the world as we know it would end by the end of 1999. Several people in Uganda claimed that this was the case, and it was also reported in various newspapers. The discovery of corpses in several mass graves seemed to confirm the interpretation of murders as a result of prophetic failure. However, documentary evidence does not tell the same story, to the extent that one wonders whether widespread expectations within Ugandan society regarding possible events at the time of the passage to the year 2000 were not projected on the group by outsiders.

The book published by the MRTCG in 1996 reported the following:

> When the year 2000 is completed, the year that will follow will not be year two thousand-and-one. The year that will follow shall be called Year One in a new generation that will follow the present generation; the generation that will follow will have few or many people depending on who will repent (MRTCG 1996, 53–54).

However, the same book mentioned the possibility that God, due to the growing disobedience of people, could "shorten the period stated and . . . close this generation before reaching to the year 2000" (MRTCG 1996, 61). Thus, some flexibility was granted: There could have been expectations of the end-times at previous dates. Although detailed evidence is lacking at present (more documents could, however, still emerge), we have reason to believe that the leaders had already expected an apocalypse a few years earlier, probably in 1997, while some sources suggest the prediction was even made twice. This could certainly have created pressure, although it would have been relatively easy to resolve it by saying that God was still granting a time of mercy.

Most extant documents indicate that the group was normally expecting events in the year 2000 and not before. Kataribaabo's handwritten history of the group states: "Our mission . . . is to invite all people to come and participate in the great feast of 'the redeemed' in the new heavens and new earth which will begin with YEAR ONE, after the year 2000."

Moreover, the certificate of incorporation of the MRTCG, dated December 1998, contains the following statement:

> Another objective for which God sent us this **NEW MOVEMENT OF TRUTH AND JUSTICE** [original emphasis] is to notify all the people in the world to prepare themselves for the closing of this generation which is already at hand at each one's door and also to prepare for YEAR ONE of the next generation after year 2000, which will consist of people who will enter new earth where sorrow and misery are absent.

During my first trip to Uganda, I met a Roman Catholic priest and teacher who had had a lengthy discussion with Kataribaabo on December 18, 1999; fortunately, he had kept the notes he had scribbled down after the interview, so we can be confident that his report is not a later reinterpretation. Kataribaabo told him that there would be no year 2001. If Kataribaabo and the followers of the movement had expected apocalyptic events at the end of 1999, he would certainly not have spoken about a later deadline twelve days before the supposed end of the world, especially to a person he would have liked to convince to join the movement. There is yet another element that shows how consistently the group expected a major change in the year 2000 and not by the end of 1999: A letter to regional civil authorities dated January 15, 2000, concludes in this way:

> When the year 2000 comes to and [sic] end, the present times or generation will be changed and there will follow a new generation and a New Earth, only those who have the Ten Commandments of God will go live in the New Earth. The year 2000 will not be followed by year 2001 but it will be followed by YEAR ONE in a NEW GENERATION.

Obviously, over the years the deadline for apocalyptic events has remained consistent. While speculation about events in late 1999 may have occurred in the movement, we have no strong evidence for it. Thus, while internal pressure may have played a role, it is by no means certain that we are dealing with a case of failed prophecy—unless the leaders wanted in some way to anticipate a possible failure. It is somewhat ironic that many media representatives and even governmental agencies in the West were busy consulting with experts about the possibility of apocalyptic groups committing violent actions at the very end of 1999, but the only group that actually exploded close to that period was not concerned with the time of transition to the year 2000 in itself. The agendas of apocalyptic groups often fail to meet secular expectations about them.

Possibly some observers did not grasp the unfolding of events as foreseen by the MRTCG. Confusion about different events might also have contributed to partly inaccurate reports by outsiders. What was expected for March 17, 2000, and possibly even for earlier dates might have been a Roman Catholic version of the rapture: The elect would be taken to heaven, while those on earth would still have a last opportunity to repent during the end-time turmoil leading to late 2000 and the ushering in of a new world.

This seems to be confirmed by a message from the Virgin Mary allegedly received by Credonia Mwerinde on April 8, 1998. The message had been written down in a local language and was roughly translated for me. It does not state clearly that core members of the MRTCG would leave this earth, but it suggests that important events would take place in the year 2000; one even wonders whether there is not an indirect reference to a death by fire since we read the following in that approximate translation: "Then start preparing in your hearts and don't be scared, because those were the experiences passed through by the first ones. Now do you think that the Uganda martyrs were forgotten by God?" This may just be a reference to expected persecutions, but considering the fact that most Ugandan martyrs of the nineteenth century perished by fire, the question should be left open.

Before these events were to take place, the members of the group were instructed to entrust their important documents to the care of the local authorities—which they did indeed do just before the events. Prominent among these important documents are land titles. And why? Because the police were supposed to make them available to former members (including Fr. Ikazire and Teresa Kibwetere), who would repent and then would come to reopen the compound, live there, and continue to preach the message. The document states that these repentant apostates should not refuse to fulfill this work because "few months" would remain to complete it. Obviously, if the repentant former members had to go to the local authorities in order to get the documents, the implication is that the faithful members would have left this earth in the meantime. The scenario seems to be perfectly consistent: expectation of the end of this world for late 2000 but rapture of the elect to heaven before the end.

External Pressure: Opposition to the MRTCG

In the discussions on violence and religious movements developed in various scholarly books over the past decade, one of the issues often raised is that of the role played by external pressure, which pushes fragile groups that perceive themselves as assaulted to resort to radical means, including self-destruction, to defend themselves (Wessinger 2000).

While most of the material suggests that this was not the primary factor leading to the end of the MRTCG, evidence can be found that serious tensions indeed existed between the group and the surrounding society. The group also believed that it had to endure much persecution.

This is revealed in a typewritten document in English signed by Kataribaabo in the name of the leadership and dated May 12, 1995. This document was given—and possibly also read aloud—to a group of officials (including the registrar for nongovernmental organizations) who visited the group on that day. The document mentions serious incidences of "persecutions." Besides the arrest of Credonia Mwerinde and other early members in 1988 and 1989 for various reasons, the most important events listed were as follows:

- In June 1990 "a team of persecutors" found them attending a Sunday service at a church, "closed all the outlets and started beating us and hurt us" until some parishioners came to their rescue. Apparently this frightened the group: "Frankly speaking on that occasion we humanly felt obliged to surrender the mission and return home. But again our Lord Jesus and His Mother Mary soothed us and replenished our fervor."
- In December 1992 a party of people from the parish in Kanungu planned to demolish the compound, but the local authorities apparently stopped them in time.
- However, the respite lasted only a few months, and then came the most important event:

On 5-10-1993 a team . . . stormed the place . . . and ordered everybody present to vacate the place within a period of three hours. The elderly and expectant mothers, especially for fear of the gun, had much suffering to experience. They all fled on foot and empty-handed. The indigenous children of the place, moved by team-spirit also went along with the rest. The home was abandoned, gardens unweeded, crops stunted and the meagre yields were eaten up by pests or harvested by thieves. . . . Practically a lot of property was looted. . . . In short every domestic article that was portable was taken.

The whole place grew wild, old houses collapsed, and so did these which were still under construction.

We had kept bees but the hives were also stolen; and the plantation of pineapples also became bushy. Obviously such a big damage retarded our progress.

From this it seems that the group was not able to return to the compound in Kanungu before late 1994 or even early 1995, which means the members apparently had to stay away from the place, at least as an organized group, for more than a year. This explains the image of total devastation and desolation described in the document.

So there was real trouble for the MRTCG at its headquarters in Kanungu. Interestingly, after the events of March 2000, apparently no media—and none of the people I spoke with in Uganda—mentioned such significant tensions, a fact that can only encourage foreign observers to remain cautious and be aware that they may not always be privy to all of the facts and thus may be missing crucial parts of the whole story. Moreover, some investigation of the group may have been planned in early 2000, although this is not very clear—if it were the case, however, it might have contributed to reinforcing the group leaders' concerns (Wallis 2005, 61–62).

An unusual interpretation was suggested soon after the events by Irving Hexham (2000), who thought that MRTCG members might actually have been victims of a witch hunt by the local populace (hence their death by fire) since there were indeed accusations of witchcraft against the group by some local residents: "[T]he possibility that people in the church were locked in from the outside and then set on fire by enemies who believed them to be witches could not be ruled out" (Hexham 2000, 7). Without dismissing outright a hypothesis coming from a scholar with expertise in Africa (though with no field research on this case), several elements plead against such an interpretation. It is striking that the group, which did not sell its property in Kanungu, entrusted the property deeds and other documents for safekeeping to the local police in Kanungu, which is certainly not the kind of behavior one would expect from a group in conflict with the local environment or authorities. In addition, there are too many indications that events were carefully planned by insiders: For instance, emissaries of the MRTCG came to visit several people who had been in touch with the group during the weeks immediately before March 17, telling them that the Virgin would come on that day to take them to heaven and later revisiting those they could not find at their homes. There was a definite desire to have every possible participant gathered in Kanungu on the fateful day, with the movement promising to pay for people's transportation costs if needed. Even former members were apparently invited. Several reliable witnesses also report that members burned belongings (e.g., clothes) during the preceding days. Even a few letters were reportedly left behind by people taking leave of their acquaintances, although I was not able to see any of them.

As in any case of this kind, mysteries remain that are unlikely to be fully elucidated unless somebody associated with the events suddenly emerges and provides explanations. One such mystery is the six bodies that were found in a pit dug in one of the rooms where members used to sleep. The bodies were those of muscular people, Ugandan policemen explained; they therefore assumed that these were probably the executioners who had strangled the MRTCG followers at other locations before the events of March 17 and were then themselves disposed of. One policeman remembers having seen the remains of a meal in a nearby room, but the bees that had been attracted by the smell had all died, which in his view was an indication that these six people had probably been poisoned (but no analysis could be carried out to identify the substance). These six people had died before the fire in the church. There is no way to know their identity. If they were the henchmen of movement's leaders, where did they come from? Were they members of the MRTCG or outsiders? Were they killers who had been involved in the Rwandan genocide of 1994 in flight to the nearby DRC and subsequently hired by the leaders of the MRTCG for a gruesome task? In any case, that the people found in the pit had been executioners is only conjecture: They could also have been killed for some other reason (Bagumisiriza 2005, 37). All such questions will probably remain unanswered, which is in itself an invitation to exercise caution before drawing final conclusions about a case loaded with so many uncertainties.

"You Will Be Hearing about Us . . ."

In the handwritten history, confirming doctrines found in the book *A Timely Message from Heaven*, it is stated that the community would "survive the year 2000 and it would begin with a new social order." The MRTCG was coming close to the time of what would prove to be a prophetic failure. In the history of millenarian movements, cases of failed prophecies abound: Most of them do not lead to deadly denouements, however. Nevertheless, it is true that the leaders might have found it a difficult task to confront disgruntled followers who had forsaken everything in expectation of the promised reward. According to a member who met a Catholic priest in early January, work had stopped at the compound because the end was very near (Bagumisiriza 2005, 96). To find a way back after a further failed prophecy and to appease people who had sacrificed everything would have been much more difficult than in possible previous cases with dates not so strongly anchored in the movement's fundamental beliefs.

Could the events of March 17 and the graves filled with bodies during the previous weeks have been an attempt to find a radical way out of their difficulties? It is quite possible, but it makes sense only with a mix of strong beliefs if the leaders also perished at that time. Other examples of violent ends show that such scenarios can indeed unfold. What is completely missing in this case, however, is a knowledge of the precise processes that led to the outcome and especially the way in which the leaders' interpersonal relations made it possible.

A credible witness who was a personal friend of Credonia Mwerinde but not a member of the movement visited Mwerinde on March 11, 2000. Mwerinde said the following to her on that day, less than a week before the finale in Kanungu:

> It is unfortunate that we have been unable to convince you to join us, but you have been adamant. For us, we shall soon be going to heaven, and you will be hearing about us on radio and reading about us in newspapers.

This is a striking statement, especially since it is reminiscent of similar attitudes in other groups that met a violent end. The leaders of the Solar Temple had wanted the group's "transit" to be "spectacular" and had taken care to send statements to a number of media (Mayer 1999). Jim Jones of the Peoples Temple stated: "We've got to go down in history. We've got to be in the history books" (Chidester 1988, 116). Leaders of such groups are not only concerned with their earthly, immediate interests: What matters to them is also their fame. They want to impress the world. They want—facing difficulties, opposition, and decline—to be recognized for what they think they are. Sometimes, even if it means sacrificing their own lives, as well as those of their followers, what they do is a consequence of a complex process of doctrinal rationalization. This would seem hard to believe if there were not some well-documented cases. Moreover, this is strangely similar to the logic found in a number of rampage shootings, such as at Columbine High School, where the killers had also wanted to impress the world and were speculating that movies would be made about them while they prepared for their deadly act. Both rampage shootings and millenarian violence may thus be ways of getting attention.

This is, however, only one possible interpretation. There are too many lingering uncertainties to allow one to be definitive. Tensions with the wider society, including the Roman Catholic Church, existed, although we have no evidence that this was the cause of the end of the MRTCG group. Other instances of failed prophecies had in all probability occurred. The hypothesis I propose, based both on the available evidence and on comparative insights gained from the study of other groups, is that all of these elements likely played a role: The murderous end of the group could have been a radical response to expressions of internal discontent along with a desire to make a radical statement to the world and to force its prophecy to be fulfilled. If the leaders all perished in the event, they had probably managed to convince themselves that they were about to go to heaven—even if this would need some human help and a fire of their own making.

NOTES

1. This observation emerges from a careful reading of the material available on the movement. Interestingly, other observers and I come to the same conclusion regarding the Order of the Solar Temple and the interaction between Jo Di Mambro and Luc Jouret, the two prominent leadership figures within the group: The "transit" of the Solar Temple would probably not have taken place without the interaction that developed between them.

2. This is taken from the handwritten history of the MRTCG, recovered from the burned-out church; for details, see the following section.

3. It is my intention to publish it in full some day. I would like to thank Terence Kinyera, at that time an officer with the Criminal Investigation Department, Southwestern Region, Mbarara, for kindly allowing me access to this document, which is an important resource for historical research on the MRTCG. I describe the untitled document as a "handwritten history," but only the first part of the document presents the origins of the MRTCG: The rest of the text deals with the various beliefs and practices of the movement,

especially related to the end-times and signs of the times. It was probably meant to become a book for spreading the message of the movement. While there is no clear title, an inscription at the top of the front page suggests that the working title at least was Obutumwa ("message").

4. Some sources external to the MRTCG claim that the date is not accurate and that Kashaku passed away several years later (Bagumisiriza 2005, 76).

5. Although the doctrinal context is entirely different, we should remember that the Japanese group Aum Shinrikyo had developed a concept of "merciful killing," and, due to the uncertainties surrounding the Ugandan case, we cannot entirely rule out such a possibility, though there is no evidence to support it.

REFERENCES

Atuhaire, Bernard. 2003. *The Uganda Cult Tragedy: A Private Investigation*. London: Janus.
———. 2005. Who Cares about Kanungu? *New Vision*. March 17. http://www.newvision.co.ug.
Bagumisiriza, Narcisio. 2005. *The Kanungu Tragedy March 17th, 2000, and Details of Related Discoveries: The Movement for the Restoration of the Ten Commandments of God*. Kabale, Uganda: Kabale Diocese.
Battiata, Mary. 1988. Ugandans Desperately Seek Miracles. *Washington Post*, July 25, A13.
Bogere, Hussein. 2009. Police Calls Off Kibwetere Hunt. *The Observer*, March 26. http://www.observer.ug.
Bwire, Robert. 2007. *Ashes of Faith: A Doomsday Cult's Orchestration of Mass Murder in Africa*. Amsterdam: Frontier.
Chidester, David. 1988. *Salvation and Suicide: An Interpretation of the People's Temple and Jonestown*. Bloomington: Indiana University Press.
Gifford, Paul. 1998. *African Christianity: Its Public Role*. London: Hurst.
Hexham, Irving. 2000. What Really Happened in Uganda? *Religion in the News* 3(2): 7–9, 24.
Introvigne, Massimo, and Jean-François Mayer. 2002. Occult Masters and the Temple of Doom: The Fiery End of the Solar Temple. In *Cults, Religion, and Violence*, ed. David G. Bromley and J. Gordon Melton, 170–88. New York: Cambridge University Press.
Kabazzi-Kisirinya, S., Nkurunziza R. K. Deusdedit, and Gerard Banura, eds. 2000. *The Kanungu Cult-saga: Suicide, Murder, or Salvation?* Kampala, Uganda: Department of Religious Studies, Makerere University.
Kassimir, Ronald. 1999. The Politics of Popular Catholicism in Uganda. In *East African Expressions of Christianity*, ed. Thomas Spear and Isaria N. Kimambo, 248–74. Oxford: Currey.
Kustenbauder, Matthew. 2009. Believing in the Black Messiah: The Legio Maria Church in an African Christian Landscape. *Nova Religio: Journal of Alternative and Emergent Religions* 13: 11–40.
Lewis, James R., ed. 2006. *The Order of the Solar Temple: The Temple of Death*. Aldershot: Ashgate.
Mayer, Jean-François. 1999. "'Our Terrestrial Journey Is Coming to an End': The Last Voyage of the Solar Temple." *Nova Religio: Journal of Alternative and Emergent Religions* 2: 172–96.

———. 2001. Field Notes: The Movement for the Restoration of the Ten Commandments of God. *Nova Religio: Journal of Alternative and Emergent Religions* 5: 203–10.

———. 2002. Endzeit in Uganda: Die Bewegung zur Wiederherstellung der Zehn Gebote Gottes. In *Afrikanisch initiierte Kirchen in Europa*, 52–71. Werkmappe "Sekten, religiöse Sondergemeinschaften, Weltanschauungen," no. 87. Vienna: Referat für Weltanschauungsfragen.

Movement for the Restoration of the Ten Commandments of God (MRTCG). 1996. *A Timely Message from Heaven: The End of the Present Times*, 3d English ed. Movement for the Restoration of the Ten Commandments of God, Karuhinda, Rukungiri and Rubiziri, Bushenyi (Uganda).

Mubangizi, Michael. 2009. Fire in the Name of God. *Observer*, March 26. http://www.observer.ug.

Nkurunziza, Andrew. 2007. I Narrowly Survive the Kanungu Inferno. *Monitor*, March 16. http://www.monitor.co.ug.

Twesigye, Emmanuel K., S. Aden, and Mollie Wollam Benedicts. 2005. The Ethics of HIV/AIDS and the Rise of an Apocalyptic Mariologist Movement for the Restoration of the Ten Commandments. *Scriptura* 89: 456–68.

Uganda Human Rights Commission. 2002. *The Kanungu Massacre: The Movement for the Restoration of the Ten Commandments of God Indicted*. http://infosect.freeshell.org/infocult/THE_KANUNGU_MASSACRE.doc.

Wallis, John. 2005. Making Sense of the Movement for the Restoration of the Ten Commandments of God. *Nova Religio: Journal of Alternative and Emergent Religions* 9: 49–66.

Wessinger, Catherine. 2000. *How the Millennium Comes Violently: From Jonestown to Heaven's Gate*. New York: Seven Bridges.

Zimdars-Swartz, Sandra L. 1991. *Encountering Mary: From La Salette to Medjugorje*. Princeton, N.J.: Princeton University Press.

PART III

Select Religious Groups Involved in Violence

10

Murder in Knutby: Charisma, Eroticism, and Violence in a Swedish Pentecostal Community

Jonathan Peste

The murder and attempted murder on January 10, 2004, in the small village of Knutby, one hour by car outside Sweden's capital, Stockholm, were immediately followed by massive media coverage not only in Sweden but also in several other countries. Both the media and the Swedish police soon realized that the violence was connected to Knutby's influential Pentecostal community, Knutby Filadelfia. The media gave considerable attention to the "strange" and somewhat exotic teachings and behaviors of the community—for example, the fact that one of the community's top leaders, Åsa Waldau (née Björk), was referred to as the bride of Christ (*Kristi brud*) in the community.

During the police investigation, the community's concepts of "coming home" (*att komma hem*) and "be taken home" (*att tas hem*) became metaphors for dying or killing members of the community as a merciful act. For some, it was a reminder that the violent potential in religion is not restricted to Islam but can also be found in contemporary Christianity. For others, certain similarities to violent new religious movements were evident. According to the police investigation, the trial, and the advice from psychologists and other experts consulted during the proceedings, Sara Svensson was manipulated by Pastor Helge Fossmo into murder and attempted murder. They had also had a sexual relationship, and at the time of the murder Sara Svensson was psychotic.

Journalist Terese Cristiansson, in her book *Himmel och helvete: Mord i Knutby* (2004), draws similar conclusions: Helge Fossmo used religious ideas to manipulate his former lover, Sara Svensson, into killing his wife. The attorney also claimed that Helge had killed his first wife, Heléne, on December 18, 1999, but the jury did not find conclusive evidence to support this allegation. The police, as well as Cristiansson, pointed out that specific circumstances in the teachings and social dynamics in Knutby Filadelfia also made the violence possible.

Journalist Jan Nordling, author of *Knutby: sanningen och nåden* (2004), maintains a generally critical attitude toward new religious movements. However, the book also contains an enlightening description of the community of Knutby Filadelfia, its history and theology, and its relations with the outside world.

Cecilia Södergren gives a balanced analysis of the violence of Knutby in her BA thesis from Göteborg University (2006), *Att tas hem: Makt och våld i Knutby Filadelfia*. She integrates a history of religious perspective with both psychological perspectives and gender-power theory when considering the impact of evolving religious ideas in Knutby. Aspects of Helge's behaviors had psychopathic features, but Knutby Filadelfia's theology and views of gender were also factors in the origins of violence there. Further, Svensson was no helpless victim; she played along and had an active role in planning, preparing for, and executing the violence.

In a book by scholar Eva Lundgren (2008), new perspectives and hypotheses are presented, many of which are speculative. Lundgren interviewed Helge Fossmo several times after his conviction. She not only points out some loose ends in the police investigation but also gives extensive consideration to how several influential pastors in Knutby Filadelfia all participated in creating a "cult of death." Lundgren's book *Knutbykoden* speculates at length on Helge's view that he is no more responsible for the violence than several other important pastors in the community. Her book shows that important ideological and behavioral elements in the inner circle of pastors in Knutby's community made violence possible. Helge's persuasive charisma, sexual ambitions, and perceptions of death were not unique among members of the inner circle of leaders of Knutby's Pentecostal community.

This chapter does not offer new answers to the question of who was responsible for these deaths. It is also beyond the scope of the present text to suggest a final account of what happened in Knutby. Instead, I present a critical overview of the history of the violence at Knutby Filadelfia and then discuss some potential explanatory perspectives on this incident.

The Story of Knutby: The Church and the Deaths

Home to one thousand residents, Knutby is sixty kilometers north of the Swedish capital, Stockholm. The town's Pentecostal community, Knutby Filadelfia, was formed in 1921. In 1934 Knutby Filadelfia had 106 members, but by 1984 the membership had dropped to 27. However, by January 2004 Knutby Filadelfia had 83 members and by January 2008, 94. Clearly a dramatic increase in the membership occurred after 1984.[1]

In 1985 Kim Wincent was elected pastor of Knutby Filadelfia.[2] He was thirty years old at the time. During his early youth he had become an alcoholic but was "saved" by Jesus Christ at the age of twenty-one. He became a member of a Pentecostal church, met his wife, Monika, and began working as a nurse. He attended several Bible schools organized by the Pentecostal movement, as well as the movement known as "the Word of Life," which was at the time—and still is—led by the charismatic and well-known leader Ulf Ekman. Soon Kim Wincent became a pastor at Knutby Filadelfia. At the same time, he continued taking courses at the Word of Life and tried to instill elements of the movement's charismatic teachings and practices in Knutby Filadelfia. Wincent's first year marked a new attitude in the community toward Knutby's nonmember population. Members started making an effort to be a part of Knutby society and to acquire a good reputation. Wincent became a part-time member of the fire department. The church also started a youth cafe and sponsored children's activities on its premises.[3]

There are important similarities between Pentecostal teachings and those of the Word of Life, which are heavily influenced by American charismatic teachings. Both movements teach the idea that the spirit of God can mediate God's will through prophecies and tongues. However, in the Pentecostal movement the new prophesies must be tested and accepted by the community or the elders. The Pentecostal movement has always worked in a democratic way: Its power resides in the board—the elders. In the Pentecostal movement everybody is equal before God. In the charismatic movement the idea of apostolic leadership is central, and God is believed to speak foremost to the leaders. Thus, a new view of prophecies was introduced into Knutby.

Some (but not all) of Knutby's more influential members opposed this new direction. One of the elders, Per-Arne Waldau, shared Kim Wincent's enthusiasm for these charismatic concepts.[4] When a power structure similar to that of the charismatic movement was established in Knutby, many of the older members left the congregation in protest.[5] Knutby's congregation was (and is still) not a typical Pentecostal community in many respects.

Kim Wincent worked to rejuvenate the community and made contacts with other Pentecostal communities close to Knutby. In 1991 Knutby Filadelfia had forty members. Per-Arne Waldau's son Patrik, at the time sixteen years old, had become close friends with ten-year-older Åsa Björk, a children's pastor in Uppsala's Pentecostal congregation. Björk was dismissed from this position the same year following allegations that she had had intimate relations with underage boys while working as a child pastor. Patrik Waldau brought Åsa Björk to Knutby after she divorced her husband.[6]

Soon Åsa was seen as a sign of God, "a fire," in Knutby.[7] She was viewed by many as a very charismatic woman. She was beautiful in her long dark hair, sang beautifully, and was able to give full attention to whomever she was speaking to.

She also claimed to have direct contact with Jesus. She did not have a religious upbringing even though her grandfather was a prominent pioneer in the Swedish Pentecostal movement (to whom she said she was proud of being related). Åsa herself sometimes mentioned her own childhood as having been a difficult one. Her mother was opposed to Åsa's involvement in the Pentecostal movement, and the conflict became so severe that she was forced to leave her parent's home.[8] Åsa Björk and Patrik Waldau married in 1994, shortly after he turned eighteen.

Åsa changed many things in Knutby Filadelfia. She was also very influenced by the Word of Life movement and combined its teachings with Pentecostal ideas. She traveled around Sweden to preach and to recruit new members. Several influential members of Pentecostal communities were recruited by her. She was appointed as pastor by Kim Wincent and developed a one-month religious education program. A new kind of apocalyptic vision was created, one that saw the "fire of Knutby" being spread all over Sweden and ultimately the whole world.[9] Knutby Filadelfia was considered to be especially chosen to mediate the will of God. Knutby's theology also included the idea that the end of times was near and that Jesus was soon to return to earth.

The demands on the members of Knutby Filadelfia increased. The church was the new family, and secular work was important only because it provided an economic base for the church. Different working teams were created, and team leaders were appointed. There were singing activities, classes, prayers, child care, and even a secondhand store. The pastors of Knutby Filadelfia traveled a good deal and were paid part-time by the congregation. China and India were chosen as strategic locations where the mission of spreading Knutby's faith would begin. Knutby Filadelfia also supported an orphanage in India. Members worked or socialized with each other almost every day of the week. Paradoxically, Knutby Filadelfia became more closed off from nonmembers living in the village.

The only way to be included was to unreservedly acknowledge the faith of Knutby Filadelfia. Some of Knutby's inhabitants were contacted by members of Knutby Filadelfia and "love-bombed"—that is, deliberately exposed to displays of friendship. The residents were contacted a number of times, but, if the overtures of the church members were not accepted, they never returned, and all contact was terminated. A dualistic teaching also developed. Sickness was seen as a sign of cooperation with the devil, and Åsa Waldau called the official Protestant Swedish State Church a tool of the devil.[10] Several of the older members and elders left the movement, especially after the elders' council was more or less replaced by the pastors' leadership.[11]

The view of the family, especially with regard to the roles of husband and wife, became very traditional and patriarchal. The husband was viewed as the head of the family, and the wife was to obey him. Åsa Waldau was to a large extent responsible for this development. At the same time, sexual activity was viewed as a source of power that would make humans free and clean.[12]

Knutby Filadelfia was said to be organized like a plow. There could be only one leader at the top because otherwise the plow would not be sufficiently sharp.

Åsa was the principal leader, followed by a trinity: her husband, Patrik Waldau; Helge Fossmo; and Urban Fält. Then came the rest of the leadership, consisting of five pastors: Kim Wincent, Emma Gembäck, Peter Gembäck, Johan Grimborg, and Per-Arne Waldau, the only member left from the elders' council. Finally came the rest of the members, the "bench padding."

At Åsa Waldau's invitation, Helge and Heléne Fossmo moved to Knutby in 1997, and Helge began working as pastor at Knutby Filadelfia. Åsa Waldau and Helge Fossmo had known each other for a long time and shared their inspiration from the Word of Life movement. They also had a creative approach to theology. Often Åsa came up with an idea that Helge, with his extensive knowledge of the Bible, could give legitimacy to. Exactly how and with whom the idea that Åsa was the bride of Christ originated is uncertain, but most likely all of the pastors accepted the idea that Åsa had a very special relation with Jesus Christ. Åsa and Jesus had a union of love, and her marriage with Patrik was only temporal. In the end Åsa would unite with Jesus for eternity. In 1999 she began wearing a special ring with seven diamonds as a symbol of this union. She also received the name Tirsa from the Song of Solomon. The book of Revelation was very important in creating a central role for Åsa in the apocalyptic theology of Knutby Filadelfia. According to Helge, Åsa was called the bride of Jesus and not the bride of Christ. Using the Jewish name was a way of showing solidarity with the modern state of Israel, according to Helge.[13]

Helge's wife, Heléne, suffered from periods of depression soon after moving to Knutby and was frustrated that Helge was spending so much time with Åsa Waldau. This made Åsa angry, and, according to Eva Lundgren (2008), Åsa warned Helge that her disobedience of God could be punished by death. Heléne was also critical of Åsa because she believed the bride of Jesus and heaven should be more generous. Heléne's lack of faith became a topic of discussion among the pastors, and Samuel Frankner was appointed to take Heléne into his pastoral care.[14] Several persons have testified that, toward the end of her life, Heléne expressed a longing for death and a desire to go to heaven.[15] At the same time, Helge became close a friend of Sara Svensson.

Sara, born in 1977, was the only child of a forty-three-year-old woman. She was overwhelmed with love by her parents but also had a life-threatening food allergy and as a child spent a good deal of time at the hospital. When Sara was twelve, her mother died of cancer.[16] After her mother's death, Sara took care of the household and her father. She cooked and cleaned but also developed a psychiatric condition. In the forensic examinations made in connection with the trial, a psychiatrist connected Sara's dependent personality disorder (*osjälvständig personlighetsstörning*) to the experience of the death of her mother.[17] Although Sara had friends and was seen as a positive and happy person, she also remained somewhat distant from others.

Sara grew up to be an ambitious, hard-working, energetic, beautiful, and charismatic woman. In 1996 she attended a Bible school and began working with persons with mental retardation. Sara met Åsa Waldau at another Bible school in 1997. Sara became convinced that Åsa was the first person who could truly guide her since her mother's death. Åsa called Sara "pure, sacred and close to God."[18] After coming to Knutby, Sara soon started working closely with Åsa as a community leader.

During the fall of 1999 Helge allegedly told Sara in confidence that his marriage with Heléne was not going well and that Heléne was impure. According to Helge, if Heléne did not improve, they would either divorce or Heléne would die. And divorce was not a good solution, according to the community. Meanwhile, without Sara's knowledge, Helge told Åsa and Patrick Waldau that he had dreamed that Heléne would die.[19]

In October 1999 Sara and Helge were allegedly sick simultaneously for forty days. They both had the task of praying for Åsa Waldau. Sara also prayed for Helge, and they were considered by the other pastors to be spiritually connected.[20]

Heléne Fossmo died on December 18, 1999, by a blow to her head. At first the police investigation concluded that Heléne had died by falling and hitting her head against the shower knob.[21] A few days later Helge announced that he was going to marry Alexandra Fossmo, the sister of Åsa Waldau.[22] Other than Helge's cold behavior, additional strange circumstances surrounded Heléne's death. She was wearing a nightgown when she fell in the bathtub and had a toxic amount of dextropropoxifen in her blood. The substance came from pain-relief medication that had been prescribed for Helge.

During the spring of 2001, Helge and Sara became more and more attracted to each other, and Sara's husband was repeatedly left alone while Helge and Sara went together into their bedroom and closed the door. On June 10 Sara drove Helge to the hospital after he began shivering. Sara stayed with him the whole night. When Sara's husband, Linus, came to the hospital to take her home, Helge suddenly had severe pains in his body, and Helge told Linus to go home without Sara—that he needed her. According to Sara, Helge told her that he was being attacked by demons and the devil and that he needed Sara to be constantly by his side for six months in his bedroom.

Helge's wife, Alexandra, moved out of their bedroom so that Sara could help him undisturbed.[23] Helge's and Sara's relationship developed until they were having frequent intercourse, and, according to Sara, their sexual relationship had a healing effect. Sara said that Helge once claimed to have become blind because of the demons' attacks but that he had regained his sight after sex. The rest of the community believed Helge and Sara were participating in spiritual battles with Helge's demons. If someone asked, which happened a number of times, Helge and Sara denied having sex.

Sara and Helge discussed whether their sexual relationship was adultery and concluded that it was not: Their love was heavenly. It was a heavenly relationship between pure siblings.[24] According to Sara Svensson's testimony in May 2001, Helge began asking leading questions about the possibility of killing in God's name.²⁵ This was, according to the testimony Sara gave during the trial, the beginning of a process in which Helge convinced Sara that she had to kill his wife and another man, Daniel Linde, whose wife Helge later fell in love with. According to Sara, Helge used different methods to influence her. He asked her different direct and indirect questions about killing and the will of God. Later he also sent her anonymous SMS messages, which requested that she kill Alexandra, messages she believed came from God. Helge allegedly convinced her that he was not the source of the messages. The later police investigation, however, proved that the messages came from Helge. When Sara once asked why she had to kill Alexandra, Helge answered that it would be an act of obedience to God.

Helge and Sara discussed what killing meant, especially the killing of Alexandra. Helge often used the words "be taken home" about the death of specific persons.²⁶ To be taken home meant that the person or the person's soul goes home to God. It was, according to Helge, a merciful act to kill someone like Alexandra, who disobeyed Helge and thus disobeyed God. At the same time, Sara and Helge told certain persons in the community, foremost among them Åsa and Patrik Waldau, about their affair. They wanted to get married, and they believed this was God's will. The other leaders of the congregation did not accept this view.

Then, suddenly, Helge changed his story and accused Sara of tempting him and of being a tool of the devil. He wanted to repent of his sexual infidelity. Sara now became the scapegoat of the congregation and felt more and more isolated from the rest of the community, while Helge convinced everyone that he had to deal with Sara's spiritual problems. During the spring of 2002 Helge gradually became less loving toward her.

The rest of the members of the congregation also changed their view of Sara. Before this, she had been a pure person with a particularly close relationship to God. Now she was believed to be connected to Satan. Helge accused her of tempting him and of leading him astray.²⁷

Helge told her that her sin could infect the other members of the congregation and directed her to stay in her room and not socialize with others. Sara felt increasingly isolated and interacted mainly with Helge, who was able to exert his influence on her undisturbed. In court, other members of the congregation testified that Sara met other people on a daily basis and that she seemed to feel all right.²⁸ Still, it was only with Helge that she talked about those things that mattered the most to her.

According to Sara, her relationship to Åsa had already declined before her sexual relationship with Helge came to light. Sara felt that Åsa made unreasonable demands on her. Sara also questioned the notion that Åsa had an especially close relationship with God.²⁹ It is not far fetched to assume a degree of competition between Sara and Åsa, both of whom were seen by the congregation as having extraordinary relationships with God.

Despite their own deteriorating relationship, Sara and Helge vacationed together in Norway during the summer of 2003. After this, however, Sara realized that Helge was having a sexual relationship with another woman, Carola, who was a married neighbor and a member of the church. By this time, Sara was convinced that the voice of Helge was also the voice of God, and she blamed herself for Helge's relationship with Carola. She was convinced that her role was to be Helge's slave. At the time, Helge was having relationships with three women; his wife, Alexandra; Sara; and Carola.[30]

On November 8 Sara attacked a sleeping Alexandra with a hammer. Sara said that she was extremely anxious on the night of the murder attempt. She knew that Helge was waiting in his car and that he was waiting for an SMS that would say that she had killed Alexandra. After the murder attempt, Sara was banished from the community and ordered to leave Knutby forever. She went back to her father's house in a distant town in the south of Sweden but maintained contact with Helge by telephone and SMSs without the knowledge of anyone in the congregation. Soon Helge and Sara began discussing another murder attempt.

Helge and Sara kept in touch by telephone. She also gave him practically all of her money, which had originally been a considerable inheritance from her mother. They also planned to kill Daniel Linde, Carola's husband. Sara was now allegedly focused on doing God's will.[31] Before the second murder attempt, Sara bought a pistol from criminals in Stockholm.

The night and early morning of January 10, 2004, Sara first shot Alexandra, who was sleeping in her bed. She then walked to Daniel and Carola's house and shot Daniel. At the same time, Carola and Helge were together in Helge's car. Daniel Linde survived the attack despite the fact that one bullet went through his chest and another through his jaw, stopping one millimeter from the aorta. Samuel Frankner, who was living in Daniel and Carola's house at that time, was awakened by the shots. He helped Daniel to phone for emergency help.

Sara Svensson was interrogated by the police on the evening of January 10 and arrested and charged with murder and attempted murder on January 11. On the evening of January 11 she confessed to the crimes. When the police asked her why she had tried to kill two persons, she explained that she had heard a strong inner voice that told her to do so. She did not mention Helge at all.[32] Helge was arrested on January 28, suspected of involvement in the murder of Alexandra Fossmo and the attempted murder of Daniel Linde. The prosecutor also decided to reopen the investigation into the death of Heléne Fossmo.[33]

The forensic psychiatric examination concluded that Sara suffered from a dependent personality disorder[34] or, more specifically, from an "unspecified psychic mental disorder with religiously colored beliefs of a psychotic variety."[35] Another suggested diagnosis was "extended psychosis."[36]

On February 16 several members of the Knutby community met with the police on their own initiative and provided new information. They had, as a group, previously refrained from revealing everything they knew. Now they jointly decided to give new testimony. The circumstances behind this decision are unclear. Initially the community members had protected Helge Fossmo.

However, they changed their testimonies in the face of the facts and their new perception of his personality. Helge was no longer a warm and loving person but a tool of the devil; the community believed that he had received "a lot of power from the devil."[37]

It was not until March 16 that Sara admitted to the police that she had had a sexual relationship with Helge.[38] The court noted in its verdict that it was the police who convinced Sara that Helge had written the anonymous text messages, not God. According to Sara, she was at first certain that she had committed the murder herself, but, after the police discovered the messages, she realized how smoothly Helge had played her.

Explaining the Violence

Some scholars claim that religious violence is inherently more vicious than other kinds of violent behavior. The inclusion of a divine or an ultimate authority makes people more willing to use extraordinary violence.[39] Others claim that religion is never the real reason behind religious violence; there are always other injustices behind it.[40] Finally, some argue that religious violence must be explained by studying the interaction between diverse religious, psychological, and social factors.[41]

Most religious persons and communities never become violent, irrespective of religious adherence. It is thus highly unlikely that religion is the only factor to take into account when explaining the origins of violence in religious communities. Particularly in small, close-knit groups that set themselves in opposition to the surrounding society for ideological or political reasons, many important factors come into play—including ideology-theology, group dynamics and behavior, personal background of the followers and leaders, as well as relationships with nonmembers and the larger society.[42]

Explanations of violence and terrorism in radical political or revolutionary movements and small groups have ranged from leaders' personal traits to volatile elements in certain ideologies and theologies (such as millenarian beliefs and dualism) to interactionist accounts. In a similar way, sociologists and religious sociologists have researched cases of violence in new religious movements. Roughly speaking, explanations have ranged from a focus on manipulative leaders to interactional approaches in which ideological development is related to group dynamics inside the movement and its interaction with mainstream society. More recently, interest in the decisive roles of charismatic leaders in the precipitation of violence has been growing.[43]

How can the violence in Knutby be related to these scholarly discussions? In the case of Knutby, the external society exerted no pressure; in fact, state authorities and other Pentecostal communities imposed no control of any kind. The community of Knutby developed freely in the Swedish countryside. It was successful in recruiting new members, and little attention was given to the few critical voices. Still, having a hundred members was a far cry from some pastors' vision that Knutby Filadelfia would spread throughout the entire world. There was no strong emphasis on millenarian expectations in the eschatology of the Knutby Filadelfia community. The teachings are postmillenarian, and salvation is to a large extent connected to personal spiritual and ethical cleansing. In direct parallel to this individualistic focus, the violence was motivated to a large extent by the personal needs of several persons—and legitimated religiously.

The principal explanation that has been offered is that the violence was committed for personal reasons, foremost Helge's own gains. After arriving at Knutby, Helge was able to retain a prominent role in the community even after the death of his first wife, Heléne. Later he managed to keep relationships going with three women: his second wife, Alexandra; Sara; and Carola, a woman who was married to another man. Helge used religious language and religious ideas to convince Sara to commit murder. The investigation of the Swedish Social Board compared Sara's experiences with those of physically abused women. Helge's alternation between love and abuse effectively caused her to break down. Simultaneously, Sara talked only to Helge about her innermost feelings, and in this situation a "traumatic binding" developed between them. Religious views, as well as perceptions of gender power, influenced the process.[44]

Finally, one more mysterious death is connected with the Knutby community. Eva Lundgren (2008) notes that Samuel Frankner was connected with the deaths of three Knutby community members. He was present when both Heléne's and Alexandra's bodies were discovered. Frankner also found the body of community member Ernest Davies in Lake Långsjön in southern Stockholm. Davies had been born in Ethiopia, was married, worked as a physical education teacher, and was physically fit. At the same time, rumors circulated that he had the "wrong" kind of sexual preferences, which was the worst kind of sin.[45]

There were teachings and socially sanctioned behaviors, especially within the inner circle of pastors in Knutby, that sanctioned certain kinds of violence. Without this social and ideological context, perhaps Helge's predictions of Heléne's death would have been questioned by the community members. Had it not occurred within Knutby Filadelfia, the police would already have been contacted following the failed hammer attack on Helge's second wife, Alexandra. Instead, the attack was handled quietly inside the community. Death, which the pastors frequently discussed, was given a deeper spiritual meaning. Death could function both as punishment and as salvation. There are strong indications that even the most important pastor, Åsa Waldau, the bride of Jesus, was expected to be taken home and united with her spiritual husband. Her earthly husband, Patrik, had a romantic relationship with another woman, and Åsa must have felt lonely in some way. The texts of SMSs presented at the trial reveal that Åsa seems to have hoped that Alexandra, who later died, would keep her company in heaven. Still, Sara and Helge had other primary motives for the killing.

Violence and religion can be connected in many different ways, but most often several interacting factors lead to the violence, as in the case of Knutby Filadelfia.[46] The Knutby Filadelfia violence is in many respects similar to cases of violence in new religious movements. Similarities to the prophetic and messianic claims of Jim Jones and David Koresh are evident, as well as to Aum Shinrikyo's perception of killing as an act of mercy. In Knutby, however, the prophetic claims were primarily connected with a woman, Åsa Waldau. Another difference is that Knutby had several strong leaders, and Åsa and Helge competed for absolute leadership. The violence of Knutby Filadelfia should perhaps be understood as a combination of lack of external control, social interaction between charismatic pastors, a theology of eroticism and death, and the egoism and psychopathic and psychotic behavior of Helge Fossmo and Sara Svensson.

NOTES

1. Lundgren (2008), 53–54.
2. Cristiansson (2004), 188.
3. Nordling (2004), 45–49.
4. Lundgren (2008), 54–56.
5. Nordling (2004), 40–45.
6. Lundgren (2008), 56–58, 67.
7. Ibid., 56.
8. Ibid., 58–59; Södergren (2006), 9.
9. Lundgren (2008), 64.
10. Ibid., 70.
11. Ibid., 68; Södergren (2006), 11.
12. Lundgren (2008), 63.
13. Ibid., 80–96.
14. Ibid., 97–118.
15. Ibid., 111.
16. Cristiansson (2004), 41.
17. Ibid., 42.
18. Ibid., 43.
19. Ibid., 33.
20. Ibid., 30.
21. Ibid., 24.
22. Ibid., 36.
23. Ibid., 44.
24. Ibid., 29.
25. Ibid.
26. Ibid., 107.
27. Ibid., 72.
28. Ibid., 74–75.
29. Ibid., 77.
30. Ibid., 84.

31. Ibid., 151.
32. Ibid., 171.
33. Lundgren (2008), 16–17.
34. Cristiansson (2004), 42.
35. Ibid., 76 ("ospecificerad psykisk störning med religiöst färgade övertygelser av psykotisk valör").
36. Ibid., 109 ("folie à deux").
37. Lundgren (2008), 17.
38. Ibid.
39. See, for example, Juergensmeyer (2000) and Avalos (2005).
40. See, for example, Pape (2005).
41. See, for example, McTernan (2003).
42. See, for example, Wessinger (2000).
43. Walliss (2006a, 2006b). See also several of the chapters in Bromley and Melton (2002).
44. Cristiansson (2004), 76.
45. Lundgren (2008), 112–13.
46. See, for example, Hall (2003) and Jones (2008), 3–28.

REFERENCES

Avalos, Hector. 2005. *Fighting Words: The Origins of Religious Violence.* New York: Prometheus.
Bromley, David G and Melton, Gordon J. 2002. *Cults, Religion and Violence.* Cambridge: Cambridge University Press.
Cristiansson, Terese. 2004. *Himmel och helvete: Mord i Knutby.* Stockholm: Månpocket.
Hall, John R. 2003. "Religion and Violence: Social Processes in Comparative Perspective." In *Handbook of the Sociology of Religion*, ed. Michele Dillon, 359–81. New York: Cambridge University Press.
Jones, James W. 2008. *Blood That Cries Out from the Earth: The Psychology of Religious Terrorism.* New York: Oxford University Press.
Juergensmeyer, Mark. 2000. *Terror in the Mind of God: The Global Rise of Religious Terrorism.* Berkeley: University of California Press.
Lundgren, Eva. 2008. *Knutbykoden.* Stockholm: Modernista.
McTernan, Oliver. 2003. *Violence in God's Name: Religion in an Age of Conflict.* London: Darton, Longman, and Todd.
Nordling, Jan. 2004. *Knutby, sanningen, och nåden.* Stockholm: Hallgren and Fallgren Studieförlag AB.
Pape, Robert A. 2005. *Dying to Win: The Strategic Logic of Suicide Terrorism.* New York: Random House.
Södergren, Cecilia. 2006. Att tas hem: Makt och våld i Knutby Filadelfia. BA thesis, Göteborg University.
Walliss, John. 2006a. Charisma, Volatility, and Violence: Assessing the Role of Crises of Charismatic Authority in Precipitating Incidents of Millenarian Violence. In *Exercising Religion: The Role of Religions in Concord and Conflict*, ed. T. Ahlbäck,

404–24. Åbo, Finland: Donner Institute for Research in Religious and Cultural History.

———. 2006b. "Millenarian Violence and Persecution: Rethinking the Role of Cultural Opposition." In *Hotbilder: Våld, aggression, och religion*, ed. Maria Leppäkari and Jonathan Peste, 177–94. Åbo, Finland: Akademi.

Wessinger, Catherine. 2000. *How the Millennium Comes Violently: From Jonestown to Heaven's Gate*. New York: Seven Bridges.

11

Modern Pagan Warriors: Violence and Justice in Rodnoverie

Kaarina Aitamurto

When Rodnovers, the followers of the Slavic pre-Christian spirituality,[1] talk about the different spiritual paths that people may choose, becoming a "warrior" is the one that is usually mentioned first. The military ethos of Rodnoverie is also manifested in the martial art fights that are usually featured in festivals and rituals. These may be symbolic representations of, for example, the victory of spring over winter, and they are considered a traditional means of honoring ancestors and sustaining and displaying the Pagan virtues of bravery and strength. The image of a warrior is also connected to the social philosophy of Rodnovers. As a this-worldly religion, Rodnovers are particularly interested in improving the society around them. Confronting injustice and oppression inevitably brings the issue of violence to the agenda even when the goal is to find alternatives to the use of physical assault. Rodnoverie is an extremely fragmented and versatile movement, and societal views of its adherents range from pacifism to right-wing militarism. A small minority also subscribes to radical racist politics, and in some cases Paganism has been connected with ethnic violence. Recently, such groups have also gained attention in media—much to the annoyance of the majority of Rodnovers and especially, of Rodnovers who consider racism and violence to be incompatible with Pagan worldview.

The focus of this chapter is an analysis of philosophical and religious doctrines that accommodate such diversity and the influence of social context on diverse interpretations of the religion. As a case study, Rodnoverie blurs the idea of distinct religious movements that are prone to violence. Despite the fact that Rodnoverie is a new religious movement, the theoretical tools elaborated in the study of violence in mainstream religiosity often seem better suited to the study of Rodnoverie. Therefore, this chapter also bridges the analytical gaps between different types of religious organization.

History

Rodnoverie belongs to the same set of movements as Wicca, Druidism, and Asatru, but it emerged and developed quite independently of contemporary Western Paganisms. Very little documented information exists on the roots of the Rodnoverie movement. The reason for this is that in Soviet times such groups of religious seekers had to function in secret. When the Soviet Union began breaking down at the turn of the 1990s, small groups and charismatic wizards cropped up. Nevertheless, the formation of the movement would not have been possible had seeds not already been sown in the final decades of the Soviet Union. In the 1970s, Pagan currents emerged in the underground ultranationalist opposition. In 1979 Valerii Emelyanov, professor of Semitic languages and one of the founding members of the notorious ultranationalist organization Pamyat, published the flagrant anti-Semitic book *Desionizatsiya* (Emelyanov 2005).[2] Emelyanov suggests that Christianity was created by Jews to subjugate other people by imposing a slave mentality on them, to make them regard Jews as the chosen people, and to convince them to "turn the other cheek" to oppression. Therefore, Emelyanov urges Russians to return to their own Pagan gods in the fight against Jewish aggression.

Ultranationalist circles were not, however, the only setting where Pagan ideas were discovered and cultivated in Soviet times. Some small communities began to reconstruct Slavic Pagan religious practices (Rodoslav' 2006, 117), but many Rodnovers also found Paganism through other forms of alternative spirituality, such as Russian cosmism.[3] Especially important was Eastern spirituality, which was very popular with the Russian intelligentsia during the last decades of the Soviet Union. For the formation of the Rodnoverie movement, a much more influential book than Emelyanov's *Desionizatsiya* was an allegedly ancient manuscript on pre-Christian Slavic history and worldview; this was the *Book of Veles*, which came to Russia in the seventies from American emigrant circles.[4] One of its leading proponents, Mirolyubov, claimed that the *Book of Veles* talked about the same ancient Vedic religion as the Indian Vedic literature. Indian spirituality was, in fact, quite commonly taken as a representative of the original Indo-European religion and thus almost native.

Until the end of the 1990s, Rodnoverie had very few followers outside the small circles of intelligentsia in the big cities of Moscow and Saint Petersburg. The later expansion of the movement was mainly due to two books: the popular version of the *Book of Veles* by Aleksandr Asov and Aleksandr Belov's *Slavyano-goritskaya bor'ba* (Gaidukov 2005, 41). The latter volume introduces martial arts, which Belov claims he has reconstructed on the basis of folkloric material. Belov founded a martial arts club that had an impressive forty thousand members in its heyday. Even though not all of the members were Pagans, the club effectively disseminated Paganism to the Russian periphery.

Belov's Paganism cannot be equated with the radical anti-Semitic extremism of Emelyanov. Nevertheless, both of them share the idea that Paganism is a religion that calls for responsibility and encourages bold confrontation with the enemy. Ideologically, Belov is close to traditionalists such as Julius Evola or Rene Guenon, both of whom are, incidentally, known to many contemporary Rodnovers.[5] Also, Belov's ideas exemplify an ultraconservative elitism that does not lack some correlation with fascism. His militant nationalism becomes apparent, for example, in his claim that the word *rus* derives from the expression for "militant person" and that Paganism is the only religion truly compatible with a warrior identity (Belov 1993, 6–7). The *Slavyano-goritskaya bor'ba* attracted some radical ultranationalist followers, including skinheads, who combined Paganism with their nationalistic agenda and military mentality. Such interpretations of Paganism were, however, decisively rejected by Belov. Disappointment in his followers, financial problems, and accusations of fascism by the media eventually led Belov to dissolve the martial arts club and to found a secluded organization of "barbarian cast" with two hundred of his most trusted followers (Meranvil'd 2004). Though the image of a warrior was prevalent within Rodnoverie from the outset, it does not characterize all of the factions of the movement. In fact, one good indication of the orientation of a given group is whether it reveres Perun, the god of thunder and militia, or Veles, the god of cattle, poetry, and mysticism (Prokofyev, Filatov, and Koskello 2006).

The contemporary Rodnoverie movement is extremely heterogeneous and includes innumerable self-designated, small, and transient groupings. Some umbrella organizations have established their position, such as the Circle of Pagan Tradition, the Slavic Union of Slavic Communities of the Native Faith, the Church of Inglings, and the Circle of Veles. The last of these has gained popularity in recent years mainly due to its charismatic leader, Veleslav, who has written several books on the philosophy and the practice of Rodnoverie. The success of this organization also reveals a general trend within the movement toward being less political and more tolerant; Veleslav is a sworn nationalist, yet he consistently argues that the nationalistic love of one's own traditions does not and should not mean disrespect for and aggression toward other traditions.

No reliable data are available on the numbers or socioeconomic background of Russian Rodnovers, but virtually all scholars agree that men outnumber women and that the majority of adherents are relatively young, many of them students. Some youth subcultures have been crucial in introducing people to Rodnoverie. Especially noteworthy is metal music, particularly Pagan and Viking metal. Another avenue to Rodnoverie for many young people has been the *rekonstruktory* [reconstructionist] movement, which refers to a hobby that resembles live role playing.[6] The difference between these is that the *rekonstruktory* focus on certain historical periods and their activities include not only games but also, for example, the regular practice of historical martial arts.

An "Open-Source" Religion

Contemporary Paganism has no generally acknowledged sacred texts or authorities that could claim the status of gatekeeper. Consequently, Cowan (2005, 30–35) characterizes it as an "open-source" religion, implying the difficulties in demarcating and predicting the future of the movement. The heterogeneity of contemporary Pagan movements can be explained by their emphasis on the freedom of individual thinking. Though Pagans are often quite proud of their permissiveness, this also instigates endless debates within the movement on the definition of the religion and who has the right to use the designation of "Paganism." The diffuse and heterogenic nature of Rodnoverie also poses great challenges to scholarly attempts to define the movement and the religion.

Rodnoverie has several features that support its classification as a religion: It has its own theology, calendar, and transitional rituals, and it ponders the questions of morality, life after death, and the ways a human being can connect to the divine.[7] However, well-founded counterarguments to such an interpretation can also be made. In their ethnographic study of nationalistic youth groups in provincial Russia, Pilkington and Popov (2009) encountered people who use Pagan gods, imagery, and slogans. The young nationalists did not, however, have any ritual activity, and on closer examination their spirituality turned out to be quite syncretistic. In conclusion, Pilkington and Popov argue that Paganism cannot be considered a religion. Even though this argument is not convincing with respect to many other Rodnoverie groups, I suggest that contemporary Paganism in Russia is a phenomenon that reaches beyond the definition of religion. Political nationalism is the domain that most often overlaps with Rodnoverie as a religion, and one could well ask whether many groups can be considered political or religious organizations.

As important as it is to distinguish political motives and goals from religious ones, drawing sharp lines between them can be difficult and even misleading. Politics and religion are typically tightly interwoven, and their separation as distinct domains is based mostly on Western social philosophy. The subjectivity of the distinction unavoidably transfers one's own cultural values and, in the worst case, evaluative judgments. A common strategy for vindicating "religion" is to label the forms of religiosity that are not approved of as a political misuse of religion (McCutcheon 2005, 4, 68–69). However, despite the fact that many Rodnoverie groups are equally interested in spirituality and societal issues and regard these as interconnected, the difference between those that are focused on politics and those that are more religiously oriented is too prominent to be ignored.

The divergent roots of Rodnoverie in the nationalistic movement and in the intelligentsia who were interested in alternative spirituality attest that the political and more spiritually oriented forms of Rodnoverie were initially at least partially distinct. Even though these different approaches to Paganism often overlap, such division is still, to a certain extent, maintained within Rodnoverie. For example, some Rodnoverie groups have little ritual activity, and their publications mainly address political issues. Furthermore, in newspapers such as *Za Russkoe Delo* the analysis of current political events regularly refrains from referencing any spiritual framework.

Violence and Rodnoverie

While it may be difficult to determine whether some organizations are more religious or political by nature, it is even more difficult to determine the motivation of an individual act. In January 2009 an attempt to blow up a McDonald's in Moscow led police to three minors (the fourth member of the group, who was an adult, was released until further investigations could be carried out) who were later found guilty of several bomb attacks and twelve racist murders. The gang identified as Pagan Rodnovers but apparently had no connection to any mainstream organization within the movement. Though Rodnoverie was mentioned in media coverage of the episode, it was also noted that the group belonged to a skinhead subculture whose religious views feature a "hodgepodge of Paganism, Hitlerism and Christianity" (Movseyan 2009).

The violent attacks to which some Rodnovers have been publicly connected are predominantly ethnic hate crimes. It is difficult, however, to estimate both their number and the role that religion played. Racist violence is rampant in Russia, but the statistics shed very little light on the issue as police are often unwilling to admit the ethnic aspect or even to investigate such cases (Amnesty International 2007). As the majority of racist assaults remain unsolved, it is virtually impossible to approximate the percentage of Pagans among the guilty. Furthermore, there can be only tentative answers to the question of the extent to which assaults carried out by Pagans are religiously motivated. In recent decades, Paganism has established itself, though it is still marginal in ultranationalist and anti-Semitic circles. For example, on the web pages of two notorious extremist organizations, the "Movement against Illegal Immigration" and the National-Socialist "Slavic Union," Rodnoverie is presented as the second legitimately native religion after Orthodox Christianity. Some smaller racist groupings are committed to Paganism, but, in most cases, the religious conviction of the members seems to be of secondary importance.

Before analyzing how Pagan religiosity can justify the use of violence or how it can accommodate it at all, I want to make two points: First, those Rodnovers and Rodnoverie groups that commit violent crimes are undoubtedly in the minority within the movement (Prokofyev, Filatov, and Koskello 2006). Second, even though radical groups such as skinheads are usually excluded from the mainstream of the movement, it would be superficial and even misleading to divide these into two distinct phenomena. Individuals easily transcend such boundaries, and, more important, the philosophical underpinnings that foster violence can also be found in the thinking of people who do not commit violent acts.

Social Justice

Social philosophy is an intrinsic component in virtually all forms of religiosity. Perhaps in Paganism, however, it holds a central position. Rodnoverie (and contemporary Paganism in general) can be regarded as exemplary cases of world-affirming religion; consequently, Pagans are very concerned about our natural environment. It is quite common that Rodnovers argue on not only theological but also social grounds about their choice of Paganism as a religion. That is, not only do Rodnovers claim that people should choose Paganism because Pagan gods exist and that to ignore them would thus be unintelligent, but they also maintain that Paganism can make more valuable contributions to contemporary society than any other religion. Ecological claims are of key importance in this argument. Pagans argue that both Christianity and Western rationalism have placed human beings above nature and subjugated it to utilitarian goals. The only solution to the impending ecological disaster is, the argument goes, to restore a more respectful attitude toward nature, which can be attained only by a profound change in our values. Given that religion is seen as one of the fundamental elements of our worldview, Paganism is presented as a religious alternative that sanctifies nature.

Other than ecological issues, social justice is the most frequent topic when Rodnovers talk about their religion. The following is wizard Velemudr's response when asked why Paganism has recently gained so much popularity: "People want to be human beings and to preserve their own sociocultural belonging. Many of them have had enough of lies and injustice. People adopt Paganism because of the Justice [sic] that neither neo-Russian democracy nor religions have been able to give them" (Izvednik 2004, 142).

Interestingly, Velemudr positions Paganism against both democracy *and* religion. Many Rodnovers claim that Paganism is not actually a religion but a worldview, a philosophy, or simply a tradition. Similar reservations about the concept of religion can be found in Western antiauthoritarian alternative spirituality, but the Rodnoverie argument implicitly invokes a Marxist criticism of religion as the "opium of the people." In Soviet times, the Christianizing of Russia was explained in the context of the emergence of hierarchical, centralized power and the concentration of wealth. In light of Russian history and contemporary politics, it is easy to posit the Orthodox Church as an ally of the ruling elite and, therefore, as an accomplice to political suppression. The link to Marxism probably reflects more the legacy of the Soviet educational system and historiography than any political alignment; though many Rodnovers subscribe to leftist ideology, the majority of the movement seems to be closer to the right wing. Correspondingly, in addition to classic Marxist approaches, the anti-Semites denounce Christianity as a part of the "Jewish plot," and the Pagan version of the Slavophil approach highlights Christianity as an *alien* influence and the Christianizing of Russia as the conquest of Russia by a foreign ideology and foreign interests. Not only is criticism of the advice to "turn the other cheek" made by anti-Semites such as Emelyanov, but it is also argued that the Christian idea of final judgment suppresses the resistance of injustice in this world and enables the domination of those who use ruthless force. According to Dobroslav (2005, 69), it is "criminal" to turn the other cheek when Mother Nature is endangered.

The political and societal views of the Rodnovers are indeed far from uniform. In her analysis of the Rodnovers' attitude toward globalization, Koskello (2005) detects that Rodnovers can be politically positioned at the very extremes of liberal tolerance and conservative fundamentalism, while very few are centrists. Rodnoverie political views also range from right-wing conservatism to semianarchist socialism, as revealed by the names of some of the social programs Rodnovers support or have founded: "Vedic Communism" (Danilov 2000), "Social-Communism" (Yakutovsky in Izvednik 2004), "Ecological Socialism" (Novikov-Novgorodets 2007), "National Democracy," "National Capitalism" (Sevast'yanov 1996), and various interpretations of "National Socialism."

With regard to the topic of the present volume, sects and violence, one of the most relevant differences in the political outlooks of the Rodnovers is their approach to confronting social injustices and, hence, to the usage of violence. The fact that this issue is so topical in many forms of contemporary Paganism is attested by the frequency with which it appears in Western Paganism as well. For example, in her "visionary novel," the *Fifth Sacred Thing*, Starhawk (1999), a feminist witch and environmental activist gives a thought-provoking model of the pacifist confrontation of aggressive occupants in the fictitious setting of San Francisco in 2048. Pacifism is also presented as a distinctly Pagan virtue by some Rodnovers. Yakutovsky, for example, explains that indigenous Siberian Pagans would rather let the roof collapse on their heads than fight back because, according to Yakutovsky (1995, 70, 74), abstinence from "vicious deeds" is considered a virtue in Paganism. Pacifists are in the clear minority within Rodnoverie, but the issue of confronting injustice has roused elegant discussions that reflect a full range of political positions.

Virtually all Rodnovers subscribe to some form of nationalism, at least in the sense that they are committed to the preservation and revival of their native tradition. An important difference is, however, whether ethnicity is predominantly used as a crucial explanatory factor in the analysis of social problems as well: Nationalists claim that Russia's problems derive from foreign oppression, while other Rodnovers reject such generalizations and encourage Russians to be more concerned with their own problems than with blaming foreigners.

The difference between these two approaches is poignantly conceptualized by Kavykin, who divides Rodnovers into tolerant and xenophobic groups. Kavykin (2007) argues that while xenophobic Rodnovers construct their identity in relation to an outside enemy, this approach is lacking in the discussions of tolerant Rodnovers. The difference is manifested in the social programs of Rodnoverie groups and even in their leaders' biographies. While the principals of the xenophobic wing often recount the narratives of their personal lives as continuous struggles against the enemy, tolerant leaders describe their spiritual growth in terms of inner conflicts (Kavykin 2007).

The Multifaceted Image of the Warrior

The differing connotations and ideological underpinnings of the symbol of the warrior in Rodnoverie discussions also reveal Kavykin's distinction between tolerant and xenophobic orientations. The idealization of militancy is easily attached to the politics of hate, but the image of the warrior may also be used as a symbol of moral agency. Militant metaphors and, especially, the symbol of the warrior can indeed be found in many religions and are cultivated in religious groups that have no connection with violent acts or with the propagation of violence. Thus, it has been suggested that symbolic violence may also be an alternative means of expressing, processing, and releasing aggression. However, such arguments have not fully satisfied all scholars. Juergensmeyer (2003, 163, 171–74) reminds us that the symbol of the warrior nonetheless always implies an enemy and therefore also bolsters the dichotomy between "us" and "them."

Both of these interpretations—symbolic religious violence as a safeguard against and as an inspiration to acts of violence—are relevant to Rodnoverie. The warrior identity can commit Rodnovers to responsibility and be used as a means of expression. Nevertheless, even when the image of the warrior is imbued with the values of bravery, honesty, and moral agency, the shadow of the enemy still often lurks in the discussion.

The social criticism of Rodnovers is often quite constructive, but it may also resort to various conspiracy theories that are current in Russia more generally. The conspiracy theories have a tendency to explain the world in very Manichean and even apocalyptic ways. According to Juergensmeyer, the interpretation of mundane social situations in the context of war totalizes struggle into the extreme options of either winning or perishing, but a cosmic war further aggravates the conflict beyond any conciliation by identifying it with the eternal fight between the forces of good and evil (Juergensmeyer 2003, 149–53, 220). In extremist Rodnoverie rhetoric, Russia is repeatedly portrayed as an "occupied country" in which the genocide of Russians is ongoing, and, consequently, the current social situation can be described as "war." Within the framework of global conspiracies, the enemy is often demonized in a way that efficiently justifies and even encourages violence.

Demonization can mean plain dehumanization. One of the wildest theories argues that Jews and the inhabitants of the Caucasus region originate from the vampire monkeys of Lemurian swamps, who managed to seduce white men in the brothels of Egypt and thereby produce offspring that can talk and appear to be human (Popov 2003).

Some extremist Rodnovers do not hesitate to champion "might is right," but, in the majority of cases, aggression is justified by shifting the blame to the victims. The Russian ultranationalist press is full of stories on crimes committed by non-Russians and detailed descriptions of their arrogant and insolent behavior. The scapegoat strategy vindicates aggression, and this explains the curious contradiction in many extremists' texts where the authors proclaim their love of peace next to the rudest attacks on their enemies. Hence, even the ideal of Paganism as a pluralistic and tolerant religion can be compatible with militant anti-Semitism. An exemplary case is that of prominent Russian wizard Dobroslav, who manages to combine ecologically oriented philosophy with pacifism and National-Socialist politics. Dobroslav 2005, 92–93) argues that Paganism means respect for nature and life. He states that killing is against human nature and that it had no justification until the advent of the Manichean Abrahamic religions. The humanism of his views is, however, watered down because he practically excludes Jews from humankind, presenting Jews and Judaism as a plague that corrupted the original paradise.

While talking about Manichean cosmic wars and demonizing the opponent, it is good to remember that some specifically Pagan doctrines oppose these. Pagans are proud of the intellectual independence their religion imparts to its followers and, consequently, of the tolerance that recognizes the validity of different spiritual paths or traditions. Rodnovers often argue that, in ancient Pagan times, all of the diverging religious traditions coexisted peacefully. For many Pagans, an inherent feature of their religion is the avoidance of evaluative dualisms such as good versus evil or light versus darkness. This is also an important component of Rodnoverie religious self-identification, as well as criticism of Christianity and other Abrahamic religions.

When one analyzes the image of the warrior in Rodnoverie, its symbolic nature cannot escape notice. When defense of the native land is discussed, it is often attached to the image of a fight with swords or martial arts. Becoming the "soldier of Perun" does not usually mean joining the army or learning to shoot but the development of the mental virtues of a warrior and disciplined practice of reconstructionist martial arts. In the contemporary world of modern warfare, an ideal of the warrior equipped with such weapons seems completely unrealistic.

The practice of old-fashioned fighting can be seen as yet another manifestation of romanticism within contemporary Paganism or as part of ritualistic activity that develops the qualities of bravery and commitment and, furthermore, contains magical qualities. Nevertheless, it also includes a comment on modern society. The direct and experiential nature of martial arts distinguishes it from impersonal and technical modern warfare. Compared with historical times, modern international politics is a complex, tangled skein. Consequently, the Rodnoverie fascination with eras when wars were fought with swords can be seen as nostalgia for simpler times, when the enemy and the goals of military action were easily understood. On the other hand, it can also be considered as a criticism of impersonal, highly technical weaponry. The same point is made by a Pagan representative of the French *Nouvelle Droit*, Alain de Benoist, whose literary works are well known to many Rodnovers. In his book *On Being a Pagan*, de Benoist charges the dualism of Christianity with introducing the demonization of the enemy. According to him, in Pagan wars the soldiers respected the opponent. He considers clinically effective modern weapons of mass destruction to be the culmination of postPagan, dualistic dehumanization of the other (Benua de 2004, 173–77).[8]

The tangibility of a traditional warrior underlies the agency of the individual and exemplifies the Pagan philosophy of responsibility. The ethics of responsibility are closely tied to the this-worldliness of Paganism, which sets different alternatives into oppositional structures: First, Pagans seek ways to reverse the modern alienation that diminishes the meaning of physical communities and the modern risk society, where complex structures are often beyond the grasp of individuals, yet still have an effect on them. Second, world-affirming Paganism stresses the immanence of the divine as opposed to the dichotomy between the mundane world and the sacred transcendent.

Unlike the modern world, responsibility is outwardly simple in a physical conflict with swords. As with global, technical modernity, which blurs the causes and agents of war, Rodnovers blame Christianity for transferring personal responsibility to the transcendent: Punishments and rewards are anticipated as being finally paid in the afterlife, and sins committed against other human beings can be forgiven by God. For Pagans, there is no divine authority that can liberate people from responsibility. The this-worldliness of Paganism means that, for the majority of Pagans, the world around us is more important and more certain than life after death. Consequently, whether or not justice or truth conquers in this lifetime is not of secondary importance. Some Rodnoverie authors regard it as even immoral to turn the other cheek because for them this would mean accepting injustice by not intervening. On the warrior ethic Belov writes: "Personally for me a fight is a direct and strict manifestation of the principle that infamousness, treachery and impudence must not be left unpunished" (Selidor 2007, 12.)

The Social Context

Rodnoverie, like contemporary Paganism in general, has emerged in societies that are predominantly Christian, and it is therefore only natural that the religion often constructs its identity vis-à-vis Christianity. Nevertheless, the "Christianity" that is challenged by Pagans is not a uniform phenomenon but is constructed in a certain context and from certain vantage points. For example, in the West the word

"Pagan" has been explained as deriving from a word that refers to civilian country dwellers as opposed to militias, the "soldiers of the Christian God" (Hardman 1995, x). The idea of the Christian as soldier has indeed been central to many forms of Christianity. Nevertheless, in the case of Rodnoverie these roles have become inverted in a way that can perhaps best be explained by societal context. In post-totalitarian Russia, Rodnovers want to identify their religion with agency and responsibility, not with humility and pacifism.

The unforeseeable boom of alternative spirituality in post–Soviet Russia has usually been explained by the sudden vacuum of values. This refers not only to disillusionment with the previously cherished ideology and values, which of course it does for some, but also to the bankruptcy of the Soviet Union, which dissolved many institutions and societal norms that had sustained the everyday life of ordinary people. During its first decade, the new Russia witnessed harsh economic depression and a privatization project that countered all of the capitalist ideals of free enterprise: Huge governmental fortunes were simply transferred into the hands of oligarchs who were also, as a rule, members of the former communist elite. Social instability nourished corruption, and the law of the jungle seemed to apply in the marketplace. In response, the urge to create not just social structures but also commonly shared morality and social solidarity has remained at the top of the agenda in Russian public discussions. The remedy most often prescribed has been nationalism. As early as 1996, President Yeltsin commissioned a group to define the national "Russian idea." The next president, Putin, has gained wide support expressly because he has distanced himself from the unpopular neoliberalism of the nineties and instead plies his audience with nationalistic appeals.

The societal diagnosis that Rodnovers make bears a striking similarity to these public trends. Also, Rodnovers see nationalism as a promise of social solidarity and responsibility that is ultimately based on feelings of interconnectedness. The stressfulness of the post-Soviet vacuum of values is echoed in conservative Rodnoverie projects that bemoan the demise of the former order, which, for example, kept pornography and prostitution out of the public eye. Rodnovers may also attempt to preserve some of the Soviet ideals. Though the Soviet Union is often perceived extremely critically, to say the least, some Rodnovers still vow to uphold what they consider Soviet or communist values, such as justice or the pursuit of the common good instead of individual interests.[9]

Western individualism is often the target of Rodnoverie criticism and is seen predominantly in terms of egoist utilitarianism. Alternatively, Rodnovers present communality and a sacrificial spirit as inherently Russian values that should be restored. At the same time, Rodnoverie social philosophy advocates a highly individualistic ethos, especially in its emphasis on individual responsibility. The new rise of Paganism can be presented as part of the evolution of humanity to maturity when rigid divine commandments or intimidation from divine authorities are no longer needed to guarantee morality. Though conservative Rodnovers certainly support tightened societal control, individual responsibility is still usually seen as the best hope for societal stability and solidarity. Symptomatically, virtually all Rodnoverie organizations actively campaign against drinking, smoking, and drugs. They present a positive approach to life as a Pagan alternative to the social apathy of drinking, which is rife in poor suburbs and villages.

Religious Violence and New Religious Movements

The nature of the violent episodes that are most often connected with new religious movements (NRMs) is poignantly described by the term *dramatic denouement* (Bromley 2002).[10] What is common to tragedies involving, for example, the Solar Temple, Aum Shinrikyo, or the Branch Davidians is that dramatic violence was resorted to as an alternative to the dead end to which the surrounding society had driven the faithful and/or as an apocalypse with the promise of a new beginning. These cases have been studied and compared to each other in an effort to find some common elements that can predict the risk of mass violence. These discussions are more thoroughly analyzed elsewhere in this book, so I here make only a few superficial comments. A number of characteristics have been identified as common to dramatic denouements, such as isolation, charismatic leadership, external persecution, and apocalyptic expectations. Exceptions to any single theory can usually be found, yet, more important, an overwhelming majority of the NRMs with such features are not at all prone to violence (Bromley 2002, 2004; Introvigne 2002; Robbins 2002). Also, as Richardson (2001, 106) suggests, violence should be seen not only as a trait of some entity but also as one that arises from relationships between individuals, groups, and the surrounding society. Nevertheless, these theoretical formulations are useful in our effort to understand why a religious group might conclude that there is "no place for us to go but up" (Introvigne 2002).

The hate crimes that were committed by the notorious gang of teenagers discussed earlier could perhaps be interpreted as a dramatic denouement. In general, however, such a model has little relevance for Rodnoverie. The movement is characterized by an antiauthoritarian and individualistic spirit that usually guarantees critical feedback to its leaders. Rodnoverie communities can be an important source of emotional support, but as a rule they are loose and ever transient by nature. Within Rodnoverie, apocalyptic imagery is bound to collide with its this-worldly philosophy and emphasis on the immanence of the divine. Rodnoverie has faced some outside persecution by hostile media, the anticult movement, the Russian Orthodox Church, and governmental officials, but so far it has enjoyed relative peace in comparison to a number of other NRMs.[11]

One of the reasons that the model of dramatic denouement seems irrelevant to Rodnoverie is that it applies only to a limited type of NRM. The term *new religious movement* indeed covers a divergent set of religious phenomena: NRMs can be conservative or radically revolutionary; some of them are based on world religions;

and others are syncretistic or are based on entirely new innovations. While some NRMs are extremely exclusive and high demand, others may be diffuse and quite inclusive. This last difference is especially noteworthy in regard to the analysis of religious violence: Dramatic denouements seem to be associated with the first category of tight, totalistic communities, while the latter traits—transience and antiauthoritarian pluralism—are more characteristic of the Rodnoverie.

Given that the analysis of violence related to NRMs has focused mainly on the high-demand, totalistic, and authoritarian form of religiosity, the question remains, What insight could the case of Rodnoverie contribute to an understanding of the violence carried out by NRMs that are characterized by antiauthoritarianism and inclusiveness?

The violence resorted to by some Rodnovers, as well as the doctrinal interpretations that excuse violence, is usually not aimed at adherents of other religions or opponents of the Rodnoverie community but at those who are seen as "enemies of Russia or Russians." Thus, the conflict is prompted by ethnic or political motives rather than religious ones. Furthermore, the violent acts seem to be based more on individual interpretations than on conclusions made by the religious community or the recommendation of an authoritative religious leader.

"Individual interpretations" cannot, however, be understood outside the societal context. An oft-neglected fact in the analysis of racist violence is that radical extremists usually do not see themselves as hateful monsters but as noble fighters, ready to sacrifice themselves for a good cause. Therefore, it is reasonable to ask, how did they arrive at such an interpretation? Naturally, there is no single answer to this question. A religious framework of cosmic war and dehumanization of the opponent is one part of the puzzle, but this must be supplemented with sociopolitical contextual factors (Juergensmeyer 2009). Though skinheads are officially denounced and undoubtedly disapproved of by the majority of Russians, there is also much silent approval when the police do not interfere in racist attacks (Amnesty International 2007) or when racist violence is publicly belittled as a small problem in comparison to criminality in general or to crimes committed by illegal immigrants.

As a nondogmatic religion, Rodnoverie is apt to function as a cultural resource and thereby also easily lends support to other ideological goals and mundane social struggles. As the episodes of racist violence attest, this feature may, in the worst cases, carry a vicious potential much more dangerous than apocalyptic sectarianism. Dramatic denouements have given a notorious reputation to exclusivist, high-demand, deviant religious minorities despite the fact that these instances are rare, especially when considered in the context of religious violence in general.

The model of religious violence resorted to by a secluded fundamentalist group can be found in mainstream religiosity in the form of, for example, terrorism. It seems quite plausible that the number of victims is much higher in incidents in which mainstream religion has been one of the elements legitimizing widely approved or state aggression (e.g., in the various holy wars that have taken place throughout history). In the attempts to explain racist violence, analysis of individual psychology is not sufficient, as pointed out by the eminent scholar of extremism, James Aho (1994). Instead, Aho encourages scholars to turn their attention to places where the psychology of the enemy is sustained: the "courtrooms, mythologies, schoolhouses, pulpits, altars, and the media" (Aho 1994, 6).

Though some studies have analyzed violence in NRMs and world religions within the same framework, these discussions often feature two different topics. First, the consideration of philosophical and symbolic representations of violence has been elaborated predominantly with regard to NRMs. Second, the social context is usually more central in discussions of violence within mainstream religiosity.[12] Such a difference in focus naturally derives from the fact that doctrinal analysis is probably more relevant when a small apocalyptic group commits mass suicide as a transitory step; correspondingly, social and political aspects are more relevant in a tangled conflict between two ethnic groups with different religions who are also struggling over resources and hegemony. Nevertheless, it might also be possible that an alien or deviant religion tempts us to seek reasons for violence in its doctrine, while in the case of a familiar tradition, the focus falls more naturally on an analysis of the conditions when a particular deviant interpretation emerges.[13]

Conclusions

During my fieldwork in Saint Petersburg, a colleague arranged for me to meet a young Rodnover who, though not belonging to the violent skinhead subculture, identified himself as National-Socialist. This student demonstrates the dualistic nature of a sacrificial saint and an extremist zealot,[14] one who is filled with passion to improve the well-being of Russians. As he described the apathy and the hedonism that he saw as troubling and destroying Russia, he told me that he had once gotten so irritated that he punched a man who asked for a cigarette. This case exemplifies both the versatility that the religious violence may encompass and the vague lines between religious and societal or political motivation: Should the punch be interpreted as an act of a fundamentalist who wishes to replace secular with religious values at the center of society, or is it better understood as a symptom of frustration in a given social situation?

One could argue that the study of the relationship between religion and violence has suffered from its topical nature. The infamous instances of mass violence connected with NRMs, as well as tragedies such as the attack on the World Trade Center, have obliged scholars to seek models to predict and thereby to prevent such incidents. However, the focus on tragic events demarcates violence, both acts of violence and the idealization of it, into small groups, and such a division (or even externalization) can be somewhat problematic. As Juergensmeyer notes, violence can be found in virtually all religions, not to mention the usage of imagery referring to violence in a positive light (Juergensmeyer 2003, 6–7). McCutcheon (2005, 4–5, 28–30) also criticizes the study of religious violence as constructing dualistic models of the incomprehensible "other" and the reasonable "us."[15]

The term *new religious movement* covers a wide range of the most divergent groups, and, in a similar vein to mainstream religions, individual NRMs may reflect various orientations. Though it is important to study the ways their religious doctrines accommodate or even encourage violence, it is perhaps paramount to study the societal context and relationships where violent behavior emerges, as Richardson (2001, 106) suggests. Rodnoverie is not a religion that would actively propagate violence, but there are Rodnovers who have committed horrendous violent acts. Some Rodnovers are pacifists, while others believe in the use of physical force in the name of some good cause. The majority, however, seem to fall somewhere in between. Such middle ground was nicely portrayed by a Finnish Wiccan who explained that Pagan morality commands one neither to turn the other cheek nor to hit back but to firmly grab the hitting hand and to convince the aggressive person that such behavior is not acceptable. The ideal of the warrior may set violence in a justified or even a positive light, but it can also be a symbol of responsible agency that is considered especially important in a posttotalitarian social context. Therefore, such an ideal may even function as an antidote against violence or as a safe means of expressing one's aggressions.

NOTES

I wish to thank Marlene Laruelle, René Gothóni, and Markku Kivinen for their valuable comments.

1. "Rodnoverie" refers to the Russian followers of pre-Christian Slavic spirituality. Similar terms, derived from the same expression, "native faith," can, however, be found in other Slavic countries (e.g., Ridna Vira in Ukraine; Rodzima Viara in Poland).

2. The book appeared as a so-called tamizdat [published abroad]. It was not, however, targeted solely at the underground opposition; the author sent copies of the book to all of the members of the central committee of the Soviet Communist Party. There is even some evidence that the KGB engineered or at least supported Paganism as a plot to break up the Orthodox nationalistic opposition. Emelyanov apparently also enjoyed some official protection (Laqueur 1993, 112–16, 210–11).

3. On Russian cosmism, see Hagemeister (1997).

4. The *Book of Veles* is regarded as forgery by the majority of academics. For more information on the book, its fascinating history, and the incredible influence it has attained, see Shnirelman (1998, 4–6.)

5. Several books by these authors have been published in Russia in recent decades. The first and the most famous is undoubtedly Aleksandr Dugin's prefaced translation of Evola's *Pagan Empire*. On traditionalism, see Sedgwick (2004).

6. Not all reconstructionists are, however, Pagans. On this youth subculture in Russia, see, for example, IA Regnum (2007).

7. Here I approach the definition of "religion" through the idea of "family resemblance," according to which religions share several common features, none of which is a prerequisite. See Gothóni (1996).

8. However, de Benoist himself is quite capable of demonizing the "other," as becomes evident in the racist nature of his texts.

9. Belief in and loyalty to Soviet values cannot be seen through the dualistic model of acceptance or rejection. As Yurchak points out, many people were highly skeptical of and disillusioned with the Soviet reality and rhetoric but subscribed to some of its values, although in a somewhat unorthodox or abstract sense (Yurchak 2006, 93–98).

10. I am using the term *new religious movements* here for two reasons. First of all, in Russia the terms *cult* and *sect* have become almost useless in the study of religion because they have been thoroughly usurped by the anticult movement, which employs concepts such as "totalitarian cults" or "destructive sects" (Shterin 2004.). Second, I find that many of the common characteristics of "sect" (e.g., exclusiveness or inward orientation) fit Rodnoverie poorly. That is not to say that I consider these concepts useless with regard to the analysis of Rodnoverie. In fact, I believe that a reflexive analysis of contemporary Paganism could contribute greatly to the theoretical discussion of the definition of "sect" and "cult." Unfortunately, such a discussion would require space beyond this chapter. Therefore, here I use the term *new religious movement*, which incorporates a wider array of religions and religious movements.

11. In 2009 the leader of the Church of Inglings was sentenced to jail for eighteen months for violating an earlier order to cease church activities because of their extremism. The verdict on extremism was based on the church's racist doctrine, which prohibited interracial marriage, and used the swastika as a religious symbol. (The church has, however, consistently disassociated itself from Nazism and claimed that the Nazis misunderstood and misused the swastika.) The teachings of the church feature esoteric prejudices but do not encourage violent acts. The verdict can be seen as an interesting case study of strict use of the law regarding religious groups in Russia: What will happen to an organization that has three thousand adherents when all of its religious activity is banned? Without commenting on this verdict, I maintain that the Russian government's actions against extremism have many bizarre features. The choices of target have often seemed either totally random or politically motivated. They include, among others, the Pagan priest of the indigenous Siberian faith and the followers of a renowned Muslim theologian, Said Nursi (Verkhovskii and Kozhenikova 2009).

12. The societal context of the form of external prosecution has been analyzed in several studies on NRMs and violence. Here, however, by "societal context" I refer to the movement's political concerns and goals and to the influence of the wider societal conflicts that the analyzed religion adopts as its own.

13. To label a conflict "religiously motivated" may lend it a sense of obscurantism much like the label of "ethnic conflict" easily overshadows the impact of genuine economic and political concerns.

14. This is a revision of the "sacrificial saint" and "suicidal zealot" by Berman and Iannaccone. In this case, the "suicidal" is better replaced with "xenophobic" (Iannaccone and Berman 2006).

15. See also Aho (1994). Both of these thinkers stress, however, that broadening such views would not mean relativism, or the vindication of violent action.

REFERENCES

Aho, James A. 1994. *This Thing of Darkness: A Sociology of the Enemy*. Seattle: University of Washington Press.

Amnesty International. 2007. *Russian Federation: Update Briefing: What Progress Has Been Made since May 2006 to Tackle Violent Racism?* AI Index EUR 46/047/2007. October 24. http://www.amnesty.org/en/library/info/EUR46/047/2007 (accessed August 11, 2009).

Belov, A. K. 1993. *Slavyano-goritskaya bor'ba: Iznachal'e*. Moscow: NKDR.

Benua de, Alen (Benoist de, Alain). 2004. *Kak Mozhno Byt' Yazychnikom*. Moscow: Russkaya Pravda.

Bromley, David G. 2002. "Dramatic Denouements." In *Cults, Religion, and Violence*, ed. David G. Bromley and Gordon J. Melton, 11–41. New York: Cambridge University Press.

———. 2004. "Violence and New Religious Movements." In *Oxford Handbook of New Religious Movements*, ed. James R. Lewis, 143–62. New York: Oxford University Press.

Cowan, Douglas E. 2005. *Cyberhenge: Modern Pagans on the Internet*. New York: Routledge.

Danilov, Vladimir. 2000. *Ariiskaya Iimperiya: Gibel' i Vozrozhdenie*. 2 vols. Moscow: Volya Rossii.

Dobroslav (Dobrovol'skii, Aleksei). 2005. *Yazychestvo kak Volshebstvo*. Mosow: Slava.

Emelyanov, V. N. 2005. *Desionizatsiya*. Moscow: Russkaya Pravda.

Gaidukov, Aleksei V. 2005. "Sovremennoe Slavyanskoe (Russkoe) Yazychestvo v Peterburge: Konfessional'naya Dinamika za Desyatiletie." In *Religioznaya Situatsiya na Severo-Zapade Rossii i v Stranakh Baltii*, ed. A. Yu. Grigorenko and A. M. Prilutskiy, 37–57. St. Petersburg: Svetoch.

Gothóni, René. 1996: Religions Form a Family. *Temenos: Studies in Comparative Religion* 32: 65–79.

Hagemeister, Michael. 1997. "Russian Cosmism in the 1920s and Today." In *The Occult in Russian and Soviet Culture*, ed. Bernice Glatzer Rosenthal, 185–202. Ithaca: Cornell University Press.

Hardman, Charlotte. 1995. Introduction. In *Paganism Today*, ed. Graham Harvey and Charlotte Hardman, ix–xix. London: Thorsons.

IA Regnum. 2007. *Istoricheskaya Rekonstruktsiya: Nauka i Igra na Vsyu Zhizn'—Interv'yu Organizatora Festivalya "Gorodetskoe Gul'bishche."* September 3. http://www.regnum.ru/news/878967.html (accessed August 19, 2009).

Iannaccone, Laurence R., and Eli Berman. 2006. Religious Extremism: The Good, the Bad, and the Deadly. *Public Choice* 128 (July): 109–29.

Introvigne, Massimo. 2002. "There Is No Place for Us to Go but Up": New Religious Movements and Violence. *Social Compass* 49(2) (June): 213–24.

Izvednik. 2004. *Vestnik Traditsionnoy Kul'tury: Stat'i, Izvednik. Vol*, no. 1, ed. A. Nagovitsyn, 56–200. Moscow: Vorob'ev.

Juergensmeyer, Mark. 2003. *Terror in the Mind of God: The Global Rise of Religious Violence*, 3d ed. Berkeley: University of California Press.

———. 2009. "Religious Violence." In *Oxford Handbook of the Sociology of Religion*, ed. Peter Clarke, 890–908. New York: Oxford University Press.

Kavykin, Oleg Igorevich. 2007. *"Rodnovery" SamoidentifikatsiyaNneoyazychnikov v Sovremennoi Rossii*. Moscow: RAN, Institut Afriki.

Koskello, Anastasia. 2005. "Sovremennye Yazycheskie Religii Evrazii: Krainosti Globalizma i Antiglobalizma." In *Religiya i Globalizatsiya na Prostorakh Evrazii*, ed. S. Filatov, 296–332. Moscow: Neostrom.

Laqueur, Walter. 1993. *Black Hundred: The Rise of the Extreme Right in Russia*. New York: HarperCollins.

McCutcheon, Russell T. 2005. *Religion and the Domestication of Dissent: Or, How to Live in a Less than Perfect Nation*. London: Equinox.

Meranvil'd, V. B. 2004. *Slavyano-Goritskoe Dvizhenie kak Odna iz Form Vozrozhdeniya Russkoi Natsional'noi Kul'tury*. Ioshkar-Ola: Mariiskii gosudarstvennyi universitet.

Movsesyan, Lyusya. 2009. *Skinkhedam-Yazychnikam Pred'yavleny Obvineniya v Ubiistvakh*. June 18. http://www.newsland.ru/News/Detail/id/387615/August 21.

Novikov-Novgorodets, B. M. 2007. *Vedicheskoe Mirovozzrenie Protoslavyan-Osnova Podlinnoi Rossiiskoi Gosudarstvennosti I Geopolitiki*. Moscow: Belye Al'vy.

Pilkington, H., and A. Popov. 2009. "Understanding Neo-paganism in Russia: Religion? Ideology? Philosophy? Fantasy?" In *Subcultures and New Religious Movements in Russia and East-central Europe*, ed. G. McKay, C. Williams, M. Goddard, N. Foxlee, and E. Ramanauskaite253-304. Oxford, New York: Lang.

Popov, Vladimir. 2003. *Obez'yany Putina (Khishchniki vo Vlasti)*. Moscow: Nasledie Predkov.

Prokof'ev, A., S. Filatov, and A. Koskello. 2006. "Slavyanskoe i Skandinavskoe Yazychestva: Vikkanstvo." In *Sovremennaya Religioznaya Zhizn' Rossii: Opyt Sistematicheskogo Opisaniya*. part 4, ed. M. Burdo and S. B. Filatov, 155–207. Moscow: Logos.

Richardson, James T. 2001. "Minority Religions and the Context of Violence: A Conflict/Interactionist Perspective?" *Terrorism and Political Violence* 13(1): 103–33.

Robbins, Thomas. 2002. "Sources of Volatility in Religious Movements." In *Cults, Religion, and Violence*, ed. David G. Bromley and Gordon J. Melton, 57–79. New York: Cambridge University Press.

Rodoslav' (Zinchenko, A. A.). 2006. *IzvilistyePputi Traditsii*. Moscow: Ladoga-100.

Sedgwick, Mark. 2004. *Against the Modern World: Traditionalism and the Secret Intellectual History of the Twentieth Century*. New York: Oxford University Press.

Selidor (Belov, Aleksei). 2007. *Udar iz Niotkuda: Azbuka Boevoi Magi*. Moscow: Russkaya Panorama.

Sevast'yanov, Aleksandr. 1996. *National-Demokratiya*. Moscow: Aleksandr Sevast'yanov.

Shnirelman, Victor. 1998. *Russian Neo-pagan Myths and Antisemitism*: Analysis of Current Trends in Antisemitism. Acta 13. Jerusalem: Hebrew University of Jerusalem.

Shterin, Marat. 2004. "New Religious Movements in the New Russia." In *New Religious Movements in the 21st Century*, ed. Phillip Charles Lucas and Thomas Robbins, 99–116. New York: Routledge.

Starhawk (Simos, Miriam). 1999. *The Fifth Sacred Thing*. London: Thorsons.

Verkhovskii, Aleksei, and Galina Kozhevnikova. 2009. *Nepravomernoe Primerenie Antiekstr emistskogoZzakonodatel'stvo v Rossii v 2008Ggodu*. SOVA Center. http://xeno.sova-center.ru/29481C8/CB5956B (accessed August 11, 2009).

Yakutovsky, G. P. 1995. *Russkii Mir i Rai Zemnoi*. http://magice.boom.ru/ray.html (accessed August 25, 2009).

Yurchak, Alexei. 2006. *Everything Was Forever, Until It Was No More: The Last Soviet Generation*. Princeton, N.J.: Princeton University Press.

12

Ananda Marga, PROUT, and the Use of Force

Helen Crovetto

Like materialism, spirituality based on non-violence will be of no benefit to humanity. The words of non-violence may sound noble, and quite appealing, but on the solid ground of reality have no value whatsoever.
—P. R. Sarkar, *PROUT in a Nutshell Part VI*

Prabhat Ranjan Sarkar (1921–1990, aka Shrii Shrii Anandamurti), founded Ananda Marga [Path of Bliss] as a new sociospiritual organization in 1955. Its motto is *Atmamoksartham jagadhitaya ca* [for the sake of self-realization and for service to humanity]. Adherents refer to their spiritual practices as tantra yoga. The organization's social service work provides underprivileged people with food, clothing, shelter, education, and medicine. Its projects usually take the form of schools, children's homes, medical clinics, and disaster relief. Together with positive contributions in the field of ecology (Crovetto 2005), Ananda Marga's social work represents an aspect of the movement that is certainly praiseworthy but has been largely overshadowed by its association with violence.

Sarkar was of the opinion that the spiritual evolution of the individual and society was tied to the use of force. He said the "main characteristic" of the tantra yoga his followers practice is that "it represents human vigor. It represents a pactless fight" that "is not only an external or internal fight, it is simultaneously both" (Anandamurti 1994, 26–27).[1] This statement has some resonance with Muslims who define *jihad* as both an internal and an external struggle (Appleby 2000). In many people's minds, those who belong to Sarkar's movement are simply terrorists. The mere mention of Ananda Marga is enough to send some South Asians literally running from the room.[2] The view that all Ananda Margiis are terrorists is untrue and an unfortunate oversimplification. It would be more precise to describe them as revolutionaries with an extremely idealistic or utopian sociospiritual agenda.

Sarkar propagated a distinctive theory of ideal, sociopolitical leadership, but the main concern of his socioeconomic and political program (and one of its defining characteristics) was the goal of collective well-being brought about by a mass movement. The other defining characteristic was his teaching that such a mass movement would take the form of revolutionary actions against exploitative conditions or regimes. Sarkar is on record as having specifically rejected terrorism. Nevertheless, debate may always accompany the labeling of a group as "terrorist" or "revolutionary" because categorization is largely the function of the person doing the naming. The question I address here is, under what circumstances did Sarkar's ideology approve of the use of force?

Sarkar's publications present doctrinal justifications for the use of force to achieve his idealistic concept of social justice. At the social level, his followers' potential use of force is limited to perceived conditions of mass exploitation. The exceptions Sarkar made for the use of force in individual life are noted as I proceed. There are allegations of several types of violence in Ananda Marga's history that have contributed to the view that Ananda Margiis may be terrorists. One is intraorganizational violence: the murder of ex-workers who wanted to start their own organizations. Another concerns terrorist incidents from the 1970s, which occurred during the period Sarkar was incarcerated. Ananda Margiis say Sarkar was jailed and wrongly convicted on politically motivated charges. What appears to have been a portion of Ananda Marga's membership responded with violence under the banner of a related organization. However, these are not sufficient grounds to assert that the entire Ananda Marga movement and its various branches utilize terrorism either systematically or sporadically. It also sheds no light on the nature of Sarkar's ideology concerning the use of force. Furthermore, there have been incidents of violence perpetrated against Ananda Margiis.

The following examination of Ananda Marga history and its ideology supporting the use of force relies primarily on Sarkar's books and secondarily on interviews with members and ex-members. These interviews took place over a twenty-five-year period from 1970 through 1995.

The examination here includes a description of the founding of Ananda Marga and its political wing, PROUTist Universal, highlights from the movement's history, a sketch of the guru, a summary of the spiritual and socioeconomic ideology, and a profile of membership. I discuss several cosmological and moral aspects of Ananda Marga's worldview and elucidate the movement's ideological approval of the use of force for the purpose of establishing a revolutionary mystic socialism it calls PROUT (Progressive Utilization Theory). The role of elite leadership in a revolutionary struggle is presented, as well as the potential use of the movement's budding paramilitaries. Allegations against the movement are considered. Ananda Marga and PROUTist Universal's political program are expressions of their revolutionary sociospiritual utopianism.

Prabhat Ranjan (P. R.) Sarkar and His Organizations

Prabhat Ranjan (P. R.) Sarkar's biography describes him as having been born on Buddha Purnima to a distinguished middle-class family from Jamalpur, Bihar state, during an era of sociopolitical turbulence (Vijayananda Avadhuta 1994).[3] He was a student at Calcutta's Vidyasagar College and a prolific linguist. Bengali was his native language, and even today some of his books are available only in Bengali. Sarkar was interested in the Indian struggle for home rule and had a maternal family tie to Indian independence fighter Netaji Subash Chandra Bose (1897–1945), who was his uncle. One of Sarkar's most important books on social philosophy, *Problems of the Day* (1959), is dedicated to Bose with the following inscription: "To the great hero Subhas Chandra Bose, whom I did love, and whom I do love even now." Like Bose, Sarkar was a believer in armed struggle, and he fashioned the ideology of his movement accordingly.

The formation of Ananda Marga may have been influenced by the nineteenth-century Bengali religious reform movement, Brahmo Samaj, and other nineteenth-century movements and figures within Hindu revivalism (Sil 1988a). Like other revivalists, Sarkar addressed socioeconomic and political issues, but he supported universalism rather than nationalism (1993a, 1993b). Ananda Marga's literature does not explicitly mention inspiration by the nineteenth-century movements; however, Brahmo Samaj and Ananda Marga share some similarities. Both oppose the caste system and image worship while believing in a single, all-pervasive divinity. Another link is that Sarkar was a great admirer of Rabindranath Tagore (1861–1941), the 1913 Nobel laureate in literature. Tagore had a well-known connection to the Brahmo Samaj through his father, who served as its leader for a time (Hopkins 2005).[4] Sarkar kept life-sized sculptures of Bose and Tagore in the garden of his Kolkata home.

In 1959, four years after starting Ananda Marga, Sarkar launched PROUTist Universal as a separate organization. The latter was meant to propagate PROUT, Sarkar's socioeconomic and political philosophy. PROUTist Universal has its international headquarters in Copenhagen, Denmark. Ananda Marga's international headquarters is at Ananda Nagar in the Purulia District of West Bengal, with a de facto headquarters in the Kolkata suburb of Tiljala. Both organizations are presently under the control of Ananda Marga *sannyasis*, members of the monastic order founded by Sarkar in 1962. While Sarkar was alive, sannyasis from both organizations met simultaneously and received directions from him on how to proceed with their work assignments. Sarkar sometimes switched the sannyasis' assignments between Ananda Marga and PROUTist Universal. All of the members of Ananda Marga and PROUT that I questioned considered themselves to be members of a large family headed by the same guru.

Despite the fact that Ananda Marga and PROUT are distinct organizations, Sarkar's socioeconomic and political philosophy should be viewed as an integral part of his spiritual philosophy. This is indicated by the arrangement of the two books that Sarkar felt represented his definitive philosophy, or *darsana sastra* (1993a). The first book, *Ananda Sutram* (1996/1962), has four chapters on spiritual philosophy and a fifth chapter on PROUT. The second book, *Idea and Ideology* (1993a/1959), contains nine articles on spiritual philosophy and two articles on PROUT. Sarkar may have created two separate organizations in the hope of shielding his sociospiritual work from the political repercussions of his revolutionary political ideology.

A Profile of Membership

The social profile of Ananda Margiis and PROUTists is not uniform. Many members are apparently well integrated into their surrounding societies as they engage in normal occupations and often perform social service. Some of these people also keep a close watch on the political scene wherever they are. Organizational workers, be they sannyasis or local full-time workers (LFTs), tend to be more socially isolated and subject to group regimentation and "intensive socialization tactics" (Bromley and Shupe 1981, 212). As noncloistered monastics, sannyasis renounce kinship ties and are controlled by a highly centralized authoritarian organization. Some Ananda Marga workers live exclusively in the organization's offices and have minimal contact with those who are not members of their movement. Other workers and members live in agrarian communities that Sarkar called "Master Units." These individuals may experience differing degrees of rural isolation.

Both sannyasis and LFTs may be described as subject to institutional and ideological totalism (Robbins 2002). That is because the members of these segments of the movement accept a firmly controlled physical and mental life in the belief that this will benefit their spiritual development. In Ananda Marga, institutional totalism and to some extent ideological totalism are accomplished through a highly centralized, authoritarian organizational structure. Ananda Marga's sannyasis and LFTs have a number of rules of conduct. One rule for sannyasis is this: "No logic, no reasoning; but the compliance of the order" (interview with a former organizational worker, June 1, 1998).

The ratio of sannyasis to married persons in the movement has varied greatly over the years. During the 1970s there were very few sannyasis in North America. When American Margiis spoke among themselves, they jokingly referred to the organization as "the incredible shrinking Marga" because its married membership was greatly reduced while Sarkar was imprisoned. According to Ananda Deviika Ma (pers. comm., January 31, 2006), a former organizational worker who cofounded a separate organization, reports from the 1990s indicate that the ratio of sannyasis to married persons is now roughly fifty-fifty in North America. This indicates that married membership declined even as the number of renunciates increased when the central Ananda Marga organization sent the latter to work in North America. Despite the fact that Ananda Marga is an international organization with a sannyasi membership of many different nationalities, the predominant organizational influence is exercised by its male Indian sannyasis.

No matter what their status in the movement, Margiis with at least a rudimentary understanding of Sarkar's ideology support the concept of the transformation of the world through spiritual, socioeconomic, and political change.

Saivite Tantra Yogis with a Charismatic Guru

Sarkar's followers believe him to be an incarnation of both Sadasiva (true Siva) and Lord Krsna. That is to say that Ananda Margiis consider Sarkar and his incarnations to be the supreme consciousness, or God. Their oral hagiography describes him as having entered the world in an enlightened state. Sarkar claimed no lineage for his authority and described his teachings as a revival of the original practices of Sadasiva. Ananda Margiis believe Sadasiva was a historical figure from seven thousand years ago who was the first to teach tantra yoga. In the sense of reviving ancient doctrines and practices, Ananda Margiis believe themselves to hold Hindu reformist views.

Sarkar wrote 264 books in various languages, many originally in Bengali and later translated into English. Some are compilations of his talks in English, Bengali, Hindi, or other Indic languages. He also composed 5,018 songs mostly in Bengali. The tunes of the songs and their lyrics are referred to as Prabhat Samgita (songs of the new dawn).

Ananda Marga's *acaryas* (spiritual teachers) initiate people into a system of nondualistic tantra yoga loosely based on Patanjali's Astanga (eight-limbed) yoga.[5] Patanjali's approach is described in his *Yoga-Sutra,* estimated to be a second-century work (Potter 1983). Many scholars consider it to be a classical arrangement and the basis of a number of other systems. However, historical analysis by David White (2003) suggests that Patanjali's system postdates tantric ritual aimed at the acquisition of *siddhis,* or supernatural yogic powers. This would challenge what I have described as Sarkar's reformism, which harkens back to Sadasiva. In line with their reformist views, Margiis practice a purely internal interpretation of the *pancamakara* (Anandamurti 1994)—or five "Ms"—five *tattvas* (items, substances) associated with tantric practice. Their significance is interpreted differently depending on the orientation and ideology of the tantric group in question.[6] Though Sarkar (1988a) proclaimed the superiority of Saivism, by his own admission his spiritual system was eclectic, combining the Sakta, Saiva, and Vaisnava systems of spiritual practice (Anandamurti 1994). The elements of *jnana* (knowledge), *karma* (action), and *bhakti* (devotion) yogas are fairly evenly weighted, but Sarkar ultimately privileged the devotional path (Anandamurti 1987d). Supreme consciousness was likened to a loving and compassionate father with a reciprocal attachment for his devotees (Anandamurti 1987b, 1987c).

An Organizational History of Conflict

During the 1960s Ananda Marga and PROUTist Universal rapidly gained popularity throughout India. In 1966 missionaries were sent to other continents to proselytize and set up social service projects (Vijayananda 1994). The first social service projects were Ananda Marga disaster-relief teams, some of which are apparently still functioning. In 2005 the Ananda Marga Universal Relief Team for Ladies (AMURTEL) had members in saffron-colored T-shirts assisting Hurricane Katrina victims in Louisiana and Texas.

Ananda Marga's popularity in India earned it the opposition of the Communist Party (Vijayananda 1994). Members of the latter probably felt that Ananda Marga's socioeconomic and political philosophy infringed upon its voter base. Margiis and PROUTists were vociferous critics of both capitalism and Communism, but the socialism of PROUT was clearly more like Communism than capitalism. In his book *Human Society*, first published in Bengali in 1959, Sarkar said that the "great Karl Marx" may have opposed the religion of his day, but he "never opposed spirituality, morality and proper conduct" (1999, 269). Sarkar and his followers described Ananda Marga as a sociospiritual organization, not a religion. Ensuing tensions between Ananda Margiis and Bengali Communists were followed by a 1967 attack on Margiis at their Ananda Nagar headquarters. Ananda Marga workers claim that local residents were incited by Communist leaders to kill several of their sannyasis.[7] An American man who visited Ananda Nagar in the early 1970s said he and several Ananda Marga sannyasis came under attack by locals.[8]

Ananda Marga faced opposition from Prime Minister Indira Gandhi's government through much of the 1970s. Organizational workers were critical of alleged government corruption during Gandhi's tenure (Alister 1997). As a response to obstruction in India, Ananda Marga increased its proselytizing in other countries, including the United States. The third Indo-Pakistani war began officially on December 3, 1971, and led to the formation of the nation-state of Bangladesh. On the same date, Indira Gandhi's government declared an emergency, which among other things signaled the activation of preventive detention laws. After the war these laws were used to imprison people suspected of leftist political activities (Amnesty International 1979).[9]

Sarkar was arrested on December 29, 1971, along with several disciples and accused of abetting the murder of half a dozen former disciples. It was alleged that Sarkar was poisoned in 1973 while in government custody at the Bankipur Central Jail. The government then tried unsuccessfully to prevent Ananda Margiis from holding government jobs (Alister 1997). On June 26, 1975, Prime Minister Indira Gandhi declared another emergency and instituted martial law, banning Ananda

Marga along with other organizations. In 1976 Sarkar was convicted. The Margiis appealed to Amnesty International (Amnesty International 1979),[10] the International Commission of Jurists in Geneva, and British lawyer William T. Wells. The secretary-general of the International Commission of Jurists criticized the Indian government's conduct in Sarkar's trial, and Wells produced a report observing that the ban on Ananda Marga was an obstruction to Sarkar's defense attorneys presenting witnesses in his case (OSL 2007).[11]

Many Margiis feared that attempts would be made on Sarkar's life either while he was imprisoned or as a result of his conviction. Seven Ananda Marga sannyasis immolated themselves in an attempt to draw public attention to their guru's case. The first two, a German man and woman named Acarya Lokesha and Acarya Uma, respectively, simultaneously self-immolated on the steps of a church in the center of Berlin. A Filipino man named Acarya Gagan self-immolated at a rural location in Texas.[12] Prime Minister Morarji Desai lifted martial law in 1977, and Sarkar was granted another trial (Alister 1997). After about seven years of incarceration, he was acquitted of all charges by the Patna High Court on August 2, 1978, and was quickly released (Kang 2000).

Before Sarkar's retrial, what appears to have been a splinter group of PROUT formed in response to Sarkar's conviction. Some outraged non-Indian Margiis were suspected of being behind its creation. This group, the Universal PROUTists Revolutionary Federation (UPRF), claimed responsibility for acts of international terrorism, including assault and bombing, against Indian interests (U.S. Department of Justice 2007b). These incidents culminated in 1978 with the bombing of the Hilton Hotel in Sydney, Australia, in which three people died.

Following the terrorist incidents, alleged to have been committed by some of his followers, Sarkar issued statements from Bankipur Central that he would not come out of jail by any means other than legal procedures and that those perpetrating terrorism did not understand Ananda Marga's ideology. The international agitations promptly ceased. The UPRF's rapid response to Sarkar's statements gives weight to assertions that some of Sarkar's followers had indeed been behind the UPRF's activities. That same year, Sarkar was acquitted by the Patna High Court (Vijayananda 1994). In 1990 a man named Evan Pederick admitted he had planted the Hilton Hotel bomb and surrendered to police (Alister 1997). Known by the Sanskrit name Om Prakash, Pederick was a Margii at the time of the incident.

Federal Bureau of Investigation documents dating from 1975 through 1984, released under the Freedom of Information Act, reveal that between November 1981 and June 1983 a full investigation of Ananda Marga was conducted (U.S. Department of Justice 2007b). The FBI concluded that during that period the organization was not involved in terrorist activities in the United States. In April 2005 the U.S. State Department released a document titled "Country Reports on Terrorism 2004," which included its latest list of "Designated Foreign Terrorist Organizations," as well as a list of "Other Terrorist Organizations." Neither Ananda Marga nor PROUT was included on these lists.

When Sarkar was exonerated and released, he was greeted by thousands of his disciples. While Indian government opposition to new religious or spiritual movements is not the norm, the perceived problem with Ananda Marga was its increasingly popular socioeconomic and political philosophy. In the early 1980s I was on my way to Kolkata's Howrah train station when a PROUT political rally happened to be crossing the Howrah bridge at the same time. Our cab driver erroneously opined that the marchers were Communists, but they were PROUTists, as far as the eye could see in both directions, carrying signs with slogans supporting PROUT and the ideology of Ananda Marga.

With the passage of time the organization reblossomed, and Ananda Marga sannyasis claimed that the High Court of India had determined that Ananda Marga was a sect of Hinduism.[13] This appears to have been an attempt to enfold a controversial organization that possessed a somewhat novel, partially antinomian, and revolutionary sociospiritual ideology into the great ocean of religious philosophies that constitute contemporary Hinduism. It can only be described as an uneasy alliance after the long-time adversarial relationship between the government of Prime Minister Indira Gandhi and the movement.

A bloody incident occurred in April 1982 near the Kolkata suburb of Tiljala, which involved local residents and zealous Ananda Marga sannyasis. The sannyasis were attacked, and seventeen were killed. This episode, described later, may have been due to Ananda Marga's proselytizing.

In the early 1990s, the Indian government accused members of the movement of dealing in arms. This case temporarily landed an American Margii in a Kolkata jail. He was a college student, and family members who flew in from Florida successfully obtained his release into their custody (interview with family friend, May 10, 1995, Melbourne, Florida).

Proselytizing and Allegations of Murder

Ananda Marga and PROUTist Universal were set up as proselytizing organizations. Sarkar's "Supreme Command," which is printed at the beginning of most of his books, states, in part, that it is the "bounden duty of every Ananda Margii to endeavor to bring all to the path of bliss." Remember that the organization's name translates as "path of bliss." During the 1970s and 1980s the organization's sannyasis were very active proselytizers, teaching what by many accounts was a very effective system of spiritual practices free of charge to all who were interested. Credit should be given to the movement for the spiritual and social services it provides. Its social service projects are often set up among the most disadvantaged people and maintained despite a wide variety of challenges. Before and after the allegations of terrorism, several governments, including the United States, Britain, and Finland, recognized the value of the movement's social service projects by assisting with grants and materials (U.S. Department of Justice 2007a).[14]

However, the missionary zeal of a number of sannyasis to establish social service projects may have turned into a liability in at least one case. On April 30, 1982, residents near Tiljala attacked and killed seventeen sannyasis in broad daylight as the Margiis attempted to cross Bijon Setu, a local bridge. The Margiis claimed that the renunciates were murdered by Communist Party of India Marxists (CPM) from West Bengal (Ananda Marga 2008). This accusation revisited a long-standing tension that Margiis say has persisted between Bengali Communists and themselves since their movement first became popular in the 1960s. A Kolkata newspaper reported that the local residents accused the sannyasis of kidnapping children (Sil 1988b).[15]

These accusations may have come about as a result of the sannyasis' trying to increase the number of children in their movement's schools and children's homes. Ex-workers report that during the 1970s and 1980s such service projects were expected to show regular increases in enrollment and that sometimes quotas were set (interview with a former organizational worker, June 1, 1988). In the early 1980s, a small children's home was established in southern Portugal for children whose parents could not afford to feed or care for them. When the situation of these families improved, they sought the return of their children. The Ananda Marga workers fought to retain them because the children's release would (and in fact did) force the closure of the project. If overzealous missionary tactics were to blame near Tiljala, it is easy to understand how they might have appeared threatening to the locals.

The organizational workers believed it was desirable to increase the number of children in their schools and children's homes for several reasons. In addition to providing a bona fide social service, they would also increase the number of converts to their spiritual philosophy and movement. Ananda Marga has a preschool curriculum titled the *Circle of Love* (1980), which teaches Ananda Marga's cosmogonic theory, monistic worldview, and meditation techniques. In poorer countries, indigent children who enter Ananda Marga service projects at a young age are likely to become lifelong members or organizational sannyasis. In this regard, Ananda Marga has conducted itself not unlike many other religious organizations that sponsor service projects. To the extent that its members also engage in indoctrination, they can be accused of having dual motives.

Allegations of the murder of former organizational workers were made by the central government of India against Ananda Marga sannyasis in 1971, when Sarkar was arrested and charged with abetting or inciting others to commit murder. No charges were proven against Sarkar or any other worker. Stories circulating within Ananda Marga and PROUTist Universal allege that a former organizational sannyasi was murdered for wanting to start his own organization (interview with a former organizational worker, April 9, 1995). The account told to me was that the sannyasi was a senior monk who resented not being assigned a particular position in the organizational hierarchy. He enlisted the support of several influential Margiis and asked Sarkar to alter his decision. When the sannyasi did not succeed in his appeal, he left to start his own organization, which was supported by the same individuals.

In the 1980s another murder allegation surfaced regarding a second former organizational sannyasi. This man was also said to have left Ananda Marga to found his own organization. Acarya Nityananda Avadhuta had once been highly placed in the movement (interview with a former organizational worker, June 16, 2006). After he was sent to the United States to teach, he married an American woman and had a child. Living in Boulder, Colorado, he was described as being very popular in the alternative community (Buhrman 2000). One man noted that Acarya Nityananda had developed a philosophy of financial self-reliance. He was working in a local grocery to support his family but continued to teach meditation free of charge. This is in contrast to the Ananda Marga requirement that its sannyasis live exclusively on donations. Former organizational workers allege that a German LFT murdered Nityananda in Sweden (former organizational worker 1998).[16]

Unfortunately, the murder of apostates is not as rare a phenomenon within some extreme new religious movements as one would hope (Wessinger 2000b).[17] In Ananda Marga's case, members with a self-justifying sense of morality may have decided to take matters into their own hands. *Avadhutas* are a type of senior monk said to be completely detached from the created universe. In the late 1980s one of them reacted angrily when questioned about the murder of apostates. He accused those who left the organization and tried to start their own groups of "taking the best that the organization had" (former organizational worker 1998). Then he walked away without explaining, but presumably he meant the system of spiritual practices Ananda Marga teaches. In the early 1980s another avadhuta was reported to have boasted that many other spiritual organizations suffer schisms, but Ananda Marga does not (former organizational worker 1998). The implication behind his claim was that Ananda Marga should be judged as spiritually superior and more authentic than other spiritual organizations because of its lack of schisms. Ironically, shortly after Sarkar's death at least two schisms led to the establishment of organizations based on the ideology propagated by Ananda Marga.[18]

The Progressive Utilization Theory

To a large extent, the controversy that Ananda Marga has generated can be attributed to PROUT, Sarkar's theory of socioeconomic and political ideas, which is summarized in the fifth chapter of Sarkar's seminal work, *Ananda Sutram* (Anandamurti 1996/1962). Its political aspect describes a social order or social cycle (Samaja Cakra) dominated by one of four classes of people in turn: laborers, military-minded individuals, intellectuals, or capitalists; called *sudras, ksatriyas, vipras,* and *vaisyas,* respectively.[19] In *Human Society* (1999/1959), Sarkar traced the historical development of the social classes and their movement within the social cycle.

What he actually depicted was an infinite social spiral, with each of the four classes dominating for a period of time and all of their social contributions being rolled into a new round of class dominances. Sarkar believed that a healthy society should change periodically, bringing improvements with the ascendency of each social class to power. If any class adopted the role of an exploiter and clung to political power, Sarkar proposed a solution. He asserted that an indispensable body of spiritual elites called Sadvipras should determine who held positions of political leadership (Anandamurti 1978b, 1996). He called this arrangement the "benevolent dictatorship of the Sadvipras" (Sarkar n.d., 3; 1993b, 45–46).

Sadvipra Society Rests on Revolutionary Ideals

Sadvipras were supposed to be intellectuals whose true (*sad*) knowledge was based on the experience of spiritual reality. This implies they would be spiritually developed or self-realized individuals. Sarkar (1999) referred to them as spiritual moralists: spiritualists with a mission to fight against immorality. On the level of collective society he described Sadvipras' work as applying varying degrees of force to the social cycle in order to change the order of dominance of the social classes (Anandamurti 1996). These applications of force could range from mild to severe, depending on what the Sadvipras thought was necessary. Great applications of force would produce revolutionary change, whereas milder applications would result in evolutionary transformation. Nonetheless, Sarkar stated in many of his books that revolution would always be necessary in order to wrest control of society away from capitalists (Anandamurti 1996; Sarkar 1987a, 1987b, 1993b). A complete rotation of his social cycle, called peripheric evolution (*parikranti*), included sudra revolution (Anandamurti 1996), which meant a popular or worker's uprising, the overthrow of government and its rulers, accompanied by basic socioeconomic changes. Sarkar believed that a greater proportion of intellectual versus military-minded people in the process would produce a revolution less inclined to bloodshed (1987b, 1999), but he said this "rarely happens" and "in most cases, popular emancipation is blood-soaked" (1987b, 5). So Sadvipra society ultimately rested on revolutionary ideals.

For Sarkar, capitalists were a special social problem. He characterized them as "immoral and anti-social" exploiters responsible for the starvation of others (1987a, 2). He criticized their "ambition to become rich by exploiting others" as a "psychic disease"(1993b, 6). In the general interests of humanity, Sarkar believed that capitalism had to be destroyed "by taking strong measures"(1993b, 4–5). The pressure of circumstances would have to be applied so that people who exploit others would be forced to stop. In *PROUT in a Nutshell*, part VI, Sarkar explains that he believes that the first Sadvipras will be created from the middle class, from a segment of dissatisfied intellectuals and military-minded people who feel especially exploited by capitalists. These Sadvipras will spearhead general or mass revolution against exploiters (Sarkar 1987b).

Sarkar envisioned Sadvipras as classless individuals whose spiritual development would ensure the protection of all group interests (1993b). They would remain in the metaphorical center of society, controlling the social cycle's rotation (Anandamurti 1996). On the concrete level Sarkar recommended organizing Sadvipras into legislative, executive, and judicial boards, with a Supreme Board acting as the ultimate authority (n.d.). He asserted that the "establishment of [social] equality is possible only by tantrics and not by non-tantrics" (Anandamurti 1994).

Sadvipras are supposed to follow spiritual morality and be the "genuine servants of mankind," (Sarkar 1991a, 73), but to date the results produced by what we may call proto-Sadvipras are mixed. There are allegations by former organizational workers that other workers engaged in various kinds of illegal activities, part of which seemed to be aimed at fund-raising.[20] One ex-sannyasi explained that organizational finances were always a problem because the sannyasis were forbidden to work for money and had to rely on donations. This situation was sometimes aggravated when sannyasis were sent to distant parts of the globe to proselytize with only their faith to rely upon.

A Socialist Ideology Produced and Supported by Spiritual Experience

The socialism of PROUT is based on Sarkar's belief in and, one would assume, his experience of cosmological patrimony. He asserted that "This universe is created in the imagination of Brahma, the Supreme Entity, so the ownership of this universe lies with Brahma and not the microcosms [people] created out of Brahma's imagination" (1987a, 1). In order for others to experience the universe in the way that Sarkar did, Ananda Marga's system of spiritual practice is aimed at providing individuals with the mystical experience of the unity of the universe. Without such an experience there is no confirmation of the validity of Sarkar's assertion, and it remains only an intellectual, cosmological idea. Consequently, PROUT is a mystic system because it desires socioeconomic justice that is based on spiritual ideals and that results from the means by which Ananda Margiis and PROUTists hope to achieve it. They seek the spiritual or mystical development of humanity as a result of the mystical experience they say regular meditation provides.

The mystical socialism of PROUT is described in the fifth chapter of Sarkar's *Ananda Sutram* as a series of principles contained in aphorisms. They grant people the right to use the wealth of the universe but not to abuse it by hoarding. Sarkar said, "No individual should be allowed to accumulate any physical wealth without the clear permission or approval of the collective body" (Anandamurti 1996, 47–48). They guarantee people the minimum necessities of life as those are conceived of during any particular time period, including food, clothing, shelter, education, and medicine. If there is a surplus, PROUT believes that people who serve society should be given more so as to enable them to serve in a better way. This type of incentive economy distinguishes PROUT from Communism, for PROUT believes that a healthy society would have an ever-increasing minimum standard available to everyone. All of the physical, mental, and spiritual resources in the universe were to be developed, utilized, and "rationally distributed" (Anandamurti 1996, 48). All individuals should be given the opportunity to contribute to society according to their most developed capacities. Finally, throughout his ideology, Sarkar allowed for changes that would occur in different time periods, at varying locations, and with disparate individuals.

When Sarkar formulated his economic ideology, he envisioned PROUT functioning at three levels: small-scale concerns (held privately), cooperatives, and "key industries" or public utilities (1988b, 13). The key industries would function as nonprofits to produce things that local governments would find impractical to make for themselves. Wherever possible, he encouraged the use of producers' and consumers' cooperatives, which he expected to represent the bulk of economic endeavors (Sarkar 1988b). At the provincial level he conceived of bioregional entities called Samaj (society/societies) with populations that shared sociolinguistic bonds. These organizations would be capable of providing their population's minimum essentials of life by employing decentralized industry (Sarkar 1990).

Given the fact that popular revolutionary action resulting in massive social change was indispensable to Sarkar's socioeconomic and political system, it is reasonable to call PROUT a form of revolutionary mystic socialism.

Sadvipra Society as a Nonapocalyptic Social System

Ananda Marga's spiritual worldview should be classified as nonapocalyptic. Sarkar said that the Sadvipras' control of the social cycle would result in "the victory of every social class" (1993b, 46). To the extent that this is interpreted as a collective social salvation, it is tempting to classify Ananda Marga as a revolutionary progressive millennial sect (Wessinger 2000b).[21] Catherine Wessinger, drawing on the work of Norman Cohn, defines a millennial movement as one that believes in "an imminent transition to a collective salvation or permanent well-being accomplished by a superhuman agent or human beings working according to a divine or superhuman plan" (Wessinger 1997, 48). In contrast, Sarkar taught that Sadvipra society would for several reasons be in a state of constant flux. First, he believed that cosmic evil would never be eliminated, only controlled (Anandamurti 1987a). Sarkar described Sadvipras as engaging in a never-ending struggle against social exploitation (1993b, 1999). If cosmic evil does not get the upper hand, the Sadvipras (and everyone else) will be considered to have achieved the victory of the moralists over the immoralists by reducing human suffering. However, the Sadvipras are fated to achieve at best only a temporary victory. Thus, Sarkar taught a doctrine of perpetual struggle. Second, his spiral concept of social history was formed by a progressive succession of class dominances. After the first sudra revolution, a second *sudra* society would be formed, a second *ksatriya* society, and so on until a second sudra revolution was necessary. Each social cycle would be different because of technological developments and human mental expansion or refinement (Sarkar

1993b). This is in contrast to the strictly cyclical pattern of social history found in many Indic religions.[22] Inasmuch as Sarkar said that "the universe is being created endlessly" and will never cease to exist (Anandamurti 1986c, 99), Ananda Margiis may be described as historical progressives, but without a concept of a terminal social destiny.

Ananda Margiis believe that the nation-states of the twenty-first century are in different stages of their social cycles (Sarkar 1999). They hope that Sadvipra societies will become established in different parts of the globe and that eventually a global socioeconomic and political configuration guided by Sadvipras will predominate (Sarkar 1993b). However, while they apparently are anxious to spiritualize the world and save it from exploitation, there is no evidence in their literature that they believe a global transformation is imminent or that a simultaneous, total, global transformation is even possible. Sarkar said, "the rule of Sadvipras will only come about through the systematic and rational application of PROUT by many highly intelligent people." This sounds like a time-consuming process whose ideal might be achieved in a distant future. Sarkar then said, "It is not possible to establish the rule of Sadvipras by blind physical force" (1988c, 36–37).

Ananda Margiis' sense of urgency to proselytize arises from their monistic philosophy, which implies that fewer people can progress spiritually if many persons are weighted down by the darkness of materialism. The most important factor in Ananda Marga's socioeconomic and political system is the self-realized Sadvipra. The role of the divine is to assure struggling human beings of their ultimate success in the cosmic plan,[23] specifically the establishment of Sadvipra society. However, the creation of Sadvipras themselves takes time because spiritual development cannot be forced. The process within Ananda Marga is for all members to do the spiritual practices of tantra yoga, making them eligible for self-realization on a soul-by-soul basis. After an individual performs spiritual practices and develops devotion toward supreme consciousness, divine grace is thought to provide final assistance in reaching the spiritual goal (Anandamurti 1987c). A self-realized individual is presented with the option of merging into unmanifested consciousness or continuing to serve others while in an embodied human form (Anandamurti 1993).[24] Sarkar called the latter *jivan-mukta* (one who is liberated while living). Sarkar did not teach an eschatology that allows for collective liberation or salvation.

Paramilitary Activity

Sarkar believed in the necessity of maintaining military preparedness. He taught that war was inevitable as long as animality was present in humans (Kusumita 1979). Therefore, he supported the concept of a world army (Sarkar 1993b). Within Ananda Marga he created a paramilitary wing called Volunteers Social Service (VSS) and a corresponding women's division named Girls' Volunteers (GV). Despite the name of the GV, both the male and female sides of the paramilitary wing were composed of adults.[25] During Sarkar's lifetime one of the duties of the VSS and the GV was to keep order at Ananda Marga sociospiritual gatherings.

The existence of the VSS and the GV caused problems for Margiis in India and Australia. Finally, some of their members tried to minimize the importance of the paramilitary activities by characterizing them as Boy Scout–style training (Alister 1997). The programs do not appear to be particularly threatening if we compare them to a large Hindu nationalist organization such as the Rashtriya Svayamsevak Sangh (RSS) [National Union of Volunteers]. The RSS, founded in 1925 by K. B. Hedgewar (1889–1940), engages in social service and military training (Rashtriya Svayamsevak Sangh 2010). It is based on "the notion of Hindu racial, cultural, and religious superiority" (Appleby 2000, 110).

The VSS and the GV may be relatively small and founded on universalism, but they function as militias. An ex-Margii alleges that in the late 1970s their European retreats included practice with firearms. In the early 1980s a document came to light that was described to a sannyasi as a mutual defense pact signed by the Sikh Khalsa and Ananda Marga (former organizational worker 1998). Sarkar's position on the use of force is more aggressive than that of the seventeenth-century Sikh luminary, Guru Gobind, who said, "When all else fails, it is righteous to lift the sword in one's hand and fight" (Appleby 2000, 89). It is very difficult to determine to what extent Ananda Marga or PROUT have created nonpublic alliances of this type. During the 1980s, VSS and GV were theoretically available if the movement had to defend itself. Sarkar is on record as saying, "You should remember it is not the barrel of a gun but the spiritual force of human beings that is the real source of power" (1988b, 24). To what extent Ananda Margiis might feel threatened by the societies in which they live is an important and interesting question. The answers are intricately tied to Ananda Marga's global history and its ideology of social justice.[26]

Sarkar's ideology concerning the use of arms seems to alarm people more than Ananda Marga's paramilitary's strength or its degree of cohesion. However, considering PROUT's revolutionary ideology, it is natural to assume that VSS and GV could play a part in future revolutionary activities launched by PROUT.

An Ideology of Perpetual Cosmic War

Sarkar stated that gurus who have the ability to grant liberation from reincarnation are called Taraka Brahma [liberating Brahma] and that one of their functions is the polarization of the good and evil forces in the world (Anandamurti 1986a). They prepare society to fight (Anandamurti 1986a). Sarkar termed an even rarer form of guru Mahakaola. This type of Taraka Brahma was said to arise periodically in human society to reinstate *dharma* (Anandamurti 1986a), the righteous, spiritual, and "correct" order of society. Sarkar is considered by followers to have been a

Mahakaola, and the predominance of the theme of "cosmic war" in the movement's history is clear.

Cosmic war refers to a universal struggle between good and evil. Scott Appleby (2000) points out that this type of dualism is at the heart of religious fundamentalism.[27] According to the ideological characteristics of fundamentalism determined by Harriet A. Harris and the University of Chicago's Fundamentalism Project, Ananda Marga fulfills only some of the characteristics of fundamentalist groups and should therefore be described as "fundamentalist-like" (2004, 412–13). Ananda Marga notably lacks a religious or historical allegiance to a particular land and millennial beliefs. However, its political activism is religiously or spiritually motivated. The following ideological characteristics from the Fundamentalism Project's list are present in the Ananda Marga movement: absolutism, elect membership, sharp boundaries, behavioral requirements, charismatic and authoritarian leadership, and moral dualism.

Sarkar said that the totality of human history is a never-ending struggle between good and evil within human society and "throughout the entire cosmos" (1993b; Anandamurti 1987a, 90; 2000). He exhorted spiritual aspirants to engage in a ceaseless struggle against evil (Anandamurti 1990). Sarkar's concept of evil was any condition, situation, or exploitative action by an individual or group that blocked the physical, mental, and spiritual development of others (Anandamurti 1978a). Such a broad definition included the lack of minimum essentials for human life. According to Sarkar, "The absence of collective outlook is the root of all evil. The strong are perpetrating atrocities and injustices on the weak; powerful human groups are exploiting powerless ones. Under such circumstances it is the duty of virtuous people to wage war on the oppressors" (1993b, 21).

Sarkar also considered the imposition of social and religious dogmas, such as the caste system, to be manifestations of evil. He discussed his opposition to dogma and various kinds of groupism in many of his books. In *The Liberation of Intellect: Neo-Humanism* (1983), Sarkar did not limit himself to humanistic concerns and defended the developmental rights of animals, plants, and even allegedly nonsentient entities such as rocks. Likewise, Ananda Margiis consider themselves to be broad-minded universalists.

Sarkar's writings demonized sociospiritual exploiters, whom he called "demons in human form" (1987c, 19), "devils," "evil forces," "fiends of hell," and "creatures of darkness." A particularly intense concentration of these colorful labels can be seen in *Ananda Vanii Samgraha: A Collection of the Spiritual Messages of Shrii Shrii Anandamurti* (1990). On the other hand and significantly, Sarkar also said, "You have no right to hate even a single living creature" (1985, 11). To what extent his followers have been able to eschew an "us versus them" mentality while engaging in the process of cosmic war is open to question. Catherine Wessinger and Mark Juergensmeyer have identified radical dualism and the dehumanization or "satanization" of others as problematic characteristics within some new religious movements, which can contribute to episodes of violence (Wessinger 2000a; Juergensmeyer 2000).

Sarkar asserted that "Peace is the result of fight. Peace-lovers of the universe must not keep themselves away from fight" (Anandamurti 1990, 9). In *Problems of the Day* and *PROUT in a Nutshell*, part III, Sarkar described his doctrine of social struggle by referring to two possible states of "peace." The first is dominated by the static principle, or *tamas*, which may be called "static" or "black" peace (1993b, 18). When people are under its influence, they refrain from acting on behalf of oppressed peoples. The second state is dominated by the sentient principle, or *sattva*, which Sarkar called "sentient" or "white" peace (1987a, 11). He thought of what people normally call peace as a static condition and said that his followers should seek a "white peace," in which they actively struggle against wrongdoing (1987a, 12). When under its influence, people courageously confronted individual aggressors or aggressor-nations, using arms if necessary (1993b).

According to Sarkar's monistic spiritual worldview, no problem was simply an individual or group affair but the collective problem of universal humanity (Anandamurti 1985). All human life was deeply interconnected, and each human being was obliged to shoulder responsibility for the well-being of every other human being or group. In his *Discourses on Mahabharata* (1991), Sarkar wrote about the Mahavisva [Great Universe] as a culture consisting of cooperative living entities. He considered the establishment of such a society the central task for moral people in the modern age.[28] Failure signified the destruction of humanity through constant fighting (1991). He placed a utopian ideal before his followers. His Mahavisva would be as perfect a sociospiritual ideal as possible. It would be relatively free from social inequalities, and all people would move forward on the path to self-realization. However, it would require a more or less constant vigilance and struggle by Ananda Marga–style spiritual moralists. The establishment and maintenance of Mahavisva would require engaging in cosmic war, a mental and physical struggle between good and evil forces in the universe.

Ananda Marga's monistic ideology requires some parsing to comprehend its moral dualism. Margiis assert the divine unity of all things and find no contradiction in their belief that cosmic evil manifests as part of that unity. Sarkar's cosmology as described in *Ananda Sutram* is monistic, with universal consciousness undergoing a temporary or relative transformation (of manifestation) to appear as the universe we know. Therefore, one of Ananda Marga's senior monks referred to Ananda Marga philosophy as *advaetadvaetadvaeta vada*—a theory (*vada*) of nondualistic, dualistic, nondualism (Vijayananda 1994). When individual souls earn liberation from rebirth, they return to their characteristic nondual state. Sarkar said that in the manifested world, divine consciousness assumes the roles of actors who take on good and evil characteristics. Under the complete control of divine will, these actors enact a cosmic struggle (Anandamurti 1986b). In other words, divine consciousness or Siva creates evil out of himself for his own purposes.

Sarkar's "Spiritual Morality"

One of Sarkar's pivotal concepts is "spiritual morality." Sarkar defined "simple morality" as following factual truth, while "spiritual morality" permits an individual to go beyond simple morality if there is an overriding justification (1991, 45–48). Of the two, he considered spiritual morality superior due to its dynamism. Simple morality should be respected as an essential human value because it imparts a tremendous moral force, but it is static in nature (1991). Sarkar cited the words and actions of Lord Krsna and the Pandavas in the *Mahabharata* as justification of his support of spiritual morality. Krsna said, "When one is outnumbered by his enemies, then destruction should be brought about by stratagem" (Narasimhan 1998, 175). Sarkar similarly endorsed strategy in the struggle against exploiters.

Sarkar said spiritual aspirants should live in such a way that others would trust them (Anandamurti 1978a). "As long as legal statutes exist, they must be obeyed. If they are found to be harmful . . . these statutes should be ground into the dust and new laws should be enacted and obeyed" (Sarkar 1990, 60). However, he also said he did not think it necessary for "rational people" to follow a country's legal codes "blindly," as these may not take into consideration the spiritual issues at stake (Anandamurti 1978b, 29). Sarkar's morality was a spiritual morality with exceptions for circumstances and a consideration of spiritual values. This is not a standard means of evaluation because it is determined by relative factors. To utilize it, Sarkar said it was necessary for a person to develop "crooked intellect" (1991, 45). He did not expand on the meaning of that phrase, but according to his interpretation of the events in the *Mahabharata*, one may conclude that it signifies "deviousness." Spiritual morality's primary concern and moral justification is the advancement of people's physical, mental, and spiritual development, while its Achilles' heel is the fact that it is so open to interpretation. Obviously not everyone would agree on a definition of *dharma* or what constitutes a threat to it. One would then determine how to act based on one's individual understanding.

Arms versus Drums and Cymbals

To win the fight against evil in society, Sarkar said *tantrikas* should acquire strength because it was "impossible for goats to establish sentient peace in the society of tigers" (1993b, 19). The real source of people's power might be their spiritual force, but organizing on the material level was indispensable. Sarkar (n.d.) observed that arms were more necessary than the drums and cymbals used for worship.[29] Not only should *tantrikas* arm themselves, but they should also go on inventing ever more powerful weapons as a counterbalance to those society has (Sarkar 1987b). Here the question may arise as to how the use of force that results in *himsa* (harm) could be sanctioned by a tantric sect claiming the moral principles of *yama* and *niyama* as the basis of their spiritual practices.[30] The answer lies in their interpretation of *ahimsa* (harmlessness) as not inflicting pain or injury on any innocent being. The immoralists are thwarting human progress by their physical, economic, and psychic exploitation. They fall into a category that Sarkar called *atatayii*, individuals or groups against whom the use of force is authorized.[31]

Sarkar encouraged military strategy by saying that as long as a group lacked power, its enemies should be patiently tolerated, but the "moment" sufficient power was achieved, the enemy had to be attacked and killed (1991, 41). There should be planning, as opposed to the "Rajput folly" of people in the *ksatriya varna* (warrior class) named Rajputs, who ruled areas of north India and were said to have marched off repeatedly to certain death even though they knew they were vastly outnumbered. With regard to taking preemptive actions, Sarkar told his followers that one needed to be sure of the enemy's intentions; then they could act with impunity (former organizational worker 1998). In the interests of humanity, Sarkar was not opposed to "mercilessly" removing theories that opposed his idea of social equality (1987c, 32). He called this principle of social equality Sama-Samaja Tattva.

In 1966 Sarkar told his followers, "Your duty will be to unite the moralists. Let there be two camps. Let there be an open fight" (n.d., 1). At this point, it is not hard to visualize the battlefield flags of the Pandavas and Kauravas from the *Mahabharata*. This time, one of the flags would be a saffron triangle (▶) with a white *svastika* on it—the flag that represents Ananda Marga. The *svastika* (swastika) is an auspicious Hindu symbol that is said to bestow good luck. Ananda Margiis highlight its literal translation as "well-being" and say it represents "permanent spiritual victory" (Tarak 1990, 32–33).[32]

Religious Violence

Some of the interactions between Ananda Marga sannyasis and others appear to have been determined by the Margiis' ideological totalism. They firmly believe that the ideology of Ananda Marga is the answer to all of the world's spiritual and material problems.

Ananda Margiis or PROUTists are alleged to have murdered apostates who left and taught independently. According to Mark Juergensmeyer's analysis of elements of religious violence, such acts could be seen as intraorganizational terrorism; the target of such murderers would be other organizational workers. Of course, these alleged acts may have been punitive as well. Nityananda was well respected, even admired, by many in the Ananda Marga organization, and his defection must have wounded the sentiments of quite a few people, not to mention that his marrying would have been seen as a betrayal of his fellow sannyasis (former organizational worker 2006). Therefore, at least some members of Ananda Marga or PROUT are not free from the allegation of terrorism. The question remains as to whether the whole organization or any branch of it should be characterized this way.

The number of positive correlations between Juergensmeyer's description of religious groups inclined toward terrorism and Ananda Marga is dramatic. They utilize images of cosmic war. They have "satanized" their opponents, which is "part of the construction of an image of cosmic war" (Juergensmeyer 2000, 182). They provide moral justifications for killing. Sarkar made different statements about whether enemies should be killed at the earliest opportunity or reformed. He seemed to prefer reformation when possible but approved the use of force in the intervening period (1987a). For Margiis and PROUTists, civil law is ultimately an option. Sarkar said that moral judgments were a concern of the material world alone and "meaningless" for supreme consciousness (Anandamurti 2000, 182). However, he did not dispute the importance of distinguishing right and wrong within society. Finally, the victory of the immoralists was unthinkable. Despite the overwhelming odds, the forces of good would prevail in the world, or everything would be destroyed. Come what may, Sarkar asserted that Mahavisva, the great universe of cooperative living entities, would have to be established:

> Not only in this small world, but also in every planet and satellite, star, meteor, galaxy and every particle of this vast creation a person has the right to live. If anybody wants to deprive people of this very birth-right, then human beings will have to establish it by the use of force. (1987a, 13)

Sarkar called his followers "spiritual soldiers" and reminded them that "victory does not come by itself. Victory has to be invited and welcomed with sweat, the warmth of the blood and fiery flames of hard labour" (Anandamurti 1990, 13, 47).

Conclusion: Revolutionary Sociospiritual Utopians

On the basis of Sarkar's books, it is more accurate to state that he and his followers, whether Ananda Margiis or PROUTists, support revolution rather than terrorism. Sarkar rejected terrorism and distanced himself from "misguided youths" who had no understanding of his ideology (former organizational worker 1998). This was an obvious reference to those who spearheaded and joined the UPRF and were alleged to have engaged in acts of terrorism. Ananda Marga's history to date indicates that the incidents of extraorganizational violence that took place while Sarkar was incarcerated were an aberration. They were mistakes by a small group of followers who later recognized their errors (former organizational worker 1998). Sarkar's followers are tantric revolutionaries with a mystical system of socialism based on their perceived experience of the unity of the universe.

Intraorganizational violence against apostates is a form of retaliation that can be classified as terrorism. The appearance in the 1990s of several organizations based on Sarkar's ideology and practices proves how futile it is to try to control the spread of ideas or to eliminate competition from other spiritual organizations.

Sarkar clearly believed that the use of force is necessary in individual, as well as collective, life and that a well-knit human society free from social injustice cannot be produced without it. Nevertheless, that did not prevent him from realizing some of the shortcomings of using a level of force that could be characterized as violent. Sarkar said violence begets further violence and tends to invite increasing levels of violence in response (Anandamurti 1978a). The extent to which this understanding may influence his followers is undetermined. It cannot be said with any certainty that the fomenting of revolution—bloody or bloodless—would be excluded from the future activities of Ananda Margiis or PROUTists. That would appear to depend on their analyses of surrounding socioeconomic and political conditions.

NOTES

1. Sarkar invented the system of diacritics that Ananda Marga uses in its publications. He chose a simplified Sanskrit transliteration that uses the accent mark almost exclusively. However, even the application of this system was not uniform from one of his books to another and sometimes was not uniform even within a single book.

2. This incident occurred as I began presenting a paper on Ananda Marga at a meeting of the North American Hindu Association of Dharma Studies (NAHADS). Two individuals who were present gasped audibly at the first mention of Ananda Marga, looked at one another, and simultaneously raced for the door. The NAHADS held what is called an "additional meeting" at the conference of the American Academy of Religion in Atlanta, Georgia, in November 2003.

3. Buddha Purnima is the full-moon day on which Buddha is believed to have been born. According to the Indian lunar calendar, this would be the lunar month of Vaesakh, which usually occurs during the Roman calendar month of May.

4. Brahmo Samaj was founded in 1828 by Ram Mohan Roy (1782–1833), who passed the leadership on to Debendranath Tagore, Rabindranath Tagore's father.

5. Its parts include *yama* (moral abstinences), *niyama* (moral observances), *asanas* (physical postures practiced without straining), *pranayama* (breath-control techniques), *pratyahara* (sensory withdrawal), *dharana* (concentration), and *dhyana* (flowing, ideational meditation). Ananda Margiis do not consider Patanjali's eighth limb, *samadhi* (a trance of absorption into divine consciousness), to be a practice but rather an experience resulting from the other seven limbs/practices.

6. Those with a yogic orientation tend to interpret them as subtle practices connected to meditation techniques. The emphasis in Ananda Marga's spiritual practices is on the psychospiritual anatomy of the *chakras* (energy centers) and *nadis* (subtle nerves) and on mantra meditation. Sarkar listed the items of the five Ms as *madya* (divine intoxication brought on by a hormonal secretion from the pineal gland), *mamsa* (control over speech), *matsya* (controlling the psychospiritual nerves of the body through *pranayama*), *mudra* (keeping spiritual company), and *maithuna* (the union of individual and supreme consciousness). Those *tantrikas* whose spiritual practices involve a sexual ritual often interpret the five Ms as *madya* (wine), *mamsa* (meat), *matsya* (fish), *mudra* (parched grain), and *maithuna* (sexual union).

7. Ananda Marga organizational workers told this story regularly in the late 1970s.

8. The man told me they had to run for their lives. He subsequently abandoned his idea of becoming an Ananda Marga sannyasi and became a monk in a different spiritual organization (former Ananda Margii 1973).

9. The "Maintenance of Internal Security Act" (MISA) and the "Defence of India Rules" (DIR) both contained detention provisions.

10. Amnesty International investigated the situation of political detainees held during the 1971 and 1975–1977 emergencies and presented a report to the Indian government on Sept. 21, 1978. While this document does not specifically mention Sarkar or Ananda Marga, Amnesty International's highlighting the plight of political prisoners held without trial probably helped resolve Sarkar's case.

11. The secretary-general of the International Commission of Jurists had received a report from Canadian jurist C. Sheppard, saying the Indian government had blocked funds coming from overseas for Sarkar's defense. The secretary-general's critical comments were reflected in the jurists' meeting minutes of Aug. 27, 1976.

12. In line with Sarkar's writings, Margiis tend to reject suicide as wasted effort that delays liberation. However, the acaryas in these self-immolation cases must have considered the well-being of their guru to be paramount.

13. Ananda Marga sannyasis told me this in the 1980s. Despite the negative, contemporary Western associations with the term, Sarkar sometimes emphasized the organization's cultic aspects and encouraged practitioners to develop a "cult of devotion" (Kusumita 1979, 32). Sarkar also explained that tantra yoga, Ananda Marga's professed system of spiritual practices, has a reputation for valuing the efficacy of practice (cultivation) over theory (Anandamurti 1994).

14. The U.S. government awarded Ananda Marga Community Education Technical Advocates (CETA) grants that supported workers at their permanent social service projects. Government assistance from Great Britain and Finland was described to me by Ananda Marga organizational workers.

15. See Sil (1988b) for an explanation of the Bengali folk attitude toward "child lifting," or kidnapping.

16. The former organizational worker who told me this story also claimed that the LFT's confession was made in the presence of four people.

17. See Wessinger (2000b) with regard to the following instances: the 1994 Order of the Solar Temple murder of apostates (Introvigne 2000) and Aum Shinrikyo's murder of dissidents (Reader 2000a). See also Reader (2000b).

18. One of these is Ananda Seva, an organization cofounded by an American, Megan Nolan. Its international headquarters is in Santa Rosa, California. The other is Modern Seers (formerly called Abhidhyan Yoga Institute), founded by a Russian man, Anatole Ruslanov. Modern Seers is registered in California and currently headquartered in Swarthmore, Pennsylvania.

19. Sarkar described the mentalities of *sudra*, *ksatriya*, *vipra*, and *vaisya* persons as dominated by black, red, white, and yellow mental color vibrations, respectively. He emphasized that these terms did not indicate caste divisions and that people could change their dominant mental vibrations by changing their activities.

20. The allegations come from a variety of former organizational workers and include fraud, forgery, and narcotrafficking, as well as trafficking in armaments. An allegation of arms trafficking also appeared in a *New York Times* article (Bonner 1998).

21. On the concepts of millennialism, catastrophic millennialism and progressive millennialism see Wessinger (2000a, 2000b).

22. Sarkar did not support the view that the universe passes through *kalpas* (ages) consisting of the Satya, Treta, Dvapara and Kali *yugas* [eras] (Anandamurti 1987c). On the fact that a nonlinear view of time is not a disqualifier for a new religion to be considered millennialist, see Wessinger (1997).

23. This comes across clearly in Anandamurti (1990).

24. Sarkar termed the first state *moksa*, a permanent or nonqualified liberation or salvation. He called the latter state a mental liberation, or *mukti* (Anandamurti 1993).

25. During the 1980s female ex-Margiis reported agitation on the women's side, up to the highest levels, to change the name to something that did not imply women's immaturity and need for perpetual supervision by the men's division. Sarkar denied the request, saying all human beings were the boys and girls of their loving father, who is the supreme consciousness.

26. An analysis of this type requires country-by-country research that I hope will be undertaken in the future. Availability of this information could defuse potentially explosive situations. Bromley and Shupe in *Strange Gods* have observed that paramilitary operations are "common among groups that feel themselves to be threatened and embattled" (1981, 64).

27. According to Appleby's definitions, Ananda Margiis and PROUTists are engaged in a struggle that falls somewhere between the Christian tradition of "just war" and the more vigorous concept of "holy war" (2000, 34).

28. At the concrete political level Sarkar believed it would be necessary to form a world government that was not based on nationalism (1993a). He preferred a decentralized bioregionalism he called Samaj.

29. Some senior male sannyasis, called *avadhutas*, carried daggers and *lathis* (staffs), while their female counterparts, called *avadhutikas*, carried *trisuls* (tridents). These were a standard part of sannyasi uniforms but have not been worn consistently. The Indian government banned them in the 1980s after a public outcry and thereafter sporadically enforced the ban. In fact, these weapons appear to be largely ceremonial and not sufficient for the purpose of insurrection. This controversy parallels that concerning the potential defensive uses of the Sikh Khalsa dagger (*kirpan*), which is banned in Denmark but legal in Canada and the United Kingdom if its size conforms to local restrictions.

30. According to Ananda Marga, the principles of *yama* and *niyama* are as follows: *Yama* (abstinences) are composed of *ahimsa* (noninjury), *satya* (right use of words), *asteya* (nonstealing), *Brahmacarya* (attachment to supreme consciousness), and *aparigraha* (nonindulgence). The items of *niyama* (observances) are *shaoca* (physical and mental cleanliness), *santosa* (mental contentment), *tapah* (penance), *svadhyaya* (spiritual study), and *Iishvara pranidhana* (surrender to supreme consciousness). See Anandamurti (1969) for an expanded explanation of these concepts.

31. *Atatayiis* include anyone who, "by the use of brute force, wants to take possession of your property, abducts your wife, comes with a weapon to murder you, wants to snatch away your wealth, sets fire to your house or wants to take your life by administering poison" (Anandamurti 1969, 10).

32. For Ananda Margiis the *svastika* implies the victory of moralists over immoralists.

REFERENCES

Alister, Paul Narada. 1997. *Bombs, Bliss, and Baba: The Spiritual Autobiography behind the Hilton Bombing Frame-up*. Maleny, Australia: Better World Books.

Amnesty International. 1979. *Report of an Amnesty International Mission to India: 31 December 1977–18 January 1978*. London: Author, AI Index: ASA 20/03/78.

Ananda Marga Pracaraka Sangha. 2008. *Justice Weeps Silently and Furtively*. Online. Available: Online. Available: Online. Available: Online. Available: http://news.indiainfo.com/publicopinion/anandamarga-justice.html. March 13 2008 2008.

Anandamitra Ac., Avadhutika, ed. 1980. *Circle of Love: A Manual for Kindergarten Teachers*. Manila, Philippines: Ananda Marga Board of Education.

Anandamurti, Shrii Shrii. 1969. *A Guide to Human Conduct*, 4th ed. Calcutta: Ananda Marga Pracaraka Samgha.

———. 1978a. *Supreme Expression I: Discourses on Spiritual Philosophy*. 's-Hertogenbosch, the Netherlands: Nirvikalpa.

———. 1978b. *Supreme Expression II: Discourses on Social Philosophy*. 's-Hertogenbosch, the Netherlands: Nirvikalpa.

———.1986a. *Ananda Vacanamrtam*, part I, 2d ed. Calcutta: Ananda Marga Pracaraka Samgha. (Orig. pub. 1979.)

———.1986b. *Ananda Vacanamrtam*, part II, 2d ed. Calcutta: Ananda Marga Pracaraka Samgha. (Orig. pub. 1979.)

———. 1986c. *Ananda Vacanamrtam*, part IV. Calcutta: Ananda Marga Pracaraka Samgha.

———. 1987a. *Ananda Vacanamrtam*, part V. Calcutta: Ananda Marga Pracaraka Samgha.

———. 1987b. *Ananda Vacanamrtam*, part VI. Calcutta: Ananda Marga Pracaraka Samgha.

———. 1987c. *Ananda Vacanamrtam*, part VII. Calcutta: Ananda Marga Pracaraka Samgha.

———. 1987d. *Ananda Vacanamrtam*, part VIII. Calcutta: Ananda Marga Pracaraka Samgha.

———. 1990. *Ananda Vanii Samgraha: Collection of the Spiritual Messages of Shrii Shrii Anandamurti*, 2d ed. Calcutta: Ananda Marga Pracaraka Samgha. (Orig. pub. 1985.)

———. 1994. *Discourses on Tantra*, vol. 2. Calcutta: Ananda Marga Publications.

———. 1996. *Ananda Sutram*, 2d ed. Calcutta: Ananda Marga Publications. (Orig. pub. 1962 Bengali; 1967 English.)

———. 2000. *Discourses on Krsna and the Giita*. Calcutta: Ananda Marga Pracaraka Samgha.

Appleby, R. Scott. 2000. *The Ambivalence of the Sacred: Religion, Violence, and Reconciliation*. Lanham, Md.: Rowman and Littlefield.

Bonner, Raymond. 1998. "The Murky Life of an International Gun Dealer." *New York Times* (July 14). http://www.nytimes.com/1998/07/14/world/the-murky-life-of-an-international-gun-dealer.html?pagewanted=all.

Bromley, David G., and Anson D. Shupe Jr. 1981. *Strange Gods: The Great American Cult Scare*. Boston: Beacon.

Buhrman, Sarasvati. 2000. Interview by author. October 7. Boulder, Colorado.

Crovetto, Helen. 2005. "Ananda Marga's Tantric Neo-humanism." In *Encyclopedia of Religion and Nature*, ed. Bron Taylor, 47–49. New York: Continuum International.

Harris, Harriet A. 2004. "Fundamentalisms." In *New Religions: A Guide: New Religious Movements, Sects, and Alternative Spiritualities*, ed. Christopher Partridge, 409–14. New York: Oxford University Press.
Hopkins, Thomas J. 2005. "Brahmo Samaj." In *Encyclopedia of Religion*, vol. 2, ed. Lindsay Jones, 1028. Detroit: ThomsonGale/Macmillan.
Introvigne, Massimo. 2000. "The Magic of Death: The Suicides of the Solar Temple." In *Millennialism, Persecution, and Violence: Historical Cases*, ed. Catherine Wessinger, 138–57. Syracuse: Syracuse University Press.
Juergensmeyer, Mark. 2000. *Terror in the Mind of God: The Global Rise of Religious Violence*. Berkeley: University of California Press.
Kang, Chris. 2000. Sarkar and the Buddha's Four Noble Truths. Paper presented at the Australian Association for the Study of Religions Annual Conference, 30 June-2 July 2000, Brisbane, Australia. http://www.metafuture.org/Sarkar-4nobletruths.pdf, accessed 6 October 2010.
Kusumita. 1979. *Baba in Fiesch: Rungsted Kyst*. Denmark: PROUTist Universal.
Narasimhan, Chakravarthi V. 1998. *The Mahabharata: An English Version Based on Selected Verses*. New York: Columbia University Press.
OSL, The. 2007. http://www.theosl.com/archives/199803/tl00107.html. January 23.
Potter, Karl H. 1983. *Encyclopedia of Indian Philosophies*, vol. 1. Delhi: Motilal Banarsidass.
Rashtriya Svayamsevak Sangh. 2010. "Rashtriya Svayamsevak Sangh." http://rssonnet.org/index.php?option=com_timeline&Itemid=56, accessed 6 October 2010
Reader, Ian. 2000a. "Imagined Persecution: Aum Shinrikyo, Millennialism, and the Legitimation of Violence." In *Millennialism, Persecution, and Violence: Historical Cases*, ed. Catherine Wessinger, 158–82. Syracuse: Syracuse University Press.
———. 2000b. *Religious Violence in Contemporary Japan: The Case of Aum Shinrikyo*. Honolulu: University of Hawaii Press.
Robbins, Thomas. 2002. "Sources of Volatility in Religious Movements." In *Cults, Religion, and Violence*, ed. David G. Bromley and J. Gordon Melton, 57–79. New York: Cambridge University Press.
Sarkar, P. R. 1983. *The Liberation of Intellect: Neo-humanism*, 2d ed. Calcutta: Ananda Marga Pracaraka Samgha. (Orig. pub. 1982.)
———. 1987a. *PROUT in a Nutshell*, part III. Calcutta: Ananda Marga Pracaraka Samgha.
———. 1987b. *PROUT in a Nutshell*, part VI. Calcutta: Ananda Marga Pracaraka Samgha.
———. 1987c. *PROUT in a Nutshell*, part VIII. Calcutta: Ananda Marga Pracaraka Samgha.
———. 1988a. *A Few Problems Solved*, part VII. Calcutta: Ananda Marga Pracaraka Samgha.
———. 1988b. *Notes on Social and Spiritual Philosophy*. Calcutta: Ananda Marga Pracaraka Samgha.
———. 1988c. *PROUT in a Nutshell*, part XIV. Calcutta: Ananda Marga Pracaraka Samgha.
———. 1991. *Discourses on Mahabharata*, 2d ed. Calcutta: Ananda Marga Pracaraka Samgha. (Orig. pub. 1982.).
———. 1993a. *Idea and Ideology*, 7th ed., ed. Ac. Vijayananda Avt. Calcutta: Ananda Marga Publications. (Orig. pub. 1959.)
———. 1993b. *Problems of the Day*, 4th ed. Calcutta: Ananda Marga Publications. (Orig. pub. 1959 English.)

———. 1999. *Human Society*, 2d ed. Calcutta: Ananda Marga Publications. (Orig. pub. 1959 Bengali; 1987 English.)

———. n.d. *PROUT in a Nutshell*, part XVIII. Calcutta: Ananda Marga Publications.

Sil, Narasingha P. 1988a. "Anatomy of the Ananda Marga: Hindu Anabaptists." *Asian Culture Quarterly* 16(2) (Summer): 1–18.

———. 1988b. "The Troubled World of the Ananda Marga: An Examination." *Quarterly Review of Historical Studies* (Calcutta) 27(4) (Winter): 3–19.

Tarak, ed. 1990. *Ananda Marga Social and Spiritual Practices*. Calcutta: Ananda Marga Publications.

U.S. Department of Justice, Federal Bureau of Investigation. 2007a. *Freedom of Information Act, Ananda Marga*, part 5 of 13, file no. 105-289420, 10. http://foia.fbi.gov/anamarga/anamarga5.pdf. March 1.

———. 2007b. *Freedom of Information Act, Ananda Marga*, part 13 of 13, references, 9–10, 19. http://foia.fbi.gov/anamarga/anamarga13b.pdf. January 16.

U.S. State Department. 2004. Country Reports on Terrorism 2004. http://www.state.gov/documents/organization/45313 (accessed March 1, 2007).

Vijayananda Avadhuta, Acarya. 1994. *The Life and Teachings of Shrii Shrii Anandamurti*, vol. 1. Calcutta: Ananda Marga Publications.

Wessinger, Catherine. 1997. "Millennialism with and without the Mayhem." In *Millennium, Messiahs, and Mayhem*, ed. Thomas Robbins and Susan J. Palmer, 47–60. New York: Routledge.

———. 2000a. *How the Millennium Comes Violently: From Jonestown to Heaven's Gate*. New York: Seven Bridges.

———. 2000b. "The Interacting Dynamics of Millennial Beliefs, Persecution, and Violence." In *Millennialism, Persecution, and Violence: Historical Cases*, ed. Catherine Wessinger, 8–11. Syracuse: Syracuse University Press.

White, David Gordon. 2003. *Kiss of the Yogini: "Tantric Sex" In Its South Asian Contexts*. Chicago: University of Chicago Press.

13

Knocking on Heaven's Door: Violence, Charisma, and the Transformation of New Vrindaban

E. Burke Rochford Jr.

I always felt that the proof of Kirtanananda's purity was New Vrindaban. The number of people there that he attracted; the buildings that were constructed; the worship of Prabhupada [ISKCON's founder]. New Vrindaban was advancing with his purity, but then he reached a point where he thought he deserves this and that he is better than everyone else. He deserves to replace Prabhupada. And as soon as he did that it was over. Finished.

—Words of a previous resident of New Vrindaban, 2007

New religious movements are prone to rapid and radical changes that promote organizational transformation (Barker 2004). An important factor influencing this volatility is charismatic leadership. Charismatic leaders face the ongoing task of sustaining their legitimacy and doing so in collaboration with followers. Charisma thus grows out of social interaction between leaders and rank-and-file members who see themselves as part of the existing system of authority. Yet as Weber argues, charismatic authority exists only during the early stages of a religious movement because it is too unstable to sustain over time. Charisma must be institutionalized or risk implosion (Dawson 2002, 85).

This chapter considers the relationship between violence, charismatic authority, and the development of one of the more significant new religious communities that emerged during the 1960s era in the United States—New Vrindaban, located in West Virginia. New Vrindaban was founded and led by Kirtanananda Swami, one of the early disciples of A. C. Bhaktivedanta Swami Prabhupada, the founder of the International Society for Krishna Consciousness (ISKCON), more popularly known as the Hare Krishna movement.[1] New Vrindaban represents a worthy case study precisely because Kirtanananda's charisma was never institutionalized, a fact that ultimately had devastating consequences for the community in the face of violence. I consider how two acts of violence in 1985 and 1986 directly and indirectly undermined Kirtanananda's authority and resulted in mass defection, financial collapse, and the decline and subsequent transformation of New Vrindaban's purpose.[2] Before turning to these issues, however, I first provide a brief history of New Vrindaban's formative years.[3]

Early History of New Vrindaban (1968–1985)

New Vrindaban was established in 1968 by two of the early American disciples of A. C. Bhaktivedanta Swami Prabhupada. Kirtanananda Swami responded to an advertisement in the *San Francisco Oracle* for people to help establish a religious community in the hills near Wheeling, West Virginia. With his friend Hayagriva he visited the owner of the property to assess the possibility of establishing ISKCON's first farm community. After initially facing opposition, the owner finally agreed to lease 132 acres of land, and ISKCON's founder Prabhupada named the emerging community New Vrindaban. In time, the community purchased a number of adjacent properties and expanded to more than 3,000 acres at its peak in the mid-1980s. Kirtanananda Swami, later known as the guru Bhaktipada, held a firm grip on the leadership of the community.[4]

New Vrindaban's early days were difficult. Under the motto of "plain living and high thinking," Kirtanananda and a handful of other devotees carved fields and pasture out of the wilderness to grow crops and provide grazing for cows. The goal from the start was to build a self-sufficient community based on spiritual principles. However, Prabhupada also wanted New Vrindaban to mirror its namesake in India. He had a vision of seven temples built on the surrounding West Virginia hilltops as found in Vrindaban, India.[5] New Vrindaban would serve as a sacred *dham* and place of pilgrimage for ISKCON devotees throughout North America. The first "temple" the community built was meant as a residence for Prabhupada, who stated that he planned to retire to New Vrindaban to work exclusively on translating and writing commentaries on the Vedic scriptures. Prabhupada visited New Vrindaban on four occasions, the last of which was in June and July of 1976. Prabhupada's "Palace of Gold" was dedicated on September 2, 1979, nearly two years after Prabhupada's death.

New Vrindaban grew rapidly until the mid-1980s. In 1975 122 people were in residence: 65 men, 43 women, and 14 children (Doktorski 2003, 38). By the mid-1980s, the community had grown to approximately 500 residents, about a 100 of whom were children attending the community's boarding school (*ashrama gurukula*). Devotees relocated to New Vrindaban from other ISKCON communities to help build Prabhupada's Palace and because Kirtanananda was known as a dynamic and charismatic speaker well versed in the Vedic scriptures. He was also admired for his dedication to Prabhupada, as symbolized by his determination to build Prabhupada's palace. As one early resident of the community recalled, "He gave such great classes and the way he would speak was inspiring. I remember the first time I heard Kirtanananda speak in Boston in 1970. I was really able to understand what Prabhupada was saying after hearing him. He helped me immensely to know Srila Prabhupada and Krishna" (interview 2007). In other cases, "problem" devotees kicked out of other ISKCON communities were sometimes sent to New Vrindaban as Kirtanananda was known to take in almost all comers as long as they worked and contributed to the community's growing success. As one devotee who lived off and on at New Vrindaban in the late 1970s and early 1980s commented, "Kirtanananda would allow people such as myself, who were not following [Krishna consciousness] very strictly, to be at New Vrindaban. He found a place for me to fit because he was so intense about building New Vrindaban" (interview 2007).

Funds to support the community came largely from traveling *sankirtan* teams that comprised devotees selling various products in public locations (e.g., candles, hats, records, stickers supporting sports teams) or who solicited funds for various fictitious charities. New Vrindaban residents solicited funds throughout North America and in a number of worldwide locations as well. *Sankirtan* revenues generated millions of dollars each year in support of the community's ambitious building projects. Yet many ISKCON leaders and members remained critical of the palace project because they believed it to be in competition with distributing Prabhupada's religious texts to the public. The latter were foundational to ISKCON's purpose, and Prabhupada emphasized book distribution from the beginning of the movement. As one long-time resident of New Vrindaban explained in a 2007 interview, "There was a schism just in regards to the building of the palace. Most of ISKCON thought that Kirtanananda was way off in wanting to build Prabhupada's palace because they thought the main focus should be book distribution. They were wondering, 'Why are you building this palace in the middle of nowhere for Prabhupada?'"

Kirtanananda saw Prabhupada's palace as one important piece of a broader project that he called a "Land of Krishna" theme park, a spiritual Disneyland capable of attracting large numbers of visitors who could then be introduced to Krishna consciousness. Soon after it was completed, the palace did attract tens of thousands of people yearly. Busloads of tourists descended on the community, and Prabhupada's palace became a major tourist attraction in West Virginia. The palace reportedly attracted more than 100,000 visitors in 1982, a number that climbed to nearly 500,000 between 1983 and 1985 (Doktorski 2003, 264). The *New York Times* declared Prabhupada's palace to be "America's Taj Mahal," and the *Washington*

Post called it "Almost Heaven." In April 1979 Kirtanananda announced plans to build the largest Radha-Krishna temple in the world at New Vrindaban. Given the community's expansive aims and the considerable income generated by palace tourism, 187 nondevotees were employed from the surrounding area as secretaries, gardeners, and construction workers, making New Vrindaban one of the largest employers in Marshall County, West Virginia (Doktorski 2003, 264).

Incidents of Violence

Things changed dramatically for New Vrindaban in the autumn of 1985, when Kirtanananda was violently attacked, suffering severe head trauma as a result. Seven months later, in May of 1986, the community faced another crisis when a former resident of the community and outspoken critic of Kirtanananda was murdered, setting off an extensive investigation by state and federal authorities. The combined consequences of these acts of violence severely undermined Kirtanananda's authority and set New Vrindaban on a course toward decline and potential failure.

On October 27, 1985, while community members were laying bricks for the temple parking lot, Kirtanananda was violently assaulted by an enraged devotee. Michael Schockman (Triyogi das), who had been an ISKCON devotee for twelve years but had lived at New Vrindaban for only two months, sneaked up behind Kirtanananda and forcefully hit him on the head and back with an iron bar. Schockman was angry because Kirtanananda had refused to give him *sannyasi* initiation, a precursor to his becoming a guru in his own right. Kirtanananda suffered severe head injuries and nearly died from the attack. He was hospitalized in intensive care in Wheeling, West Virginia, where an emergency craniotomy was performed to relieve hemorrhaging in the brain. After being transferred to the Allegheny General Hospital in Pittsburgh, a second operation was performed to remove a blood clot from Kirtanananda's brain. He remained in a coma for ten days and was in critical condition for three weeks. Not surprisingly, devotees at New Vrindaban and throughout the movement were gravely concerned about whether Kirtanananda would survive. Confidence in his recovery grew, however, when devotees saw a scan of Kirtanananda's damaged brain with an image that appeared to be that of Lord Nrisimhadeva, the half-man, half-lion incarnation of Krishna. The image was evidence to many that Krishna was looking after the well-being of their beloved leader. Devotees throughout the world performed twenty-four-hour *kirtans* (i.e., chanting and singing accompanied by music) in Kirtanananda's honor. They also prayed for his recovery. As one of his followers put it, "He almost left his body, and actually all of ISKCON was praying for him. If he had died at that point, he would have been a saint historically. But that is not what happened" (interview 2007).

When Kirtanananda returned to New Vrindaban after nearly a month in the hospital, he had trouble walking and talking as he remained partially paralyzed from his brain injury. He also suffered permanent hearing loss in his right ear, problems with his vision and memory, and lasting cognitive impairments that would interfere with his ability to lead the community. Yet Kirtanananda continued to make decisions and provide spiritual leadership. As one resident of New Vrindaban observed, "He didn't seem to have much choice; New Vrindaban residents practically demanded that he continue to lead the community" (Doktorski 2003, 260). Thus, Kirtanananda's brush with death initially elevated his authority, as well as the amount of affection showered on him by members of the community. As one of his disciples remembered:

> We thought of his smiling face, his sweet words and his past affectionate dealings with us and petitioned Lord Nrisimhadeva, "If it is your will, please return Shrila Bhaktipada to us." It was during this time that we began chanting *jaya jagad-guru shrila bhaktipada* in the temple. We had always considered Bhaktipada to be a "jagad-guru," a world-class spiritual master, but we were never bold enough to chant that refrain during kirtans until he was nearly taken away from us. It is said that one often doesn't appreciate the object of one's love until it is taken away. Our love for our spiritual master became stronger and stronger due to the fire of separation. For all we knew, we might never see him again. (Doktorski 2003, 79) (italics in the original)

It became clear early on to some at New Vrindaban that Kirtanananda was acting out of character following his head injury. Because of his spiritual status and authority, however, no one questioned him about his health. As one Prabhupada disciple and thirty-year resident of New Vrindaban recalled:

> He was in a coma for some time, and it must have been very damaging. And I felt that when he came back again, the devotees were again listening to every word he said. It was just the gospel truth as far as they were concerned. But I began to notice a difference in his behavior. I felt he needed to go back and get some follow-up [medical] care. He never went back [to the hospital] and got any rehabilitation, follow-up. Nobody in the community knew what the long-term symptoms would look like from this type of damage. No one even mentioned it. And whatever he said was like the absolute truth. And that bothered me. And it seemed that it didn't bother other people. Here he is preaching as always, but it didn't look right to me. (interview 2007)

In the months and years to follow it became increasingly evident that Kirtanananda's head injury had left him mentally unstable and spiritually weakened. However, before this became widely understood another act of violence occurred that would have far-reaching consequences. Things changed dramatically for

Kirtanananda and New Vrindaban after May 22, 1986, when a former resident of the community was murdered near the Los Angeles ISKCON temple. Stephen Bryant (Sulocana das) had been on a crusade against Kirtanananda after Kirtanananda initiated Bryant's wife without Bryant's consent. Later Kirtanananda gave his approval for Bryant's wife to divorce and marry another member of the community. Kirtanananda became alarmed when Bryant mailed him a one-hundred-page statement listing numerous and serious allegations against him and threatened to release the document to the press. This initial statement was subsequently elaborated on by Bryant and became his controversial manuscript, "The Guru Business." While Bryant was highly critical of all of ISKCON's new gurus, his harshest criticism was directed at Kirtanananda:

> [Kirtanananda] was the first to attack Srila Prabhupada trying to usurp the ISKCON movement for himself. Shortly thereafter he was the first to sit on a throne and accept worship of himself even during Srila Prabhupada's physical presence and of course he was the first to jump on the throne right after Srila Prabhupada's departure [death]. He was the first to begin a drug dealing operation (the KSS: Krsna's Secret Service) and later to set up a counterfeiting operation. He was the first to organize a woman's sexploitation party and encourage the leader of that party, [name], to keep the women satisfied as their gigolo (1986, 105).

Kirtanananda asked ISKCON's Governing Body Commission (GBC) to stop Bryant. The GBC responded by excommunicating Bryant from ISKCON. To the residents of New Vrindaban, Bryant was little more than a crazed fringe devotee out to get Kirtanananda. In fact, Bryant had gone to local authorities with allegations of drug smuggling, child abuse, and fraud at New Vrindaban (Hubner and Gruson 1987, 54). Some in the community believed that Bryant was involved in Schockman's attack on Kirtanananda.[6] Fearing for Kirtanananda's safety and worried about Bryant's threats,[7] a surveillance team was formed to keep an eye on Bryant and to track his whereabouts. One member of the surveillance team followed Bryant to California and shot him at close range while he sat in his van a short distance from the Los Angeles ISKCON temple. Bryant died as a result. A few days later Thomas Drescher (Tirtha) was arrested in Kent, Ohio, and charged with killing Bryant. Following Bryant's murder, law enforcement and ISKCON's leadership began to take his accusations against Kirtanananda more seriously. This situation intensified a few months later, when Bryant's accused killer was sentenced to life in prison for the 1983 murder of another New Vrindaban resident, Charles St. Denis (Chakradhari). By now, many within ISKCON, as well as local law-enforcement officials began to wonder whether Kirtanananda was behind the two murders. Bryant's murder set off an extensive government investigation by the FBI, the Internal Revenue Service, and the police in Los Angeles and West Virginia. As the Marshall County (West Virginia) sheriff proclaimed, "This is the beginning of the end of

New Vrindaban as we now know it" (quoted in Doktorski 2003, 261). The end certainly did seem near after FBI and Internal Revenue Service agents, in conjunction with the local police, raided the community on January 5, 1987. Moreover, several months earlier, on September 15, 1986, a federal grand jury met to investigate a possible connection between members of New Vrindaban and the deaths of Bryant and St. Denis. ISKCON authorities were anxious to distance the organization from Kirtanananda's and New Vrindaban's legal problems and, in 1987, excommunicated Kirtanananda.[8] A year later, New Vrindaban and its satellite temples and centers were also expelled from ISKCON.

Religious Innovation, Malfeasance, and the End of Charisma

In the midst of controversy and growing legal problems, in 1986 Kirtanananda initiated a radical and controversial change in New Vrindaban's religious culture, blending Christianity and other religious belief systems and practices with Krishna consciousness. At the end of the year, it was revealed that Kirtanananda had sexually molested an adolescent devotee male. Thereafter, rumors persisted about Kirtanananda's sexual behavior until 1993, when he was caught in a sexual encounter with one of his young disciples. This incident led some of the community members to openly challenge Kirtanananda's authority and leadership.

In the spring of 1986, as his and the community's legal troubles were beginning to unfold, Kirtanananda began incorporating Western literature and music into New Vrindaban's religious culture. In the summer of 1987 he detailed his plans for Westernizing Krishna consciousness and transforming New Vrindaban into an interfaith community. These and other changes were expressly meant to make Krishna consciousness more attractive to the average American. As Kirtanananda stated, "[O]ur principle is to encourage nonsectarian love of God and material detachment. Details that are favorable for this are to be adopted, and unfavorable ones abandoned. We are not meant to be a sectarian Indian cult" (quoted in Doktorski 2003, 226). In July of 1988 Kirtanananda began modifying traditional temple worship by incorporating elements of Christianity into temple services. He also eliminated many of the cultural and religious elements of Krishna consciousness that Prabhupada had brought to the United States.[9] No longer affiliated with ISKCON, Kirtanananda reorganized New Vrindaban under the name the "Eternal Order of the Holy Name, League of Devotees International."

Some of the changes Kirtanananda instituted included devotees' exchanging *dhotis* and saris for Franciscan type robes, men wearing short beards and short hair, interfaith preaching and conferences, silent chanting, Western music and instruments, including a pipe organ, and the use of English in temple worship in place of traditional Bengali and Sanskrit. Fifteen interfaith conferences held at New Vrindaban brought some new recruits to the community, yet, in the end, nearly all of them left with bitter feelings toward Kirtanananda. Two protest demonstrations were held at New Vrindaban, in 1991 and 1993, by interfaith members who claimed they were defrauded by Kirtananda (Doktorski 2003, 271).

New Vrindaban's Indian supporters were baffled and alienated by both Kirtanananda's interfaith experiment and his legal troubles, and some were reportedly outraged when they realized their financial contributions to build a Vedic-style temple were being used instead to construct the "Cathedral of the Holy Name." A large portion of New Vrindaban's Indian Hindu supporters subsequently withdrew their financial support of the community, especially after Kirtanananda publically declared, "I do not care about Indian people" (quoted in Doktorski 2003, 267).

In January 1986, just months after being attacked, Kirtanananda sexually molested a young man who was serving as his personal secretary during his period of convalescence. In December the young devotee revealed this information to two senior members of the community. He also voiced his suspicions that other young men in the community were being molested by Kirtanananda. A meeting was held with some of the more influential members of the community to discuss the allegations. Those present were sufficiently convinced that they decided to confront Kirtanananda with the allegations the next day, but someone at the meeting alerted Kirtanananda. The following day Kirtanananda denied any wrongdoing and claimed there was a conspiracy against him. The young man who claimed he had been molested by Kirtanananda was forced to flee New Vrindaban when some of Kirtanananda's disciples threatened violence against him (Rochford 2007a, 36–38).

Although rumors and specific allegations about Kirtanananda's sexual activity persisted, it was not until a 1993 incident that large portions of the community mobilized against his leadership. As one of Kirtanananda's disciples stated, the "allegations of sexual impropriety grew too believable to dismiss" (Doktorski 2003, 282).[10]

On Kirtanananda's fifty-sixth birthday (September 6, 1993), a devotee who had chauffeured Kirtanananda to the World Parliament of Religions centennial celebration in Chicago reported that he had witnessed Kirtanananda in an inappropriate sexual encounter with a young Malaysian adult male in the back of the Winnebago mobile home he was driving back to West Virginia. Rumors about the allegations spread quickly throughout the community. When confronted by two well-respected senior godbrothers, Kirtanananda confessed to his sexual indiscretions. He admitted that he was experiencing spiritual difficulty and agreed to discontinue initiating new disciples for a time and asked to meet with other senior members of the community in the hope that they might help steer him toward a path of purification (Doktorski 2003, 283; Rochford and Bailey 2006, 11). A meeting was agreed to, and a spokesman was designated to inform community members about Kirtanananda's spiritual problems and his decision to take a leave of absence from his guru responsibilities. Many of those who attended the community meeting expressed support for Kirtanananda during his time of tribulation, but others responded with anger (Doktorski 2003, 283).

Following the meeting, several of Kirtanananda's disciples visited him to gain assurance that the allegations of misconduct were false. Making a complete about-face, Kirtanananda denied that he had engaged in any inappropriate behavior and declared, once again, that there was a conspiracy against him. After hearing Kirtanananda's denial, some of his disciples became bitterly angry at those who had brought such serious allegations against their guru. One of Kirtanananda's disciples proclaimed that "coffins should be procured for the 'blasphemers' who dared to spread slanderous lies about the spiritual master, Krishna's pure devotee" (Doktorski 2003, 283). Tensions rose to such a level that many feared violence would break out. Radhanath Swami, one of the community leaders who confronted Kirtanananda about the Winnebago incident, fled New Vrindaban, fearing for his life.

As Kirtanananda continued to deny any wrongdoing, a number of Prabhupada disciples in the community defiantly returned to an ISKCON style of worship, first at Prabhupada's palace and then in the temple, when two morning programs were held to accommodate the split between devotees still committed to Kirtanananda's interfaith practices and others determined to return to Prabhupada's program of Krishna consciousness. Those turning away from Kirtanananda and his interfaith experiment reverted to traditional dhotis and saris, abandoning their Franciscan robes. In March 1994 a petition was circulated to end interfaith practices and return to Prabhupada's standards of worship and practice, and in July 1994 Kirtanananda terminated his radical experiment. By then it was clear that Kirtanananda's authority had been fatally weakened. Symbolizing both the end of interfaith practice and the downfall of Kirtanananda's rule, New Vrindaban's board of directors gave its blessing for the huge and controversial statue of Prabhupada with a crown on his head to be bulldozed and destroyed. The statue had been crafted in 1990 at the height of Kirtanananda's interfaith experiment. Many Prabhupada disciples in particular took offense at the statue because it depicted Prabhupada as a Buddha-like figure. The statue thereby epitomized the community's mistaken turn away from Prabhupada and his teachings under Kirtanananda's leadership.[11] As one Kirtanananda disciple who left New Vrindaban in 1994 concluded about the failure of the interfaith experiment:

> [T]he greatest impediment to Bhaktipada's mission of de-Indianizing Krishna consciousness was probably himself. He was undoubtedly hindered by his inability to cooperate with his ISKCON godbrothers. He was hindered by his gangster style of removing undesirable or antagonistic elements in the community even to the extent of authorizing beatings and murder. He was hindered by his disregard for women and children and his reluctance to remove pedophiles from the community. He was hindered by his reawakened lust for the illicit pleasure of touching the virile bodies of attractive men. And he was especially hindered by a deep-rooted passion for fame and adoration, to be Prabhupada's successor. (Doktorski 2003, 312)

In May of 1990 a federal grand jury indicted Kirtanananda on three counts of violating the RICO statute for illegally using copyrighted and trademarked logos during fund-raising, six counts of mail fraud, and two counts of conspiring to murder. The government also sought forfeiture of all properties owned by New Vrindaban.[12] After a three-week trial, Kirtanananda was convicted on the RICO and mail fraud counts, but the jury failed to reach a verdict on the murder charges. Kirtanananda appealed the verdicts and hired well-known lawyer Allen Dershowitz to represent him in the Court of Appeals. In July of 1993, his 1991 conviction was overturned when the Appeals Court ruled that the District Court had wrongly allowed evidence of child molestation and other controversial but irrelevant matters to be presented, thus prejudicing the jury (Rochford and Bailey 2006, 11).

Kirtanananda's second trial took place in 1996 after he refused a plea bargain by the government. This time, however, Thomas Drescher—who at the time was serving a life sentence for murdering both St. Denis and Bryant—decided to provide incriminating evidence against his former guru. Drescher reportedly turned against Kirtanananda when he learned of his guru's immoral sexual behavior. Drescher testified that he had carried out both murders under Kirtanananda's order. Following Drescher's testimony, Kirtanananda agreed to plead guilty to one count of federal racketeering and was sentenced to twenty years in prison. In 1997, because of Kirtanananda's failing health the sentence was reduced to twelve years.[13]

The Transformation of New Vrindaban

In response to the events that began in 1985, when Kirtanananda was tragically attacked and Stephen Bryant was murdered, residents of New Vrindaban began defecting from the community in ever-growing numbers. The first wave of defections occurred soon after the introduction of interfaith practice as many in the community believed that Kirtanananda had betrayed Prabhupada and his teachings. This became all the more apparent to many Prabhupada disciples in the community when Kirtanananda insisted that they surrender to his authority as if they were his disciples. Beyond this, the introduction of the interfaith experiment simply bewildered many New Vrindaban residents who had dedicated large portions of their spiritual lives to practicing Krishna consciousness under Prabhupada's guidance. Not surprisingly, large numbers of devotees defected after the January 1987 FBI raid on the community in the aftermath of Bryant's murder. Still others left New Vrindaban when word circulated that Kirtanananda had molested several young men in the community. However, for those who had otherwise remained loyal to Kirtanananda, the Winnebago incident and Kirtanananda's denial after first admitting to his untoward behavior destroyed their faith in his leadership. One Prabhupada disciple who has remained living at New Vrindaban since 1974 analyzed the situation in the following terms:

So there was a bank account that Kirtanananda had built up because of his devotion and the way that Prabhupada treated him. There was that bank account which had been built up with devotees [at New Vrindaban]. After a time there were some things that Kirtanananda did that may have seemed strange or a bit off, but he had the bank account that he could draw off of. That's credibility. But after a while the bank account became depleted. Before it was like, I am going to follow Kirtanananda because the bank account is there. You gave him that trust. And after a while you had given out so much trust, but now the reciprocation is no longer there. There is nothing going into the bank account. It is all being depleted. I think that is exactly what happened at New Vrindaban. (interview 2007)

Community census data demonstrate the consequences of Kirtanananda's downfall. In July 1986 New Vrindaban had 377 adults; by July of 1991 that number had dropped to 131. In five years New Vrindaban lost a total of 246 adult members, a reduction of 65 percent (Doktorski 2003, 263). Many of those who left New Vrindaban rejoined ISKCON and moved to one of its temple communities. In 1998 30 devotees resided in temple-owned buildings, although many more lived independently in the surrounding area. In 2009 approximately 50 devotees lived full-time within the temple community, and an additional 75 were living in independent households near the temple community. A large portion of the latter group, however, maintains little or no contact with the temple community.

As Kirtanananda's legal troubles mounted and he was ultimately convicted and sent to prison, New Vrindaban faced growing and serious financial troubles. Revenues from *sankirtan* for all intents and purposes dried up. When Kirtanananda was out on bail awaiting the appeal of his case, the court barred him from returning to New Vrindaban when an ISKCON leader warned of possible violence should Kirtanananda be allowed to return. Kirtanananda moved into a rented house with a small number of his disciples at Silent Mountain, just north of Wheeling, West Virginia. Thereafter, funds raised by his disciples were given directly to Kirtanananda rather than used to support New Vrindaban. Without *sankirtan* revenues and having lost the contributions from Hindu pilgrims and visitors, New Vrindaban's communal structure rapidly disintegrated. Beginning in 1990, householders at New Vrindaban were required to support their families independently. Many purchased property from the community or in the surrounding area, where they set up their own households. Householders working at New Vrindaban began receiving salaries and stipends for their efforts. Many, however, were forced to find employment in the outside labor market or start up small businesses to support themselves and their families. Desperate for funds, the community began selling off heavy construction equipment, the printing presses of Palace Press after it shut down, a pipe organ and an electric organ, and six large bronze bells that had hung on a bell tower. The community also sold parcels of land from its extensive holdings. By 1998 the community retained about fourteen hundred acres of land. Lacking sufficient funds, in 1995 the community began downsizing its extensive dairy operation, limiting breeding and allowing older cows to die off naturally to limit the size of the herd. In 1999 the community's day school closed. Financial pressures intensified further in 2000, when New Vrindaban was named as a defendant in a child abuse case filed in Dallas, Texas, by former students who attended ISKCON schools, including the one at New Vrindaban (*Children of Krishna et al. vs. the International Society for Krishna Consciousness et al.*). In 2002 the community filed for bankruptcy protection in an effort to secure its assets from what was expected to be a substantial payout to settle the child abuse lawsuit.[14]

As financial hardship grew and members of the community began defecting in ever larger numbers, the leadership once again reached out to the immigrant Indian Hindu community for support. This was made possible by the abandonment of the interfaith experiment in 1994 and the imprisonment of Kirtanananda in 1996. In addition, beginning in 1998 ISKCON and New Vrindaban formally renewed their relationship. Thereafter, Hindu pilgrims once again began regularly visiting New Vrindaban and contributing much-needed resources. Struggling to survive, the community refocused its mission, emphasizing pilgrimage at the expense of what remained of New Vrindaban as a residential community. As a result, many of the community's few remaining householders relocated to other ISKCON communities. Among full-time and congregational members surveyed at New Vrindaban ($n = 36$), in 2003 nearly three-quarters (73 percent) agreed that "New Vrindaban is more concerned with pilgrims of Indian descent than with its local congregation." Labor to maintain the temple, Prabhupada's palace, and the community lodge is largely provided by devotees with religious visas from India, South America, Eastern Europe, and elsewhere hoping to secure permanent residence in the United States (Rochford and Bailey 2006, 15–16). However, as one community member pointed out, "People coming for a green card really don't strengthen the community. They create a transient atmosphere, especially for those of us who want to stay and create something permanent for our families" (Rochford and Bailey 2006, 16).

Conclusion

Charismatic authority is one of the hallmarks of new religious movements (Barker 2004; Dawson 2002, 80; Rochford 2007b, 165–68, 2007c, 271–74). At the group level, charismatic authority translates into high levels of organizational commitment, religiosity, and task performance directed toward furthering the goals of the leader and the organization (Dawson 2002, 82; Rochford 2007b, 165–66). However, these can be reversed should charismatic leaders make "wrong," "immoral," and/or "controversial" choices and decisions from the perspective of the followers. In extreme instances, the charismatic bond may be broken altogether should followers feel betrayed by a fallen leader (Jacobs 1987). This, in turn, can destabilize the group and increase the potential for violent behavior (Dawson 2002, 81). Building on these critical insights, this study has demonstrated how acts of violence both against and by Kirtanananda provoked a series of events that undermined his authority and sent New Vrindaban into rapid decline as members defected and the community faced a life-threatening financial crisis. The prospect of collective violence also increased as hostility and factionalism emerged within the community, prompted by the implementation of interfaith practices, as well as Kirtanananda's examples of corrupt and immoral behavior. New Vrindaban may have survived in the end only because it was able to create a new market niche as a place of pilgrimage for immigrant Hindus and their families. By so doing, however, it gave up the radical project of sustaining a residential community dedicated to the practice of Krishna consciousness.

My discussion and analysis raise three additional issues worthy of brief consideration:

1. It is not uncommon for charismatic leaders to suddenly and without explanation change existing doctrines and policies in order to deflect the possibility that their authority might be institutionalized. Such disruptive changes may also represent strategic decisions by charismatic leaders who are attempting to reassert their authority by refocusing the members' commitment, opening up new avenues for recruitment, and/or pushing out marginal members from the group (Dawson 2002, 92). However, implementing new doctrines and religious practices can be a risky proposition, as the present case demonstrates. Kirtanananda's interfaith experiment failed in part because it ultimately robbed New Vrindaban's residents of years of accumulated religious capital. Religious capital is based upon members' "mastery of and attachment to a particular religious culture" (Stark and Finke 2000, 120). The longer and more actively people practice a particular religious faith, the stronger their preferences are for that religion (Sherkat 1997). By radically altering the community's core teachings and religious practices, Kirtanananda undermined the Krishna worldview and way of life, which were central to New Vrindaban's identity and mission. As their existing religious capital weakened under the weight of Kirtanananda's interfaith experiment, many New Vrindaban devotees found reason to question Kirtanananda's authority, as well as their place within the community.
2. Given the hostilities that emerged at New Vrindaban, the question arises as to why the community did not experience violent confrontation between supporters and opponents of Kirtanananda's leadership. Such a possibility clearly existed, especially in 1993, when tensions escalated after Kirtanananda's sexual wrongdoing created a split within the community.

One answer is suggested by Hirschman's (1970) exit-voice hypothesis. Exit and voice represent two ways that dissent can be expressed. If circumstances afford dissenters with little opportunity to successfully promote change, their only options are to "exit," or to lower their voice and give in. If, on the other hand, success seems possible or the benefits of confrontation outweigh the costs, insurgents may decide to stand and fight. A critical situational factor that shapes choices, however, is the availability of acceptable and parallel alternative situations. In the face of potential collective violence, such alternatives may appear particularly inviting. Yet the possibilities for religious switching are far less numerous for cults and new religions given their unique and often deviant religious cultures. Because New Vrindaban had its beginnings in ISKCON, those leaving had like-minded communities available in which to relocate. Without this exit strategy, it is possible and perhaps likely that tensions would have escalated to the point where dissenters to Kirtanananda's rule would have collectively organized in an attempt to seize power from within.

3. Social movement organizations generally fail when their legitimacy as an instrument is discredited in the eyes of the followers (Zald and Garner 1987, 131). Failure, however, can also bring innovation as movement leaders seek alternative means to keep the group viable into the future. Often this necessitates a transformation of goals in the direction of organizational maintenance and greater accommodation to the dominant society. Goals of social change recede in favor of mobilizing resources capable of maintaining the group. When New Vrindaban teetered on the edge of financial collapse during the 1990s, pilgrimage came to dominate the community's overall mission. Economic necessity demanded that the community again reach out to immigrant Indian Hindus for support. By so doing, however, the business logic associated with spiritual tourism overwhelmed the idea of New Vrindaban as an alternative spiritual community (Rochford and Bailey 2006). As such, the radical project that once defined New Vrindaban as a new religious community succumbed to goal displacement in the interest of maintaining the community as a viable enterprise. However, New Vrindaban hardly stands alone in this regard as ISKCON's other North American communities also experienced significant change when the leadership actively encouraged the development of an Indian Hindu congregation to help support its financially impoverished temples. Given the different religious orientations found within this immigrant congregation, ISKCON's religious culture has been reshaped (i.e., Hinduized) at the expense of its traditional Vaisnava beliefs and its mission of preaching and spreading Krishna consciousness to the Western world (see Rochford 2007a, 181–200).

NOTES

1. ISKCON's historical roots are traced to Bengal, India, in the sixteenth century. The Krishna Consciousness preached by ISKCON's founder is part of the Krishna *bhakti* movement of Caitanya Mahaprabhu (1486–1533). A distinctive feature of the Gaudiya Vaisnava tradition to which ISKCON belongs is that Caitanya is believed to be an incarnation of Krishna. The movement was brought to the United States in 1965 by A. C. Bhaktivedanta Swami Prabhupada, or Srila Prabhupada, as he is commonly called by his disciples and followers. ISKCON was incorporated as a religious organization in 1966 in New York City and is dedicated to spreading Krishna consciousness with communities and preaching centers throughout the world. The aim of the Krishna devotee is to become self-realized by chanting "Hare Krishna" and living an austere lifestyle that requires avoiding meat, intoxicants, illicit sex, and gambling. While young Westerners were drawn to the movement in the 1960s and 1970s, today the largest portion of ISKCON's North American and Western European membership comprises immigrant Indian Hindus and their families (see Rochford 2007a, 181–200). For a discussion of the movement's growth and development in North America and internationally, see Brooks (1989); Knott (1986); Rochford (1985, 2006, 2007a); Shinn (1987); and Squarcini and Fizzotti (2004). For descriptions of New Vrindaban's history, see Hayagriva Dasa (1985); Doktorski (2003); and Rochford and Bailey (2006).

2. The incidents of communal violence that I describe and analyze represent two among a number of others. In 1973 residents of New Vrindaban were terrorized when a group of armed men on motorcycles stormed the temple. They destroyed temple deities and threatened to kill Kirtanananda. In the summer of 1980 Jadurani dasi was physically assaulted at New Vrindaban by two devotee women loyal to Kirtanananda because she was challenging the qualifications of Kirtanananda and the other gurus who succeeded Prabhupada after his death in 1977. In 1983 Charles St. Denis (Chakradari) was shot and stabbed to death by another New Vrindaban resident. One report suggests that St. Denis was pressing Kirtanananda for the return of thousands of dollars he had previously given him. He was killed after he was accused of raping a woman in the community. In addition, an unknown number of children in the community's school (*ashram-gurukula*) were abused and sexually molested by teachers and others in the community. In March of 1987 a former *gurukula* headmaster was indicted on four counts of first-degree sexual assault, and a teacher's aide was indicted on two counts of third-degree sexual assault. For a discussion of child abuse at New Vrindaban and within ISKCON more generally, see Rochford (1998; 2007a,74–96).

3. I have researched the New Vrindaban community since 1993. In addition to field research there, I formally interviewed seventeen current and former residents of New Vrindaban, as well as three community leaders—including Kirtanananda. In 2003 I completed a survey to assess the views, concerns, and hopes of the local congregation. Survey findings are reported in Rochford and Bailey (2006).

4. Kirtanananda Swami was known as "Bhaktipada" after 1979 in recognition of his guru status. The honorific can be translated as "he at whose feet the *bhaktas* [devotees] sit." To avoid confusion, the name "Kirtanananda" is used throughout the chapter except where others make reference to "Bhaktipada" in quoted material.

5. Vrindaban (or Vrndavana) is a town in northern India located on the Yamuna River in present-day Uttar Pradesh. The town and the surrounding area are considered the

locations of Krishna's childhood and adolescence. Vrindaban is thus a sacred place and attracts multitudes of pilgrims to the many temples located there. See Charles Brooks (1989) for a detailed description of Vrindaban, India, and ISKCON's presence there. Also see Carney (2007), who chronicles how the town has been transformed into a center for spiritual tourism.

6. Despite rumors that Bryant was involved in the assault on Kirtanananda, no evidence has linked him to the attack.

7. Kirtanananda did acquire two guard dogs after being assaulted.

8. An ISKCON news release dated March 16, 1987, outlined the charges against Kirtanananda and the rationale for his excommunication from ISKCON. It read in part as follows:

> For months the Swami has been at the center of controversy centered around the West Virginia community he heads (known as New Vrindaban) in which bodies have recently been exhumed and former members convicted of murder and charged with child molestation. Recently the GBC and ISKCON temple presidents throughout the world had been pressuring Kirtanananda to resign due to his continued defiance of ISKCON policies, the vilification of the GBC and other members of ISKCON, [and] his practice of accepting lavish public demonstrations of worship . . . Of particular significance were his attempts to establish himself as the sole spiritual heir to ISKCON by which he systematically obscured and minimized the pre-eminent position of His Divine Grace A. C. Bhaktivedanta Swami Prabhupada, the founder-acarya of ISKCON. The GBC's decision also took into account repeated instances of dishonesty and actions which encourage division and factionalism within the religion.

9. This was not Kirtanananda's first attempt at making such radical changes. In 1967, in defiance of Prabhupada, Kirtanananda sought to Westernize the devotees' style of dress and appearance. Kirtanananda grew a beard and long hair and preached to the devotees in New York that the practice of men shaving their heads and wearing *dhoti* (lower garment of cloth worn by devotee men), *tilak* (clay markings on the forehead and body), and *sikha* (tuft of hair at the back of a male's head) were impediments to spreading Krishna consciousness in the United States. It appears that very few New Vrindaban devotees were aware of these transgressions until the 1990s, however.

10. Many of the current and former residents of New Vrindaban that I interviewed expressed the view that Kirtanananda's interfaith experiment, as well as his illicit sexual behavior, were products of his head injury. They believed that Kirtanananda was consumed by religious ideas and sexual desires that had defined his interests and life before and just after he became a devotee. As already mentioned, Kirtanananda attempted to introduce interfaith elements into ISKCON in 1967 before Prabhupada stopped him. It is also well known that Kirtanananda was in a homosexual relationship prior to his ISKCON membership. Despite this presumption of causality, it is possible that Kirtanananda would have experimented with interfaith elements and become sexually active independently of his injury.

11. Guru authority within the Hindu tradition comes from teaching without alteration the spiritual knowledge transmitted by one's own guru. By crafting a new religion,

Kirtanananda broke from the *parampara* (i.e., the succession of gurus going back in time to Krishna) and thus lost any claim to authority in the eyes of many devotees at New Vrindaban, especially among Prabhupada's disciples.

12. Kirtanananda aggressively asserted that persecution was behind his legal problems. He undertook a year-long "First Amendment National Freedom Tour," on which he defiantly alleged government persecution of himself and New Vrindaban. He visited numerous cites, spoke to millions of radio listeners and TV viewers, and appeared on national television shows such as Larry King and Sally Jesse Raphael.

13. On June 16, 2004, Kirtanananda was released from federal prison after serving an eight-year sentence. With a small group of devoted followers, he moved to his New York City temple, Sri Sri Radha Murlidara. Virtually all of the disciples who had remained committed to Kirtanananda while he was in prison abandoned him shortly after his release however in the midst of conflict and infighting. Having virtually no followers left in North America and having been shunned by ISKCON, in 2008 Kirtanananda relocated to India after completing his probation and procuring a passport.

14. The child abuse lawsuit was settled in May of 2005 by U.S. bankruptcy courts in West Virginia and California. A total of 535 former *gurukula* students received compensation ranging between $2,500 and $50,000 from the $9.5 million settlement (Rochford 2007a, 95–96). New Vrindaban was responsible for paying a substantial but unspecified amount as part of the final settlement.

REFERENCES

Barker, Eileen. 2004. "Perspective: What Are We Studying? A Sociological Case for Keeping the 'Nova.'" *Nova Religio* 8(1): 88–102.

Brooks, Charles. 1989. *The Hare Krishnas in India*. Princeton, N.J.: Princeton University Press.

Bryant, Stephen (Sulocana das). 1986. The Guru Business: How the Leaders of the Hare Krishna Movement Deviated from the Pure Path as Taught and Exemplified by Its Founder: His Divine Grace A. C. Bhaktivedanta Swami Prabhupada, Founder/Acarya ISKCON. Unpublished manuscript. http://www.harekrsna.org/pada/gurubiz.htm (accessed July 23, 2009).

Carney, Gerald T. 2007. "From Ashram to Condo: Transformation of a Religious Ideal." *Southeast Review of Asian Studies* 29: 137–56.

Children of Krishna et al. vs. International Society for Krishna Consciousness (ISKCON) et al. 2000. Law Offices of Windle Turley, P.C. http://www.rickross.com/reference/Krishna/complaint0606.pdf (accessed October 11, 2010)

Dasa, Hayagriva. 1985. *The Hare Krishna Explosion: The Birth of Krishna Consciousness in America (1966–1969)*. New Vrindaban, W.Va.: Palace.

Dawson, Lorne L. 2002. "Crises of Charismatic Legitimacy and Violent Behavior in New Religious Movements." In *Cults, Religion, and Violence*, ed. David Bromley and J. Gordon Melton, 80–101, New York: Cambridge University Press.

Doktorski, Henry. 2003. The Great Experiment: Sacred Music and the Christianization of the New Vrindaban Hare Krishna Temple Liturgies. Unpublished manuscript.

Hirschman, Albert. 1970. *Exit, Voice, and Loyalty: Response to Decline in Firms, Organizations, and States*. Cambridge, Mass.: Harvard University Press.

Hubner, John, and Lindsey Gruson. 1987. "Dial Om for Murder." *Rolling Stone* (April 9), 53-58, 78-80, 82.

———. 1988. *Monkey on a Stick: Murder, Madness, and the Hare Krishnas*. New York: Harcourt.

Jacobs, Janet. 1987. "Deconversion from Religious Movements: An Analysis of Charismatic Bonding and Spiritual Commitment." *Journal for the Scientific Study of Religion* 26(3): 294–308.

Knott, Kim. 1986. *My Sweet Lord: Hare Krishna Movement*. San Bernardino, Calif.: Reginald.

News Release. 1987. Excommunication of Kirtanananda from ISKCON. March 16. http://surrealist.org/pdf/k swami expelleda.pdf (accessed July 21, 2009).

Rochford, E. Burke., Jr. 1985. *Hare Krishna in America*. New Brunswick, N.J.: Rutgers University Press.

———. 1998. "Child Abuse in the Hare Krishna Movement: 1971–1986." With Jennifer Heinlein. *ISKCON Communications Journal* 6: 43–69.

———. 2006. "The Hare Krishna Movement: Beginnings, Change, and Transformation." In *Introduction to New and Alternative Religions*, vol. 4, ed. Eugene V. Gallagher and W. Michael Ashcraft, 21–46. Westport, Conn.: Greenwood.

———. 2007a. *Hare Krishna Transformed*. New York: New York University Press.

———. 2007b. "Social Building Blocks of New Religious Movements: Organization and Leadership." In *Teaching New Religious Movements*, ed. David G. Bromley, 157–85. New York: Oxford University Press.

———. 2007c. "The Sociology of New Religious Movements." In *American Sociology of Religion*, ed. Anthony J. Blasi, 253–90. Boston: Brill.

Rochford, E. Burke, Jr., and Kendra Bailey. 2006. "Almost Heaven: Leadership, Decline, and the Transformation of New Vrindaban." *Nova Religio* 9(3): 6–23.

Sherkat, Darren. 1997. "Embedding Religious Choices: Integrating Preferences and Social Constraints into Rational Choice Theories of Religious Behavior." In *Rational Choice Theory and Religion: Summary and Assessment*, ed. Lawrence A. Young, 65–86. New York: Routledge.

Shinn, Larry. 1987. *The Dark Lord: Cult Images and the Hare Krishnas in America*. Philadelphia: Westminster.

Squarcini, Federico, and Eugenio Fizzotti. 2004. *Hare Krishna*. Salt Lake City: Signature.

Stark, Rodney, and Roger Finke. 2000. *Acts of Faith: Explaining the Human Side of Religion*. Berkeley: University of California Press.

Zald, Mayer N., and Roberta Ash Garner. 1987. "Social Movement Organizations: Growth, Decay, and Change." In *Social Movements in an Organizational Society*, ed. Mayer N. Zald and John D. McCarthy, 121–41. New Brunswick, N.J.: Transaction.

PART IV

Rhetorics of Violence and Peaceful Denouements

14

The Nation of Islam and Violence

Martha F. Lee

Because of America's evil deeds against these twenty-two million "Negroes," like Egypt and Babylon before her, America herself now stands before the "bar of justice." White America is now facing her Day of Judgment, and she can't escape because today God himself is the judge. God himself is now the administrator of justice, and God himself is to be her divine executor!

—Malcolm X, "God's Judgment of White America"

In the United States, the African American struggle for identity, freedom, and equality was expressed in a variety of religious and political movements during the twentieth century. This chapter examines one of the most important of those movements: the Nation of Islam, which emerged in the late 1920s and continues to exist today. American society has often perceived the Nation of Islam as a violent threat to its stability and security, and the Nation of Islam, in its outspoken criticism of white America, has often implied that it would not hesitate to use violence to achieve its goals. Despite this context, however, the actual incidents of violence in which the Nation of Islam was involved have been limited in both number and intensity. This disjunction is interesting, for pre–civil rights America—and the social and political upheaval of the 1960s in particular—provided a situation that was ripe for violent conflict between African Americans and the political community that had for so long denied them equality. The U.S. government and the media clearly expected the movement to be violent. A reasonable question, therefore, is why did the Nation of Islam engage in so little violence? This chapter argues that a possible reason lies in the structure and development of the religious faith of the Nation of Islam.

The History and Doctrine of the Nation of Islam

The Nation of Islam began in 1930s' Detroit, a city that, like many of the United States' northern urban centers, experienced rapid growth of its African American population in the early twentieth century. Between 1900 and 1930, 2,250,000 African Americans moved from the rural South to the urban North; a significant percentage of those individuals moved to Detroit, where the African American population grew by more than 611 percent in that twenty-year period (Lincoln 1973, xxiii–xiv). While the motivation for this mass migration was reasonable—for many, the conditions in the South were simply intolerable—its timing could hardly have been worse. By migrating, individuals hoped to better their lives in a region where they anticipated employment in burgeoning manufacturing industries, better housing and education for their families, and less prejudice and intolerance. The Great Depression, however, intervened. Many were left without employment and decent housing and without an extended support network of family and friends. In addition, the North proved less welcoming than they had perhaps anticipated. Membership in the Detroit Ku Klux Klan increased from 3,000 to 22,000 between 1921 and 1923 (Turner 1997, 155). In such an environment, it is perhaps not surprising that many individuals turned to religious faith.

Historically, African Americans had evidenced a high level of participation in religious institutions. Church communities provided opportunities to "experiment in activities such as business, politics, social reform, and social expression" (Fauset 1944, 107–108). A variety of African American religious movements emerged in this period, including Noble Drew Ali's Moorish Science Temple and Marcus Garvey's United Negro Improvement Association (UNIA). Among the most successful of these groups was the Nation of Islam.

In the summer of 1930 a man by the name of Wallace Fard appeared on the streets of Detroit. He declared himself to be on a mission from God, "who wanted his chosen people back" (Gardell 1996, 51). Preaching an apocalyptic message that combined elements of Islamic and Christian religious mythologies, Fard quickly attracted a large following. Among those he converted was Elijah Poole, who soon changed his name to Elijah Muhammad. When Fard disappeared in 1934, Muhammad assumed leadership of the movement and moved its headquarters to Chicago.

Elijah Muhammad preached that Fard was Allah incarnate and that he, Elijah Muhammad, was his last messenger. Allah had appeared on earth to gather Black Americans and teach them self-respect, self-knowledge, and the ability to "do for self" in preparation for the end of time. Elijah Muhammad understood his prophetic mission to be the facilitation of that end, and he carried with him the authority that Fard, God incarnate, had given to him. As Allah's last messenger, it was he who shaped and defined the movement's doctrine.

Elijah Muhammad used religious myth to interpret African Americans' political history. In *The Message to the Blackman in America*, he explained that Blacks were the earth's original inhabitants, the tribe of Shabazz, and that they were Allah's chosen people. They were the first inhabitants of Mecca, where they had lived in perfect peace and harmony. Six thousand years ago their idyllic life was destroyed by Yakub, an evil child who was destined to "break peace, kill and destroy his own people with a made enemy" (Muhammad 1965, 127). Yakub was deported from Mecca to the island of Pelan, where he conducted genetic experiments aimed at creating a population of white people. He succeeded and found that "as they [grew] lighter and lighter they grew weaker and weaker. Their blood became weaker, their bones became weaker, their minds became weaker, their morals became weaker" (X 1971a, 56). Yakub returned to Mecca with these truly evil people. Through their treacherous deeds, they conquered the world; the worst of their atrocities was the enslavement of Blacks. According to Elijah Muhammad's prophecy, however, six thousand years of white rule was about to end. Muhammad prophesied that the "Fall of America" would be initiated by an apocalyptic "battle in the sky," wherein the giant "mother of planes"—a UFO foretold in the story of Ezekiel's wheel—would confront Allah's enemies (Muhammad 1965, 270):

> The years 1965 and 1966 are going to be fateful for America, bringing in the "Fall of America" . . . this is the setting of the nations for a showdown to determine who will live on earth. The survivor is to build a nation of peace to rule the people forever under the guidance of Almighty God, Allah. (Muhammad 1965, 145)

Although Elijah Muhammad also demanded a separate state for Black Americans on the North American continent, it is not clear that he ever truly believed that this was a viable option for his followers. As Lincoln notes, Elijah made no concrete plans for the separation of the races, and the Nation of Islam owned properties across the United States (Lincoln 1973, 100–102). In fact, this demand was instead often presented as the final opportunity for white America to save itself. The leadership of the Nation of Islam, however, believed this was extremely unlikely to occur. In any event, in the context of the anticipated millennium, this demand was trivial; believers anticipated that, within their lifetime, white America would fall, and they would rule the continent. Muhammad's prophecy can therefore be characterized as millenarian.

Scholars identify movements that anticipate the end of time as apocalyptic or millenarian (see, for example, Cohn 1970 and Talmon 1968). Groups that have this belief as the defining element of their doctrine anticipate a salvation that is imminent (it will happen within the believers' lifetime), ultimate and perfect (it will bring about the final, perfect stage of history), collective (only the community of true believers will be saved), and this-worldly (salvation will occur on this earth, not in some heavenly afterlife). While we might think of this type of belief structure as religious, millenarian beliefs span both the religious and the political sphere. The term itself is taken from the book of Revelation and its promise of a thousand-year reign of Christ on earth (RSV 20:4, 6), and millenarian themes are found today in a wide variety of religious movements, from Protestant faiths like the Branch Davidians at Waco to Aum Shinrikyo in Japan. Millennialism can also be found in the political sphere, however, in social movements, including Brazil's Contestado rebellion (Diacon 1991) and Christian Exodus in the United States (Sweet and Lee 2009) and established totalitarian regimes such as National Socialism in Germany (Rhodes 1980). Although the line between these two forms of millennialism seems clear—in religious millenarian movements, believers anticipate God's intervention in human history and political movements, and they take upon themselves the task of remaking the world—in fact, it is not. Religious believers, in their anticipation of a perfected worldly community are making a political claim, and secular millenarians assume an absolute, transhistorical good and pursue their goals with a religious fervor.

Religious and political millenarian beliefs therefore overlap, and both have the potential to become problematic for political authorities. Most of the research on millenarian movements is in the form of case studies, but the limited comparative research that exists suggests that movements that are predominantly political tend to be more violent than their religious counterparts. Secular millenarians are prepared to initiate the end of time themselves, whereas religious believers are content to wait for God to fulfill that role (Lee and Simms 2007, 100–27).

For all millenarian belief systems, the possibility that believers may engage in violence therefore exists. In particular, it is present because of the way individuals understand the development of history and because of the way they view nonbelievers. Millennial belief systems understand the history of the world to be the history of the struggle between good and evil and assert that believers live at the moment of culmination of that struggle. Individual believers are therefore actors in the ultimate battle in human history. In the case of religious doctrines, they may understand themselves to be God's soldiers, and in the case of secular millenarian beliefs, they may likewise understand themselves to be fulfilling a critical role in the ultimate resolution of human history. From both of these perspectives, however, nonbelievers present a practical problem. They are the enemies of God and/or pawns of the earthly powers, which must be overcome. From their perspective, believers can ignore the humanity of those individuals to commit acts of violence that might otherwise be unthinkable. Their cause becomes the guiding force of their lives. Following the Oklahoma City bombing, for example, Timothy McVeigh's attorneys commented that "his conscious mind knew that the people killed in the Oklahoma City bombing had families, that the children killed had mothers, and he fully realizes the consequences of his actions, but he was able to 'turn it off' in order to perform his mission" (Clay 2007).

Specific elements of the millenarian belief structure might incline adherents to violence. First, believers understand themselves to be living at a decisive moment in history; they are in the midst of the ultimate battle of human existence and on the threshold of a new and perfect era. They may feel it is their duty to contribute to that final battle in order to bring about its conclusion and perfected human existence. Second, millenarian visions are collective in nature. These types of belief systems emphasize the community of believers and in so doing also emphasize the distinction between "us" and "them." As suggested earlier, this emphasis on one's own purpose and community, coupled with the tendency to understand people who stand in the way of achieving one's goal as merely obstacles, can facilitate violence.

Finally, as Michael Barkun points out, the environment of a movement is important. Millenarian groups, although they may sometimes prefer isolation, are located in preexisting communities and as a result must interact with other religious and/or secular groups and often with government authorities. In these interactions, Barkun argues, two features are of particular importance: First, each side will have a preexisting interpretive framework that assigns meaning to the other's behavior, and second, that framework is often marked by a dualistic view of the world (Barkun 1996, 4–5). On the part of millenarians, this worldview sees only two domains, "that of the pure, which they inhabit, and that of the impure, in which their adversaries dwell" (Barkun 1996, 6), and it emphasizes the opposition between those two groups (Flanagan 1996, 171).

Barkun notes, however, that state authorities' interpretive frameworks may also be problematic. In reference to conflicts between colonial powers and aboriginal populations, for example, he points out that cultural differences may mean that state authorities might attribute characteristics of "savagery, superstition, and ignorance" to the communities they intend to subdue (Barkun 1996, 6). When state authorities are of the same culture, they may term those groups *cults*, imply that their leaders are disingenuous, and assume that believers are irrational or have been brainwashed. In this way, authorities and millenarian believers often possess a kind of mirror image understanding of one another (Barkun 1996, 6). Both sides possess an absolutist view of each other, which leaves little room for compromise or negotiation. The standoff between the millenarian Branch Davidians and federal agencies at Waco exemplifies this situation. The Bureau of Alcohol, Tobacco, and Firearms and the Federal Bureau of Investigation suspected that the Davidians were a religious cult led by a madman and that they were stockpiling weapons and abusing children (Reno 1995). Many of the Davidians perhaps believed the U.S. government and its representatives to be the embodiment of the Antichrist and their arrival a sign that the end of time had arrived. These interpretive frameworks are mutually exclusive and so disparate as to be effectively two different languages. In such a situation, it is perhaps unsurprising that no compromise could be reached and violence ensued.

Scholars suggest that certain social, political, and economic circumstances foster the development of millenarian movements. These circumstances include relative deprivation, a situation wherein individuals are unable to achieve socioeconomic success in the context of a larger population that does achieve those successes; multiple deprivation, a situation wherein individuals are deprived of a range of social goods (Talmon 1968, 364); the experience of some form of disaster that threatens a society's physical and/or cultural existence (Barkun 1996); and, among oppressed communities, a quest for a sense of identity, dignity, and self-respect (Lee 1996, 5; Talmon 1968, 355). As Lee and Simms point out, in each of these circumstances, communities consider themselves under threat, and in such situations, violence is always a possibility (Lee and Simms 2007, 109–10).

Arguably, each of these elements played a role in the emergence and success of the Nation of Islam. At the movement's origins—and for much of the twentieth century—the larger community in which African Americans lived denied them political rights and economic and social opportunities, while other minority groups flourished. African Americans had moved from the rural South to the urban North in the hope of building better lives for themselves and their families, but despite early successes, their hopes were dashed by the Great Depression and its economic impact. Of particular importance here is slavery's effect on identity. In the words of James Baldwin:

> It is a fact that every American Negro bears a name that originally belonged to the white man whose chattel he was . . . they are both visibly and legally the descendants of slaves in a white, Protestant country, and this is what it means to be an American Negro. (Baldwin 1962, 114)

African Americans had effectively lost both their individual and their community identity. The Nation of Islam's doctrine proclaimed that African Americans were not oppressed victims but instead Allah's chosen elect, and it offered a vision of the future wherein they would be masters of the world. It also provided the community with a history and an identity, most famously symbolized in the myth of Yakub (discussed earlier) and adherents' adoption of "X" as a surname. This was because believers were "ex-" what they were prior to conversion, their nature and potential were mysterious, and they could never know their real names, only their slave names (Lee 1996, 37; Karim 1971, 9).

In their anticipation of the Fall of America, however, the Black Muslims were not advised to engage in violence against American society. Whereas organizations such as the Black Panthers sometimes expressed militancy through violence, the Nation of Islam expressed its militant nationalism through its religious faith. As a result, its members focused on community development as they anticipated the Fall of America. Elijah Muhammad advised his followers that the Fall was partly under way (it had begun with World War I) but cautioned that it would occur according to Allah's timetable and when the Muslims were ready (Muhammad 1965, 142). Before the white race could be destroyed, Black Americans had to come to a knowledge of self and prepare their community. Contact with white Americans was strongly discouraged, and Elijah preached a strict moral code that emphasized the importance of the family unit and prohibited smoking, drinking, gambling, and the use of drugs. Members were also expected to adhere to strict dietary regulations, which included a general prohibition against eating pork and also forbade the "slave diet" of Southern blacks, which included foods such as cornbread and black-eyed peas (Lincoln 1973, 83). Elijah Muhammad advised the following:

> (1) Recognize the necessity for unity and group operation (activities). (2) Pool your resources, physically as well as financially. (3) Stop wanton criticisms of everything that is black-owned and black-operated. (4) Keep in mind—jealousy destroys from within. (5) Observe the operations of the white man. He is successful. (Muhammad 1965, 174)

In addition to strengthening its members' sense of community, these behaviors saw the Nation of Islam and its membership become economically successful; during the course of its history, the organization has owned and run schools, businesses, farms, and a hospital. While they demanded their own state and waited for the Fall of America, paradoxically, the members developed an increasing stake in American society.

History and Violence

The Nation of Islam's history can be divided into stages: (1) from 1930 until 1959, the early years of Elijah Muhammad's leadership and the emergence of the Nation of Islam as an important political entity; (2) from 1959 to 1975, the years for which the Fall of America was projected, until Elijah Muhammad's death; (3) from 1975 until 2000, the years during which Wallace Muhammad and Louis Farrakhan led separate but related religious movements, and (4) from 2000 until the present. In none of these periods did the Nation of Islam engage in organized violence directed against Americans or the United States. While there is no denying that its leaders often warned of the violence about to befall America and its citizens, these warnings were always in the context of the movement's apocalyptic belief system. Elijah Muhammad told his followers that the white race was "a race of devils" whose time on earth was limited (Muhammad 1974, 89). In the words of Malcolm X:

> [T]he white man, a race of devils, was made six thousand years ago. This doesn't mean to tell you that this implies any kind of hate. They're just a race of devils ... The only reason God didn't remove them then was because you and I were here in their clutches and God gave them an extension of time—not them an extension of time, but they received an extension of time to give the wise men of the East the opportunity to get into this House of Bondage and "awaken" the Lost Sheep. Once the American so-called Negroes have been awakened to a knowledge of themselves and of their own God and of the white man, then they're on

their own. Then it'll be left up to you and me whether we want to integrate into this wicked race or leave them and separate and go to our own. And if we integrate we'll be destroyed along with them. (X 1971a, 64-5)

These types of comments, which predict the complete destruction of the white race, were a consistent feature of Elijah Muhammad's *Message to the Blackman in America* and his speeches and often dominated Elijah's columns in the movement's paper, *Muhammad Speaks*. Always, however, they referred to *Allah's* initiation of the Fall of America and did not encourage Muslims to take up arms against their fellow citizens, although they often contained clear statements that, if attacked, Muslims should engage in self-defense.

Federal law-enforcement agencies, however, did not find this distinction meaningful. Federal Bureau of Investigation (FBI) surveillance of the Nation of Islam began in 1939; its security index, a list of prominent dissidents to be detained in the event of a national emergency or war, listed only 476 communists but 673 Nation of Islam members, the largest category on the register (O'Reilly 1989, 275). During an era when, many argue, America's greatest fear was the Soviet Union and communist ideology, this FBI index suggests that law-enforcement agencies had other concerns. Indeed, in December of 1956, J. Edgar Hoover, director of the FBI, requested permission from the attorney general to engage in technical surveillance of Elijah Muhammad with this explanation:

> The Muslim Cult of Islam is composed entirely of Negroes. Its leader, Elijah Mohammed, claims to have been sent by Allah, the Supreme Being, to lead the Negroes out of slavery. Members fanatically follow the teachings of Allah, as interpreted by Mohammad; they disavow allegiance to the United States; and they are taught they need not obey the laws of the United States. Allegations have been received that its members may resort to acts of violence in carrying out its avowed purpose of destroying non-Muslims and Christianity. (FBI 1966, cited in Gardell 1996, 72).

The FBI's files on the Nation of Islam stretch from the initial and very brief leadership of Wallace Fard in the early 1930s, through Elijah's leadership and the 1960s. These files include the COINTELPRO investigations of the 1950s and 1960s, which were carried out "against perceived domestic threats to the established political and social order" (U.S. Senate Select Committee 1976, 1A). The Nation of Islam was pursued under the FBI's Black Nationalist program, which, according to its supervisor, included "a great number of organizations that you might not today characterize as black nationalist but which were in fact primarily black" (U.S. Senate Select Committee 1976, 2). Included among them, for example, was the nonviolent Southern Christian Leadership Conference, which was labeled a Black Nationalist "hate group" (U.S. Senate Select Committee 1976, 3A).

The FBI's counterintelligence program against the Nation of Islam was therefore significant. The organization's files on the group have yet to be fully declassified, and those that have so far been made public indicate a consistent and decades-long campaign to limit the influence of the Nation of Islam, divide its leadership, and destroy it (Gardell 1996, 71–98). The full extent of this operation is still not known; a range of authors, however, have linked the FBI to the most significant act of violence related to the Nation of Islam: the assassination of Malcolm X (see, for example, Gardell 1996 and Breitman, Porter, and Smith 1976).

The intense surveillance of the Nation of Islam as a national security threat was unwarranted, but it is certainly true that members of the movement did engage in violence against one another. The degree to which those acts of violence were meaningfully related to the movement's doctrine is debatable. The first major instance of violence related to the group occurred in 1932, when a man by the name of Robert Harris, also known as Robert Karriem, murdered his lodger, James Smith. Harris, a member of the Nation of Islam, told the police he had committed the murder for religious reasons. Although Elijah Muhammad once commented that "W. D. Fard did teach us that everyone kills four devils at the proper time he ... will have free transportation to Mecca" (Sahib 1951, 95), there is no other documentary evidence to suggest that Harris's actions were anything more than the result of a serious psychiatric disorder.

For the Nation of Islam, the 1960s were a time of upheaval and change. The Muslims' anticipation of the Fall of America was encouraged by the upheaval occurring in American society. Within the movement, however, discord was also brewing. The charismatic Malcolm X had become a significant recruiter for the group, and his power in the New York region was perceived by some—most notably the group's leadership, headquartered in Chicago—as a potential threat (Lee 1996, 39). On March 8, 1964, Malcolm was expelled from the Nation of Islam, and on February 21, 1965, he was assassinated. Talmadge Hayer, Norman 3X, and Thomas 15X were convicted of Malcolm's murder; Hayer later claimed that Malcolm was assassinated for his attacks on Elijah Muhammad, for X had learned of the leader's extramarital affairs and publicly criticized him. As Gardell convincingly suggests, however, it is conceivable that the FBI played a decisive role in these events. The agency sent evidence of Muhammad's affairs to several in the Nation of Islam, including Malcolm, and FBI files suggest that well-placed agents exacerbated the conflict. While not every FBI file has yet been opened and theories regarding this issue must therefore rely on "indications and speculation," Gardell concludes that Malcolm's murder "fits into the pattern of covert FBI actions to remove black dissidents in the 1960s" (Gardell 1996, 85).

Aside from this high-profile murder, the second period of the history of the Nation of Islam saw a relatively low level of intragroup conflict and intermittent violence. The prophesied Fall of America did not occur in the mid-1960s, and Elijah Muhammad and the Muslims seemed to be moving toward a more metaphorical interpretation of the prophecy through the late 1960s and early 1970s. A number of shootings occurred during 1971 and 1972, some of which involved prominent members of the group (including Raymond Sharrieff, Elijah's son-in-law and bodyguard), but these appear to have been related to an internal power struggle.

Elijah Muhammad died on February 25, 1975, and his son Wallace Muhammad assumed leadership, initiating the third stage of the movement's history. By June of 1975, he had moved the Nation of Islam away from his father's strident millenarianism to a moderate reinterpretation of the group's doctrine. Wallace termed his father's role and mission the "First Resurrection" of American Blacks. His own call was for a "Second Resurrection." He wrote, "We now have the power to move on earth as a people. Our new birth into the Total Light of Divine makes the world recognize us for the first time as a people" (Muhammad 1975a, 12–13). At a June 1975 meeting of the movement in Chicago Wallace announced, "What was good teaching for yesterday was good for yesterday . . . the same is not good for today" (Muhammad 1975b, 1), and initiated a significant change in the its doctrine. From that point onward, "whites would be considered fully human" (*Time* 1975, 74). Through the next decades, Wallace worked to move the Nation of Islam to traditional Sunni Islam. The movement went through several name changes during this period and eventually dissolved to become part of the larger American Muslim community. Wallace Muhammad died on September 9, 2007.

Alongside Wallace's community, however, another movement was growing. By the late 1970s several members of the Nation of Islam were concerned about Wallace's leadership and changes in the movement's doctrine. The most vocal of these was Minister Louis Farrakhan. He left the movement in 1978 and began the revitalization of the original Nation of Islam, returning to Elijah Muhammad's original message. During the three decades of his movement's existence, Farrakhan has been extremely controversial. His statements recall Elijah Muhammad's criticisms of the U.S. government and his predictions of the Fall of America. Notably, however, Farrakhan, too, has become more moderate. Whereas Elijah forbade his followers to vote, Farrakhan encouraged African Americans to participate in the political system. This transition was initially awkward. Farrakhan's involvement in Jesse Jackson's 1984 campaign for leadership of the Democratic Party, for example, came to an abrupt end when he cautioned the reporter who revealed Jackson's reference to New York as "Hymie Town" that "One day soon we will threaten you with death" ("Farrakhan Denies Threatening Writer" 1984). Again, however, this was only the suggestion of violence.

For a number of years, therefore, Wallace Muhammad and Louis Farrakhan led what were essentially competing movements. The two groups had critical theological differences, but no major outbreaks of violence occurred. A number of factors likely contributed to this relatively peaceful coexistence. First, a consequence of the two groups' differing theologies was that they tended to attract new recruits from different populations. Wallace Muhammad's message appealed more to those of the African American middle class, whereas Louis Farrakhan's Nation of Islam drew adherents who were less well off. In addition, it was in neither community's interest to engage in violent conflict. Both leaders and many of their respective followers no doubt recalled when divisions in the movement had led to the assassination of Malcolm X, and this perhaps moderated their relationships with one another. Finally, as Gardell notes, at the moment when antagonistic rhetoric seemed the most heated and conflict between the two groups seemed the most possible (1983–1984), Wallace Muhammad and Louis Farrakhan met and negotiated an agreement whereby they would "endeavor to ignore each other" (Gardell 1996, 138). In recent years Farrakhan has become increasingly moderate, moving ever closer to traditional Islam and even suggesting that, with the election of Barack Obama, the United States had changed (Farrakhan 2008). In light of this evolution, it seems unlikely that the Nation of Islam will engage in doctrinally related violence in the near future.

In many ways then, the Nation of Islam provides a case study of why and how a religious movement with a radical belief system did not engage in violence related to its doctrine. Indeed, the most notable act of violence in its history—the assassination of Malcolm X—appears to have been linked to the very secular and common problem of political jealousy, perhaps fostered by government agents.

During much of its almost one-hundred-year history, the Nation of Islam has not been a particularly likeable movement. Its leaders and membership have often engaged in racist and anti-Semitic language, and their criticisms of the American state have sometimes challenged Americans' self-understanding in uncomfortable ways. The movement's doctrine and history, however, suggest that the Nation of Islam was not particularly concerned with a violent overthrow of the American state. Its members waited in faith for Allah to destroy the forces that oppressed them. Instead, it was law-enforcement agencies that more actively fostered violence in the hope of destroying the Nation of Islam.

REFERENCES

———. 1975. "White Muslims?" *Time*. June 30, 1975, 74.
Baldwin, James. 1962. *The Fire Next Time*. New York: Dell.
Barkun, Michael. 1996. "Understanding Millennialism." In *Millennialism and Violence*, ed. Michael Barkun. London: Cass, 1-9.
Breitman, George, H. Porter, and B. Smith. 1976. *The Assassination of Malcolm X*. New York: Pathfinder.
Clay, Nolan. 2007. "Papers Show McVeigh Had Little Remorse." The Oklahoma City Bombing. December 30. http://bombing.newsok.com/article/3186671/ (accessed November 3, 2009).
Cohn, Norman. 1970. *The Pursuit of the Millennium*, rev. ed. New York: Oxford University Press.
———. 2001. *Cosmos, Chaos, and the World to Come*, 2d ed. New Haven, Conn.: Yale University Press.
Diacon, Todd. 1991. *Millenarian Vision, Capitalist Reality*. Durham, N.C.: Duke University Press.

"Farrakhan Denies Threatening Writer." 1984. *Chicago Tribune* (April 7), 4.
Farrakhan, Louis. 2008. "BET's Jeff Johnson Interviews the Honorable Minister Louis Farrakhan." http://video.google.com/videoplay?docid=-3837967150963317895# (accessed November 17, 2009). December 18.
Faucet, Arthur Huff. 1944. *Black Gods of the Metropolis: Negro Religious Cults of the Urban North*. Philadelphia: University of Pennsylvania Press.
Flanagan, Thomas. 1996. "The Politics of the Millennium." In *Millennialism and Violence*, ed. Michael Barkun, 164-175. London: Cass.
Gardell, Mattias. 1996. *In the Name of Elijah Muhammad: Louis Farrakhan and the Nation of Islam*. Durham, N.C.: Duke University Press.
Karim, Imam B. 1971. *The End of White World Supremacy*. New York: Seaver.
Lee, Martha F. 1996. *The Nation of Islam: An American Millenarian Movement*. Syracuse: Syracuse University Press.
———, and Herbert Simms. 2007. "American Millenarianism and Violence: Origins and Expression." *Journal for the Study of Radicalism* 1(2): 100–27.
Lincoln, C. E. 1973. *The Black Muslims in America*, rev. ed. Boston: Beacon.
Muhammad, Elijah. 1965. *The Message to the Blackman in America*. Chicago: Muhammad's Mosque No. 2.
———. 1974. *Our Saviour Has Arrived*. Chicago: Muhammad's Temple of Islam no. 2.
Muhammad, Wallace. 1975a. *Muhammad Speaks*. April 11 Vol. 14, No. 31.
———. 1975b. *Muhammad Speaks*. July 4 Vol. 14, No. 43.
O'Reilly, Kenneth. 1989. *"Racial Matters": The FBI'S Secret File on Black America, 1960–1972*. New York: Free Press.
Reno, Janet. 1995. Attorney General Janet Reno's Opening Statement before the Crime Subcommittee of the House Judiciary Committee and the National Security International Affairs and Criminal Justice Subcommittee of the House Government Reform and Oversight Committee. http://www.pbs.org/wgbh/pages/frontline/waco/renoopeningst.html (accessed November 7, 2009).
Rhodes, J. M. 1980. *The Hitler Movement: A Modern Millenarian Revolution*. Stanford: Hoover Institute Press.
Sahib, Hatim. 1951. *The Nation of Islam*. Master's thesis, University of Chicago.
Sweet, Joanna, and Martha F. Lee. 2009. "Christian Exodus: A Modern American Millenarian Movement." *Journal for the Study of Radicalism* 4(1): 1–23.
Talmon, Yonina. 1968. "Millenarism." *The International Encyclopaedia of the Social Sciences*, vol. 10, ed. David C. Sills, 349–62. New York: Macmillan.
Turner, Richard Brent. 1997. *Islam in the African American Experience*. Bloomington: Indiana University Press.
U.S. Senate Select Committee. 1976. Final Report of the Select Committee to Study Governmental with Respect to Intelligence Activities. April 23. http://www.icdc.com/~paulwolf/cointelpro/churchfinalreportIIIa.htm (accessed November 7, 2009).
X, Malcolm. 1971a. "The Black Man's History." In *The End of White World Supremacy: Four Speeches by Malcolm X*, ed. Imam Benjamin Karim, 23–66. New York: Seaver.
———. 1971b. "God's Judgment of White America." In *The End of White World Supremacy: Four Speeches by Malcolm X*, ed. Imam Benjamin Karim, 121–48. New York: Seaver.

15

Cultural Capital, Social Networks, and Collective Violence at Rajneeshpuram

Marion S. Goldman

Rajneeshpuram, the short-lived communal city in central Oregon, was built around charismatic spiritual leader Bhagwan Shree Rajneesh, who later became known as Osho. The community lasted for less than six years—from 1981 to 1986—and for much of that time internal intrigues and external threats plagued its members. Despite possibilities for large-scale bloodshed, however, violence never escalated to the point of mass murder, suicides, or sweeping violence within the communal city.

Both external support and personal resources that were shared by most of the devotees, called sannyasins, militated against possibilities of external intervention and extensive internal violence. Rajneeshpuram is a case that makes it possible to explore the utility of the concepts of social and cultural capital to add to theory and research about contemporary collective religious violence.

Violence and New Religions

While large-scale, collective cult[1] violence is uncommon, popular discussions of new religions in the United States and stereotypes about them concentrate on the few most violent groups: the Peoples Temple and the Branch Davidians (Bromley and Melton 2002; Barker 2002). The 1997 group suicides of thirty-nine members of the isolated UFO cult, Heaven's Gate, also drew popular and academic attention but not to the same extent as Jonestown or Waco (Balch 1980; Balch and Taylor 2002). Large-scale collective violence engages the majority of movement members and has lasting physical and emotional effects on both perpetrators and victims. The violence ultimately defines the group to outsiders and frames its historical significance.

Dramatic conflict represents the end of a continuum within new religious movements and between them and their host societies. The fact that extreme external and internal tension at Rajneeshpuram did not erupt in massive violence allows us to better understand how conflicts may be mitigated even though the potential for violence exists.

The mutual accommodation in the high-tension situation in central Oregon reflected a number of variables. Among them were the sannyasins' educational levels and their external networks: in other words, their cultural and social capital (Bourdieu 2005). This extreme case of violence that was averted illuminates the hidden dynamics of more common and taken-for-granted social relationships (Goffman 1963; Bromley and Melton 2002, 3). The case of Rajneeshpuram allows us to better understand the many avenues for accommodation between new religions and their host societies and the reasons that most new religions in the United States remain relatively peaceful.

The case of Rajneeshpuram makes it possible to identify and elaborate possibilities for accommodation in terms of the three central multidimensional variables that earlier research has identified as generating violence: apocalyptic doctrine, social isolation, and external emphasis on sustaining the existing social order. This case underscores the importance of those three variables and also indicates how the sannyasins' personal attributes and the practices that reflected and supported their social privilege helped define the movement's doctrine, social boundaries, and external relationships.

The potential for large-scale collective violence involving new religious movements in the United States is rare, but the groups in which it occurs merit extensive examination, as do revolutions and other extraordinary social events that have lasting impact on their societies (Ragin 1981; Skocpol 1979). Understanding of the ways that the social composition of a movement may affect its violent potential is a further elaboration of earlier considerations of violence and new religions.

Rajneeshpuram Methods, Sources, and History

This chapter is based on participant observation at Rajneeshpuram from 1983 through 1985, life-history interviews with twenty-five devotees, additional visits to Rajneeshpuram/the Big Muddy Ranch in 1986 and 1998, and follow-up interviews with devotees in 1997. Between 1999 and 2000 I also interviewed ten individuals active in local Wasco County resistance to Rajneeshpuram.

Every issue of the *Rajneesh Times* (published biweekly between 1983 and the end of 1985) was used to supplement interviews and observation. In addition, I had access to legal documents and manuscript collections of letters, private papers, and ephemera of both sannyasins and their opponents in the University of Oregon Special Collections at the Knight Library.

Relatively recent primary sources include a set of 1997 and 2004 interviews with the former Oregon attorney general. In 2004 I spent two consecutive days recording interviews with Ma Anand Sheela, a central figure in Rajneeshpuram's history, who is now known as Sheela Birnstiel. We met at her residence in Switzerland, where she owns and runs two convalescent homes.

In 2008 I interviewed a former member of Rajneesh's household at Rajneeshpuram who had opposed Sheela and spoke about the ways that informal social networks made it possible for her and others to counter Sheela's exhortations to violence.

Rajneeshpuram began in the early 1980s, when Bhagwan Shree Rajneesh and about two thousand of his devotees created the communal city of Rajneeshpuram on the Big Muddy Ranch in Wasco County, Oregon. The men and women who settled there were primarily from the United States, although there were small contingents of Western Europeans and Australians. They hoped to blend spirituality and materialism while building an intentional community that could also serve as a destination resort and luxurious pilgrimage center for sannyasins from all over the world, supplanting the group's previous ashram in Pune (Poona), India.

Since the establishment of his ashram in Pune in 1974, Rajneesh had primarily attracted affluent seekers from North America and Western Europe. Capable, accomplished adults in their late twenties and early thirties flocked to him. Most of the sannyasins that lived at the communal city in Oregon in the '80s were more than thirty years old, and less than 5 percent of them were people of color. Two-thirds reported that they had degrees from four-year colleges. A substantial proportion of these sannyasins represented the best and brightest of the baby-boom generation, who had excelled in college and in their later careers (Goldman 1999, 11–12).

They brought their skills to help build Rajneeshpuram and also contributed money to support their guru's vision. However, devotees with substantial wealth kept most of their holdings in trust, although they contributed significant amounts to the community. Many others with less money had professional skills that they could use to reestablish their careers, should that be necessary.

In Oregon, Rajneesh kept a vow of public silence for three years, but he appeared for a daily afternoon drive in one of his ninety-six Rolls Royces, waving to sannyasins that lined the road. With the exception of the drives, the guru retreated from public view, delegating organizational leadership to Ma Anand Sheela, his personal secretary.

From the moment sannyasins settled in Oregon, they challenged established laws and customs, which generated a range of opposition throughout the state (Fitz Gerald 1986; Milne 1987). The most controversial incidents occurred in autumn of 1984, when Sheela and her inner circle bused in hundreds of homeless individuals, mostly men, in a futile effort to control county elections. Massive negative publicity, state monitoring of voter registration, and legal opposition doomed the plan. By the end of 1984 almost all of the estimated fifteen hundred homeless visitors had departed.

Less than a year after the "share a home" debacle, Sheela and her inner circle fled Rajneeshpuram for Europe. As his community disintegrated, Rajneesh spoke publicly once again, accusing Sheela and her cadre of drugging dissident sannyasins, wire-tapping, arson, attempted murder, and embezzlement of Rajneesh movement funds.

In a shocking revelation, Rajneesh publicly asserted that Sheela ordered a few members of her inner circle to sprinkle salmonella in almost a dozen restaurant salad bars located in the Wasco County, poisoning at least 750 individuals. It was a test run for a more massive effort that could temporarily incapacitate large numbers of anti-Rajneesh voters on election day (Carter 1990,: 224–26; Epps 2001).

All of the evidence suggests that only Sheela and her small circle were directly responsible for these actions, but Rajneesh's support of their criminality remains in dispute. After leaving Oregon, Rajneesh traveled all over the world until his representatives bargained with the Indian government. He resettled in the old Pune ashram, now renamed Osho International Meditation Resort (Sannyas News). By January of 1986, the Big Muddy Ranch was up for sale, and only Rajneesh and a skeleton crew of sannyasins remained.

Large-scale collective cult violence generates conflicting accounts and interpretations, so it is critical to prioritize primary sources and observation. After a group's demise, disappointed devotees, former members, and outsiders weigh in with their versions of what happened (Wright 1991). Less intentional data, such as direct observations, material artifacts, letters, and legal documents may be more accurate than retrospective accounts or published histories, where competing interests tell different stories (Bloch 1953).

After Rajneesh denounced Sheela, his accusations grew increasingly extreme as he absolved himself of any knowledge of her misdeeds. For example, he alleged, with no material proof, that Sheela and her cohorts planned to sprinkle salmonella or add psychotropic drugs to food in Magdalena Cafeteria in the communal city.

In contrast to accusations about the cafeteria, material evidence and other sources later confirmed other ostensibly fantastic allegations. For example, in 1998 I observed evidence of hidden microphones and elaborate switchboards that supported Rajneesh's descriptions of Sheela's sophisticated surveillance arrangements. I also entered two hidden laboratories where Sheela and her assistants had mixed the salmonella poisons that were distributed in salad bars.

Direct observation and gun-registration records were also important in weighing questions about weapons at Rajneeshpuram. I saw that Rajneesh's bodyguards and the 150-sannyasin Peace Force were well supplied with weapons, including Uzi submachine guns, other semiautomatic weapons, and handguns in public. In addition, there were a few unregistered firearms in a semiprivate residence on the ranch.

Rajneeshpuram is a useful case to facilitate understanding of how violence is usually avoided because, while the group exhibited many characteristics associated with large-scale collective violence, it never erupted. A capricious charismatic leader and his volatile surrogate, Ma Anand Sheela, governed the communal city (Dawson 2006, 154–62). The community was geographically isolated, at least a forty-minute drive down a narrow road to the neighboring town of Antelope. Moreover, Sheela and her circle had access to many weapons, prescription drugs, and cultured biological warfare agents that could have been used in large-scale collective violence.

Like Rajneeshpuram, the vast majority of intentional communities or more informal group-living arrangements developed by novel religions rise and disappear in the United States without large-scale collective violence (Bromley and Melton 2002; Kanter 1972). In part, their survival reflects the fact that advantaged individuals have predominated in most alternative religions in the Western world (Stark 1996a, 29–48), although most of these groups have never approached the potential for violence that characterized Rajneeshpuram. Groups that survive for more than a generation, even when they are controversial, tend to move toward the mainstream, as the sannyasins did when they reopened their Pune ashram as a destination resort and began marketing Osho Rajneesh's works in American bookstores like Barnes and Noble (Goldman 1999, 249–68).

Over a generation, almost all cults gradually minimize tension with the surrounding environment and sustain ties with outsiders (Stark 1996b; Dawson 2006, 144–46). A few, like the Golden Temple American Sikhs or Dr. Moon's Unification Church develop multimillion-dollar enterprises, and others, like the sannyasins and Scientologists, create niche markets for their spiritual goods and services. These long-term economic and cultural successes also reflect the cultural and social capital that many first-generation movement members bring to their groups.

Theoretical Approaches

The research on large-scale collective violence, as well as group suicides or murders by cults, identifies three important interdependent variables that produce violence: world-rejecting movement doctrine, physical and/or social isolation from their host societies, sustained external opposition (Hall, Schuyler, and Trinh 2000). These findings carry across cultures, although the shape of the external opposition and the specifics of internal doctrine vary in different social contexts.

Dramatic collective violence associated with new religions in the past fifty years is by no means limited to the United States. However, Dawson (2006) notes that it is particularly difficult to compare exogenous factors such as stigmatization and law-enforcement responses across cultures. I discuss Waco and Jonestown in some detail because they shared the same broad cultural and legal context as Rajneeshpuram, although their members were drawn primarily from the working class.

Theories about large-scale collective cult violence and new religions suggest that internal group processes and interactions with the external social environment must converge in order to generate extreme outcomes (Robbins and Anthony 1995, 237; Bromley and Melton 2002, 42–56). As internal strains meet external pressures, potential for disaster accelerates (Galanter 1989, 113–21).

Because of its American orientation, this chapter does not deal with other important, relatively recent incidents of large-scale collective violence in new religions. The Solar Temple in Quebec and Western Europe experienced a series of murders and suicides from 1995 through 1997 (Wessinger 2000; Introvigne and Mayer 2002). Aum Shinrikyo in Japan developed a violent, ascetic organization that initiated sarin gas attacks on outsiders, resulting in a dozen deaths and thousands of injuries (Lifton 1999; Hall, Schuyler, and Trinh 2000; Reader 2000). The Movement for the Restoration of the Ten Commandments of God in Uganda also generated large-scale collective bloodshed (Walliss 2004). Despite their many differences from each other and from the American groups considered in this chapter, these new religions shared experiences of world-rejecting doctrines, social and physical isolation from the larger culture, and external hostility.

Some research on religious violence notes charismatic leadership as an important variable in the development of large-scale collective violence. Wright (2002) asserts that a dominating charismatic leader may polarize a movement internally and also exacerbate external hostility toward a group (106). Johnson (1992) and Dawson (1999, 2002) also consider the importance of charismatic leadership in precipitating group crises. However, charismatic leadership is necessary to the formation of almost all new religious movements, and it is inherently unstable (Dawson 2006, 28–29). Thus, it is less a central element in the development of large-scale collective violence than a necessary part of almost every new religion in its first generation.

When devotees are not entirely dependent on a charismatic relationship and have strong connections with other members and outsiders, the influence of leaders who encourage violence may be considerably diminished (Jacobs 1989). External social networks allow devotees to find rewards beyond their group and its leader and can also stimulate external support for their group as a whole, thereby diminishing their dependence on a charismatic chief.

Movement doctrine is another variable that supplements or detracts from devotees' willingness to engage in large-scale collective violence. Life-embracing belief systems that promise a better life on earth seldom encourage collective violence. These doctrines often appeal to people who have access to material comforts and expect that they can discover personal and spiritual fulfillment while they are still alive (Coles 1977).

In the case of Rajneeshpuram, the devotees' external social networks, personal affluence, professional skills, and familiarity with the wider culture diminished Sheela's ability to exhort them to violence and the power of Rajneesh's apparent support for her. Their skills and networks also empowered them to generate goodwill toward their communal city.

To explore the social psychology of cult violence, Wallis (1979) developed a cumulative, interactional model that described a cycle of members' alienation, increased external pressure, and finally intense religious conflict. Bromley (2002) constructed a more precise framework that posited four stages of interactions between movements and their host societies that had led to large-scale collective violence and also group suicides in the United States and elsewhere. Bromley's model deals with dominant patterns, while recognizing that each phase may involve varied, sometimes inconsistent interactions (Bromley 2002, 12). Within each stage, including the denouement, are possibilities for peaceful resolution or conflict.

Verter's (2003) conceptualization of spiritual capital and its impact on individuals' religious decisions further refines models of cumulative interactions that lead to cult violence. He considers religious knowledge and experience as elements of spiritual capital that individuals can amass as part of their larger store of cultural knowledge (2003, 152). This application of Bourdieu's (2005) theories of cultural capital illuminates the way in which accumulated religious capital does not diminish larger stores of cultural capital. Sannyasins' religious capital added to their cultural capital because their doctrines and practices supported material success and professional accomplishment in the larger society (Goldman 1999). Their cultural capital and external social networks allowed them to negotiate relatively peaceful resolutions in a context that could have produced large-scale violence.

Peaceful Resolutions

Case studies of three other groups in the United States provide important insights into nonviolent resolutions for new religions that had periods of high tension with their surrounding society and experienced internal difficulties as well. Like Rajneeshpuram, all three exhibited many elements associated with large-scale collective violence.

Rosenfeld (1997) advocated more extensive research on groups that dispersed without violence, while describing the peaceful dissolution of a nativist, millennial group, the Justus Freemen in Montana. Kleiver (1999) considered the peaceful exodus of all 150 members of Chen Tao, a Taiwanese group that arrived in a Dallas suburb in August 1997 to anticipate God's arrival on a flying saucer in March 1998. Police and popular media in Garland, Texas, developed ongoing dialogue with Chen Tao representatives that facilitated the group's calm departure after their prophecy failed. Members of these groups did not have the sannyasins' economic and cultural resources, but they avoided violence because they cultivated external social networks and diminished their social isolation.

The third case, the Church Universal and Triumphant's (CUT) survivalist enclave on the Grand Teton Ranch in Paradise Valley in Montana, resembled Rajneeshpuram in many ways. The CUT generated considerable national attention in the late 1980s and 1990s because its members had stockpiled firearms to protect themselves during a possible apocalypse. External opponents also feared the environmental impact of their community, which was located at the edge of Yellowstone National Park. The group did not engage in large-scale collective violence despite national media attention, their cache of weapons, and a hostile social environment.

State and local law enforcement tried to reach accommodation by explicitly modeling the emphasis on peaceful legal solutions that had militated against large-scale collective violence at Rajneeshpuram. Internally, the Church Universal and Triumphant instituted organizational reforms and developed outreach to surrounding communities to reduce the group's social isolation (Whitsel 2003). Most of its members, like the sannyasins, were educated and affluent, and they hoped to find rewards within the present material world. Thus, they were willing to negotiate in order to continue their lives on earth.

These three cases of peaceful resolution in volatile situations could be examined in terms of a systematic, comparative framework in the same ways that Rajneeshpuram is considered in the following sections. By extending Bromley's (2002) model, which was derived from cases of violent denouements, it is possible to consider the more peaceful, more common instances of cult accommodation or dispersal. The ways in which social and cultural capital contribute to peaceful denouements are added to this analytic framework.

Conflict, Accommodation, and Exodus at Rajneeshpuram

Almost all alternative religions in the United States experience latent tension (Stark 1996b). Cults must differentiate themselves from the larger society and from other religions in order to appeal to potential members. However, doctrines and practices that are extremely deviant from social norms or are possibly criminal, such as polygamy or extreme promiscuity, may precipitate a second stage of nascent conflict and progressive polarization between the small culture of the movement and its host society as opponents mobilize public opinion and mount legal challenges (Bromley 2002).

This nascent conflict may lead to intensified conflict as both the movement and its opponents recruit supporters, trade accusations, and consider the use of force. Finally, a denouement may occur, which can take the form of large-scale collective violence, attacks on outsiders, group suicides, capitulation and redefinition of the movement, or relatively sudden, mass departures.

Potential resolution or diminution of conflict exists at every stage, even at denouement. There are many possibilities to avoid conflict, and that is why large-scale collective violence is rare. Avoiding violence is easier when group members retain their stake in the host society because of their social networks, doctrine, education, and cultural knowledge.

The Rajneesh devotees' continued contact with networks outside Rajneeshpuram, their life-embracing beliefs, and law enforcement's commitment to due process, which involved positive communication with sannyasins, militated against large-scale collective violence at every stage. The following sections consider each of these three variables and the ways that sannyasins' social and cultural capital influenced peaceful resolution in central Oregon.

Social Capital and External Networks

New religions that erupt in large-scale collective violence or collective suicides are physically, socially, and symbolically isolated from their host societies (Dawson 2006, 162–66). They create strong boundaries, and members depend on the leader and other devotees to define their identities (Galanter 1989). Devotees renounce their emotional ties to their former friends and families outside their group and have very little contact with them. Communication with the outside world is limited even when members work outside their religious enclaves (Balch and Taylor 2000).

When a group isolates itself, outsiders may overlook it, deliberately avoid it, or develop elaborate negative stereotypes. Isolation leads law enforcement to rely solely on disaffected members or the anticult movement for information (Hall 1987). Moreover, the media may sensationalize negative accounts of the groups. Mutual isolation can fuel hostility that creates even further social distance and mistrust.

Although Rajneeshpuram was physically remote, its residents were not socially isolated. A public-relations department staffed by professional journalists and community hosts, some of whom had been fashion models, lauded their communal city to the media and interested visitors from the outside. Cultivating outsiders' goodwill, Rajneesh's purchasing agents hosted local suppliers and placed six-figure orders for everything from farm machinery to additions to Rajneesh's Rolls Royce collection.

Even as tension mounted, Rajneesh's representatives continued to meet with sympathetic politicians and members of the ACLU in Eugene and Portland and also conferred with newspaper and television reporters. Some of them were old friends or professional mentors of the Rajneesh representatives.

Individuals with powerful positions in the Rajneesh organization initiated covert conversations with the Oregon State attorney general's office. In turn, representatives from that office moderated responses from state police and federal authorities. Sannyasins who disagreed with Sheela's confrontational policies recognized that the community's survival depended on their neighbors' goodwill and on politicians' sympathies.

The maintenance of old external networks and the development of new ones reflected the fact that the movement never required full separation from the larger society. Becoming a sannyasin did not force devotees to shun their families or old friends. After taking sannyas, in the '70s and '80s, sannyasins were supposed to meditate at least once daily, wear sunrise colors (which included a whole spectrum of red-based shades), don a *mala* of 108 beads with a locket housing Bhagwan's likeness, and become vegetarian. In terms of Kanter's (1972) paradigm, devotees did not have to renounce their old lives. They could transform themselves without giving up their old identities or sacrificing previous relationships.

Devotees could also sustain close personal bonds with people outside the group. They invited their parents, adult children, old friends, and, in a few cases, financial advisors to visit Rajneeshpuram and attend carefully orchestrated visitors' weekends. They retained their social and cultural capital and much of their economic capital, as well (Bourdieu 2005).

As Sheela rose to power, she ostracized a number of vocal dissidents from the movement. Some formed sects of the Rajneesh movement, such as the "Wild Geese" or the "Camels." These dissidents, however, rarely criticized Rajneesh or his desire to build a communal city. Instead, they blamed Sheela long before Rajneesh condemned her, and they continued to support Rajneesh's vision (Goldman 1999, 248–68; Franklin 1992). No large group of apostates or sannyasins' families formed to attack Rajneesh publicly and stigmatize or symbolically isolate the communal city.

The community was never symbolically isolated, and positive perceptions balanced the increasingly negative public sentiment that grew in the wake of political conflict in Wasco County.

Life-Affirming Doctrine and Individualism

Bhagwan Shree Rajneesh embraced the delights of materialism and supported enlightened capitalism. Occasionally he veered toward dire predictions, but the guru's emphatic celebration of individualism and independence allowed sannyasins to reject and even laugh at his occasional apocalyptic musing about everything from AIDS to a nuclear bombing of Rajneeshpuram (Gordon 1987, 186–87; Goldman 1995).

In 2004 Sheela Birnstiel, formerly Ma Anand Sheela, explained her role at Rajneeshpuram and disclaimed any malevolent intent. Addressing the issue of whether something like Jonestown could have happened in central Oregon, she noted, "Bhagwan was life positive. His whole movement was life positive. Where [a] life negative situation happens, you can see suicide happening" (Sheela Birnstiel interview by author, August 2004).

In nearly six hundred books, most of which were transcriptions of his lectures and initiation talks, Rajneesh discussed almost every major religious and philosophical tradition. These approaches came together in a spiritual stew dominated by Zen Buddhism and spiced with exhortations to fully enjoy every aspect of life.

Individual choice was the essence of the philosophy, although the ultimate freedom of enlightenment involved the disappearance of ego through surrender to

Rajneesh's teachings. As with almost everything else in the movement, there was considerable latitude for individuals to construct their own meanings of surrender. In the changed movement of the 1990s, meditation, not surrender, came to be defined as the bridge to enlightenment.

Rajneesh built flexibility into his doctrine by calling for highly individualized interpretations of his lectures and writings. Adopting the role of a therapist, he told sannyasins that they had to discover the true meaning of his words in terms of their own personal experience and understandings.

The guru emphasized his ideal of a new human being who synthesized the worldly and the godly in an imaginary hero that he called Zorba the Buddha, who blended full enjoyment of worldly pleasures with spiritual growth. Zen, tantric tradition, and prosperity spirituality came together in a vision that enticed many privileged Americans:

> A new human being is needed on earth, a new human being who accepts both, who is scientific and mystic. Who is all for matter and all for spirit. Only then will we be able to create humanity, which is rich on both sides. I teach you the richness of body, richness of soul, richness of this world and that world. To me that is true religiousness. (Rajneesh 1983, 14).

In contrast to the Rajneesh movement, the Branch Davidians and the Peoples Temple had explicit apocalyptic belief systems that contributed to dramatic collective violence by both exhorting members' sacrifice and disconcerting outside opponents.

The Branch Davidians grounded their apocalyptic visions in the book of Revelations in the New Testament, as have many other groups (Wessinger 2000). Their leader, David Koresh, maintained that the world was already experiencing the end-time period of tribulation, which would inevitably precede Armageddon and the Second Coming (Hall 2002; Wright 1995). Koresh interpreted the BATF's precipitous raid on their compound as the inauguration of the final battle.

Secular works and broadly interpreted liberation theology fueled Jim Jones's apocalyptic vision for the Peoples Temple and framed the collective violence erupting in 1978 (Hall 1987). French Marxist philosopher Regis Debray's *Revolution in the Revolution?* (1968) and Black Panther Huey P. Newton's *Revolutionary Suicide* (1974) particularly influenced Jones's call to his devotees to die fighting or kill themselves as revolutionary martyrs rather than surrender to evil capitalist opponents. Thus, the arrival of Congressman Leo Ryan and his assistants at the Jonestown community in Guyana precipitated massive violence.

While Koresh and Jones rejected the contemporary world and criticized American's greed, Rajneesh and his sannyasins embraced it (Mehta 1985). Their doctrine allowed them to reject Sheela's corrosive leadership and also to seek earthly delights. The communal city of Rajneeshpuram reflected the foundational beliefs in choice, individualism, and earthly satisfaction. There, in the middle of the high desert ranch land, the sannyasins enjoyed boutiques, bookstores, restaurants, and wine bars. In the '80s, Rajneeshpuram housed central Oregon's first gourmet pizza restaurant and espresso bar.

Journalist Win McCormick, a persistent public opponent of Rajneeshpuram, was often alarmed at the growing potential for large-scale collective violence at Rajneeshpuram. However, he reflected on the sannyasins' love of luxury and came to a prescient conclusion:

> Someday, in my opinion, the Rajneesh cult will break asunder. Since all cults have the inherent potential to end in violence, it may end that way; or, as is perhaps more likely in this case, it may end peacefully, with Bhagwan and his top assistants departing for a South Sea island or the Riviera (McCormack 1985, 262).

Due Process, Informal Contact, and the Rule of Law

In the United States, a tension exists between the emphasis on maintaining established social order through interventions and that on facilitating the rule of law, which protects due process and the rights of minority groups (Skolnick 1967). The rule of law moderated outside intervention at Rajneeshpuram. The sannyasins' large internal legal staff, its public-relations group, and its hired political lobbyists tried to ensure that federal, state, and local government representatives paid attention to due process.

When law-enforcement agents heed only the pleas of cult opponents while also stereotyping a group because of its unfamiliar doctrine, the rule of order prevails (Barker 2002; Wright 2002). Richardson's (2004) analysis of legal responses to Rajneeshpuram indicates that lawsuits put pressure on the communal city. However, other formal legal responses and informal communication limited the possibilities for precipitous external interventions.

The Oregon attorney general grounded his strategy for diminishing possibilities of violence in the Establishment clause of the U.S. Constitution, which calls for the separation of church and state. That strategy limited formal intervention based on stereotyping and general fear of the Rajneeshees, and it curtailed informal anti-cult attacks proposed by some opposing groups and the local media. Throughout the escalating conflict, the state of Oregon actively pressed for legal solutions to all accusations of criminal activities and violation of civil laws at Rajneeshpuram. This was a principled legal position that also reflected respect for the social and legal skills of the Rajneesh representatives.

In addition to public positions, the attorney general, his staff, and personal associates privately negotiated with Rajneeshpuram's opponents and with state and local law-enforcement officials to ensure that they respected the sannyasins' civil liberties. They also worked with the sannyasins to create mutual accommodations to avoid confrontations.

Until 1983, when Sheela began attacking her opponents in the press, Rajneesh's attorneys and their hired outside legal advisors and public-relations representatives enjoyed cordial informal interactions with the Oregon attorney general and his staff. His office facilitated discussions between Rajneesh attorneys and attorneys from the U.S. Office for Civil Rights about anti-Rajneesh harassment. Sannyasin attorneys also talked privately with the Oregon attorney general and the U.S. Department of Justice Mediation and Conciliation Service in their attempts to resolve conflicts (e.g., water rights disputes) that involved Rajneeshpuram and neighboring communities.

Throughout the sannyasins' sojourn in Oregon, the attorney general's representatives carefully monitored activities at Rajneeshpuram and at the same time tried to calm insurgent local opponents. A handful of antagonists posted signs that said "Rajneesh hunting season," but this was a symbolic rather than an actual call to arms. The local gun culture centered around hunting, and from an early age, gun owners were taught to raise their guns only when they planned to use them. When tensions between the communal city and the surrounding communities began escalating, representatives from the Oregon attorney general's office persuaded one influential rancher to urge other locals to follow him in locking his firearms in a bank vault.

In 1984, as sannyasins reeled from Sheela's growing irrationality, the Oregon attorney general issued his legal challenge to the city of Rajneeshpuram itself, arguing that the incorporated city represented the unconstitutional merger of church and state. This opinion would not apply to other religious communities unless they had also incorporated city governments and received state and federal funding.

The federal district court enjoined the city of Rajneeshpuram to cease exerting governmental power in December 1985 after the Big Muddy Ranch was already up for sale. The state pushed for accommodation and peaceful resolution by emphasizing the rule of law instead of the maintenance of traditional social order.

In a 1997 interview, former Oregon attorney general David Frohnmayer noted the following:

> I had persons from central Oregon who were ready to go right over the river [into Rajneeshpuram] with guns blazing. Part of our job was still to keep the peace with people who agreed with the legal position we took but were impatient and even furious with the slow pace of the courts. . . . And not withstanding [the sannyasins'] extreme reaction to my opinion, within hours of its issue, my assistants were on the phone to Rajneesh officials saying, "Above all, we've got to keep the peace with this!" (Rajneesh Manuscript Collection, University of Oregon Library Special Collections, 1997)

The attorney general's opinion on the ostensibly limited question of whether or not the city of Rajneeshpuram could control or prevent travel on county roads implicitly addressed a number of constitutional issues. The opinion affirmed the separation of church and state as ultimately more important than individuals' rights to free exercise of religion.

The opinion limited the sannyasins' ability to control the public roads through their community, create their own police force, and administer the public schools that all of the children in their district attended. It diminished the sannyasins' influence in Wasco County in terms of election procedures and street naming, as well (Frohnmayer 1985).

On the other side, the legal opinion on separation constrained state, local, and federal agencies' commitment to mainstream religions. They were informed that sannyasins were entitled to the same religious freedom as any other Americans. Despite widespread law-enforcement hostility to sannyasins' doctrine and practices, agents at every level adhered to the rule of law and did not act precipitously to support social order.

Implications

In order to understand how accommodation or retreat may overshadow conflict, it is important to consider three interrelated variables: the nature of a group's doctrine, the group's and its members' formal and informal connections to outsiders, and whether or not a rule of law with attention to due process overshadows concern for sustaining the dominant social order. Because the sannyasins possessed and utilized their cultural and social capital in terms of all three variables, they were able to facilitate accommodation and avoid collective violence.

Rajneeshpuram represents more than a curious incident in the histories of Oregon and the Friends of Osho/Rajneesh. There was an armed communal city that was in high tension with the surrounding culture, but the group did not disintegrate because of extreme collective conflict.

The gradual accommodation and final exodus from central Oregon was not a matter of chance. Along with the structural contexts and group interactions that shape large-scale violence involving new religious movements, we must continue to examine the resources of cultural and social capital that religious actors employ to avert violence and create relatively peaceful resolutions to potential tragedies.

NOTES

1. While some sociologists argue that the term *cult* may be pejorative, they use it in the titles of books and articles because it is known to most audiences. It is used in this chapter because "cult" is a synonym for other, more cumbersome terms, and scholars have begun to reintegrate it into academic usage (Goldman 2006).

REFERENCES

Balch, Robert W. 1980. "Looking behind the Scenes in a Religious Cult: Implications for the Study of Conversion." *Sociological Analysis* 41: 128–36.

———, and David Taylor. 2002. "Making Sense of the Heaven's Gate Suicides." In *Cults, Religion, and Violence*, ed. D. G. Bromley and J. G. Melton, 209–28. New York: Cambridge University Press.

Barker, Eileen V. 2002. "Watching for Violence: A Comparative Analysis of the Roles of Five Types of Cult-watching Groups." In *Cults, Religion, and Violence*, ed. D. G. Bromley and J. G. Melton, 123–48. New York: Cambridge University Press.

Bourdieu, Pierre. 2005. *The Social Structures of the Economy*. New York: Polity.

Bromley, David G. 2002. "Dramatic Denouements." In *Cults, Religion, and Violence*, ed. D. G. Bromley and J. G. Melton, 11–41. New York: Cambridge University Press.

———, and J. Gordon Melton, eds. 2002. *Cults, Religion, and Violence*. New York: Cambridge University Press.

Carter, Lewis F. 1990. *Charisma and Control in Rajneeshpuram*. New York: Cambridge University Press.

Coles, Robert. 1977. *Privileged Ones: The Well-Off and the Rich in America*. Boston: Little, Brown.

Dawson, Loren L. 1999. When Prophecy Fails and Faith Persists: A Theoretical Overview. *Nova Religio* 3(1): 60–82.

———. 2002. "Crises of Charismatic Legitimacy and Violent Behavior in New Religious Movements." In *Cults, Religion, and Violence*, ed. D. G. Bromley and J. G. Melton, 80–101. New York: Cambridge University Press.

———. 2006. *Comprehending Cults: The Sociology of New Religious Movements*, 2d ed. New York: Oxford University Press.

Debray, Regis. 1968. *Revolution in the Revolution? Armed Struggle and Political Struggle in Latin America*. New York: Pelican.

Epps, Garrett. 2001. *To an Unknown God: Religious Freedom on Trial*. New York: St. Martins.

FitzGerald, Frances. 1986. *Cities on a Hill: A Journey through Contemporary American Cultures*. New York: Simon and Schuster.

Franklin, Satya Bharti. 1992. *The Promise of Paradise: A Woman's Intimate Story of the Perils of Life with Rajneesh*. New York: Station Hill.

Frohnmayer, David. 1985. *Opinions of the Attorney General of the State of Oregon, July 1, 1983–June 30, 1985*.

———. 1997. "Oral History of Role as Attorney General." Rajneesh Manuscript Collection, University of Oregon Library Special Collections.

Galanter, Marc. 1989. *Cults: Faith, Healing, and Coercion*. New York: Oxford University Press.

Goffman, Erving. 1963. *Stigma: Notes on the Management of Spoiled Identity*. Englewood Cliffs, N.J.: Prentice-Hall.

Goldman, Marion S. 1995. "From Promiscuity to Celibacy: Women and Sexual Regulation at Rajneeshpuram." In *Sex, Schemes, and Sanctity: Religion and Deviance*, ed. M. J. Neitz and M. S. Goldman, 203–29. Greenwich, Conn.: JAI.

———. 1999. *Passionate Journeys: Why Successful Women Joined a Cult*. Ann Arbor: University of Michigan Press.

———. 2006. "Cults, New Religions, and the Spiritual Landscape." *Journal for the Scientific Study of Religion* 45: 86–96.
Gordon, James S. 1987. *The Golden Guru*. Lexington, Mass.: Grenne.
Hall, John R. 1987. *Gone from the Promised Land*. New Brunswick, N.J.: Transaction.
———. 2000. *Apocalypse Observed: Religious Movements in North America, Europe, and Japan*. With Philip Schuyler and Sylvaine Trinh. New York: Routledge.
———. 2002. "Mass Suicide and the Branch Davidians." In *Cults, Religion, and Violence*, ed. D. G. Bromley and J. G. Melton, 149–69. New York: Cambridge University Press.
Introvigne, Massimo, and Jean-François Mayer. 2002. "Occult Masters and the Temple of Doom: The Fiery End of the Solar Temple." In *Cults, Religion, and Violence*, ed. D. G. Bromley and J. G. Melton, 170–88. New York: Cambridge University Press.
Jacobs, Janet Liebman. 1989. *Divine Disenchantment: Deconverting from New Religions*. Bloomington: University of Indiana Press.
Johnson, Benton. 1992. "On Founders and Followers: Some Factors in the Development of New Religious Movements." *Sociological Analysis* (suppl.): S1–S13. Vol 53 (suppl): S1–13.
Kanter, Rosabeth Moss. 1972. *Commitment and Community: Communes and Utopias in Sociological Perspective*. Cambridge, Mass.: Harvard University Press.
Kleiver, Lonnie D. 1999. "Meeting God in Garland: A Model of Religious Tolerance." *Nova Religio* 3: 45–53.
Latkin, Carl D. 1992. "Seeing Red: A Social-psychological Analysis of the Rajneeshpuram Conflict." *Sociological Analysis* 53: 257–71.
Lifton, Robert Jay. 1999. *Destroying the World to Save It: Aum Shinrikyo, Apocalyptic Violence, and the New Global Terrorism*. New York: Metropolitan.
McCormack, Win. 1985. *The Rajneesh Files: 1981–1986*. Portland: New Oregon.
Mehta, Gita. 1979. *Karma Kola: Marketing the Mystic East*. New York: Simon and Schuster.
Melton, J. Gordon. 1992. "Violence and Cults." In *The Encyclopedic Handbook of Cults in America*, 2d ed., ed. J. G. Melton, 361–93. New York: Garland.
———. 1995. "The Changing Scene of New Religious Movements: Observations from a Generation of Research." *Social Compass* 42: 265–76.
Milne, Hugh. l987. *Bhagwan: The God That Failed*. New York: St. Martin's.
Newton, Huey P. 1974. *Revolutionary Suicide*. New York: Ballantine.
Ragin, Charles C. 1981. "Comparative Sociology and the Comparative Method." *International Journal of Comparative Sociology* 22: 102–30.
———, and David Zaret. 1983. "Theory and Method in Comparative Research: Two Strategies." *Social Forces* 61: 731–54.
Rajneesh. 1983. *Rajneeshism: An Introduction to Bhagwan Shree Rajneesh and His Religion*, ed. Ma Anand Sheela. Rajneeshpuram: Rajneesh Foundation International.
Reader, Ian. 2000. *Religious Violence in Contemporary Japan*. Honolulu: University of Hawaii Press.
Richardson, James T. 2004. "State and Federal Cooperation in Regulating New Religions: Oregon versus the Bhagwan Shree Rajneesh." In *Regulating Religion: Case Studies from around the Globe*, ed. J. T. Richardson, 477–88. New York: Kluwer Academic/Plenum.
Robbins, Thomas, and Dick Anthony. 1995. "Sects and Violence: Factors Enhancing the Volatility of Marginal Religious Movements." In *Armageddon in Waco: Critical*

Perspectives on the Branch Davidian Conflict, ed. S. Wright, 236–59. Chicago: University of Chicago Press.

Rosenfeld, Jean E. 1997. "The Importance of the Analysis of Religion in Avoiding Violent Outcomes: The Justice Freeman Crisis." *Nova Religio* 1: 72–95.

Sannyas News. http://www.sannyasnews.com/index.html.

Skocpol, Theda. 1979. *States and Social Revolutions: A Comparative Analysis of France, Russia, and China*. New York: Cambridge University Press.

Skolnick, Jerome H. 1967. *Justice without Trial: Law Enforcement in a Democratic Society*. Berkeley: University of California Press.

Stark, Rodney. 1996a. *The Rise of Christianity: A Sociologist Reconsiders History*. Princeton, N.J.: Princeton University Press.

———. 1996b. "Why Religious Movements Succeed or Fail: A Revised General Model." *Journal of Contemporary Religion* 11: 133–46.

Wallis, Roy. 1979. *Salvation and Protest: Studies of Social and Religious Movements*. New York: St. Martins.

Walliss, John. 2004. *Apocalyptic Trajectories: Millenarianism and Violence in the Contemporary World*. Oxford: Lang.

Wessinger, Catherine. 2000. *How the Millennium Comes Violently*. New York: Seven Bridges.

Whitsel, Bradley C. 2003. *The Church Universal and Triumphant: Elizabeth Clare Prophet's Apocalyptic Movement*. Syracuse: Syracuse University Press.

Wright, Stuart A. 1991. "Reconceptualizing Cult Conversion and Withdrawal: A Comparative Analysis of Divorce and Apostasy." *Social Forces* 70: 125–45.

———, ed. 1995. *Armageddon in Waco: Critical Perspectives on the Branch Davidian Conflict*. Chicago: University of Chicago Press.

———. 2002. "Public-agency Involvement in Government–Religious Movement Confrontations." In *Cults, Religion, and Violence*, ed. D. G. Bromley and J. G. Melton, 102–22. New York: Cambridge University Press.

16

"Strong as Steel, Steady as Stone": Skirting Pitfalls in 3HO/Sikh Dharma

Constance Elsberg

Stand as the Khalsa—strong
As steel, steady as stone.

—L. S. Khalsa 1976

The Healthy, Happy, Holy Organization (3HO) has not received as much attention as some of the more volatile new religions, yet it provides a revealing point of comparison. It is particularly interesting because its members have typically either been initiated as Khalsa Sikhs (participated in the ceremony of *khande de pahul khand*) or have at least adopted beliefs and practices from the Sikh Khalsa. Thus, they inherit a militant tradition, which could conceivably provide justification for or predisposition to violent action. However, the group has not been involved in violent clashes with outside groups, nor has internal factional violence occurred. Like any group, 3HO[1] has its blemishes, but here it is of interest as a group that has avoided the extremes that we have seen in the discussion of some alternative religions.

The opening epigraph is taken from a song written by a young convert in the 1970s, in the early years of the organization, and it was sung enthusiastically in ashrams at the time. It goes on to say that when things are the darkest, that's when the Khalsa stands tallest, and

Until the last star falls, we

Won't give an inch at all. (L. S. Khalsa 1976)

The lyrics convey the devotion and enthusiasm with which the new young Sikhs embraced the Khalsa tradition. Strength, determination, a refusal to back down, and courage—these were values they found in Sikh history. As portrayed in the song, these are not nonviolent values, but the words do not necessarily suggest a very aggressive stance, either. They infer power and willingness to act, as well as dignity and strength held in reserve. They are indicative of 3HO/Sikh Dharma interpretations of the Khalsa tradition, and the version(s) members have settled upon may be among the factors that have worked against violent action. To understand their interpretations of the traditions they have adopted, it is necessary to have some historical background.

The organization coalesced around Harbhajan Singh Puri, who traveled from India, arrived first in Canada in 1968, and then moved to the West Coast of the United States, where he began teaching yoga at a YMCA and at the East-West Cultural Center in Los Angeles. He had worked as a customs officer in India before he moved to North America but had also pursued an interest in yoga. In fact, he claimed to be the mahan tantric, the only person authorized to teach techniques that he referred to as white tantric yoga (to distinguish it from yoga practices with a sexual component). His arrival coincided with a surge of interest in Eastern religions as youth who had been active in the countercultural and political movements of the time turned toward spiritual pursuits. Puri appealed to just this audience. So, while many of his original students at the East-West Cultural Center were older, his classes were soon populated by hip young students. Eventually these students and Puri decided to create their own community in Los Angeles, where they established themselves as the Healthy, Happy, Holy Organization in 1969. They, in turn, were dispatched to establish new centers. Among these were ashrams in San Francisco; Vancouver; Española, New Mexico; Millis, Massachusetts; and Washington, D.C.

Their new teacher offered the young seekers a disciplined way of life and a guarantee of spiritual empowerment if they pursued his version of yoga. They dubbed him Yogi Bhajan (the name by which he is best known) and set about building a community and a lifestyle based on his teachings. Bhajan had himself experienced serious disruption as a youth during the partition of India, when he and his family were relocated from what had just become Pakistan to New Delhi. According to a biographical sketch (Singh 1979, 44–46), Bhajan was a college student at that time and a leader among his peers. Thus, he had some understanding of the needs of his rootless and sometimes disillusioned American students, and this was probably one of the building blocks of his charisma.

For the first two years of its existence 3HO was dedicated to yoga and healthy living. However, a few of his Los Angeles students began attending a Sikh study circle with Bhajan, and in 1971 a group traveled with him to India, where some were initiated at the Golden Temple. It does not appear that Bhajan originally intended to foster Sikhism, but once his students expressed serious interest Bhajan seems to have responded quickly. He began to formalize his leadership position by meeting with leaders of Indian Sikh organizations. When he and his entourage returned to the United States, they did not immediately urge conversion to Sikhism. This happened instead as a gradual process, encouraged by the leadership but not enforced. The first of their *gurdwaras* [places of worship] was inaugurated in Los Angeles in 1972. Within a year Sikh prayers were added to morning devotions, and Bhajan had created a ministry (something that is not usually associated with Sikhism) and incorporated a new organization, the Sikh Dharma Brotherhood (in April 1973).

At first glance one might think that Sikhism would have held limited appeal for many of the youth who had embraced 3HO and yoga. In the past, Sikhs had to arm themselves in order to resist India's Mughal rulers, and Sikh leaders were martyred in that effort. The tenth and last guru, Gobind Singh (1666–1708), established the Khalsa brotherhood, whose ideal was the soldier-saint who is at once a pious man and a fearless fighter. Young people from the counterculture tended to distrust formal religion, and they had emerged from a milieu in which America was viewed as dangerously militaristic, a milieu in which opposition to the Vietnam War was often a given. Thus, their decision to align themselves with a long-established warrior tradition required that they either rethink some of their previous values or find ways to align Sikh traditions with their countercultural backgrounds.

3HO took shape throughout the 1970s and '80s, a period when renewed Sikh militancy was spreading rapidly in the Indian Punjab. For the Sikh people, the Punjab is a special and sacred place with a considerable history: "[T]he land of Guru Nanak's birth and Guru Gobind Singh's vision of the Khalsa Raj combined in the minds of their followers, resulting in the eighteenth-century myth of the land of the Punjab as a divine gift to the Sikhs" (Mann 2004, 91). In fact, a Sikh, Ranjit Singh, did rule a significant area in the early nineteenth century. However, after his reign, Sikh power waned, and the Sikhs maneuvered for position first under the British and then the Indian governments. When, at the time of the partition, the Hindu and Muslim communities each gained territories in which they were dominant, the Sikhs were left without such an area. Treatment of the Sikhs as a "sect" of Hinduism (rather than as an independent religion) in the 1950 Constitution of India did little to ease anxieties (Dusenbery 1999, 133). A Sikh political party, the Akali Dal, made demands for greater recognition, and one route that Sikhs, at least those who belonged to the Akali Party, took was to lobby for a state in which Punjabi would be the dominant language. Although the demand was generally phrased in terms of the rights of a language community, political protections and opportunities for Sikhs were clearly the underlying motivation for the demands.

Eventually Punjab was divided into a Punjabi-speaking area (the state of Punjab) and a Hindi-speaking state (Haryana), but desires for Sikh autonomy never disappeared. By the 1980s this desire was taking the form of a claim that the Sikhs constituted a nation, or *qaum*. By then, the language of nationhood had become the dominant narrative for ethnic and religious groups seeking increased rights, autonomy, or power in many parts of the world (Dusenbery 1999). The Akali Dal demanded that Punjab be redefined to include Punjabi-speaking areas of neighboring states and proposed the Anandpur Sahib Resolution (1978) to address a number of grievances, including economic issues, identity, and autonomy. This intensified local feelings, and later, when Indira Gandhi instituted emergency rule in October of 1983, the Akali Dal answered with mass actions. At the same time, sectarian divisions were increasing within the Sikh community (Grewal 1990, 218). Sant Jarnail Bhindranwale rose to the attention of the Punjab and, in time, the world, with his opposition to one group, the Nirankari sect. He and his followers clashed with the Nirankaris in the Golden Temple complex, and in December 1983 Bhindranwale and his followers occupied the Akal Takht (the seat of Sikh secular authority) there. Efforts at compromise failed, and Indira Gandhi sent troops to dislodge him. Her actions incensed Sikhs around the globe. The situation spun out of control when two of her Sikh security guards assassinated Gandhi, and Hindu mobs reacted by massacring thousands of Sikhs. One Sikh response was intensified agitation for the formation of Khalistan, an independent Sikh state, although this goal was never universally shared (e.g., Puri, Judge, and Sekhon, 112–14). In the long term, however, the revival of this old dream proved more of a nightmare than a boon as militancy spread and thousands died. As Juergensmeyer describes it:

> During its heyday, from 1981 to 1994, thousands of young men and perhaps a few hundred women joined the movement. They were initiated into the secret fraternities of various rival radical organizations . . . their enemies were secular political leaders, heads of police units, some Hindu journalists, and other community leaders. Over time the distinctions between valid and inappropriate targets became blurred . . . By January 1988, more than a hundred people a month were killed in the Punjab's triangular battle among the police, the radicals, and the populace. (2000, 89)

Victims of the violence—and others who feared it—fled Punjab, and the United States and Canada were among their destinations. Many brought the attendant passions with them and supported the idea of an independent Khalistan. Political differences (as well as caste differences) led to intense and occasionally violent confrontations at gurdwaras. Even Punjabis' versions of Sikh history were reconstructed at that time to highlight the martial tradition of the Khalsa and its periods of "violent struggle" (e.g., Puri, Judge, and Sekhon 1999, 41; Dusenbery 1999). This was the environment in which the new American Sikhs had to come to their own interpretation of the tradition they had adopted.

One can imagine scenarios in which the newly minted Sikhs could have become deeply embroiled in the ongoing struggles in India or at least in the related activities in the United States and Canada. However, significantly, Bhajan did not support the movement for an independent Khalistan. According to rumor, some Sikh Dharma people became involved, but it appears that there was no formal encouragement. Presumably, official involvement on the part of Bhajan or Sikh Dharma would have provoked unwelcome interest on the part of U.S. agencies or local governments and certainly would not have been a good strategy for nurturing 3HO and Sikh Dharma.

It is also conceivable that their reading of Sikh history could have led Bhajan's students to take a highly aggressive stance when confronted by any opposition or intolerance—something they certainly encountered. They were sometimes harassed once they began wearing Indian-style clothing and the turban. They also encountered opposition to their turbans when they applied for jobs in education or in the military. They had some limited contact with the anticult movement as well, but Lewis finds that "Sikh Dharma received relatively little attention from the anti-cult movement. Few deprogramming attempts took place. In the early 1980s, militant Sikhs announced a policy of actively opposing any attempts by deprogrammers to attack their organization. No further attempts were reported" (Lewis 2009, 3; also see Bromley 2002; Introvigne 2000).

This kind of firm approach to opposition became typical. People in 3HO have made it clear that they will defend themselves in court, even physically if need be, while also establishing an effective image that tends to discourage confrontations. They employ courtesy and rather scripted depictions of themselves and their organization as a frontline defense, and often avoid contacts if they think that these will not lead to positive publicity. They have also sought political influence, and Bhajan reached out to local politicians like Bill Richardson and Pete Domenici (Bhajan's ranch and headquarters were outside of Española, New Mexico). On an even firmer note, some members have taken gatka training, and others have taken firearms training as well. In the early years, for example, women received handgun training at their "ladies' camp" (e.g., Sukhmandir Kaur Khalsa 1976, 14). The summer (1983) that I attended a 3HO camp for women, Bhajan always had security guards around him, and we took turns being on night guard duty (our presence was supplemented by that of male 3HO guards). I was told that the guards were necessary because some of the neighbors had threatened the camp and young men would drive by and shout at the residents. The mood when we were on guard duty was actually quite relaxed, but the presence of Bhajan's armed guards at various events left me feeling uncomfortable.

The guards' presence was indicative of one major occupational direction in 3HO – security work. Akal Security, started by a 3HO member, has had considerable success. Obviously this means that some members have more than just a little training and access to weapons. Here one ex-member, on condition of anonymity, describes some of his training: "I trained with a small group of armed 3HO militia. I trained with martial arts masters. I studied Shotokun Karate in Hawaii. . . . I trained in Lee Jun Fan, Kali, Escrima and Arnis. . . . A small hand picked group of us studied tactical combat small arms fighting skills at a desert training facility near Lancaster, Calif. . . . For two years I was part of a small security detail who's [sic] sole purpose was to provide armed protection to Yogi Bhajan . . . . There were lots of threats on his life. Many of his classes were covered with armed riflemen on the rooftop and always two armed Sikhs at his side and one in the back, everyone was in radio contact." (email 5/22/2009)

I do not know all of the sources of these threats, but the upheaval in India was one factor. Given the threats against Bhajan's life, there was a potential for the members to depict the external world as very dangerous, to turn inward, and even to respond violently to that perceived danger. They had the wherewithal, but their training may also have provided confidence that Bhajan and the community were adequately protected, that the best offence was a strong defense. This is in keeping with the 3HO way of meeting the world. In fact, they have mostly framed the militant Sikh tradition in terms of standing up for justice and defending basic values, rather than in terms of physical confrontation.

Similarly, their organizations have developed some of the characteristics that have been hypothesized as factors associated with violence in alternative religions, but these traits have not reached extreme expression. 3HO reflects what one might call a strain of millenarian thinking, a trait that is sometimes, but certainly not inevitably, associated with violent actions in new religious movements (Lewis 2005; Robbins 2002; Wessinger 2000a), and at times it has exhibited a tendency toward encapsulation and distrust of the outer world, traits that might also have predisposed the organization toward violence, particularly defensive or internal violence. In addition to charismatic leadership and encapsulation, Hall and Schuyler (1998) suggest that apocalyptic views may be particularly conducive to violence. For thirty-five years[2] the American Sikhs followed a charismatic leader who predicted future upheaval, and times of tribulation, and these predictions were associated with some periods of intense communal solidarity and strong group boundaries.

However, the routes that 3HO members took and the interpretations they came to favor seem to have led to a stance that, while assertive, has generally worked against the group's actually becoming involved in violent action. Some internal acts of violence may have occurred[3] but the group as a whole has not engaged in violent contact with the outside world. In fact, if asked to predict any violence connected to 3HO, I would expect it to be internal, related to rivalries over businesses or status, but also unlikely, given members' tendency to turn to the courts when facing controversy.

Before going further, it is worth noting that this is not necessarily surprising since most new religions have not been the instigators of violence. Melton and Bromley (2002) challenge the frequently made assumption that new religions are generally violence prone. They also suggest that any comparison between small new religions and the large established ones is likely to be biased simply because violence by established religions tends "to be treated as political in nature," while the acts of the new religions "tend to be defined as simply deviant or criminal" (45). This distinction is particularly interesting given the differing experiences of Sikh Dharma and the Sikhs in Punjab, and a brief comparison of the two highlights some of the factors that may lead to violence.

Robbins (2002) notes that "some scholars have stressed the dynamic factor of external opposition and persecution" (58). Punjabi Sikhs faced these conditions in a way that 3HO did not. An upswing in religious nationalism among Hindus, Sikhs, and Muslims left each community jockeying for position (e.g., Catherwood 2002). Fearing fragmentation, the central government of India portrayed the Punjab as secessionist. Feelings were intensified by the way in which Indira Gandhi handled the occupation of the Golden Temple and a number of other gurdwaras. As Mann notes, "it is not clear why the date selected for this move was the martyrdom day of Guru Arjan, when a large number of Sikhs had gathered to celebrate the event at these places" (2004, 68). Many Sikhs wanted to see Bhindranwale removed from the Akal Takht but not with such disregard for life and sacred space (Gupte 1985). Before this, there were financial differences with the central government: Punjab was contesting the way in which the central government allotted funds and was also involved in disputes over water rights with neighboring Indian states.

Some have suggested that the degeneration of the Khalistan movement was also due to another variable: the absence of effective leadership. After Bhindranwale was killed, "the militant movement petered out for want of centralized leadership and an evolving ideology. . . . His flag-bearers failed to control the mindless violence of a purely criminal nature that engulfed the Punjab in the 1980s and eroded the very basis of their movement" (Mann 2004, 70). In the end, the Punjabi movement ceased to be about nationhood or dignity. A survey of individuals involved in the terrorism found that the most common reasons given for participating were (1) "adventure, thrill, or 'the fun of it,'" (2) "smuggling or looting," and (3) "influence or persuasion of other terrorists" (Puri, Judge, and Sekhon 1999, 68). Whatever romance the young people in Sikh Dharma might have attributed to the early stages of the Khalistan movement, they found little left to inspire them in the end.

Beyond the simple absence of some of the external challenges that Punjabi Sikhs faced, a number of other factors may account for the relative nonviolence of 3HO, and I discuss these in greater depth. Some of these are cultural traits, and others are structural. Some of the cultural factors include members' counterculture backgrounds, their distinctive syncretic belief system, and the ways in which members have framed Punjabi Sikhism and aligned it with their own belief systems. In addition, a narrative that might readily justify violence is absent. This contrasts with Punjabi and diaspora Sikhs who did construct such narratives. As Axel (2001) notes, "[A]fter 1984, the term *nation*, or *qaum*, was transformed, referring to the 'peoplehood' not only of Sikhs in India but also of Sikhs around the world. On the basis of the claim that Sikhs were already a *qaum* . . . Khalistanis . . . justified their call for the creation of a separate Sikh state where all Sikhs may live free from discrimination" (5). This was a goal that was deemed worth fighting and dying for, but the *gora* (white 3HO) Sikhs did not necessarily fit into this model of an ethnic nation. They, in fact, often preferred the image of a spiritual path (or *panth*), which is more suggestive of a loose community.

Structural factors are tied to the institutionalization of 3HO and Sikh Dharma. Thus, Bhajan instituted a governing structure, formal Sikh vows, and a ministry and encouraged the creation of businesses and foundations under the 3HO umbrella. He kept a tight hold on many of these creations and arguably institutionalized his own charisma as he built them, but the structures required some sharing of authority and a diminution of his capacity to act unilaterally (Dawson 2002; Elsberg 2003; Wallis 1984). Moreover, Bhajan's readiness to join in interfaith activities probably lessened outsiders' distrust of 3HO. Most important, perhaps, is the generally accommodative character of the group (Bromley 2002; Wallis 1984). In spite of their early alienation from American culture, members found ways to work within the political system and even to affirm their patriotism. Members of 3HO have also, in a number of cases, become successful entrepreneurs with a stake in a peaceful status quo.

Factors That Predispose to Nonviolence

New-Age Beliefs and Yoga Lifestyle

The 3HO piece of the lifestyle reflected many devotees' interest in the nature of consciousness and their hunger for meaning, which they brought with them from their countercultural experiences and the youth culture of the late 1960s and early '70s. Bhajan's teachings spoke to their need for a meaningful sense of empowerment, for a form of personal power that was not based on externals such as money and titles but on something deeper and less dependent on life's vagaries. In 3HO, yoga students were encouraged to investigate the processes and peculiarities of their own minds by participating in regular meditation. They drew from the tradition of Kundalini yoga, which claims to raise energy from the base of the spine to the body's higher chakras, and practitioners were told that, in time, this would unite them with God and with pure consciousness. The boundaries of self and ego would be transcended. Bhajan said that this was a rapid route to enlightenment, something that was required given the struggles of the times. He said that Kundalini yoga would "fry" the subconscious mind—purge it of fears, negative attitudes, and past traumas and neuroses. Over time meditation would not only lift the individual into oneness with the "superconsciousness" but also develop the "neutral mind." In the neutral state, his students would be able to look upon life without being swayed by personal needs and desires or by others' opinions. Bhajan also claimed that the chants he taught would strengthen each individual's energy field and protect each meditator from "negative energy." In addition, on a more positive note, meditation would render each person more proactive, better able to "create environments." No longer merely responding to the external world, the individual would be able to shape reality, to intuitively know what to do and say, and to act with full awareness (e.g., Gurucharan Singh Khalsa 1978).

Thus, from its inception 3HO was about power, but power often conceived in spiritual and psychological terms, with the possibility of holding social and political power in the future. It was often described as a power that enabled the individual to resist external influences and to maintain clarity. Bhajan held up the ideal of a calm, balanced, focused, and aware individual. He encouraged positive thinking and appears to have borrowed from New Thought, with its emphasis on using positive thoughts to create a satisfying and successful life. He urged his students to become "those who change environments to increase the beauty and comfort for each other" (1973, 3). As he put it, "one white-clad follower of the life to be healthy, happy and holy should be enough to take away the loneliness, the sickness from the whole locality" (1974, 8). He taught that individuals must change themselves before they can expect to change the external world (see Kent 2001). These goals and ideals could appeal to idealistic young people seeking a way of living within the dominant culture on their own terms. They are not the goals and ideals one might associate with a violent organization, and they moderate the image of the Sikh warrior.

Sanatan Tradition

Bhajan appears to have drawn creatively from a variety of traditions in addition to the Khalsa. The effect of this was to balance Khalsa militancy with other strains of thought (which were incorporated in 3HO more than in Sikh Dharma). A number of former members who have attempted to research and understand Bhajan's background have suggested that he drew not only from Khalsa Sikhism but also from the Sanatan tradition. The Sanatan tradition favors diverse sources, not only the Sikh scriptures, but also Hindu scriptures and epics, yogic traditions, the practices of various sects, and some Sufi practices: "[T]he basic belief of Sanatan Sikhism is inclusivity, i.e., religious diversity is natural and Sikhism can be composed of a variety of different forms and practices, since boundaries are inherently fluid" (University of Cumbria). According to some of his former students, Bhajan often spoke of Baba Virsa Singh in the early years of 3HO. Virsa Singh is a teacher who leads communities in the United States and India and claims to have had visions of Nanak's son, Baba Siri Chand, founder of the Udasi order. Udasis and Baba Virsa Singh emphasize the use of mantras, yoga, and diet, as did Bhajan (e.g., McLeod 2009). In order for the Sikh Dharma converts to be accepted and respected by the Punjabi Sikhs it was probably necessary, in the militant climate of the times, for them to be true Khalsa Sikhs, but the eclectic practices subsumed under 3HO balanced the Khalsa ideals with practices more in tune with many members' New-Age tendencies.

Sikhism and Interpreting Sikhism

As 3HO evolved and a number of its members adopted their Sikh teacher's religion, many were initiated and took on all of the trappings of the Khalsa, including the "five Ks": *kes* [uncut hair]; *kangha* [a comb]; *kara* [a steel bracelet]; *kirpan* [a short sword]; and *kachha* [shorts]. They also began wearing the turban, but in the 3HO case it was worn by both men and women (in India it is generally worn only by Sikh men).

For administrative purposes the country was divided into five regions, each with an official in charge, and Bhajan created a governing body, the Khalsa Council, which was tasked with suggesting policies, seeing that Bhajan's decisions were executed, and ensuring "unity and strict adherence to the Guru's teachings" (3HO Foundation 1976). Each ashram (3HO centers were originally called ashrams, not a Sikh term but one familiar to Americans) had a director, a man, and if he was married, his wife was supposed to share his responsibilities. Over time most ashram residents adopted the turban, along with the Sikh texts and prayers, regardless of whether they had been initiated. They also took the last name of Khalsa, with women adapting Kaur as a middle name and men taking the name Singh, as is practiced in India. Many of Yogi Bhajan's students asked him to give them Indian first names as well.

As Sikhism was introduced, Bhajan sought to align it with members' preexisting beliefs and practices. Kundalini yoga, he said, developed the individual consciousness and empowered the individual. Sikh practices would develop "group consciousness" (Bhajan 1973, 9; Gardner 1978, 131). The Sikh lifestyle would channel the energy raised by Kundalini yoga and provide discipline, commitment, and direction. The transition was eased by the fact that a number of Sikh practices and beliefs were congruent with those of the students. The most visible similarity was the preference for uncut hair, but there were other less obvious points of overlap. Deeply concerned about issues of social justice, many of Bhajan's students readily embraced the Sikhs' egalitarian ethos and the Sikh emphasis upon living one's values. 3HO was founded at a time when the United States was deeply divided, and Nanak's message of a common humanity also found willing ears (N. Singh 1993, 28). The warrior tradition and the Sikh sword came to represent opposition to injustice, materialism, and impersonal institutions. The following quotation from an early magazine, *Sikh Dharma Brotherhood*, offers a (perhaps strained) vision of the young American Sikhs as a continuation of the Khalsa heritage:

> Look around us and see the true state of the modern world. See the millions of people without true identities, lost in the vain pursuit of a trumped-up god of money and sex. Hear the groans of the millions whose life-sparks are being snuffed out by de-humanizing institutions. View the carnage of families broken by lust and insecurity, the children orphaned by parents hooked on drugs, booze, sex, and the lust for power. And hear the echo from all sides of deceit and dishonesty. Is this not the battlefield of Guru Gobind Singh? (Gurubanda Singh Khalsa 1976)

Bhajan also used Sikhism to move students closer to mainstream life. He told his followers that Sikhs live the life of the householder, and he arranged marriages for them. The hip look and lifestyle rapidly faded and were replaced by the 5Ks, Indian dress, and suburban living. The Sikh tradition was interpreted in ways that enabled young people who were weary of battling U.S. culture and politics to create a new, less confrontational, and spiritual path that led them back toward the American mainstream (Robbins, Anthony, and Curtis 1975), while still providing sufficient distance and a critical perspective. This is particularly striking in the case of the Sikh Dharma move toward patriotism. If they saw contemporary America as in many ways a soulless, militarist, and materialist culture, they concluded that, originally, it was built on ideals that were readily associated with the Sikh tradition. Thus, in the journal quoted earlier, one writer, inspired by the nation's bicentennial, assures her readers that there are "parallels that can be drawn between the principles of the Founding Fathers and the teachings of the Ten Gurus" and that the "basic teachings of Guru Nanak, which are the foundations of Sikhism, are the same truths upheld by the Declaration of Independence and the Constitution of the United States" (Khalsa, Amar Kaur 1976, 2–3). Going even further, the Khalsa Council that year made a formal statement that, in part, "Khalsa, the Pure Ones, feel a debt to America. . . . Khalsa offers to give their lives . . . to aid any innocent person in the attainment and fulfillment of the treasured American values of life, liberty and the pursuit of happiness." (Khalsa Council of Sikh Dharma 1976) The new Sikhs had found a way to be cultural critics and patriots at the same time. Robbins suggests that the "apocalyptic movements that demonize the state may be particularly volatile" (2002, 67). This is clearly not such a movement; early in its history, members were urged to choose patriotism.

The armature of Sikh beliefs and practices also made it easier to institutionalize the nascent organization. It provided a rationale for rules and positions, and if one were to become a Khalsa Sikh, one had clear requirements to fulfill. Bhajan's position was enhanced and strengthened. He returned from his first meetings with Sikh authorities in India endowed with a new term of respect, Siri Singh Sahib. On later visits, further honorifics were added until the organization claimed that his title was "Chief Religious and Administrative Authority of Sikh Dharma of the Western Hemisphere." Bhajan and the ashram heads became quite strict as they taught Sikh practices; they allowed ashram residents to work their way into conformity but made it clear that this was now a Sikh community. Bhajan was increasing his stature vis-à-vis his students and changing the organization from an experimental New-Age community into a branch of a major religion.

The early and mid-1970s were a period of rapid expansion. Toward the end of the decade, however, growth tapered off in the face of a recession, as it did in other new religions (Kirpal Singh Khalsa 1986; Wallis 1984; Wuthnow 1986). Faced with new constraints, the organization sought to solidify its base, and members focused on gaining knowledge of Sikh beliefs and traditions and on creating "prosperity consciousness." They established businesses, and many decided to further their education. In the 1980s ashrams were consolidated, and a number relocated from urban to suburban or rural locations as members sought space and safety for their children. Individuals and families grew more autonomous and communal arrangements less common. Children of grade-school age began attending a school in India chosen by Bhajan.

By the 1980s the major pieces of the lifestyle were in place, and people were focused on their family lives. The distinctive 3HO blend of Sikhism and yoga was firmly established. Bhajan's Sikhs held Sunday gurdwara, but they started their days with yoga and meditation, employing some chants that were adopted from the *Guru Granth*. They sought oneness with *Vahiguru* (God), an essential Sikh goal, but they also believed that their meditations based on the *Guru Granth* would bring clarity, success, and health—a more New-Age, results-oriented use of the religion. They still believed that the New Age was coming, but now Sikh Dharma would usher it in.

Throughout this period, the eyes of other Sikhs who were living in North America and the Punjab were on them—they were never entirely independent actors. As the most recent extension of an international religion, they wanted to set an example and prove that they were particularly "righteous," disciplined, and inspired. In fact, they went so far as to criticize ethnic Sikhs who did not choose to let their hair grow or to wear a turban, and they were quite critical of the traditional Sikh attitudes about gender and caste. 3HO people roundly rejected what they called "Sikh politics" and generally chose not to become embroiled in the complex struggles of ethnic Sikhs (Dusenbery 1989, 1990,1999; Elsberg 2003). At the same time, they interpreted Sikhism in ways that could limit the influence of events in India. It was in their interest to separate the religion from its homeland and its troubles. If Sikhism could be seen as a world religion that was not associated with a particular place or ethnicity, this normalized and supported their conversion and their position. This also would mean that they had no obligation to take on the battles of ethnic Sikhs; indeed, they could take a highly principled stand and criticize the other Sikhs for bringing politics into the gurdwara, for continuing their attention to caste, or for failing to practice as Khalsa Sikhs.

Accommodation and Entrepreneurship

Bromley describes three "response levels" to tensions between religious movements and representatives of the broader society: contestive, accommodative, and retreatist (2002, 12). Although 3HO is essentially accommodative, it inclines somewhat to retreatism. Given their belief that religion must be enacted in everyday life, members are expected to participate actively in society. The devotee takes time to meditate and to experience the "nectar" of oneness with God, but this must be taken further. That unity must be made manifest in the world and in daily life. Asceticism and separation from the world are not considered desirable. One may feel some tension with the world or with aspects of it, but still one must live within it. Nor does 3HO/Sikh Dharma take a stand in opposition to other religious paths. Members generally portray theirs as one alternative among many, not as the only true path (although I have certainly heard individuals take a very rigid approach as well). They develop their businesses and work in a variety of fields. They vote and watch television and go to movies. And sometimes they decide that engagement and accommodation are not the ideal path and choose the retreatist option instead. They send their children to school in India rather than doing battle with local school systems in the United States. They have their own rather isolated sites for solstice celebrations. Rather than deal with local harassment, early on they closed the smaller ashrams and consolidated their centers. These two modes of response are, according to Bromley, least likely to lead to violent confrontations with the outside world.

A look at several businesses provides a further sense of the accommodative side of 3HO. The leadership encouraged entrepreneurship from the 1970s' recession on. This seemed to be a promising approach. If Sikhs created their own businesses, they would not have to encounter outright discrimination based on their clothing and turbans; nor did they have to work in bureaucracies, which many found unappealing. Also, many did not have the credentials that would enable them to find jobs in existing corporations; a number had left college without completing a degree or had simply turned their backs on the "straight" world of careers and résumé enhancing. The early recruits may have been bright, thoughtful, and aware, but they didn't typically come equipped with MBAs. A 3HO member, writing in 1986, described some of the businesses:

> 3HO Foundation members are found nationwide in many professional and technical fields. Some have started manufacturing businesses such as health food products, furniture, and massage tools; others have become very successful in sales and distribution of products such as insurance, health food, shoes, and school supplies; and 3HO Foundation restaurants can be found in many cities in the country. Small businesses have been started in areas such as construction, janitorial service, landscaping, painting, auto mechanics, T.V. repair, security, and small business computers.
> (Kirpal Singh Khalsa 1986, 236)

Today the businesses are still numerous and include Akal Security, Yogi Tea, and Peace Cereal. 3HO trains Kundalini yoga teachers. Akal Security, started in Santa Fe by Guru Tej Singh, holds a lucrative contract with the U.S. Marshall Service and guards the Reagan Building in Washington, D.C. The firm makes a financial contribution to Sikh Dharma, although it primarily hires personnel from outside of 3HO. Guru Tej has attributed some of his success to Sikh teachings. For example, here he is describing a situation that occurred some time ago, when the organization was smaller, in which he and employees of the company calmed a crowd at a concert:

> [W]e took the approach that we were the neutralizing element and we're not going to be defeated. It's the concept of the warrior. The concept of the warrior is not excellence in arms and all that. It's that whatever

challenge you have to face, whatever battle you have, you will overcome the opposition and be victorious. That positivity is contagious. It carries over in running the business and dealing with personnel. Whatever the problem, we go in with the attitude that we will find a solution. (quoted in Power 2003, 4)

He has adapted the warrior image to business and to the exercise of nonviolent strength and authority. One more quotation from Guru Tej also captures the application of a principle in yoga—the importance of the breath: "We apply a technique called 'modeling' in our field work. In modeling, I stand, speak, and act in such a way as I want the disputant to act. I very rarely tell the person to breathe deep, but what I do is very noticeably take long deep breaths myself. That inevitably makes the person begin to breathe deeply" (quoted in Power 2003, 6).

Another success story, this one of a business that is no longer under the 3HO umbrella, is that of Kettle Chips, originated by Nirbao Singh Khalsa, who later left 3HO and resumed his given name, Cameron Healy. The company was sold to a private equity group in 2006 and was put up for sale in December 2009, with an asking price of around $700 million (*Portland Business Journal*). The company's Oregon plant uses extensive green technology. When he was in 3HO and running the business, Nirbao Singh says that he often thought in terms of Sikh tradition and about Bhajan's advice to maintain a balanced life and a neutral mind. Here he is referencing the first Sikh guru, Nanak:

> There was a situation where he confronted a . . . mountain man in the Himalayas. . . . Through Nanak's interaction with this entity he neutralized and put an element of peace in him. . . . To me, that's an inspiration. The Sikh tradition goes on to a martial period which is physical confrontation in defense of truth. Certainly, there's inspiration there in terms of standing for your position and defending it but, for me, I get more juice from the early-stage Nanak approach. (quoted in Power 2003, 60)

Not all of the businesses have proved successful, of course. Golden Temple restaurants have failed, for example. Nirbao's earlier efforts were not as successful as Kettle Chips proved to be. A Sikh Dharma man who ran a telemarketing business in California was found guilty of "grand theft, money laundering and illegal telemarketing" (*Monterey County [Calif.] Herald* 1992a, 1992b, 1992c; *State of California v. Kirpal Singh Khalsa* 1991; *World Sikh News* 1992). However, while there may well have been a fair share of the "old freak spirit," as it was called in the counterculture (which included a belief that it is fine to "rip off the establishment"), the general trend in Sikh Dharma affairs seems to have been in the direction of moving closer to mainstream culture.

Factors That Could Predispose to Violence

Millennialism

Bhajan, like a number of New-Age figures, talked about the waning of the Piscean age and the transition to the Aquarian age. He depicted the present age of Pisces as a time of social inequality, insecurity, and greed. The Aquarian age, he predicted, would replace this with a new ethos. With its coming, knowledge would be more equitably distributed, and spiritual awareness would be widespread. The transition, however, would be difficult. He predicted "great tidal waves of insanity," for which his students must prepare: "Your little families, your little world, your little home, your little money, your little ego—man, you are just talking like idiots! Your dead bodies will lie on these roads, your children will be orphans and people will eat them alive. That is the time we are going to face" (1974, 8).

This may not be millennialism in the strict sense, as defined, for example, by Catherine Wessinger in *Millennialism, Persecution, and Violence*: "belief in an imminent transition to the millennial kingdom (the collective salvation)" (2000b, 7). A clear picture of a millennial kingdom or the means of collective salvation is lacking. The assumption is that a better time will definitely come, but it is "better" in a sense that is perhaps more closely associated with New-Age thought than Christian theology (see Lewis 2005; Robbins and Palmer 1997). As a device, the prediction seems to have been a response not only to the New-Age proclivities of many of Bhajan's early students but also to the survivalist mentality of the 1970s and the strong sense of a dark time ahead, which was associated with parts of the counterculture. It was also a means by which Bhajan could provide his students with an intense sense of purpose and significance. They would be prepared, strong, and ready to minister in the coming hard times. All of the discipline, deprivations, and struggles associated with becoming part of 3HO and Sikh Dharma were given an aura of absolute necessity. And this, in turn, contributed to Bhajan's authority and to his students' willingness to follow his lead.

Bhajan and the leadership added a piece to this prediction when Sikhism was adopted. Bhajan framed the Khalsa in the language of the New Age. The Khalsa "nation of steel" would revitalize the United States. The Khalsa would grow strong, and "we will have our own industries, our own businesses, and we will provide our own jobs and our own culture. We will grow to be a nation [of] 960,000,000 Sikhs"(Premka Kaur Khalsa 1972, 343). Bhajan puts this prediction in an explicitly nonviolent context, although it is interesting that he finds it necessary to make a point of doing so: "We will run the factories and establishments . . . So just relax and feel good, and let us not be aggressive or destructive. . . . Are you going to break the glass windows of our universities which we are going to run tomorrow? . . . calmly and quietly assure your future, work hard, sweat and build and live up to it. You must. Time has given you a call" (1972, 33). His predictions were darker in 1984. Aside from the literary significance of the year, it was also the year of

"Operation Bluestar," when Indian troops went into the Golden Temple. There is an audiotape of a talk Bhajan gave that year; here is his paraphrased message (the quality is not very good): "War is set—nothing can stop World War III or the death of Indira Gandhi. Because the Golden Temple has been desecrated, humanity faces a tremendous end" (Bhajan, November 20, 1984). This tape was forwarded to me by a group of former members. It sounds exactly like Bhajan in voice, pacing, and phrasing, but I cannot attest to its authenticity.)

As in the above example, some of Bhajan's predictions approximate Wessinger's category of catastrophic millennialism: "[T]he belief is that the millennial kingdom will be accomplished by a great catastrophe . . . that destroys the currently evil world so that a collective salvation will be accomplished for the saved" (2000b, 8). She suggests that this can take different forms—with believers being more or less active in promoting the change. In the least active scenario, adherents "believe that they must prepare themselves with faith and ethical living, and watch for the catastrophic change; they are waiting in faith to be included in the millennial kingdom" (2000b, 9). This may come closest to the 3HO view since members are supposed to strengthen themselves for the hard times ahead. In the early years they were told to prepare via the practice of yoga, meditation, and disciplined living, but they were also supposed to help by their calm, centered, spiritual presence. The emphasis was often on the hard times, however, rather than on the coming Aquarian Age.

Sometimes, however, the tone is more upbeat, closer to Wessinger's "progressive millennialism," a "belief that humans working in harmony with a divine or superhuman plan can progressively build the millennial kingdom" (2000b, 9). This is the tone Bhajan takes when he suggests that Sikh Dharma will reform the society and run its institutions. Although Wessinger suggests that progressive millennialism is less likely to be associated with violence, applying these concepts on the ground can be difficult. A group can move back and forth between progressive and catastrophic millennialism depending on circumstances. This, indeed, is my picture of the dynamic in 3HO/Sikh Dharma.

I have the impression that this millennial strain of belief was most significant in the early years. It still holds considerable potential today, however, because, according to organizational predictions, we are now in the midst of the transition period. Thus, in 1996, one of the early leaders, Shakti Parwha Kaur Khalsa, wrote that on "November 11, 1991, we entered into twenty-one years of transition into the Aquarian Age, which comes into full force in the year 2013. The twenty-one years are divided into three-year periods of increasing intensity" (62). In this prediction 3HO/Sikh Dharma is in step with a number of contemporary groups that predict a major change in 2012—although their timing differs by a year.

Encapsulation

Members speak of the early years as a time when they created a sharing community, loved their new way of life, were deeply bonded to Yogi Bhajan and to one another, and felt that they had found a true home. As a 3HO writer described it, "[A] magical, mystical, and miraculous reality was our standard frame of reference.... A feeling of mutual admiration and kinship developed between us.... The atmosphere made us feel comfortable enough to try new roles" (Guru Darshan Kaur Khalsa 1991, 10–11).

But then, as Sikhism became the dominant note and organizational structure was formalized, commitment and discipline were increasingly valued. In some cases leaders exercised their authority with considerable zeal. Here, for example, the head of a Massachusetts ashram (no longer a member) describes his methods:

> When the new student moves in, I consider it important for him to make a clean break with the past. It is part of my office to give permission for trips to visit friends or home. I often exercise that right of refusal. As the head of the house I sometimes feel it is necessary to criticize someone publicly. I do this only when circumstances or peers have not provided the proper teachings. (Josephs 1974, 5–20)

The early solidarity and sense of common identity gave way to increased individualism as the ashram residents married, moved out of communal residences, and started families. The recession loomed. Communal economic arrangements were not always successful. Nirbao Singh, for example, describes early communal arrangements in Oregon: "People would live in the ashram and work in the business. Their needs would be taken care of. Board and room. Doctor bills. There were communal cars." However, in his view, "because it wasn't a lump sum check every month, they didn't see it as a motivator. They didn't feel they were being paid enough, ever.... It was a great experiment but I would never do things that way again" (quoted in Power 2003, 52). He ran his next enterprise according to a more conventional capitalist model.

In an article about alterations in the 3HO lifestyle, Guru Darshan Kaur also attributes the changing atmosphere to cultural trends: "We began to echo the trends of our national culture in the '80s; we were less interested in flights of fancy and became more materialistic.... Many of us no longer get to know each other well.... We are not sure how far we can trust one another. Inter-group politics and manipulation are common" (Guru Darshan Kaur Khalsa 1991, 10–11).

In the 1980s beliefs and practices were standardized. Bureaucracy proliferated. This way of living did not necessarily please all of the members, many of whom were strong believers in self-expression and experimentation. The organization showed signs of fragmentation. Much of the leadership of the Española ashram left the organization in the mid-1980s, complaining of "intense discipline" (Lewis 1998, 113) and of resistance to their efforts to forge new groupings and creative forms of leadership. The emphasis on "prosperity" produced problems, as well as income. A number of businesses failed, and, rather than go into bankruptcy, the ashrams did what they considered the "righteous" thing and attempted to settle accounts with creditors. However, as previously suggested, not all businesses were so honorable. The head of the Washington ashram and an associate were indicted in a sting operation and accused of "engaging in a continuing criminal enterprise involving the importation of multi-ton quantities of marijuana during the 1983–1987 time period" (*United States of America v. Gurujot Singh Khalsa*). Many ashram residents left in the aftermath. In addition, in the midst of these challenges, two female former members accused Bhajan of assault and battery and a number of other crimes. Although several of the charges were dismissed, the assault and battery charges were not. The case was settled out of court.

The organization's response was a circle-the-wagons mentality. Bhajan insisted that any attack on him was an attack on all. He requested that anyone who showed signs of doubts about 3HO teachings be reported to him. Any criticisms of the lifestyle or leadership were attributed to *shaktipod*, a moment in a convert's life when pride and other personal flaws lead to doubt. There was no loosening of routines or rules or requirements, and criticism was generally not tolerated. Those who remained in the organization shunned those who left. This was a period when 3HO and Sikh Dharma were quite vulnerable—to further fragmentation, to excessive discipline from the top, and to external suits and criticism. In the end, the organizations managed to survive and to continue to shift in accommodative directions as some businesses prospered and new forms of ashram leadership allowed more participation and gave women a larger role.

One way to describe 3HO's evolution is to use a typology developed by Jean-Paul Sartre (see Hayim 1980; Sartre 1976). While certainly not a new model, it remains useful for depicting the organizational dynamics of an evolving movement. Sartre looks at the way that an organization may develop out of a type of collectivity that he calls a praxis group. A *praxis group* is the product of its members' disenchantment with a society in which relationships between persons and things appear to be valued more than those between people, a society where commodities and externally imposed rules prevail. People manage to find one another and act together so as to change both themselves and the outside world. Their joint action is enlivening and creates an empowering unity. Sartre believed that membership in a praxis group is typically drawn from marginalized groups, from people who have experienced feelings of powerlessness and isolation. Research on the new religions indicates that members are often drawn from middle-class families, and this is the case with 3HO, whose members are also better educated than the average individual in the United States (Barker 1984; Elsberg 2003, 146; Wallis 1984). Converts to 3HO were not marginal in an economic sense, but a significant segment experienced a deep discontent with the nature of power, materialism, and rationalization in the United States, and their descriptions of the early years sound much like Sartre's depiction of a praxis group.

The unity of the praxis group does not in any way overwhelm the individual members. Each individual thrives, and "each member of the group feels that he has the same share of rights, sovereignty and leadership as every other member"

(Hayim 1980, 91). This is a precious and fragile form of solidarity, and those who share it understandably wish to maintain it. As the group expands, its members begin to fear the possibility of losing what they have created, of returning to the old ways, and so they seek to formalize the social bonds they have created. Formal oaths or pledges may be instituted. Loyalty is expected. Freedom is circumscribed with an "implicit right of everyone over everyone else" (Hayim 1980, 97). Individuals may even be accused of betrayal. A "pledge group" has replaced the praxis group. "Permanency becomes the group's objective. . . . Unity, rather than praxis, becomes the aim. . . . This is the stage of transition from praxis to routinization" (Hayim 1980, 94). For Sartre, who was looking at political violence in the twentieth century, this represents a dangerous period: "[T]he transition to the pledge group leads to the rise of violence." (Hayim 1980, 97).

Without assuming the inevitability of violence, one can conclude that this period of intense concern with enforcing loyalty and conformity may be a dangerous and difficult time. Whether it actually leads to violence and whether that violence is directed outward or inward must depend on a number of variables, including the nature of the interaction with external groupings (e.g., Bromley and Melton 2002). One would probably need extensive access to the leadership to know just how 3HO sidestepped the worst dangers embedded in this stage. However, a number of factors may have contributed, in addition to those already discussed.

3HO was not under attack to the degree that some groups have experienced. Hall (2002), for example, convincingly argues that the Branch Davidians' apocalyptic theology and the group's internal dynamics are not sufficient explanation for their final end. Rather, he finds that the FBI and the Bureau of Alcohol, Tobacco, and Firearms accepted a version of reality supplied by the anticult movement and adopted by parts of the media. This contributed to, as Bromley and Melton (2002) describe it, "an alliance between an oppositional movement of former members and relatives, the media, and various governmental agencies" (8). Bhajan and his students did not face such an array of forces. Moreover, Bhajan was able to find people to help him pay his court fees, so he was not subject to extreme isolation and economic fragility. 3HO did not become a "fragile millennial group"—one that "initiates violence because of a complex combination of internal weaknesses and cultural opposition that threatens its religious goal" (Wessinger 2000b, 25).

Members were also maturing throughout this time. They had children to raise, jobs to see to, and a variety of commitments. They had only limited time and energy available for confrontations and factional loyalties. Furthermore, judging by the attitudes expressed by people I interviewed during this time, they were not as willing to accept the leaders' dictates as they were when they were younger. Moreover, the growing role of women in leadership may have mitigated tendencies toward violence, given the 3HO belief that women should be nurturing and "graceful." Axel suggests that the historical creation of a Sikh *qaum* has been accompanied by "the masculinization of the *amritdhari* body" (*amritdhari* are men who have taken Khalsa initiation and wear the five Ks) and that "Sikh subjectification, through masculinized symbolism and imagery, has been intimately related to the takeover of Punjab by the British, nation-state formation, and the development of a fight for a Sikh homeland" (2001, 35–36). In an intricate line of argument, Axel ties this masculinization to violence. It is a trend for which many in 3HO feel little sympathy, and their greater valorization of the feminine principle may be a further cultural element that limits violence.

Given the events of the 1980s, Bhajan was open to criticism and probably had little choice but to move in the direction of institutionalizing and routinizing his charisma. Because his milieu included Sikhs in the United States and in the Punjab, Bhajan had to prove himself as a leader not only to his disciples but to a variety of Sikh groupings. Sikhs, particularly Khalsa Sikhs, do not take kindly to an individual's claiming to be a guru, although one can become a *sant*, or teacher. Khalsa Sikhs believe that, with the passing of the tenth guru, a period of Sikh history ended. From then on, truth was to be found in the writings of the gurus and in the Sikh *sangat*. Thus, any individual who claims special knowledge or an extraordinary right to leadership is treading on dangerous ground. Bhajan had to restrict his claims (although he sometimes hinted that he was as close to being a guru as one could be without claiming the status); he could not step too far out of bounds and continue to claim a place within the national and international Sikh leadership.

This is not to suggest that he ceased to make claims that would support his charismatic qualities, which he certainly did not, only that his construction of charisma was constrained by the potential reactions of Sikhs who were not under the 3HO umbrella. Thus, Bhajan claimed to be able to "control water," to read auras, and to be mentally in contact with his students no matter how far away they might be. He claimed to know the right partner for an individual seeking to marry. He told people which careers to follow (if they asked). He told some people where to live, moving them about from one ashram to another, supposedly in order to develop their spiritual lives. He assigned duties and diets and yoga regimes. He publicly criticized and humiliated individual students, and, as Dawson notes, "dissent may be increasingly stifled through the careful control of information and the public use of ridicule and other means of peer pressure" (2002, 93). He remained a dramatic and changeable personality. Even today he is supposedly present as mahan tantric at tantric yoga classes (which were taped before his death). He, to a considerable degree, managed the process of routinization of charisma, retaining his central place in the organization and exerting considerable control over others' lives, but not going to the extremes that we have seen in a few cult leaders.

A brief comparison with Aum Shinrikyo is useful in further highlighting the differences between 3HO and some of the groups that have resorted to violence. Some parallels exist between Aum and 3HO/Sikh Dharma. Both taught Kundalini yoga, with their leaders saying that it was the fastest way to enlightenment. Both began as yoga and meditation groups and then adopted a formal religion (Buddhism and other teachings in the Aum case). The leaders of both claimed telepathic and other special powers (Reader 2000, 167) and the capacity to take on disciples' "karmic ills." Each claimed that his interpretation of religious tradition was "scientific" (Repp 2005). Both predicted future warfare and a significant future role for their followers. But there the parallels end. Bhajan, however much he stressed obedience to the spiritual teacher, did not, like Asahara, justify killing if ordered by a guru (Repp 2005). In addition, although he cultivated politicians, Bhajan did not attempt to field a political party, as did Asahara, and did not experience the kind of rejection and withdrawal that followed when this was not successful. He did not enjoin asceticism, as did Asahara. He did not require celibacy (although he said that sex should be only within marriage). Furthermore, unlike Asahara, he did not say that suffering was to be expected; his approach was sufficiently worldly that he told his followers that happiness and self-acceptance are desirable goods. He did not consistently paint himself as the one man with the true way, and he did not attract the intense media attention and condemnation that contributed to Aum's extreme actions (See Repp 2005; Reader 2000).

Dawson maintains that in order "to sustain their legitimacy, charismatic leaders must strike a dynamic balance between asserting too much dominance and not asserting enough. To err in either way brings instability. It is too much dominance, however, that tends to bring violence" (2002, 85). Bhajan avoided extreme dominance. He did, however, leave a legacy of divided authority that is now creating volatility.

In fact, 3HO seems to have reached a major crisis. The directors of a board created by Yogi Bhajan (presumably in anticipation of his own death), the Unto Infinity board, which was set up to oversee the businesses, have ceased to live as Sikhs and have removed their turbans (which is considered quite a major step in Sikh Dharma). They have fired people on a number of other related boards of directors and have taken over one of the major organizational entities, Sikh Dharma International. Bhajan named his widow and Guru Amrit Kaur (whom he appointed "director of spiritual trust") to lead Sikh Dharma International, so this pits the business-oriented boards against the Sikh Dharma bureaucracy and Bhajan's wife. Since the businesses have provided significant financial support to Sikh Dharma International (in the millions of dollars), this is a major rift. According to a blog posted on December 13, 2009, two of the members of the Unto Infinity Board:

> visited the Sikh Dharma Offices in Española at Hacienda de Guru Ram Das and informed all the employees of Sikh Dharma International that they were no longer employed unless they immediately sign a paper recognizing the current Unto Infinity's authority, the existence of their surrogate board SDS and disassociating themselves with what is being described as an unauthorized complaint filed in the Oregon Courts. (Mukhtiar Singh Khalsa 2009)

According to this account, most of the employees refused to sign. The incident seems to have come close to violence (Gurujot Kaur Khalsa 2009). The employees were removed from office. Since then, Sikh Dharma International and Unto Infinity have filed opposing lawsuits and a new director of Sikh Dharma International, a lawyer, has been appointed by Unto Infinity[4].

It is obviously difficult to predict the future in the midst of the current upheaval, but it is hard to imagine that events will reach a conclusion without protracted legal wrangling and realignment of the current entities. The officers of Unto Infinity clearly aim to take over the management and resources of Sikh Dharma International. They have just sued the previous directors of SDI for resources which they claim the directors took with them when they were evicted. Whether UI will succeed is largely up to the courts at this point. If they do succeed they may continue SDI's spiritual functions, but will be in a position to apportion and perhaps limit funds for these. It is possible that those most angered by the Unto Infinity takeover, if they lose their lawsuit, will leave the currently existing sangats (congregations) and organizations to create alternatives, or the individual *sangats* may affiliate more closely with local ethnic Sikhs. Many individuals will face difficult choices: to spend years in court, to accept a new status quo and make the best of it, to start over again and create a new spiritual community, or to simply disaffiliate. It seems reasonable to predict, however, that this controversy will be settled in an essentially nonviolent, if painful and contentious, way.

NOTES

1. I refer to a number of organizations under the general heading of 3HO because the group is best known by this title.

2. Bhajan died in 2004.

3. Former members maintain, for example, that Bhajan abused a woman and that a member was murdered in questionable circumstances.

4. Possible sources for updates on these events include the *Santa Fe Reporter* – Corey Pein has recently produced an article in that paper; and Eugene Oregon's *Register-Guard* – see articles by Sherri Buri McDonald.

REFERENCES

Axel, Brian Keith. 2001. *The Nation's Tortured Body: Violence, Representation, and the Formation of a Sikh "Diaspora."* Durham, N.C.: Duke University Press.
Barker, Eileen. 1984. *The Making of a Moonie.* Oxford: Blackwell.
Bhajan, Yogi. 1972. "Yogi Bhajan Speaks." Beads of Truth (Summer Solstice Souvenir Issue): 33:. Reprinted as "Reverse the Times" in *A Man Called the Siri Singh Sahib*, ed. Premka Kaur Khalsa and Sat Kirpal Kaur Khalsa, 341. Los Angeles: Sikh Dharma.
———. 1973. "Scriptures of the World." Beads of Truth 17 (March): 9–11.
———. 1974. "Expand." Beads of Truth 23: 8.
———. 1975. "Solstice Sadhana: A Lecture by Yogi Bhajan." *Journal of Science and Consciousness for Living in the Aquarian Age* 1 (May): 1–7. (Orig. pub. 1973.)

Bromley, David G. 2002. "Dramatic Denouements." In *Cults, Religion, and Violence*, ed. David G. Bromley and J. Gordon Melton, 11–41. New York: Cambridge University Press.

———, and J. Gordon Melton. 2002. "Violence and Religion in Perspective." In *Cults, Religion, and Violence*, ed. David G. Bromley and J. Gordon Melton, 1–10. New York: Cambridge University Press.

Catherwood, Christopher. 2002. *Why the Nations Rage: Killing in the Name of God*, rev. and updated ed. Lanham, Md.: Rowman and Littlefield.

Dawson, Lorne. 2002. "Crisis of Charismatic Legitimacy and Violent Behavior in New Religious Movements". In *Cults, Religion, and Violence*, ed. David G. Bromley and J. Gordon Melton, 80–101. New York: Cambridge University Press.

Dusenbery, Verne A. 1989. "Of Singh Sabhas, Siri Singh Sahibs, and Sikh Scholars: Sikh Discourse from North American in the 1970s." In *The Sikh Diaspora: Migration and Experience beyond Punjab*, ed. N. Gerald Barrier and Verne A. Dusenbery, 90–119. New Delhi: Chanakya.

———. 1990. "Punjabi Sikhs and Gora Sikhs: Conflicting Assertions of Sikh Identity in North America." In *Sikh History and Religion in the Twentieth Century*, ed. Joseph T. O'Connell, Milton Israel, and Willard G. Oxtoby, with visiting editors W. H. McLeod and J. S. Grewal, 334–55. New Delhi: Manohar.

———.1999. "'Nation' or 'World Religion'?: Master Narratives of Sikh Identity." In *Sikh Identity: Continuity and Change*, ed. Pashaura Singh and N. Gerald Barrier, 127–44. New Delhi: Manohar.

Elsberg, Constance. 2003. *Graceful Women: Gender and Identity in an American Sikh Community*. Knoxville: University of Tennessee Press.

Fenton, John Y. 1988. *Transplanting Religious Traditions: Asian Indians in America*. New York: Praeger.

Gardner, Hugh. 1978. *The Children of Prosperity: Thirteen Modern American Communes*. New York: St. Martin's.

Grewal, J. S. 1990. *The Sikhs of the Punjab*. New York: Cambridge University Press.

Gupte, Pranay. 1985. *Vengeance: India after the Assassination of Indira Gandhi*. New York: Norton.

Hall, John R. 2002. "Mass Suicide and the Branch Davidians." In *Cults, Religion, and Violence*, ed. David G. Bromley and J. Gordon Melton, 149–69. New York: Cambridge University Press.

———, and Philip Schulyer. 1998. "Apostasy, Apocalypse, and Religious Violence." In *The Politics of Religious Apostasy*, ed. David G. Bromley, 141–70. Westport, Conn.: Praeger.

Hayim, Gila J. 1980. *The Existential Sociology of Jean-Paul Sartre*. Amherst: University of Massachusetts Press.

Introvigne, Massimo. 2000. "The Magic of Death: The Suicides of the Solar Temple." In *Millennialism, Persecution, and Violence: Historical Cases*, ed. Catherine Wessinger, 138–57. Syracuse: Syracuse University Press.

Josephs, Gurushabd Singh. 1974. "Education of the Spirit: The Dynamics of Personal Growth in a Sprityal Commune." Ph.D. diss., Univ. of Massachusetts. Ann Arbor: UMI, 74–25, 847.

Jurgensmeyer, Mark. 2000. *Terror in the Mind of God: The Global Rise of Religious Violence*. Los Angeles: University of California Press.

Kent, Stephen A. 2001. *From Slogans to Mantras: Social Protest and Religious Conversion in the Late Vietnam War Era*. Syracuse: Syracuse University Press.

Khalsa, Amar Kaur. 1976. "Sikh Dharma and the Spirit of 76." In *Sikh Dharma Brotherhood: The Magazine of Sikh Dharma in the West* 2 (Summer): 2–3.

Khalsa Council of America. 1976. "Our Pledge to America." In *A Man Called the Siri Singh Sahib*, ed. Premka Kaur Khalsa and Sat Kirpal Kaur Khalsa,292. Los Angeles: Sikh Dharma.

Khalsa, Guru Darshan Kaur. 1991. "The Healthy, Happy, Holy Organization through the Years." *Khalsa Family Visions* 3 (December): 10–11.

Khalsa, Gurubanda Singh. 1976. Editorial. *Sikh Dharma Brotherhood: The Magazine of Sikh Dharma in the West* 2 (Spring).Inside front cover.

Khalsa, Gurucharan Singh. 1978. "Morning Sadhana: The Foundation of a Spiritual Life." In *Kundalini Yoga Sadhana Guidelines*, ed. Gurucharan Singh Khalsa, 14–29. Pomona, Calif.: Kundalini Research Institute.

Khalsa, Gurujot Kaur. 2009. Recent SDS Communication regarding SDI Board. Spiritual Forum, December 4. http://www.gurusant.com/forum/index. (Accessed 1/4/2010)

Khalsa, Kirpal Singh. 1976. "Stand as the Khalsa." In *Sikh Dharma Brotherhood: The Magazine of Sikh Dharma in the West* 3 (Fall): 8–9.

———. 1986. "New Religious Movements Turn to Worldly Success." *Journal for the Scientific Study of Religion* 25: 233–47.

Khalsa, Mukhtiar Singh. 2009. "Stewardship Has Removed Board and Taken Over Sikh Dharma International." Spiritual Forum, December 4.http://www.gurusant.com/forum/index. (Accessed 1/4/2010).

Khalsa, Premka Kaur. 1972. "Birth of a Spiritual Nation." In *A Man Called the Siri Singh Sahib*, ed. Premka Kaur Khalsa and Sat Kirpal Kaur Khalsa, 343. Los Angeles: Sikh Dharma.

Khalsa, Shakti Parwha Kaur. 1996. *Kundalini Yoga: The Flow of Eternal Power*. Los Angeles: Time Capsule.

Khalsa, Sukhmandir Kaur. 1976. "Handguns." *Beads of Truth* 32 (Fall), 14–15.

Lewis, James R. 1998. *Cults in America*. Santa Barbara: ABC-CLIO

———. 2005. "The Solar Temple 'Transits': Beyond the Millennialist Hypothesis." In *Controversial New Religions*, ed. James R. Lewis and Jesper Aagaard Petersen, 295–317. New York: Oxford University Press.

———. 2010. "Autobiography of a Schism." *Marburg Journal of Religion 15*. http://www.uni-marburg.de/fb03/ivk/mjr/pdfs/2010/articles/lewis_2010.pdf

Mann, Gurinder Singh. 2004. *Sikhism*. Upper Saddle River, N.J.: Prentice Hall.

McDonald, Sherri Buri. Mar. 3, 2010. "Money trail at heart of Sikhs' legal battle." *Register-Guard*, Eugene, Ore. http://special.registerguard.com/csp/cms/sites/web/news/cityregion/24501955-41/sikh-community-golden-temple-roberts.csp.

———. May 9, 2010. "Yogi's legacy in question. Former followers say he abused his position for power, money and sex." *Register-Guard*. Eugene, Oregon. http://special.registerguard.com/csp/cms/sites/web/news/cityregion/24671927-41/yogi-khalsa-bhajan-leaders-members.csp.

———. May 9, 2010. "Rift threatens business empire." *Register-Guard*, Eugene, Ore. http://special.registerguard.com/csp/cms/sites/web/news/cityregion/24578583-41/yogi-bhajan-golden-community-temple.csp.

———. Oct 14, 2010. "AG files against Golden Temple." *Register-Guard*, Eugene, Ore. http://www.registerguard.com/csp/cms/sites/web/news/cityregion/25403282-41/attorney-information-lawsuit-court-general.csp.

McLeod, Hugh. 2009. Udasis. http://www.sikh-heritage.co.uk/movements/Udasis/udasis.htm (accessed August 13, 2009).

Melton, J. Gordon, and David G. Bromley. 2002. "Challenging Misconceptions about the New Religions–Violence Connection." In *Cults, Religion, and Violence*, ed. David G. Bromley and J. Gordon Melton, 42–56. New York: Cambridge University Press.

Monterey County (Calif.) Herald. 1992a. "Khalsa Gets 3-Year Jail Sentence" (October 28).

———. 1992b. "Man Pleads Guilty in Phone Fraud." Peninsula ed. (August 25), 1c–2c.

———. 1992c. "Seaside Man Cleared in Bilking Scheme" (October 15), 3c.

Pein, Corey, July 7, 2010. "Khalsa vs Khalsa: A simmering lawsuit could decide the fate of a $ 1 billion Sikh Empire." *Santa Fe Reporter*, Santa Fe, New Mexico. http://www.sfreporter.com/santafe/article-5502-khalsa-vs-khalsa.html? (Accessed Oct. 15, 2010)

Portland Business Journal. Dec. 72009. "Kettle Foods for Sale." http://portland.bizjournals.com/portland/stories/2009/12/07/daily38.html. This worked for me

Power, Stephen Burns. 2003. *Spirit Warriors: Interviews with American Sikhs: The First Generation*. Lincoln: iUniverse.

Puri, Harish K., Paramjit Singh Judge, and Jagrup Singh Sekhon. 1999. *Terrorism in Punjab: Understanding Grassroots Reality*. New Delhi: Har-Anand.

Reader, Ian. 2000. "Imagined Persecution: Aum Shinrikyō, Millennialism, and Legitimation of Violence." In *Millennialism, Persecution, and Violence: Historical Cases*, ed. Catherine Wessinger, 158–82. Syracuse: Syracuse University Press.

Repp, Martin. 2005. "Aum Shinrikyo and the Aum Incident: A Critical Introduction." In *Controversial New Religions*, ed. James R. Lewis and Jesper Aagaard Petersen, 153–94. New York: Oxford University Press.

Robbins, Thomas. 2002. "Sources of Volatility in Religious Movements." In *Cults, Religion, and Violence*, ed. David G. Bromley and J. Gordon Melton, 57–79. New York: Cambridge University Press.

———, Dick Anthony, and Thomas Curtis. 1975. "Youth Culture Religious Movements: Evaluating the Integrative Hypothesis." *Sociological Quarterly* 16(1): 48–64.

Robbins, Thomas, and Susan J. Palmer, eds. 1997. *Millennium, Messiahs, and Mayhem: Contemporary Apocalyptic Movements*. New York: Routledge.

Sartre, Jean-Paul. 1976. *Critique of Dialectical Reasoning*. Trans. Alan Sheridan-Smith. Atlantic Highlands, N.J.: Humanities.

Sikh Dharma. "Status Update for SDI Corporation: September 24, 2010. http://www.sikhdharma.org/pages/status-update-sdi-corporation-september-24-2010 (accessed Oct 16, 2010)

Singh, Nikkey-Guninder Kaur. 1993. *The Feminine Principle in the Sikh Vision of the Transcendent*. New York: Cambridge University Press.

Singh, Shamser. 1979. "The Fruits of Inner Searching." In *The Man Called the Siri Singh Sahib*, ed. Premka Kaur Khalsa and Sat Kirpal Kaur Khalsa, 44–46. Los Angeles: Sikh Dharma.

State of California v. Kirpal Singh Khalsa. 1992. No. MCR 8425. Superior Court of California.

3HO Foundation. 1976. *Sikh Dharma Brotherhood: The Magazine of Sikh Dharma in the West* II (Spring).

United States of America v. Gurujot Singh Khalsa. 1998. No. 88–210-M. Order of Detention, U.S. District Court, Alexandria, Va.

University of Cumbria, Division of Religion and Philosophy, Sanatan Singh Sabha. Overview of World Religions Project. http://philtar.ucsm.ac.uk/encyclopedia/sikhism/sanatan.html.

Wallis, Roy. 1982. "The Social Construction of Charisma." *Social Compass* 29(1): 25–39.

———. 1984. *The Elementary Forms of the New Religious Life.* London: Routledge and Kegan Paul.

Wessinger, Catherine. 2000a. *How the Millennium Comes Violently: From Jonestown to Heaven's Gate.* New York: Seven Bridges.

———. 2000b. "The Interacting Dynamics of Millennial Beliefs, Persecution, and Violence." In *Millennialism, Persecution, and Violence: Historical Cases*, ed. Catherine Wessinger, 3–39. Syracuse: Syracuse University Press.

World Sikh News. 1992. "Yogi's Crooked Crew Held in Bilking Scam." *Stockton, Calif.* 8(30) (August 21).

Wuthnow, Robert. 1986. "Religious Movements and Counter-movements in North America." In *New Religious Movements and Rapid Social Change*, ed. James A. Beckford, 1–28. New York: Sage /Unesco.

17

"Smite Him Hip and Thigh": Satanism, Violence, and Transgression

Jesper Aagaard Petersen

1. Introduction

Judging by the conversations I have had in the past, two questions always seem to lurk in the back of people's minds whenever I mention that I study modern Satanism: "Why him?" and "Why that?" As an instance of guilt by association, I must be a Satanist or at least a pervert even though I usually wear cheerful Hawaiian shirts, not black from head to toe; I must be one of those *subversive* Satanists. In addition, depending on the person the subject matter is often deemed too trite, vulgar, or dangerous for academic study. To quote the conclusion to Chris Mathews's recent study, Satanism is "an immature, intolerant, and hateful ideology" with "odious and repugnant" doctrines, "founded on bluster and insecurity" and appealing "to inchoate minds." If that were not enough, it is "often little more than a soft entry point for the doctrines of neo-Nazism and neo-fascism" that should be declared "intellectually, scientifically, and morally bankrupt" (Mathews 2009, 204–205). In the same vein, David Frankfurter lumps "[m]ost forms of self-defined Satanism" together as "a self-conscious (if usually quite inarticulate) critique of social fears and their mythical representations in satanic terms" and concludes: "This social criticism, of course, is no more subtle than appropriating and parodying symbols" (Frankfurter 2006, 201).

To be fair, the connection between Satanism, Satanists and violent subversion is not grasped out of thin air. Contemporary Satanism is a complicated hodgepodge of discourses, relations, and practices relating to the appropriation of the name. First of all, there is a *mythological link* between Satan and evil in the Christian tradition that is transmitted into the secularized Western reinterpretations of that tradition (cf. Kelly 2006; Medway 2001; Murchembled 2003; Russell 1977, 1981, 1984, 1986). Although the role of the devil is often ambiguous in mainstream society, it is not surprising that people have knee-jerk reactions to the name Satan, especially if it is connected to subcultural subversions of naturalized values not easily grasped by outsiders. Second, many *moral entrepreneurs* outside modern Satanism itself actively promote claims and scenarios connecting Satanism, crime, and violence. The discourse of "satanic panic" is recurrent, although it seldom reaches the heights of the Satanism scare and satanic ritual abuse cases of the 1980s that spiraled from a fringe existence in evangelical milieus to a mainstream presence across many sectors until discredited by a wave of popular and academic research in the 1990s (cf. Ellis 2000; Lewis and Petersen 2008; Richardson, Best, and Bromley 1991; Victor 1993). Both of these discourses on Satanism play on a narrative of evil and violence related to society's normative compass and could be termed a mythical use of Satan and Satanists.

Third and most important for the present study, antinomianism is actively cultivated by *arange of actors* calling themselves Satanists or describing their project as satanic; serial killers like Richard Ramirez, rock stars like Marilyn Manson, and subcultural celebrities like Anton LaVey all play with societies association of Satan with evil, transgression, and violence, as do their respective fans (cf. Baddeley 2000; Mathews 2009; Moynihan and Søderlind 1998; Partridge 2005, chapter 6). While they have very different ideologies (not to mention practices), it is no wonder that Satanism and violence are conflated into one, as the typical uninformed onlooker often rolls them all into one homogenous group and takes their actions as connected and the most radical as representative. Even if taking a less naïve look at popular culture, I can understand some people's unease when confronted with Marilyn Manson's cultural critique and sonic assault or their stumbling over interviews with declared Satanists Boyd Rice and Nikolas Schreck on Tom Metzger's right-wing TV show *Race and Reason* on YouTube.[1]

In other words, a large gray area exists between the demonological mythologies prevalent in society and the satanic discourse of actual Satanists. Sometimes this gray area is exploited explicitly, sometimes implicitly; sometimes strategies of exclusion and inclusion solidify the boundaries between blasphemous and violent acts on one side and sanitized satanic rituals and self-development on the other. But not always. Spokespersons such as LaVey himself and "disciples" such as Manson, Schreck, and Rice are notoriously ambivalent in their play with gray, often formulated as the "third side" or "satanic alternative" to established social dichotomies. In can be very difficult to discern when it is serious and when it is irony, play, stupidity, or plain provocation, especially when moving to the fringes of the margins, so to speak, among one-man groups and nebulous networks.

Nevertheless, this chapter is a critique of easy conflations such as Mathews's through an elaboration of my classification of modern Satanism as rationalist, esoteric, and reactive in a "satanic milieu" (Petersen 2005, 2009a, 2009b), conceptualized along the same lines as the cultic milieu of Colin Campbell (Campbell 1972). Hence it is a sociological entity of actors in intermediate social spaces that are anchored in discursive networks and driven by a common "ideology of seekership" rather than a sense of belonging to one particular group. By analyzing a choice of discourses on Satanism and violence, I expand on the trait of antinomianism or nonconformity through the concept of transgression, an expansion with theoretical consequences for the first and most general feature, self-religion. Transgression is in fact a common denominator of the three Satanisms of my typology, but it is strategically dissimilar *in practice*; it is articulated and deployed differently, a point that should be related to Olav Hammer's understanding of structurally conservative and structurally radical disembedding processes (Hammer 2001a, 2001b; Petersen 2009a) and the related conception of sanitization of practices (Urban 1995). For example, Anton LaVey's understanding of magical transgression in the ritual chamber is a sanitized and secularized version of more radical practices of transgression that are prevalent in the esoteric milieu, in various reactive subcultures such as Black Metal masculinity culture and indeed in segments of the Church of Satan's "constituency" itself.

Things are thus seldom what they seem in this milieu, and any blanket reduction, while strengthening polemics, makes for bad sociology. On the one hand it is important to *discern* the actual violence of serial killers, neofascists, and marginalized teens using Satanism as an alibi (a demonological use of violence and transgression that in essence is confirming social mores) from the "symbolic violence," "aesthetic terrorism," or "transformational psychodrama" that satanic groups and individuals use to challenge the self-evident and decondition the self. On the other hand, it is significant to *acknowledge* the similarities and analyze the specific inclusion and exclusion processes in the territory of the satanic milieu. These relate to pathways to and from popular culture and complicated socialization processes that are as determined by esoteric practices as by broader religious and societal trends such as conspiracy theories, radical politics, and avant-garde art (cf. Dyrendal 2008; Dyrendal 2008). How different formulations of Satanism articulate transgression, self, and society can say a lot about the practices actually used—popularly speaking, where they place themselves on LaVey's scale of "nine parts social respectability to one part outrage" (Barton 1990, 16; cf. Alfred 1976, 187; Mathews 2009, 145, 166–67).

2. Historical Violence and Mythical Realities

> *We are fuelled by Satan/Yes we're schooled by Satan/Fuelled by Satan!*
> *Writin' those tasty riffs/just as fast as we can./Schooled by Satan!*
> (Tenacious D, "Explosivo")

Before tackling the intricacies of transgression within the satanic milieu, I find it prudent to step back and systematically examine the extant depictions of "satanic" violence available in cultural narratives. Broadly speaking, Satanism, transgression, and violence are linked through three interfaces today: the alleged violence of mythical Satanism, the actual violence of ostensive acts, and the symbolic violence of religious Satanism.

A. Mythical Violence and "Satanists": The Christian or Demonological Model

An entire library can be filled with sources to and studies of moral panics, folk devils, and social imaginations of deviant violence.[2] The violent transgressions associated with Satanists in contemporary Satanism scares are many and quite colorful; we might call them "atrocity catalogues" in line with the "atrocity tales" of David Bromley and Anson Shupe (e.g., Bromley and Shupe 1981). Ritually, blood, excrement, and other substances abound; sacrifices, cannibalism, and various perverse (often sexually charged) acts are practiced, frequently involving children as victims; and a mélange of religious and "occult" trappings are reported:

> I was carried to the toolbench where gibberish was spoken by the four robed adults around me. Rather than water sprinkled, a small, black, wriggling cocker spaniel was held over me and disemboweled with a dagger-like instrument . . . the long white taper was lit and ceremoniously held over me, wax dripping carefully onto each of my nipples. It was then inserted, still lit, into my vagina. In this way I was welcomed into the faith. (Anne Hart, "A Survivor's Account," quoted in Frankfurter 2001, 357–58).

Socially, satanic crime networks of the rich and influential wield political, legal, and media power in vast conspiracies; the unsuspecting are lured through fronts such as legal satanic churches, daycare centers, and popular culture into prostitution, drug abuse, pornography, or "cultism"; mass sacrifices are covered up with mobile crematoria; commercials, corporate logos, children's television, and rock music are infused with satanic messages, and so on:

> I have been told it is a common occurrence for these groups to kidnap their victims (usually infants and young children) from hospitals, orphanages, shopping centers and off the streets. I have been informed that Satanists have been successful in their attempts to influence the Boy Scouts. I can say that there is a network of these people across the country who are very active, they have their own rest and relaxation farm, they are in contact with each other, it ties in loosely to the drug

operation, it ties into motorcycle gangs and it goes on and on. (Ted Gunderson, quoted in Jenkins 2004, 222).

These atrocity catalogues are most explicit in evangelical material such as Bob Larson's *Satanism: The Seduction of America's Youth* (1989), but narratives of evil do not have to be embedded in religious contexts; the complex can be readily secularized from an evangelical to a psychiatric or legal framework without losing the quality of totality, as with Michelle Smith and Laurence Pazder's *Michelle Remembers* (1980) and Lauren Stratford's *Satan's Underground* (1988). In addition, they are distributed in and strengthened by popular culture: Television talk shows and "documentaries," most notably Geraldo Rivera's "Devil Worship: Exposing Satan's Underground" (1988); Dennis Wheatley's novels and the Hammer film adaptations; the unholy trinity of *Rosemary's Baby* (1968), *The Exorcist* (1973), and *The Omen* (1976), with scores of sequels; Alan Parker's *Angel Heart* (1987), which highlights the connection to exotic voodoo stretching back to colonial times through W. Seabrook's *Magic Island* (1929) and H. P. Lovecraft's backwater swamp cultists (with their "tom-tom poundings"); *Evilspeak* (1981), which incorporates computers and flesh-eating pigs into the time-proven mold, and so on.[3] Not all of these products portray Satanists explicitly, but all of them partake in the telling of atrocities of a "satanic" nature (Frankfurter 2006, 65, 84; Jenkins 2004, 228–32; Partridge 2005, chapter 6).

From a social scientific standpoint, these demonological narratives stem from political, social, and religious articulations of a perceived "problem" in periods of heightened anxiety (Richardson, Best, and Bromley 1991) and seem to reinforce boundaries between neighbors or actualize latent fissures in a collective as a solution (cf. Appadurai 1996; Lincoln 1989). Jews, Christians, Catholics, Communists, Masons, Witches, white slavery rings, pedophiles, and other "others," whether these groups actually exist or not, have been used to make manifest moral threats and mobilize to the cause of defeating the danger. While the cognitive, narrative, and social mechanisms seem to be universal in time and space (e.g., Frankfurter 2006; Stevens 1991; cf. Lewis and Petersen 2008, part 2), the discourse of a secret conspiracy of Satanists that grows in Christian regions seems to be particularly paradigmatic as they are allied with the supreme source of evil and are thus monstrous practitioners of absolute transgression (Frankfurter 2006; Harvey 2009; Smoczynski 2009).

Secret satanic conspiracies do not exist, and atrocities are usually committed in the name of cleansing evil rather than doing it. However, as David Frankfurter has convincingly argued, these "Satanists" are mythical elements in "performances of evil" that reflects society through inversion and subversion. So, the perversions and violence reported in satanic ritual abuse cases and broader "occult panics" have a mythical existence; that is, they exist as culturally framed scripts that have formative power. Groups can act as if they exist, making them discursively real (Frankfurter 2006, 169, 205; cf. Jenkins 2004). While not Satanism as such, Frankfurter calls these social acts mimetic and divides them into direct and indirect mimesis, highlighting the difference between people actually claiming to be witches, Satanists or demons (an enacting) and the experts on and victims of these conspiracies telling us about them or the hunters eradicating them (an acting as if). Both types are framed by performances that ritualize purification, consequently reasserting social values through the negotiation of evil (Frankfurter 2006, chapter 5). This takes us into the realm of ostensive violence.

B. Ostensive Violence and Reactive Satanists: Appropriating "Dark Occulture"

Contrary to the mythological violence of indirect mimetic performance, ostensive violence does exist outside cultural narratives, as both adolescents and marginalized, confused individuals play with the atrocity catalogues and enact the image of Satanists in popular culture and dark "occulture" (Partridge 2004, 2005). These self-declared Satanists are thus necessarily *reactive*. Ostension refers to "legends as behavior," here reflexive performance of Christian mythology as direct mimesis, which in turn becomes enrolled in social negotiations of Satanism through pseudo- and quasi ostension or impersonation and mistaken attribution (Ellis 1991, 281ff; cf. Frankfurter 2006, 176–77). Nonetheless, a line must be drawn between the criminal violence "legitimized" through references to Satan and the relatively benign oppositional violence of legend tripping and metal subcultures, for example.

Regarding criminal violence, many examples spring to mind. Charles Manson's Family, for one, obviously integrated hard crime and what seems like a very idiosyncratic and flexible ideology appropriated from popular culture (such as the Beatles), the cultic milieu (the Process Church, LaVey's Church of Satan, Hubbard's Scientology), hippy culture (freak-outs and drug use), and apocalyptic conspiracy culture (race war, war on the system) (Lachman 2001; Lyons 1988). Ostension of Christian and occult discourse on evil certainly played a part, but to create a category of "acid-culture eclectic Satanists" or the like to describe the acts of Manson and his followers seems to me to stretch Satanism too far (Truzzi 1974). The Tate–La Bianca murders are not satanic; if anything, they are a radicalized expression of hippy counterculture and the ever-present war on the "fascist" establishment. As Philip Jenkins succinctly states:

> [W]e should be very cautious about accepting such claims. By definition, multiple killers are not normal people, and they might have odd motivations for their acts.... These [murders attributed to divine command] were the work of disturbed individuals whose psychiatric conditions chanced to be expressed in the language and rhetoric of a belief system widespread in their social background. (Jenkins 2004, 237)

The same can be said of teenage murderers such as Sean Sellers, adult killers such as Richard Ramirez, or the small, hardened core of Norwegian black metal vandals such as Varg Vikernes (the famous "Count Grishnackh") and Bård Eithun (Baddeley 2000, 137–39; Moynihan and Søderlind 1998, chapter 7). Although an ostension of cultural scripts, killing friends, family, or complete strangers, dabbling in Nazism, or setting medieval churches on fire have very little resonance even within their own social background, and the personal Satanism adopted is an expression rather than a cause of their sociopathic tendencies.

A wide gulf separates violent crime and the transgressions of reactive young Satanists to proper behavior, assessments of cult cops notwithstanding. David Frankfurter denotes this specific modern variant of direct mimesis as parodic (Frankfurter 2006 198–203), a youthful rebellion "plucking" symbols from "a more grotesque cultural reservoir" (199). Their use of the monstrous, morbid, violent, and satanic is necessarily reactive to society, dependent on group dynamics, and motivated by "psychological impotence and social deviance," but it is also playful, both as a mocking of social expectations and as "experiments with evil" (201). As I said earlier, their acts are usually benign, although provocative: Through aesthetic choices they signal a distance from mainstream style (Lowney 1995); sometimes they stray into vandalism of cemeteries or public buildings, sometimes they smoke pot, drink alcohol, and have sex, and sometimes they play on social conceptions of danger in legend tripping, playing with the "occult," or enacting "Satanism" (Ellis 1991, 2000, 2004).[4] Most often this is "satanic tourism" as "identity work" (Fine and Victor 1994).

Sometimes they gain a level of social coherence, as with the black metal scene and its combination of inverted Christianity, nature worship, and violent masculinity (Dyrendal 2008; Moynihan and Søderlind 1998; Mørk 2009); aside from the crimes committed by a small minority, violence usually takes a sonic form, with blast beats on grotesquely distorted guitars, growling or shrieking vocals, and fast-paced drums. Both the performances and lyrics support the satanic style, with pyrotechnics, inverted crucifixes, and animal carcasses on stage to underscore the violent message (at least in the old days). Gry Mørk has described black metal's "worship of darkness" as an example of "creative violence," parallel to similar projects such as David Fincher's movie *Fight Club* (1999), where existential issues of gender identity, alienation, and self-fulfillment interact with cultural critique. Accordingly Violence assumes "formative, healing, structuring . . . and/or balancing functions . . . for the individual"—it is progressive (Mørk 2009, 172–73; cf. Kolnar 2003).

Keith Kahn-Harris's study of extreme metal (Kahn-Harris 2007) provides another useful analytical framework for understanding the use of violence and Satanism through transgression, both as a negotiation of "transgressive" and "mundane subcultural capital" and as "reflexive anti-reflexivity" or "knowing better but deciding not to know" (145). Regarding capital, the use of ostensive violence through enacting cultural scripts must be understood as an interaction between members of the scene and the wider public; transgression thus becomes a way of gaining status by asserting individuality (Kahn-Harris 2007, chapter 6). "Reflexive anti-reflexivity," while primarily used to understand the ironic play with radical politics, can then be said to be constitutive of the *ambiguous* use of cultural others to express the values of the scene (Kahn-Harris 2007, chapter 7).

This combination of dark occulture and creative violence as direct mimesis is actually quite established as cultural practice, as Evelyn Lord's historical study of hellfire clubs can demonstrate (Lord 2008). The earliest clubs were direct and indirect mimetic performances of violence—directly, as when young aristocrats such as John Wilmot, second Earl of Rochester and his Ballers (or Bawlers) got into fights, threw bottles of urine on passersby, imported Dutch leather dildoes, or performed other transgressions as "an extension and inversion of [official] street theatre . . . creating violence instead of spectacle" (Lord 2008, 5; cf. 8, 11, 33), and indirectly, as when moral panic gripped early eighteenth-century London because of the mythical Mohocks "that play the Devil about town every night, slit people's noses and beat them" (Jonathan Swift, quoted in Lord 2008, 30). Again, what is a cultural script (here the fear of primitive violence and savages) can be enacted, which then again provides the scripts with further elaboration. The same can be said of the later blasphemous clubs, such as the Duke of Wharton's Hellfire Club (1721–1722) and the more classicist-paganist sexuality clubs epitomized by Francis Dashwood's Medmenham Friars (1751).

What is true of aristocrats in Enlightenment Britain might not be so for adolescents today. Much of the essentializing "history of antimorality" found in studies of Satanism (e.g., Ashe 2003; Lachman 2001) makes the mistake of seeing multiple expressions of antinomianism as one reified tradition (imitating emic Christian or satanic historiographies). Nevertheless, the various stages of clubs in Lord's study do give us a historical foundation of understanding the uses of violence, blasphemy, and sexuality in expressions of gender and identity if we are attentive to the historical and social differences in context. In this sense, libertine self-dramatizations, whether public or private, point back to the transgressions of carnival grotesques and forward to reactive "satanic" violence of middle-class teenage "scenes."

Reactive Satanism rarely distances itself from inverse Christianity and popular conceptions of Satan and Satanists but is actually an appropriation of these stereotypes in the construction of individual and collective identity (Schmidt 2003). Nevertheless, we should acknowledge some complexity here: It is always an appropriation; it is not a passive reception devoid of any possibility of or interest in interpretation and combination. Indeed, it can be deeply meaningful, whether a phase or a longer engagement, and is not *necessarily* criminal or shallow (Lowney 1995; Mørk 2009). Although ostensive violence such as that found in reactive expressions of Satanism can be explained by psychological or social factors (as with David Frankfurter earlier), it is useful to understand the inner workings of the different uses to which these practices are put. Whereas they sometimes spring from "impotence" or "deviance," they just as often enact cultural scripts in an ironic or playful manner. When combined with a systematic discourse on Satanism and transgression, the ostensive acts of young adults shade into the next category of "symbolic" or "aesthetic" violence.

C. Symbolic Violence and Modern Religious Satanists: Self-Religion and the Third Alternative

In opposition to both mythical and reactive Satanism, modern religious Satanism is a distinctive phenomenon in the satanic milieu fueled by self-religion (Heelas 1982, 1996), as well as the practice of antinomianism, a positive appropriation of a cluster of Satan-related words and a formulated ideological genealogy (Petersen 2009a, 7–10). Satan is understood as a symbol of oneself, a model of practice, or a principle or force not to be worshipped but to be emulated and understood. This is a structurally radical use of a disembedded figure of Satan in identity construction, only superficially resembling the Christian devil and more in line with Romantic reappraisals (Petersen 2009a, 10–14). The locus of authority is the self, and the project is one of liberation or empowerment even though the conflict between self and society and the "authentic human" is articulated in a variety of ways (Dyrendal 2009).

In my typology I outline two discrete interpretations (Petersen 2009a, 7). *Rationalist Satanism* is an atheistic and philosophical Satanism often associated with Anton LaVey and the Church of Satan, although it has developed beyond the specific formulations found there (barring names such as "LaVeyan Satanism"). Nevertheless, all acknowledge their roots in LaVey's work and the practice of explicitly using Satan as a symbol for the human condition as a carnal, emotional, and rational being. Hence, Satan is an ideal figure of adversarial practice, the practice of the accuser, and a name for the self that expresses oneself rather than something or someone else (e.g., LaVey 1969). This materialistic outlook is expressed in the goals of "rational self-interest" and "indulgence," and support is found in rationalist, secular, and individualist arguments based on science, philosophy, and the arts (cf. Petersen 2009b, 226–34).

Conversely, *esoteric Satanism* is a more mystical and initiatory formulation of Satanism as antinomian self-deification (e.g., Flowers 1997). Thus, Satan is associated with traditional left-hand path conceptions of magical practices and mystical experiences, whether considered a literal entity or a symbolic being (Granholm 2009; Sutcliffe 1996). The gnostic or esoteric outlook is supported by ritual experience, widespread syncretism, and scientism; appeals to and appropriations of exotic magical systems such as tantric practices, Aleister Crowley's Thelema, and chaos magick give this type of Satanism a more prototypical esoteric character (cf. Petersen 2009b, 234–39).

How do these religious Satanists articulate and perform violence? At least two trajectories are possible: on the one hand the pragmatic analysis of violence as a *natural necessity* and on the other the symbolic and aesthetic interpretation of violence and blasphemy as *performative transgression*. In both senses, violence must be seen through the emic scripts of modern Satanism itself. In the following I focus on rationalist Satanism, but there is significant subcultural overlap as the practices and arguments are frequently the same, although they are legitimized differently.

In the online text "Satanism and Violence," Vexen Crabtree, a prolific Internet Satanist of rationalist persuasion, describes violence as a natural given that a Satanist must understand and accept (Crabtree, "violence"). The human species is confronted with violence in both natural and cultural senses and should therefore be willing and able to give back; hence the Satanist is ideally trained in martial arts or "combat science" to be "emotionally and physically capable of dealing with antagonizers" and is willing to support wars to protect "the developed world." This is tied to concepts of self-preservation and "responsibility to the responsible" that ultimately rest on Anton LaVey's analysis of social Darwinism and retributive justice—"man is just another animal" (LaVey 1969, 25; 1992, 93–94). Crabtree's rationalist Satanism seems to posit the Satanist not only as an agent of necessary violence but also as an intelligent analyst of the state of affairs that reserves violence to proper situations: "The Satanist may never engage in violence . . . [but a]s a religion of the Earth, Satanism in the name of intelligence and responsibility requires us to make ourselves capable of physically defending both ourselves and what we consider to be good" (Crabtree, "violence").

From an impressionistic view of the satanic milieu (such as message board discussions and informal conversations), this seems to be a standard ethical view of most religious Satanists (as well as common sense). Satanism is about life, self-expression, and balance in alignment with nature:

> Satanism has been thought of as being synonymous with cruelty and brutality. This is so only because people are afraid to face the truth—and the truth is that human beings are not all benign or all loving. Just because the Satanist admits he is capable of both love and hate, he is considered hateful. On the contrary, because he is able to give vent to his hatred through ritualized expression, he is far more capable of love—the deepest kind of love. (LaVey 1969, 65)

Balance is indeed a core concept. In a rationalized reorientation of the unification of opposites in Western esotericism and dialectical thought, LaVey offers a satanic *third* perspective and solution to all aspects of life—ontology, epistemology, anthropology, aesthetics, ethics, and religion. As presented in an analysis of the material (or "inverted") pentagram in "The Third Side: The Uncomfortable Alternative" (LaVey 1998, 29–33), "the essence of Satanism is in the answers and solutions evoked by the THIRD side—the lower point representing the sword plunged into the earth, the beard of wisdom seen on the goat of the inverted star" (LaVey 1998, 30). He continues: "This central lowest point represents a rational resolution to the established but often extraneous opposing premises symbolized by the lateral two points" (LaVey 1998, 32). As a third alternative to love and hate, LaVey mentions venting hatred through "ritualized expression," pointing to the second trajectory of symbolic violence, which is tied up with ritual practice. As we will see, all material can be appropriated in and reframed by this project, from

Nazi occultism and fascist aesthetics to dark occulture and popular stereotypes of anti-Christianity.

In what is dubbed "phase-one Satanism" (Barton 1990, 15–16, 29, 68, 119, 123) of the early Church of Satan (roughly 1966–1972), marked anti-Christianity was enacted in public and private blasphemies without slipping into reactive Satanism as such (although ostension and mimesis were definitely present) (Alfred 1976; Barton 1990; Moody 1974). The performances balanced between positive empowering ceremonies such as a wedding, a baptism, and a burial and more "cathartic" rituals such as Black Masses. After 1972, rituals were privatized as the church reoriented itself to be a forum or cabal for "productive aliens" who "use their alienation" to practice what they preach (Barton 1990, 30), effectively strengthening the elitist aspect of rationalist antinomianism. However, "phase-one Satanism" remains in the ritual practices found in the literature, ready to be reactivated in new contexts.

For example, "The Book of Satan" in *The Satanic Bible* is a performance "clearing the air"; the violent rhetoric of the text is a "diatribe" of "diabolical indignation" praising the strong, the doubting of certainties, the law of the jungle, and the material world, ending with a blessing of the antithesis to Christian morality (LaVey 1969, 27–35). The rest of *The Satanic Bible* is a practical "implementation" of these statements in considerably less violent terms, first in intellectual prose ("The Book of Lucifer") and second in magical practice ("The Book of Belial" and "Leviathan"). In rituals such as the "Black Mass" (LaVey 1969, 99–105; 1972, 31–60) and the "Invocation Employed towards the Conjuration of Destruction" (LaVey 1969, 114–18, 149–50), violence is definitely present, but it is framed through the ritual space as an "intellectual decompression chamber": "The formalized beginning and end of the ceremony acts as a dogmatic, anti-intellectual device, the purpose of which is to disassociate the activities and frame of reference of the outside world from that of the ritual chamber, where the whole will must be employed" (LaVey 1969, 120). Similarly, the "Shibboleth" ritual (Moody 1974, 378–79; cf. Aquino 2009, 458, quoting from LaVey's original "Satanic Monograph") is a symbolic "psychodrama" to rid the participants of perplexing persons or types through a symbolic role playing and the subsequent ritual "killing" of them (by selling their soul to the devil [Aquino 2009, 458]).

As such, blasphemy (of all conventions) and human "sacrifice" (through curses and role playing [LaVey 1969, 87–90]) are appropriated as symbolic acts. Inspired by Hugh Urban's analysis of the Kapalikas, we could call this a sanitization of practices; the bloody violence of Vedic ritual is "sanitized" in the brahminical tradition, a process explaining the complicated myths surrounding early tantric mythology (Urban 1995, 70). As such, rationalist Satanism can be understood as a *sanitized* reframing of mythological and reactive scripts, as well as a secularized version of esoteric Satanism, sharing an appeal to antinomianism "that has more to do with the overcoming of one's own inhibitions and limitations, which are seen as bound up with socialisation, than with any ill-conceived anarchism" (Sutcliffe 1996, 111).

This sanitization of blasphemy and violence is very influential in the satanic milieu. Violence and transgression become tools for identity work, but they do so in a sense that twists the ostensive performances described earlier. Understood along the lines of Michel Foucault's "hermeneutics" or "technologies of the self" (Carrette 2000; Foucault 1999; Martin, Gutman, and Hutton 1988), Satanism becomes the *practice* of Satan as an adversarial project in an emic sense, a positive affirmation of self through negative deconditioning rather than the *belief* in or *impersonation* of Satan. To understand this point, we have to understand transgression.

3. Satanism and Transgression: A Provisional Analytics

Be ye angry, and sin not: let not the sun go down upon your wrath: Neither give place to the devil. (Ephesians 4: 26–27)[5]

Transgression can be found in many different contexts: political, ethical/normative, anthropological, and philosophical. As outlined in various introductions to the subject, the concept has shifted from the binaries of a legal and moral context over an anthropological systemic approach to a poststructural disruption (Jenks 2003; Jervis 1999; Julius 2002; Taussig 1998). Generally, poststructural models question the normativity of the moral framework of good and evil, the philosophical framework of high and low transgression, and the rigidities of structural coding. As described by George Bataille and later Michel Foucault, what is important is not the act itself but the play around the limit. In the words of Hugh Urban:

> [I]ts power lies in the dialectic or play (*le jeu*) between taboo and transgression, sanctity and sacrilege, through which on[e] systematically constructs and then oversteps all laws.... "The prohibition is there to be violated"; for it is the experience of overstepping limits that brings the blissful sense of continuity and communion with the other. (Urban 2003, 301, quoting from Bataille, *Erotism: Death and Sensuality*, 1986)

Unfortunately, these models do not transcend the ethnocentric core of philosophy. Transgression is the play of norm and other that simultaneously shows and supersedes the limit; there is thus ambivalence in Bataille's work, as well as in the reception by Foucault as to whether transgression ultimately *transcends* or *confirms* what is transgressed (Bataille 1985; Foucault 1977). It is one thing that the limit or norm is needed *in order* to transgress—that is a logical proposition; it is something entirely different whether the goal lies in mystical, ineffable, and apophatic experiences, as with Bataille, or in normative interrogation, as at least some of Foucault's arguments indicate (cf. Jenks 2003).

The consequence of this ambivalence is that inheritors of this model, similar to established anthropological models such as M. Gluckman's "rites of reversal," V. Turner's "liminality", and even M. Bakhtin's "temporary liberation" (Bakhtin 1984; cf. Stallybrass and White 1986; Taussig 1998) axiomatically assume that transgressor, transgressed, and outside observer all belong to the same normative and epistemic framework or ideological formation. An example could be the terrorist acts of September 11, 2001, which Chris Jenks sees as the *ultimate* transgression, one that actually confirms the norm by totally transcending it. A concrete expression of that confirmation is the coming together of world leaders and peoples of the free world in combating the threat of terrorism (Jenks 2003, 1–3). He concludes:

> To transgress is to go beyond the bounds or limits set by a commandment or law of convention, it is to violate or infringe. But to transgress is also more than this, it is to announce and even laudate the commandment, the law or the convention. Transgression is a deeply reflexive act of denial and affirmation. (Jenks 2003, 2; cf. 7–9)

What Jenks obviously neglects is the hermeneutic framework of the terrorists themselves; they see these acts as a holy duty inasmuch as our moral order is patently false (Lincoln 2006). Murder might be wrong, but not if the cause is right—and it is not transgression at all if the end is justifiable. What Jenks does is to provide an unnecessarily monological understanding of something that is inherently polyvocal.

Thus, all transgression is either ultimately impossible or necessarily part of the system itself as a simultaneous surpassing and confirmation of the norm, as it is evaluated from within the system and from the categories of the system itself. Translated into the categories of the present discussion, all Satanism is necessarily anti-Christian because Satanism is a denial of Christianity. When stated this way, it is clear that this understanding of transgression is too simple. We need an etic level of explanation, an anthropological reflexivity to correct this "emic" theorizing. From the viewpoint of historical-critical analysis there is good sense in assuming either that what the system, the norm, or indeed society judges as transgressive not *necessarily* seems that way from the viewpoint of the transgressor or that this judgment call seems like an irrelevant after-effect (as with September 11). Transgression must be understood along polyvocal lines with multiple discursive positions. I propose a simple heuristic dichotomy of transgression *from* and transgression *to*.

Transgression *from*, or reactive transgression, should be understood as the systemic transgression outlined earlier, a simultaneous confirmation-in-transgression. Violent black metal antics, excesses of various hellfire clubs, ostension of Christian scripts, and other reactive Satanisms actually confirm Christianity as a normative system with their practices. Transgression *to*, on the other hand, must be understood through its own premises of transgression—it is a transgression of something, of course, but with a goal entirely outside the normative system so transgressed. Most elaborated rationalist and esoteric Satanisms and indeed modern left-hand path practices as a whole are not framed by Christianity as much as by an external ideology of practice that demands transgression for the sake of the self (Flowers 1997; Granholm 2009). These types of Satanism cannot be understood as a structural transgression-as-confirmation of Christianity's normative framework that is just another normative Christianity;[6] they must be analyzed as practices of deconditioning to attain something else, something more, whether defined as liberation, gnosis, empowerment, or realization, to name a few goals. This could be seen in light of Hugh Urban's astute description of classical Tantra as built upon an elitist double norm (Urban 2003, 278f, 303–304). He quotes Douglas Brooks:

> Tantrism . . . does not intend to be revolutionary in the sense of establishing a new structure of social egalitarianism . . . it opens its doors only to a few who . . . seek to distinguish and empower themselves. (Brooks in Urban 2003, 278n23)

Transgression is a necessary means of attaining worldly power while simultaneously attaining liberation, something only a few can do because of the countersystemic character of this project. The rest of us are limited to (anti)systemic acts (Urban 2003, 304). Transgression *from* plays with the norm as both means and end, while transgression *to* constructs a new affirmative space where the norm is but a means to a new end. Satanic transgression is thus context dependent.

When it comes to the construction of tradition, that is, the genealogical discourses prevalent in the satanic milieu, it is both an ideological context and a practical act. Hence, the individual biography and the collective ethos are related to "historical metaphors and mythical realities" (Sahlins 1981) that facilitate a satanic practice. This returns us to the point of sanitization of violence discussed earlier, as it is obvious that the mutual exclusion of, for example, black metal from a rationalist discourse and Anton LaVey from a radically reactive genealogy points to different traditions of excess; where reactive Satanism is directly related to the negotiation of masculinity and subversive spectacle found in theater metaphor, there is no explicit *ideology* of transgression, only an agreement on opposition. On the other hand, this ostensive practice is more of an ambiguous "other" in the traditions constructed by rationalist and esoteric Satanists as it is not the opposition in itself but the non-symbolic direction it takes that is judged wrong.

It is evident that there is a definite congruence of my Satanism typology and the categories of transgression from and to. Although both can be found in rationalist and esoteric groups, reactive Satanism necessarily involves transgression from; when it is not, it is one of the other two types. This is as much due to mutual exclusion processes as a process of sanitization not in time but in space; one of the conditions set when moving from reactive to religious Satanism is indeed the distancing of explicit violence and transgression *from* something. This is easier said than done, however, as we will see.

4. Art from Marginality, Art as Marginality?

> Q: *"God Hates Us All," How does that fit in? A: God doesn't hate. But it's a great fucking title* (Tom Araya (Slayer) in S. Dunn's documentary *Metal: A Headbanger's Journey*, 2005)

Art That Kills: A Panoramic Portrait of Aesthetic Terrorism 1984–2001 by George Petros (2007) is an example of the "play with gray" seen in the combination of second-generation rationalist Satanism and more expressive violent forms of post-punk, which can be contrasted with the sanitization strategies previously discussed. This book constructs both an *ideological* transgressive tradition with a noteworthy element of Satanism in it (the content: images, text, interviews, manifestos, etc.) and an actual *articulation* of transgressive practice (the book itself and the individual projects described). In it, significant links between popular art, art theory, esotericism, and Satanism are proposed that illuminate the fine lines between symbolic and ostensive violence.

"Aesthetic terrorism" is the guiding metaphor for this project and is defined as "[u]sing the element of surprise through the usage of past clichés, knowledge and 'home truths' being flung out of joint, and therefore used as a weapon or subversive force" (J. G. Thidwell 1984, quoted in Petros 2007, 7). It is associated with John Aes-Nihil's "aesthetic nihilism," an "art that is so extreme it verges on destruction. It's a way of reacting to society. It is a reaction against mass culture by doing a vicious satire of it. It's extreme devotion to the creation of extremely intense art" (John Aes-Nihil, quoted in Petros 2007, 132–33). We can learn a lot from the self-presentation of the book:

> "Art That Kills" examines the point where art meets crime. The book documents a *diabolical* era, 1984–2001. It chronicles the evolution of a *new aesthetic movement*, a terrifying fringe of Underground Art where enlightenment and depravity combined. Murder, rape, torture, pedophilia, cannibalism, drugs, sedition, racism and blasphemy mixed with literature, history, politics, news, movies, TV, punk rock, philosophy and science. The book profiles a *pantheon* of dissidents and deviants, presents excerpts from their work, re-lives their crimes, and attempts to analyze an elusive era. The scene described herein is essentially the *"second generation"* of American Underground Art (the "first generation" ran from '66 through the '70s). All varieties of taboos and criminal advocacy found confluence, beyond "confrontation" or

"shock." Pure sadism drove it. Sexual psychosis flavored it. Frustration with politics, big business and mass entertainment fueled it. . . . (from the Amazon promo; my emphases)[7]

Basically, it looks like a huge collection of fanzine material loosely structured in the categories of "precursors," "soundtrack to 1984," "soundtrack to 1994," "mags and 'zines'" and "gallery of transgression"; between these categories are assorted biographies of luminaries in the "movement." Self-declared Satanists included in this genealogy of aesthetic terrorism include Nick Bougas, Shane Bugbee, Peter H. Gilmore, Anton S. LaVey, Marilyn Manson, Michael Moynihan, Adam Parfrey, Boyd Rice, Nikolas and Zeena Schreck, Stanton LaVey, and Szadora. Esoteric luminaries include Kenneth Anger and Genesis P-Orridge, both of which have distinct cross-over presences between avant-garde art scenes and the left-hand path and satanic milieus.

And that is exactly my point. Through the double move of constructing a tradition, indeed a "new aesthetic movement" in a generational and geographical perspective (Petros 2007, 9) while simultaneously articulating a transgressive program, a link is forged between the ideology of rationalist Satanism and the expressivism of postpunk. They are effectively lending authority to each other and supplying the necessary legitimacy in the two fields. Although I can find little in common between, for example, Anton LaVey and G. G. Allin, they are both recruited into the genealogy of aesthetic terrorism in a move similar to Anton LaVey and Peter Gilmore's identification of "de facto Satanists" (e.g., LaVey 1969, 104). They are both in opposition; it matters less to what. Further, but in contrast to that, it is no coincidence that Anton LaVey appears right at the start as the second precursor (alongside W. Burroughs, K. Anger, and C. Manson), while grandson Stanton LaVey and Szadora are the very last entries in the book (just after M. Manson) (Petros 2007, 14–20, 312–17, respectively). A fruitful alliance is forged between two vanguards—an "alien elite" of productive Satanists on one hand and the ultimate "misfits," the transgressors of the American punk scene, on the other. The salient factor is not the specific transgressions but the general nonconformist lifestyle and bohemianism exemplified by both.[8]

This linkage not without problems, of course. I believe LaVey would raise an eyebrow or two at the amount of drugs taken (overdose seems like a typical way to go), and the law-and-order mentality of the Church of Satan has a hard time sanitizing "murder, rape, torture, pedophilia, cannibalism, drugs, sedition, racism, and blasphemy." Indeed, the book is an individual project and not a total statement of the satanic milieu, rationalist Satanism, or even the second-generation Satanists within the Church of Satan, which seem to be core constituents of the book (such as Peter Gilmore, Boyd Rice, Zeena Schreck, and Nikolas Schreck).

Rather than seeing this book as a transparent source of Satanism or postpunk, I suggest looking at it as an artifact or a monument exemplifying the link between aesthetics and religion. Content-wise, the violence and perversion often mimics the reactive transgressions of ostensive Satanism, but they are now discursively integrated in an avant-garde *aesthetics*. Indeed, the very existence of the book is an analysis, one step away from the raw performance of postpunk. It is an intellectualization or sanitization after the fact. That doesn't necessarily take away its shock value, but it may lead us to broaden the scope to the links between art and transgression on a more general level.

First of all, it might be useful to compare the notion of aesthetic terrorism with similar tactics in the neo-avant-garde, especially the Situationist International. Founded in 1957 to reawaken the radical potential of dada and surrealism, its influence has been wide. In many ways, the critique of *récupération*, or co-optation by the capitalist mainstream, and the resultant tactic of *détournement*, or subversive appropriation of artistic and mass cultural commodities, are parallel to both the general stance of rationalist Satanism and the punk movement. In fact, some critics see punk rock as an experiment in practical situationism later recuperated by the mainstream (Solvang 1995; cf. Duguid 1995).[9] Although allied to Marxism and later the radical Left, their project is almost prototypical to the general stance of the avant-garde in conflict with both mass culture and high culture. It would be safe to say that this very persistent myth of "counterculture" is one link between Satanism, punk, and the avant-garde (cf. Heath and Potter 2005).

The use of postpunk and violent iconography and discourse gives the aesthetic and satanic milieus a common discursive ground that activates conformity as the common enemy. At the same time, the use of the floating signifier "Satan" is in itself a transgressive practice used to distinguish Satanists and "poseurs" and a strategy to reveal tacit assumptions in others. This is in turn related to the shift in the use of Satan as an emblem of the self, a shift that shows a structurally radical use of Satan today (Hammer 2001b, 33; Petersen 2009a, 10–14). Satan and Satanism are no longer primarily associated with the structurally conservative Christian context (as an evil entity) except when transgressing this very context as a practical intervention. In the ideological sense, a new romantic and self-religious hermeneutics of "purely personal drama of salvation and redemption to be acted out within the confines of the self" (a "biodicy") has replaced the Christian "theodicy" (Campbell 1987, 182). Today this drama can be acted out through a variety of means—aesthetics, consumption, and self-religion among them.[10]

Second, following that angle we might ask ourselves whether Foucault and Bataille indeed have a point with regard to Satanism as transgression; the problem lies in the traditional equation of Satanism and anti-Christianity, however. Both Christianity and Satanism exist as parts of a different system, namely a sociological and cultural one: late modernity with its specific cultural logic of capitalism. If we understand all religion as, differentiated yet dedifferentiating fields of practice, Satanism could indeed be described as a transgression *from* late modern society (cf. Dyrendal 2009, 72). Hence, all Satanism in the satanic milieu is potentially a transgression-as-confirmation of the conditions of late modernity, a role it shares with Christianity and indeed all modern religion even if the more "developed" Satanisms within the milieu are transgressions *to* something outside the nexus of Christianity. In this sense, all religion in modernity express the aims of "identity politics" broadly understood as detraditionalized political projects (Zaretsky 1994, 1995). Satanism in all forms can thus be conceptualized as "cultural avant-gardes" (Dunn 1991), "concerned less with aesthetic innovation than with contestation of meaning and innovative systems of cultural representation" (Dunn 1991, 130).

This brings us to an entirely different aspect of symbolic violence and sanitization. In *Modern Satanism: Anatomy of a Radical Subculture*, Chris Mathews presents a critique of modern Satanism (practically identical to LaVey's rationalist Satanism and offshoots) based on the premise that one vector in LaVey's writings, which draws on social Darwinism, misanthropy, and political extremism, is in fact *the core* of Satanism. The "play with gray" found in modern religious Satanism is not ambiguous at all; it is pseudooccult neo-fascism, "a discriminatory ideology of bigotry and intolerance that legitimates and glorifies violence" (Mathews 2009, 79). There is no doubt that this vector is there, as can be seen in "The Book of Satan" in *The Satanic Bible* (LaVey 1969, 27–35), Blanche Barton's biography, *The Secret Life of a Satanist* (Barton 1992), and essays such as "Pentagonal Revisionism: A Five-point Program" (LaVey 1992, 93–96); there is also little doubt that it can be activated by Satanists interested in the interface of Darwinism, cultural critique, and right-wing politics (Baddeley 2000, 148–66, 212–45; Mathews 2009, 139–59, 177–95; cf. Parfrey 1990, 2000; Petros 2007). However, his textual bias and curious neglect of everyday lived religion miss some very important points.

First of all, the movement texts of modern Satanism are not all philosophical tracts aiming at consistency. They must be seen in relation to genre and context, whether they are critical essays, ritual texts, or rhetorical interventions. Even when they postulate to be coherent philosophy, actual Satanists appropriate them according to need (Lewis 2002). For example, Vexen Crabtree, discussed earlier and mentioned by Mathews, clearly distances himself from LaVey on the issue of social Darwinism: "I do not agree with LaVey that such a police state or entire master race culture is possible. I do believe in forbidding the most pathetic people from breeding, but I know that there is no valid way to measure who *is* unworthy..." (Crabtree, "Elitism"). Hence, it is very problematic to move from text to milieu without tracing the use to which they are put; LaVey's assertions are not unequivocally "accepted as fact by Satanists" (Mathews 2009, 79), just as rationalist Satanism is not the totality of modern Satanism.

Second, the elaboration of one dimension of LaVey's work, the social Darwinist, ignores other strands or downplays them as confusion or hazy ad hoc statements (Mathews 2009, 76, 78). Just as Al-Qaeda is not Islam or even fundamentalist Islam, Darwinism, neo-Nazism, and fascism are not Satanism. The logical fallacy of the undistributed middle, which Mathews accuses LaVey of committing, is precisely what he himself commits: "That the two groups can be described with a middle term—in this case, 'outsider'—does not make them equivalent" (Mathews 2009, 227n33).[11]

Third, his righteous (and sometimes appropriate) indignation of the explicit use of fascist and Nazi aesthetics misses the fact pointed out by Keith Kahn-Harris: More often than not, "reflexive antireflexivity" informs ideological commitment. In other words, selective appropriation can utilize these elements to provoke, to rile up, or to transgress, and there is no slippery slope from aesthetic to ideological Satanism (at least not in the sense of political radicalism) (Mathews 2009, 169–72, 174, 192, 204). In fact, LaVey's own appropriation of Ragnar Redbeard's *Might Is Right* in the "Book of Satan," which is a key aspect of Mathews's thesis, is selective, editing out the anti-Semitism and toning it as a "satanic" work (Mathews 2009, 64–66; cf. Gallagher 2009; Lewis 2009).

Nevertheless, Mathews might have a valid, if undeveloped point. The ritual transgressions of "phase one Satanism" described earlier, which were powerful modes of transgression in the late 1960s, primarily targeted Christian morality and middle class complacency through sinister (but often amusing) antics and symbolic inversions. Twenty years later, the activities of the second-generation "Abraxas clique," namely Adam Parfrey, Boyd Rice, and the Schrecks, seems much more brutal and uncompromising (Baddeley 2000, 148–53; Mathews 2009, chapter 8; Petros 2007, 198–200). The "8-8-88 rally", for example, although nominally a concert with Boyd Rice's NON and a screening of a Charlie Manson movie called *The Other Side of Madness*, was a cross between a political rally and performance art that celebrated the death of the 1960s in full fascist style (August 8 was the date of the LaBianca murders, as well as a reference to "Heil Hitler") (Baddeley 2000, 148). While there was a significant amount of ambiguity in the actual ideological investment (from the interviews it seems like much was chosen to "mak[e] people anxious" [Petros 2007, 199]), there is no doubt that the Church of Satan had a harder time sanitizing the elements of fascist aesthetics and hard-core transgression; in addition, it seems like the second generation just didn't care to sanitize anything, making the division between reactive ostension and rationalist Satanism rather slim.

It is evident that Charles Manson and Adolf Hitler represent greater transgression than the Prince of Darkness himself today, a fact that underscores the obvious potential for transgression in these emblematic figures (and which is obvious if one leafs through *Art That Kills* and counts swastikas, Nazi salutes, and paraphernalia). Although the content changed, the aesthetic terrorism of the Art That Kills group was thus a return to very public and very blasphemous practices gone from the Church of Satan for twenty years; perhaps it could even be called a deprivatization and desanitization of transgression in contrast to LaVey's sanitization of blasphemy and violence in private ritual spaces as he moved on from "phase one". In this sense, while distasteful, they are still transgressions *to*, if we look beyond the surface aesthetics and into the contestation of meaning indicated by the public taboo-breaking of cultural avant-gardes.

In any case, the apocalypse culture of the second generation was not the endpoint of ideological development or transgressive practice, as a contemporary example might demonstrate. The "6-6-2006" High Mass of the Church of Satan, held on the most diabolical day of the millennium at the Steve Allen Theater in Los Angeles, was a publicized private gathering of satanic luminaries celebrating the 40th anniversary of LaVey's creation (Farren 2006). Reporter Mick Farren describes the Mass (which included the invocation of compassion, destruction, and lust in a Black Mass) as distinctly lacking, "turning depressingly middle-class, a self-realization seminar with occult trappings" (4). Apparently the powerful politico-aesthetic charge of the "8-8-88 rally" and the fascist current of the Church of Satan have been sanitized once again, after LaVey's death and the consolidation of Peter Gilmore as high priest. This is very much in tune with other media appearances where the Church of Satan is presented as approachable, even benign. Nevertheless, straight-arm horned salutes and "Hail, Satan!" concluded the ceremony, making the reporter somewhat ill at ease (Farren 2006, 4–6), indicating that an element of symbolic violence indeed has remained, whether couched in satanic or other trappings.

6. Conclusion

In contrast to the conflation of David Frankfurter and the dismissal of Chris Mathews, I suggest we analyze the permutations of self-declared Satanism as a variety of satanic discourses in a satanic milieu. Within this milieu are discrete groups with websites and local chapters, spokespersons with movement texts (in whatever form), and seekers with various interests, all participating in a community of sentiment around darker aspects of the cultic milieu. Nevertheless, the actual coherence of doctrine, adherence to practices, and seriousness of organization differ widely. Hence I work with a categorization of modern Satanism into rationalist, esoteric, and reactive Satanism that should be understood as narratives of self-image and as dynamic categories, not as absolutes or reified roles.

Reactive Satanism is in fact expressing similar goals of "street theater," masculinity, public violence, and blasphemy as other gang cultures then and now. Paradoxically, though, the very public practices of ostension are in fact playing with the limit and so confirm the norms with which they play. In rationalist and esoteric Satanism, on the other hand, actions ideally transcend social boundaries to redress the balance and express the self. Their identity work is ideally building another norm—it is a transgression *to* something rather than a transgression *from*. In practice, though, these categories should rather be seen as discursive positions in a milieu that stretches from the narrowly religious to the broadly transgressive, highlighting Anton LaVey's scale of "nine parts social respectability to one part outrage." Although logically incongruent, religious and reactive Satanism are often closer than either might acknowledge, as we saw in the apocalypse culture of aesthetic terrorism.

The mythical realities of esotericism, hellfire clubs, devil worship, and fascist aesthetics are a necessary backdrop to rationalist practices of lesser and greater magic, artistic transgression, and personal empowerment. In the same vein but much more ambivalently, the symbolic violence and aesthetic terrorism so popular both as an intellectual strategy and as a performative assertion are sanitized versions of the dialectic private-public transgression and violence found in medieval Bengal, seventeenth-century London, British football casuals, and the 1990s' Norwegian music scene. One reason that LaVey and almost all rationalist and esoteric Satanists vehemently reject black metal church burnings and the advocacy of sacrificial "culling" of the herd (besides the senselessness of these acts from a self-preservation perspective and their lack of subtlety) is that their detraditionalized acts have the same roots; even Satanists "other" what is close. Let us not make the same mistake.

NOTES

This chapter is based on a paper with the same name presented at the conference "Satanism in the Modern World," Nov. 19–20, 2009, Norwegian University of Science and Technology, Trondheim, Norway. I want to thank Asbjørn Dyrendal for valuable comments.

1. See http://www.youtube.com/watch?v=wsKbbIybtVM&;feature=related (Rice) and http://www.youtube.com/watch?v=4IC8QJ408Kg&;feature=related (Schreck), both from the blog http://raumfahrer.wordpress.com/manson/, which discusses Marilyn Manson and the nexus of Satanism and Nazi chic. Much of this goes back to the fascination with Charles Manson of second-generation Satanists in the Church of Satan in the late 1980s and early 1990s, of which more later.

2. Regarding Satanic panic, recent studies include Frankfurter (2006); Jenkins (2004); and Medway (2001); classics include Ellis (2000); La Fontaine (1998, 1999); Lewis and Petersen (2008); Richardson, Best, and Bromley (1991); and Victor (1993), all with links to general literature such as Stanley Cohen, Norman Cohn, and Nachman Ben-Yehuda.

3. I could include role-playing games such as *Nephilim*, *Call of Cthulhu*, and the *World of Darkness* series, supplements to Dungeons & Dragons such as the *Book of Vile Darkness*, the *Tome of Corruption* for Warhammer Fantasy Roleplay, computer games like the *Diablo* series, as well as music and television. It is actually somewhat odd that evangelicals have targeted the Smurfs and Pokemon with that much *explicitly* violent material (Best 1991; Martin and Fine 1991).

4. Sometimes they even cut themselves or commit suicide. However, again, this is an expression of deeper problems where Satanism actually can be of some help (Lowney 1995; Moody 1974; Moriarty 1992).

5. King James version. Electronic Text Center, University of Virginia Library.

6. Comparable to Randall Alfred's proposition of LaVeyan Satanism as the ultimate Protestant sect, as it sanitizes hedonism into hard work but also legitimizes worldly enjoyment (Alfred 1976, 199–200).

7. See http://www.amazon.co.uk/Art-That-Kills-Panoramic-Aesthetic/dp/1840681403/ref=sr_1_1?ie=UTF8&s=books&qid=1258383612&;sr=8-1.

8. The same basic strategy can be found in Adam Parfrey's collections of "apocalypse culture" (Parfrey 1990, 2000) blending social critique, necrophilia, pedophilia, and other

entertainment with an undercurrent of Satanism, or, in Matt Paradise's blog "Diabologue" found online (a part of Paradise's media company Purging Talon), where Satanism is quite explicit, while the aesthetic terrorism is limited to horror movies and freak culture in general.

9. We could compare this with the explicit use of situationism by the punk icon Frank Discussion and his band the Feederz, as well as the prankster movement, with roots in Ken Kesey's Kool-Aid acid tests which pioneered the use of sampling in their total experiences.

10. Cf. Randall Alfred's proposition of LaVeyan Satanism as the ultimate consumer capitalism (Alfred 1976, 200), secularizing the private responsibility for salvation into a modern autonomous, imaginative hedonism found in self-religions, romanticism, advertising, and consumer culture (Campbell 1987).

11. The same can be said about his charge of confirmation bias—one tends to notice and to look for whatever confirms one's beliefs (Mathews 2009, 168). For example, even though he is presented with counterevidence, Mathews can dismiss two presentations of modern Satanists as politically plural by asserting that "Satanists are typically politically conservative, tending towards the extremes of conservatism. Its natural political affinities are with the far right" (Mathews 2009, 141; cf. 171), citing no evidence outside textual material.

REFERENCES

Alfred, Randall H. 1976. "The Church of Satan." In *The New Religious Consciousness*, ed. C. Y. Glock and R. N. Bellah, 180–202. Berkeley: University of California Press.
Appadurai, Arjun. 1996. *Modernity at Large: Cultural Dimensions of Globalization*. Minneapolis: University of Minnesota Press.
Aquino, Michael. 2009. *The Church of Satan*, 6th ed. San Francisco: Temple of Set.
Ashe, Geoffrey. 2003. *The Hell-fire Clubs: A History of Anti-morality*. Sparkford, UK: Sutton. (Orig. pub. 1974.)
Baddeley, Gavin. 2000. *Lucifer Rising: Sin, Devil Worship, and Rock 'n' Roll*. London: Plexus.
Bakhtin, Mikhail. 1984. *Rabelais and His World*, trans. H. Iswolsky. Bloomington; Indianapolis: Indiana University Press. (Orig. pub. 1965.)
Barton, Blanche. 1990. *The Church of Satan*. New York: Hell's Kitchen Productions.
———. 1992. *The Secret Life of a Satanist*. Los Angeles: Feral House.
Bataille, Georges. 1985. *Visions of Excess: Selected Writings 1927–1939*, trans. A. Stoeckl. Manchester: Manchester University Press.
Best, Joel. 1991. "Endangered Children and Antisatanist Rhetoric." In *The Satanism Scare*, ed. J. T. Richardson, J. Best and D. G. Bromley, 95–107. New York: de Gruyter.
Bromley, David G., and Anson D. Shupe. 1981. *Strange Gods: The Great American Cult Scare*. Boston: Beacon.
Campbell, Colin. 1972. "The Cult, the Cultic Milieu, and Secularization." In *A Sociological Yearbook of Religion in Britain*, vol. 5, ed. M. Hill, 119–136. London: SCM.
———. 1987. *The Romantic Ethic and the Spirit of Modern Consumerism*. Oxford: Blackwell.
Carrette, Jeremy. 2000. *Foucault and Religion: Spiritual Corporality and Political Spirituality*. London: Routledge.

Crabtree, Vexen. N.d "Satanism and Violence." http://www.dpjs.co.uk/violence.html. (accessed August 1, 2010).

Crabtree, Vexen. N.d. "Satanism and Elitism: The Alien Elite." http://www.dpjs.co.uk/elitism.html. (accessed September 28, 2010).

Duguid, Brian. 1995. "A Prehistory of Industrial Music." EST magazine [online], at http://media.hyperreal.org/zines/est/articles/preindex.html. (accessed January 7, 2010)

Dunn, Robert. 1991. "Postmodernism: Populism, Mass Culture, and Avant-garde." *Theory, Culture, and Society* 8: 111–35.

Dyrendal, Asbjørn. 2008. "Devilish Consumption: Popular Culture in Satanic Socialization." *Numen* 55(1): 68–98.

———. 2009. "Darkness Within: Satanism as a Self-religion." In *Contemporary Religious Satanism: A Critical Anthology*, ed. J. A. Petersen, 59–73. Burlington, Vt.: Ashgate.

Ellis, Bill. 1991. "Legend-trips and Satanism: Adolescents' Ostensive Traditions as 'Cult' Activity." In *The Satanism Scare*, ed. J. T. Richardson, J. Best, and D. G. Bromley, 279–96. New York: de Gruyter.

———. 2000. *Raising the Devil: Satanism, New Religions, and the Media*. Louisville: University Press of Kentucky.

———. 2004. *Lucifer Ascending: The Occult in Folklore and Popular Culture*. Lexington: University Press of Kentucky.

Farren, Mick. 2006. "The Devil's Advocates." Citybeat 158. Originally accessed at http://www.lacitybeat.com/article.php?id=3916&issueNum=158. (now defunct). An abstract can be found at http://www.altweeklies.com/aan/the-devils-advocates/Story?oid=166070. (accessed September 29, 2010)

Fine, Gary Alan, and Jeffrey S. Victor. 1994. "Satanic Tourism: Adolescent Dabblers and Identity Work." *Phi Delta Kappan* 76(1): 70–72.

Flowers, Stephen E. 1997. *Lords of the Left-hand Path: A History of Spiritual Dissent*. Smithville, Tex.: Runa-Raven.

Foucault, Michel. 1977. "A Preface to Transgression." In *Language, Counter-memory, Practice*, ed. D. F. Bouchard, 29–52. Ithaca, N.Y.: Cornell University Press. (Orig. pub. 1963.)

———. 1999. *Religion and Culture*, ed. Jeremy Carrette. New York: Routledge.

Frankfurter, David. 2001. "Ritual as Accusation and Atrocity: Satanic Ritual Abuse, Gnostic Libertinism, and Primal Murders." *History of Religions* 40(4): 352–80.

———. 2006. *Evil Incarnate: Rumors of Demonic Conspiracy and Satanic Abuse in History*. Princeton, N.J.: Princeton University Press.

Gallagher, Eugene V. 2009. "Sources, Sects, and Scripture: The 'Book of Satan' in the Satanic Bible." Paper presented at the conference *Satanism in the Modern World*, November 19–20 2009, Norwegian University of Science and Technology, Trondheim.

Granholm, Kennet. 2009. "Embracing Others than Satan: The Multiple Princes of Darkness in the Left-hand Path Milieu." In *Contemporary Religious Satanism: A Critical Anthology*, ed. J. A. Petersen, 85–101. Burlington, Vt.: Ashgate.

Hammer, Olav. 2001a. *Claiming Knowledge: Strategies of Epistemology from Theosophy to the New Age*. Boston: Brill.

———. 2001b. "Same Message from Everywhere: The Sources of Modern Revelation." In *New Age Religion and Globalization*, ed. M. Rothstein, 42–57. Aarhus, Denmark: Aarhus University Press.

Harvey, Graham. 2009. "Satanism: Performing Alterity and Othering." In *Contemporary Religious Satanism: A Critical Anthology*, ed. J. A. Petersen, 27–39. Burlington, Vt.: Ashgate.
Heath, Joseph, and Andrew Potter. 2005. *The Rebel Sell: How the Counterculture Became Consumer Culture*. Chichester: Capstone.
Heelas, Paul. 1982. "Californian Self-religions and Socializing the Subjective." In *New Religious Movements: A Perspective for Understanding Society*, ed. E. Barker, 69–85. New York: Mellen.
———. 1996. *The New Age Movement: The Celebration of the Self and the Sacralization of Modernity*. Oxford: Blackwell.
Jenkins, Philip. 2004. "Satanism and Ritual Abuse." In *Oxford Handbook of New Religious Movements*, ed. J. R. Lewis, 221–42. New York: Oxford University Press.
Jenks, Chris. 2003. *Transgression*. Key Ideas, series ed. P. Hamilton. New York: Routledge.
Jervis, John. 1999. *Transgressing the Modern: Explorations in the Western Experience of Otherness*. Oxford: Blackwell.
Julius, Anthony. 2002. *Transgressions: The Offences of Art*. London: Thames and Hudson.
Kahn-Harris, Keith. 2007. *Extreme Metal: Music and Culture on the Edge*. New York: Berg.
Kelly, Henry A. 2006. *Satan: A Biography*. New York: Cambridge University Press.
Kolnar, Knut. 2003. *Det ambisiøse selv*. Unpublished doctoral thesis submitted to the Dept. of Philosophy, Norwegian University of Science and Technology, Trondheim.
Lachman, Gary. 2001. *Turn Off Your Mind: The Mystic Sixties and the Dark Side of the Age of Aquarius*. New York: Disinformation.
La Fontaine, Jean S. 1998. *Speak of the Devil: Tales of satanic abuse in contemporary England*. Cambridge; New York: Cambridge University Press.
———. "Satanism and Satanic Mythology." In *The Athlone History of Witchcraft and Magic in Europe, Vol. 6: The Twentieth Century*, ed. B. Ankarloo and S. Clark, 81–140. London: The Athlone Press.
LaVey, Anton S. 1969. *The Satanic Bible*. New York: Avon.
———. 1972. *The Satanic Rituals*. New York: Avon.
———. 1992. *The Devil's Notebook*. New York: Feral House.
———. 1998. *Satan Speaks!* New York: Feral House.
———. 2009. "Infernal Legitimacy." In *Contemporary Religious Satanism: A Critical Anthology*, ed. J. A. Petersen, 41–58. Burlington, Vt.: Ashgate.
———, and Jesper Aagaard Petersen, eds. 2008. *The Encyclopedic Sourcebook of Satanism*. Amherst, N.Y.: Prometheus.
Lincoln, Bruce. 1989. *Discourse and the Construction of Society: Comparative Studies of Myth, Ritual, and Classification*. New York: Oxford University Press.
———. 2006. *Holy Terrors: Thinking about Religion after September 11*, 2d ed. Chicago: University of Chicago Press.
Lord, Evelyn. 2008. *The Hell-fire Clubs: Sex, Satanism, and Secret Societies*. New Haven, Conn.: Yale University Press.
Lowney, Kathleen. 1995. "Teenage Satanism as Oppositional Youth Subculture." *Journal of Contemporary Ethnography* 23(4): 453–84.
Lyons, Arthur. 1988. *Satan Wants You: The Cult of Devil Worship in America*. New York: Mysterious.

Martin, Daniel, and Gary Alan Fine. 1991. "Satanic Cults, Satanic Play: Is 'Dungeons & Dragons' a Breeding Ground for the Devil?" In *The Satanism Scare*, ed. J. T. Richardson, J. Best, and D. G. Bromley, 107–23. New York: de Gruyter.

Martin, Luther H., Huck Gutman, and Patrick H. Hutton. 1988. *Technologies of the Self: A Seminar with Michel Foucault*. Amherst, Mass.: University of Massachusetts Press.

Mathews, Chris. 2009. *Modern Satanism: Anatomy of a Radical Subculture*. Westport, Conn.: Praeger.

Medway, Gareth J. 2001. *Lure of the Sinister: The Unnatural History of Satanism*. New York: New York University Press.

Moody, Edward J. 1974. "Magical Therapy: An Anthropological Investigation of Contemporary Satanism." In *Religious Movements in Contemporary America*, ed. I. I. Zaretsky and M. P. Leone, 355–82. Princeton, N.J.: Princeton University Press.

Mørk, Gry. 2009. "'With My Art I Am the Fist in the Face of God': On Old-school Black Metal." In *Contemporary Religious Satanism: A Critical Anthology*, ed. J. A. Petersen, 171–98. Burlington, Vt.: Ashgate.

Moriarty, Anthony. 1992. *The Psychology of Adolescent Satanism: A Guide for Parents, Counselors, Clergy, and Teachers*. Westport, CT: Praeger Publishers.

Moynihan, Michael, and Didrik Søderlind. 1998. *Lords of Chaos: The Bloody Rise of the Satanic Metal Underground*. Venice, Calif.: Feral House.

Murchembled, Robert. 2003. *A History of the Devil: From the Middle Ages to the Present*, trans. J. Birell. Malden, Mass.: Polity. (Orig. pub. 2000.)

Parfrey, Adam, ed. 1990. *Apocalypse Culture*, 2d ed. Los Angeles: Feral House. (Orig. pub. 1987.)

———, ed. 2000. *Apocalypse Culture II*. Los Angeles: Feral House.

Partridge, Christopher. 2004. *The Re-enchantment of the West: Alternative Spiritualities, Sacralization, Popular Culture*, and Occulture. Vol. 1. London: T and T Clark.

———. 2005. *The Re-enchantment of the West: Alternative Spiritualities, Sacralization, Popular Culture and Occulture*. Vol. 2. London: T and T Clark.

Petersen, Jesper Aagaard. 2005. "Modern Satanism: Dark Doctrines and Black Flames." In *Controversial New Religions*, ed. J. R. Lewis and J. A. Petersen, 423–457. New York: Oxford University Press.

———. 2009a. "Introduction: Embracing Satan." In *Contemporary Religious Satanism: A Critical Anthology*, ed. J. A. Petersen, 1–24. Burlington, Vt.: Ashgate.

———. 2009b. "Satanists and Nuts: Schisms in Modern Satanism." In *Sacred Schisms: How Religions Divide*, ed. S. Lewis and J. R. Lewis, 218–47. New York: Cambridge University Press.

Petros, George. 2007. *Art That Kills: A Panoramic Portrait of Aesthetic Terrorism 1984–2001*, ed. J. L. Williams. London: Creation Books.

Richardson, James T., Joel Best, and David G. Bromley, eds. 1991. *The Satanism Scare*. New York: de Gruyter.

Russell, Jeffrey Burton. 1977. *The Devil: Perceptions of Evil from Antiquity to Primitive Christianity*. Ithaca: Cornell University Press.

———. 1981. *Satan: The Early Christian Tradition*. Ithaca: Cornell University Press.

———. 1984. *Lucifer: The Devil in the Middle Ages*. Ithaca: Cornell University Press.

———. 1986. *Mephistopheles: The Devil in the Modern World*. Ithaca: Cornell University Press.

Sahlins, Marshall David. 1981. *Historical Metaphors and Mythical Realities: Structure in the Early History of the Sandwich Islands Kingdom*. ASAO Special Publ. 1. Ann Arbor: University of Michigan Press.

Schmidt, Joachim. 2003. *Satanismus: Mythos und Wirklichkeit*. Marburg: diagonal-Verlag. (Orig. pub. 1992).

Smoczynski, Rafal. 2009. "Cyber-Satanism and Imagined Satanism: Dark Symptoms of Late Modernity." In *Contemporary Religious Satanism: A Critical Anthology*, ed. J. A. Petersen, 141–51. Burlington, Vt.: Ashgate.

Solvang, Per. 1995. "No Future." Originally published in *Samtiden* 4 (1995); accessed November 12 2009 at http://www.annelorentzen.no/salong/articles/nofuture.htm.

Stallybrass, Peter, and Allon White. 1986. *The Politics and Poetics of Transgression*. Ithaca: Cornell University Press.

Stevens, Phillips, Jr. 1991. "The Demonology of Satanism: An Anthropological View." In *The Satanism Scare*, ed. J. T. Richardson, J. Best, and D. G. Bromley, 21–39. New York: de Gruyter.

Sutcliffe, Richard. 1996. "Left-hand Path Ritual Magick: A Historical and Philosophical Overview." In *Paganism Today*, ed. G. Harvey and C. Hardman, 109–37. Glasgow: Thorsons.

Taussig, Michael. 1998. "Transgression." In *Critical Terms for Religious Studies*, ed. M. C. Taylor, 349–364. Chicago: University of Chicago Press.

Truzzi, Marcello. 1974. "Towards a Sociology of the Occult: Notes on Modern Witchcraft." In *Religious Movements in Contemporary America*, ed. I. I. Zaretsky and M. P. Leone, 628–45. Princeton, N.J.: Princeton University Press.

Urban, Hugh B. 1995. "The Remnants of Desire: Sacrificial Violence and Sexual Transgression in the Cult of the Kapalikas and in the Writings of Georges Bataille." *Religion* 25(1): 67–90.

———. 2003. "The Power of the Impure: Transgression, Violence, and Secrecy in Bengali Sakta tantra and Modern Western Magic." *Numen* 50(3): 269–308.

Victor, Jeffrey S. 1993. *Satanic Panic: The Creation of a Contemporary Legend*. Chicago: Open Court.

Zaretsky, Eli. 1994. "Identity Theory, Identity Politics: Psychoanalysis, Marxism, Poststructuralism." In *Social Theory and the Politics of Identity*, ed. C. Calhoun, 198–215. Cambridge, Mass.: Blackwell.

———. 1995. "The Birth of Identity Politics in the 1960s: Psychoanalysis and the Public/Private Division." In *Global Modernities*, ed. M. Featherstone, S. Lash, and R. Robertson, 244–59. Thousand Oaks, Calif.: Sage.

PART V

Violence Against NRMs

18

State-Fostered Violence against the Falun Gong in China

James T. Richardson and Bryan Edelman

On April 25, 1999, more than ten thousand Falun Gong adherents gathered in a peaceful "appeal" around Zhong-nanhai in the People's Republic of China (PRC). The protestors wanted the PRC central government, the majority of whose members reside there in the new "forbidden city," to recognize the movement as a legitimate form of spirituality.[1]

A few months later, on July 22, 1999, the State Council, the executive branch of the central government, officially banned Falun Gong, labeling it an "evil cult," an act that concluded nearly three months of intense preparation, described in great detail by James Tong.[2] This included a massive intelligence-gathering operation to find out more about the Falun Gong, including the names and locations of all leaders across the country, many of whom were arrested just prior to July 22. Also, the government was intent on stopping all further demonstrations by the Falun Gong and did so very effectively throughout the country. A major propaganda campaign was quietly organized as well that resulted in a huge outpouring of negative media once the campaign against the Falun Gong was announced on July 22.[3] The Standing Committee of the National People's Congress (NPC) then passed ex post facto legislation banning "evil cults" on October 30, 1999. In the months that followed, the government took several other actions in an effort to exert social control over the Falun Gong movement and to garner support in the international arena.

These official actions resulted in considerable punitive actions against Falun Gong leaders by various arms of the Chinese government.

It was estimated in February 2000 that 35,000 practitioners had been detained, 300 jailed, 5,000 sent to labor camps, and 50 committed to mental hospitals.[4] Estimates at that time also place the number of deaths in prison at more than two hundred, and there were eleven confirmed deaths. Current reported numbers of those detained, jailed, and committed are even higher. James Tong reports the following numbers through 2005 and says, "These reports appear verifiable":[5] 14,474 cases of physical torture and psychological abuse, including 4,724 cases of severe physical beatings or other physical trauma such as 1,732 cases involving use of electric shocks, and 2,895 deaths of imprisoned practitioners.

These statistics clearly show that state-fostered violence against the Falun Gong has been thorough and effective. Individual practitioners have been dealt with harshly, and the overall effect of this massive campaign is the near termination of the movement itself in China. Thus, the overall impact has been to use the apparatus of the state to deny the Falun Gong movement the right to exist within Chinese society. The movement has not been totally stamped out in China, but it has been forced underground, and it is much smaller than was the case before the persecution started.[6]

The key questions of this chapter are, how are such high levels of violence against members of a minority religious group justified by those in positions of power in China, and how is the apparatus of the state used to effect this violence? It is one thing for a state to *allow* discriminatory behavior toward minority faiths that are out of step with dominant values and parties in a society. That happens with regularity around the globe. However, when the state itself becomes an instrument of violence toward minority faiths, this demands explanation.

Before describing the unique structure of government in China, which contributes to violence against a minority faith, We present a short discussion of how religion is officially defined there, as well as some analysis of the justifications for exerting social control on those groups that contravene official approaches to religion.

Religion in China: Official and Unofficial, "Normal" versus "Cult"

Religious freedom is enshrined in the PRC constitution with language that appears to be consistent with customary international law, which appears in many modern constitutions. Article 36 incorporates freedom of choice and belief, as well as a prohibition against discrimination on the basis of religion (emphasis added):

> Citizens of the People's Republic of China enjoy *freedom of religious belief*. No state organ, public organization, or individual may *compel citizens to believe in, or not believe in*, any religion; nor may they *discriminate against* citizens who believe in, or do not believe in, any religion.

However, the article places certain restrictions on religious practice that are somewhat unusual (emphasis added):

> The state protects *normal*[7] religious activities. No one may make use of religion to engage in activities that *disrupt public order*, impair the health of citizens or interfere with the educational system of the state.

Although the PRC constitution protects religious freedom in principle, the reality is quite different. Only five religions have been sanctioned by the state—Catholicism, Protestantism, Islam, Buddhism, and Taoism—and those only through state-approved organizations. Such state-controlled religions apparently represent what the constitution considers to be "normal religions." All other religions, which operate as underground "house churches," are subject to government suppression and the whims of the political leadership. According to Human Rights Watch, government oversight of officially registered religions includes scrutinizing membership, ceding some control over the selection of clergy, opening financial records to the government, allowing censorship of religious materials, interfering with doctrinal thought, and limiting religious activities to religious sites.[8]

Much of the danger to these unregistered religions and organizations lies in the abstract term *cult* identified in the recent legislation (discussed later), the ease with which this label can be applied to an organization, and the absence of objective criteria that can be applied to determine whether a group should be classified as a cult or a "normal" religion in accordance with PRC law.[9]

"Cults refer to illegal organizations that promote and deify their leaders in the name of religion, qigong or other establishments," according to Professor Zhou Zhenxiang, criminal law expert and vice president of the China Youth Political Science Academy:

> [They] try to delude and hoodwink others, recruit and control members, and jeopardize social order through the fabrication and spread of superstition and heretical ideas. They are characterized by leader worship, spiritual control, fabrication of heretical ideas, accumulation of wealth by unfair means, formation of secret societies, perpetration of harms to society, and so on.[10]

The characteristics that supposedly characterize a "cult" were later changed to create an even more abstract definition. During the government-sponsored International Symposium on Evil Cults in Beijing on November 9–10, 2000, local authorities were urged not to debate whether a group is a genuine religion or not. Rather, they should consider whether it is harmful to society.[11]

This evolving definition demonstrates that the government was rapidly developing criteria for use by the appropriate ministries to determine which groups are valid religions and which are "evil cults." But the effects are not vague: Groups that are labeled "evil cults" may be officially disbanded, and members of the groups may be prosecuted by the state apparatus with impunity, especially if they persist. Moreover, these groups have no objective legal basis or process for refuting the "evil cult" label.

This ambiguous standard has some house church leaders fearing that their groups will be classified as cults. Shortly after the legislation passed in October 1999, fourteen Christian sects were labeled "evil cults," their facilities destroyed, and their leaders arrested.[12] According to the Information Center for Human Rights and Democracy, twelve hundred temples and churches were destroyed in Zhejiang Province alone within a few months in late 1999. Government officials said they were destroyed because they were not approved by the authorities.[13]

Ideological Underpinnings of Violence against Nonapproved Religions

The philosophical basis underlying the conception of legality in the contemporary PRC is known as *socialist legality*. A conservative conception of this philosophy is that law is the reification of class willpower and that law reflects the dominance of the ruling class over the ruled. Socialist legality is not restrained by the notion of law but uses law as a tool to strengthen its dictatorship.[14]

According to Lenin, the legal establishment serves two purposes in the socialist state. First, courts play a role of coercive deterrence by suppressing potential threats to the government. Second, the suppression of the enemy educates the proletarian masses.[15] Both political and legal establishments of coercion, suppression, and dictatorship can develop only if the dictatorship is successful at eliminating the bourgeois enemy.[16] Moreover, if an organization or movement is defined as deriving from the "bourgeois enemy," this allows any and all means to be used against them.

Unlike in the West, where law is usually seen as a constraint on the power of the state, the PRC views law as a means to maintain stability, regulate society, protect the interests of the communist ruling class, and strengthen and enforce the government's authority. The content of law focuses on preserving the social order through the imposition of duties upon citizens. Law is not a method to constrain the state's actions but a means to guarantee that the people will perform their duties.[17] The ruling communist elite may use law to enforce its policies, but the elite class itself is not easily constrained by law. This reflects a system known as the *rule by law*, where "officials handle public affairs according to relevant laws without questioning the nature of these laws."[18] The rule by law enables the power holders to use law enforcement to exert social control over the populace.

In sharp contrast, the *rule of law* refers to both the content and the underlying principles of law. Democratic societies create procedures for making and implementing the law of the land, which all persons, regardless of class position, must follow. These laws and procedures restrict lawmakers and law enforcement, as well as ordinary citizens. Everyone is required to respect both the law and the rule of law.[19] Such is not the case in China today, the many protestations of the Chinese government to the contrary, and the Falun Gong have suffered greatly as a result.

Governmental Structures Implementing Violence

The strength of the people's dictatorship is manifested throughout the People's Congress in the form of democratic centralism, a key concept underlying socialist rule of law. Because the Communist Party represents the laboring people of the country, it is assumed that no need exists for sharing power with other political parties or other entities. Democratic centralism supposedly guarantees stability, ensuring that any minority obeys the majority, subordinates obey superiors, and local governments obey the central government.[20]

Just as the executive organs of the state must yield to the NPC as the ultimate authority, so, too, must the courts. Although the constitution identifies the Supreme Court as the highest judicial organ, responsible for supervising the administration of justice by the people's courts at various local levels, it also provides that the Supreme People's Court is responsible to the NPC and its standing committee, and the local people's courts at various levels are responsible to the organs of state power that created them. These provisions mean in practice that judicial autonomy is a myth in modern China.

Moreover, the ultimate power to interpret the law and the constitution is *not* granted to judges, who are trained in the legal profession, but to legislators, who may have no expertise in doing so, a process fraught with potential problems. If the judiciary finds a defendant not guilty, the verdict can be overridden politically. Thus, if the Communist Party has control over the state legislative apparatus, then the judiciary can be used as a tool of suppression by party leadership, a situation far from one that could be described as functioning under the rule of law. More than 60 percent of the NPC's body and the majority of the key government positions are held by Communist Party members, making such control more than a possibility.[21]

The top-down structure created by democratic centralism and the large number of party members holding key government positions, coupled with the doctrine of these members adhering to party policy, gives the central Chinese Communist Party (CCP) leadership the ability to control most of the state's decisions and brings into serious question the idea of separation of party and state. The CCP leadership can easily turn party policy into state policy, as it has demonstrated with Falun Gong, regardless of what is stated in the PRC Constitution and the CCP constitution. James Tong amply demonstrates how the CCP-dominated governmental structure has initiated, sanctioned, and directed the violence against the Falun Gong and by so doing has effectively strengthened its own position in Chinese society.[22] Indeed, observers might be tempted to believe that the campaign against the Falun Gong might have had as a major focus the rejuvenating of the CCP in China.

Detailed Timeline of Official Actions against the Falun Gong

Given the monolithic and unchecked political structure just outlined, the full power of the state was turned on the Falun Gong very quickly and efficiently, as shown by this timeline of official actions taken.

On July 22, 1999, three months after the original demonstration at the "forbidden city" and after much secretive planning and organization by the government, the Ministry of Civil Affairs under the State Council issued a decision that banned "the Research Society of Falun Dafa and the Falun Gong organization under its control." The Ministry of Security issued a notice that prohibited the displaying of "public marks"—signs or advertisements—promoting Falun Dafa, distributing of promotional materials, gathering to perform exercises or promotional activities, and participating in sit-ins, petitions, demonstrations, and other activities that opposed the decision to ban the group's activities.[23] These decisions led immediately to the arrest of thousands of Falun Gong leaders across China.[24]

On August 29, 1999, the General Office of the State Council issued notice no. 77/1999, which expanded the ban to other similar *qigong* groups and activities. It designated such activities as "illegal gatherings" that "endangered public security, disrupted social order and harmed social stability."[25] In October 1999 thousands of Falun Gong practitioners went to Beijing after hearing that the PRC parliament would debate a bill to criminalize Falun Gong and other religious groups labeled as "evil cults" by the government.[26]

On October 30, 1999, the Standing Committee of the NPC passed a "Decision on Banning Heretical Organizations and Preventing and Punishing Heretical Activities." This called for a major crackdown on "heretical organizations such as Qigong and other forms." It has since been applied retroactively to practitioners who engaged in banned activities prior to that date.[27]

On the same day, the Supreme People's Court *and* the Supreme People's Procuratorate issued a joint judicial interpretation titled "Explanation on Questions concerning the Concrete Application of Laws Handling Criminal Cases of Organizing and Making Use of Heretical Organizations." The interpretation applies Article 300 of the criminal code to those illegal groups that have been found using religion, *qigong*, or other things as a camouflage, deifying their leaders, recruiting and controlling their members, deceiving people by creating and spreading superstitious ideas, and endangering society. The interpretation goes on to detail the punishment for those found guilty of violating the law. Some of the violations include besieging government organizations, enterprises, or institutions, holding demonstrations to disrupt public places for religious activities, resisting the ban, or publishing or distributing illegal material. The interpretation goes on as follows:

The offences of establishing or using sects to organize, scheme, carry out and instigate activities of splitting China, endangering the reunification of China or subverting the country's socialist system should be handled according to relevant laws on endangering state security offences, as stipulated in the Criminal Law.[28]

On November 5, 1999, the Supreme People's Court issued Notice 29, which instructed local and military courts in how to handle cases of people involved in crimes for "organizing or using heretical organizations, particularly Falun Gong." It also called on the courts to "unify their thinking" and to "grasp the heretical character of Falun Gong" and the "threat" it posed, as well as to "fully understand" the spirit of important directives given to central authorities about "how to deal with and resolve the Falun Gong question." The notice further states that:

Courts at all levels must be "fully aware" of the "important, complex, and long-term" nature of this "struggle" and they must make it their "serious political duty" to punish "every kind of heretical organization crime." Courts at all levels must handle these cases under the leadership of the party committees. Higher courts are to supervise lower courts and use the media to publicize significant cases in order to increase the social impact of the trials. Other means should also be found to publicize the trials so as "to educate the large masses of people" and to make them aware of the "heretical organizations" that were "opposing science, humanity, society and the government."[29]

This decree seems to fit into the conception of socialist legality and the use of the court system as an instrument to suppress dissent and "educate" the masses. The tone of the notice seems to convey the message "vigorously convict." It also makes reference to the court's political duty, even though the state and the party are supposedly separate entities, according to the PRC constitution. Finally, the notice refers to the importance of educating the masses about the heretical nature of Falun Gong and its posited opposition to science, society, and government.

On November 24, 1999, the Ministry of Public Security issued "Regulations on Managing Mass Cultural and Sports Activities." This was intended to ban large public gatherings, especially those involving *qigong* groups that "threaten national security and public order." Nine specific types of gatherings are forbidden under the regulations, including those that:

violate principles of the constitution, or endanger national security and public order, infringe upon customs of ethnic minorities, violate ethnic unity and instigate national separatism, propagate superstition and heresy, pornography and violence that are detrimental to the health of the people.[30]

Virtually any group's activities could be suppressed under these provisions. The regulations also state that "mass congregations shall not be held near places of governmental agencies above the local level, at radio or television stations, foreign embassies and consulates, military establishments and other vital institutions."[31] The regulations empower the police to detain and fine people found in violation of them.

The Chinese Government in Action against the Falun Gong

As already noted, the announcement of the systematic and carefully planned campaign against the Falun Gong on July 22, 1999, led directly to many actions, including the arrest of thousands of movement leaders, a "media tsunami" of articles and programs attacking the Falun Gong, and many other efforts to suppress the movement.[32] The efforts involved governmental entities at every level and all of the resources of the mass media in China. These immediate actions were followed by very systematic and effective programs to force Falun Gong practitioners to recant and renounce the movement, and some of the program involved severe violence against participants.

In February 2001, less than two years after the massive demonstration at party headquarters that provoked the campaign against Falun Gong, President Jiang Zemin summoned more than two thousand top party officials to Beijing for a rare closed-door meeting. All of the senior central officials, top party leaders from each province, and leaders of the military, the judiciary, and government ministries attended. The reason for the meeting was to ensure that the "Party remained united against the campaign to crush the Falun Gong, as well as supportive of the decision in 1989 to use troops against the democratic protesters in Tiananmen Square."[33]

All seven members of the standing committee of the party's politburo stood up at this unusual meeting to endorse the anti–Falun Gong campaign as an "urgent necessity." President Jiang and other top leaders made it clear that they planned to crush the Falun Gong movement before the end of their terms at the 2002 party congress. Jiang went on to accuse local officials of not enthusiastically stamping out the movement and of allowing practitioners to go unhindered to Beijing to protest. After the meeting, government officials briefed party organizations and government agencies throughout the PRC about the official anti–Falun Gong policy.

This meeting serves as an indication of how important these two issues are to the PRC political leadership. According to Erik Eckholm and Elisabeth Rosenthal, whose article draws heavily on interviews with two officials who disagree with the party's approach, party leaders asserted that *Falun Gong had become a tool of the West and the CIA*, which they believed were directly nurturing and protecting the Falun Gong organization. James Tong agrees with this assessment as well.[34] This was apparently the major justification given for the entire ad hoc process that had been implemented to exert control over Falun Gong.

In December 2001 Beijing imposed a ban on using the Internet to organize or coordinate the activities of "evil cults."[35] Coupled with the state council's ban on the Falun Dafa organization in July, the regulations and Internet ban seem to contradict several rights guaranteed in the PRC constitution, including citizens' rights to enjoy freedom of speech, press, assembly, association, procession, and demonstration, which are protected under Article 35. These other actions of the Chinese government clearly show the level of concern about the Falun Gong and the immense power of the state when it focuses on the suppression of a minority faith.

Framing the Falun Gong as an "Evil Cult" and the Influence of the Western Anticult Movement

On November 13, 2000, the China Anticult Association (CACA)—a nonprofit organization purported to have no relationship with the government—was established to support the government's anticult position. Comprising scholars, religious leaders, and journalists, the group was charged with educating the public about the threat posed by "evil cults."[36] Systematic efforts have also been made to define so-called cults as political, not spiritual, groups. In a memorandum on the Falun Gong, CACA outlined the international threat that "evil cults" pose to society. According to the document:

> [T]he influence of cults has been spreading throughout the world . . . and poses an international public hazard, a reverse tide to the progress of social development.
>
> Falun Gong and other cults do their utmost to deify their leaders, fabricate heretical fallacies, profane human dignity, endanger social stability, and deceive kind-hearted people in order to realize their evil goal of opposition to mankind, society and science.[37]

The international threat was expanded upon by Li Dongsheng, special advisor of the Chinese delegation, at the fifty-seventh session of the UN Commission on Human Rights. Li called upon the international community to act together to eradicate "evil cults," which he identified as a danger to women's rights and interests. According to Li, Falun Gong practiced inhumane mind control upon women, thereby depriving them of their freedom of expression.[38]

Efforts have also been made to recast the government's crackdown as a legitimate action against criminals, not religious followers. Yao Chenglin, deputy director of the Shandong provincial judicial department, laid out the legal argument against the Falun Gong. According to Yao, at least six laws and regulations have been violated. Several of these violations are directly related to Falun Gong doctrine, falling within the realm of religious belief. According to Yao, the group publicized fallacies of idealism, feudalism, and superstition and spoke against modern science. These fallacies conflict with Articles 20 and 24 of the constitution, which require the state to promote the development of natural and social sciences and to oppose feudal and other corrosive ideas.[39] The arguments put forth by Yao may be seen as an attempt to limit the fundamental right of freedom of belief and are thus illegitimate under customary international law. However, other violations cited by Yao relate to illegal practices pursued by the Falun Gong. Crimes included failing to register with the proper department; organizing demonstrations; and publishing materials advocating feudalism, superstition, theism, and idealism.[40]

As described earlier, anticult movement (ACM) ideology asserts that the cult threat poses a serious danger to society. However, most of the claims put forth by the ACM lack empirical verification or general acceptance within the scientific community.[41] Nonetheless, China has incorporated many ACM theories into its campaign against the Falun Gong. The China Association for Science and Technology concluded the following (emphasis added):

> Li [founder] and his cult took advantage of the *psychological vulnerability* of Falun Gong practitioners and tried all out to *dominate their minds*. The cult not only *harmed the practitioners and their families*, but also threatened the political and *social stability* of China.[42]

According to CACA, the Falun Gong uses "evil fallacies to control its followers' minds with the aim of doing severe harm to society." Using a much-disputed statistic, the organization cites government claims that "more than 1,700 people have died from the cult's mental control."[43] Not surprisingly, no scientific evidence is presented to support the notions that Li is able to control his followers' minds.

The most compelling evidence concerning China's adoption of the ACM's theories is found in a CACA book that was put together after an international symposium in Beijing in November of 2000.[44] Attendees included several proponents of anticult government intervention, particularly from France. Alan Vivian, then head of the Center against Mental Manipulation, was among those in attendance. Vivian, then president of France's Interministerial Mission for the Fight against Cults, played an important role in the push for anticult legislation in the 1990s.[45]

Five characteristics promoted by the American Family Foundation, a prominent anticult organization, can supposedly be used to identify a cult:

1. pyramid structure with authority at top
2. charismatic or messianic leader
3. use of deception to recruit and to raise funds
4. isolation from society
5. use of mind-control techniques[46]

These criteria were incorporated into the interpretation of the October 30 anticult legislation.[47] In addition, the CACA conference proceedings book (2000) is filled with allusions to these factors and other ACM theories. Examples include references to leader worship; the secretive nature of the cult; the belief that only the cult knows the truth; psychological manipulation and mind control; dictatorial organizational structure; the severing of family ties; the prohibition of criticism; and so on.[48]

The use of mind control by the Falun Gong is described further by another CACA (2001) publication: "A fraction of addicts have degenerated into slaves under Li's mental yoke."[49] A member's suicide note is quoted to bolster this claim: "With my brain under control of Li Hongzhi the bastard, I felt his mental torture and persecution every day. I can not stand any longer and survive such mental torture."[50]

The influence of the ACM on China's official policy toward the Falun Gong appears to be strong. Its claims have been used to support the government's position that legitimate spiritual groups have not been targeted for suppression. Thus, the government asserts that religious freedom has not been jeopardized by the crackdown. It is not clear whether the government's attempt to start an international campaign against cults is merely the product of a perceived political threat or a genuine acceptance of the ACM's views.[51] Another possible interpretation is that the campaign was launched in part to rejuvenate the Chinese Communist Party, using the Falun Gong as a focus of the effort.

A Specific Case of Death in Prison

The PRC government press agency has claimed that all government acts concerning Falun Gong have been in accordance with the law.[52] The PRC has dismissed claims by Amnesty International that torture of Falun Gong practitioners is occurring. Moreover, officials have stated that none have been beaten to death in labor camps. At the same time, the government has forbidden foreign media and human rights observers from investigating any accusations of torture.[53]

The case of Chen Zixiu, which has received considerable international attention, calls the PRC's assertions into question. Chen's death and the controversy surrounding it were brought up by the UN's Committee against Torture, when the PRC's compliance with the treaty came up for review.[54] This is but one of possibly hundreds, even thousands, of claimed deaths since the crackdown on Falun Gong began.[55]

Chen was arrested in Beijing for being in violation of the July and October 1999 government ban on protesting the crackdown on Falun Gong. She had just arrived in Beijing and was arrested when she admitted to the police that she was a Falun Gong practitioner. According to cellmates, Chen was told that her beatings would continue until she renounced her faith. Chen eventually died in custody. She was fifty-eight years old. Chen's daughter, Ms. Zhang, was told that her mother's death was the result of a heart attack. Zhang was herself eventually arrested for pursuing the case with authorities and sentenced to fifteen days in jail for "distorting facts and disturbing social order."[56]

Chen Zixiu lived and eventually died in Weifang, a city in Shandong Province about 250 miles southeast of Beijing. James Tong claims that in this province in the six years after the ban was established there have been 282 deaths in prison, one of the highest totals of all provinces.[57] This appears to show that the violence is systematic and stems from policies adopted by Beijing.[58] Office 610, a government bureau that has been coordinating the crackdown on Falun Gong, issued an order in December 1999, telling officials of local governments that they would be held responsible if they did not stem the flow of protesters to Beijing. Weifang officials were under strict orders to eliminate, by any means possible, the large number of protesters coming from their district. According to Falun Gong practitioners, Weifang officials told Chen that they had been told by the central government that "no measures are too excessive in wiping out Falun Gong."[59]

The Government's Reaction to Claims of Prison Deaths

During a news briefing on March 21, 2000, PRC ambassador Qiao Zonghuai publicly defended the PRC's ban of Falun Gong. Qiao labeled Falun Gong as a cult that has harmed society with its antihumanity, society, and science rhetoric and said that the ban was justified and was being carried out in strict accordance with the law and international human rights requirements. The PRC was following the common practices of all governments regarding cults, he added.[60] Qiao reiterated that the PRC is a country that follows the rule of law and that no legitimate *qigong* activities would be suppressed.[61]

The statements made by Ambassador Qiao and the PRC delegation run counter to the well-documented crackdown taking place in the PRC. Judicial interpretations passed down to the lower courts encourage the judiciary to convict Falun Gong defendants in an effort to educate the masses. Attorneys are discouraged from taking Falun Gong practitioners' cases. In addition, the freedom of belief espoused by the PRC delegation and protected by law does not extend to Falun Gong practitioners. In sum, the Communist Party's and the government's response to the Falun Gong movement violates citizens' right to a legal defense, freedom of religion, speech, and assembly, which are enshrined in the constitution and in treaties to which the PRC is a party.

Finally, the deaths that have taken place in Chinese prisons indicate that torture is occurring in PRC detention facilities with the approval of party leadership. The PRC's refusal to investigate these claims does not support the party's stated dedication to protecting citizens' rights.

Conclusions

China's political apparatus, which is dominated by the Chinese Communist Party, has mounted a massive and unprecedented campaign against the Falun Gong, and that campaign has apparently sanctioned violence against practitioners, especially those incarcerated as part of the government's reeducation efforts toward more recalcitrant leaders of the movement. The coordinated effort to involve the entire political and governmental apparatus, including the courts, in China in this campaign of repression was impression, as was management of the state-controlled media in China. As a result, the Falun Gong movement is much smaller and now functioning underground in China to a much more limited extent.

The extent of the violence against the Falun Gong may be surprising to observers from the West, who are more accustomed to less direct and punitive actions against minority religions. Indeed, in some Western nations, particularly the United States, efforts to exert control over minority faiths has often been relegated to the realm of self-help actions and private organizations that have carried out limited efforts against "cults." Some checks and balances were available to the participants, usually through the use of the courts and other private organizations (such as the ACLU) to defend themselves and their members. In China, however, the actions were organized by the state and were pervasive in their effects. There were no checks and balances operating in China, and the will of a small cadre of CCP leaders was implemented with a vengeance—and very effectively—as the statistics cited earlier demonstrate.

Why this massive campaign was launched remains a question. It could be that CCP leaders were genuinely concerned about the possibility of a massive movement emerging from the Falun Gong that would attempt to overthrow the government. It could also be that they were genuinely concerned about the health and welfare of the millions of practitioners who were involved in the movement. However, more cynical explanations suggest that the effort to suppress the Falun Gong was otherwise motivated and included an effort to demonstrate what might happen to anyone or any group that questioned the authority of the CCP leadership. Also, the massive reeducation effort that was a part of the suppression of the Falun Gong involved many thousands of party members, who were themselves led to rededicate themselves to the maintenance of the place of the CCP in Chinese society. Perhaps we will never understand the full motivations of those who organized and directed the suppression of the Falun Gong in China, but we do know that it was very effective and that it led directly to the harming of thousands of practitioners.

NOTES

This chapter makes use of and updates some of the material contained in Bryan Edelman and James Richardson, "Falun Gong and the Law: Development of Legal Social Control in

China," *Nova Religio* 6(2): 312–31 (used with permission). Moreover, some of this material (also used with permission) is taken from Bryan Edelman and James Richardson, "Imposed Limitations on Freedom of Religion in China and the Margin of Appreciation Doctrine," Journal of Church and State 47(2) (2005): 243–67.

1. See James W. Tong, *Revenge of the Forbidden City: The Suppression of the Falungong in China, 1999–2005* (New York: Oxford University Press, 2009), 32–51, for a thorough discussion of the events leading up to this fateful decision to demonstrate at Chinese Communist Party headquarters. Also see Ian Johnson, "China's Rigid Policies on Religion Helped Falun Dafa for Years," *Wall Street Journal* (Dec. 13, 2000). The April 25, 1999, demonstration was one of a dozen or more mass demonstrations that Falun Gong launched against media outlets and governmental bodies that had been critical of the movement. Most of the earlier demonstrations had been successful in that the authorities had capitulated to Falun Gong's demands. Johnson won a Pulitzer Prize in 2001 for his thorough coverage of the Falun Gong movement and efforts to suppress it.

2. See Tong (32–51) for details of the covert actions that took place over this three-month period and an analysis of why the campaign was organized in this manner.

3. See Tong (78–101) for details of this impressive effort, which made use of all forms of media. Tong notes, for example (211), that during this three-month period thirty-one anti–Falun Gong books were produced and appeared in bookstores within a week of the July 22 ban. Another fifty titles were available within a month. He also reports (78) that within four weeks of the official ban the state news agency issued 1,650 press releases and 290 articles promoting the government's view of the Falun Gong. In addition, the China Central Television Corporation aired 1,722 news items totaling more than one hundred hours of programming on the Falun Gong.

4. Falun Gong practitioners, comp. and ed., *A Report on Extensive and Severe Human Rights Violations in the Suppression of Falun Gong in the People's Republic of China, 1999–2000* (Buford, GA.: Golden Lotus, 2000).

5. Tong (122–26).

6. Tong (209–11) discusses the revealing fact that, years after the ban of the Falun Gong, law-enforcement entities remain geared to take actions against the Falun Gong, which suggests that the movement still exists. He also notes that a number of practitioners are still choosing prison instead of recanting, plus thousands who had recanted have renounced their recantations.

7. No explanation is given as to what constitutes "normal" religions. However, it can be assumed that all groups that fall outside of the five officially recognized religions and their accompanying registered organizations are outside of this parameter. These organizations include the China Buddhist Association, the China Taoist Association, the China Islamic Association, the Chinese Patriotic Catholic Association, the National Administration Commission of the Chinese Catholic Church, the Chinese Catholic Bishop's College, the Three-self Patriotic Movement of the Protestant Churches of China, and the Christian Council. See Evans, C. (2002). "Chinese law and the international protection of religious freedom," *Journal of Church and State*, 44 (4), 758. Chinese Law, 9. The eight organizations are under the oversight of the Office of Religious Affairs. Registration requirements and other measures prevent these religious organizations from spreading easily, particularly to the countryside. There has been, however, discussion in China over the utility of the registration process. For example, according to Liu Peifeng of Tsinghua University, "The

registration of religious groups should be considered only for corporations. Those who are not registered should also be recognized with legal status." See Liu Peifeng, "On the Registration of Religious Groups," in *Comparative Approaches to Regulating Religion and Belief: State Authority and the Rule of Law* (Beijing: Chinese Academy of Social Sciences).

8. Elliott Abrams, Testimony on Religious Freedom in China and the May 1, 2000, Report of the U.S. Commission on International Religious Freedom, 2000WL19304286 (Washington, D.C.: Federal Document Clearing House, 2000), para. 7.

9. See James T. Richardson, "Definitions of Cult: From Sociological-Technical to Popular-Negative," *Review of Religious Research* 34 (1993): 348–56, and Jane Dillon and James T. Richardson, "The Cult Concept: A Politics of Representation Analysis," *Syzygy: Journal of Alternative Religion and Culture* 3 (1994): 185–97, for discussions of the politicization of the term *cult*.

10. Niu Aimin, "Organizing and Using Cults for Criminal Activities Must Be Punished—Criminal Law Expert Zhou Zhenxiang on Falun Gong's Cult Nature and Applicability of Criminal Law," Xinhua News Agency, Nov. 4, 1999.

11. This conference was attended by more than one hundred supposed experts from eight nations: the United States, Republic of Korea, Japan, France, Uganda, Canada, and Russia. The goal was to focus on promoting international cooperation and academic studies for the prevention and control of destructive cults. See Alex Buchan, "Fears Grow That China Will Class House Churches as Cults: Authorities Urged to Determine Whether Cults Are Harmful to Society," Compass News, Dec. 8, 2000. http://www.worthynews.com/726-fears-grow-that-china-will-class-house-churches-as-cults.

12. John Pomfret, "China Expands Crackdown on Religions Not Recognized by the State," *Washington Post* (Sept. 5, 2000).

13. Frank Langfitt, "Places of Worship Razed in Chinese Crackdown: Campaign Focuses on Heavily Christian City of Wenzhou," *Baltimore Sun* (Dec. 15, 2000); Abrams, Testimony on Religious Freedom, para. 11.

14. Chih-yu Shih, *Collective Democracy in China* (Hong Kong: Chinese University Press, 1999), 3–16.

15. Some scholars now claim that the focus of socialist legality has shifted away from the suppression of the ruled class and toward resolving conflicts among the ruling class and its allies in the unified front. Under this newer development, law is no longer simply a tool of the ruling class. Instead, legislative power enables the state to regulate the behavior of both the ruled and the ruling class. See ibid.

16. It is not the ruling class but the state that must write the laws. Under such a system, laws are no longer a tool of the ruling class. Because legislative power enables the state to regulate the behavior of the ruled and the ruling class, the ruling class must maintain supervisory power over state institutions. See ibid.

17. Ibid., 40.

18. Ibid., 52.

19. In the PRC, the legal system is measured by its ability to provide a legal basis for the proletarian ownership of the means of production. According to the scientific socialist principles of the rule by law, the will of individuals cannot be formed into law. If the will of a leader is exercised against the interests and the will of the ruling class, his class will abandon him. The Western interpretation of rule of law views democracy as a means for individuals to participate in politics and protect their rights. The socialist view of the rule

of law sees democratic participation as a means to harmonize the contradictions among the people through consultation. The PRC ruling party associates democracy with rule by law. Western democracies equate the concept with the rule of law. See ibid., 56–57, for a discussion on the rule of law and the rule by law in PRC and the West.

20. Ibid., 59.

21. Chen, *Restructuring Political Power in China*, 163.

22. Tong, 19–20, 137–40, 157–64, and especially 213–19.

23. The following piece of legislation can be found in Amnesty International, "China: The Crackdown on Falun Gong and Other So-called 'Heretical Organizations,'" Mar. 23, 2000, http://www.amnesty.org/en/library/info/ASA17/011/2000 (accessed Aug. 2, 2010).

24. Tong (52–78) gives great detail about the massive number of arrests that occurred just before and after the July 22 set of edicts.

25. Amnesty International, "Crackdown on Falun Gong," 18.

26. Ian Johnson, "China's Crackdown Feeds Falun Dafa's Defiance," *Wall Street Journal* (Oct. 29, 1999).

27. Amnesty International, "Crackdown on Falun Gong," 19.

28. Ibid., 20.

29. See ibid., 21. The term translated here as "heretical organization," *xiejiao zuzhi*, is often translated into English as "evil cult" or "destructive cult." Amnesty International explains that *xiejiao zuzhi* "refers to a large variety of groups and has a far broader meaning than 'cult.' 'Xiejiao zuzhi' is the expression used in Chinese legislation, in official statements and by the state media to refer to a wide range of sectarian and millenarian groups, or unorthodox religious or spiritual organizations, and other groups, which do not meet official approval. 'Xiejiao zuzhi' can be translated as 'heretical organization,' or 'evil,' 'heterodox' or 'weird religious organization.'" See ibid., 43, note 1. "Heretical organizations" spread superstitious beliefs that threaten the development of the socialist state and hinder efforts to educate the people in the sciences.

30. Ibid., 22.

31. Ibid., 22.

32. See Tong (52–78) for details, and Tong (100) for the phrase "media Tsunami."

33. Erik Eckholm and Elisabeth Rosenthal, "China's Leadership Pushed for Unity," *New York Times* (Mar. 9, 2001). Meetings such as this are rare. With the president (Jiang), the premier (Zhu), and the NPC chairman (Wan) set to step down from power in 2002, it was important for the ruling conservative faction of the party to maintain its control over the party and for Jiang to solidify his legacy.

34. Tong refers to this justification in several places in his book.

35. Tyler Marshall and Anthony Kuhn, "China Goes One-on-One with the Net," *Los Angeles Times* (Jan. 27, 2000).

36. The CACA was founded by He Zuoxiu, a famous seventy-three-year-old physicist with the Chinese Academy of Sciences. It is interesting to note, like Mr. He, that a large proportion of listed academics within CACA are in fields (e.g., aerodynamics, hydroelectric engineering, optics) that have no relationship to the study of religion or new social movements; one member is curator of the Chinese Museum of Science and Technology. For a list of CACA's membership see China Anticult Association, "Memorandum on 'Falun Gong' Proposal for Establishment of a China Anticult Association," Nov. 13, 2000,

http://web.amb-chine.fr/flg/07/004.htm. Tong (117) also talks about the involvement of university scholars in the reeducation enterprise that was organized by the government.

37. China Anticult Association, "Memorandum on 'Falun Gong' Proposal for Establishment of a China Anticult Association," Nov. 13, 2000, http://web.amb-chine.fr/flg/07/004.htm.

38. Xinhua, "Delegate: China Bans Falun Gong to Protect More Women from Danger," *China Daily* (Apr. 4, 2001); http://www.zhihui.com.cn/storydb/news/0410.htm.

39. H. Wang and X. Zhang, "What Laws, Regulations Has Illegal 'Falun Gong' Organization Violated?" *China Daily* (Aug. 17, 1999).

40. Ibid.

41. See James T. Richardson, "Regulating Religion: A Sociological and Historical Introduction," and other chapters in James T. Richardson, ed., *Regulating Religion: Case Studies from around the Globe*, 4 (New York: Kluwer Academic, 2004).

42. Xinhua, "Scholars Probe into Psychological Effect on Falun Gong Practitioners," *China Daily* (July 6, 2001).

43. Xinhua, "China Anti-cult Association Condemns Falun Gong's Inhumanity," *China Daily* (Dec. 19, 2001).

44. This conference was attended by more than one hundred supposed experts from eight nations: United States, Republic of Korea, Japan, France, Uganda, Canada, China, and Russia. The goal was to focus on promoting international cooperation and academic studies for the prevention and control of destructive cults. Alex Buchan, "Fears Grow That China Will Class House Churches as Cults: Authorities Urged to Determine Whether Cults Are Harmful to Society," Compass News, Dec. 8, 2000, available online at: http://www.hrwf.net/English/china2000.html#Fearsgrowthatchinawilclasshouse.

45. Cyrille Duvert, "Anti-cultism in the French Parliament," in Richardson, *Regulating Religion*, 43.

46. American Family Foundation; http://www.csj.org/studyindex/studycult/study_whatisdescult.htm (accessed Aug. 2, 2010).

47. The Supreme People's Court and the Supreme People's Procuratorate issued a joint judicial interpretation titled "Explanation on Questions concerning the Concrete Application of Laws Handling Criminal Cases of Organizing and Making Use of Heretical Organizations." The interpretation applies Article 300 of the criminal code to those illegal groups that have been found using religion, qigong, or other things as a camouflage, deifying their leaders, recruiting and controlling their members, and deceiving people by creating and spreading superstitious ideas, and endangering society (Edelman and Richardson, "Falun Gong and the Law," 317).

48. Bryan Edelman and James Richardson, "The Crackdown on the Falun Gong: Western Influence and the Development of the Anti-cult Movement in China," paper presented at the 2002 conference of the Society for the Scientific Study of Religion, Salt Lake City, Utah.The conference was held from October 31 through November 3, 2002.

49. Chinese Anticult Association, *Combat Evil Cults, Safeguard Human Rights* (Beijing: China Science and Technology Press, 2001), 20.

50. Ibid., 21.

51. The Chinese government's attempts to use the post-September 11 environment to label the Falun Gong as "terrorists" suggest that the use of the ACM's theories is a product of political opportunism, not conviction. See Willy Wo-Lap Lam, "Widening the

Definition of Terrorism," Jamestown Foundation, 2000; http://www.jamestown.org/programs/chinabrief/single/?tx_ttnews%5Btt_news%5D=3759&tx_ttnews%5BbackPid%5D=191&no_cache=1. (accessed Oct. 14, 2010).

52. Ian Johnson, "China Describes Its Punishment of Falun Dafa Followers," *Wall Street Journal* (Jan. 19, 2001).

53. Ian Johnson, "China Reports Suicide by Sect Adherent," *Wall Street Journal* (Feb. 20, 2001).

54. Ian Johnson, "China Tells U.N. It Did No Wrong in Death of Falun Gong Member," *Wall Street Journal* (May 8, 2000).

55. Tong (125).

56. Ian Johnson, "A Grieving Daughter Traces a Tortuous Path," *Wall Street Journal* (Oct. 2, 2000).

57. Tong (123).

58. Ian Johnson, "How One Chinese City Resorted to Atrocities to Control Falun Dafa," *Wall Street Journal* (Dec. 26, 2000).

59. Ian Johnson, "Practicing Falun Gong Was a Right," *Wall Street Journal* (Apr. 25, 2000).

60. This claim may be related to the PRC's interest in a number of actions taken by other governments around the world, including even some Western democracies, to exert control over "sects and cults." See James T. Richardson and Massimo Introvigne, "'Brainwashing' Theories in European Parliamentary and Administrative Reports on 'Cults' and 'Sects,'" *Journal for the Scientific Study of Religion* 40(2) (2001): 143–68.

61. "Chinese Ambassador Defends Government Banning of Falun Gong," Xinhua News Agency, Mar. 21, 2000; http://miksa.ils.unc.edu/sgbrowser/btrec/doc_show.cgi?id=28135&id2=XIE20000321.0164 (accessed Oct. 14, 2010).

19

Deprogramming Violence: The Logic, Perpetration, and Outcomes of Coercive Intervention

Anson Shupe

Violence directed against individual members of unconventional religious groups (as opposed to actions directed specifically against collectivities) in order to discourage their further membership, at least as far as North America is concerned, has been an inevitable component of the post–World War II "new religious movements" (NRMs) controversies. Predominant among those NRMs generating concern were ones of Eastern (e.g., the Divine Light Mission, Transcendental Meditation, the Hare Krishnas), sectarian Christian (e.g., the Children of God, the Unification Church), and quasi-therapeutic (e.g., est, the Church of Scientology, Synanon) origins. Indeed, violent reaction accompanied the growth and visibility of such movements beginning roughly in the late 1960s and early 1970s and eventually winding down during the first decade of the twenty-first century.

One brief chapter cannot begin to provide an adequate bibliography of the context of what I have previously termed a "culture war," a war or struggle for public legitimacy in which the tactics used included propagandistic accusations and counteraccusations rich in hyperbole and occasionally violence against persons. Over the aforementioned time period a wide variety of social scientists, historians, and religious scholars from various countries have analyzed numerous specific movements (such as the messianic Unification Church of the Rev. Sun Myung Moon [e.g., Bromley and Shupe 1979] or the Church of Scientology International [e.g., Lewis 2009]), as well as the reasons that persons joined (Barker 1984) or defected (Wright 1987; Barker 1988; Bromley 1988, 2004). They have also analyzed groups and movements that opposed those NRMs, what is hereafter termed the "anticult movement" (ACM) (Shupe and Bromley 1980; Beckford 1985; Bromley and Shupe 1993; Shupe and Darnell 2006), while various lawyers and legal experts (e.g., Delgado 1977, 1979–1980; Lemoult 1978) sought these groups' legal definitions and the status of various related issues.

However, here my purpose is narrower. I examine deprogramming as a form of violence, the targets of which were (most often) individual NRM members. Such violence accompanying the NRM controversy was "inevitable" for a three-stage syllogism of reasons:

First, the persistent emergence and operations of new and/or culturally unconventional religious groups seeking/competing for adherents and resources are both historically "normal" and to be expected in large pluralist societies with constitutional assurances that the federal government (with ultimate monopoly on the means of force) will neither establish any official state-sponsored religious denomination nor interfere with the (relatively) free exercise of religious tenets.

Writing on the broad sweep of religious diversity in North America, historian Philip Jenkins (2000, 4, 5) observes in *Mystics and Messiahs* that "there is no period, including colonial times, in which we cannot find numerous groups more or less indistinguishable from the most controversial movements [today]." He further adds, on the "normalcy" of such religious innovation, that "far from being a novelty, cults and cultlike movements have a very long history on American soil. Extreme and bizarre religious ideas are so commonplace in American history that it is difficult to speak of them as fringe at all."

Second, the resulting competition (and frictions) among struggling NRM groups and with more traditional established entities (which usually disapprove of the latter), not to mention the family institution (among others), the goals, lifestyle, and boundaries of which often run counter to those of NRMs, together virtually ensure the existence of countermovement organizations opposed to specific NRMs or more generally the entire category of such spiritual alternatives (Bromley and Shupe 1993). The emergence of such countermovements is as "normal" under the conditions of laissez-faire religious practice as the NRMs themselves and in fact predictable. Jenkins (2000, 10) reminds us that "Just as no era lacks its controversial fringe groups, so no era fails to produce opponents to denounce them; anti-cult movements are also a long-established historical phenomenon."

Third, in a religiously pluralist society with a constitutionally enshrined tradition that proscribes government interference with any but the most egregious religious practices (i.e., ones that threaten state interests) and with no particular government agencies (or ministries) that are responsible for oversight of any religious bodies, those persons, families, or groups with grievances against NRMs find themselves thrown back on their own grassroots measures, such as the following: personally initiated and underwritten litigious actions on behalf of individuals; lobbying politicians, officials, and agencies, denouncing NRMs as dangerous and pushing for selective legal strikes against NRMs to inhibit the latter's activities; attempting to sway and enlist mass media to promulgate negative, alarming images of such groups; and/or directly seeking to extract particular individuals, usually loved ones and family members, from such groups, usually against their free will while simultaneously cultivating ideological justifications or rationales for what are desperate and (if the group members are adults) illegal measures.

This in fact is what happened and led to the practice of deprogramming, the focus of this chapter. In sum, as I have previously noted (Shupe 2009, 271):

> Attempts to work through existing social control agencies, such as law enforcement agencies and political representatives at every level, to remedy their situations by finding assistance to remove their (frequently) adult family members from NRMs often proved futile. Thus the ACM was established in grassroots fashion as a third-party social control institution. When families tried to remove by force loved ones from these controversial groups they resembled the vigilante committees of America's frontier past.

The Domain of Deprogramming

What is deprogramming? The answer has varied according to the audience; it has alternately been cast as heroic, altruistic intervention or as predatorily mercenary kidnapping. As deprogramming attracted notoriety for violating religious liberties and during the 1970s gained for its practitioners the unsavory reputation of being ersatz, unaccredited mental health adventurers, what advocates and critics have meant by the term has shifted over time.

Deprogramming's essential definition is succinctly stated in the following excerpt from an essay by sociologist David G. Bromley (1988, 203): "[t]he practice of forcibly separating individuals from religious groups for the purpose of inducing them to remove their memberships." According to ACM spokespersons of the 1970s–1990s, deprogramming is the logical antidote to a presumed process of "programming" (i.e., manipulative personal autonomy-stealing mind control that is presented as poorly understood except by supposedly nefarious "cult" leaders and also by a small corps of enthusiasts who claim to be able to reverse its effects). The element of violence and the essence of deprogramming begin with the adverb "forcibly" in Bromley's definition. To suggest deprogramming without violence, I maintain, is not really deprogramming but rather posing a fatuous dodge by those who wish, perhaps, to neutralize their own association with the activity. Otherwise, the term makes no logical sense seen in terms of the ACM since mind-controlled NRM members should be incapable of disobeying NRM leaders and of independently considering disaffiliating.

Both academic and anticult movement advocates have typically traced the origins and practice to Theodore Roosevelt ("Ted") Patrick. During the early 1970s

Patrick was a special representative for community relations living in San Diego, California, and that post-Watts riot state. He first began forcible abductions of family members who fell under the influence of Children of God missionaries. The word "deprogramming" initially appeared in Patrick's coauthored book, *Let Our Children Go!* (Patrick 1976), and, according to Patrick, as well as many who experienced the technique, it basically followed a four-step strategy: (1) orchestrate the abduction of an unsuspecting NRM member, often with the assistance of associates and the collusion of family members (who are the true clients of the procedure); (2) secure that NRM member under restraint and/or guard at a remote place (such as a motel, rural home, or farm); (3) argue and through one-sided harangues, often in the emotional context of tearful family members and their repeatedly stated benevolent fiduciary concerns, demand a recantation; and (4) threaten never to allow the target's return to the NRM, occasionally intimating violence or actually committing it. The goal in social psychological terms is to force the family NRM member to contemplate the cost-benefit equation of standing steadfast in the new faith membership in the face of such relentless pressure versus abandoning the faith in question and returning "to the fold" of a forgiving, appreciative family and, of course, being released.

This description is, of course, an ideal type since many deprogrammings never went beyond stages (1) and (2); other deprogrammings were abandoned at stage (3) in the face of the member's complete intransigence; and more than a few members eluded and escaped the deprogrammers somewhere during stages (1), (2), or (3). In addition, in some deprogrammings, as I indicate in the final section of this chapter, events did indeed escalate into further psychological and physical violence beyond the initial abductions. It is unnecessary to present a lengthy history of the deprogramming phenomenon since these exist elsewhere. For more detailed descriptions of deprogramming's rationale and practice, as well as its associated controversies, see Bromley (1988), Bromley and Shupe (1993), Shupe, Bromley, and Darnell (2006), and Shupe (2009).

Moreover, it has been documented from organizational newsletters, inner-organizational memoranda, organizational telephone records, budgetary evidence, and correspondence among activists that the practice of coercive (i.e., violent) deprogramming was inextricably involved in the goals, operations, and/or concerns of the earliest-to-mature social-movement organizations, finances, and ideologies of the ACM, from the earliest FREECOG (Free the Children of God) to the California-based CFF (Citizens Freedom Foundation) to the later Chicago-based CAN (Cult Awareness Network) and AFF (American Family Foundation). During the late 1980s and 1990s, for example, the two largest ACM groups, AFF and CAN, while two distinct operations, nevertheless held joint annual meetings at which coercive deprogrammers and sympathizers recruited clients and held their own openly advertised/scheduled caucuses at convention sites. The AFF and CAN also possessed closely interlocking directorships, enjoyed overlapping financial/legal arrangements and frequent cordial correspondence, and championed each other's activities, though CAN lionized deprogrammers more than AFF (for details of these assertions see Shupe and Darnell 2006, 47–67, 79–184; for a history of the ACM's first decade during the 1970s, see Shupe and Bromley 1980.)

As noted, the term *deprogramming* has not always been used consistently. At times critics of the ACM countereffort have seemed to refer to almost any activities of the latter that involved contact, persuasion, or discussion with NRM members. Likewise, ACM activists could assert that simply chatting with a "cultist" on the remote chance it would engender doubt about the person's faith, whether or not it ever did, could be considered a form of deprogramming. Such usages muddy the water, however. When reading ACM newsletters beginning in the early 1970s and their editors' frequent paeans to deprogrammers like Patrick (and later others such as Joe Alexander Sr. and Galen Kelly), one clearly sees that both early and later advocates of the practice unabashedly assumed it entailed a dramatic element of psychological intimidation, physical abduction, and eventual confinement.

Later ACM advocates rather disingenuously tried to distinguish between "coercive" deprogramming and, apparently somewhat euphemistically, a noncoercive (i.e., nonviolent) form. Some even imply it can be voluntary and, curiously, "contractual" between deprogrammer and target. (For such a description of this imagined possibility see the statement of two ACM psychologists, Michael D. Langone and Paul R. Martin, in Shupe and Darnell 2006, 97.) For another example, see the writings of Steven Hassan (1988, 1994), an ex-Unificationist who underwent coercive deprogramming and later became a bona fide degreed counselor and who describes himself as once a proponent and practitioner of the coercive type. Later Hassan publically repudiated the coercive variety and turned to a "gentler" form, which he calls "strategic intervention therapy," though he still maintains that the targeted groups are inherently "destructive." With Hassan's nonviolent intervention technique, however, one wonders how many members of NRMs would willingly enter into such "discussions" with the foreknowledge that the "counselor's" entire purpose is not to ascertain their religious sincerity or their full understanding of the extent of their spiritual decisions but rather is to convince them to abandon their faith. (Recall that the "counselor's" client is not the NRM member but rather someone else who hired the "counselor.")

Toward the end of the twentieth century, as academic writings, legal decisions in punitive lawsuits, and some media reporting began to move toward an awareness and even condemnation of the civil liberties implications of violent kidnappings and involuntary confinement of legal adults, some (though not all) former ACM deprogrammers began to relabel themselves "exit counselors" or "interventionist specialists and counselors" and seek at least the color of professionalization with proposed codes of ethical conduct during their interventions (Shupe and Darnell 2006, 96–101). Thus, by the early 1990s "few of the persons practicing coercive deprogrammings, even if they continued to conduct them, cared to be known as deprogrammers" (Shupe and Darnell 2006, 100). The term was simply becoming too odious.

Finally, by what social science standard could deprogrammings—discounting the persons who claimed professional fees for their services to arrange and manage such intervention using force, as well as the client families who, out of the best of benign motives, paid for these activities—be technically considered violence? Iadicola and Shupe (2003, 23), after an exhaustive review of previous sociological (and other) definitions of violence, present their own: "Violence is any action or structural arrangement that results in physical or nonphysical harm to one or more persons." In an elaboration of this succinct yet inclusive delineation, they take into account that the action in question must be willingly or deliberately committed (even without full knowledge of its harmful consequences), may be justified or unjustified from the standpoints of various actors, may be purely physical or purely psychological or entail both dimensions, and may or may not be recognized as violence per se by the perpetrating actors or recipients.

As I elaborate in the final section, deprogramming meets each of these criteria and can thus be considered violence.

A Brief Note on the Prevalence of Coercive Deprogrammings

Narrowing the definition of deprogramming to episodes that involved abductions and nonvoluntary confinement, we encounter obstacles to estimating with any accuracy their prevalence since the early 1970s. The situation is analogous to attempting to estimate total occurrences of clergy malfeasance across denominations in North America or even within a single centralized case such as the Roman Catholic Church during any given time frame (Shupe 2007, 7–8). In both situations there is no private or state agency monitoring or compiling ongoing independent statistics. When deprogrammings with negative outcomes have been reported (usually but not always by victim targets) to law enforcement, these instances would usually either be subsumed under broader law-enforcement categories of kidnapping, assault, or criminal confinement or (as when family members' involvement complicates things) surface in civil suits against ACM groups and individual deprogrammers, minus the criminal label. Thus, their uniqueness is statically lost and we have to turn to very incomplete alternatives sources.

The deprogrammers' own claims, when available, seem boastful and unrealistic. For example, as early as 1976 Ted Patrick claimed to have performed 1,600 deprogrammings, while his protégé, Joe Alexander Sr., variously claimed in newspaper articles only two months apart during the late 1970s "career" totals of 1,000 and then later 600 deprogrammings (Shupe and Bromley 1980, 138). Bob Brandyberry claims to have deprogrammed approximately 500 persons between 1980 and 1989, 150 of which he labeled "illegal" deprogrammings or "false imprisonments" (his words), and 75–85 percent of those were direct CAN referrals (Shupe and Darnell 2006, 85). Meanwhile, CAN staff member Marty Butz, on the witness stand under oath in a civil suit, estimated that he had made 400–500 referrals to deprogrammers, often over the telephone (Shupe and Darnell 2006, 88). There is no immediate way of verifying these figures, and they may be only loose estimates.

In fact, deprogrammings, successful or otherwise, would *not* be reported for a number of reasons. A major one is the obvious embarrassment of the family clients, often parents. The rhetoric of mind control may have somewhat exonerated parents of any responsibility for a member's NRM affiliation (e.g., "I am not the type of parent who would raise the type of child who would join a strange cult; therefore, my child must have been brainwashed into it."), but public knowledge of a deprogramming would nonetheless create a minor scandal and call awkward attention to internal family strains. While some deprogrammers have staged press conferences and showcased their intervention successes before the media (both for self-aggrandizement and to bolster the entire ideological edifice of deprogramming and anticultism), we have good reason to think that this embarrassment factor is the reason that many families, reunited after an abduction and "restoration," have virtually disappeared from public view as ex-NRM members got on with their lives. This supposition is circumstantially supported by the fact that ACM organizations were always strapped for cash, "head office heavy," and "rank-and-file light." Many, if not most, families simply ceased financial donations, subscriptions, and contacts with ACM groups once their loved ones had abandoned the NRMs (Shupe and Bromley 1980, 196–97). (Membership in NRMs also indicated a parallel high turnover; see Bromley and Shupe 1979, 70–71; Wright, 1987). It is safe to conclude that many, if not most, successfully deprogrammed targets did not in turn become moral entrepreneurs or later ACM crusaders. Along the same lines of embarrassment, of course, deprogrammers would not want to widely advertise their ineffectiveness, whether the fault lies in their theory or their bungling of details, when deprogrammings go bad.

A further reason for silence could also be the logical fear of NRM groups' retaliation in the event of publicizing attempted or successful deprogrammings, though this seems improbable given the relative lack of resources and limited time/attention span of most groups that could be devoted to such ACM harassment.

Two relevant but limited studies of deprogrammings with samples of convenience deserve mention here. Psychologist Trudy Solomon (1981) examined one hundred cases of ex-NRM members, not all of whom had been deprogrammed as a means of exit, and found that those who had been deprogrammed later showed more evidence of adopting ACM rhetoric and explanations of their previous NRM behavior than did the "walkaways" (i.e., those who simply disaffiliated on their own). However, Solomon was unable to extrapolate the size of the larger population of either group beyond her sample.

Sociologist David G. Bromley (1988) has performed the most detailed analysis of deprogrammings with a relatively large sample of 397 cases of Unification Church members, taken from January 1973 to July 1986. While Bromley acknowledges that a "complete census" of coercive deprogrammings, successful or otherwise, will probably never exist, his triangulation of sources to construct his saturation sample uncovers a number of interesting patterns for a single NRM during a specified time period. Among them are the following: The average age of those deprogrammed was twenty-two years, and more than 20 percent were twenty-six years of age or older; the most successful deprogrammings occurred with those who had been members for the shortest time and were the youngest; and of the deprogramming cases he amassed, deprogrammers had a two-thirds success rate. Most significant, despite "outside" assumptions that these members of one of the highest-profile NRMs were strongly attached to their membership status, Bromley observes that most were either in the process of newly affiliating *or disaffiliating already*.

Finally, a wealth of deprogramming cases are known from published accounts, such as newspaper and popular magazine articles, ACM newsletters, social science monographs, journal articles, and available court testimonies (including transcripts, depositions, notarized statements, and affidavits). Some comments on these sources are relevant.

The social science sources, which have most often critically analyzed deprogramming logic and procedures, are biased in the direction of offering spectacularly unsuccessful intervention episodes. Furthermore, it is not unusual to see the same cases repeated anecdotally in more than one source. Examining three of my own coauthored writings on the ACM (*The New Vigilantes*, Shupe and Bromley 1980; *Strange Gods*, Bromley and Shupe 1981; *Agents of Discord*, Shupe and Darnell 2006), I enumerated forty-five in-depth discreet cases from a variety of groups, including the Hare Krishnas, the Alamo Foundation, the Unification Church, and the Church Universal and Triumphant, almost all of which were deprogrammings that failed or went seriously awry. I was reminded, however, that dozens of other cases in our files had to be editorially discarded and never used for publication because of their redundancy with ones used and/or limitations of page space. Likewise, the cases that appear in attorneys' offices and in court in civil suits understandably involve failed deprogrammings and are brought by angry NRM members.

On the other hand, cases covered in newspaper and magazine articles have typically involved successful interventions, particularly during the 1970s and 1980s, when the alleged "cult menace" and sensational "mind-control" themes made lurid copy. However, innumerable examples of local media coverage of successful interventions that never made the national wire services, in which both the "rescuers" and the "rescued" were without national stature and quickly faded into oblivion, are no longer available.

Perusal of ACM newsletters, such as complete sets from the existence of the Citizens' Freedom Foundation (1974–1985) and the Cult Awareness Network (1986–1996) reveals more issues than not touting the efficacy of deprogramming with success stories and portrayals of deprogrammers as heroic humanitarians. When they do mention deprogrammings that fail, it is not the fault of the technique but rather of some other outside (perhaps misguided) interference.

So what can we conclude about the prevalence of deprogrammings? During the "culture war" of NRMs versus the ACM from the 1970s to the 1990s, one would get the impression from the mass media that the occurrence of deprogrammings was extensive. Yet the same media coverage also misled many, including ACM enthusiasts, to believe that the "cult presence" in North American was also alarmingly extensive and growing. We know now that the latter was much exaggerated. Thus, based on more than thirty years of personal familiarity and more than forty years of work with all of these types of materials, I would conservatively estimate that the total number of cases of deprogramming violence against members of various NRMs, whether the technique succeeded or not, involves three thousand to four thousand persons (plus or minus five hundred), some of whom were deprogrammed more than once. Depending on how nuanced one's definition of "violence" is, of course, the number could be somewhat higher.

The Harms of Deprogramming

Elsewhere (Shupe and Darnell 2006, 76–92), a typology of roles in the anticult social movement economy has been developed to place various actors who helped amass, monitor, and/or distribute its resources:

player-mavericks: the actual deprogrammers, who had no (or only minimal) ties to the various ACM organizations (e.g., CFF, CAN)
operatives: these people also performed entrepreneurially in deprogrammings but were more integrated into the formal ACM as a result of referrals from deprogramming clients; they in turn paid kickbacks from their deprogramming fees
managers: full-time staff members, officers, board members, and network regulars who served as ACM spokespersons and ran the groups' daily affairs
counselors and *experts*: academic, law-enforcement, clerical, financial, and legal professionals whose important function was to validate ACM claims and/or provide fiduciary expertise to aid the managers

In this final section, however, the focus is on a sampler of outcomes of quintessential deprogrammings that illustrate a typology of actual (not hypothetical) harms. Because of extensive primary-source documentation for even the following short collection of cases, readers are referred here only to more readily available publications containing extensive citations of those sources. In addition, because so many of the harms that occur often covary simultaneously with others, this sample consists, for the sake of manageability, of a relatively small number of cases.

Following the Iadicola-Shupe definition of violence, I present two broad categories of harm, psychological and physical, subdivided by discreet varieties of each with brief selected cases. Other varieties of psychological and physical violence are certainly possible, but those presented here are grounded in available cases.

Psychological Violence

ONGOING FEARFULNESS. Abductions occur abruptly and unexpectedly from the target's perspective. Thus, the shock component is compounded for the target by the mystery (at least in the beginning) of what is happening and (later) how long the loss of freedom is to continue. This prolonged uncertainty is a potent psychological tool for deprogrammers. For example, thirty-three-year-old Karen Lever, president of her own Sunyata Systems, Inc. (a computer consulting firm she founded in Redmond, Washington) was returning to Seattle by airplane from a Southern California business trip in late May 1990. Her parents, who were afraid she was falling under the influence of the late Dr. Frederick Lenz's Rama seminars, hired deprogrammers to abduct her in the parking lot of Seattle's SeaPac airport as she was putting her luggage in her car. Without warning or explanation she was grabbed and shoved into a van, and a hand was clamped over her mouth as the van passed by the parking lot toll booth. She underwent eights days of confinement. Understandably anxious about both her own safety and pending business affairs in her self-run corporation (which meanwhile went unattended), she was told that her deprogramming was more important than the success of her business (Shupe and Darnell 2006, 56–57).

In a second case that demonstrates the cultivation of ongoing uncertainty, during the late 1970s Unification Church member Arthur Roselle was abducted by lead deprogrammer Steven Hassan and manhandled during an initial escape attempt (he suffered cuts and bruises). Hassan corroborated Roselle's version that, because of Roselle's escape attempt and his continued resistance, Hassan had to have Roselle's hands and feet tied, yet the latter still managed to kick a hole in a wall while being held down on a bed. When Roselle refused to eat during the confinement, Hassan told him that he (Hassan) had a registered nurse ready to give Roselle intravenous glucose to sustain his life (Shupe and Darnell 2006, 150–51).

In a third case, in which parental responsibility and anxiety were used as "hooks" to break down resistance, thirty-year-old LaVerne Collins-Macchio, a member of the Church Universal and Triumphant (CUT) and a single mother, was violently abducted from her Boise, Idaho, home one November evening at 8:30 P.M. in 1991. She had just put her four young sons to bed. Lured to the front door of her home by a deprogrammer posing as a pizza delivery man, she, clothed only in her nightgown, was abruptly seized, dragged into the street, and thrown into a van waiting at the curb. Her mother had feared a millennial Jonestown-like aspect of CUT and hired the deprogrammers. During her seven-day confinement, Collins-Macchio was moved to three different locations (a remote cabin, then two motel rooms). She resisted harangues about her church and others successfully but spent much of the time worrying about her children's safety (Shupe and Darnell 2006, 171–72).

SHOCK OF VIOLATED TRUST. Family relations ideally and in reality are often grounded in implied trust. Loss of this trust is a psychological injury. Three years after two failed deprogrammings orchestrated by her parents, during one of which they tried unsuccessfully to have her committed to the Menninger Clinic at Topeka, Kansas), college graduate and Unification Church member Pam Fanshier told Bromley and Shupe (1981, 177–80) during an interview in the spring of 1978 that she believed her parents had finally come to accept and appreciate her new sectarian religious commitment. Therefore, she felt confident inviting them to her June graduation ceremony at the Unification Theological Seminary at Barry town, New York. She was first to go home to visit for a few days, and then she and her parents were to return to Barrytown for graduation. Instead, they drove her to a trailer in the woods nowhere near her home, intending to hold her for an indefinite period until, this time, the intervention finally "took." But she escaped again, more distrustful of her parents than ever.

DEHUMANIZATION AND ABASEMENT. Besides having one's autonomy stolen and legitimate anger dismissed as simply "that's only the cult talking," verbal abuse has been common. Perhaps the most famous string of invectives was unleashed by deprogrammer Ted Patrick during an intervention with Unificationist Wendy Helander (the target of several previous deprogrammings) when he accused her of being a prostitute for the Rev. Sun Myung Moon and called her "a vegetable, a dog, a bitch" (Bromley and Shupe 1979, 232). Likewise, during the five-day abortive deprogramming of Henry Kuegel, a member of the Church Universal and Triumphant, three deprogrammers (and several assistants) mocked Kuegel's determination to observe his church's norm of celibacy before marriage. One of the deprogrammer's girlfriends came down to the basement where Kuegel was confined, laughed at his beliefs about celibacy, flirtatiously touched his body, and contemptuously told him, "In the church, you men don't have genitals!" (Shupe and Darnell 2006, 94).

ESTRANGEMENT FROM LOVED ONES. In the Pam Fanshier case, Fanshier in 1975 had to obtain a lawyer to defend her against her parents' claims that, as a Unificationist "cult" member, she was therefore mentally incompetent. It took a psychologist and a court-appointed psychiatrist to declare her in good mental health. *But she still was able to reconcile with her parents at that point.* After the 1978 failed deprogramming prior to her preseminary graduation, however, the wedge of distrust was driven further in the direction of estrangement.

In the case of Janet Schumacher, a thirty-one-year-old woman who had *not* joined any sectarian religious group, her mother simply disapproved of her daughter's fiancé, Charles Connefax, and hired Ted Patrick to deprogram Janet out of the engagement. The deprogramming failed miserably, Janet married Connefax anyway, and then she had both her mother and Patrick charged with second-degree kidnapping (Shupe and Bromley 1980, 134).

INTIMIDATION AND THREAT OF PHYSICAL HARM. This dimension of psychological harm is so pedestrian (i.e., so common in accounts of deprogrammings and certainly in the many interviews that my colleagues and I have conducted over the years) that it needs little illustration. The threat of physical harm to the deprogrammee or damage to one's possessions, coupled with the uncertainty of the confinement factor, are potent psychological issues in the minds of deprogrammees who continue to resist, at least as they report their experiences. For example, Walter Robert Taylor, a member of the Old Catholic Order, was abducted by four deprogrammers, physically threatened repeatedly, and had not only his monastic clothes ripped off his body but also his vestments and rosary beads destroyed in front of him (Shupe and Darnell 2006, 154).

Physical Violence

CONFINEMENT: BINDING, GAGGING, SMOTHERING, AND BATTERY. Physical confinement is an indispensable element of deprogramming violence. The deprogramming procedure is, after all, involuntary, so in order for the deprogrammer to launch a verbal attack on a person's NRM of choice, the deprogrammee must be held still or forced to listen. This means loss of physical freedom and mobility. The removal of the target to a secure, often rural, place out of normal earshot of curious neighbors or passers-by is therefore often necessary.

Thus, Ted Patrick's attempted deprogramming of a LaGrange County, Indiana, Old Order Amish wife in 1990 involved shuttling the woman (and, most uncharacteristically, also her adolescent daughter, who was *not* the target of an intervention) through Indiana, Ohio, Michigan, and finally to a secluded farmhouse in Illinois, from which she escaped when he let her go to the bathroom by herself. (The wife was in no NRM but had been reconsidering the Amish biblical basis for not operating gas-combustion engines, which worried her husband, Patrick's client. See Shupe and Darnell 2006, 169–70). Likewise, Pam Fanshier on her third deprogramming was taken to the remote Kansas countryside (from which she escaped and had to tramp to a phone barefooted through dense woods; see Bromley and Shupe 1981, 179). Pentecostal Jason Scott, in the case that ended up bankrupting the Cult Awareness Network after a lawsuit in 1996, was driven to an oceanside cottage. He was taken from the getaway van in handcuffs, and one of his deprogrammers held him by a nylon strap as a "leash." In the cottage the deprogrammers installed thick nylon straps over windows in a meshlike pattern, guarded the two doors of the cottage, and after removing Scott's shoes installed motion detectors in the room where he was held (Shupe and Darnell 2006, 182).

However, deprogrammers also have an immediate need to hold and silence the target at the moment of abduction since these initial acts of intervention frequently take place in public or quasi-public areas. Hence, Karen Lever had to be silenced and her struggles immediately discouraged when deprogrammers seized her in Seattle's airport parking lot. She stated that "One man sat on me and clamped his hand over my mouth to prevent me from screaming as we passed through the airport parking pay booth. I could hardly breathe" (Shupe and Darnell 2006, 56).

Before his longer five-day confinement, Jason Scott was abducted outside his grandparents' home, where he had been living apart from his mother (client of deprogrammer Rick Ross). Three men (one weighing three hundred pounds) sat on his arms, legs, and torso after he was dragged into a van. He was handcuffed at the wrists, his ankles were tied with rope, and his mouth was gagged with duct tape from ear to ear (Shupe and Darnell 2006, 181).

In the same way, Debra Dobkowski, who in 1992 was mistakenly abducted by Galen Kelly, a former private investigator who turned deprogrammer, instead of the intended target, was held down and immediately silenced in the van into which she was thrown (Shupe and Darnell 2006, 94–95). James Boland, a Roman Catholic who converted first to Baptist and then Pentecostal, and LaVerne Collins-Macchio were both smothered and silenced with hands covering their faces. Collins-Macchio was thrown face down onto the floor of a van, and two men sat on her while keeping the palms of their hands over her mouth. According to later court records, when finally released after a week's confinement, she still had finger-shaped bruises around her mouth, one arm, and a leg (Shupe and Darnell 2006, 55–56, 171).

Later injuries from targets who resisted their abductions are legion, as well as stories of minor batterings during deprogrammings (e.g., shoving, slaps to the face). Jason Scott and Karen Lever, for example, received numerous cuts, scratches, and bruises from just their abductions, as did Collins-Macchio. Many targets have reported temporary circulation problems in limbs caused by binding. Given that so many targets, when abducted and confined as legal adults, feel outraged at their treatment, it is understandable that they would receive injuries.

INAPPROPRIATE SEXUAL CONTACT AND ABUSE. There had been rumors of sexual abuse, sexual harassment of targets by deprogrammers, and deprogrammers having sex with targets held in confinement ever since the early days of the ACM (Shupe and Darnell 2006, 93–95), but it was not until the demise of the Cult Awareness Network in 1996 and various previous lawsuits against CAN, as well as the accompanying release of the group's internal memoranda, correspondence, and evidence of deprogrammer contacts (thanks in part to a Chicago bankruptcy court), that evidence corroborating these rumors could be collected. Consider, for example, the earlier 1981 case of Stephanie Reithmuller, a twenty-year-old Cincinnati woman whose parents feared she was in danger of becoming a lesbian. Presumably as some sort of radical sexual-orientation intervention, Stephanie was repeatedly raped, even gang-raped by deprogrammers, during her confinement of several days (Shupe and Darnell 2006, 56).

Less dramatic examples exist as well. Stories of sexual advances by deprogrammers and deprogrammers having sex with their targets seem to have been endemic, according to the testimonies of ex-CFF and ex-CAN staff members (Shupe and Darnell 2006, 92–93). I have already mentioned Henry Kuegel of the Church Universal and Triumphant, whose deprogrammers mocked his belief in sexual abstinence before marriage. James Boland, a Roman Catholic, was not alone in having his genitals fondled by deprogrammers, while Debra Dobkowski was repeatedly groped during her confinement in a van during an abortive deprogramming attempt (Shupe and Darnell 2006, 93–95). More examples can be found in the earlier sources and their primary references. Suffice it to point out, finally, that Cynthia Kisser, executive director of CAN, when she was expressly asked under oath during a lawsuit about deprogrammers having sex with targets (i.e., as sexual assault) would not condemn it as a perversion. (On the climate of tolerance for deprogrammers and sexuality, see Shupe and Darnell 2006, 96ff.)

HYGIENIC NEGLECT. Something *never* openly discussed in the mainstream social science literature is the issue of deprogrammers allowing in some cases an almost total suspension of targets' hygienic needs. This harm is as much a psychological issue of self-esteem and debasement as a form of physical abuse. It has occurred during extended deprogramming confinement, either chosen by targets to avoid the deprogrammers' sexual harassment or forced on the targets. This is truly an unsavory form of violence, one that causes obvious physical discomfort for the targets. It is worth providing a few examples to illustrate this aspect of deprogramming harms.

Karen Lever was guarded twenty-four hours a day and denied privacy either to use the toilet or to shower. The door to the bathroom was nailed open, and she was never out of the direct view of at least one deprogrammer. For eight days she refused to take a shower under these conditions (Shupe and Darnell 2006, 57). After being fed greasy, undercooked foot that induced diarrhea and stomach cramps, Jason Scott was forced to use a toilet in a bathroom with the door nailed open, always accompanied by two male deprogrammers (Shupe and Darnell 2006, 93). Former Unification Church member Arthur Roselle (who eventually left the church voluntarily sometime after his attempted deprogramming) recalled his hygienic treatment by deprogrammer Steven Hassan. Roselle had his hands bound constantly during the confinement and was always escorted to the bathroom, not allowed to wash or shave, and was "helped" while he was urinating. Because of embarrassment, Roselle forced himself not to have bowel movements during that time (Shupe and Darnell 2006, 93–94). Claire Kelley, another Hassan target, spent three days confined in a New Hampshire log cabin and always had a guard present when she used the bathroom.

Undoubtedly the grossest illustration of hygienic neglect/abuse and deprogrammer insensitivity toward a target occurred with Debra Dobkowski, the unfortunate young Virginia woman who was mistakenly abducted instead of the intended target, whom she apparently resembled. During a long drive to the intended target's mother's home, who confirmed the mistake after seeing the wrong woman in custody, Debra's menstrual period began. During that trip and the long return to where she was first abducted, Debra was forced to sit in her own menses despite appealing to one of the deprogrammers (a woman) for tampons. She was not allowed to clean herself but finally given tampons after a special stop was made to obtain some; however, she was not allowed to leave the van to use them. The deprogrammers, after stealing money from her purse, dumped her in the original parking lot in her soiled clothing (Shupe and Darnell 2006, 95–96).

After the Cult Awareness Network declared bankruptcy in 1996, the North American anticult effort lost its national-level clearinghouse for deprogramming referrals. The American Family Foundation has always continued to operate more as a think tank and an educational foundation and did not engage in such referrals. Thus, individual deprogrammers have had to rely almost exclusively on word-of-mouth referrals and posting sites to advertise their services on the Internet. As a result, it appears that the prevalence of deprogrammings has since fallen precipitously.

Conclusion

In this chapter I have surveyed the logic of deprogramming from the standpoint of its advocates, identified its objective status as a form of violence, provided a rough idea of its prevalence, and offered illustrations of various forms of psychological and physical harms incurred by various targets of the procedure. It should be obvious that the concept of a gentle, voluntary, or nonviolent deprogramming is semantic waffling, a form of what in the sociology of deviance is termed *neutralization* and ultimately an oxymoron. Such interventions are hardly unique in the history of North American religion and an understandable, if desperate, strategy employed in predictable ways by anticult countermovements.

REFERENCES

Barker, Eileen. 1984. *The Making of A Moonie: Brainwashing or Choice?* New York: Blackwell.
———. 1988. "Reflections from the Unification Church." In *Falling from the Faith: Causes and Consequences of Religious Apostasy*, ed. David G. Bromley, 166–84. Newbury Park, Calif.: Sage.
Beckford, James A. 1985. *Cult Controversies: The Societal Response to the New Religious Movements*. New York: Tavistock.
Bromley, David G. 1988. "Deprogramming as a Mode of Exit from New Religious Movements." In Bromley, *Falling from the Faith*, 185–204.
———. 2004. "Leaving the Fold: Disaffiliating from New Religious Movements." In *The Oxford Handbook of New Religious Movements*, ed. James R. Lewis, 298–314. New York: Oxford University Press.
———, and Anson D. Shupe Jr. 1979. "Moonies." In *America: Cult, Church, and Crusade*, ed. David G. Bromley and Anson D. Shupe Jr. Beverly Hills, Calif.: Sage.
———. 1981. *Strange Gods: The Great American Cult Scare*. Boston: Beacon.
———. 1993. "Organized Opposition to New Religious Movements." In *The Handbook on Cults and Sects in America*, ed. David G. Bromley and Jeffrey K. Hadden, vol. A, 177–98. Greenwich, Conn.: JAI.

Delgado, Richard. 1977. "Religious Totalism: Gentle and Ungentle Persuasion under the First Amendment." *Southern California Law Review* 51 (November): 47–58.

———. 1979–1980. "Religious Totalism as Slavery." Special Issue: "Alternative Religions: Government Control and the First Amendment." *New York University Review of Law and Social Change* 9(1): 35–56.

Hassan, Steven. 1988. *Combatting Cult Mind Control: The #1 Best-selling Guide to Protection, Rescue, and Recovery from Destructive Cults*. Rochester, Vt.: Park Street.

———. 1994. "Strategic Intervention Therapy: A New Form of Exit-counseling for Cult Members." In *Anticult Movements in Cross-cultural Perspective*, ed. Anson D. Shupe Jr. and David G. Bromley, 103–25. New York: Garland.

Iadicola, Peter, and Anson D. Shupe Jr. 2003. *Violence, Inequality, and Human Freedom*, 2d ed. New York: Rowman and Littlefield.

Jenkins, Philip. 2000. *Mystics and Messiahs: Cults and New Religions in American History*. New York: Oxford University Press.

LeMoult, John. 1978. "Deprogramming Members of Religious Sects." *Fordham Law Review* 46: 599–640.

Lewis, James R., ed. 2004. *The Oxford Handbook of New Religious Movements*. New York: Oxford University Press.

———. 2009. *Scientology*. New York: Oxford University Press.

Patrick, Ted. 1976. *Let Our Children Go! With Tom Dulack*. New York: Ballantine.

Shupe, Anson D., Jr. 2005. "Deprogramming." In *Encyclopedia of Religion*, editor in chief Lindsay Jones, vol. 4, 2291–93. New York: Thomson.

———. 2007. *Spoils of the Kingdom: Clergy Misconduct and Religious Community*. Urbana: University of Illinois Press.

———. 2009. "The Nature of the New Religious Movements–Anticult 'Culture War' in Microcosm: The Church of Scientology versus the Cult Awareness Network." In *Scientology*, ed. James R. Lewis, 269–81. New York: Oxford University Press.

———, and David G. Bromley. 1980. *The New Vigilantes: Deprogrammers, Anticultists, and the New Religions*. Beverly Hills, Calif.: Sage.

———, and Susan E. Darnell. 2004. "The North American Anti-cult Movement: Vicissitudes of Success and Failure." In Lewis, *Oxford Handbook of New Religious Movements*, 184–201.

Shupe, Anson D., Jr., David G. Bromley, and Joseph C. Ventimiglia. 1979. "Atrocity Tales, the Unification Church, and the Social Construction of Evil." *Journal of Communication* 29 (Summer): 42–53.

Shupe, Anson D., Jr., and Susan E. Darnell. 2006. *Agents of Discord: Deprogramming, Pseudo-science, and the American Anticult Movement*. New Brunswick, N.J.: Transaction.

Solomon, Trudy. 1981. "Integrating the 'Moonie' Experience: A Survey of Ex-members of the Unification church." In *In Gods We Trust: New Patterns of Religious Pluralism in America*, ed. Thomas Robbins and Dick Antony, 275–95. New Brunswick, N.J.: Transaction.

Wright, Stuart. 1987. *Leaving Cults: The Dynamics of Disaffiliation*. Washington, D.C.: Society for the Scientific Study of Religion (monograph).

Afterword

In the introduction I raised the issue of how difficult it was to predict NRM violence in the context of a discussion of 3HO, a new religion in which I was involved for three years. The 3HO contained all of the endogenous factors found in the NRMs that explode (or implode) in dramatic ways, plus a martial tradition that seemed custom made for a violent outcome. Yet 3HO was never involved in violence.

As a number of contributors discuss in their respective chapters, another set of considerations for assessing an alternative religion's potential for violence includes exogenous factors such as embittered apostates and hostile parents of current members, "anticult" organizations, sensationalized media coverage, and provocative interventions by state control agencies (such as child protective services and law enforcement). As Elsberg discusses in her chapter, 3HO was able to respond to pressure from these various groups and agencies so that conflicts never escalated out of control. A raid by law enforcement is arguably the single most provocative act by outside forces, and 3HO communities were never raided. However, even the incorporation of such exogenous factors does not necessarily add up to a recipe for disaster.

For example, in 1984, acting on allegations of child beating, the Vermont State Police, armed with a court order and accompanied by fifty social services workers, raided the Island Pond Community homes and took 112 children into custody. The district judge ruled that the search warrant issued by the state was unconstitutional, and all of the children were returned to their parents without undergoing examinations. Island Pond was one of the Twelve Tribes Messianic Communities, a group that in 1984 was known as the Northeast Kingdom Community Church. A totalistic group with an apocalyptic theology, the Twelve Tribes/Northeast Kingdom had emerged from the Jesus People Revival in 1972 under a charismatic leader. Hostile ex-members, an antagonistic local press, and direct intervention by members of the Cult Awareness Network (then known as the Citizens Freedom Foundation) came together to convince state law-enforcement officials to undertake the raid. In other words, the Island Pond raid contained all of the ingredients—endogenous, as well as exogenous—that analysts have put forward as factors contributing to violent outcomes. Yet there was no violent outcome (King 2008).

Similarly, the Family International, originally known as the Children of God, had all of these endogenous and exogenous components. Additionally, the group had been highly confrontational in its early years and condoned unusual sexual practices such as the controversial practice of "flirty fishing." After having avoided the public spotlight for years, it was subjected to a new wave of intensive negative media attention in the summer of 1993, following raids on members' homes in France and Argentina to investigate charges of child abuse. Like the Twelve Tribes, the members remained nonviolent, worked within official channels, and had their children returned. They were eventually exonerated of all charges (Oliver 1994).

Another, more recent parallel case is the Fundamentalist Church of Jesus Christ of Latter-day Saints (FLDS) in Texas. Like the Twelve Tribes and the Family International, the FLDS was also raided, with a similar outcome. It was obvious that no one in the relevant law-enforcement agencies had ever heard about the Short Creek Raid—a historically earlier law-enforcement fiasco that had taken place in Arizona (Bradley 1993)—much less bothered to learn the hard lessons that state of Arizona officials were forced to learn from that raid. Given these disconfirming examples, does it make any sense at all to try to predict NRM violence?

Current Models and Directions for Future Research

In May 2009 I had the pleasure of speaking with members of the National Centre for Terrorist Threat Assessment in Sweden. This center is charged with assessing the potential for violence of a wide variety of political and religious groups—not just alternative religions—in Sweden. A number of my colleagues in NRM studies had already spoken to this same group and had informed its members that there were no definitive criteria for predicting which New Religions might commit violent acts. In general, I have to agree with these colleagues, but that does not mean our research is completely bereft of insight.

In a number of different publications, Bromley and Melton have assessed the state of our knowledge about the NRM-violence connection and indicated directions for future research (Bromley and Melton 2002; Melton and Bromley 2009). In addition, Bromley has directly offered suggestions for public-policy makers and law-enforcement officials (2005). In this afterword, it seems appropriate to bring together elements of these assessments and suggestions with insights that can be derived from the chapters in the current collection.

As a preface to this discussion—and although there is near-universal agreement among mainstream scholars on this point—it still bears repeating that the popular stereotype of dangerous "cults" (or, in European parlance, "sects") is neither predictive nor explanatory. On the one hand, anticultists are typically willing to label hundreds of religious groups "cults," the vast majority of which will never become violent. On the other hand, asserting that a religious organization that has been involved in an act of violence is a "cult"—as if nothing else needed to be said—is rather like asserting that an individual involved in a violent incident is a member of a certain "violent" ethnic group. In other words, the structure of the assertion has the appearance of offering an interpretation, but it is an "explanation" that does not explain.

As discussed throughout this volume, prior research has called attention to two sets of factors—endogenous (internal characteristics of the religious group) and exogenous (external individuals, agencies, and organizations)—that regularly play a role in violent events involving alternative religions. These elements are not static. Rather, violence is almost always the result of a process of *polarization* that arises from an interaction between internal and external elements (Melton and Bromley 2002, 241–43). This interaction proceeds through a series of stages, and violent outcomes can be averted at any stage (Bromley 2002). What we can draw from this research is a model of NRM violence consisting of internal factors, external factors, and interactions among them. For ease of reference, we might refer to this as the internal/external interaction model.

This construct seems neat enough, except that the groups that have been involved in violence have demonstrated enough variability that we are forced to discuss them in terms of a spectrum or continuum (Melton and Bromley 2009, 39). Thus, for example, Heavens Gate represents a group that had minimal interaction with exogenous forces before its tragic demise, whereas Falun Gong represents precisely the opposite situation. The extreme variability among incidents of NRM violence recently prompted Melton and Bromley to speculate that "scholars may conclude that it is necessary to develop a typology of violent episodes for which related but distinct theoretical explanations are required" (2009, 40).

Another problem with the internal/external interaction model is that it is not reliably predictive. As we saw with the ill-considered law-enforcement raids carried out against the Twelve Tribes and The Family International, every factor can be present, and authorities can even initiate a confrontation with no one getting killed or seriously injured. As Melton and Bromley observe, "Both The Family and the Twelve Tribes were the targets of police raids against their communities, with The Family experiencing a number of raids in several different nations. In both instances the groups relied on judicial processes to resolve their disputes, and both groups were exonerated of the charges brought against them" (2009, 39).

In "Violence and New Religious Movements," Bromley (2004) indicates several directions for future research that might help us refine our current models. These include the observation that, thus far, research has focused on movements and not on agencies of social control such as law enforcement. Because control agencies are capable of escalating tensions or even initiating conflicts, they should be an integral part of researching NRM violence.

Another important observation is that, to date, researchers have focused their studies on rank-and-file members and low-level leaders of new religions (here Bromley is referring to studies of NRMs in general, not just studies of violent ones). He encourages social scientists to place greater emphasis on researching and understanding how movements work at the upper echelons, particularly the inner circle, where decisions are made and from where violent initiatives are likely to originate.

Other topics for research are movements and incidents in which violence was avoided. In different but related ways, Goldman's and Elsberg's chapters provide examples of this kind of research. One observation from these studies that might be extended to other situations is that members of both Rajneeshpuram and 3HO had economic and cultural resources that contributed to deescalating the potential for violence. In other words, members of these two groups were invested in the social order in ways that the members of Peoples Temple and the Branch Davidians were not.

Finally, social scientists are encouraged to study a greater diversity of groups involved in violence. Bromley mentions NRMs in non-Western contexts, such as the MRTCG, and different types of violent religious groups. Once again, the present collection takes a step in the direction suggested by Bromley.

Early Warning Signs and Suicide Cults

To shift the discussion back to public policy and law-enforcement issues, when I spoke with members of the National Centre for Terrorist Threat Assessment, I noted that several observable indicators that we might call "early warning signs" can indicate that a specific religious group might be dangerous or "going bad." I say "*going bad*" because NRMs tend to be dynamic and changing. Thus a problematic, potentially threatening group might transform into a much more stable, unproblematic group. On the other hand, in response to a variety of internal and external forces, a new religion that had previously been a relatively peaceful group might quickly develop into a threat. Along these lines, I believe the clearest danger sign is when religions—and, more specifically, when religious leaders—place themselves above the law, though certain nuances make this point trickier than it might first appear.

All of us, in some sphere of life, place ourselves above the law if only when we go a few miles per hour over the speed limit or fudge a few figures on our income-tax returns. Also, when push comes to shove, almost every religion in the world would be willing to assert that divine law takes precedence over human law—should they ever come into conflict. Hence, a group that, for example, solicits donations in an area where soliciting is forbidden should not, on that basis alone, be viewed as a potential danger to society. Exceptions should also be made for groups or individuals who make a very public protest against certain laws judged as immoral, as when a conscientious objector goes to jail rather than be drafted into the military.

On the other hand, it should be clear that a group leader who violates serious laws has already developed a rationale that could easily be used to legitimate more serious antisocial acts. Examples that come readily to mind are the following: Marshall Hertiff, founder/leader of Heaven's Gate, who regularly ducked out on motel bills and was once arrested for stealing a rental car; Luc Jouret, coleader of the Order of the Solar Temple (OTS), who was arrested after he illegally tried to purchase guns with silencers only two years before the first OTS murder-suicide incident; and Swami Kirtanananda, founder of the New Vrindavan community, who was caught authorizing the theft of computer software and raising money for fake charities before being arrested for ordering the murder of a community critic. Based on this pattern, I would certainly be inclined to take rumors about a religious group more seriously if I knew the leader had a history of trouble with the law.[1]

Another point I made to members of the National Centre for Terrorist Threat Assessment is that, though there is too much variability to delineate a set of clear criteria for predicting violence in the broader spectrum of nontraditional religions, the situation is different for NRMs involved in group suicides. In my chapter (Lewis 2005b) in *Controversial New Religions*, coedited with Jesper Petersen, I argue for the existence of a set of factors that *could* identify potential suicide groups.

The question I ask in that analysis is, What if, instead of seeking commonalities among the "big five" NRMs involved in violence, one focused instead on the three groups that imploded in group suicides—People's Temple, Solar Temple, and Heaven's Gate? While it is true that both the People's Temple and the Solar Temple also engaged in acts of murder, one could argue that these violent acts were aspects of the suicide event. It is thus possible to distinguish such suicide-related murders from the otherwise comparable violence initiated by the leadership of Aum Shinrikyo and other groups.

Though it is often more illuminating to complexify rather than to simplify certain phenomena, for my purposes I focused on distilling the details of these three groups down to a common core of shared traits. Though this approach is open to criticism—and would certainly never do for a comprehensive explanation—it nevertheless bears fruit as an analytical strategy. These traits are outlined and briefly discussed on pages 140–141 of Henrik Bogdan's chapter, "Explaining the Murder-suicides of the Order of the Solar Temple," in this volume.[2]

However, despite major areas of overlap with the other two members of the "big five," Aum Shinrikyo and the Branch Davidians, these latter groups lack several of the seven essential traits outlined by Bogdan on page 141. Specifically, David

Koresh did not segregate himself from unbelievers (Dawson 2002, 86–87) and was in good health immediately prior to the ATF raid on Mount Carmel. Koresh had also fathered a number of children he believed would eventually rule the earth—in effect, his successors. Asahara seems to have been in reasonably good health as well, plus he had already indicated to followers that his children would be his spiritual successors (though this successorship was rather vague at the time of the subway attack and clarified only later). Finally, though neither Aum Shinrikyo in 1995 nor the Davidians in 1993 were experiencing rapid growth, they were also not stagnant; both could have reasonably anticipated future growth.[3] In other words, the Davidians lacked four of these traits, whereas Aum Shinrikyo lacked three.[4]

In contrast to recent theorizing on the relational and processual aspects of violence (e.g., Bromley and Melton 2002), the approach of distilling a list of traits may strike some observers as static and regressive. Also, confining the discussion to specific internal factors seems to reproduce the flaws of anticult theorizing about cults (Hall 2002, 167), especially when that theorizing focuses on charismatic cult leaders (Melton and Bromley 2009, 46–47). So, to make certain my analysis is not misinterpreted, let me explicitly restate that my goal here is a very narrow one and is not intended to constitute a general theory—either of NRM-related violence or, for that matter, of suicide cults. Producing a truly comprehensive account of religious groups that have committed acts of mass suicide would necessarily go beyond the factors discussed earlier.

Triangulation and "Quadrangulation"

Though we lack a comprehensive model of NRM violence in general, we still have room to describe how those who are charged with handling a situation with a potentially violent NRM might best go about fulfilling their responsibilities. The manner in which law-enforcement officials responded to the Freemen standoff in Montana (Wessinger 1999) and the eschatological fervor of the Chen Tao UFO religion in Texas (Szubin, Jensen, and Gregg 2000) have been cited as exemplary models of sensitive police work that defused potentially volatile situations. In both cases, law-enforcement officials sought information from researchers, established a "meaningful dialogue" with the respective groups, and actively tried to sort out misinformation.

In his "Violence and New Religious Movements" (2004), Bromley explicitly advises law-enforcement agencies to establish three lines of communication—with members of the NRM, with former members, and with what he refers to as "cult-watching" groups (CWG). This "triangulation" (Carter 1998) of information allows officials to make better judgments about the actual situation. In principle I agree with Bromley, though in practice the different possible sources of information he mentions do not present themselves to officials as straightforwardly as his brief discussion might suggest.

To begin with, he refers to Eileen Barker's (2002) discussion of five different CWGs, implying that law enforcement might be receiving information from multiple organizations. However, unless a situation develops like the Branch Davidian siege that goes on week after week, it is unlikely that authorities will be approached by more than two kinds of CWGs, namely anticult groups (or individual anticult "consultants") and academic researchers (probably one or more individuals rather than an organized group). Another issue to take into account is that former members can be neutral or hostile. In some cases, extremely hostile apostates are little more than spokespeople for the anticult movement. Though it would be preferable to consult with neutral ex-members, these can be difficult to locate. Finally, depending on the social organization of the NRM in question, it might be possible to communicate with distinct segments of the organization, such as with NRM spokespeople *and* current members of the NRM who are communicating independently of official spokespeople.

In a worst-case scenario, of course, events take place rapidly, and the only available line of communication is with the NRM itself. However, for the sake of analysis, let us imagine a less urgent scenario in which concerns have been raised about a group I will refer to as Badmash Meditation International (BMI). The Badmashees practice an exotic religion, live in a rural commune in Kudzu County, and have been a mild irritant to their neighbors for the past six or seven years. Critics accuse them of being a survivalist, doomsday "cult," and the local newspaper occasionally runs critical stories about the group, but no major incidents have occurred. Most of the locals who have actually interacted with the commune members think they are "a little weird but okay."

Then, after years of low-level tension, the situation begins to escalate. One of the Badmashees falls into a piece of farm machinery and dies. The surrounding community begins to spread rumors that the dead Badmashee was executed, implicitly accusing Badmash leaders of staging his death to look like an accident. Around the same time, the commune runs afoul of a local ordinance that seems to have been passed with the express purpose of harassing BMI. The group refuses to recognize the ordinance, so the sheriff eventually arrests Billkuhl Baykahr, the Badmashee whose name is on the commune lease, and throws him into jail.

As concern about the group increases, a former member surfaces and alleges that group leaders sexually abuse BMI children with impunity. The allegations, initially reported in the local newspaper, get picked up and repeated by news outlets in larger towns. In the wake of this media coverage, a group of concerned Kudzu County residents invite an "expert" from the Free Minds Foundation to speak at a community center on "the cult menace." The Badmashees react by very publicly purchasing firearms at the local gun store, an action they know will quickly become known throughout the entire community. Rumors subsequently begin to spread that the Badmashees intend to assault the county jail in order to free Baykahr by force. Other, wilder rumors begin to circulate, such as the accusation that commune members plan to pour poison into the local reservoir in a plot to kill off the locals. The situation has become volatile. A special state police task force that was created in the wake of the 9/11 attacks is finally called in to manage the BMI situation. How should this task force proceed?

Though some alarmed county residents might be urging immediate police action, on the surface, anyway, the only law the Badmashees have broken is the ordinance for which Baykahr has already been arrested. Everything else is allegation and rumor. Until further information has been gathered and substantiated, the situation does not appear to warrant provocative police intervention. After an initial briefing by the sheriff's office, the task force then attempts to establish respectful, nonconfrontational communication with the BMI leadership. It tries to gather as much relevant information as possible. Whether the group's response is friendly or hostile, some sort of communication line will be established so that the task force can always call someone at the commune in the event of any new development.

Simultaneously, other task force investigators gather the same kind of information about the commune members—particularly about Badmash leaders—that one would normally gather on criminal suspects. Though clean records do not prove innocence, criminal records might provide clues to understanding aspects of the current case. This is standard police work and does not require further commentary.

As has already been noted, anticult groups are not neutral observers. However, there is always a possibility that anticultists have essential items of information that other parties to the confrontation do not possess. Let us imagine a situation where, for example, a disenchanted current commune member has anonymously leaked the location where the water-supply poison is being stored to the Free Minds Foundation. In this hypothetical case—and despite the fact that most of the foundation's views on nontraditional religions might be hopelessly flawed—it is clearly worth communicating with this kind of organization on the off chance it has valuable information.

At first glance, former members—and especially recent defectors—appear to have the greatest veracity. However, apostates from tight-knit religious communities are rather like divorced persons: Sometimes they can be objective about their ex-spouse, but often they are not. In particular, research has demonstrated that apostates who associate with anticult organizations are inclined to be far more negative than other former members (e.g., Solomon 1981; Lewis 1986, 1989) However, like anticult groups, even the most negative ex-member might have valuable information. Additionally, and though they are typically far more difficult to locate, apostates without axes to grind can be the most helpful sources of information.

Finally, our hypothetical state task force should seek out academic researchers. The British government funds a neutral, academic "cult-watching" group, the Information Network Focus on Religious Movements (INFORM), which makes it easy to obtain this kind of information in the UK. In sharp distinction to the British situation, France actually adopted a French anticult organization, the Association de Défense des Familles (ADFI), and transformed it into an arm of the government—an unwise decision, given the extreme nature of the ADFI's views on "the sects." It would be ideal to have an INFORM-like organization in every nation. Without one, however, it might be possible to find a researcher who had written a scholarly study of Badmash Meditation International, though this is not likely if the Badmashees are a small group. In lieu of a BMI specialist, it would still be useful to find a university researcher who specializes in the study of NRMs, as that person would have some insights into the dynamics of high-demand religious groups.

To summarize, I would reconceptualize the triangulation of sources discussed by Bromley into what we might call "quadrangulation": In addition to the kinds of information one derives from standard police work, law-enforcement officials who are attempting to manage a situation involving an intensive religious group should establish an ongoing relationship with the group and seek information from four sources:

1. the NRM
    a. the group's official channels
    b. individual members (if the NRM's organizational structure permits)
2. anticult organizations
3. apostates
    a. negative apostates (often allied with anticult groups)
    b. more neutral apostates
4. academic researchers
    a. scholarly groups like INFORM (if available)
    b. academicians who have researched the NRM in question (if available)
    c. academicians who are NRM specialists (in lieu of the availability of the other two categories)

One Direction for Future Research

Three decades ago, one could count the number of new religions specialists on one's fingers and read everything that had been published in the field in about one month. Since that time the field has expanded radically and even given rise to a number of subspecialities (e.g., Pagan studies; New Age studies). The explosive growth of NRM studies has been matched by explosive growth in the number of new publications. Major academic presses are now publishing an increasing number of NRM titles.

Despite this rapid expansion, a number of specialists in the field, including this author, have complained about the lopsided state of the literature. Studies of specific groups tend to cluster around a dozen or so of the highest-profile NRMs while leaving hundreds of smaller alternative religions unstudied. Prior to their respective tragedies, no academic research had been carried out on the People's Temple, the Branch Davidians, or the Movement for the Restoration of the Ten Commandments of God. One descriptive paper had been published on the Order of the Solar Temple. The only NRM that had received more than token attention was Heaven's Gate, but the field research on this group was more than two decades old at the time of its group suicide.

One effective way of addressing this imbalance would be to encourage graduate students to write theses and dissertations on understudied NRMs, particularly those groups that have already aroused controversy. This would serve not only the field of NRM studies but also law enforcement by, on the one hand, contributing to a de facto database on controversial religions and, on the other hand, creating "experts" on specific groups. New studies of alternative religions would also provide a broader base from which to theorize about NRMs.

Having recently moved from North America to Europe, I am acutely aware of the different position of NRM studies in the academic establishments of the two continents. In North America, the current cohort of NRM scholars consists mostly of aging academicians who became involved in the study of alternative religions in the 1970s and early 1980s. (I include myself in this group.) Though most of these researchers continue to be quite active, relatively few younger scholars (with the exception of the many students of contemporary Paganism) are in line to replace the first generation of NRM specialists.

In northern Europe by contrast—particularly in the Scandinavian countries and the UK—the field appears to be flourishing, with many new scholars working on NRMs. Even Germany, which formerly discouraged graduate students from writing their dissertations on NRMs, has finally recognized the importance of this field of study. Funding sources in these countries provide grants for doctoral students to research and write their theses and dissertations and often specify the topic area. If one or more of these funding bodies provided fellowships for doctoral students to research understudied NRMs, it would greatly enhance the field, as well as provide an important public service, especially to public policy bodies and law enforcement agencies.

Notes

1. I have elsewhere discussed criteria for distinguishing harmless from potentially *harmful* (not just potentially *violent*) groups (Lewis 2005a, 2001, 1998).

2. If I could retroactively redo this model, I would collapse the first two factors into something like "totalistic social environment," but discussing these kinds of modifications here would distract from the focus of this afterword.

3. Though not growing—or growing only very slowly—in Japan, Aum Shinrikyo had been expanding in Russia (Reader 2002, 195).

4. In the original work that I am here summarizing, "The Solar Temple 'Transits': Beyond the Millennialist Hypothesis" (Lewis 2005b), I also address the apparent challenges to this model represented by the MRTCG suicides and by the suicides of members of OTS and Heavens Gate, which took place some time after the original suicide events.

REFERENCES

Barker, Eileen. 2002. "Watching for Violence: A Comparative Analysis of the Roles of Five Types of Cult-watching Groups." In *Cults, Religion, and Violence*, ed. David G. Bromley and J. Gordon Melton. Pp123–148. New York: Oxford University Press.
Bradley, Martha Sonntag. 1993. *Kidnapped from That Land: The Government Raids on the Short Creek Polygamists*. Salt Lake City: University of Utah Press.
Bromley, David G. 2002. "Dramatic Denouements." In Bromley and Melton, *Cults, Religion, and Violence*. Pp11–41. New York: Cambridge University Press.
———. 2004. "Violence and New Religious Movements." In *The Oxford Handbook of New Religious Movements*, ed. James R. Lewis Pp143–162. New York: Oxford University Press.
———, and J. Gordon Melton, eds. 2002. *Cults, Religion, and Violence*. New York: Cambridge University Press.
Carter, Lewis. 1998. "Carriers of Tales: On Assessing Credibility of Apostate and Other Outsider Accounts of Religious Practices." In *The Politics of Religious Apostasy: The Role of Apostates in the Transformation of Religious Movements*, ed. David G. Bromley. Pp221–238. Westport, Conn.: Praeger.
Dawson, Lorne L. 2002. "Crises of Charismatic Legitimacy and Violent Behavior in New Religious Movements." In Bromley and Melton, *Cults, Religion, and Violence*. Pp80–101. New York: Cambridge University Press.
Hall, John R. 2002. "Mass Suicide and the Branch Davidians." In Bromley and Melton, *Cults, Religion, and Violence*. Pp149–169. New York: Cambridge University Press.
King, Thomas. 2008. *The Island Pond Raid, the Inside Story: Factual Account of the Infamous Island Pond Raid*. Bloomington, Ind.: AuthorHouse.
Kleiver, Lonnie D. 1999. "Meeting God in Garland: A Model of Religious Tolerance." *Nova Religio* 3. Pp45–53
Lewis, James R. 1986. "Reconstructing the 'Cult' Experience: Post-involvement Attitudes as a Function of Mode of Exit and Post-involvement Socialization." *Sociological Analysis* 42(2) (Summer).Pp151–159
———. 1989. "Apostates and the Legitimation of Repression: Some Historical and Empirical Perspectives on the Cult Controversy." *Sociological Analysis* 49(4) (Winter). Pp386–396.
———. 1998. *Cults in America*. Santa Barbara: ABC Clio.
———. 2001. *Odd Gods: New Religions and the Cult Controversy*. Amherst, N.Y.: Prometheus.
———. 2005a. *Cults: A Reference Handbook*. Santa Barbara: ABC-Clio.
———. 2005b. "The Solar Temple 'Transits': Beyond the Millennialist Hypothesis." In *Controversial New Religions*, ed. James R. Lewis and Jesper A. Petersen. Pp295–318. New York: Oxford University Press.
Melton, J. Gordon, and David G. Bromley. 2009. "Violence and New Religions: An Assessment of Problems, Progress, and Prospects in Understanding the NRM-Violence Connection." In *Dying for Faith: Religiously Motivated Violence in the Contemporary World*, ed. Madawi Al-Rasheed and Marat Shterin. Pp27–41. New York: Tauris.
Oliver, Moorman, Jr. 1994. "Today's Jackboots: The Inquisition Revisited." In *Sex, Slander, and Salvation: Investigating the Family/Children of God*, ed. James R. Lewis and J. Gordon Melton. Pp137–151. Stanford: Academic.

Reader, Ian. 2002. "Dramatic Confrontations: Aum Shinrikyo against the World." In Bromley and Melton, *Cults, Religion, and Violence*. Pp189–208. New York: Cambridge University Press.

Solomon, Trudy. 1981. "Integrating the 'Moonie' Experience: A Survey of Ex-members of the Unification Church." In *In Gods We Trust*, ed. Thomas Robbins and Dick Anthony. Pp275–294. New Brunswick, N.J.: Transaction.

Szubin, Adam, Jensen, Carl J., III, and Rod Gregg. 2000. "Interacting with 'Cults': A Policing Model." *FBI Law Enforcement Bulletin* 69. Pp16–24

Wessinger, Catherine. 1999. "Religious Studies Scholars, FBI Agents, and the Montana Freeman Standoff." *Nova Religio: The Journal of Alternative and Emergent Religions* 3. Pp36–44.

Index

15X, Thomas, 303
3X, Norman, 303
6-6-2006 High Mass, 370
8-8-88 rally, 369
Abrahamic religions, 239
acaryas (spiritual teachers) in Ananda
    Marga, 253
  Acarya Lokesha, 255
  Acarya Uma, 255
  Acarya Gagan, 255
  Acarya Nityananda Avadhuta, 258,
    267
accommodation between new
    religions and society, 308, 314,
    319–20
Accommodation, as response to wider
    society, 332, 334, 336–37, 342
accounts, 51n12
ACLU, United States, 391
Adams, Elliott, 393
advaetadvaetadvaeta vada, 265
Aesthetic Terrorism, 365–70. See also
    Petros, G.
African independent churches, 193
Age of Aquarius, 138, 143
Age of Pisces, 138
Ahdar, Rex, 57n111
ahimsa (non-injury), 266
Aho J., 244
Aho, James, 53n32, 55n55

AIDS
  divinely revealed cure for, 197–98
  punishment, seen as divine, 199, 200
Aitamurto, Kaarina, 9
Akal Security, 329, 337
Akali Dal, 327–28
Åkerbäck, Peter, 141–42, 144
Alamo Foundation, 297, 201
Alexander, Jr., Joe, 402
Ali, Noble Drew, 296
aliens—*see* extraterrestrials
Amenta Club, 136
America, Fall of, 297, 300
American Academy of Religion, 269n2
American Family Foundation (AFF),
    388, 395n46, 400–1, 411
American values
  and 3HO/Sikh Dharma, 335
Americans, African,
  and lack of political rights, 300
  participation in religious
    institutions, 296
  slave names of, 300
  struggle for identity, 295, 300
  20th Century migration of, 296, 300
Amnesty International, 255, 270n10,
    389, 394n23, 394n25, 394n29
AMURTEL (Ananda Marga Universal
    Relief Team for Ladies), 254
An Chen, 394n21

Ananda Deviika Ma, 252
Ananda Marga, 9, 35, 249–58, 260–65, 267
  agrarian communities, 252
  authoritarianism in, 252
  authoritarian leadership in, 264
  Ananda Marga in North America, 252–54, 267–69
  animals, attitude towards, 264
  atatayii, concept of, 267, 271n31
  behavioral requirements for members, 252, 264
  charismatic leadership in, 253, 264
  civil law, attitude towards, 266, 268
  collective outlook in, 264–65
  cosmology in, 250, 257, 260, 265
  crooked intellect in, 266
  ecology in, 249
  education in Ananda Marga schools, 257
  eschatology of, 262, 265
  finances within, 258, 260
  flag of the organization, 267
  hatred, attitude towards, 264
  humanism, concept of, 264
  membership profile of, 252
  military readiness, 266–67
  motto, 249
  murder, allegations of, 250, 257
  mysticism in, 260
  ownership concept, 260
  paramilitaries, 251, 262–63, 271n26
  peace, concept of, 265
  plants, attitude towards, 264
  religious reformism in, 253
  self-immolations, 255, 270n12
  schisms, 258, 258n18, 268
  spiritual morality versus simple morality, 266
  spiritual soldiers, 268
  strategy in war, 266–67
  struggle/ fight, concept of, 249, 264–67
  suicide, attitude towards, 270n12
  universalism in, 264
  use of arms ideology, 263, 265
  world army ideology, 262
Ananda Nagar, headquarters of Ananda Marga, 251, 254
Ananda Seva, 270n18
Ananda Sutram, 252, 258, 260, 265
Ananda Vanii Samgraha: A Collection of the Spiritual Messages of Shrii Shrii Anandamurti, 264

Anandamurti, Shrii Shrii, 249
Ancient and Mystical Order Rosæ Crucis (AMORC), 136
Anson, R.S., 54n40
Anthony, Dick, 7, 20, 50n3, 51n14, 52n23, 55n53, 58n117, 74–75
antiauthoritarianism, 236, 242–43
Anti-Catholic sentiment, 45
anti-cult literature, 151
Anti-Cult Movement (ACM), 33, 35, 46–47, 329, 388–89
anticult movement
  as totalistic, 64, 72–78
  attempts to criminalize religious belief, 76–78
  legislation in France, 63, 77–78
  legal testimony, 74–79. *See also* brainwashing; deprogramming; Delgado, Richard; Ofshe, Richard; Singer, Margaret
Anticult
  Anticult Movement (ACM), 5, 7, 420, 419, 421
Anticult movment, 134
antinomianism, 20
anti-Semitism, 232–33, 235, 237, 239
Apocalyptic, 114
apocalyptic doctrine, 308, 316–17
apocalyptic images and rhetoric, 238, 242
  expectations, 242–44
Apocalyptic views, 330, 335, 343
Apocalypticism, 63, 66, 67, 70, 72, 78, 80–81
Apostates, 420, 421
apostates from Ananda Marga, 257–58, 267–68
Apostates, 22, 26, 45
apostolic socialism, 97
apparitionism. *See* Marian visionaries
apparitions of the Virgin
  apocalyptic views, often linked to, 201
  Kibeho (Rwanada), 194, 198
  Mbuye (Uganda), 197–98
Applewhite, 41–42
Applewhite, Marshall Herff, 176, 184
Applewhite, Marshall, 140
Aquarian Age, 339–40. *See also* New Age
Archédia Club, 136
Ardas, 4
Armageddon, 149, 152, 162
armaments, Ananda Margiis trafficking in, 256, 270n20

armed struggle in Ananda Marga, 251,
    265–67. *See also* sudra revolution
    entries
  invention of new weapons, 266
  preemptive actions, 267
Asahara Shoko (Matsumoto Chizuo), 148,
    149, 151, 152, 153, 157, 160–61
Asahara, Shoko, 8, 141, 345, 418
Asahara, Shôkô. *See* Aum Shinrikyo
Asatru, 232
Asov A., 232
Assassins, 36
Association de Defense des Familles
    (ADFI), 420–1
Association of Aum Shinrikyo Victims, 148
Astanga yoga, 253
ATF (Bureau of Alcohol, Tobacco &
    Firearms), 121, 123, 126
atrocity tales, 43–45, 57n98
Atuhaire, Bernard, 192–93
Aum incident, 147, 151–57, 161–65
Aum Shinrikyo, 7, 8, 17–18, 21–25, 31–36, 41,
    61n145, 71, 81, 107, 133–37, 140–43,
    175, 242, 270n17, 312, 344–45, 417–18
  merciful killing, 213
Australia, 137
Authoritarianism, 66–67, 71–73, 75. *See also*
    totalism
avadhutas (senior renunciates), 258

Babies were being beaten, 44
Backman, Carl, 34, 52n21
Baffi, C.R., 54n45
Baingana-Muntu, Msgr. Edward, 198
Balch, Robert, 41, 53n28, 56n86, 56n87
Baldwin, James, 300
Ball-Rokeach, Sandra, 32, 51n10, 52n24,
    55n54
Bangladesh, 254
Bankipur Central Jail, 254–55
Barker, Eileen, 52n23, 59n120, 60n139, 419
Barkowski, John, 54n46, 57n105
Barkum, Michael, 50n2, 52n20, 55n53, 55n64
Barrett, David V., 136, 144
Barrie-Anthony, Steven, 7
Bataille, G., 362
Bauer, Bernard, 53n34
Becker, Howard, 51n12
Beckford, James, 43–44, 50n3, 51n12, 54n47,
    57n100, 57n99, 57n104, 60n139

Belov A., 232–33, 240
Bengali language, Sarkar as speaker of, 251,
    253
Bernard, Raymond, 136
Bhagwan Rajneesh (Osho), 10
Bhajan, Yogi, 326, 329, 334, 340, 345
  Predictions of future social upheaval,
    330, 339–40. *See also* Puri,
    Harbhajan Singh
bhakti (devotional) yoga in Ananda Marga,
    253–54
Bhaktivedanta Swami Prabhupada: 276,
    289n1
Bhindranwale, Sant Jarnail, 328, 331
Biermans, John, 58n117
Bijon Setu incident, 256–57
bioregionalism in Ananda Marga, 261,
    271n28
Black metal, 353, 356–58, 363–64
Black Panthers, 38
black peace, 265
blood-letting in revolution, 259, 268–69
Bock, D.C., 55n55
body, nature of, 180
Bogdan, Henrik, 7, 136, 142–44, 417
Book of Veles, 232
Bose, Netaji Subash Chandra, 251
boundary control, 158–59
Bourdieu, Pierre, 308, 313, 316
Brahmo Samaj, 251, 269n4
brainwashing, 61, 63, 74–79, 151–57, 396n60.
    See also coercive persuasion; mind
    control
Branch Davidians, 7, 11, 17–18, 22–25, 31–36,
    40–44, 72, 77–82, 92, 107, 113–15,
    118–20, 122–27, 133, 137, 140, 143, 154,
    158, 161–63, 175, 186, 242, 416–19,
    422
Brazil, 298
Breyer, Jacques, 136
Bromley, David, 5–6, 15, 18–19, 43, 46, 61,
    51n14, 52n23, 53n27, 54n47, 57n101,
    57n102, 57n110, 57n112, 57n98, 57n99,
    58n116, 58n117, 59n120, 59n124,
    59n125, 59n127, 414–16, 418
Bromley, David G., 139, 144, 403–4
Bryant, Stephen (Sulochan): murder of,
    279–80, 284
  role in assault on Kirtanananda, 290n6
Buddha Purnima, 269n3

Buddhism, 152, 159, 160, 165, 167
　Mahayana, 149
　Tantric (Esoteric), 149, 153, 155
　Tibetan, 153, 155
Buhunga (Uganda), 204
Bureau for International Narcotics and Law Enforcement Affairs (U.S. State Department), 162
business enterprises (Aum), 150, 165
Businesses
　and accommodative stance of 3HO/Sikh Dharma
　and communal economic arrangements
　and criminal activity
　development of encouraged by Yogi Bhajan
　and legal contests over control of names of businesses created by 3HO members
　and recession
　warrior image adapted to business
Buziga (Uganda), 204

Calcutta (Kolkata), India, 251, 256
California, 133
Campion, Jane, 58n118
Canada, 134, 137
capitalism, view within Ananda Marga, 254, 259
Carroll, Jerry, 53n34
Carter, Lewis, 42, 47, 56n91, 56n92, 60n136
catastrophic millennialism, 20
Caucasus region, 239
Center against Mental Manipulation, France, 388
CESNUR, 53n31
chakras (bodily energy centers) in Ananda Marga philosophy, 269n6
Chang, Maria, 61
Change
　altering one's environment, 333, 342
　changing one's self, 333, 342. *See also* Aquarian Age
characterological approach, 33
Charisma, 326, 332
　routinization of, 344
Charismatic authority: 275, 286–87
Charismatic leadership, 16–19, 23–26, 307, 311, 312, 330, 344, 345
chemical agents, 117

chemical pneumonia, 117, 119
chemicals, 150, 161–62, 164, 168n35
Chen Tao, 418
Chen Zixiu, 389–90
Chicago, 296
Chidester, David, 50n1, 55n64
Chih-yu Shih, 393n14
child-lifting. *See* kidnapping children *entry*
Children of God, 35–6, 54n45, 397, 400
China Anti-Cult Association (CACA), 387–89, 394n36, 395n37, 49
China. 379–96
Chinese Communist Party (CCP), 383, 389, 391
Christ, 179, 184
Christianity, 232, 235–37, 239–41
　Orthodox Christianity, 235
Church of Inglings, 233
Church of Scientology, 397
Church Universal and Triumphant, 35, 42, 401, 406, 409
Ciarn, R.B., 52n16, 52n23
Circle of Love, 257
Circle of Pagan Tradition, 233
Circle of Veles, 233
Citizens Freedom Foundation (CFF), 400, 404, 409
Clark, John, 58n115, 59n120
Clayton, Stanley, 102
Clement V, Pope, 135
coercive persuasion, 77. *See also* brainwashing
cognitive distancing, 152, 155
Cohn, Norman, 261
collective violence, 307, 311–15, 317–18, 320
communication, 157, 162–63, 165
Communism, 237, 241, 260
Communist Party, 254, 256
　Bengali Communists, 254, 257
　Communist Party of India Marxists (CPM) from West Bengal, 257
Community Education Technical Advocates (CETA) grants, 270n14
Concerned Relatives, 97, 106–7
Conference, Southern Christian Leadership,
　and FBI, 302
conspiracy theories, 177, 237–38
Constitution, PRC, 380–81, 383, 385
contrast symbols, 68, 71

Controversial New Religions (2005), 417
Copenhagen, Denmark, headquarters of PROUT, 251
cosmic evil, 261
cosmic war, 264–65, 268
   constructing an image of cosmic war, 268
Counterculture, 327, 331, 338–39
Country Reports on Terrorism 2004, 255
Cowan D. E., 234
crisis negotiators, 124, 126
Crovetto, Helen, 9
crucifixion, 182
CS, 115–20, 126
cult, 151, 156
Cult Awareness Network (CAN), 400–2, 404, 408–11
Cult Awareness Network (formerly the Citizens Freedom Foundation), 414
cult, 379, 381–82, 393n9
cultic aspects of Ananda Marga, 270n13
cults, 31, 33
Cults, Religion, and Violence (2002), 8
Cultural avant-garde, 368
cultural capital, 307–8, 311, 313–16, 320
Cult-watching groups, 418
cyanide, 117–18, 120

daggers carried in Ananda Marga, 271n29
Daly, R, 58n115
Daniels, Ted, 139, 144
Darendorf, Ralf, 32, 51n11
darsana sastra, 252
Davidians, Branch, 298
   and United States government agencies, 299
Davis, David, 57n112, 57n113
Davis, James, 55n69
Davis, Winston, 42, 53n28, 56n88, 56n89
Dawson, Lorne, 17, 23, 55n53, 56n76, 61
Day, James, 59n129
de Benoist, Alain, 240
death, 148, 151, 153–55, 158
deaths, 380, 389
Defensive violence, 330
Delgado, Richard, 58n115, 74, 76–77
democratic centralism, 383
Demonology, 352–53, 354–56
demonstration, the, 179, 182
Depression, Great, 296, 300

Deprivation,
   multiple, 299
   relative, 299
Deprogramming, 11
deprogramming, 43, 45–46, 49, 64, 73–74, 77–78. *See also* brainwashing; Delgado, Richard; Singer, Margaret
   as coercion, 399–402
   as violence, 398–9, 402, 406–11
   defined, 399
   origins, 399–400
   prevalence of, 402–5
   publicity about, 402–4
   rationale for, 399–406
Derks, Franz, 51n12, 58n117
Desai, Morarji, 255
Designated Foreign Terrorist Organizations list, 255
Detroit, 296
   and Ku Klux Klan, 296
deviance amplification, 66, 78–82
dharma, 263, 266
Di Mambro, Joseph, 134, 136, 140
diacritics in Ananda Marga literature, 269n1
DiMambro, Joseph, 41
disaster relief in Ananda Marga, 249, 254
   Hurricane Katrina, 254
Discourses on Mahabharata, 265
divine authority, 240–41
Divine Light Mission, 35, 397
Do—*see* Applewhite, Marshall Herff
Dobroslav, 237, 239
Dramatic denoumets, 6, 15–16, 19, 25, 27, 242–43
Drescher, Thomas (Tirtha): 280, 284
drugs, 150, 162, 165, 168n35
Druidism, 232
Durkheim, Emile, 38
Duvert, Cyrille, 395n45
Dymally, Senator Mervin, 53n35, 54n45

earthquake (Kobe 1995), 150, 157
East-West Cultural Center, L.A., 326
Eckholm, Elizabeth, 386, 394n33
ecological concerns, 236–37, 239
Edelman, Bryan, 11, 395n48
Egypt, 239
Ellison, Christopher, 54n46, 57n105
Ellwood, Robert, 55n51
Elsberg, Constance, 5, 10, 413, 416

Emelyanov V., 232–33, 237
Emmanuel, Christopher, 134
Emory, Meade, 60n133
Encapsulation, in 3HO/Sikh Dharma, 330, 340
Endogenous (internal) factors, 415
endogenous factors, 16–19, 26–27
Entrepreneurship, and 3HO/Sikh Dharma, 332, 336, 337. *See also* businesses
Erikson, Erik, 64–68, 70, 72, 74–75, 79, 81
est, 397
Evans, Carolyn, 392n7
"evil cult," 379, 381–82, 384, 387, 394n29
evil, Sarkar's concept of, 264
Evola J., 233
Evolutionary Level Above Human, 183
evolutionary transformation in Ananda Marga's social cycle, 259
exemplary dualism, 20, 66, 68
exit counseling, 46, 401
Exodus, Christian, 298
Exogenous (external) factors, 415
exploitation, concept in Ananda Marga, 250, 259
    demonization of exploiters, 264–65. *See also* satanization of opponents *entry*
    strategy aginst exploiters, 266
External opposition to alternative religions and 3HO/Sikh Dharma, 330–31, 343
extraterrestrials, 174, 177, 179
extreme case of violence, 308

Fabré-Palaprat, Bernard-Raymond, 136
Faivre, Antoine, 135, 144
Falun Gong, 11, 26, 79, 379–96, 415
    as tool of the West, 386
    as terrorists, 395n51
Family International, The (formerly the Children of God), 414–15
Family, The, 54n44
Fanon, Franz, 38, 55n66
Fard, Wallace, 296, 303
    and FBI, 302
Farrakhan, Louis, 300
    resurrects the Nation of Islam, 304–5
    and anti-Semitism, 304
Father Divine, 97
Fautre, Willy, 60n140
FBI (Federal Bureau of Investigation), 115–23, 125–26

FBI, 154–55, 162–63. *See* United States Government, Federal Bureau of Investigation
Federal Bureau of Investigation documents, 255
Ferme des Rochettes, 134
Fire, 113–24
Firearms training, in 3HO/Sikh Dharma, 329, 337
"Five Ks," 333
Flinn, Frank, 59n129
Flirty fishing, 414
flying saucer—*see* UFO
forbidden city, 379
Foucault, M., 362
Fragmentation in 3HO/Sikh Dharma, 341
France, 47, 134, 137
Frankfurter, D., 351, 355–58, 370. *See also* mimesis, mimetic performance
free exercise cause in U.S. Constitution, 318, 320
FREECOG (Free the Children of God), 400
Freedman, A., 58n115
Freedom of Information Act, 255
Freeman standoff, 53n32, 56n96
Freemasonry, 135–37, 142
Freemen (Montana Freemen), 418
Frohnmayer, David, 319–20
Fundamentalist Church of Jesus Christ of Latter-day Saints (FLDS), 414

Gaines M.J., 54n45
Galanter, Marc, 17, 50n6
Gallagher, Eugene, 49n1, 52n18, 53n27, 56n78, 57n106, 57n108, 59n126
Gamson, William, 52n24, 59n120
Gandhi, Indira, 254, 256, 328, 331, 340
Garrison, Omar, 47, 54n41, 60n135
Garvey, Marcus, 296
Girls' Volunteers (GV), 262–63
Gnosticism, 178
Golden Temple, 326, 328, 331, 340
Golden Way Foundation, 136
Goldman, Marion S., 10, 416
Goode, Eric, 51n12
government, 148, 150–51, 155, 157–58, 162, 164
Government misfeasance, 122–24
Graham, Hugh, 50n5, 55n61
groupism, 264
Gruson, 53n38

Guenon R., 233
Gurr, Robert, 50n5, 55n61
Guru Gobind, 263
guru of Ananda Marga, 250, 252–53
Guyana, 97–98, 103

Hadden, Jeffrey, 52n23
hagiography in Ananda Marga, 253
Hale-Bopp Comet, 42, 177, 187
Hall, John R., 137, 139, 141, 144
Hall, John, 18, 37, 50n1, 53n30, 55n57, 55n64, 56n75
Hanegraaff, Wouter J., 135, 144–45
Hardman, Charlotte, 54n44, 54n45, 54n46
Hardon, Bert, 60n139
Hare Krishna, 9
Hare Krishnas, 397, 404
Hargrove, Barbara, 57n110
Harris, Harriet A., 264
Harris, Robert, 302
Hassan, Steven, 401, 405–7, 410
Hayer, Talmadge, 303
He Zuoxiu, 394n36
Healthy, Happy, Holy Organization (3HO), 4, 5, 10, 413, 416
Healthy, Happy, Holy Organization
  administrative structure of, 334
  assertive stance of, 330
  beliefs about women in, 343
  businesses associated with, 337–38
  combining Sikhism and yoga, 336
  compared to Aum Shinrikyo, 344
  compared to a fragile millennial group, 343
  history of, 326, 327, 333
  individualism and materialism in, 341
  institutionalization of, 331, 335
  interpretations of Sikh and Khalsa traditions, 326, 328, 330, 336, 338, 339
  martial arts training in, 329
  middle class membership of, 342
  and millennialism, 330, 340
  militia, 329
  and *New Age beliefs*, 332
  as pledge group, 343
  and power, 332
  as praxis group, 342
  and Punjab, 330, 344
  recent events in, 345
  and relations with other Sikhs, 336, 344
  response to external pressures of, 342, 343
  retreatist response to tensions with external society, 336, 337
  Sanatan influence on, 333
  and Sikh Khalsa, 326, 333
Healy, Cameron, 338
Heaven's Gate, 5, 7, 8, 17–18, 21, 25, 31–36, 41, 133, 137, 140–43, 307, 415, 417, 422
Heaven's Gate, history of, 174, 176–77, 180, 183–84
Hedgewar, K. B., 263
Hellfire clubs, 358, 363, 370
Heretical organization, 394n29
Hermetica Fraternitas Templi Universali, 137
Hertiff, Marshall, 417
Hexham, Irving, 61n140, 210
Hilton Hotel bombing, 255. See also Pederik, Evan, *entry*
himsa (injury), 266
Hindu reformism in Ananda Marga, 253
Hindu revivalism in Ananda Marga, 251
Hitlerism, 235
Holy Smoke, 58n118
holy war, 271n27
homeless at Rajneeshpuram, 309, 310
house churches, 381, 393n11, 395n44
HRT (Hostage Rescue Team), 124–25
Huber, John, 53n38
Huguenin, Thierry, 135
Human Individual Metamorphosis—see Heaven's Gate
Human Society, 254, 258

Iadicola, Peter, 402, 405
Idea and Ideology, 252
identity confusion, 70, 72
Identity politics, 368
ideological totalism, 252, 267
Ikazire, Fr. Paul, 195, 200, 208
illegal activities, allegations against Ananda Marga, 260
immoralists, concept in Ananda Marga, 268
Indian emergency declarations, 254
Indo-Pakistani war, 254
Information Network Focus on Religious Movements INFORM, 420–21
institutional totalism, 252
intensified conflict, 16, 19
intensive socialization tactics, 252

Interministerial Mission for the Fight against Cults, France, 388
Internal Revenue Service, 47
International Commission of Jurists, 255, 270n11
International Society for Krishna Consciousness (ISKCON): history of, 289n1
internet, 387
interviews of Ananda Margiis, 250
Introvigne, Massimo, 41, 51n15, 53n30, 56n81, 56n82, 57n99, 57n113, 59n126, 59n128, 60n129, 60n140, 61n140, 61n141, 135–37, 140, 144
ISKCON, 35, 36
Islam, Nation of
  doctrine, 297, 300–1
  history, 296–97, 301–5
Islam, Sunni, 304
Island Pond Community—see Twelve Tribes Messianic Communities
Island Pond, 47

Jackson, Jesse, 304
Jamalpur, India, 251
Japan, 147–48, 150–56, 159, 160–64, 298
Japanese new religion(s), new religious movements, 147, 152, 155, 158–59, 161–63, 166n16
Jehovah's Witnesses, 20, 47
Jenkins, Philip, 76, 79–80
Jews, 232, 237, 239
Jiang Zemin, President of China, 386
jihad, 249
jivan-mukta (living-liberated individual), 262
jnana (knowledge) yoga in Ananda Marga, 253
Johnson, Ian, 392n1, 394n26, 396n52, 396n53, 396n54, 396n56, 396n58, 396n59
Jones, 38–40
Jones, James Warren (Jim), 96–98, 100–110
Jones, Jim, 25, 140
Jones, Marceline, 96–97, 102–4
Jonestown, 5, 72, 78–79, 82, 97–98, 101
  deaths in, 98, 109–10
  People's Rallies, 102 (*See also, White Nights, revolutionary suicide*)
Jonestown/People's Temple, 307, 311, 316–17

Jouret, Luc, 134, 136, 140, 417
Joyu Fumihiro, 163
Judah, Stillson, 55n52
Judaism, 239
Juergensmeyer M., 238, 244–45
Juergensmeyer, Mark, 264, 267–68
  intraorganizational terrorism, 267
  characteristics of religious groups inclined towards terrorism, 268
Juergensmeyer, Mark, 62
just war, 271n27
Justus Freemen, 313

Kamikuishiki (village), 157, 160, 168n35
Kamushwa, Gaudia, 198
Kanungu
  headquarters of the group, 195
  land given by Kashaku family, 197
  March 17, 2000, events on, 204
  persecutions, compound temporarily left in 1993 due to, 209
  refuge during apocalyptic events, seen as place of, 202
Kaplan, H., 58n115
Kaplan, Jeffrey, 51n7, 61n146
Kariya Kiyoshi, 151
Karl Marx, 254
karma yoga in Ananda Marga, 253. *See also* social service *entries*
Karriem, Robert. *See*, Robert Harris
Kasapurari, Fr. Joseph, 195, 205
Kashaku, Paulo
  persecutions against him and his family, 197
  place in the history of the MRTCG, 196
  visions and revelations, recipient of, 196–97
Katariibaabo, Fr. Dominic
  author of handwritten history of the group, 196
  biography, 195
  death in Kanungu, probable, 204–5
  year 2001, says there will be no, 207
Kauravas, 267
Kavykin O. I., 238
Kelley, Harold, 51n13
Kelly, Galen, 401
Khalistan, 328, 331
Khalsa Council, 334, 335

Khalsa
  history of, 327, 344
  inititation into, 325, 336, 333, 343
  interpretations of its traditions within
    3HO/Sikh Dharma, 333–35
  as last name, 334
  and revitalization of U.S., 339
  and Sikh gurus, 344
Khande de pahul khand, 325
Kibwetere, Joseph
  biography, 194–95
  Mwerinde, meets with, 195, 197
  visionary groups, contacts with other, 198
  wife. See Kibwetere, Teresa
Kibwetere, Teresa, 194–95, 198, 209
kidnapping children, allegations against
    Ananda Marga, 257
Kilbourne, Brock, 45–46, 49, 50n6, 51n8,
    51n9, 52n23, 58n114, 59n121, 59n123
Kim, Byoung-Suh, 58n117
King, Christine, 52n24, 57n99
Kinyera, Terence, 212
Kirtanananda Swami: 275–76
  assault on, 278–79, 290n7, 290n10
  challenges to authority, 282–83,
    290–91n11
  charisma, 276–77, 287
  excommunication from ISKCON, 281,
    290n8
  interfaith, 290n9, 290n10
  legal issues, 284–86, 291n12, 291n13
  sexual malfeasance, 282, 284, 287
Kirtananda Swami, 9, 417
Kituse, John, 51n13
Klan, Ku Klux, 296
Kliever, Lonnie, 56n96
Knights Templar, Order of, 135–36
Knutby community, 6
Komuhangi, Ursula, 197
Kono Yoshiyuki, 150, 166n13
Koresh, David, 23–25, 44, 120–26, 154,
    168n34
Krakauer, Jon, 62
Krsna, 253, 266
Krylova, Galina, 61n142
ksatriyas (military-minded individuals) in
    Ananda Marga social order, 258, 261,
    270n19
Kuhn, Anthony, 394n35
Kundalini Yoga, 4, 10, 332–37, 344

Lang, Gladys, 51n12
Lang, Kurt, 51n12
Langfitt, Frank, 393n13
Langone, Michael D., 401
Langone, Michael, 58n115
Langrod, John, 51n6
language (religious), 162
latent tension, 16, 19
lathis (staffs) carried in Ananda Marga,
    271n29
Laufer, William, 59n129
LaVey, A. S., 352–53, 359–61, 364, 366,
    368–70, 370–71, 371n6, 372n10
  The Satanic Bible, 361, 368
  Church of Satan, 356, 359, 361, 366,
    369–70
Law enforcement, 56n78
Layton, Carolyn, 105
Layton, Deborah, 101
leadership, concept in Ananda Marga, 250
Lee, Martha F., 10
leftist political activities, 254
Legion of Mary, 193
LeMoult, John, 59n124
Lemuria, 239
Les Granges sur Salvan, 134
Levi, Ken, 50n1, 54n50, 59n121, 59n123, 55n53
Lewis James, 50n1, 54n42, 54n46, 56n96,
    58n117
Lewis, H. Spencer, 136, 145
Lewis, James R., 139–41, 144
LFTs, local full-time workers, 252, 270n16
Li Dongsheng, 387
liberalism, 237
Lifton, Robert L., 50n1, 52n17, 55n56, 56n84,
    64–68, 70–71, 73–75, 77–78, 81–82
Lilliston, Lawrence, 54n46
Liu Peifeng, 392–93n7
Lobov, Oleg, 150
London, Perry, 58n114
Lyman, Stanford, 51n12
Lynn, Monty, 51n8

Maaga, Mary, 50n1, 55n62, 55n71
Mahabharata, 266
Mahakaola, 263–64
Mahan tantric, 326, 344
Mahavisva (Great Universe), 265, 268
Maintenance of Internal Security Act
    (MISA), 270n9

Makerere University, research by, 192, 198
Malony, Newton, 55n55
Manson Family, 16, 21, 25, 27
Marian visionaries, 193
   change, revelations offering space for, 201
   Mbarara diocese, groups in, 198
   visionary milieu, 194, 200
Marshall, Tyler, 393n35
martial arts, 231–34, 239
   reconstructionist, 233, 239
martial law, 254
Martin, Paul, 401
Martinique, 137
Marx, Gary, 51n15, 61n147
Marxism, 236–37
   criticism of religion, 236
Masada, 186–87
Masculinization, 344
   and masculine symbolism, 344
   and violence, 344
mass movement in Ananda Marga, 250
mass suicide, 113–16
Master Units, 252
materialism, material world, concept in Ananda Marga, 249, 268
Matheson, Peter, 52n24
Mathews, C., 351, 368, 370, 372n11
Matsumoto (city), 150, 155, 158, 162
Mayer, Jean-François, 8
Mayer, Jean-François, 41, 53n30, 56n80, 137, 140–45
McBride, James, 51n14, 58n115, 59n129, 60n133
McCarthy, James, 51n15
McCutcheon R. T., 245
McVeigh, Timothy, 298
Mecca, 297
media, 149, 150–57, 161–64, 166n13, 167n31, 168n37, 174, 295
Media coverage, China, 386, 392n2
Melton, Gordon, 52n25, 54n42, 54n46, 61n141, 139, 144
Melton, J. Gordon, 6, 414–15
membership in Ananda Marga, 250, 252
metal music, 233
metaphysical religious tradition, 176
Michela, J. L., 51n13
militant images and metaphors, 233, 238
militia groups, 125
millenarianism, 63, 66, 70, 79–80
   definition of, 297
   moral dualism in, 299
   overlap of religion and politics in, 298
   relationship of ultimate purpose to violence in, 298–99
   and search for identity, 300
   secular more violent that religious, 298
Millenialism, 264, 271n21, 330, 339–40
   catastrophic millennialism, 340
   progressive millennialism, 340
millennialism, 16–17, 19–21, 24–26, 175
Miller, Christine, 98
Miller, Donald, 57n112
Mimesis, mimetic performance, 355–58, 361
mind control, 63, 74, 75–80, 151–52. *See also* brainwashing; coercive persuasion
Ministry of Civil Affairs, China, 384
Ministry of Security, China, 384–85
misguided youths, 268
Moberg, David, 51n8
Modern Seers, 270n18
modern technical warfare, 240
moksa (salvation), 271n24
monasticism in Ananda Marga, 251
monism in Ananda Marga, 257, 262, 265
monk warriors (Buddhist), 164
Moon, Rev. Sun Myung, 397, 407
Moore, Annie, 106
Moore, Rebecca, 7, 38–39, 50n1, 50n4, 50n5, 55n58, 55n60, 55n68, 56n72, 57n109
Moorish Science Temple, 296
moral philosophy in Ananda Marga, 250, 261
   immoralists, 268
   moral dualism, 264–65
   moral justifications for killing, 268
   moral judgments, 268
   simple morality, 266
   spiritual morality, 260, 265–66
morality, 254, 258
Mori Tatsuya, 156
Mormons, 36
Morrison, D.E., 55n69
Moscow, 232, 235
Mount Carmel, 115–16, 118, 12–122, 124
Mountain Meadow Massacre, 36
Movement Against Illegal Immigration, 235
Movement for the Restoration of the Ten Commandments of God (MRTCG), 5, 7, 8, 416, 422

AIDS as factor in development of the MRTCG, 200
apostles, selection of, 195–96
comparison with other cases of apocalyptic violence, 212
corpses, identification of, 204
documents entrusted to local authorities before the end, 208
end, members expecting the, 211
failure, discussions on prophetic, 206–7, 211
former members during the endtimes, role attributed to, 208
Judicial Commission of Inquiry, 192
killings of members in 2000, 204
leaders, interaction between, 195
leaders, death or survival of, 205–6
opposition to the MRTCG, 208–10
origins, 196–200
persecution, sense of, 199, 209
properties sold before the fire, 205
rapture of the elect, apparent belief in the, 208
relatives of the members, tensions with, 203
Roman Catholic Church, critical of modern developments in, 200–201
school for children, 203
traditionalism, selective, 201
training of members, 202
victims, number of, 191–92
way of life, 202–3
witch-hunt, hypothesis about the MRTCG being victim of, 210
year 2000, place of, 206–8
Mt. Carmel, 5, 7, 418
Muffler, John, 5n6
Muhammad, Elijah, 296
 prophesies the Fall of America, 297, 300, 301n3
 and *Message to the Blackman*, 296–97, 302
 death of, 304
 emphasizes support for Black community, 301
 and white Americans as devils, 301
Muhammad, Wallace, 301
 assumes leadership of the Nation of Islam, 304
Mukantabana, Specioza, 198
mukti (liberation), 271n24
murder, 147–49, 153–55, 158–59, 161–62

Muslims, 249
Mwerinde, Credonia
 father. *See* Kashaku, Paulo
 expecting the final events to have a big impact, 211
 jailed, being, 197
 Kibwetere, meets with, 195
 survival, allegations of, 205
 Nyabugoto rock, visits to, 198
 rumors about her, 194
mystic socialism, 250, 260–61, 268
mysticism, 178

nadis (spiritual nerves) in Ananda Marga philosophy, 269n6
Namino-son (village), 149, 150, 160, 163
Narrative, 327, 331
nascent conflict, 16, 19
Nation of Islam, 6, 10
National Centre for Terrorist Threat Assessment (Sweden), 414, 416, 417
National People's Congress, 379, 380, 383
nationalism, 233–34, 237, 241
nationalism, opinion of Sarkar, 251, 271n28
national-socialism, 235, 239, 244
Nationhood, 327, 331, 339. *See also* Qaum
Negative summary events, 43–44, 54n47
neoliberalism, 241
Neo-Templarism, 135–36
Nettles, Bonnie Lu, 176, 180–82
Neutral mind, 332, 338
New Age, 135–38, 143, 173, 177, 182, 332–36, 339
New religions, 31
 Conflict voer, 61n146
new religious movements, 175
New Thought, 333
New Vrindaban: 9, 275–91, 417
 child abuse and bankruptcy, 296, 291n4
 community census, 285
 defection from, 284–85, 286, 288
 early history, 276–78
 expelled from ISKCON, 281
 funding, 277, 285–86
 government investigation of, 280–81, 284
 Indian supporters, 282, 285, 286, 287, 288
 interfaith, 281–82, 286, 283–84, 287
 number of residents, 276–77, 285
 renewed relationship with ISKCON, 286
 transformation of, 284–86, 288
 tourism and pilgrimage, 277–78, 286, 288

New West Magazine, 97
Newport, Kenneth, 113–14, 119–20, 122, 127
Newport, Kenneth C. G., 7
Newton, Huey, 38, 55n64
Niu Aimin, 393n10
Nolan, Megan, 270n18
nondualism in Ananda Marga, 253
nonviolence, opinion of Sarkar, 249
Nordquist, Ted, 55n52
"normal religion", 381, 392n7
North American Hindu Association of Dharma Studies, 269n2
Nostradamus, 152
Nouvelle Droit, 240
Nyabugoto rock (Uganda), 198

Obama, Barack, 304
Objects, Unidentified Flying (UFOs), and Ezekiel's Wheel, 297
Ofshe, Richard, 54n40, 58n115, 74–75. *See also* brainwashing; deprogramming; Singer, Margaret
Oklahoma City bombing, 53n32, 125
Oklahoma City, 298
Old Amish Order, 408
Old Catholic Order, 408
Oleson Theodore, 62
Order of the Solar Temple, 63, 77, 270n17
Order of the Solar Temple, l'Ordre du Temple Solaire, or OTS, 133–45
Order of the Solar Temple Ugandan case, comparison with, 191, 192, 212
orgacide, 52n24
organizational structure of Ananda Marga, 252
Osho, 307, 310–11, 320
Ostension, 356–57, 361
Other Terrorist Organizations list, 255
Outremer, 135

pacifism, 231, 237, 239, 241, 245
Paganism, 422
Palmer, Susan J., 137, 139, 144–45
Palmer, Susan, 50n2, 52n20, 54n44, 54n45, 54n46, 56n77, 56n95, 57n113
Pamyat, 232
pancamakara (5 Ms), 253, 269n6
Pandavas, 266
Panthers, Black, 300

Paris, 135
Partition of India, 326–27
Patanjali, 253, 269n5
Path of Bliss. *See also* Ananda Marga *entries*
Patna High Court, 255
Patrick, Jr., Theodore (Ted) Roosevelt, 399–402, 407–8
Patrick, ted, 59n119
patriot groups, 125
Patriotism, in 3HO, 332, 335
Peace Cereal, 337
Peace Mission, 97
peaceful resolution, 313–15, 319–20
Pederik, Evan (Om Prakash), 255
Pelan, 297
People's Protectorate, 384, 395n47
People's Republic of China (PRC), 379, 382, 389–90
Peoples Forum, 103
Peoples Temple, 5, 7, 16–22, 25, 35–40, 55n57, 55n70, 137, 141, 143, 158, 175, 416–17, 421
Peoples Temple, history of, 96–98
Peoples Temple, The *See* Jonestown
Peoples Temple, Jim Jones concerned about future fame, 212
peripheric evolution (*parikranti*), 259
Perun, 233, 239
Peste, Jonathan, 8
Petersen, Jesper Aagaard, 10, 417
Petros, G., 365
   Art That Kills, 365–68. *See also* Aesthetic Terrorism
Petrowsky, Marc, 53n28
Philip IV, "the fair," of Bourbon, 135
Pilkington H. and Popov A., 234
poa, 153–54, 157, 162
Poewe, Karla, 61n140
poison gas (attack), 147, 150, 154–55, 161–62
   nerve gas, 162
   VX gas, 158
police, 149, 150–51, 154–59, 161–62, 164
Politburo, CCP, 386
political philosophy of Ananda Marga, 250–54, 256, 258–59, 262, 269
   political program in Ananda Marga, 250–51
political strategy, 32
Pomfret, John, 393n12
Poole, Elijah. *See* Muhammad, Elijah

popular Catholicism
 Uganda, 193
Port Kaituma, 98
Post-punk, 365–67. *See also* Petros, G.
Prabhat Samgita, 253
Prabhupada's palace: 276–77, 286
preventive detention laws, 254
Problems of the Day, 251
progressive millennialism, 20
Progressive utilization theory (PROUT), 9
Progressive Utilization Theory, 250. *See also* PROUT *and* PROUTist Universal *entries*
projection, simple, 68–69
projective identification, 66, 68–72, 78–79, 81–82
Prokes, Mike, 101
proselytizing by Ananda Margiis, 254, 256–57
 proselytizing by Ananda Margiis in the United States, 254
 proselytizing through social service, 256–57
 urgency to proselytize, 262. *See also* Supreme Command *entry*
PROUT, 249–52, 255–56, 258, 260, 262, 267, 269
 cooperatives, 261
 decentralisation of industry, 261
 incentive economy, 260
 key industries (public utilities), 261
 principles of PROUT, 260–61
 small scale industries, 261
PROUTist Universal, 250–51, 254, 256–57
Prus, R.C., 51n13
pseudospeciation, 67–68, 73, 75, 78, 82
psychoanalytic theory, 66, 68–69, 82. *See also* splitting; projective identification
Psychological society, 45
psychological warfare, 126
public prosecutors, 154, 155
Punjab
 history of, 327–28, 331
 militancy in, 327–28, 331, 344
 Sikh Dharma experience compared to that of Sikhs in Punjab, 330–31
Puri, Harbhajan Singh, 326. *See also* Bhajan, Yogi
Putin V., 241

Qaum, 327, 331, 343
qigong, 384–85, 390

racist violence, 231, 235, 243–44
 bomb attacks, 235
 murders, 235
Rahn, Patsy, 62
Rajneesh group, 42, 47
Rajneesh, Bhagwan Shree, 307–9, 310–12, 315–16, 318–19, 320
Rajneeshpuram, 10, 307–9, 310–20, 416
Rajput folly, 267
Rama Seminars, 406
Ramsay, Michael, 135
Rancho Santa Fe, California, 174, 187
Rapoport, David, 33, 36, 51n17, 54n48, 55n55
Rashtriya Svayamsevak Sangh (RSS), 263
Reader, Ian, 50n1, 51n7, 52n17, 53n29, 55n56, 56n84, 56n85, 61n145
Rebellion, Contestado, 297
recantations, 392n6
Redican, K.J., 54n45
Reflexive anti-reflexivity, 357–58, 369
reformation of exploiters, 268
Registration process, China, 392n7
rekonstruktory, 233–34
religion, 254, 256–57
 religious and social dogmas, 264
Religious Capital: and New Vrindaban, 287
Religious freedom
 China, 380, 390
religious fundamentalism and its characteristics, 264
 fundamentalist-like characteristics in Ananda Marga, 264
Reno, Janet, 44
renunciation, 159f
Reparatrix-group, 198
Repp, Martin, 8
Republics, Union of Soviet Socialist, 302
Restoration of the Ten Commandments of God, 17–18, 25, 27
Revelation, Book of, 179, 297
Reverend Moon, 47
revolutionaries, 250, 268
Revolutionary millennial movements, 33
revolutionary philosophy in Ananda Marga, 250–52, 256, 259, 261, 263, 268–69
 revolutionary action in Ananda Marga, 250
 revolutionary transformation in Ananda Marga's social cycle, 259

revolutionary progressive millenialism, 261
  Catherine Wessinger, 261
revolutionary suicide, 95, 106–8
rhetoric in Peoples Temple
  confession, 105
  martyrdom, 108
  persecution, 104–6
  suffering, 104–6
Richardson J., 242, 245
Richardson, Herbert, 57n110, 60n134
Richardson, James T., 6, 11, 42, 45, 47, 50n3, 50n6, 51n8, 51n9, 51n12, 51n14, 52n23, 52n25, 53n37, 54n44, 54n46, 55n51, 55n59, 55n64, 56n78, 56n91, 56n93, 57n99, 57n103, 57n107, 57n109, 57n110, 57n111, 58n114, 58n116, 58n117, 59n120, 59n124, 59n126, 60n129, 60n131, 60n133, 60n134, 60n138, 60n139, 60n140, 61n142, 61n143, 61n144, 61n146, 61n148, 62, 76, 80–81, 393n9, 395n41, 395n48, 396n60
Robbins, Thomas, 7, 20, 49n1, 50n2, 50n3, 51n7, 52n20, 52n23, 55n53, 56n77, 56n95, 57n113, 58n115, 58n117, 59n129, 60n133, 61n146, 62, 66, 139, 144, 145
Rochford, Burke, 54n43
Rochford, E. Burke, 9
Rodnoverie, 9
Roller, Edith, 99–100
Roman Catholic Church
  Uganda, 193
Rosenfeld, Jean, 49n1, 53n30, 53n32, 56n79, 56n96
Rosenthal, Elizabeth, 386, 394n33
Rosicrucianism, 135
Rothchild, John, 54n45
Ruby Ridge, 72, 125, 186
Rugazi (Uganda), 204
Ruhesi, Hilda, 198
Ruiz, Pedro, 51n6
Rukungiri (Uganda), 191–92, 197
rule by law, 383, 393n19
rule of law, 383–84, 393n19
Ruslanov, Anatole, 270n18
Russia, 47–48, 150
Russian Orthodox Church, 47, 236, 242
Ryan, Leo Congressman, 38, 39
Ryan, Rep. Leo J., 97–98, 104, 107–8

Sadasiva, 253
Sadock, B., 58n115
Sadvipra leadership in Ananda Marga, 259–62
  benevolent dictatorship of the Sadvipras, 259
  proto-Sadvipras, 260
Saint Petersburg, 232, 244
Saivism in Ananda Marga, 253
Sakamoto Tsutsumi, 148–49, 154–55, 158–59, 161–63
Saktism in Ananda Marga, 253
salmonella poison, 310
Sama Samaja Tattva, 267
Samaj, 261, 271n28
Samaja Cakra, 258
San Francisco Chronicle, 97
Sanatan tradition, 333
Sanitization, 353, 361–62, 364, 367–69
sannyasis (renunciates) of Ananda Marga, 251–52, 256–57, 267
  financial support of sannyasis, 258
  male Indian *sannyasis* in Ananda Marga, 253
Sanskrit transliteration in Ananda Marga literature, 269n1
Sarkar, Prabhat Ranjan, 249–51
  allegations he was poisoned in custody, 254
  exonerated of legal charges, 256
  incarceration, 250, 254
Sartre, Jean Paul, 342–43
Satanic milieu, 353, 359, 362, 364, 366–67, 370
Satanism, 10
  Atrocity catalogues, 354–56
  Esoteric, 353, 359, 364, 370
  Mythological, 351–52, 354–56
  Rationalist, 359, 361, 364, 366, 368, 370
  Reactive, 353, 356–58, 363–64, 367, 370
  Religious, 359–62, 364
  Typology of, 352–53, 359, 364, 370
satanization of opponents, 264–65, 268
scapegoat strategies, 239
Schacht, Larry, 105
Schecter, R.E., 58n115
Schuyler, Philip, 137, 139–40, 144
Scientology, 35, 47
Scotland, 135
Scott, Jason, 408

INDEX 439

Scott, Marvin, 51n12
Secord, Paul, 34, 52n21
Seiwert, Hubert, 61n140
self-violence, 173
separation of church and state, 318, 320
Seventh-Day Adventists, 20
Shabazz, tribe of, 297
Shakers, 45
Shaktipod, in 3HO/Sikh Dharma, 342
Shambala, 152
Shapiro, Eli, 58n115
Sharrieff, Raymond, 304
Sheela, Ma Anand, 309–12, 315–17, 319
Shepherd, Gary, 54n46, 58n115
Shepherd, William, 58n115, 59n120, 59n129, 60n133
Sherwood, Carlton, 60n134
Shinrikyo, Aum, 297
Short Creek Raid, 414
Shterin, Marat, 59n126, 60n129, 61n142, 61n143, 61n144
Shupe, Anson, 11
Shupe, Anson, 46, 53n26, 54n47, 57n99, 57n112, 58n116, 58n117, 60n130, 60n132, 60n139
Siberian Paganism, 237
siddhis (yogic powers), 253
Sikh Dharma Brotherhood, 334
Sikh Dharma International, 345–46
Sikh Dharma. *See* Healthy, Happy, Holy Organization
Sikh Khalsa, 263
  daggers (*kirpan*) carried by Sikh Khalsa, 271n29
Sikhism
  conversion to by 3HO members, 326–27
  and process of institutionalization in 3HO/Sikh Dharma, 334–35, 339
  interpretations of in 3HO/Sikh Dharma, 331, 333–34, 336
  and Sanatan tradition, 333
  and yoga in 3HO/Sikh Dharma, 336
Sikhism
  Sikh, 4, 10
Simmonds, Robert, 55n51
Singer, Margaret, 58n115, 74–77, 79. *See also* brainwashing; deprogramming; Richard Ofshe
Singh, Baba Virsa, 333
Situationist International, 367

skinheads, 233, 235–36, 243–44
Slavic Union, 235
Slavic Union of Slavic Communities of Native Faith, 233
Slavyano-goritskaya bor'ba, 233–34
Smith, William, 54n46, 56n95
social capital, 307–8, 311, 314, 315–16, 320
social exploiters, Sarkar's opinion, 259
social injustice, 264, 269
social isolation, 308, 311–15
Social justice, and 3HO, 334
social justice, philosophy in Ananda Marga, 250, 263
  social equality, 260, 267
  social inequality, 265
social networks, 308–9, 312–15
social order theory in Ananda Marga, 258–59
social service, concept in Ananda Marga, 249, 252
  social service projects in Ananda Marga, 249, 254, 256–57. *See also* kidnapping children, allegations *entry*
Social weapon, 32
socialism in Ananda Marga, 254, 260, 268. *See also* mystic socialism
Socialism, National, 298
Socialist legality, 382, 385, 393n15
socioeconomic philosophy in Ananda Marga, 250–54, 256, 258–62, 269
  socioeconomic program in Ananda Marga, 250
sociopolitical philosophy in Ananda Marga, 250
  sociopolitical leadership in Ananda Marga, 250
sociopolitical turbulence in India, 251
sociospiritual philosophy in Ananda Marga, 249–52, 254, 256, 265, 268
Solar Temple, 17–18, 21–23, 25, 31–36, 41, 242, 312
Solar Temple
  Order of the Solar Temple (OTS), 5, 7–8, 417, 422
Solomon, Trudy, 58n117, 403
soul, 183
Soviet Union, 232, 236, 241
Spain, 137
Spector, Malcolm, 51n13
Spielman, Roger, 57n99

Spiritual path, 331, 335
spiritual philosophy, 249, 252–54, 260, 263
    spirituality, concept in Ananda Marga, 249
Spiritual power, and 3HO, 326, 332
spiritual practices in Ananda Marga, 249, 256–58, 269n5–6
Splitting, 66–70, 81
Starhawk, 237
Starr, J.M., 55n55
Stewart, Mary, 55n51
Stigal, Sam, 57n99
Stmody, 185–86
Stone, Alan, 118
Strange Gods, 271n26
Structurally radical, structurally conservative disembedding processes, 353, 359, 367
subway(s), 151, 154–55, 159, 162,
sudras (laborers) in Ananda Marga social order, 258, 270n19
    sudra revolution, 259, 261
suicide, 120
suicide, promotion of, 185–87
Suicide
    altruistic, 38, 55n70
    revolutionary, 38, 55n70
    theology of, 38
    rejection of, 175, 179
    rhetorical transformation of, 183–84, 187
    views of, 173–74, 177
Sunday Mainichi (newspaper), 148, 152, 155, 159, 161, 163
Supreme Board in Ananda Marga, 260
Supreme Command of Ananda Marga, 256
Supreme People's Court, China, 383–85, 395n47
survivors, 121
svastika (swastika), 267, 271n32
Swantko, Jean, 47, 54n44, 57n107, 59n126, 60n137, 61n140
Switzerland, 134, 137, 142
Sydney, Australia, 255
Symbolic violence, 231, 238–39, 244–45, 359–65
Symposium on Evil Cults, 381
Synanon, 35, 397

Tabor, James, 49n1, 52n17, 53n27, 56n78, 57n106, 57n108, 59n126
Tagore, Rabindranath, 251

tantra yoga, 249, 253, 262
tantra, 249, 253, 262
    struggle as an aspect of, 249
    tantric ritual, 253. See also *pancamakara* (5 Ms) entries
Taraka Brahma, 263
tattvas (items/ substances), 253
Ten Commandments group, 31, 35
terrorism, 243
Terrorism and Political Violence, 49
terrorism, 250, 255–56, 267–68
    Sarkar's opinion of, 250
    allegations of terrorism against Ananda Marga, 250, 255–56
    allegations of terrorism against only some members of Ananda Marga, 267
    allegations of terrorism against UPRF, 255. See also UPRF *entries*
    Country Reports on Terrorism 2004, 255
    Designated Foreign Terrorist Organizations list, 255
    intraorganizational terrorism in Ananda Marga, 267–68
    Other Terrorist Organizations list, 255
Testa, Bart, 57n110
Texas Department of Public Safety, 122, 124
The Family, 47
The Liberation of Intellect: Neo-Humanism, 264
The Two, 176
The Way, 35
Theosophical religious tradition, 186
Therapeutic effects, 32
Third Reich, 52n24
this-worldly religiosity, 231, 242
thought reform, 64–68, 73, 75, 77
Thugs, 36
Ti—*see* Nettles, Bonnie Lu
Tiananmen Square, 386
Tiljala, headquarters of Ananda Marga in Kolkata (Calcutta), 251, 256
Tipton, Steve, 51n8
Tokyo Broadcasting System (TBS), 149, 155, 161–64
Tokyo, 133, 140
Tong, James, 379, 383, 386, 392n1, 392n2, 392n3, 392n5, 392n6, 394n22, 394n24, 394n32, 394n34, 395n36, 396n55, 396n57

Torture, 380, 389–90
totalism, 19, 21, 24, 26
　and anticult, 77
　and religious fundamentalism, 66
　as therapeutic, 72–73
　defined, 64–70
　ideological totalism, 67–68
　totalism begets totalism, 73. *See also* exemplary dualism
Totalitarianism, 64–67, 77, 79
Tracy, Phil, 56n73
Transcendental Meditation, 397
transformation, bodily, 177–78
Transgression, 359, 362–65, 367–70
"trial and error" method, 160
Tribe, Laurence, 60n134
Trinh, Sylvaine, 139–40, 144
trisuls (tridents) carried in Ananda Marga, 271n29
Tropp, Richard, 96
turning the other cheek, 232, 237, 240, 245
Twelve Tribes Messianic Communities (formerly the Northeast Kingdom Community Church), 413–15

U.S. Department of Justice, 255, 256n14
U.S. State Department, 255
U.S. Supreme Court, 47
UFO, 8, 418
ufology, 177
UFOs, 179, 181–82, 184, 186
Uganda Human Rights Commission, 192, 204–5
UN Commission on Human rights, 387
UN Committee against Torture, 389
Underwood, Grant, 54n49
Ungerleider, J.T., 59n120
Unification Church, 43, 47, 397, 401, 403–7, 410
United Negro Improvement Association, 296
United States government, 295
　Bureau of Alcohol, Tobacco and Firearms (ATF), 299
　Federal Bureau of Investigation (FBI), 299
　　and assassination of Malcolm X, 302–3
　　Black Nationalist Program of, 302
　　COINTELPRO, 302
　　and surveillance of Nation of Islam, 302–3
　　detains Nation of Islam members, 302
　　files on Wallace Fard, 302

United States, 137, 391
universalism versus nationalism in Ananda Marga, 251
University of Chicago's Fundamentalism Project, 264
Unto Infinity Board, 345
UPRF (Universal PROUTist's Revolutionary Federation), 255, 268
　bombing by UPRF, 255
Urban, Hugh, 53n28
use of force in Ananda Marga, 249–50, 265, 268–69
　defense pact with Sikh Khalsa, 263
　doctrinal justification for, 250, 264
　physical force and Sadvipra rule, 262
　use of force in individual life, 250. *See also atatayi* entry
utopian philosophy in Ananda Marga, 250–51, 265, 268

Vaisnavism in Ananda Marga, 253
vaisyas (capitalists) in Ananda Marga social order, 258, 270n19
Vajrayana, 149, 153
van den Broek, Roelof, 135, 145
Van der Lans, Jan, 51n12, 58n117
Van Driel, Barend, 50n3, 51n8, 57n103, 60n139
Vedic tradition and Russian Paganism, 232, 237
Velemudr, 236
Veles, 233
Veleslav, 233
Ventimiglia, J.C., 54n47
Vermont State Police, 413
violence, 147, 152–54, 157–58, 161, 163–65
　legitimation (justification), 164–65
　"religious violence", 163f, 165
violence in Ananda Marga, 249–50
　intraorganizational violence in Ananda Marga, 250
　violence against Ananda Margiis, 250. *See also* Bijon Setu incident *entry*, 257
violence in Peoples Temple, 98
　discipline, 99
　behavior control, 100–102
　behavior modification, 99–100
　terror, 100, 102–4
violence in Sarkar's view, 269

Violence, 31–61
    and interactionist perspective, 33, 36, 41, 48
    against new religions, 34, 43–48, 60n131
    amplification of violence, 33, 40
    as property of a relationship, 34, 48
    as reaction to external threats, 33, 39
    atrocity tales as form of, 43–45
    "background violence," 32
    beliefs and violence, 34, 36
    by religious groups, 34–43
    characteristic of group culture, 36
    children, 36, 39
    collective violence, 34, 52n24
    conflict perspective, 32, 46
    conflict/interactionist approach, 31, 41
    context of violence, 31, 33, 36, 40, 48–49
    cultural expectations, 37
    exacerbation of, 37
    genocide, 52n24
    group beliefs justifying violence, 33, 36
    individual violence, 34
    interdependence of violence and context, 33, 40
    legitimate actions, 49
    low frequency in NRMs, 32
    mass media, role of, 46, 48
    non-violence of most NRMs, 37, 48
    organizational level, 43, 46–49
    predictions of, 40
    theology of, 37
    traditional religions and violence, 36
violence, against Falun Gong, 380
violence, religious, 107–8
Violence: and authority, 287
    exit-voice hypothesis, 288
    factionalism, 287–88
    fear of, 283
    incidents of, 278–81, 289n2
vipras (intellectuals) in Ananda Marga social order, 258, 270n19
Vivian, Allen, 388
Volunteers Social Service (VSS), 262–63

Waco, 113–17, 124–25, 127
Waco, Texas, 133
walk-ins, 182
Wallace, A.F.C., 59n122
Wallenstein, H.J., 54n45
Wallis, Roy, 33, 52n19

Walliss, John, 18, 62, 140–41, 145
Wang, H., 395n39
War 1, World, 300
war, 149, 151–52, 154, 156–57, 164
warfare narrative, 126
Warren, N.C., 55n55
Watanabe, Manuba, 56n84
weapons, 150, 154, 162
Wellisch, K.K., 50n120
Wells, William T., 255
Wessinger, Catherine, 20, 33, 38, 41, 49, 50n2, 50n4, 52n17, 52n20, 52n22, 53n27, 53n29, 53n30, 54n49, 55n53, 55n55, 55n56, 55n65, 55n67, 56n75, 56n77, 56n78, 56n83, 56n84, 56n90, 56n95, 56n96, 56n97, 57n106, 61n145, 62, 71, 138–39, 141, 144–45, 264
West, Louis, 58n115
Western esotericism, 135
White Nights, 103–4, 109 (*See also*, Jonestown, *deaths in*)
white peace, 265
White, David, 253
Wicca, 232
Wilson, M.A., 54n45
Wknody, 185
Wolf, Susan, 54n45
Women, in 3HO leadership, 342–43
Woodin, Kenneth, 55n70
World Trade Center, attack on, 244
Wright, Stuart A., 7
Wright, Stuart, 25–26
Wright, Stuart, 50n1, 52n18, 53n27, 55n53, 55n57, 56n78, 58n117

X, Malcolm, 295, 305
    and white Americans as devils, 301
    as effective recruiter, 303
    assassination of, 302–3
    criticizes Elijah Muhammad, 303
xenophobic forms of Paganism, 238
Xinhua News Agency, 395n38, 42–43, 396n61

Yakub, 297, 300
Yakutovsky G. P., 237
yama and *niyama* (abstinences/observances) in Ananda Marga philosophy, 266, 269n5
    yama and *niyama* enumerated, 271n30. See also *ahimsa* and *himsa* entries

Yao Chenglin, 387–88
Yeltsin, B., 241
yoga, 147–48
Yoga
    and businesses, 338
    Kundalini yoga, 332, 334
    and Sanatan tradition, 333
    and Sikhism, 327, 334
    as taught by Yogi Bhajan, 326, 332, 334, 344
    white tantric yoga, 326, 344

Yoga-Sutra, 253
Yogi Bhajan, 4–5, 10
yugas (eras), 271n22

Za Russkoe Delo, 235
Zald, Mayer, 51n15
Zang, X., 395n39
Zeller, Benjamin, 8
Zellner, William, 53n28
Zhou Zhenxiang, Professor, 381